Introducing
the Apocrypha

Introducing the Apocrypha

Message, Context, and Significance

David A. deSilva

Foreword by James H. Charlesworth

Baker Academic

Grand Rapids, Michigan

© 2002 by David A. deSilva

Published by Baker Academic
a division of Baker Publishing Group
P.O. Box 6287, Grand Rapids, MI 49516-6287
www.bakeracademic.com

Paperback edition published in 2004
ISBN 0-8010-3103-6

Printed in the United States of America

The Library of Congress has cataloged the hardcover edition as follows:
DeSilva, David Arthur.
    Introducing the Apocrypha : message, context, and significance / David A. deSilva.
        p.   cm.
    Includes bibliographical references (p.) and indexes.
    ISBN 0-8010-2319-X (cloth)
    1. Bible. O.T. Apocrypha—Criticism, interpretation, etc. I. Title.
    BS1700 .D44 2002
    229'.061—dc21   2001056532

In honor of the God
who was never without a witness
in the world

Contents

Foreword

Bending the Knee of the Heart in an Apocryphon: A High-Water Mark in Jewish Theology

One of my close colleagues at Duke University for over twenty years was the dean of the chapel, Dr. James Cleland. Pondering whether he was a Christian Jew or a Jewish Christian, Dr. Cleland liked to refer to the Prayer of Manasseh. He would frequently tell the story of a Southern Baptist minister who opened the pulpit Bible and read from this early Jewish prayer. The members of the congregation were amazed at the "Christian" character of the prayer and later told him that it was one of the most insightful and meaningful prayers they had ever heard. They confessed, however, that they could not find the text in their Bibles. He told them it was in their pulpit Bible.

Cleland and these Christians had a point. The Prayer of Manasseh is indeed one of the greatest penitential prayers ever composed. Samuel Sandmel once told me that it should have been "canonized" within the liturgy of the Day of Atonement (Yom Kippur). We do not have the fluid liturgy of Yom Kippur that was directed by the high priest and the Levites in the Jerusalem temple before 70 C.E., yet I can imagine that perhaps the Prayer of Manasseh was read at that time of year—not only privately but also publicly in synagogues, both in the land and in the Diaspora. Perhaps some in the temple read it, calling on God as they confessed their sins and asked forgiveness.

Those who have focused their lives on the study of prayers frequently tell me that the most deeply spiritual prayers are those composed by early Jews. Subsequently, I often hear the Prayer of Manasseh cited. Once, when I thought my interlocutor was only superficially informed about early Jewish prayers, I was startled to hear the following answer: "Well, I do not memorize the titles of prayers you scholars give them. My interest is in the spirituality in a prayer." The individual then quoted the Prayer of Manasseh from memory:

> And now behold I am bending the knees of my heart before you;
> and I am beseeching your kindness.
> I have sinned, O Lord, I have sinned;
> and I certainly know my sins.

I beseech you:
    forgive me, O Lord, forgive me! (Pr. Man. 11–13)

Despite what may be heard in sermons and published in books, Jews during the time of Jesus did acknowledge their sinfulness and confess their sins. In fact, in the temple they established a yearly liturgy and ritual for confessing sins and seeking God's forgiveness. During this ritual, Yom Kippur, even the high priest, having immersed himself in purifying waters and put on elegant and expensive garments, openly confessed his sins. Centuries later Jews remembered his words:

O Lord, I have committed iniquity, transgressed, and sinned before you, I and my house.
O Lord, forgive the iniquities, transgressions, and sins, which I have done by committing iniquity, transgression, and sin before you, I and my house. (*m. Yoma* 3.8)

Manasseh was ancient Israel's most wicked king. The Prayer of Manasseh assumes that he recognized and acknowledged his sin. Most scholars, however, conclude that a Jew shortly before the time of Jesus composed this prayer and placed it on the lips of Manasseh. The work is thus both apocryphal (not contained in the canon represented by the Hebrew Bible) and pseudepigraphical (attributed to an ancient Israelite or Jew). Hence, the Prayer of Manasseh has been included in collections of the Old Testament Apocrypha and in the larger corpus of early Jewish religious texts called the Old Testament Pseudepigrapha. As we become more globally aware, we need to know that the Prayer of Manasseh is in the Greek Orthodox Bible and in the Slavonic Orthodox Bibles and—of course—widely available to Roman Catholics since it is deuterocanonical. As we ponder the borders of the canon and the texts that contain God's Word in the words of Scripture, we hear the cry from the heart of the human who prayed the Prayer of Manasseh, someone so distraught and in need of God's healing forgiveness that he bent the knees of his heart.

Jews and Christians who wish to learn about their ancient roots need to know about—indeed read—the so-called apocryphal books. Virtually all of the Old Testament Apocrypha are now included in the New Revised Standard Version of the Bible. Others, along with many more Jewish religious texts, are conveniently collected in *The Old Testament Pseudepigrapha* (2 vols., Anchor Bible Reference Library [Garden City, N.Y.: Doubleday, 1983–85]).

David deSilva's *Introducing the Apocrypha* is the best introduction to this ancient corpus. He wisely refuses the glib pronouncement of some professors that the Old Testament Apocrypha are the books added in the Septuagint. This claim fails to observe that such a list varies according to the contents of the ancient manuscripts of the Septuagint. DeSilva thus opts for an inclusive definition of the Apocrypha. He helps the interested reader to comprehend the message, context, and significance of these ancient Jewish compositions. With living and captivating prose, and with erudition and insight, he leads the reader into the thoughts of some great Jewish minds that were imbued with revelation from above. As deSilva makes clear, the Apocrypha are not a threat to faith; they are "a vital witness to faith, specifically the faith of Jewish people living in the period between the third century B.C.E. and the first century C.E."

What is unique and important about deSilva's *Introducing the Apocrypha*? I have found the following features especially helpful:

- it indicates the importance of the Dead Sea Scrolls, especially in clarifying the transmission of such documents as Ben Sira and Tobit;
- it enriches our perception of the Apocrypha by incorporating social-scientific and socio-rhetorical methodologies and insights;
- it discloses the pervasive adaptation of the Deuteronomistic explanation of why the wicked prosper and the righteous suffer: that is, a viable explanation of theodicy, especially in light of national woes;
- it shows why these texts are commentaries on sacred Scripture;
- it helps us comprehend that the authors of the New Testament were reacting not so much to ancient texts as to roughly contemporaneous documents intimately filled with God's continuing revelation;
- it exposes the fact that the roots of Jesus' teaching lead deep into the soil of early Jewish theology.

Many Jews and not a few early Christians perceived God's Word in the words of the Apocrypha. During the time of Jesus, there was no closed and clearly defined canon of sacred writings. One might imagine that the Apocrypha are not only the byways of ancient Scripture but also part of the highways. The list of geniuses who knew and admired the Apocrypha as depositories of God's Word reads like a Who's Who of the early church: Tertullian, Origen, Eusebius, Jerome, and Augustine. This way leads to spiritual nurture and a better understanding of whose we are.

Did God hear the prayer of the wicked Manasseh? As with virtually all early Jewish prayers, this one affirms that God always answers an honest and contrite prayer. Note how the Prayer of Manasseh ends: affirming that God is "the God of those who repent," the author concludes with these words:

> In me you will manifest all your grace;
> and although I am not worthy,
>   you will save me according to your manifold mercies.
> Because of this (salvation) I shall praise you continually

all the days of my life;
because all the hosts of heaven praise you,
    and sing to you forever and ever. (Pr. Man. 14–15)

Professor deSilva rightly stresses that the Prayer of Manasseh "shows the boundless forgiveness of God."

James H. Charlesworth
Princeton Theological Seminary

Preface

My journey with the Apocrypha began as a thirteen-year-old when I noticed, leafing through the *Book of Common Prayer* during a not-so-engaging sermon, that there were several Scripture readings prescribed for special days from books that I did not recognize as coming from the Bible. I finally found the titles listed as "Apocrypha" in the church's "Articles of Faith," being recommended therein as edifying literature. So I borrowed a copy of the RSV Apocrypha from the church library and skimmed through Wisdom of Solomon and Wisdom of Ben Sira. I was aware that I was reading special books, even though they were not part of my Bible, and I made a mental note to return to that collection in earnest some day. Twenty years later, I had my chance.

The reader of this book is urged to have a copy of the Apocrypha at hand and to use this book as an aid to reading those primary texts. When this volume refers to a passage from the Apocrypha, the reader would do well to look up the verses and read them. While this will make for a slower read through the present text, it will be far more rewarding in the long run.

I wish to thank those who have been most instrumental in supporting me in the writing of this volume. I had the benefit of excellent teachers who cultivated in me a love and zeal for intertestamental Jewish literature, J. H. Charlesworth and C. R. Holladay being the most influential in this regard. Jim Weaver received my proposal graciously and conveyed the publisher's commitment to the project. Jim Kinney, his successor at Baker Academic, was kind and generous in his support of a project he inherited rather than chose. His editorial and production staff, of course, deserves high praise for their efforts in turning the manuscript into this handsome book. The trustees and president of Ashland Theological Seminary granted me a quarter's leave to begin this project, and for their support of this, as well as all my academic endeavors, I am truly thankful. My research assistant, Rev. Jeffrey Vanderhoff, labored many hours gathering the books and articles I requested and helping to prepare the bibliographies. Finally, I thank my wife, Donna Jean, and my three sons for allowing me the hours of the workday to devote to this book. The evenings, of course, belonged to light-saber duels, dinosaurs, and LEGO!

Abbreviations

General

AB	Anchor Bible
b.	Babylonian Talmud
Bib	*Biblica*
CBQ	*Catholic Biblical Quarterly*
JB	Jerusalem Bible
JBL	*Journal of Biblical Literature*
JSHRZ	*Jüdische Schriften aus hellenistisch-römischer Zeit*
JSJ	*Journal for the Study of Judaism in the Persian, Hellenistic, and Roman Periods*
JTS	*Journal of Theological Studies*
KJV	King James Version
LXX	Septuagint
m.	Mishnah
MT	Masoretic Text
NEB	New English Bible
NJB	New Jerusalem Bible
NRSV	New Revised Standard Version
RSV	Revised Standard Version
t.	Tosefta
TEV	Today's English Version

Apocrypha

Tob.	Tobit	Sus.	Susanna
Jdt.	Judith	Bel	Bel and the Dragon
Add. Esth.	Additions to Esther	1 Macc.	1 Maccabees
Wis.	Wisdom of Solomon	2 Macc.	2 Maccabees
Sir.	Wisdom of Ben Sira	1 Esd.	1 Esdras
Bar.	Baruch	Pr. Man.	Prayer of Manasseh
Let. Jer.	Letter of Jeremiah	Ps. 151	Psalm 151
Add. Dan.	Additions to Daniel	3 Macc.	3 Maccabees
Pr. Azar.	Prayer of Azariah	2 Esd.	2 Esdras
Sg. Three	Song of the Three Young Men	4 Macc.	4 Maccabees

Introduction

1

The Value of the Apocrypha

Why study the Apocrypha? The answer to this question may not be obvious to many Christians. After all, were these texts not excluded from the canon held sacred by the Jews? Were they not excluded from the canon promoted by the Protestant Reformers, who held that Scripture alone contained the revelation of God's way of salvation and thus took great care to purge those Scriptures of these marginal books? To many other Christians, however, the question will be equally incomprehensible—but for a very different reason. The Catholic or Orthodox Christian might reply, "Are they not, after all, part of our Scriptures? Have they not been read, used, and valued by the towering figures of our tradition for two millennia?"[1] It is perhaps the internecine strife between these great limbs of the body of Christ that has led to the disuse, neglect, and eventual suspicion of the Apocrypha among many Protestant Christians, while at the same time leading to a more decisive elevation of these texts among Roman Catholic Christians. One of the goals of this volume is to move readers past seeing the Apocrypha as one more thing that separates one group of Christians from another and toward seeing these books for what they are in and of themselves and to value them on that basis.

1. Catholic and Orthodox Christians would not refer to these books as "apocrypha." Instead, the term "deuterocanonical" is used to distinguish this supplementary collection of "canonical" works from the "protocanonical" books of the Old Testament. Catholic and Orthodox Christians tend to use the word "apocrypha" for "pseudepigrapha," that wealth of Jewish literature produced between ca. 200 B.C.E. and 200 C.E. which lies beyond even the expanded canon. This corpus includes *1 Enoch, Testaments of the Twelve Patriarchs, Jubilees, 2 Baruch,* and many others. The word "pseudepigrapha" means "bearing a false attribution of authorship." The real author assumed the identity of a notable Old Testament worthy such as Enoch, Abraham, or Baruch and wrote in his name. This is a common, though by no means universal, characteristic of this corpus, but it is not limited to noncanonical books. Ecclesiastes surely was not written by Solomon, the son of David, nor is it likely that Isaiah of Jerusalem wrote all the oracles collected in Isaiah.

What Are the Old Testament Apocrypha?

To many people, particularly Protestant Christians, the Apocrypha are a collection of forbidden or heretical books scrupulously to be avoided. The word itself means "hidden things" (*apocrypha* singular, *apocryphon*), but the adjective "hidden" has taken on a pejorative nuance—"hidden for a good reason," "suspicious," "heretical." Such an evaluation, however, is more the work of centuries of unfamiliarity with the actual texts than a balanced assessment of the texts' meaning and value.

Far from being a threat to faith, the Old Testament Apocrypha are a vital witness to faith, specifically the faith of Jewish people living in the period between the third century B.C.E. and the first century C.E. The different writings come from Palestine, Alexandria (Egypt), Antioch (Syria), and possibly even Persia (from the large Jewish community that settled and remained in Babylon after the deportation under Nebuchadnezzar). Some were written originally in Greek, the common language of the Mediterranean world from the third century B.C.E. on, others in Hebrew or Aramaic.

These books bear witness to what it meant to remain faithful to the God of Israel during a tumultuous period of history. It was a time of political upheaval, as powerful empires vied for domination; it was a period of peril for Judaism itself, as the enticements of Greek culture led many away from persevering in the Mosaic covenant (Torah) and as forceful attempts were made to bring Jews into conformity with the customs and culture of Hellenism (the "Greek way of life"). The Apocrypha contain the testimony of faithful Jews who sought to live out their loyalty to God in a very troubled (and often hostile) world. While it is difficult to identify a single common theme running through the whole collection, a major concern addressed by many of these texts involves how Jews are to respond to the challenges of Hellenism and of persevering as a minority culture in a Greek world. It is perhaps this aspect of the Apocrypha that most draws me to these texts, since a similar question continues to face the community of disciples: What challenges threaten the commitment of the contemporary people of God, and how can we find a faithful response to God in our world?

The books of the Apocrypha certainly answered timely concerns and inspired the Jews of their period, as they enjoyed a wide circulation and were preserved for posterity. These books had a greater importance for Diaspora Jews than for Palestinian Jews, although a few books that originated in Palestine continued to be read and even quoted (like Ben Sira) or their stories told (like Judith and 1 and 2 Maccabees) well into the rabbinic period despite their "noncanonical" status. Perhaps this is because the challenge to remain a faithful Jew was more keenly felt outside the Jewish ancestral homeland, despite the advance of Hellenism in Palestine as well.

The early Christian church also received these texts as profitable writings. Their influence on the New Testament and early church fathers will astound those who are accustomed to thinking of the Apocrypha as worthless or dangerous. The measure of their usefulness is attested also in their inclusion in the major manuscripts of the Greek translation of the Old Testament (called the Septuagint, abbreviated LXX). The Septuagint began as a translation of the Torah, the first five books of the Bible, into Greek around 250 B.C.E. As fewer and fewer Diaspora Jews learned Hebrew, translations of the Prophets and the Writings became essential. The body of texts grew finally to include all the books of the Hebrew Bible but came to include several intertestamental books as well.[2] The Roman Catholic and Greek Orthodox canons of the Old Testament represent basically the Septuagint collection, while the Protestant Old Testament has returned to the consensus of early rabbinic Judaism concerning the limits of Scripture.

What Do the Writings of the Apocrypha Contain?

The Apocrypha represent a fine collection of Jewish literature from the intertestamental period. First, the collection contains contributions to historiography of the period, providing essential information about a formative period for the Judaism within which the early church grew. First Esdras is a retelling of the events in our canonical Ezra and Nehemiah, which speak of the return of Jewish exiles from Babylon and the reestablishment of the Jerusalem temple. The issues of ethnic purity present in the canonical books are also emphasized in 1 Esdras. First and Second Maccabees tell the story of the attempt in 175–167 B.C.E. to dissolve Jewish identity and make the population of Judea "like the nations" through Hellenization and of the successful resistance movement headed by Judas Maccabeus and his brothers. This traumatic period left an impression on the Jewish people that rivaled the deportation to Babylon under Nebuchadnezzar. Third Maccabees (which is more fictive than historical) recounts a similar trial that befell Jews in Alexandria, as these Jews likewise struggled to remain loyal to their God and traditions in a hostile environment. All three books of Maccabees speak to the concern of

2. We cannot be certain, however, that the Jewish communities that used the Septuagint are responsible for this innovation, since the only manuscript evidence we have for this expanded collection comes from the fourth- and fifth-century Christian community. In fact, second-century-C.E. Jews moved away from the tradition of the Septuagint version of their Scriptures in favor of the more recent, more officially sanctioned translations by Jewish scholars such as Aquila and Theodotion. These translations were limited to those books included in the Hebrew canon and thus did not include the books of the Apocrypha (although Theodotion's Daniel does include the additions). For a finely nuanced introduction to the formation of the Septuagint, see Jobes and Silva 2000: 23–104.

Jews for maintaining their very Jewishness in the face of a sometimes alluring, sometimes coercive, Greek culture.

The collection also contains several books of wisdom literature, similar to the canonical Proverbs, Ecclesiastes, and several psalms (like Psalm 1, 19, and 119, which praise the "fear of the Lord" and the Torah). Wisdom of Ben Sira (also called Sirach or Ecclesiasticus) is a lengthy collection of the instructions of a Jerusalem sage from the early part of the second century B.C.E., just a few decades before the Hellenization crisis that gave birth to the Maccabean literature. Wisdom of Solomon is the product of a Diaspora Jew writing in Greek, in close contact with Greek thought, yet unwilling to relinquish Jewish values and loyalty to Torah. Unlike Proverbs, these are not collections of short sayings but of much more developed arguments and instructions. These two books (together with 2 Maccabees 6–7) have had the most widespread influence on Christian writers of the first six or seven centuries of the church—and hence on the exposition of Christian theology—of all the Apocrypha. The Book of Baruch contains a Wisdom poem (together with a series of penitential prayers and a prophecy of deliverance). In all three works, wisdom is essentially equated with knowledge of and obedience to Torah. Again, this shows an intense interest in preserving Jewish identity and fidelity to the One God in a world of powerful enticements to abandon the ancestral ways.

This collection also contains a number of what might be called "historical romances," taking "romance" in the older sense of "edifying story." Tobit is a tale about Jewish piety in the Diaspora and about God's providential ordering of life, even in the domestic matters of arranged marriages. Judith preserves a tale about a female military hero who delivers her people by a cunning plan, exploiting a Gentile general's moral weakness. It, too, is a tale that emphasizes the efficacy of prayer and fasting and lifts up God's providential care for God's people in times of distress. The Greek versions of Esther and Daniel also contain numerous episodes not found in the Hebrew text. The Greek additions to Esther provide a theological and religious dimension that is lacking in the original Hebrew (canonical) version. The additions to Daniel comprise two additional court tales, supplementing canonical Daniel's first six chapters: Daniel displays his divinely given wisdom in exposing a conspiracy (Susanna) and twice shows the Gentile king the worthlessness of his putative gods (Bel and the Dragon).

The Apocrypha include several beautiful liturgical pieces. Some of these are further additions to Daniel, namely, Prayer of Azariah and Song of the Three Young Men. The former is a penitential psalm, confessing Israel's sins and imploring God's forgiveness and restoration, and the latter is a psalm of praise and deliverance. Both were placed within the canonical tale of the ordeal of the fiery furnace in Daniel 3. Another penitential psalm is included as Prayer of Manasseh, which shows the boundless forgiveness of God. Finally, Psalm 151 preserves a liturgical reflection on God's choice of

David over his six brothers and a brief mention of David's defeat of the Philistine enemy Goliath.

Two books are more akin to thematic essays. Letter of Jeremiah explains the folly of Gentile religion, focused on the topic of idolatry. Fourth Maccabees focuses on the firmness of nine Jewish martyrs from the period of 167–166 B.C.E. (whose story appears also in 2 Maccabees 6–7). It holds up for a new generation these models of resistance to the enticements of Hellenism and promotes strict observance of the law of Moses as the way to embody the ideal person of virtue prized even by the Greeks.

The last book included in this collection is an apocalypse called 2 Esdras (chs. 3–14 = 4 Ezra). Written at about the same time as Revelation (ca. 95–96 C.E.), 2 Esdras seeks to make sense of the destruction of Jerusalem by a far more ungodly people, those of the Roman Empire. It is extremely valuable as an example of how apocalyptic literature functioned as theodicy (seeking out God's justice behind an unjust state of affairs), as another sample of this mysterious literary genre (of which Daniel 7–12 and Revelation are the only fully developed canonical examples), and as an expression of Judaism's solution to the destruction of the temple, namely, renewed interest in Torah.

At this point, it would be proper to admit that this way of delineating the collection of the Apocrypha is somewhat artificial. Indeed, defining where "Apocrypha" ends and "old Jewish literature" begins has always been a problem. This is reflected as early as the three great uncial manuscripts of the Septuagint, Codices Sinaiticus (fourth century C.E.), Vaticanus (fourth century C.E.), and Alexandrinus (fifth century C.E.). All three contain Apocrypha mingled in with the other books of the Old Testament, but each one contains a different collection of texts. Alexandrinus even goes beyond the collection to list *Psalms of Solomon* as an appendix (although this appendix has been removed). Likewise, different Christian communities today set different limits on the collection called (by Protestants and Jews) Apocrypha. The Roman Catholic canon includes all of the above except 3 and 4 Maccabees, 1 and 2 Esdras, Prayer of Manasseh, and Psalm 151. The Greek Orthodox Bible omits only 2 Esdras and 4 Maccabees (included as an appendix, however). The Slavonic Bible contains all but 4 Maccabees. The present volume adopts the widest delineation of Apocrypha for three reasons. First, it allows this book to be used effectively as a companion to those texts included as the "Apocryphal/Deuterocanonical Books" in the New Revised Standard Version. Second, it is in keeping with the ecumenical scope of biblical scholarship at the turn of the millennium. Third, it would be a shame to miss what some of the more marginal texts have to offer, especially in a context where our primary goal is to gain as rich an immersion as possible into the world of intertestamental Judaism and the matrix of early Christianity.

The Value of Studying the Apocrypha

Whatever one's position concerning their canonicity, the books of the Apocrypha richly reward readers in several important ways. Catholic and Orthodox readers will be interested in these texts as Scripture, while other readers will also find much of value from the careful study of these texts as documents providing windows into the period formative for both modern Judaism and Christianity and as devotional literature that still has a word for people of faith.

A first reason that motivates us to study these books is that they contribute to a fuller, more reliable picture of the Judaism of 200 B.C.E. to 100 C.E. The issues with which Jews in Palestine and abroad were wrestling during this period demonstrate continuity with issues that can be found in the Hebrew Scriptures but always represent a later stage of development and often some important modifications of what we see in the older literature. The books of the Apocrypha close that gap. As such, they are invaluable as a means of approaching a closer understanding of the Judaism within which Jesus carried out his ministry and within which the early church grew both in Palestine and throughout the Mediterranean. To begin with, 1 and 2 Maccabees provide critical information regarding the historical developments of this period, particularly the Hellenization crisis and the Maccabean Revolt, both of which left indelible marks on Jewish consciousness and ideology. Also, the texts of the Apocrypha bear witness to the esteem in which the Torah was held and to the promotion of (and motivations for) the strict observance of its laws. Jewish (and Jewish-Christian!) resistance to Paul's mission becomes more comprehensible when read in light of the continuous pressure on Jews to loosen the bonds of Torah and allow for freer interaction with Gentiles. To many, Paul looked more like an apostate and a Hellenizer rather than a loyal Jew proclaiming the messianic age. In addition, these texts provide insight into important developments in Jewish theology and ideology, preparing the reader for what he or she will encounter in the New Testament. For example, the messianic ideal of a military conqueror—which led to the frequent misunderstanding of Jesus' ministry by would-be followers and by opponents—came to full expression during the Hasmonean period (the rule of Israel by the family and descendants of Judas Maccabeus). The notion of substitutionary atonement, assurances about the individual's afterlife (whether resurrection of the body or immortality of the soul), speculations about angels and demons, and the personification of Wisdom (which provided the early church with language to speak of the Son's relationship with the Father and his preincarnate history) are greatly developed and refined in this literature, showing how concepts from the Hebrew Scriptures were passed along, with developments, to the early church. Finally, these texts mediate to us something of the life of Jews in the Diaspora—something of great importance for understanding the early Christian mission, yet something of which the Hebrew Scriptures say very little. The Apocrypha offer windows into the prayers and liturgies of these Jews, into the ethos of the pious life embraced by them, and into the ways in which they used the literary, conceptual, and rhetorical forms of the Greek world but in such a way as to enhance commitment to Jewish values—something that continues in the Christian literature. The Jewish apocryphal literature becomes an important vehicle for bringing Greek thought and rhetoric into the Christian culture.

A second compelling reason for studying these texts is that the authors of the New Testament themselves show signs of a high degree of familiarity with this literature. While the Apocrypha are never explicitly cited as Scripture, there are many places where the relationship between New Testament text and Apocrypha text goes beyond echo or parallel into influence. This relationship can be overstated, as in an article by Elias Oikonomos (1991: 17):

> Jesus himself, the apostles Peter, Paul, and James, and the Book of Revelation, use the deuterocanonical writings in a way similar to Jewish practice. The quotation of them in the New Testament is evidence that the deuterocanonical writings were used in the same way as the "protocanonical."

Oikonomos supports this claim in a footnote directing the reader to the tables of quotations and allusions given in critical editions of the Greek New Testament, which do show an impressive number of references to the Apocrypha. He does not distinguish carefully enough, however, between actual quotation and other kinds of intertextual reference, such as recontextualization, echo, and allusion. In a quotation, an author indicates that he or she is introducing some other text into the new one, usually with a formula such as "as it is written," "as the Spirit says," "as the Scripture says," or merely a "for." In this sense, the New Testament authors never quote an apocryphal book in the manner that they quote texts from what came to be known as the Hebrew canon.[3] Their reticence to do so makes Oikonomos's claim that they treated the "deuterocanonical" books the way they did the "protocanonical" ones highly suspect.

3. Stuhlmacher (1991: 2) claims to have found a few quotations; e.g., Sir. 4:1 in Mark 10:19, and Sir. 17:26 in 2 Tim. 2:19. In the first example, the words "do not defraud" appear to have been taken out of Sir. 4:1 and included in a summary of the commandments. This may not indicate direct and conscious borrowing, however, since this injunction ("do not defraud") became a standard part of ethical summaries of the Torah, a very convenient formulation by which to capture in a nutshell Deuteronomy's interest in economic justice and integrity. In the second example, the author appears to have created his own "Scripture" out of phrases known to him from LXX Joel 3:5 and Sir. 17:26. The result is so different from the originals, however, that it is difficult to see these as clear signs of "quotation" comparable to what one finds in the use of Psalms, for example, in Hebrews 1. Nevertheless, Stuhlmacher's emphasis on the importance of the Apocrypha and Pseudepigrapha for understanding the New Testament and its Christology remains unimpeachable.

The relationship can be understated as well, however. Those who speak of the New Testament authors only rarely alluding to the books of the Apocrypha or admitting only "an occasional correspondence of thought" (Beckwith 1985: 387)[4] are saying more about their ideological convictions about the Apocrypha than about actual usage and influence, which actually are quite substantial. Although it is true that no book of the Apocrypha is quoted or identified as such, recontextualizations and reconfigurations abound. That is, New Testament authors weave phrases and recreate lines of arguments from Apocrypha books into their new texts. They also allude to events and stories contained in these texts. The word "paraphrase" very frequently provides an adequate description of the relationship.

This happens to such an extent that one may conclude that the New Testament authors (and, one might add, Jesus, whose sayings resonate strongly with Ben Sira and the pseudepigraphic *Testaments of the Twelve Patriarchs* at a number of meaningful points) valued much that they had learned from these resources. Because of the nature of paraphrase and allusion, it frequently becomes impossible to prove that a New Testament author is drawing directly from an Apocrypha book itself. In many cases, it could be asserted that the thought of an Apocrypha text has entered the Jewish culture and thus been carried less directly into the mind of an author. In such cases, one could at least say that the author values the content of what can be found also in the earlier Jewish texts, even though it might be too much to say that he or she specifically valued that text. I will provide a number of examples to demonstrate the kind of usage and influence I am suggesting.

The authors of Matthew and James appear to have had some familiarity with Ben Sira. For those inclined to view the Jesus tradition in Matthew as historically reliable, this means also that Jesus himself drew on Ben Sira's sayings in his preaching. Since Ben Sira was a Jewish sage resident in Jerusalem—and one whose work was well known to the first- and second-century rabbis—it is not surprising that those ministering in a Palestinian setting should show some familiarity with this wisdom collection. Jesus' emphasis in the Lord's Prayer that our forgiving other people's sins against us goes hand-in-hand with God's forgiveness of our sins against God (Matt. 6:12, 14–15) is not attested in the Jewish Scriptures. It is, however, a noteworthy emphasis in Ben Sira:

> Forgive your neighbor the wrong he has done,
>   and then your sins will be pardoned when you pray.
> Does anyone harbor anger against another,
>   and expect healing from the Lord?

---

4. Beckwith (1985: 388) claims, for example, that 4 Maccabees is never even referred to by any New Testament or second- or third-century Christian writers, but he is overlooking or suppressing many correspondences (especially between 4 Maccabees, the Epistle to the Hebrews, and Origen; see deSilva 1998: ch. 7).

> If one has no mercy toward another like himself,
> can he then seek pardon for his own sins? (Sir. 28:2–4)

Knowledge of this background is very instructive. It shows that some of the highest ideals of Jesus were formulated neither de novo nor in opposition to Jewish sages but in keeping with their finest expression.

Further, when Jesus invites, "Come to me, all you that are weary and are carrying heavy burdens, and I will give you rest. Take my yoke upon you, and learn from me; . . . and you will find rest for your souls. For my yoke is easy, and my burden is light" (Matt. 11:28–30), he uses language and a literary form very similar to that of the earlier wisdom teacher:

> Draw near to me, you who are uneducated,
> and lodge in the house of instruction. . . .
> Put your neck under her yoke,
> and let your souls receive instruction;
> it is to be found close by.
> See with your own eyes that I have labored but little
> and found for myself much serenity. (Sir. 51:23, 26–27)

Jesus' use of similar language may have invited the hearers to view him as a teacher of wisdom and of interpretation of Torah and to view attaching themselves to his group of disciples as a kind of attachment to a wisdom school.

Another noteworthy correspondence between sayings attributed to Jesus and the Apocrypha involves the means by which one shows oneself to be a wise investor. In the Book of Tobit, the aged Tobit gives ethical instruction to his son, Tobias:

> If you have many possessions, make your gift from them in proportion; if few, do not be afraid to give according to the little you have. So you will be laying up a good treasure for yourself against the day of necessity. For almsgiving delivers from death and keeps you from going into the Darkness. (Tob. 4:8–10)

Jesus likewise promotes the giving away of possessions to the needy as the means by which to lay up a treasure for oneself: "Sell your possessions, and give alms. Make purses for yourselves that do not wear out, an unfailing treasure in heaven, where no thief comes near and no moth destroys" (Luke 12:33; cf. 18:22). The combination of the paradoxical claim that giving is actually saving in the best way and the rationale drawn from the extreme of human experience (mortal danger in Tobit, survival after death in Luke) suggests that Jesus draws not only on scriptural resources for his promoting of almsgiving but also on the logic of Tobit (whether or not he got this from reading Tobit himself or from hearing teachers who had read Tobit). Again, it shows how deeply rooted Jesus' message was in the ethics of his time.

James, located in Jerusalem for most of his ministry, also appears to be familiar with the sayings of Ben Sira. This is not surprising, since the Epistle of James resembles a wisdom collection more fully than any other book in the New Testament, and the author no doubt enjoyed a broad acquaintance with Jewish wisdom tradition. When James speaks of the impossibility of God tempting human beings to sin, he uses a much older tradition:

> No one, when tempted, should say, "I am being tempted by God"; for God cannot be tempted by evil and he himself tempts no one. But one is tempted by one's own desire, being lured and enticed by it. (James 1:13–14)

> > Do not say, "It was the Lord's doing that I fell away";
> >   for he does not do what he hates.
> > Do not say, "It was he who led me astray";
> >   for he has no need of the sinful. (Sir. 15:11–12; cf. 15:20)

In both, the theological problem of why temptation must exist in a world ruled by an omnipotent and righteous God is solved in precisely the same way: distancing God as the cause or source of any evil and placing the responsibility squarely on the individual person (see Sir. 15:14–17).

Paul's letter to the church in Rome shows that the apostle enjoyed an intimate knowledge of Wisdom of Solomon. The opening indictment of Gentiles in Rom. 1:18–32 reproduces to a large extent the earlier critique of Gentile ignorance of the One God and description of the resulting moral chaos found in Wis. 13:5–10 and 14:22–27 (which the reader is encouraged to read). Paul shares with this author the view that contemplation of creation ought to have led to acknowledgment and worship of the Creator and that idolatry is the cause of all the moral ills of the Gentile world. The correspondences between their lists of these vices are notable. Similarly, Paul's argument for God's sovereignty over human beings in Rom. 9:19–24 reiterates the similar claims of Wisdom of Solomon concerning the impossibility of the creature condemning the actions of the Creator, even using the same image of the potter's rights over the pot (Wis. 12:12; 15:7). Paul also shares with this same author the image of the body as the earthly tent, a perishable thing that weighs down the soul (2 Cor. 5:1, 4; cf. Wis. 9:15).

The author of Hebrews knows of the Maccabean martyrs, those who chose to be executed rather than transgress the Torah during the thick of the Hellenization crisis in 167–164 B.C.E. These, who "were tortured, refusing to accept release, in order to obtain a better resurrection" (Heb. 11:35), are included among the examplars who define what faith looks like in action (see 2 Macc. 7:9; 4 Macc. 9:13–18). Hebrews also shares much in common conceptually with the author of 4 Maccabees, defining faith in similar terms, showing a concern for firmness with regard to the hearers' commitment to God.

Finally, we may note that the author of Jude goes beyond even our Apocrypha to cite verbatim several lines from *1 Enoch*, an apocalypse written down in several parts from the third century B.C.E. possibly to the first century C.E. Jude 14–15 is a direct quotation of *1 Enoch* 1.9:

> And behold! He comes with ten thousands of His holy ones to execute judgment upon all, and to destroy all the ungodly; and to convict all flesh of the works of their ungodliness which they have impiously committed, and of all the hard things which ungodly sinners have spoken against Him.

Such examples could easily be multiplied, particularly if we were to include echoes of shorter phrases or to trace shared concepts and rhetorical commonplaces. It is therefore important for students of the New Testament to pursue familiarity with the contents of the Old Testament Apocrypha, if only in order to know what was in the New Testament authors' library and cultural inheritance. These books constitute a valuable cache of primary texts for deepening our appreciation of the intellectual, theological, rhetorical, and social milieu of early Christianity.

A third reason that impels us to study these writings is that they were formative for early Christian theology, a heritage shared by Protestant, Catholic, and Orthodox Christians. Even early authors who questioned the status of these writings as Scripture per se, such as Origen and Jerome, used the texts in their exposition of the books of the New Testament and in their clarification of Christology, soteriology, and the life of faith. We see this influence beginning within the New Testament as early as the Epistle to the Hebrews, which uses concepts from the depiction of the figure of Wisdom in Wisdom of Solomon to elaborate on the relationship of Jesus, the Son, to God.

> In these last days [God] has spoken to us by a Son, whom he appointed heir of all things, *through whom he also created the worlds. He is the reflection of God's glory and the exact imprint of God's very being*, and he sustains all things by his powerful word. (Heb. 1:2–3)

> Wisdom, *the fashioner of all things*, taught me. . . .
> [Wisdom] is a breath of the power of God, and *a pure emanation of the glory of the Almighty*. . . .
> She is *a reflection of eternal light, a spotless mirror of the working of God, and an image of his goodness*. . . .
> She is an initiate in the knowledge of God
> and *an associate in his works*. (Wis. 7:22, 25–26; 8:4)

The italicized words show the correspondence between these two texts. The author of Hebrews has paraphrased the Jewish text's description of the figure of Wisdom and reconfigured it now as a description of the nature and work of the Son, not only as he was experienced in the flesh but also before and beyond the incarnation.

Moreover, these texts are held to be canonical and fit for public reading in worship by two-thirds of the world's Christians. Out of respect for them and in a spirit of solidarity with brothers and sisters across the world, Protestant Christians would do well to have at least a basic grasp of these texts' meaning and an appreciation for their content, as one might for any widely read devotional or inspirational literature that has exercised a profound influence on Christian thought and culture (e.g., Augustine's *City of God*, à Kempis's *Imitation of Christ*, or Bunyan's *Pilgrim's Progress*).

These benefits become dangers when books of the Apocrypha are ignored. Without the Apocrypha, the modern student of Scripture has a skewed view of the Judaism into which Jesus was born and within which his followers moved. With only the Hebrew Scriptures for comparison, we attempt to place the early Christian movement within a much older form of Judaism and proceed without an adequate awareness that Judaism developed and grew considerably in the five centuries between Malachi and Matthew. We are left without the documentation of the streams of thought and practice that provided continuity, but also development, between the Testaments. This problematic approach to the New Testament was astutely criticized nearly a century ago by W. M. F. Petrie (1909: 168): "As we should certainly be wrong in attributing to teachers of our own day all the change from the mediaeval position, so we are equally wrong if we ascribe to Christianity every fresh thought that is not to be found in the prophets."[5] In sum, we need to pour ourselves into these books at least, and indeed would do well eventually to look at several more besides, in order to arrive at a proper understanding of the Jewish environment of early Christian thought, community life, and ethics.

The Apocrypha and the Canon

In all that has been said here, no suggestion has been made that Protestant Christians or Jews should revise the limits of their canons. Fundamentally, the need for studying the Apocrypha is not based on decisions about their status as Scripture. It is based on the fact that these texts open up to our view the three centuries concerning which the Protestant and Jewish canonical Scriptures are almost completely silent. In so doing, they become indispensable for a more accurate grasp of the world of the New Testament, as well as the world of emerging rabbinic Judaism.

Nevertheless, the issue of canon is not completely irrelevant. It is only because of ongoing canonical debates, and differing views regarding the canon,

---

5. I am indebted to Mr. Henri Goulet for bringing this quotation to my attention.

that we can identify these books as a discrete corpus. The principle of selection for the Apocrypha, and hence the discussion here of these specific books (and the exclusion of other vitally important resources for the authors and environment of the New Testament, such as *1 Enoch, Psalms of Solomon,* and *Testaments of the Twelve Patriarchs*), rests in the discussion of their status as Scripture, their secondary status as deuterocanonicals, or their exclusion. To use a gross oversimplification, if it were not for Augustine, these books might have been lost to the church; if it were not for Jerome, we might never have distinguished them as a collection separate from the Old Testament.

The church's interest in these books sets the Apocrypha apart from the rest of the material written during the same time period. The early church held on to these books while Jewish communities forgot most of them, preserving them carefully and conscientiously whereas so many other Jewish texts of the period survived more by chance than design. In so doing, the church set them apart from the remainder of noncanonical Jewish literature as texts possessing the greatest value and even authority for the disciple. This fact of history demands our attention and justifies our treating them apart from the Pseudepigrapha, the sectarian documents among the Dead Sea Scrolls, and even the bodies of literature left to us by Philo and Josephus.

The discussion of the canonicity of the books of the Apocrypha in early Judaism and early Christianity has been fraught with difficulties. First and foremost, there is the very term "canonical," for the word "canon" applied to a set of books is a Christian innovation of the fourth century (Eissfeldt 1964: 560). Earlier than this, one finds terms such as "sacred writings," "scriptures," books that "defile the hands" (that is, books that are sacred and communicate sacral power to the hands of those who touch them, which must be washed away). Among the rabbis of the late-first and second centuries, one finds discussions of whether or not certain books, such as Esther, Ecclesiastes, and Ben Sira, "defile the hands," that is, are holy in a way that other books are not. So the very use of the term "canonical" when investigating these early communities is already misleading, although unavoidable.

Second, many mistakenly assume that an author's *use* of a work implies that the author and addressees regarded the work as canonical.[6] To say that the author of Jude regarded *1 Enoch* as canonical simply because he quotes it (and appears to have accepted it as indeed ancient, coming from the hand of Enoch!) is a fallacious conclusion. All that can be said about Jude's use of this pseudepigraphon is that he regarded it as a valuable resource for the exhortation and edification of Christians, a suitable quotation from an ancient authority to advance his rhetorical goals.[7]

---

6. This has been helpfully critiqued in Beckwith 1985: 435.
7. Quotation from an ancient text was an important and basic argumentative strategy in the Greek and Roman eras. The opinion of a respected voice from the past carried great weight.

Third, there has been confusion between "canonical" and "authoritative." A book does not have to be canonical or even claim to be inspired in order to be authoritative for a community of readers. Indeed, it is perhaps from the aspect of the "authoritative" and degrees of authority that one might more authentically approach the question of the Apocrypha in the early church and synagogue. Although the early rabbis discussed what books "defile the hands"—that is, what books were at the core of their access to the divine mind—this distinction does not restrict what books are considered authoritative. As commentary on the holy texts, the Mishnah (ca. 200 C.E.) and the Talmud (compiled by the sixth century C.E.) remain authoritative for the rabbinic Jewish community, even though not at the same level as the biblical texts. Conversely, lack of canonicity—even having canonicity denied or rejected—does not imply lack of authority. This can be seen in the use of sayings from Ben Sira quoted by the rabbis in their debates long after the question of Ben Sira's canonicity was answered in the negative.

If we turn to the Jewish sect at Qumran, for another example, we find a community that appears to distinguish between classical authoritative texts, namely, the books of the Old Testament (notably, Esther is lacking at Qumran, a book disputed also in rabbinic circles), and many other texts, some shared beyond Qumran (like *1 Enoch* and *Jubilees*), some peculiar to Qumran (like the *Community Rule*, the *Thanksgiving Psalms*, and the *War Scroll*). This distinction is reflected in the way in which the sacred texts are written on more durable materials, the way they are quoted, and the fact that these texts become the basis for commentaries—a sign that these texts are, in some way, a special collection set apart from and above others. Nevertheless, *Jubilees* and the *Community Rule* were highly authoritative, regulating the calendar of Jewish feasts and Sabbaths observed at Qumran and regulating multiple aspects of community life there as well. Functionally, these "extrabiblical" texts carried as much weight as biblical texts. Also at Qumran, divine inspiration was not bound to what we would call canonicity. The Teacher of Righteousness, the mysterious figure who gave the sect its distinctive form, also gave his community *the* inspired, authoritative commentary on several of the Scriptures. The existence of the genre of commentary, still, attests to the distinction between a core collection of texts and a secondary body of literature that is derivative in some way from that core.

A fourth challenge in this discussion is somewhat more specific and technical, having to do with the differences between the Hebrew and Greek forms of the same canonical book (as it would come to be called). Daniel and Esther, for example, exist in two forms: the shorter, Hebrew texts and the longer, Greek texts. If Daniel, then, is considered sacred, in which form will it be thus considered? There is evidence that the Greek-speaking Jew, while not regarding books such as 1 Maccabees and Ben Sira as sacred or as part of that core of authoritative texts, would nevertheless regard the Greek form of Daniel this way. This is seen from the fact that translations of Daniel produced by Jews in the first centuries B.C.E. and C.E. (notably, the reading that came to be attributed to Theodotion, a Greek-speaking Jew of the late first century C.E.) contain the additions rather than follow what we now know as the Masoretic Text. Baruch and Letter of Jeremiah, moreover, were seen as appendices to the Book of Jeremiah and so might easily have been regarded by Greek-speaking Jews as part of the core body of texts (canon) (see Beckwith 1985: 339–41).[8]

A fifth persistent factor that has clouded this discussion is the concept of an "Alexandrian Jewish canon" of Scripture that was broader than the Palestinian Jewish canon. This is based on a lack of clarity about the meaning of the term "Septuagint" and can be illustrated by considering a severe misstatement of the facts (Oikonomos 1991: 17 [cf. Constantelos 1997: xxvii]):

> Both Judaism and Christianity began by simply using the deuterocanonical writings as part of the biblical canon. It is hard to say when this kind of usage began; it was certainly not later than the translation of the Septuagint (from 285–247 B.C.) since this translation, made by Jews for Jews and Gentiles, includes the deuterocanonical writings.

The author of this quotation has assumed that the "Septuagint" in the sense of that collection of texts known from Codices Alexandrinus, Sinaiticus, and Vaticanus (or in the sense of the critical editions available today) was the "Septuagint" of the Jewish community of the third century B.C.E. This is, however, a grave misstep, because the work undertaken in the third century B.C.E. in Alexandria involved only the Greek translation of the Pentateuch (clearly the scope envisioned by *Letter of Aristeas*). Moreover, the quotation involves its author in a paradox: it would be impossible for the third-century-B.C.E. version of the Septuagint to contain the Apocrypha books, since they were all written between 185 B.C.E. and 100 C.E. (with the possible exception of Tobit, which may predate the second century B.C.E.)! Also telling in the argument against an Alexandrian Jewish canon is that Philo, the Jewish commentator in Alexandria par excellence, never quotes from the Apocrypha (Beckwith 1985: 384). Indeed, his focus is overwhelmingly on the Torah, with occasional references to the Prophets, Psalms, and other texts that would become known as the Jewish canon.

The "Septuagint" codices mentioned above cannot be used as evidence for an Alexandrian Jewish canon that included the Apocrypha.[9] These manuscripts are fourth- and fifth-century Christian works, fail to agree on the ex-

---

8. This is simply an expanded version of the typical question of Old Testament textual tradition facing the modern student of the Bible, who frequently finds that the authors of the New Testament used the Greek version (the LXX) as Scripture rather than the Hebrew version. One place where this difference appears most dramatically is in Heb. 10:5–10, where the author makes a stunning theological point that is possible *only* on the basis of the Greek text.

9. This has been decisively refuted in Sundberg 1964.

tent of the extra books, and seem to have been compiled more with convenience of reference in mind than as the standards of canonical versus noncanonical books (the fact that one even contained, at one point, *Psalms of Solomon* strongly suggests this). As "church books," they may have sought to contain what was useful rather than what was strictly canonical. These manuscripts do bear witness, however, to usage in the church in the fourth century (differing from one region to another or even within a single region). The fact that the books of the Apocrypha are interspersed among the (other) Old Testament books also suggests that the communities that produced these manuscripts did not share a consciousness of a closed Old Testament canon corresponding to the rabbinic canon. With these considerations in mind, we can begin to sort out the history of the use and status of the Apocrypha books in the early synagogue and early church.

By the second century B.C.E., there is clear evidence of an awareness of a three-part set of sacred, authoritative writings. The prologue to the Greek translation of Ben Sira, provided by Ben Sira's grandson, speaks of the grandfather's zeal in studying "the Law and the Prophets and the other books of our ancestors" and notes the difference between the Hebrew original and Greek translations of "the Law itself, the Prophecies, and the rest of the books." We find a similar way of referring to the core authoritative texts in Luke 24:44, where Jesus exclaims, "Everything written about me in the law of Moses, the prophets, and the psalms must be fulfilled." Readers of Matthew will be familiar with the frequent reference to the first two parts of this core: "the law and the prophets" (Matt. 5:17; 7:12; 22:40).

It would seem, then, that well before the turn of the era there was a consensus that the five books of Moses (the Law) and the corpus of Prophets (which may have contained the "historical books," referred to by Jews as "the earlier, or former, prophets," but which did not contain Daniel) were held up as the core body of sacred texts.[10] These texts gave Jews their identity and heritage, providing a fixed point of reference through centuries of change. Because of their importance, their antiquity, and their universal use and acceptance by Jews, there would never be a question concerning their place at the core.

Alongside the Law and the Prophets stood the less well defined "rest of the books"—what would come to be called the Writings (*Kethubim*). Luke 24 suggests that the psalms had precedence of place in this collection, which is

---

10. Ben Sira himself provides evidence for the shape of the Prophets section. In his praise of the ancestors, he speaks of the major figures known from Joshua through 2 Kings and mentions Isaiah, Jeremiah, Ezekiel, and "the twelve prophets" (Sir. 49:10), thus showing an awareness already of a single grouping of the minor prophets. The absence of Daniel from the list is telling: though the court tales may well have been told earlier, Daniel in its present form dates from the Maccabean period and was not known to Ben Sira. The fact that Daniel is finally placed in the third division of the Jewish Scriptures, the Writings, also bears witness to its later date, since the body of the Prophets had already taken its final shape.

not surprising given their importance for the corporate and individual worship life of Jews. The discovery of the Psalms Scroll at Qumran with a 151st psalm (as well as some fourteen other previously unknown hymns interspersed throughout the collection) suggests that we should not assume this collection to have been completely fixed in the first century B.C.E. Proverbs and Job also were likely to have received high esteem rather early. It is mainly about books in this category that we find discussion or debate in early rabbinic literature. The Mishnah shows that even as late as the discussions of the rabbis at Jamnia (in the 90s C.E.) there was debate concerning the status of Esther, Ecclesiastes, Song of Songs, and even the prophetic book Ezekiel—that is, whether or not they were sacred writings that would "defile the hands." The Mishnah records debates toward even the end of the second century C.E. about Song of Songs and Ecclesiastes (*m. Yadayim* 3.5) (de Lange 1978: 8). Esther appears to have been debated even longer.

By the end of the first century C.E., we find an awareness of a closed canon in Judaism. When Josephus enumerated the sacred books at twenty-two (*Against Apion* 1.38) and the author of 4 Ezra (= chs. 3–14 of 2 Esdras) enumerated them at twenty-four (4 Ezra 14:45), they gave expression to the conviction that there was a fixed number of sacred Scriptures (even though that precise number would continue to be debated for another century).[11] In these enumerations, the twelve Minor Prophets are counted as one book (or scroll), Ezra and Nehemiah count as a single book, and the dual books of Samuel, Kings, and Chronicles each count as a single book.

At this point we may inquire into the status of the books of the Apocrypha in Judaism. Among the rabbis, only Ben Sira received attention as a possible candidate for a sacred text, but the only evidence we have is negative (*t. Yadayim* 2.13). It was read and quoted by rabbis and apparently continued to carry weight in their debates, but it was not to be held in the same esteem as the older, sacred texts. Baruch also commanded great respect, even being read in some synagogues. Baruch's association with Jeremiah (Baruch was the prophet's scribe and held by some to share in the prophetic gift) gave the text ascribed to him a special status in the eyes of many readers, but it too failed to achieve the recognition of a sacred book.

In Palestine at least, none of the other Apocrypha books attracted the attention of rabbis debating sacred status. Judith and 1 Maccabees were, of course, popular stories linked with the celebration of Hanukkah. Their survival in Jewish culture, if not in canon, was assured by their connection with this festival. The Dead Sea Scrolls include five copies of Tobit, two fragments

11. Many scholars reconcile Josephus's count of twenty-two with the more common count of twenty-four by asserting that he counted Lamentations as part of Jeremiah and Ruth as part of Judges. While this is quite possible, it is equally possible that he and his circles held fewer books among the Writings to be sacred. Josephus's division of books into the historical/prophetic corpus and writings was also different from what became standard, several writings having to be included among his prophets.

of Ben Sira (to which can be added the fuller fragments found at Masada and at the Cairo Geniza), one copy of Letter of Jeremiah (in Greek), and Psalm 151 at the conclusion of the Psalms Scroll. This remains evidence of use but does not tell us of the status of these texts. They were sufficiently valued to be copied, studied, and preserved, but nothing in the other texts composed at Qumran indicates their status (in the way that the *Community Rule* indicates the binding authority of *Jubilees*, for example).

The impression one gets from the foregoing discussion is that of ripples in a pond, with the Torah standing unambiguously at the center (the rock dropped from above, as it were), the Prophets forming the next ripple, and then several ripples of "the rest of the books," some of which stand in great esteem (like Psalms and Proverbs), some of which lack sufficient esteem to avoid being disputed later (like Esther and Ecclesiastes), and others of which are pushed farthest out from the central core. Although this last group may be read, studied, and even cited, they are not at the center of the community's reflection upon itself, its calling, its identity.

Many suggestions have been offered for the failure of the Apocrypha to rise to the status of sacred Scripture in Palestine. One may exclude works written originally in Greek outright (such as Wisdom of Solomon, 3 and 4 Maccabees), since these are obviously products of Diaspora Jews writing in the Hellenistic and Roman periods. Cohen (1987: 178) suggests that a major factor is the Jewish community's awareness during this period of living in a postclassical age, in a time when the high-water mark of Jewish literature is long past. The literature of the Jewish classical age is held in greater esteem than more recent imitations, commentaries, and derivative works and rather naturally emerges as canon.[12]

This awareness of living in a "silver age," as it were, is articulated in Jewish texts as the cessation of the prophetic voice (see 1 Macc. 4:46; 9:27; 14:41; Josephus, *Against Apion* 1.40–41; and perhaps indirectly the fact that Ben Sira's inspiration derives mainly from study of classical Jewish [and other] texts). The conviction that the prophetic voice had ceased during the reign of Artaxerxes probably accounts for the tendency to view as canonical only what derives (or purports to derive) from that period. Hence, an Ecclesiastes or Daniel could sneak by, and a Baruch could command some consideration, but a 1 Maccabees or Ben Sira—obviously dating from well after the prophetic voice had ceased—would not come to be reckoned as canonical. Others, the origins of which could not be confirmed (Judith, Tobit) or which are obviously derivative works (like Letter of Jeremiah or Prayer of Manasseh), likewise did not command serious consideration for ranking alongside the Law, Prophets, and Writings. This is the logic found in the ruling in *t. Ya-*

---

12. Chapter 6 of Cohen 1987 offers a fine discussion of the emergence of an Old Testament canon.

dayim 2.13: "The book of Ben Sira and all books written from that point on do not defile the hands."

Beyond this, there is only speculation as to why particular books failed to command greater assent and esteem. Orlinsky (1974: 277) suggests that certain apocrypha failed to become Scripture in Palestine because something in them violated Pharisaic-rabbinic halakhah (such as Judith not having Achior immersed as well as circumcised at his conversion or Tobit's reflection of the practice of the bride's father, rather than the groom, writing the marriage contract). Another explanation may be found in the Jewish response to Hellenism, the Hellenization crisis, and the Hasmonean (Maccabean) dynasty. First, in the wake of the political messianism and spirit of revolt that resulted in the desolation of both the temple and the population of Judea, the adulation of the family of Judas Maccabeus must have seemed dangerous. A new model for the messianic era was needed to avoid such active and self-destructive revolt against the Gentile empire. With the revolts of 115–117 C.E. in the Diaspora and the rise of Simon ben Kosibah and the renewal of political messianism around him in 130 C.E., the need to distance Judaism from all forms of divinely legitimated revolt was all the more urgent. Hence, the ideology of 1 and 2 Maccabees was not deemed safe for the survival of Judaism. Second, rabbinic Judaism sought to define itself around Torah and reflection upon Torah and not around the Hellenization crisis and the successful Maccabean Revolt (the focus of much of the Apocrypha), especially in light of the widespread disillusionment with the Hasmonean and Herodian dynasties. These factors may well have motivated a turning away from the whole intertestamental period and back to the Torah and the prophets of Judaism's classical age.

Evidence for Diaspora Judaism is more difficult to find. We have already noted the problematic assumption that the Christian collection commonly called the Septuagint actually reflects Diaspora Jewish views of Scripture (see Anderson 1970: 145–49). The fact that neither Philo nor any New Testament author (most of whom wrote in the Diaspora) unambiguously quotes a text from the Apocrypha as Scripture also weighs heavily against this assumption. The evidence from Josephus is also striking: while he knows 1 Esdras and 1 Maccabees, he lists a canon similar to that embraced in Palestine at the same time. G. W. Anderson has even suggested that the Alexandrian Jewish community had more restrictive views of canon than their Palestinian coreligionists held, elevating the Torah above all others as inspired and normative, while being less clear about the Prophets and the Writings. Certainly, Philo's preoccupation with Torah (with no concern to apply his allegorical interpretations to any passage outside this corpus) might be seen to support this thesis. The Samaritans, a Jewish sect familiar from the pages of the New Testament, took the most extreme view, holding only to the Torah as canon. In sum, perhaps the most balanced statement would be to affirm again the central place of Torah for Diaspora Jewish communities, followed by the former and later

Prophets, followed at last by the Writings. If there was a special emphasis on Torah (with a corresponding de-emphasis on the third part of the Scriptures), this might help to explain how other books could rise to prominence alongside the Writings. If the lines of the normative were most clearly drawn at the inmost circle, the distinction between the Writings and what would come to be called the Apocrypha might the more easily have been blurred.

Regarding the early church, we find that although the books of the Apocrypha are not recited as Scripture in the New Testament, Jesus, Paul, James, and others show their familiarity with the contents of much of the Apocrypha, especially Ben Sira, Wisdom, Tobit, and 1 and 2 Maccabees. It may be that these resonances, noticed by early Christians who came into contact also with, say, Wisdom of Solomon, contributed to the status that Wisdom of Solomon enjoyed in the church. At the end of the first century and beginning of the second, Christian authors refer more and more to these texts and even ascribe to them the status of Scripture (shown usually in the way the quotation is introduced, as in "as it is written"). Thus, the *Didache*, a church manual written at the turn of the first century, paraphrases Tob. 4:15 (*Didache* 1.2; this is the negative form of the Golden Rule) and Sir. 4:31 (*Didache* 4.5; an instruction about almsgiving) as rules binding for Christians. The pseudonymous *Epistle of Barnabas* quotes as "another of the prophets" 4 Ezra (= chs. 3–14 of 2 Esdras). The quotation (*Epistle of Barnabas* 12.1) is a compilation of 4 Ezra 4:33 and 5:5, embellished with a phrase whose source cannot be identified. Here, the fairly recent Ezra apocalypse rises to instant esteem as a prophetic witness to the cross, "when blood drips from a tree." *First Clement*, written by Clement of Rome around 96 C.E., incorporates Wis. 2:24 (*1 Clement* 3.4) and 12:12 (*1 Clement* 27.5). In the former passage, Clement assumes Wis. 2:24 to provide accurate information about "envy" as the origin of death and uses this tradition to interpret the significance of the story of Cain and Abel. Polycarp of Smyrna (*To the Philippians* 10.2) has learned from Tobit (4:10; 12:9) that "almsgiving delivers from death." Irenaeus accepted the Greek form of Daniel, with its additions, as the canonical prophet (*Adversus haereses* 4.26.3), as would Origen (along with Esther and Jeremiah, to which were linked Baruch and Letter of Jeremiah). Clement of Alexandria (d. 216 C.E.) quotes Wisdom and Ben Sira as Scripture; the Muratorian Canon and Tertullian both indicate an acceptance of Wisdom as Scripture.[13]

This broadening of the scriptural base in the early church extended even past what we call the Apocrypha. Held in especially high regard was *1 Enoch*. The *Epistle of Barnabas* quotes *1 Enoch* 89.56 specifically as Scripture ("for Scripture says" [*Epistle of Barnabas* 16.5]) as a prophecy of the destruction of the temple in 70 C.E. Tertullian argued that *1 Enoch* be accepted as Scripture (*De cultu feminarum* 1.3). His criteria are worth noting: the book's usefulness

---

13. The Muratorian Canon (or Fragment) includes Wisdom within its list of New Testament books, indirectly showing evidence of a reluctance to include it in the Old Testament.

for edification, particularly where testimonies about Jesus are concerned, and its use by a New Testament author argue for its authority. He even suggests that its absence from the Jewish Scriptures is due to its usefulness as a witness to Jesus.

Origen, the influential Alexandrian Christian from the first part of the third century, provides an important window into the status of the Apocrypha books in his *Letter to Africanus*. Africanus had raised suspicions about the tale of Susanna in the Greek text of Daniel (which would have included the Additions to Daniel: Susanna, Bel and the Dragon, and Prayer of Azariah and Song of the Three Young Men). He notes that this episode contains puns that work only in Greek and thus would not work in a Hebrew original, if such existed. Hence, he questions the episode's place in the text of Daniel and suggests that it ought to be excised. Origen, who by this point has had extensive experience comparing the Hebrew to the available Greek translations as he compiled his *Hexapla*, replies first by admitting the differences between Daniel in the Greek and in the Hebrew, citing the above listed additions as such. He goes on to do the same not only with Esther (see the chapter on the Additions to Esther) but also with Job, Jeremiah, Genesis, and Exodus. With these latter books, however, it is no longer a question of apocryphal episodes but of differences in arrangement of material and the absence or addition of verses or even paragraphs in one version or the other.[14] With regard to the crucial question, namely, whether or not the church is to follow the text accepted by the Jews, Origen says this:

> So, then, when we notice such things, are we forthwith to reject as spurious the copies in use in our Churches, and enjoin the brotherhood to put away the sacred books current among them, and to coax the Jews, and persuade them to give us copies which shall be untampered with, and free from forgery?! Are we to suppose that the same Providence that in the sacred Scriptures has ministered to the edification of all the Churches of Christ, had no thought for those bought with a price, for whom Christ died; whom, although His Son, God who is love spared not, but gave Him up for us all, that with Him He might freely give us all things? In all these cases consider whether it would not be well to remember the words, "Thou shalt not remove the ancient landmarks which thy fathers have set." (*Epistula ad Africanum* 4–5)

Origen cannot countenance abandoning the text that has been known to and used by the Christian church for two centuries. He puts forward two arguments for accepting the form of the text known and used by the church as canonical: God's providential care for the new Israel and respect for the practice

---

14. Jeremiah is an important witness to the fact that the Greek translations did not always end up being longer and hence include "noncanonical" material. The Greek text of Jeremiah is only seven-eighths the length of the Hebrew, and it is quite likely that it is the Hebrew text that has undergone imaginative expansion at certain points.

that has already been established in the church. A similar logic undergirds his views on Tobit:

> Tobias (as also Judith), we ought to notice, the Jews do not use. They are not even found in the Hebrew Apocrypha, as I learned from the Jews themselves. However, since the Churches use Tobias, you must know that even in the captivity some of the captives were rich and well to do. (*Epistula ad Africanum* 13)

Usage by the church determines the authority and reliability of Tobit, which Origen can then use as evidence for a particular point he wants to make against Africanus's criticism of Susanna.

Origen's student Athanasius makes his views on the extent of the Old Testament canon known in the thirty-ninth of his *Festal Letters*. In this he enumerates as part of the canonical Old Testament only the books known also from the Hebrew canon. What is striking about his list is that Baruch and Letter of Jeremiah are listed as appendices to Jeremiah and therefore as part of the canon. It can be inferred from Origen and Athanasius that the early church, though aware of differences of textual tradition between the Hebrew and the Greek, was nevertheless rather uniformly reading the longer forms of Daniel, Esther, and Jeremiah as canonical Scriptures. Tobit, Wisdom, and Judith were also recommended for edification, but there was not yet the same uniform practice of the churches in accepting these as authoritative (Beckwith 1985: 394–95). Melito of Sardis also produces a list of Old Testament books coinciding with the rabbinic canon (except for the omission of Esther; the list is preserved in Eusebius, *Historia ecclesiastica* 4.26.7). These voices express reserve concerning the status of the Apocrypha,[15] even while other voices, such as Clement and Tertullian, had promoted the canonical status of many of these books.

The debate concerning the status of these books became part of the permanent tradition of the church universal on account of the work of two weighty authorities in the church: Jerome, who was responsible in large measure for the translation of the Vulgate, the Latin Bible that would be used by the Western church for more than a millennium, and Augustine, whose theological works became foundational for Christian theology. In order to undertake the task of Bible translation, Jerome devoted himself to learning Hebrew, refusing to rely merely on the Greek version of the Old Testament. He undertook these studies in Palestine, moreover, under a rabbi. In his prefaces to the books of the Bible, therefore, he notes carefully the differences between the Hebrew and the Greek texts—thus making clear the additions to books like Daniel, Esther, and Jeremiah—as well as between the Hebrew and Septuagint canons. He advocated a division of the broader Old Testament canon into

---

15. It can be assumed, however, that they still followed the longer, Greek text of Daniel, Esther, and Jeremiah. In the case of Athanasius, the latter is made explicit.

works that were "canonical," which would be used to inform doctrine and practice, and works that were "ecclesiastical," which would be read in churches and used for edification but not for the confirmation of doctrine. He was joined in this regard by his near-contemporary Rufinus (see Rufinus, *Commentarius in symbolum apostolorum* 37–38) (Sparks 1970: 533–34).

Augustine vehemently opposed Jerome's attempts to reform the more popular usage of the church. He advocated following the Septuagint text, in part due to its common use in the Eastern churches and Augustine's desire to maintain unity with them. He also advocated quite explicitly the broader canon of the Old Testament, which was to include Tobit, Judith, 1 and 2 Maccabees, Wisdom, and Ben Sira (*De doctrina christiana* 2.8.12–13), and one would assume the additions to Esther, Daniel, and Jeremiah (which were not distinguished by Augustine as additions but as natural parts of those books). Augustine knew, however, that not all churches recognized this fuller canon, and so he instructed his readers to allocate to the various books authority in keeping with the number of churches that regarded them as canonical together with the respective weight and authority of those churches (i.e., a deuterocanonical book would have great authority either if the more important churches regarded it as Scripture or if the majority of churches did so). Moreover, Augustine used the Apocrypha texts in the same manner as the other Scriptures. The frequency of his use of Wisdom and Ben Sira, for example, in discussing such weighty matters as the Trinity, shows that he regarded them as quite suitable for establishing points of doctrine.

Augustine's authority resulted in the affirmation of his canon by several church councils, including the Council of Carthage (397), and in the more general acceptance of these books as canonical. This view was never unanimous, however. Many Catholic ecclesiasts questioned the place of the books of the Apocrypha in the Old Testament canon. Jerome's position was followed by Gregory the Great, John Damascene, Hugh of St. Victor, and Nicholas of Lyra (Collins 1997a: xxxi). The last of these is remembered to have influenced Luther's own thinking on the Apocrypha. Cardinals Ximenes and Cajetan, both contemporaries of Luther, also promoted a distinction between the Hebrew canon and the Apocrypha, books which they held to be useful for edification but not for establishing official doctrine (Collins 1997a: xxxi–xxxii).

The question of the status of the Apocrypha was brought to the forefront once more, however, by the Protestant Reformers. The principle of *sola Scriptura* (according to which Scripture alone, and not church tradition, was to be the source for all doctrine) and doctrinal objections to the contemporary use of the Apocrypha texts in the Roman Catholic church motivated a new inquiry into the canonical status of the disputed books. These doctrinal debates mainly concerned the great emphasis on works of mercy in Tobit as having salvific effect (though this is not a necessary reading of Tob. 4:7–11) and the use of 2 Macc. 12:43–45 as a legitimation of the saying of Masses and prayers on behalf of the dead.

The weight of these doctrinal concerns continues to be invoked as evangelical Protestants, especially, speak of the Apocrypha. To consider but one example: "Since evangelicals strongly insist that their beliefs and doctrine be grounded in Scripture, to exclude the Apocrypha is to unseat, say, the doctrine of purgatory, which finds precious little support outside the Apocrypha" (Carson 1997: xlvi). It would be a mistake, however, to overstress this point. First, 2 Maccabees does not necessarily support the idea of purgatory, although it does support the thought of making atonement for the deceased and thus ensuring their experience of the resurrection of the just. Paul encounters a similar practice in Corinth, however, without stopping to correct it (and he was hardly reticent about correcting belief and practice in those churches; see 1 Cor. 15:29). Additionally, the words of Jesus in Matt. 25:31–46 or Luke 12:32–34 and 14:13–14 could be adduced with equal effectiveness as those in Tobit 4, were one inclined to promote works of mercy as having saving efficacy. The Apocrypha as a whole have suffered considerably on account of the excesses of interpretation applied to but a few passages. Nevertheless, the New Testament has been subjected to far more outrageous interpretations, and few would countenance throwing out that baby with the bathwater.

Both Andreas Bodenstein (better known as Karlstadt, after his birthplace) and Luther show exceptional reserve in dealing with the Apocrypha. Karlstadt follows Jerome's distinction (also promoted by Wyclif in the prologue to his English translation of the Vulgate) between books suitable for use as the basis of doctrine and books to be read for moral instruction. Karlstadt shows a more critical side when it comes to Baruch, 1 and 2 Esdras, and the Additions to Daniel, suggesting that these are worthy of the censor's knife but is quite positive in his assessment of the edifying value of the other Apocrypha (Metzger and Murphy, eds., 1991: vii). In his German Bible, Luther removes the Apocrypha, including the apocryphal Additions to Daniel, to a section between the Testaments. His verdict on them, found in his preface to the Apocrypha, echoes Jerome: "These are books that, though not esteemed like the holy Scriptures, are still both useful and good to read."

Calvin was more forthright in his rejection of the Apocrypha from canonical consideration (though he was nonetheless well read in them). Following his lead, the framers of the Westminster Confession (1646) stated, "The books commonly called the Apocrypha, not being of divine inspiration, are no part of the canon of the Scripture; and therefore are of no authority in the Church of God, nor to be in any otherwise approved, or made use of, than other human writings." This statement relegates the Apocrypha to the level of human writings as opposed to divinely inspired Scriptures; it should be noted, however, that use of Apocrypha is not proscribed. Indeed, the Westminster Confession's statement might be seen to agree with Jerome's, Wyclif's, and

Luther's judgment that these texts may be used as edifying literature, just as one would use any devotional classic.

In response to the positions advanced by these Reformers, as well as to quiet doubts about the extent of the canon raised by voices within the Catholic church, the Council of Trent in 1546 ruled all the books of the Apocrypha canonical (this would not include 3 and 4 Maccabees, Prayer of Manasseh, or 1 and 2 Esdras; the last three still appear in an appendix to the Vulgate, however). This largely put an end to all debate within the Roman Catholic church and is the practice reflected today.

A peculiarly Protestant innovation was the printing of Bibles without the Apocrypha—a move made not even by Luther or by the printers of the first editions of the King James Version. This went far to actualize and even radicalize Protestant opinion about (or against) the Apocrypha, which came rather quickly to be lost to the view of the devout Protestant, except in the Anglican and Lutheran traditions, which continued to draw from these books for lectionaries and special services.

The place of the Apocrypha in the Eastern Orthodox churches has also been rather varied. Indeed, important synods and councils, including the Trullan Council (619), seem to show a great deal of toleration for local custom and an unwillingness to impose a decision about the status of these texts. That is to say, if a particular see (episcopal region) viewed them as canonical, that was a venerable position; if another see viewed them as "permitted to be read" but not canonical, that also would be respected. The tendency in modern Greek Orthodox churches is to view the books as canonical. Perhaps the most prominent of these books is Wisdom of Solomon, which is as closely woven into Greek Orthodox liturgies as Psalms (Constantelos 1997: xxvii–xxix).

Among Protestant churches today, the status of the Apocrypha remains varied. In the Anglican communion, including the Episcopal church, readings from the Apocrypha are not uncommon in the Sunday lectionary, the daily lectionary, and the lists of possible readings for special offices such as funerals and weddings. Several of the canticles (scriptural hymns) used during the service of Morning Prayer are taken from the Apocrypha (notably, Prayer of Manasseh and Song of the Three Young Men). The sixth article from the Articles of Religion, the closest thing we find to a "Confession" in the Anglican church, includes a clear statement concerning the Apocrypha: "And the other Books (as Hierome saith) the Church doth read for example of life and instruction of manners; but yet doth it not apply them to establish any doctrine." The article then lists all the books of the Apocrypha except 3 and 4 Maccabees. The use of the Apocrypha entered a great recession during the eighteenth and nineteenth centuries but experienced a resurgence in the early twentieth century as part of the Oxford Movement and the renewal of appreciation for the church's Catholic heritage (Callaway 1997: xxxix).

The Apocrypha are not represented, however, in the common lectionary used by United Methodists, Presbyterians, and other Protestant denominations or in the Lutheran lectionary (although Song of the Three Young Men is retained as a canticle). As one leaves these mainline denominations for the more independent, evangelical, or charismatic churches, no trace is left of the Apocrypha. As the reader will by now have surmised, this book is written from the perspective of Jerome, Wyclif, Luther, and the sixth Article of Religion of the Anglican church: the conviction that the Apocrypha, while not of the status of sacred Scripture, have much to teach us about God, ethics, challenges to faithful living, and the developments in Jewish history, culture, and thought that provide the matrix for the early church. Other texts do as well but the Apocrypha have preeminence among them on account of the high regard the church has had for them throughout the millennia; and the fact that two of the three major branches of Christianity regard them as sufficiently important to be included in every printed Bible continues to witness to this importance.

Instructive in this regard is the publication by Collins Publishers of the *Common Bible*, by the United Bible Societies of interconfessional editions of the Bible containing the Apocrypha between the Testaments, and by Oxford University Press and HarperCollins of major study edition Bibles including the Apocrypha (expanded to include 1 and 2 Esdras, Prayer of Manasseh, and 3 and 4 Maccabees), which allows Greek Orthodox, Roman Catholic, and Protestant all to use the same edition. The proliferation of such Bibles with the Apocrypha also has the advantage of inviting Protestant Christians to become more familiar with their content. Including them in the printed edition is a reminder of their historic importance for the church from its inception and an opportunity for the Christian to have ready access to these edifying texts. Placing the Apocrypha between the Testaments is a reminder that they have always stood at a second level of authority in the church taken as a whole. It is also a visible expression of the conviction that God's people have always been left with a witness to God's Self, the way to live before God, and the hope that God gives—even if the prophetic voice had a long hiatus, the people of faith still had ongoing, living witnesses to their God.

This leads us back to our purposes in studying them here: not to reconsider the question of canonicity, but to get deeper into the world of Judaism at the turn of the era and into the matrix of early Christianity. In the words of D. A. Carson, "However strongly evangelicals, as part of the larger Protestant tradition, reject the Apocrypha as Scripture, they can no more dismiss this corpus from all consideration than they can write off the world and culture into which the Christ was born, and in which the New Testament was written" (Carson 1997: xlvii).

I would also emphasize at this point, however, that the value of the Old Testament Apocrypha is not merely historical. These texts have not only informed people of faith but also have inspired them throughout the millennia.

Many of the ethical ideals taken up by Jesus and his disciples and promoted in the New Testament find their roots here and so are reinforced and strengthened by the reading of them. But even more, these texts add fuel to the fire in the soul sparked and fed by the canon shared by all Christians. The zeal to walk faithfully before God in the face of adversity, the commitment to choose obedience to God over succumbing to the passions or weaknesses of the flesh, the experience of God's forgiveness and expectation of God's deliverance—all these are strengthened by these texts, which one can approach with confidence at least as the best devotional literature to have withstood the test of time.

Historical Context

2

"The Yoke of the Gentiles"

Critical historical research continuously disproves the maxim that "hindsight is 20–20." Our view into the past is also a view through a glass darkly. Archaeological, epigraphic, and numismatic remains, where these exist, are subject to a wide variety of interpretation. Literary sources reflecting the history of a particular people and period do so through the lens of their authors' own biases and ideologies. Frequently, yawning gaps exist with no reliable evidence for the reconstruction of spans of decades or even a whole century. The modern historian can easily fall into one of two traps. On the one hand, extreme skepticism and caution can leave one with no picture of the contours of a period; on the other hand, one may be so intent on creating a picture of "the way it was" that one will ignore the contradictions between sources, fail to take into account their biases (or one's own), and produce a history that is little more than the revival of old ideological propaganda or the creation of new propaganda. One important lesson of historiography in the last half of the twentieth century is that history is often what we make it, shaped to serve and support modern agendas.

Since our texts are shaped by and speak to people in a particular historical situation, facing the challenges and wrestling with the questions of that moment in time, it is necessary to attempt to sketch some picture of the historical context of the Second Temple Period, especially of the events and conditions that concerned the Jewish authors and readers of the books of the Apocrypha, shaping the world in which they lived and within which they sought to live as faithful Jews. The purpose of this overview is to provide the reader with the basic contours of the history and the challenges faced by Jews during this period, so that he or she will be better able to place each individual book of the Apocrypha and the contribution it seeks to make to Jewish life within a meaningful framework. Because this treatment must be brief and because it is written with the aim of illumining particular texts (and not the examination of history for its own sake), the reader must refer to the studies cited in the notes for fuller accounts and more critical treatments of the period.

The End of Judean Independence

In 721 B.C.E., Sargon II, king of Assyria, conquered the northern kingdom of Israel. Many Israelites were deported to Assyria and Media, while the king resettled foreigners (probably military retainers and veterans of his campaigns) among the remaining Israelites (2 Kings 17). The southern kingdom of Judah survived for another 125 years until Nebuchadnezzar, king of the Babylonian Empire, defeated the Assyrians and sought to secure his rule over all their former holdings. This brought him into Judah. In 597 B.C.E., Jerusalem surrendered; its royal family and many of its noble families were resettled in Babylon and its environs. Zedekiah, the uncle of the former Judean king, was appointed regent. Once Nebuchadnezzar had left the region, however, Judah attempted to throw off the yoke of foreign domination, with the disastrous results well known to all from 2 Kings 24–25 and Jeremiah 52. The temple was destroyed, the city burned, and its remaining elite deported or executed. Gedaliah, a Judean supporter of surrender, was appointed governor of the province. Again, once the Babylonian presence was removed, an uprising claimed the governor's life. Many Jews fled to Egypt (against Jeremiah's advice; see Jer. 42:7–43:7) where there was already a sizable Jewish presence; still others were deported to Babylon after the uprising was put down.

The destruction of the temple and the end of Jewish independence were a tremendous blow. The temple had been the place of God's dwelling and the place where mediation between the divine and human could occur. Now this was gone, as was the political independence that had always been a sign of God's favor and an assurance of the people's election. During this time, the Deuteronomistic History and its interpretation of exile as punishment for disobedience to God's Torah took its shape and profoundly influenced the exiles' understanding of their history. Exile became an occasion for reexamination and for reshaping what it meant to be Jewish.

Some Jews kept their hearts' focus on their ancestral land. The author of Psalm 137 was such a person: "How could we sing the Lord's song in a foreign land? If I forget you, O Jerusalem, let my right hand wither!" (Ps. 137:4–5). For these people, the promises of restoration and return found in Second Isaiah (Isaiah 40–55) provided a sure hope and a positive program for reclaiming their faith: remain obedient in exile, and prepare for the day of the Lord, when a way would be made through the wilderness, when God would vindicate God's Self and people by bringing them home, reestablishing their nation, and restoring their temple on God's holy mountain.

Other Jews, however, put down roots in Babylon. During their generations of exile, they had become less strangers and more citizens of this new land, following Jeremiah's own advice (Jer. 29:4–14). They prospered, built houses, planted farms and vineyards, and advanced in Babylonian politics. The stories of Daniel and his three companions, for example, reflect a context in which Jews could hold together the double goal of retaining their ancestral religion and achieving success in a new political environment (see Grabbe 1992: 120–21). Babylon remained, in fact, a primary center of Diaspora Judaism throughout the next millennium. It would become so important that, in later centuries, the Talmud compiled by its sages and students of Torah would become the normative corpus for Judaism at the end of antiquity and the beginning of the Middle Ages.

The Period of Persian Domination

In 539 B.C.E., Cyrus conquered Babylon and became king of the Persian Empire. His policy of allowing conquered peoples to remain in their native land or to return to their native land made him the fulfillment of the Jewish exiles' hopes (see Isa. 44:24–45:13). A certain Sheshbazzar, who is called the "prince of Judah" in Ezra 1:8, is made governor (Ezra 5:14) of Judah and leads back the first group of exiles to settle in Jerusalem and its environs, along with some portion of the vessels that had been plundered from the Jerusalem temple. The reconstruction of the stages of the rebuilding of the Jerusalem temple is a matter of considerable debate. The main part of the work is credited to Sheshbazzar's successor, Zerubbabel, and the priest Jeshua, with the prophets Haggai and Zechariah goading the people to take up the task in earnest.

The finished second temple allowed for the resumption of cultic worship but also brought disillusionment—and this not just because its size and grandeur paled in comparison to that of its predecessor. The Jews who had remained in Judea during the exile appear to have been at odds with the returnees at a number of points. The "people of the land" are presented in Ezra and Nehemiah as non-Jews, but in fact they appear to have considered themselves fully Jewish. The concern of Nehemiah and Ezra with keeping Jewish bloodlines "pure" (Ezra 9–10; Neh. 13:23–27) established entrance requirements to join the "congregation of the exile" that not every self-declared Jew could meet. This is the birth of sectarianism in Judea, conceived with the formation of different answers to the question "What makes one a Jew?" There was some question, then, as to whether or not this temple would be a temple for all who called themselves Jews or just for those Jews who had returned from the exile (whose pedigree was meticulously recorded) or who could join themselves to that group (see Cohen 1987: 137–41).

Ezra, whose mission is traditionally dated to 458 B.C.E., appears to have been mainly concerned with establishing a particular interpretation of the Mosaic law as the law of Judea and with insulating the congregation of the exile from the erosive influences of "non-Jews," which, again, would have included many self-professed Jews. His major accomplishment in this latter regard was rousing the congregation of the exile to dismiss "foreign" wives and disown their children by these wives. Nehemiah, who came to Judea in 445 B.C.E., rebuilt the defensive walls around the perimeter of Jerusalem as well as shored up the ideological walls separating Jew from "non-Jew." He registered the people by ancestral family, a means by which the constituency of "Israel" could be defined and delimited (Neh. 7:5–69). He bound the registered families to an oath to practice endogamy and to observe rigidly the laws of Sabbath and tithing (Neh. 10:28–39; see also 13:1–3, 23–27) (Grabbe 1992: 134). The rest of Jewish history up to the time of Alexander remains shrouded in the silence (or absence) of sources.

Already within the Persian period we find Jews asking questions that will continue to reverberate throughout the Second Temple period. As different answers are formulated, sects are born, Jews fashion divisive labels, and the variegated forms of Second Temple Judaism take shape. First, the restored temple emerges as a major focus not only of Jewish unity but also of Jewish disunity. Who should administer the temple cultus: Zadokites or other priestly families? What role should Levitical priests play? Second, the question of Jewish identity and distinctiveness comes to the fore. How and how far can Jews relate to their non-Jewish neighbors? What defines a Jew: genealogical or religious criteria or both? A third question concerns the reality of the restoration achieved during the Persian period as compared with the idealistic visions that had been set forward in Isaiah and other prophets of restoration. Has the nation been restored, or do the people look forward to new interventions of God in the future? If the latter, when and by whose agency will the final restoration take place?

The Period of Domination by the Hellenistic Kingdoms

The balance of power shifts westward with the rise of Philip II of Macedon, who united the city-states of Greece and Macedonia into a force capable of competing with the Persian Empire. His son, Alexander III, pushed the Persian armies and their king, Darius, back from the western tip of Asia Minor to their capital cities of Persepolis and Ecbatana in just four years, during which time he also secured Syria, Palestine, and Egypt. A pupil of Aristotle and lover of the Greek way of life, Alexander carried with him Hellenic culture, which he spread throughout the new Greek Empire by founding cities with Greek institutions (like the gymnasium, the lyceum, and Hellenistic forms of worship). Forty cities from Egypt to India bearing the name Alexandria attest to his energy and success. He encouraged his troops to intermarry with women from the conquered peoples, thus literally wedding the new cultures to his own, and he spread Greek throughout the Mediterranean and into the Near East as the language of political and cultural expression. Through his efforts, the influence of Greek culture could be felt in cities throughout the known world. Learning the Greek language was often regarded as the pathway to power and influence for indigenous elites, the means by which they might break into and find a place within the hegemony of the dominant culture (Hengel 1980: 62). It is not that Greek culture and language *replaced* native languages and cultures; rather, the two now coexisted, each influencing the other (Grabbe 1992: 156–58, 161). Travel throughout this vast empire was facilitated, and, consequently, the Jewish Diaspora grew under Hellenistic rule. Egypt and Babylon remained major centers, and Syria and Asia Minor witnessed significant growth in their Jewish population.

Alexander died in 323 B.C.E. at the age of thirty-three, leaving no heir except a son born shortly after his death. The empire was torn apart by Alexander's generals. Ptolemy was entrenched in Egypt, Seleucus in Syria and Babylon, Cassander in Macedonia and Greece, Lysimachus in Thrace, and Antigonus in Asia Minor. Although these generals vied with one another, only the power plays between the dynasties of Ptolemy and Seleucus were of immediate concern to Judea, since Palestine was the prize each wanted to control.

Under Ptolemaic rule, which ran from 319 to 198 B.C.E., the Judeans enjoyed relative freedom and peace, the Ptolemies being satisfied as long as the taxes were flowing in. The house of Tobias rose to great power and influence beginning with Joseph, who secured the office of tax collector for the province of Palestine—a privilege that formerly belonged to the high priest.[1] The Tobiad family shows, from its very beginnings, a greater degree of openness to the non-Jewish world than their conservative coreligionists would have approved of, although the former would hardly have considered themselves as going against their ancestral tradition. In a letter to an official, Joseph writes, "Many thanks be to your gods." Even if this is a formal ending added by a scribe in Joseph's employ, it is a remarkable concession for a henotheist to make. He also appears to have sold a Jewish girl slave to a Gentile and to have kept some male slaves uncircumcised—two practices forbidden in Torah. Joseph shows his indifference toward Jewish sensibilities in his maintenance of good relations with Samaritan Jews, who help finance his first visits to Alexandria. Joseph is remembered as one who helped Judea move toward economic prosperity, but it would appear that he did so—and advanced his own status—through his willingness to embrace nonexclusivist policies. It is likely that the supporters of Jason, to whom we shall soon turn, would have had similar sensibilities.

Antiochus III, the great-great-grandson of Seleucus I, wrested Palestine from Ptolemaic control in 198 B.C.E. He continued the tolerant policy that Judea had enjoyed under Persian, Greek, and Ptolemaic rule. Josephus preserves a document written by Antiochus III in which the king gives Jews the

---

1. The story of Joseph ben Tobias is recorded in Josephus, *Jewish Antiquities* 12.157–236; see also Grabbe 1992: 192–98.

legal right to continue self-regulation under the Torah (*Jewish Antiquities* 12.138–146). Even if this document has been doctored, it preserves the essence of Antiochus's concessions to the new subjects. When Antiochus III attempted to annex the coastlands of Asia Minor, he was stopped by the representatives of the Roman Republic, already a force to be reckoned with and a power making itself felt in the eastern Mediterranean.

Antiochus III died on his return trip and was succeeded by his son, Seleucus IV. Because of heavy financial obligations, Seleucus sent his agent Heliodorus to confiscate certain treasuries deposited in the Jerusalem temple. The Jewish people, apprised of his intentions, took to the streets en masse. The demonstrations turned Heliodorus away from his mission, and he eventually murdered his ruler. No doubt, the threatened violation of the temple treasury reminded the people of the dangers of Gentile domination. Antiochus IV, a son of Antiochus III who had been sent to Rome as a hostage after his father's defeat, now seized the throne. Here begins the story of the most significant and well-documented crisis of Second Temple Judaism before Pompey's invasion.

Judea had already been a part of a Hellenistic kingdom for 150 years. In what follows, we will speak of the "Hellenization crisis," but we should also consider how the Hellenization of Palestine advanced in ways that were not seen as critical or threatening to the survival of Judaism.[2] The first and most basic kind of Hellenization was the introduction of the Greek language into the region. No doubt, this was a slow process, with only the elites showing much interest in gaining an education in Greek for themselves and especially their children. Merchants and artisans may also have picked up some Greek, at least enough to facilitate doing business. Greek did not replace Aramaic, and the majority of the population probably learned little or no Greek during the Hellenistic period (Grabbe 1992: 167).

A second trend is the introduction of Greek names, especially among the elite class. This is particularly well documented from the period of Antiochus IV on. This is at least a concession to the Greek-speaking people with whom these elites would have had (or sought to have) contact; at most, it is a desire to present themselves as more a part of the dominant culture than a part of a subjugated people.

Hellenism is also marked by a closer and more invigorated interaction between people of different cultures. Native cultures are not lost,[3] but the degree

2. See Hengel 1974 and 1980. The second book is especially important, since Hengel modifies a number of the conclusions in his earlier study that were rightfully critiqued as being overdrawn. See Barclay 1996: 88–91 for an excellent analysis of aspects of the Hellenization of Jews. Barclay invites careful analysis of ways in which Jews adopted or interacted with the political, social, linguistic, educational, ideological, religious, and material aspects of Hellenistic culture, calling for attention to be given both to the distinct elements of Hellenization and to the degree of Hellenization to be observed in a given aspect in a given location.

3. Grabbe (1992: 170) raises this important caveat. All ethnic groups would be concerned to preserve their own ancestral heritage and customs, while adapting and acculturating to the new environment.

of exposure to other cultures increases. Thus, a third element of Hellenization occurs at the level of sharing philosophical ideas, the traditions and stories that constitute cultural literacy, and the like. This was to have a profound impact on Judaism, as Jewish authors would now begin to weave into their own work ideas and references learned from outside the cultural heritage of Judaism and even begin to write literature patterned no longer after the genres represented by the Hebrew Scriptures but in imitation of genres learned from other cultural traditions. Closely related to this is the degree to which Jews had access to and made use of Greek education, which would have involved a systematic exposure not only to Greek language but also its literature, art of argumentation, ethics, and other important facets of Greek culture.

It is critical to bear in mind that Hellenization progressed slowly on all these fronts, not only in Judea but in most areas.[4] The cultural and rhetorical resources available to Josephus in the first century C.E. were not yet available to the chroniclers of the Maccabean Revolt (1 and 2 Maccabees); the Greek philosophical content of Wisdom of Solomon (from first-century-C.E. Egypt) was not yet available to Ben Sira (from second-century-B.C.E. Palestine). Nevertheless, it was a process set in motion quite early in the Second Temple period.

In all these areas, Hellenizing would not necessarily be antithetical in and of itself to remaining a faithful Jew.[5] As one explores the whole spectrum of intertestamental Jewish literature, one discovers that the simple equation of resistance to Hellenism with fidelity to Judaism is false. Wisdom of Solomon and 4 Maccabees, for example, at once show the greatest degree of Hellenistic influence and the greatest passion for remaining faithful to Torah and the Jewish way of life.[6] The Maccabean Revolt was not, therefore, a cultural war against the influence of Hellenism; it was, however, fueled by zeal for preserving the Jewish way of life, the ultimate solution for which appears to have been political independence—a lesson that history has rather recently rediscovered.

The Hellenization Crisis

The period between 175 and 161 B.C.E. is one of the most well-documented and yet most difficult periods to understand.[7] All our sources evi-

4. Hengel (1980: 53–54) views the Roman period as the time of the greatest strides in Hellenization.

5. Feldman (1986) often speaks as if these were incompatible and is rightly criticized by Grabbe (1992: 151).

6. Such texts from the Diaspora during the early Roman period can be expected to show an advanced degree of Hellenization, as do the writings of Philo. The point remains, however, that such a high degree of acculturation to Greek language, rhetoric, and philosophy does not necessarily correlate with a departure from rigorous observance of the Jewish Torah.

7. Some material from this and the previous section has been adapted from deSilva 1998: 37–42.

dence some bias or program of their own that filters the data and colors the framework. Piercing through the veil of partisan legend to historical fact has challenged scholarship for decades. As one reads the earliest sources (1 Maccabees, 2 Maccabees, Daniel 7–12), one should bear in mind that the authors, and the Jewish people by and large, would have regarded the events of this period differently than did the Syrian king Antiochus IV and therefore would probably not understand or accurately reflect his motives. One should also not expect them to know where the real source of the trouble was, for the Hellenizing Jewish leaders acted in the king's name, and the king gave these leaders rather free rein (as long as taxes and peace were maintained). Thus, 1 Maccabees' portrait of a tyrant's conscious attempt to impose Greek culture and to suppress Judaism will have to be tempered with an awareness of other struggles surrounding the actual prohibitions against Judaism that sparked the Maccabean Revolt.[8]

Jeshua, who took the name Jason, was the more progressive brother of the high priest Onias III. When the latter's reputation was tarnished by accusations made against him by members of the Tobiad family (the Jewish rivals of the Oniad family), Jason appealed to Antiochus IV to be made high priest in his brother's place. He secured this by promising a massive bribe to Antiochus IV, who was always in need of money to supply his tribute to Rome (after his father's defeat in Asia Minor) and to finance his ongoing campaigns against the Ptolemies in Egypt. In the review of aspects of Hellenization above, I deferred mention of the political and administrative sphere. It is this element that the high priest Jason sought to bring to Judea. An additional bribe of 150 talents bought Jason the right to re-create Jerusalem as a Greek *polis*, a Greek city with a new constitution.

Jason established a list of citizens, confirming the privileges of the aristocracy (Grabbe 1992: 268) (and probably limiting the list to those who would be in support of his political renovation). He established a gymnasium with a list of young men ("ephebes") enrolled to take part. This would become the educational and cultural center of the new Jerusalem. This policy of voluntary Hellenization had a lot of support, especially among the upper classes. All our sources agree that a group of "renegade" Jews sought after the Hellenization of Judea and secured the right to become a Greek city from the Syrian king at their own initiative. The sources also agree that many in Jerusalem enthusiastically took part in the Greek institutions (although this was lamented, as in 2 Macc. 4:13–15). While this change might be viewed as only affecting the political sphere and not affecting the day-to-day religious life of the temple or the people (Grabbe 1992: 256, 278–79), it cannot have escaped notice that the Torah was no longer the legal basis for government in the land. The theocratic state had been replaced, a fact recalled in 2 Macc. 4:10–11. That text

---

8. Laying the initiative for these reforms at Antiochus's feet continues to mar treatments of the history of the period (as in Wylen 1996: 51).

need not be read as a reaction to (or slanderous invention of) violations of Torah per se so much as to the displacement of Torah as the constitution of Judea (and not merely as a religious text that could still regulate cultic and other religious functions). Thus, while this move did not directly threaten traditional observances or occasion violent reactions, it would have justifiably made uneasy those who captured the significance of it.

Nevertheless, Jason commanded widespread support among the Judean elite, since his reforms promised them participation in the larger cultural life of the Mediterranean and unimpeded access to both economic and political advancement in the larger arena of the Hellenistic kingdoms. Antiochus IV, moreover, would welcome such enthusiasm for Hellenistic ways and support it in whatever ways he could. The de-emphasizing of native culture, customs, and hopes, and their replacement with Hellenistic culture and ambitions, would make Judea a more pacified possession. Antiochus had designs on conquering Egypt itself, and a secure Judea was a necessary prelude to his imperial aspirations. The formation of Antioch-at-Jerusalem no doubt seemed to him a step in the right direction.

Matters became more complicated in 172 B.C.E. when a certain Menelaus, supported by the Tobiad family, made a bid to Antiochus IV for the high priesthood, raising Jason's annual tribute by three hundred talents. Antiochus, always looking for more income to finance his planned campaigns against Egypt and other activities, accepted. This was a highly problematic setup for the Judeans. While they might have been appalled at his having purchased, in effect, the high priesthood, Jason was at least a Zadokite and, therefore, an acceptable incumbent. Menelaus, however, had no such claim to the high priesthood. The question of what priestly line occupied the high priesthood appears to have been of decisive significance for the mysterious group known as Hasideans, who first appear as pious devotees of the Torah (unwilling even to defend themselves on the Sabbath), join the Maccabean struggle, and leave the Maccabean party when Alcimus, a Zadokite, is appointed high priest. It can be assumed that their split from the center of Jewish worship became decisive when the non-Zadokite Menelaus entered the office. This change of priesthood appears also to have split the upper class and military personnel; Jason fled Jerusalem but retained a large number of supporters. The induction of an unacceptable high priest, then, plants the seeds of dissent, and his unacceptable actions water those seeds into rebellion.

Menelaus, unable to pay Antiochus the amounts he promised, had been summoned to Antioch to answer the king. A revolt in Tarsus, however, bought Menelaus a reprieve. He appropriated funds from the temple treasuries to bribe Syrian officials and to increase his own liquid assets, a move that deeply alienated the local population. When Antiochus is at last free to hear charges against Menelaus, the latter has the wherewithal to pay Antiochus and get his accusers executed. The situation worsens against the backdrop of Antiochus's unsuccessful campaigns to take Egypt. After his first defeat, Antiochus himself raided the temple treasury to replenish his war coffers, which no doubt increased anti-Seleucid sentiments in Jerusalem. While Antiochus is on his second campaign against Egypt, a false rumor of his death rouses Jason to seize this long-awaited opportunity to regain control of the high priesthood. He attacks Menelaus in Jerusalem, besieging him in the citadel. Menelaus seeks help from Antiochus, who regards this as a revolt against his own rule by pro-Ptolemaic factions in Judea. He responds brutally by slaughtering thousands.[9] Menelaus himself led Antiochus into the temple so as to pay the latter his due tribute from the treasury, an act of desecration that deeply galled the populace.

After Antiochus restored Menelaus, resistance again flared up with the result that, in early 167 B.C.E., troops under the command of Apollonius again had to enter Jerusalem. Apollonius fortified the Akra, a fortress adjacent to the temple, with Jewish and Syrian mercenary soldiers. Many residents of Jerusalem fled into the countryside; many more were dispossessed of houses and property in order to furnish the settled soldiers. The temple itself now became the common property of the Jewish and Gentile inhabitants of Antioch-at-Jerusalem, and the worship was altered to suit the syncretistic practices of the inhabitants of the Akra. This change in cult practice would be remembered in the sources as the "abomination of desolation." The precise nature of the cult established there remains a mystery (Bickerman 1979: 61–75; Wenham 1992; Grabbe 1992: 258–59); suffice it to say that it was unacceptable to the majority of Jews, including, no doubt, many who were avid promoters of Hellenism.

Moreover, the practice of Judaism itself was, in some way, proscribed. Again, it is difficult to discern the facts behind the sources. Did Antiochus IV settle on the suppression of Judaism in Judea himself? Was the program of overturning the Jewish Torah and religion a measure invented by Menelaus or other members of the party of extreme Hellenizers and supported by Antiochus IV as a plausible plan to rout resistance?[10] Whatever the answer, we can be sure that the suppression of Torah observance was local to Judea. Samaria was unmolested and, apart from some agitation against Jews in the cities of Philistia, Jews in the Diaspora were unaffected. The cultic symbols of Jewish exclusivism appear to have been particularly targeted, at least in the remembrance of the authors of 1, 2, and 4 Maccabees: circumcision of infants brought death to the family; the sign of acquiescence to, and acceptance of, the religious pluralism of the new Antioch-at-Jerusalem was eating a morsel of pork; possession of a copy of the Torah also was punished with execution,

9. Jason appears to have fled Jerusalem before Antiochus's armies had arrived, leading Tcherikover (1999: 188) to posit an intermediate revolt in which some conservative party ousted Jason shortly after Jason ousted Menelaus.

10. Bickerman (1979: 76–90) argues that the proscription of Jewish observances and the persecution of those who resisted was the brainchild of Menelaus and his party.

since as long as people outside the regime had access to Torah, the legitimacy of the inclusivistic cult promoted under Menelaus (and symbolizing the peaceful coexistence of Jew and Gentile in Judea) would be threatened. So began the first systematic attempt to enforce the abandonment of an exclusivist form—the traditional form—of Judaism. At this point, the process of Hellenization had overstepped the limits of the people's tolerance, and a revolution against Menelaus's priesthood and Syrian rule ensued.

These developments had a profound and lasting impact on the Jewish people, one that is renewed annually in the celebration of Hanukkah. The repression of Judaism and the response of the Torah-observant Jews dominate 1, 2, and 4 Maccabees and are mirrored in 3 Maccabees (a work patterned rather closely after 2 Maccabees). The "abomination of desolation" is so traumatic that it becomes a topic of apocalyptic expectation (see Mark 13): the atrocities committed under Menelaus against God and God's people would be repeated in the future, prior to God's final visitation. On the whole, Jews certainly had cause now to be impressed with the dangers of Hellenization as well as its promise. This leads to a concern or challenge that reverberates throughout the literature of the period: the attempt to discern how far is too far. In what ways and to what extent could the Gentile nations' contributions to language, rhetoric, philosophy, and culture safely be used? At what point is the line of holiness calling Israel to remain separate from the nations breached, thus incurring the wrath of God? The central challenge could be summarized not as resisting Hellenization but as discovering how to maintain fidelity to the Jewish way of life in the midst of Hellenization.

The Maccabean Revolt

The details of the campaign waged by Mattathias and his sons, often called the "Hasmoneans," because of their descent from an ancestor named Hashmonai, or the "Maccabees," after the nickname given to the most prominent hero of the actual war, Judas Maccabeus, are the subject of 1 and 2 Maccabees and need not be rehearsed in detail at this point. This priestly family rallied a guerilla army, which at first included the enigmatic Hasideans, and began their cleansing of Judea by attacking Jews who had already abandoned observance of the exclusivistic commands of Torah. Uncircumcised boys were forcibly circumcised; Jews who had accommodated too much were left to fear for their lives (1 Macc. 2:44–48; 3:5–6). The threat was not taken sufficiently seriously by the Greco-Syrian government, with the result that insufficient forces were dispatched at first to crush the revolt. This resulted in some early victories that fueled the fire of resistance and demoralized the Syrian occupying forces, more or less setting the tone for the campaigns that followed.

The Seleucid administration continued to send out increasingly larger forces, but Judas's army also grew on account of his initial victories. Embattled on several fronts, Antiochus could not sustain a suppression of revolution as well and so rescinded the decrees against the practice of Judaism. Judas and his revolutionaries had thus brought an end to the attempt to reform and reshape religion in Judea, restoring the traditional, exclusivist form of Yahwism to the temple and the region. The pagan paraphernalia were removed from the temple, which was purified and rededicated to the Torah-regulated service of God.

The military campaigns could have stopped there if religious freedom were the sole motive of the Maccabees and their supporters. Nevertheless, Judas continued to besiege the Syrian garrison in the Akra and made raids on the neighboring Gentile cities where, we are told, Jews were being mistreated and required rescuing. At this point, Antiochus IV dies. The sword will never depart from his house, as his descendants (and claimants to the throne pretending to be descendants) will fight over the throne until the dynasty comes to an end. Lysias, the guardian of the boy who would come to be Antiochus V, responds to the continued unrest in Judea by executing Menelaus and installing Alcimus as high priest. At this point, many Jews were willing to lay down their arms. Alcimus was a Zadokite and therefore an acceptable high priest; and they were certainly glad to have the apostate Menelaus, who came to be remembered as an agent of apostasy, out of that hallowed office.

Judas and his brothers, however, together with a sizable army, refused to abandon the field. What began as a war for the restoration of Torah had become a war for political independence. Judas himself would die on the battlefield. In the decades that followed, however, the Seleucid kingdom was weakened internally by rival claimants to the throne moving against one another in court intrigues and civil wars. Jonathan, Simon, and their successors were able to exploit this, playing one rival off against another, amassing royal concessions and favors. Jonathan, a younger brother of Judas, became high priest of Judea, a title that would remain in the Hasmonean family for a century and mark them as the political leaders of Judea. Simon, the last of the brothers, succeeded Jonathan. Under his leadership, the Seleucid garrison in the Akra was expelled and "the yoke of the Gentiles" lifted (1 Macc. 13:41). Whatever the Seleucid monarch's opinion of their relationship, the Judeans saw themselves once more as an independent state—for the first time since 597 B.C.E.

Simon's son, John Hyrcanus I, would push the borders of the newly independent Judea to annex Samaria and Idumea, even forcing the latter to convert to Judaism and accept circumcision. John Hyrcanus's son, Aristobulus I, would annex Iturea, likewise requiring the inhabitants to convert to Judaism. These pursued as policy what Antiochus IV had accepted as an extreme measure to stamp out resistance. With Aristobulus I, the Hasmonean high priests also began to assume the title of king. After a brief reign of a year, the throne passed to Aristobulus I's brother, Alexander Janneus, who expanded the borders of the Hasmonean state to the original extent of the Solomonic kingdom. It is also under Alexander that one finds the most ardent opposition to Hasmonean rule and the most brutal reprisal enacted by a Jewish king upon his subjects (prior to Herod). Alexander, having suppressed a revolt, crucified eight hundred of his countrymen while slaughtering their families before their eyes.

Upon Alexander's death, the crown passed to his widow, Alexandra Salome, and the high priesthood to his elder son, Hyrcanus II. This is a period in which the Pharisaic party first moves into the limelight in Judea, and they appear to have had a strong influence over the queen. The dynasty ends amidst the same kind of civil strife that had plagued the Seleucid dynasty during this period. Hyrcanus II succeeded his mother as king, but his brother Aristobulus II hotly contested that claim and, for a time, replaced Hyrcanus II. The latter, however, gained the support of the Nabatean ruler and returned to besiege Aristobulus in Jerusalem. At this point, Rome intervenes in Jewish history. Both sides appealed to Pompey the Great, a Roman general, but Aristobulus appears to have been unhappy with the slowness of the general's deliberations. The end result was Pompey's arrival at Jerusalem itself. While Aristobulus presented himself humbly before Pompey, his followers closed the city gates to the Romans and secured themselves on the Temple Mount. Hyrcanus's followers were able to open the gates and admit Pompey and his army, who besieged the temple for three months and finally took it. Pompey himself entered the temple precincts, including the Holy of Holies, a violation remembered bitterly in *Psalms of Solomon*. Pompey finally decided in favor of giving Hyrcanus the high priesthood but not giving either brother the title of king. Instead, Judea would become a client state of Rome, falling under the yoke of the Gentiles again, after not even a century of independence.

The period of the Hasmonean state generated its own questions and challenges, and several Apocrypha can be read as responding to its concerns. There were attempts to legitimate Hasmonean rule by remembering (and, to some extent, idealizing) the story of Judas and his brothers, the saviors of Israel. Nevertheless, a major question continued to focus on the legitimacy of the high priest and the proper functioning of the temple. Indeed, the sect at Qumran appears to have taken its definitive shape in opposition to the Hasmonean high priest[11] and the regulating of the temple under his leadership. Although disaffection with the Hasmonean dynasty grew as the line contin-

---

11. The majority of scholars regard Jonathan or John Hyrcanus as the archenemy of the Teacher of Righteousness. It has also been suggested that Alcimus or his immediate successor was labeled the Wicked Priest in the Dead Sea Scrolls, who opposed and pursued the Teacher of Righteousness, the enigmatic personality who gave shape to the Qumran community. In any case, Qumranite disaffection with, and critique of, the Jerusalem temple and priesthood continued throughout the Hasmonean and Roman periods until the community was destroyed in 68 C.E.

ued, the enduring legacy of the Maccabeans was a renewed zeal for the restoration and secure establishment of the kingdom of Israel. Even if Jews might no longer view the Hasmonean kings as worthy or faithful leaders, they would now continue to hope for a worthy king in the future who would take the best achievements of the Hasmoneans and combine them with the perfect embodiment of traditional Jewish virtues. Thus, messianism and the fostering of hopes for God's perfect restoration of Israel (seen in shadowy form in the Hasmonean restoration) also flourished during this period. Of course, the advent of a new Gentile empire on the Judean scene—the Roman Republic—renewed all the old questions and concerns about how to live securely as Jews under the domination of non-Jews.

The Period of Roman Rule

The most important source for Judean history during this period is the work of Josephus, who treats the subject in books 14–20 of his *Jewish Antiquities* and in his *Jewish War*. This history is, of course, greatly enhanced by the work of Suetonius, Tacitus, Dio Cassius, and by the wealth of archaeological, epigraphic, and numismatic evidence from the Roman period. Since few of the Apocrypha are likely to have been written in Palestine during this period (those written during the Roman period, such as Wisdom of Solomon and 4 Maccabees, most likely come from outside Palestine), our treatment of this period will be even more skeletal.

The new arrangement under Pompey, in which the Hasmonean Hyrcanus II enjoyed only the title of high priest, left open an opportunity for the enterprising Antipater and his sons Phasael and Herod to distinguish themselves in the administration of the vassal state of Judea. These had been appointed as governors of Judea and Galilee by the Roman governor of Syria and so filled the void created when the kingship was taken from the Hasmoneans (Levine 1998: 470–71). Aristobulus's son, Antigonus, however, continued to try to win back the throne and priesthood by force. With Parthian support, he captured Hyrcanus II and had his uncle's ears clipped so as to disqualify him from ever holding the high priesthood again. Herod fled to Rome while the Parthians established Antigonus as a short-lived king of Judea (Levine 1998: 471). Preferring a loyal vassal in charge of Judea to a Parthian presence at their eastern border, the Roman consuls Octavian and Marc Antony appointed Herod king of Judea and recaptured Jerusalem on his behalf.

Thus began the reign of Herod the Great, "King of the Jews" from 37–4 B.C.E. Josephus speaks well of Herod's building projects, the most celebrated of which was the renovation of the temple but perhaps the most astounding of which was the creation of a human-made harbor at Caesarea Maritima. He also established many cities in which Greek and Jew felt equally at home and even sent gifts of regal proportions to foreign cities, making Judea less of a second-class part of the Mediterranean region. His brutality toward opponents, whether revolutionaries among the people or members of his own family, earned him popular hatred, as did his tendency to pour resources equally into projects that the Jews endorsed (such as the Jerusalem temple) and that they abhorred (such as a temple to Augustus in Samaria).

After Herod's death, his kingdom was divided among his sons, none of whom received the title of king. After the removal of Archelaus from the ethnarchy of Judea in 6 C.E., Roman governors exercised direct rule of Judea until 41 (after which Agrippa I, son of Herod and friend of the emperors Caligula and Claudius, enjoyed a brief reign as king of Judea) and then again from 44 until the Jewish Revolt of 66–70.

In principle, Roman rule should have been no more grievous than the domination of Judea by the Persians, the Ptolemies, and the first Seleucids. Augustus confirmed the rights of Jews throughout his empire to observe their ancestral laws without molestation (although, in practice, sporadic pogroms occurred against Jews in the Diaspora). The Roman governors were not to interfere in the religious life of Judea, although their custody of the garments of the high priest during the times they were not in use was a potent reminder of the dependence of that freedom of religion on Roman good will. Nevertheless, short-lived rebellions against Roman rule erupted during this period, always put down with ruthless efficiency. Varus, for example, executed over two thousand revolutionaries by crucifixion shortly after Herod's death. Rome's contributions to Judean society were extolled by some Jews, whereas those who focused on the heavy-handed administration of justice, the burden of taxation, and the occasional indiscretions by governors or their soldiers rejected the legitimacy of Roman rule.

An incident during the reign of Gaius Caligula (37–41), a poor emperor even in the best attempts at revisionist history, confirmed the dangers of Roman rule in the eyes of many Jews. Perhaps as a reprisal for the failure of Jews to respect a sacred place of their Gentile neighbors in non-Judean Palestine (Grabbe 2000: 578), Caligula determined to place a statue of himself in the Jerusalem temple. Jews had been free from participation in the imperial cult, offering sacrifices on behalf of the emperor rather than to the emperor, but this impending innovation suggested a change in that policy and the loss of an important religious privilege. All the memories of the desecration of the temple by pagan cult in the time of Antiochus IV flood the minds of Jews as they take to the roads, fall to the ground, and bare their throats before the advance of the governor, Petronius, who understands that the Jews would rather be exterminated than suffer the desecration of their temple. Only his delay in carrying out the emperor's orders and Gaius's timely assassination save the day.

When the indiscretions of the early governors gave way to the injustice of the later ones (who do appear to have sought to use their stay in the province to enrich themselves and even to have provoked incidents and uprisings so as to cover their tracks), the anti-Roman sectors of the population led Judea into a full-scale revolution against Roman rule in a futile fight for independence. Fueled by the sacred history of God giving victory to God's faithful no matter how numerous and strong the enemy, by an ideology of "no king but God," and by messianic fervor for the restoration of the Jewish State, the Zealots emerged and, in cooperation with people from every stratum of Jewish society, declared war on Rome.

The legions of Vespasian quickly regained control of Galilee and most of Judea. After the suicide of Nero, Vespasian halted his advance, waiting to hear of news from Rome and eventually marching on Rome himself as his troops' candidate for emperor. The civil wars of 68–69, in which Roman army fought Roman army, gave rise to hopes in Judea that the beast called Rome would devour itself. They also gave the factions in Jerusalem time to lose sight of their common enemy and begin to make war on each other. When the emperor Vespasian dispatched his son, Titus, to finish the retaking of Jerusalem, he had little to do but wait for internal strife and famine in the besieged city to do the work for him. In 70, he took the city, destroyed its walls, and razed its temple.

The impact upon Jews of the destruction of the second temple was momentous and devastating. An unwelcome recapitulation of the events of 587 B.C.E., the very institutions of temple and sacrificial cult would no longer be part of Judaism. Within the Apocrypha, only 2 Esdras 3–14 (= 4 Ezra) bears witness to one Jew's response to the challenges of living as a Jew in the shadow of a burnt temple and unpunished Rome. What is the theological meaning of this history? Where is the justice of God, who allows the worse sinners to prosper while chastising so severely the one people who had a care for God? What will give meaning and hope to life as a Jew in these sadly changed circumstances? Outside the Apocrypha, of course, responses are far more numerous. Other apocalypses, such as *2 Baruch*, respond directly to this crisis as well (also from a vantage point of several decades later). Josephus's *Jewish War* is not merely a history of the period but an attempt to make sense of the destruction and to exonerate the majority of Jews from guilt in a revolt against Rome. The work of the sages in Palestine, giving shape to a Judaism centered on Torah instead of temple, on prayer and charitable acts instead of sacrifice, would eventually give birth to rabbinic Judaism, the major form in which Judaism survived its revolts against Rome.

As punishment for a second revolt—the Bar Kokhba Revolt of 132–135 C.E., in which messianism and apocalypticism played a large role and thus fell largely from favor among Jews who survived—the very city of Jerusalem was declared off limits to Jews and reestablished as a pagan city, Aelia Capitolina, by the emperor Hadrian. Hadrian had also proscribed circumcision for a time and so comes to be remembered as a second Antiochus IV in rabbinic stories.

Jews in the Diaspora

According to Strabo (his testimonies are gathered in Josephus, *Jewish Antiquities* 14.114–118), Jews were already to be found in every region of the Roman Empire by the early part of the first century B.C.E. In all likelihood, Diaspora Jews produced Tobit, the Additions to Esther and Daniel, 3 and 4 Maccabees, and Wisdom of Solomon. Moreover, 2 Maccabees preserves letters sent to Diaspora Jews from their Palestinian coreligionists, and the book itself may well have been written for the benefit of a Diaspora audience. Beyond the Apocrypha, moreover, a great corpus of Jewish literature can claim to have originated outside Palestine. While each of the texts mentioned above will be used to illumine the situation and responses of Diaspora Jews to the challenges they encountered, a brief orientation to their context will provide some useful mental hooks on which to hang those more extended explorations.

Nebuchadnezzar's deportations of Jews from Judah established a strong Jewish presence in the major cities of Babylonia, one that continued to flourish and grow long after the edict of Cyrus granting permission to Jews to return to their ancestral land. Jews also immigrated to Egypt to escape the fall of Jerusalem in 587 B.C.E. A military colony of Jews existed in Elephantine in the Upper (that is, southern) Kingdom of Egypt from before the fifth century B.C.E. The Jews of this colony were rather open to native Egyptian influences on their religious life and intermarried with non-Jews. More Jews were brought to Egypt, some to serve in the armies, some as slaves, by Ptolemy I after he secured Palestine. Under Ptolemy II, all Jewish slaves and prisoners of war were freed. Soldiers remained with the army; others took up agriculture. Many were settled in military colonies, Ptolemy providing land, the Jews remaining on call for military service. Their loyalties were thus clearly toward the Greek overlords of Egypt, a factor that contributed to the mutual animosity between them and the indigenous population. Jews, of course, remembered Egyptians as their former oppressors. The Egyptians, however, told a different story of the exodus—for example, that the Hebrews were a criminal, leprous lot banished from Egypt.

Jews appear to have been allowed to observe their traditional religious practices and even to regulate the life of their own communities according to their own laws. Under Ptolemy II, the translation of the Torah from Hebrew into Greek was initiated. This translation became the authoritative Torah for Diaspora Jews, whose knowledge of Hebrew had faded as successive generations were raised under Hellenistic rule. Stories about the translation, such as the one found in *Letter of Aristeas*, promoted the divine inspiration of the translation itself and, in some cases, the superiority of the Septuagint version to the Hebrew original. The Seleucid advance on Palestine prompted another immigration of Jews to Egypt, including Onias and the high priestly family.

Onias IV built a temple in Leontopolis, where sacrifices and priestly services were carried out until Rome closed the temple in 73 C.E., for fear it might become a center for rebellion like the Jerusalem temple had. This temple, like the one in Elephantine, was surrounded by a military colony of Jews entrusted with the defense of a strategic location against Seleucid aggression. Onias's sons were high-ranking officers in the Ptolemaic army. The Jews in Diaspora Egypt appear by and large to have enjoyed good relations with their Ptolemaic overlords. The one notable exception appears to be a short period of persecution under Ptolemy VIII, which was due, however, not so much to anti-Judaism as to the fact that the Jewish soldiers had been caught up in a dynastic power struggle. The Jews had risen to great political and military prominence under Ptolemy VI and probably supported his heir, Ptolemy VII. When, after a few short months, Ptolemy VIII wrested control of the state from his weak brother, he engaged in reprisals against his rival's supporters. This was, at the most, a short interruption in an otherwise peaceful existence under Ptolemaic rule.

Under Roman administration, the Jewish communities in Egypt flourished, especially at Alexandria, which had become a major center of culture, learning, and commerce in the Mediterranean region. Individual Jews associated with this city (such as Philo and, perhaps, the author of Wisdom of Solomon) show an astounding degree of Hellenization in terms of their linguistic and cultural fluency. Philo estimates the number of Jews in Egypt at one million. While this is, no doubt, an exaggeration, the fact that Jews occupied two of the five districts of the city of Alexandria suggests that this was the largest Jewish community outside of Palestine.

Although officially granted toleration by the empire, the Jews were not free from hostility. A particularly severe pogrom erupted in 38 C.E., the result of decades of Jewish-Gentile tension coming to a head around the issue of whether or not Jews were "equal citizens" of Alexandria. Similar issues led to similar anti-Jewish riots in several other cities. Claudius ordered the cessation of violence against the Jews but also admonished the Jews not to seek to advance their status in "a city not their own."[12]

Rome itself was host to a thriving Jewish community (see Leon 1995). The Jewish presence in Rome caught the attention in 59 B.C.E. of Cicero, who speaks of them as an identifiable element in Roman and Italian society (*Pro Flacco* 66–69).[13] Many Jews were taken to Rome as slaves and prisoners of war by Pompey, but many Jews were present in Rome as free persons as well. They took part in Roman society, spoke Greek, took Latin and Greek names, and were influenced by Roman culture in their artistic expression. Leon's careful study shows, however, that the Jewish community at Rome was itself quite

12. Josephus (*Jewish Antiquities* 19.280–285) relates only that half of the edict favorable to Jews; the edict itself, in effect, censures both sides in the dispute (see Barclay 1996: 70–71).
13. Discussed in Leon 1995: 5–7; Barclay 1996: 286–88.

diverse in terms of degree of acculturation to its environment (Leon 1995: 258). Their relatively peaceful coexistence with Roman society was occasionally disturbed during the principate. Tiberius, for example, drafted four thousand Jews to serve in the army and banished many others in response to proselytizing activity in Rome, which was deemed corrosive to good Roman values (Barclay 1996: 298–99). Claudius appears to have banned Jewish meetings in 41 C.E. and to have expelled some portion of the Jewish population from Rome in 49 C.E., quite probably because of internecine Jewish unrest between Jewish Christians and non-Christian Jews.[14] Any disturbance of the peace of Rome was unwelcome. Even these would eventually be allowed to return, and the Jews as a whole continued to thrive in Rome.

Jewish communities also existed in Syria and Asia Minor (perhaps owing their origins to immigration of Jews under the early Seleucids, particularly as part of the army), Cyrenaica (modern Libya), Cyprus, and Greece. About their history less is known, although again there are some outstanding examples of cultural achievement from among their numbers. Jason of Cyrene, for example, composed a five-volume history of the Maccabean Revolt, which provided the basis for the abridged version we call 2 Maccabees.

The primary challenge facing Diaspora Jews was living as a minority group in the midst of, and in daily proximity to, a dominant Gentile culture—one that frequently made the Jew feel inferior or unwelcome in proportion to the extent that such a Jew stood apart from the dominant culture. The Jews had to negotiate a path between two potentially contradictory principles: the desire to survive and thrive in this Gentile world and the desire to remain faithful to and to preserve their Jewish heritage and identity (Tcherikover 1999: 346). John Barclay has provided students of this period with some useful tools for thinking about the responses of Jews to the Hellenistic-Roman environment in which they lived and thus charting out more precisely the course followed by individual Jews between these two guiding principles. These tools are the scales of assimilation, acculturation, and accommodation.[15]

The assimilation scale reflects the degree to which a Jew has become socially integrated into the life of the dominant culture. At the low end of the scale stands the Jew who restricts his or her social life to the Jewish community and avoids traffic with non-Jews as far as possible. Moving up the scale, one will find Jews who enjoy daily interactions with non-Jews through commerce, Jews who not only work but also play with their non-Jewish neighbors (e.g., through attending the theaters and games), Jews who seek a gymnasium education, and, at the high end of the scale, Jews who abandon those markers that make them distinct from non-Jews. It is indeed rare to find Jews at the high end of this scale, but some did reverse the marks of circumcision, accept

14. See Barclay's judicious review of the conflicting evidence (1996: 302–6).
15. The three paragraphs that follow summarize Barclay 1996: 92–101.

induction into pagan cults, and, in short, eliminate all that separated them from their non-Jewish neighbors.

The second scale measures acculturation, or the degree to which a Jew has internalized the culture of the Hellenistic-Roman world—its language, values, and traditions. At the low end of the scale, one finds the Jew with no knowledge even of the Greek language. Further up the scale are Jews with a basic acquaintance with Greek and with the moral values of the Hellenized world. Beyond that, one finds Jews with a more direct grasp of Greek literature, philosophy, rhetoric, and ethics. At the high end of the scale stand those whose mastery of Greek language and education is nothing less than expert, as in the cases of Philo and Josephus.

The third scale measures accommodation, or the use to which Jews put whatever facility in Greek language and learning they have. This scale moves out from a center in which Jews use their facility in the dominant culture to reinterpret their tradition in ways congenial to being understood within that dominant culture while still maintaining the uniqueness and distinctiveness of their tradition. From this center, one moves to one side where the distinctiveness of Judaism is completely submerged and the Jew seeks to project Jewish tradition as essentially the same as the dominant culture. At the other end of the spectrum, the Jew uses facility in the intellectual traditions of the dominant culture to assert the supreme value of the Jewish way of life and to denigrate the Gentile way of life.

Barclay's conceptual tools are of great value for analyzing not only the location of the author of a particular book of the Apocrypha (or any other Jewish text from the Second Temple period) but also for analyzing where along those three scales that particular author wishes to fix readers (moving them, if they do not begin where the author wants them; confirming them, if they are in substantial agreement with the author). They are also helpful in and of themselves for assisting the student to see that Hellenization is not simply a process antithetical or alternative to remaining a Jew. Rather, Jews can be Hellenized in a variety of ways, to a variety of degrees, to a variety of ends. The most acculturated of the authors of the Apocrypha, for example, are also the least assimilated and the least supportive of assimilation (at least at the point of abandoning the practices and other visible marks that distinguish Jew from non-Jew).

The Jews outside Palestine had several supports for their efforts to retain their distinctive identity and to preserve a distinctive social body with a distinctive culture. These anchors are important to bear in mind as one also considers the influences from the dominant culture. First, Jews developed the institution of the synagogue as one means by which they could renew their bonds as a community and remain in touch with the essential elements of their heritage. The rational worship of the One God in the synagogue aided, no doubt, by the more philosophical interpretation of Judaism and its Scriptures, such as one finds in Philo's works or in 4 Maccabees, attracted some

Gentiles to this oriental cult much as other Gentiles were attracted to the worship of Isis or Mithras. The initiative for such movement (which would hardly be called conversion in most cases, since circumcision remained a stumbling block to all but the hardiest) need not come from Jewish missionary work, since many Gentile inhabitants of the Greco-Roman world appear to have been of a curious disposition and attracted to new and foreign rites (just as others despised all such cults as barbarian superstition).

The Jews also had the bond of ethnicity. Common descent from Abraham, and being commonly identified by outsiders by their racial identity as "Jew," remained a common topic in the cultivation of communal care and mutual support—so much so, that Jews would face the charge of being *misoxenoi*, haters of those not belonging to their race. They had, and tended to maintain, the distinctive practices by which they set themselves apart from the Gentile community, particularly Sabbath observance, circumcision, the observance of the Mosaic dietary laws, and the avoidance of all forms of idolatry. So effective were these practices in the maintenance of Jewish distinctiveness that every Gentile author indulging in anti-Jewish slander mentions these in particular. Finally, the Jews had Torah and the other Scriptures. Even a Jew such as Philo, who could quote Homer, Hesiod, and Euripedes, looked to the Pentateuch as the basis for life in this world under God.[16] It is no accident, then, that it is those authors most concerned to help their fellow-Jews maintain a positive evaluation of their cultural heritage and resist the pressures to assimilate completely who return again and again to these distinctives.

Other challenges facing Diaspora Jews included retaining a sense of connectedness with the land of Israel—their heritage celebrated in the Torah—from which they were removed. The corollary of this was the tension between understanding life in the Diaspora as exile and punishment, and celebrating their lives in the Diaspora as a place where God's favor and presence was fully known and enjoyed. Indeed, there seems to have been some tension between Palestinian Jews and their Diaspora sisters and brothers on these points. The growing linguistic alienation of Greek-speaking Diaspora Jews from their ancestral language of Hebrew meant that they now read as Scripture a translation that was at many points substantially different from the Scripture read in Hebrew in the synagogues in Palestine (and from the Aramaic paraphrases thereof). The continued existence of a Diaspora is assumed to be a sign of God's displeasure with Diaspora Jews, judging from a portion of the letter preserved in 2 Macc. 1:4–6. Nevertheless, contact with the land of Israel through pilgrimage, through the collection and sending of the temple tax, and through eschatological hope continued to provide Diaspora Jews with a reminder of that larger people and lasting heritage to which they belonged.

16. See Barclay 1996: 399–444 for a fuller discussion of these resources for Diaspora Jewish identity.

Tobit

3

"Better Is Almsgiving with Justice"

Tobit successfully mixes the pleasant with the useful (the recipe recommended in Horace, *Ars poetica* 343–344), proving that ethical instruction can be entertaining as well. The author promotes an ethos for Jewish readers that will lead them to safeguard their distinctive heritage and preserve their group identity but does so through the vehicle of a delightful story, rife with the three-dimensional characterizations, irony, and the reversals that make for entertaining narrative. The story reflects quite honestly how fidelity to God's way can result both in secular advancement and in temporal ruin. It affirms nevertheless that adherence to God's way in all circumstances gives one's life an honorable integrity that cannot be gainsaid and that results in the enjoyment of God's favor in the end. Ethics is developed in a way that directs the reader particularly toward the strengthening of the law-observant Jewish community through endogamy (marrying within one's people, within one's tribe if possible), charitable support of the righteous poor, duty toward one's parents and kin, and giving the dead a proper burial. This ethos resonates deeply with the wisdom literature of the Second Temple period and, ultimately, with the early church.

Structure and Contents

The story opens in the land of Israel with Tobit, a pious and Torah-observant Jew, remembering his life in the northern kingdom of Israel. When his neighbors abandoned the cult center of Jerusalem in favor of Jeroboam's alternative temples, Tobit remained faithful to the commands in Deuteronomy concerning worshiping only at the site designated by God. There he would take his triple tithes for the priests and Levites, the poor, and the enjoyment of the festivals in Jerusalem. After the tribe of Naphtali had been taken into exile in Assyria, he remained faithful to the dietary laws of Torah, even though the majority of his fellow Jews "ate the food of the Gentiles" (1:10–

11). As would be the case for Daniel and his companions, observance of dietary regulations was no obstacle to Tobit's rise to prominence in the court of Shalmaneser. Indeed, his mindfulness of God is explicitly named as the cause of this success (1:12–13).

In exile, Tobit continued to give alms to the righteous poor and left no Jewish corpse unburied. This latter act of piety brought about a reversal of fortunes under the hostile Sennacherib, one of the archvillains in the history of Israel (see 2 Kings 19). Tobit connects with this story after Sennacherib's defeat in Judah and return to Nineveh. Enraged against the Jewish people, he begins to execute Israelites as enemies of the state and sentences their corpses to lie unburied as the final disgrace. Tobit buries these bodies as well for piety's sake, making him a hunted criminal. His property is confiscated, and he becomes a fugitive (1:16–20).

After Sennacherib's assassination by his sons, Tobit's nephew Ahikar, who is well placed in the Assyrian court, intercedes for him with Esarhaddon, and so Tobit is able to return to Nineveh and to his wife and son. As the family was about to enjoy the Pentecost dinner (now a domestic observance, since access to the Jerusalem temple is denied), Tobit sends out his son, Tobias, to invite the righteous poor to enjoy the meal with them. Tobias returns with the disturbing news that a Jew has been murdered and left unburied. Tobit abandons the table and buries the corpse after sunset, to the mockery of neighbors who think that Tobit has not yet learned his lesson (2:1–8). That night, after washing himself (presumably as an improvised purification for corpse defilement), he sleeps outside in the courtyard of his house. As he sleeps, sparrows drop their excrement into his eyes, leaving white films. Going from physician to physician, his eyesight declines until he is totally blind. Ahikar supports him for a while, but he ultimately becomes dependent upon his wife, who must now earn money doing "women's work" (2:9–11). One day, Anna's employers were so pleased with her work that they sent her a goat as a bonus. Tobit accused Anna of stealing the goat, and she retorted by taunting him with his fall from a prosperous man who performed charity to a man who must depend on the charity of others (2:12–14). Now that insult has been added to injury, Tobit prays to God to release him from life (3:1–6).

This provides a segue to another person in distress in distant Ecbatana. Sarah, the daughter of Raguel and Edna, had lost each of seven husbands on their wedding nights on account of the jealous demon Asmodeus. One day, after Sarah scolded one of her servant girls, the maid retorted by blaming her for the deaths of seven men and by wishing that Sarah would follow them childless (3:7–9). Sarah, too, prays for release from the reproaches she must endure, asking for either death or help (3:10–15). The scene shifts to the heavenly realm: the prayers of both Tobit and Sarah are brought before God, who sends the archangel Raphael to rescue both (3:16–17).

Tobit, eager to set his affairs in order, tells Tobias about ten talents of silver he left in trust with Gabael in Media. He instructs Tobias about duty toward his parents and God, almsgiving, selecting a wife from among his kin, and justice in human interactions, and commissions him to retrieve the money after finding a trustworthy companion for the journey (4:1–5:3). Tobias finds Raphael, disguised as an unemployed but well-traveled Jew named Azariah, and presents him to Tobit. Learning that Azariah is a relative and that his father, Hananiah, was a Torah-observant Jew, Tobit hires him to assist his son. Tobias and Azariah depart (5:4–17), leaving Tobit to console his wife, who is afraid for her son's fate (5:18–6:1).

The two men camp the first night by the Tigris River, where Tobias is attacked by, but captures, a large fish. Azariah instructs him to keep the gall, which can be used to remove white films from a person's eyes, and the heart and liver, which can be burnt over incense to drive away demons (6:1–9). When they enter Media, Azariah tells Tobias about Raguel and of his intention to secure Sarah as a wife for Tobias. Tobias fears her fatal marriage bed, but Azariah instructs him again on the technique for defeating the demon (6:10–18).

Tobias and Azariah are welcomed most hospitably by Raguel and Edna, who agree happily to the union (7:1–16). Alone with Sarah, Tobias performs the exorcism, and Raphael chases Asmodeus to the far side of Egypt and binds him. The couple prays together for God's mercy on their union and go to sleep (8:1–9a). Meanwhile, Raguel had a grave dug for Tobias so that he could be buried quickly and the family spared more disgrace and reproach. Learning, however, that Tobias survived the night, he blesses God and orders the grave filled in quickly (8:9b–18). During the fourteen-day wedding feast, Azariah is dispatched to Ecbatana to complete the original mission of retrieving the funds, returning with Gabael as a wedding guest (8:19–9:6).

Back in Nineveh, Tobit and Anna are trying to hold on to the hope that their son is still alive, despite the fact that the time for his return has long since elapsed (10:1–7a). Mindful of his parents, Tobias and Sarah leave Raguel and Edna at the end of the fourteen days (10:7b–13). As they approach the city, Azariah and Tobias run ahead, anoint Tobit's eyes with the fish gall, and restore his sight. Tobit praises God loudly and publicly for his mercy as he goes out to meet his new daughter-in-law. Tobit and Anna give a second wedding feast for the couple, this time with Ahikar and Nadab on the guest list (11:1–18).

Tobit and Tobias decide to offer Azariah half of what they brought back out of gratitude for his deliverance of Sarah and Tobit. Azariah reveals privately to the men that he is one of the seven angels of the Presence. Instructing them to bring honor to God with their testimony and persevere in giving alms, Raphael ascends back to heaven (12:1–22). Tobit offers a lengthy psalm of thanksgiving, in which he applies what he has learned of God's mercy and restoration to the future of Israel (13:1–17). The book closes with Tobit's testament, a deathbed speech in which he instructs Tobias to take his family and leave Nineveh before its inevitable destruction and predicts the glorious restoration of Jerusalem and conversion of the nations. He reminds Tobias and his children of the importance of serving God faithfully and giving alms, which, after all, saved Ahikar from the plot set against him by his ungrateful nephew, Nadab (14:1–11a). After burying father and mother, Tobias takes his family back to live with Raguel and hears of Nineveh's destruction before his death (14:11b–15).

The story is artfully structured, cutting from scenes in Nineveh to scenes in Rages of Media with expert montage. The way in which the author brings together the predicaments of two very different people in different places and provides for their resolution through the journey of Tobias and the angel has delighted readers and hearers across the millennia. The complete loss of suspense at 3:16–17 and 6:6–8 is compensated for by the possibilities for irony that this opens up, since the author and reader share information that the characters do not. Tobit accepts Azariah on the basis of his kinship and lineage, but what makes him trustworthy is actually part of a false identity. When Tobit assures Anna that "a good angel" will accompany Tobias (5:22), the audience knows that this is indeed the case. With subtle irony, Raguel urges Tobias with the first half of a proverb to "eat and drink, and be merry tonight" before his entry into the bridal chamber (7:10), since, for all Raguel knows, tomorrow Tobias may be dead. Though the audience knows that all will be well, they still delight to watch the characters learn that their story, as Raguel says to God, "has not turned out as I expected, but you have dealt with us according to your great mercy" (8:16).

The literary unity, or integrity, of Tobit had been disputed in the late nineteenth and early twentieth centuries, the heyday of reconstructive surgery on ancient texts. In particular, chapters 13 and 14 were thought to be later additions to the original book. This view has been largely discredited. Fragments of Tobit found at Qumran show chapters 13 and 14 to have been part of the work before 100 B.C.E.; so if in fact they were added, they were added very early. Literary arguments add considerable weight to the case for unity. The book, taken as a whole, begins and ends with concern for the Temple. The plight of Tobit and his family is only fully reversed, albeit proleptically, in chapters 13 and 14 as the return from exile is contemplated and affirmed (Soll 1988: 39–53; Moore 1996: 77). Moreover, echoes of 1:3 in 14:9 with the recurrence of "truth," "justice," and "almsgiving" in that same order suggest that the author has intentionally used a literary device to link the beginning and ending of the story (Di Lella 1979: 386):

"I, Tobit, walked in the paths of truth and justice . . . and I practiced many acts of almsgiving." (1:3)

"Serve God in truth . . . and command your children to practice justice and almsgiving." (14:9)

Taken together, these considerations strongly favor the literary unity of Tobit as we have it.

Textual Transmission

Tobit survives in two different Greek editions (or recensions). Codices Vaticanus and Alexandrinus (B and A) preserve the shorter edition, while Codex Sinaiticus (א) preserves the longer version.[1] Although in most cases it is easier to understand how a longer version is derived from a shorter through scribal expansions and clarifications, with Tobit priority is to be given to the longer text (Nestle 1899: 22–35; Simpson 1913b).[2] Sinaiticus has two major gaps (4:7–19 and 13:8–10) that need to be supplied from the Old Latin, the version that most closely corresponds to א. The English reader has easy access to these two editions: the RSV follows the shorter recension, the NRSV follows Sinaiticus (as do the NEB and NJB). The discovery of dozens of fragments of five separate manuscripts of Tobit at Qumran has served to confirm the priority of א, the longer Greek version, over A and B. The Qumran manuscripts have also been of use in correcting א, sometimes in favor of a reading preserved in A or B, sometimes in favor of a reading preserved in none of the Septuagint codices.

Tobit has also been passed down in Latin translations. The Old Latin was based on a Greek version very similar to א and thus can be used to confirm readings in א and supplement its gaps. The Vulgate is based on the Old Latin, Jerome having access to this at the same time as access to an Aramaic manuscript. Jerome employed a bilingual Jew to provide him with a running Hebrew translation of the Aramaic as he revised the Old Latin based on that oral translation. The whole process took them a day (Jerome, *Preface to Tobit*), which suggests that the work was not so careful. A few peculiarities of the Latin versions are worth mentioning. The Old Latin and the Vulgate give both father and son the name Tobias, thus adding to the confusion of the story. More significantly, the Vulgate (perhaps Jerome's own pious addition) includes a report of Sarah and Tobias abstaining from intercourse for three days after their wedding, devoting themselves instead to prayer. This became a mark of piety promoted in the Roman Catholic Church. There are also versions in Syriac, Ethiopic, Sahidic, Armenian, and Aramaic, all based on one of the Greek editions.

1. Rahlfs 1979 and Zimmermann 1958a provide both the shorter and longer Greek texts. The preferred critical edition is Hanhart 1983.

2. Recent supporters include Moore 1996: 68; Di Lella 1979: 380 n. 2. Deselaers (1982) argues that Vaticanus and Alexandrinus have priority and that the original language was Greek, but both of these conclusions are rejected by the majority of Tobit scholars.

Scholars had long debated whether the original language was Greek or a Semitic language (Aramaic or Hebrew). Pfeiffer (1949: 272–73) correctly notes the Semitisms behind the Greek and so posits a Semitic original, favoring Aramaic (given the author's familiarity with Aramaic literature such as the tale of Ahiqar). His opinion has been confirmed by Fitzmyer (1995a: 671), whose examination of the five Qumran manuscripts proved that Greek was not the original language but rather, that the original was Semitic and probably Aramaic.[3] The Qumran manuscripts have helped less than scholars had hoped with regard to settling the question of a Hebrew or Aramaic original. The fact that "at Qumran a Hebrew text may contain Aramaisms just as an Aramaic text may contain Hebraisms" (Moore 1996: 33) complicates matters, as does the fragmentary state of the Tobit manuscripts. Moreover, there are very few verses surviving in both Aramaic and Hebrew, with the result that comparative study is hindered (Moore 1996: 34–35).[4]

Author, Date, and Setting

The anonymous author was a pious Jew concerned with keeping covenant and maintaining Jewish identity and solidarity within a Gentile-dominant culture. Where the author wrote remains a mystery. Pfeiffer (1949: 273–75) favors Palestine, having ruled out the eastern Diaspora on account of the book's gross geographical errors where that part of the world is concerned, having ruled out Egypt on account of the book having been written in Aramaic,[5] and having underscored the fact that Tobit and Ben Sira share a common set of values. A more judicious opinion is ventured by Moore (1996: 43), who acknowledges that one cannot be certain even whether the work originates from the Diaspora as opposed to Palestine, although, if pressed, he would opt for an eastern Diaspora setting. The book's interest in exilic life, with only dim recollections of life in the land of Israel, could suggest an origin beyond Palestine; the fact that five copies of Tobit were found at Qumran suggests, however, that its message was equally appropriate in Israel and may

3. Fitzmyer (1995a: 671–72) also brings new support for the view that Sinaiticus is the older recension, given its correspondences with the Qumran fragments and the presence of Semitisms in א where A and B have smoothed out those translational infelicities in favor of better Greek.

4. The contents of the five manuscripts are as follows: 4Q196 (4QTobA): 1:17; 1:19–2:3; 2:10–11; 3:5, 9–15, 17; 4:2, 5, 7, 21; 5:1, 9; 6:6–8, 13–18; 7:1–6, 13; 12:1, 18–22; 13:1–2 (?), 3–18; 14:1–3, 7; 4Q197 (4QTobB): 3:6–8; 4:21; 5:1, 12–14, 19–21; 6:1–18; 7:1–10; 8:17–21; 9:1–4; 4Q198 (4QTobC): 14:2–6, possibly also 10; 4Q199 (4QTobD): 7:11; 14:10; 4Q200 (4QTobE, the Hebrew manuscript): 3:3–4 (very fragmentary), 6, 10–11; 4:3–9; 5:2; 10:7–9; 11:10–14; 12:20–22; 13:1–4, 13–14, 17–18; 14:1–2. See Abegg, Flint, and Ulrich 1999: 637–46 for English translations of these manuscripts; Fitzmyer 1995a: 657–58.

5. The discovery of an Aramaic papyrus of the tale of Ahiqar in Elephantine, Egypt, dating from the fifth century B.C.E., seriously undermines this objection, however.

well have originated there. Tobit reflects Jewish values so broadly and addresses the challenges of living as a Jew at such a basic level, that it is indeed difficult to determine its geographical setting from hints in the narrative.

Dating the book is also difficult, since the narrative does not seem to reflect current events as it tells the story. The formation of the canonical collection of Prophets is often taken as a *terminus a quo* (the earliest date) for the composition of Tobit, but 14:4 does not really demand that this collection be final and complete. Tobit does not speak of the Law and the Prophets, as if to denote two categories of Scripture, but only of the "prophets of Israel" whose words must prove true. The author evidences knowledge of their works individually but not of their collection.

Since the law is known as "the book of Moses" or "the law of Moses" (6:13; 7:11–13), the work must certainly postdate the fifth century, when the formation of the Pentateuch was nearly complete. It seems reasonable to set the earliest date of composition as sometime during the third century B.C.E. The book reflects the same ethos as in Ben Sira and Judith with regard to dietary laws, burial of the dead, endogamy, and piety. Formerly, the use of the book in *2 Clement,* Polycarp, and Clement of Alexandria had established this *terminus ad quem* (the latest date) as 100 C.E. This endpoint has been now set with much greater precision based on the discovery of the fragments of Tobit at Qumran, the earliest of which dates from 100 B.C.E. Tobit's failure to reflect any knowledge of the issues surrounding the Hellenization crisis and Maccabean Revolt suggests that the book was written sometime between 250 and 175 B.C.E.

Genre and Purpose

What kind of book is Tobit? Confusion about its genre is evident as early as the Septuagint codices themselves, where Sinaiticus treats it as a historical book but Vaticanus as a wisdom book (Delcor 1989: 474). Catholic scholars had defended its historicity until the eighteenth century. Nevertheless, Tobit's historical and geographical errors,[6] together with the fact that the story concerns ordinary people rather than the rulers of a people (the usual subjects of history), strongly suggest that the author did not compose or present this work as historiography. Rather, the work falls most nearly into the category

6. These are summarized in Moore 1996: 9–11 and, more briefly, in Levine 1991: 48. Tobit, being of the tribe of Naphtali, would more likely have been deported earlier, with the rest of his tribe, when Tiglath-pileser took that region (2 Kings 15:29); Tobit could not have been a young man when the northern tribes seceded from the kingdom in 922 B.C.E. (see Tob. 1:4) *and* alive at the time of their deportation under Tiglath-pileser sometime between 740 and 731 B.C.E. (see Moore 1996: 107); Sargon II, not Shalmaneser, was the father of Sennacherib; Rages and Ecbatana are 180 miles apart, not a two-day journey; Tobias and Raphael would not have sat on the banks of the Tigris on their journey from Nineveh to Ecbatana, unless they got lost (the Tigris is west of Nineveh, not east).

of "romance" (Moore 1996: 18–19), defined by Perry (1967: 44–55) as "an extended narrative . . . which relates . . . for the sake of entertainment or spiritual edification, and for its own sake as story . . . the adventures or experiences of one or more individuals in their private capacities and from the viewpoint of their private interests and emotions." The sapiential (wisdom) aspects of Tobit are at home in this genre, since instruction was one of its aims.

In composing this romance, the author has incorporated many literary forms. Notable among these are prayer, psalms, benedictions, and the testament genre. Tobit's final discourse in chapter 14 resembles other testaments both in form (a deathbed speech to kin) and content (moral instruction and predictions about the future). The popularity of this genre in the intertestamental period is evident from the surviving examples, such as *Testaments of the Twelve Patriarchs, Testament of Moses, Testament of Job*, and *Testaments of the Three Patriarchs* (see Collins 1984; Kolenkow and Collins 1986). The author's twofold aim of entertaining and edifying, delighting and teaching, has been often noted (Levine 1991: 42; Metzger 1957: 30). It is clear from the amount of ethical and sapiential material in Tobit that the author wished to promote or reinforce a set of values. These values sought to dispose the audience to engage in behaviors that would sustain the Jewish minority culture in the midst of the Gentile world. Attempts to get more specific than this concerning the author's purpose—for example, to combat the divine powers attributed to the Egyptian god of healing with a rival story (Simpson 1913a: 188)—falter on the inability of scholars to fix with any precision the provenance and date of the work.

Formative Influences

Scholars have sought out the author's inspiration and source material primarily in two places: secular folktales and Jewish Scripture. In the history of interpretation, the importance of the former has been rather overstated, to the detriment of the analysis of the ways in which Jewish Scripture has informed and shaped this story, but this pendulum has been swinging toward correction during the last quarter of the twentieth century.

It is often said that the author drew on folktales about the "Grateful Dead" and the "Poison Maiden" or "Dangerous Bride." In the first archetypal tale, a person buries a corpse, whose grateful ghost then delivers that person from some peril or bestows some type of reward. In the second type, a man attains a beautiful woman as his wife only by defeating some curse or supernatural lover. Pfeiffer (1949: 269) regards Tobit's dependence on these tales as demonstrated fact, drawing his support from Cicero (*De divinatione* 1.27; which only resembles the Grateful Dead motif),[7] "a modern Armenian tale," and a Bohemian variant "heard near Adrianople," both of which may no doubt claim to be several centuries old.

Tobit, however, predates all of Pfeiffer's examples, and it is unclear how far back one should assume these folktale traditions to stretch without written attestation. Although one should not jump to the other extreme and suggest that Tobit is *the* source for *all* other similar tales, it is certainly possible that Tobit itself exercised some influence on the development of the folktales cited by Pfeiffer. The Cicero tale is a perfectly natural development in a culture in which reciprocity is a core value, a value believed to transcend the grave. Piety toward the deceased is held to be rewarded. This is a pillar of domestic cults in Italy, where libations and prayers keep the spirits of the deceased beneficent and disposed to give aid to the living family. The two oral tales cited by Pfeiffer, however, could very well be popular derivatives of the Tobit story, given the pervasive telling of Tobit (thanks to the church fathers' interest in the book) and the tendency to assimilate such stories with one's pre-Christian worldview.

The reading of the Grateful Dead tale as a foundation for Tobit is especially suspect because the dead are never said to be grateful (Glasson 1959: 276–77).[8] In Jewish culture, though not Greek and Roman culture (where honor shown the dead resulted in some numinous favor toward the living), charity toward the dead was said to be pure because there was no hope for reciprocity. Thus Simpson (1913a: 190), although himself an advocate of the Grateful Dead tale as a source for Tobit, quotes Rashi's comment on Gen. 47:29 to the effect that "the kindness that a man shows the dead is *kindness of truth* for the doer has no hope of (receiving) a reward (from the corpse)." The folktale of the Grateful Dead would thus not be as congruent with Jewish beliefs as with Greco-Roman beliefs. Vermes (in Schürer 1986: 1.226) pronounces the most judicious sentence on this issue: the author's use of this folktale cannot be established with any certainty.

Even if one assumes these folktale types to predate Tobit, the author's departures from, or modifications of, the type remain equally impressive as the points of similarity. This is especially true vis-à-vis the Grateful Dead tale, since burying the dead actually brings Tobit twice into ruin and since recompense comes in the story from God rather than from the ghosts of the dead (who never even

7. Recounting how dreams are channels for the voices from beyond, Cicero cites one story "concerning Simonides who having found the dead body of a man who was a stranger to him lying on the road, buried it. Having performed this office, he was about to embark in a ship, when the man whom he buried appeared to him in a dream at night and warned him not to undertake the voyage, for that if he did he would perish by shipwreck. Therefore he returned home again, but all the other people who sailed in that vessel were lost."

8. Glasson's own suggestion that Tobit is based on the Greek myth of Apollo and Admetus (the former acting as the latter's servant and helping him defeat Artemis's serpents, which barred his way to his marriage bed with Alcestis) has not won a following.

appear). The element of the Dangerous Bride tale has more to commend itself as a source that might have spurred on the author's thinking.[9]

Unquestionable, however, is the author's acquaintance with the tale of Ahiqar, which existed by the fifth century B.C.E. and was probably composed in Aramaic (as the discovery of a fifth-century Aramaic fragment from Elephantine suggests). The numerous points of contact with this story (Tob. 1:22; 2:10; 11:18; 14:10–11) show the author's familiarity with the whole of the Ahiqar story, from his rise to prominence under Sennacherib and Esarhaddon, to his betrayal by his nephew Nadin (Nadab in Tobit), to his ultimate vindication and Nadin's punishment. The author of Tobit, however, reflects a version of the Ahiqar story in which the hero is a Jew (being Tobit's nephew) rather than a polytheist and an embodiment of Jewish values such as almsgiving (this may be the author's own addition). Several sayings in Tobit reflect sayings of Ahiqar in one or another of the different versions of that tale (see Lindenberger: 1985: 489–90).

The author lives primarily, however, within the world of the Jewish scriptural tradition, and it is within that world that he firmly anchors his characters. Tobit's story is embedded in the Deuteronomistic History. Tobit is taken into exile in Nineveh along with the northern tribes (Tob. 1:3; 10; cf. 2 Kings 17:5–18; 18:9–12). Tobit 1:18–21 locates Tobit's acts of charity toward the dead in the aftermath of Sennacherib's defeat in Judea, in the period between Sennacherib's disgraceful return and his assassination by his two sons (see 2 Kings 19:35–37). The book is deeply infused with Deuteronomy's ideology and phraseology. Tobit understands his people's misfortunes strictly from the viewpoint of Deuteronomy 28–29 (see Tob. 3:2–5), and his hope for the reversal of their fortunes resonates deeply with Deuteronomy 30–32 (Tob. 13:2, 5–6).

Deuteronomy is an especially important background for the closing chapters of Tobit. Weitzman (1996: 55–57) cogently argues that the audience of Tobit would recognize quotations from the Song of Moses, noting the reading of the song as a "song of praise" rather than a witness against Israel in the intertestamental period, its incorporation into liturgy, its quotation beyond Tobit, and the general tendency of intertestamental hymns to pattern themselves after classical models. The angel's command to Tobit in 12:20, "Write down all these things that have happened to you," and Tobit's writing and speaking his hymn in 13:1a[10] could therefore recall God's command to Moses

9. Another tale alleged to have influenced the author of Tobit is the "Story of Khons," an agent of the Egyptian god of healing, who exorcised a demon that had possessed a princess (the text can be found in Pritchard, ed., 1950: 29–31). Simpson (1913a: 187–88) regarded Tobit as written specifically as a Jewish rebuttal to this story. Unless Tobit was written in Egypt (and the fact that the demon is driven away to Egypt as if to the farthest reaches of the earth suggests that the place was far from the author's home [see Moore 1996: 14]), it is unlikely that the author would have known of this tale.

10. This is one place where the Qumran text 4QTobHeb[a] can supplement or correct Sinaiticus, as the latter speaks only of Tobit singing the psalm, not writing it down as well.

to write down the song that God would teach him (Deut. 31:19) and Moses' obedience in doing so (Deut. 31:22, 24) before he speaks the song to the people (Deut. 31:30) (Weitzman 1996:51–52). Tobit 13:2 loosely paraphrases the first part of Deut. 32:39 ("I kill and I make alive") and more closely recontextualizes the second part ("no one can deliver from my hand").[11] Tobit 13:5–6 reflects the promise of Deut. 30:1–5 but even more specifically recalls the language of Deut. 32:20. The direction of the pronouncement "I will hide my face from them" (Deut. 32:20) is reversed in Tob. 13:6: "If you . . . do what is true before him, then he will turn to you and will no longer hide his face from you." "If you turn to him with all your heart and with all your soul" (Tob. 13:6) recalls the Shema itself (Deut. 6:5).

Di Lella (1979: 381–85) has also shown the importance of Deuteronomistic thought and vocabulary for Tobit's testament, particularly Tob. 14:3–11: (1) Long life and prosperity in Israel depend on fidelity to the covenant, whereas infidelity leads to destruction and expulsion. Tobit 14:7 expresses this negative aspect, recalling Deut. 28:63–65. Calling Israel "the good land" (Tob. 14:4) recalls Deuteronomy's title for Israel (see Deut. 1:35; 3:25; 4:21–22). (2) Tobit 14:4–6 recontextualizes Deut. 30:1–4, affirming that God will extend mercy when punishment has run its course. (3) The promise that the faithful will dwell in the land "with security" is affirmed in both Tob. 14:7 and Deut. 12:10–11 (*oikēsousin/katoikēsete meta asphaleias*). Other points of contact include the promise of joy as a result of loving and obeying God (Tob. 14:7; cf. Deut. 12:12); the linking of fearing God, loving God, and serving God (Tob. 14:6–7, 9; cf. Deut. 10:12–13; 6:13); the command to "bless" God "with all their strength" (Tob. 14:9; cf. Deut. 32:3, 43; 6:5); the elevation of mindfulness of God as a core value; and the insistence upon Jerusalem as the single, central cultic center for the Jewish people (Tob. 1:4–6; 14:5–7; cf. Deut. 12:1–14).

The author of Tobit also drew upon the narratives of Genesis 24 and 29, two journeys undertaken to procure a wife, for Tobias's journey. Although Tobias is sent out for a different purpose (as was Jacob), the result is that he finds his bride within the family, as his father instructed.[12] The undeserved suffering of Tobit, a man who has shown himself righteous in every way, also recalls the story of Job, as does the scene of marital disharmony in Tob. 2:11–14 (although Anna merely defends her honor, whereas Job's wife urges Job to attack God's honor). Weitzman (1996: 59) rightly points out that Job was regarded as a figure from the patriarchal period in early Judaism and that the author of Tobit was particularly drawn to that era. These allusions to patriarchal stories are a part of the author's response to the threat of exile and life in

11. Compare 1 Sam. 2:6, in Hannah's Song, as a text utilizing motifs from the Song of Moses. That verse both recontextualizes the phrase "I kill and I make alive" and then paraphrases it using the same geographical imagery of going down to and returning from Sheol that is found in Tobit's paraphrase of Deut. 32:39.

12. Moore (1996: 8–9) offers a detailed analysis of similarities between Tobit and Abraham's quest for a bride for Isaac.

Diaspora to Jewish identity. The patriarchal narratives affirm that God encounters Israel, intimately relates with Israel, and works on Israel's behalf beyond the borders of its land (Weitzman 1996: 60). Such a strategy behind the author's choice of allusions would indeed make Tobit a pertinent word to Jews in Diaspora.

The author also drew upon the prophetic literature of Israel. He quotes Amos 8:10 at Tob. 2:6, as Tobit, having learned of an unburied Jew on the eve of Pentecost, connects this sorrowful reality with Amos's prophecy against Bethel, a prophecy that came true in the exile and continues to come true in new experiences of sorrow in exile. Tobit also makes a general reference to Nahum's oracles against Nineveh (Tob. 14:4),[13] providing an interesting window into the way the author read the words of the prophets (i.e., that they would inevitably come to pass at the time designated by God). The author recontextualizes other prophetic texts, such as the prediction that Jerusalem will become a light shining "to all the ends of the earth" with the result that "many nations" will come to Jerusalem with gifts for God (Tob. 13:11; cf. Isa. 2:3; 60:3) or the prediction of the rebuilding of Jerusalem with precious stones (Tob. 13:16; cf. Isa. 54:11–12). One also sees the unmistakable imprint of the biblical psalms and prayers upon the form, phraseology, and content of the prayers, frequent benedictions, and final hymn in Tobit.

Tobit and the Values of Intertestamental Judaism

Tobit preserves an outstanding witness to the values cherished by Jews in the Second Temple period. These values are also, strategically, such as will maintain the solidarity and distinctive identity of the Jewish community in the face of the threat of assimilation into the dominant Gentile culture. The author conveys moral instruction through the deeds of the characters as well as through their speech. Tobit is a model of integrity, practicing first what he preaches to his son and, eventually, to his grandchildren. Tobias and Sarah are models of honorable children, who make caring for their parents a primary concern. The audience receives instruction, then, in the way of life promoted by the author not only in the lengthy speeches of Tobit (chapters 4 and 14) but also throughout the story as they observe the noble motives and actions of the characters with whom they are led to sympathize.

Perhaps the most outstanding value in this book is care for the pious Jews through almsgiving and provision for burial. Nurturing this value produces a supportive community that defines itself by ethnic heritage and shared commitment to the distinctive culture shaped by the law of Moses. Tobit distinguishes himself by his acts of charity toward poorer, righteous Jews and his

---

13. Alexandrinus and Vaticanus read "Jonah" rather than "Nahum," but I agree with Moore (1996: 290) against Metzger (1957: 36) that the latter is to be preferred.

pious burial of exposed Jewish corpses (1:3, 16–18; 2:2–7). His commitment to doing works of kindness gains Tobit notice in the court of God (12:12–14), resulting both in God's decision to test Tobit's commitment and in God's commitment to bring healing to the whole family of Tobit and Raguel. It is noteworthy that Tobit restricts his alms to the *righteous* poor, who are "wholeheartedly mindful of God" (2:2; cf. 4:6b), a practice advocated also in Sir. 12:1–7. Charity thus becomes one more instrument for encouraging commitment to Jewish core values (like Torah observance), since these values are what make one fully a part of the group and its mutual assistance.

Tobit gives almsgiving a prominent place when instructing Tobias (4:6–11, 16–17), including several motivations for almsgiving. Generosity in giving to the poor will result in God's generosity toward the giver (4:7). It is an intelligent investment against the uncertain future. When one might be in need of assistance, the reputation for being virtuous and generous is the best credit line (4:9). Almsgiving is approved by God as an "excellent offering," which becomes all the more important where Jews are separated from the temple (4:11). Finally, it provides the best insurance against a premature death (4:10). Almsgiving is also underscored by the angel Raphael in his revelation speech (12:8–9) and by Tobit in his testament (14:2, 9–11). In fact, 14:10–11 specifically uses the secular story of Ahikar as a proof of the claims made for almsgiving's power to deliver the giver in 4:10 and 12:9. In the original Ahiqar tale, Ahiqar escapes execution because he had previously spared the executioner when an unjust sentence was given. In Tobit, however, it is his charitable acts in general that save Ahikar from the machinations of his wicked nephew.

A second noteworthy value is the preservation of kinship duties. First among these is one's duty toward one's parents, honoring them during life and providing for a proper burial after death (4:3–4; 10:12–13; 14:10a, 11b–12a). When a couple marries, each partner gains a second set of parents to which the same duties are owed (8:21; 10:12–13)—quite a different vision from the modern Western concept of the "in-law." Kinship duties extend far beyond the parent-child relationship. Ahikar is kin (nephew, 1:22) to Tobit and so naturally comes to Tobit's aid as advocate and, in the early years of his blindness, provider (1:21–22; 2:10). By way of contrast, Nadab's treachery is multiplied because, in plotting against Ahikar, he does it to his kinsman and benefactor (14:10–11). Tobit's charity is basically directed to his "kindred" (1:3), even when he extends this to all Israelites. The Jewish community itself continues to be regarded as an extended kinship group to whom certain duties (notably assistance) are owed, in distinction from the many other peoples of the world (1:16–18, 2:2–3).

Kin are presumed to be trustworthy. The fact that Azariah is (in his assumed identity) a kinsman gives Tobias hope that he will prove to be an acceptable and reliable traveling companion, and so he hastens to introduce him to Tobit (5:9). Tobit needs only discover Azariah's lineage to evaluate whether or not Azariah will be a trustworthy companion for Tobias's mission (5:11–12). Since Tobit knows Azariah's father and uncle to be noble Jews who observed Torah faithfully, he is also confident of Azariah's character (5:14). The child inherits the moral credit rating of the parent.

Nestled within this larger value of kinship is the third prominent value, endogamy—a social-scientific concept indicating marriage within one's own group, tribe, or family. Such a marital strategy was crucial to preserving the Jewish people in the midst of non-Jewish nations, part of the author's desire to give Israel definition and shape "by genealogy rather than geography" (Levine 1991: 48) once removed from Israel's land. The actual form urged by Tobit—marrying within the pool of one's father's relatives—is rather impractical for the intertestamental period, being ultimately rooted in the pentateuchal concern that the property allotted to each of the twelve ancestral divisions of Israel remain in the particular tribe (Num 36:1–9). In going to the extreme, however, it certainly reinforces the more basic impetus to marry fellow Jews rather than to court assimilation through intermarriage with non-Jews. Such intermarriage was one of Alexander's strategies for mingling the peoples of the world into one, a practice that his armies took to heart. It would have been regarded as socially, politically, and economically advantageous by many Jews to seek a union with a well-placed Gentile family.

The author of Tobit combats this tendency both through the story and through the character's speeches, reminding the hearers of the divine viewpoint on whom Jews should marry. Tobit marries a fellow Jew, a kinswoman (1:9), and Sarah's marriage partners all were male relatives from her father's side. When the known list of available suitors from that pool is exhausted by the tireless efforts of the demon, Sarah assumes that the pool of potential marriage partners is exhausted (3:15). There is simply no one left for whom she should be kept for marriage, as far as she is aware.

Tobit, in 4:12, presents marriage with those of other races as a kind of fornication: the first way to avoid fornication is to marry a woman of Israelite stock. He cautions Tobias, and through him the audience, against pride and contempt for one's race, which are identified as motives for mixed marriage. This is, again, a product of the Hellenistic setting (both in the Diaspora and in Palestine), where marriage into a Gentile family would provide more potential for advancement through entering the mainstream of the dominant culture. Azariah speaks of endogamy as the norm for marriage (6:12), such that Tobias has a hereditary claim on Sarah's hand, being next in line. This is anchored in no less an authority than the "book of Moses" (6:13; cf. Num. 36:6–9). The issue of inheritance is an important background here: since Sarah will inherit Raguel's estate, it must remain within the ancestral tribe.

The author also promotes an ideology of marriage, revealed mainly in the prayer of 8:5–7 (which is an optional Old Testament reading in Catholic, Anglican, and United Methodist marriage services). Marriage exists not for the purpose of sexual gratification or lust but for mutual help throughout life.

Edna's parting words to Tobias are also relevant here, as the groom is commissioned, "Do nothing to grieve her all the days of your life" (10:12). The author shows a sensitivity to marriage as a partnership, not as an opportunity for sexual exploitation or emotional domination.

An overarching value that holds all the others together is fidelity to God's law to the full extent that one's context permits. Tobit scrupulously heeds cultic law while in Israel (1:4–8), worshiping only at the proper site (1:4; cf. Deut. 12:13–14), even though his kin in the tribe of Naphtali worshiped the golden calves Jeroboam erected in Dan (1:5) and at Bethel as alternative cult sites for the northern kingdom after the division of Solomon's kingdom (see 1 Kings 12:25–33). He observed the tithe laws meticulously, setting apart a first tithe for the priests and Levites, a second to spend in Jerusalem at the festivals, and a third to give away to the poor in Jerusalem (1:6–8). Once removed from the land of Israel, however, Tobit no longer could observe these aspects of Torah, and so he moved his emphasis doubly to almsgiving and acts of charity as "excellent offerings" (4:11).

Tobit also observes Torah's dietary regulations. After the deportation to Assyria, Tobit refrained from eating the "food of the Gentiles," again in contrast to the majority of his fellow-Jews (1:10–11). By his example, the reader is confirmed in the commitment to abide by what is right when even one's fellow Jews go another way. Tobit's examples and instructions promote mindfulness of God (1:12; 14:7–9), which is nothing other than honoring God by following God's commandments (4:5). The author promotes the fear of the Lord, the avoidance of sin, and the doing of what is right as "true wealth" (4:21; 12:8b), because ultimately this keeps one in the center of God's favor and God's design to restore Israel (14:7–9).

The connections between Tobit and Ben Sira are numerous and suggest the importance and pervasiveness of these values (rather than literary interdependence).[14] Both uphold duty toward parents (Tob. 4:3; Sir. 3:1–16); view fear of the Lord and observance of Torah as the core values of this life and as the path to a good future (Tob. 4:5–6, 21; Sir. 1:11–13); promote almsgiving, particularly toward those who share one's commitment to Torah (Tob. 2:2; 4:7–11, 17; Sir. 3:30; 4:4–5; 7:32–33; 12:1–7); and view obedience to God's law as the source of true wealth and honor (Tob. 4:21; 12:8; Sir. 10:19–24; 40:26). Tobit's practical advice likewise resonates with Ben Sira, who promotes not withholding wages from a worker (Sir. 34:22; Tob. 4:14 directly recontextualizes Lev. 19:13); moderation in the use of wine (Sir. 31:25–31; Tob. 4:15); and seeking counsel from worthy sources, especially God (Sir. 37:7–15; Tob. 4:18–19).

Tobit also provides a window into the personal piety and prayer life of Second Temple Jews. The prayers of Tobit and Sarah resemble the individual laments and prayers of Psalms, except that the psalmists never seek deliverance

14. A number of these are noted in Moore 1996: 21 n. 49, 46.

in death but rather *from* death. Tobit begins with a declaration about God's just character, moves into a historical reminiscence about the exile, again acknowledging God's justice, and finally presents his petition. Sarah begins with a benediction, follows this immediately with a request, adds a protestation of virtue (as is characteristic of the biblical psalms), and resumes her request. Noteworthy about both prayers is the openness and honesty before God, as both petitioners pour out quite plainly what troubles them most about their situation and ask God to intervene. The assumption behind such prayers is that God is intimately concerned not only with the fate of the people as a whole but also with the plight of each individual.

The prayer of Tobias in 8:5–7 also exhibits an artistic and rhetorically apt form. It begins, as with most biblical prayers, with declaration of God's praise. This is followed by a statement anchoring the request in God's purposes (here, revealed in creation) and a declaration of intent to act in conformity with God's purposes. Only at this point is the request actually made. In a sense, this prayer provides a model for "praying according to God's will," since God's own purposes are considered first, before Tobias's wishes, and the request embedded in God's purposes.

The form of the benediction ("Blessed are you, O God") is especially common in Tobit, and it is likely that this reflects the prayer life and practice of pious interjections experienced by the author (Tob. 3:11; 8:5, 15, 16, 17; 11:14; 13:1, 17; see also Jdt. 13:17; Pr. Azar. 3; Sg. Three 29; 1 Macc. 4:30; 2 Macc. 1:17; 1 Esd. 4:40, 60; 3 Macc. 7:23). There is an interesting mix of prayer and magic in the exorcism of the demon in 6:17–18, a mix that would be greatly embellished in, for example, *Testament of Solomon* but is notably absent from exorcisms in the New Testament. The response to receiving benefits from God is public testimony to the Benefactor, honoring God and increasing God's fame in the world (11:16–17; 12:6–7a, 20a). This is rooted in the practice of honoring and increasing the reputation of human benefactors in the ancient world (see deSilva 2000b: 113–14, 141–43).

Theology

The Book of Tobit reaffirms Deuteronomy's basic explanations of prosperity and suffering. Obedience to Torah and commitment to virtue are assumed to result in prosperity (4:6; cf. Ps. 1:1–3), whereas departure from Torah is the source of misfortune. Tobit's prayer in 3:3–5 and the testimony to the general lawlessness of Tobit's neighbors in chapter 1 both support the basic dictum of Deuteronomy that sin leads to exile. Tobit also interprets his own predicament of being an exile and an impoverished blind man as the punishment for his own sins (3:3, 5), perhaps merely by virtue of being a part of a sinful people who have, as a whole, renounced God's protection. He has no other model by which to understand these developments, at least until Raphael presents an alternative. Raphael claims that he was sent to test Tobit (12:13–14), recalling the testing of Job by a more insidious angelic being, although we are not explicitly told why. Perhaps, like Job, his ongoing fidelity to God and God's values (as seen in his instructions to Tobias) is given the opportunity to be proven and to shine the more brightly for being preserved amidst adversity.[15]

Tobit makes a greater contribution in the realm of angelology and demonology. Intertestamental texts such as Tobit provide the bridge from the spare presence of angels and virtual nonappearance of demons in the Old Testament to their ubiquity in the New Testament. The author of Tobit speaks of seven archangels of the Presence (12:15), referring thus to an especially distinguished order of angels (as in *Testament of Levi* 3.5 and Rev. 1:4; 4:5; 8:2). The author also shares with *Testament of Levi* the view that angels bear petitions to God and that archangels function on behalf of the righteous (see *Testament of Levi* 3.5–7), resulting in a somewhat bureaucratized theology of prayer in which petitions are brought from humans through angelic intermediaries to God for the Almighty's attention (3:16–17; 12:12–15). The author shares with *1 Enoch* and *Jubilees* a worldview in which fallen angels wreak havoc on humankind (here in a very personalized way, and one reminiscent of Gen. 6:1–4, which is the basis for *1 Enoch*'s development of an extensive theology of fallen angels and their demonic offspring). There is also a correspondence between human acts of exorcism and spiritual warfare: Tobit causes Asmodeus to flee, but Raphael overpowers and binds the demon (8:3). This active spiritual realm is very much the world in which the New Testament authors and their audiences live and move.

Another major theological concern of Tobit is the destiny of Israel. Just as Tobit and Sarah move from tragedy to a restoration of happiness and a sense of being restored to God's favor, so the story of the larger people of God will also move from the tragedy and desolation of exile to a glorious restoration. Again, Deuteronomy 28–32 undergirds the closing chapters of the book, where reversal and restoration are promised as the result of renewed fidelity to God in the land of exile. Tobit's experience—"Though he afflicted me, he has had mercy upon me" (11:15)—will yet be the experience of the whole people of God.

Tobit's final psalm and testament contain the book's eschatology. The first part of the testament's predictions (14:4–5a) is largely "prediction after the fact," since the author writes in the late third or early second century B.C.E. The statement about the inevitability of the fall of Nineveh reveals a specific doctrine of prophecy: "Everything that was spoken by the prophets of Israel,

---

15. Harrington (1999: 25) is correct, however, to critique the work for failing to delve deeper into the meaning in the several forms of suffering that it raises (save for the exile, of course, for which the old Deuteronomic explanation is amply attested: see 3:2–5; 13:3–9).

whom God sent, will occur. None of all their words will fail, but will come true at their appointed times" (14:4). Thus, Nahum's oracles (especially Nah. 1:1; 2:13–3:19) against Nineveh must become reality, and Tobias and Sarah plan for their future accordingly. This is a conviction shared by the early Christians, as they read their own past, present, and future history from those same oracles of God. Indeed, the claims of 14:4 and 8 are vindicated in the world of the narrative, which does not close with the death of Tobit but with the fall of Nineveh in 14:15.

Tobit goes on to "predict" dereliction of duty toward the covenant (14:4b), the exile and destruction of Jerusalem as God's righteous response (13:5a, 9; 14:4b), but also the promise of return and restoration (13:2, 5–6; 14:5b), especially featuring a splendidly restored Zion and temple (13:16–17; 14:5).[16] The final stage of this eschatology reaffirms the vision of Isaiah and Jeremiah: the final conversion of the nations from their idolatries to the worship of the One God (14:6–7; cf. Isa. 2:2–3; 60:2–3) and the gathering together of all the dispersed Jews in the promised land (13:5b, 13; 14:7; cf. Isa. 11:12; 43:5–7; 54:7; Jer. 29:13–14; 31:7–10; 32:37). Tobit's theological contributions are thus mainly conservative, reinscribing the theology found in Deuteronomy and the eschatology announced by the prophets.

Women in Tobit

The prominence of women in this romance has invited scholars to examine how they are characterized and what that might reveal about women in the world of the author. Sarah and Tobit stand equally in God's focus as God sends the angel to rectify their situations (although Sarah's introduction is briefer).[17] Other female characters are also well developed. We see Anna's predicament as a result of her husband's blindness, her deep love and anxiety about her son, and her noble preference to let go of the money rather than risk the life of her son (2:11–14; 10:4–7; 5:18–20). Edna is prominent in the initial interview with Tobias and Azariah on the eve of the wedding night and in blessing the newlyweds at their departure (7:2–4, 15–16; 10:12–13). Tobit was orphaned, and it is his grandmother Deborah who is credited with his education in Torah (1:8). His pious lifestyle is a great tribute to her effectiveness.

We should not read more into the presence of women in Tobit than warranted, however, so as to make it appear more "modern" than it is. Schuller

16. This is itself a process, since the temple will be rebuilt in a lackluster way until the final age, when it will be restored to its full splendor (14:5).

17. In an uncharacteristic lapse, Harrington (1999: 10) says that Sarah's only words are "Amen, Amen" in 8:8, overlooking the prayer and soliloquy in 3:10–15 by which we are given such a concise, yet effective, window into her character and plight.

(1992: 239), for example, envisions Edna also setting her seal on the marriage contract, but this is nowhere implied. Anna's role as the breadwinner strains relations with her husband, as is seen in the quarrel that provided the straw to break Tobit's back. This reversal of the norm (see Sir. 25:22) sits uneasily at Tobit's home. The exclusion of Sarah and Anna from the angel's self-revelation suggests again a lack of parity between genders in the world of the story.

Despite the prominence of women in the story, the place of women remains the same in the story as in the world from which it arose (Bow and Nickelsburg 1993: 143). As with many other women in the Apocrypha, Sarah's virtue is measured by her chastity (virginity before marriage and containment of sexual activity to a single married union, never again to have sexual relations after her husband's death, as in Judith and 4 Maccabees; 3:14–15a). This reflects the predominant cultural elevation of sexual exclusiveness as the area of a woman's honor, part of a double standard that is constructed to keep women hidden, secret, and private. Levine has noticed how the male characters have names related to God and God's manifestations in the world. Thus, the names Tobit and Tobias (Tobiyahu) mean "God is my good," the name Raphael means "God heals," Azariah "God helps," and Raguel "God's friend" (Levine 1991: 51; Moore 1996: 25). The women, on the other hand, have names connected with sexuality and procreation, whether by etymology or association. Sarah's name recalls the barren wife of Abraham, the name Edna means "sexual pleasure," and the name Anna (Hannah) recalls the once barren mother of Samuel, whose position in the household was jeopardized by her inability to conceive, as this Hannah regards the loss of Tobias to be the loss of her own future well-being.

While the Book of Tobit does at least acknowledge the feelings, contributions, and roles of women in the families of which they constitute so important a part and even promotes a positive view of marriage as a partnership that is not to make the spouse the vehicle for sexual gratification or become grievous to the woman, it is modest in its contributions to moving Judeo-Christian culture toward that vision in which "there is no longer male and female" (Gal. 3:28).

Influence

The most noteworthy connections between Tobit and the New Testament center on the teaching concerning alms found in both. Both Raphael and Jesus assume that prayer, fasting, and almsgiving will be part of the life of the righteous (Tob. 12:8; Matt. 6:1–18). Alms are to be given cheerfully, without begrudging the gift (Tob. 4:16; 2 Cor. 9:7), and are to be given in accordance with one's means. Whether one has much or little, one can still help the less fortunate in proportion to what one has (Tob. 4:8; 2 Cor. 8:12). Aid is not to be refused the poor (Tob. 4:7; Luke 6:30). Almsgiving is especially encouraged toward the company of the righteous: in Tobit the Law-observant Jews, in the New Testament the "household of faith" (Tob. 4:6b–7a; Gal. 6:10; cf. Heb. 13:1–3).

The New Testament shares not only Tobit's practical advice but also its ideology of almsgiving, intensifying that the latter as one's eternal destiny, not just temporal future, is connected with almsgiving. Giving charity and relief to the poor is the way by which one lays up a true treasure, one that can prove truly helpful in the day of adversity (Tob. 4:9). Giving alms is better than laying up gold (Tob. 12:8), since almsgiving can deliver a person from death, presumably because God's favor will be available when needed (Tob. 4:7b, 10; 12:9). Jesus clearly approved this teaching, since he is remembered to have promoted almsgiving as the way to build up "treasure in heaven" (Luke 12:33–34). The author of 1 Timothy develops this, urging Christians of means to engage in charity, thus "storing up . . . the treasure of a good foundation for the future, so that they may take hold of the life that really is life" (1 Tim. 6:18–19).

The "day of necessity" becomes, in the New Testament, the "day of judgment," and almsgiving is still an essential part of being found prepared for that day. Matthew 25:31–46 promotes clothing the naked and feeding the hungry as the means by which one renders Jesus his due service and so finds deliverance on that day. Similarly, the parable in Luke 16:19–31 portrays the giving of alms as the way a certain rich person might have avoided "going into the Darkness" (Tob. 4:10), now in the framework of an afterlife of conscious torment or happiness. The parable gives the sense, as does Tobit, that this is a major and essential lesson to be learned from the law of Moses and from the prophets.

Two passages in Acts also show the influence of Tobit in regard to the importance and efficacy of almsgiving. The newly deceased Tabitha is praised for her "acts of charity" (*eleēmosynai*, Acts 9:36; cf. Tob. 1:3), and the clothing she made for the widows is shown to Peter, who is urged to restore her to life. Her acts of charity become a witness to her devotion to God and neighbor, and thus her worthiness to receive this benefit. Almsgiving does, in fact, work toward delivering her from death (cf. Tob. 4:10) in a more dramatic way than the author of Tobit envisioned. Also, Cornelius is known for his devotion to acts of charity, with the result that an angel appears to him and says, "Your prayers and your alms have ascended as a memorial before God" (Acts 10:4). This is a very close paraphrase of Raphael's words in Tob. 12:12, with the same result: the sending of an angel to give the doer of alms some benefit from God.

Beyond the New Testament, Polycarp, the second-century bishop of Smyrna, recontextualizes the advice of Tob. 4:10 to give alms because "almsgiving delivers from death" (*To the Philippians* 10.2). Moreover, the *Shepherd of Hermas*, an early-second-century Christian work, continues to share the view of Tobit, as modified by Luke, that giving alms is the way to lay up a treasure for the future, now specifically the eternal future in God's kingdom (*Similitude* 1).

Tobit also includes the negative version of the Golden Rule (Tob. 4:15; cf. Matt. 7:12; Luke 6:31). This precept is quite common in the moral teaching of the ancient world, being found also in Hillel (*b. Shabbat* 31a), the Targumim (*Targum Pseudo-Jonathan* Lev. 19:18), Confucius (*Analects* 12.2), Epictetus (*Fragmenta* 38), and, in its positive form, in Diogenes Laertius (*Lives of the Philosophers* 5.21, attributed to Aristotle) (Zimmermann 1958a: 159–60).[18] This negative version appears again in *Didache* 1.2, probably as a rephrasing of Jesus' saying in the negative rather than a sign of direct dependence on Tob. 4:15. That a Jesus saying would be thus modified at the close of the first century (and also in the scribal addition to Acts 15:29 found in late-second-century fathers and some later manuscripts) shows the persistence of the negative formulation.

Raphael's revelatory discourse in 12:17–20 might well have provided a model for the New Testament authors who spoke of Jesus' mission, his return to the Father, and his ascension from the sight of the disciples. Jesus' statements in John to the effect that he came to do not his will but the will of the Father (John 5:30; 6:38) resonate with the angel's similar claim: "I was not acting on my own will, but by the will of God" (Tob. 12:18). Raphael's declaration "See, I am ascending to him who sent me" (Tob. 12:20) finds a later echo first in the frequent designation of God as "him who sent me" in John's Gospel (John 1:33; 4:34; 5:30, 38; 6:29, 38–39) and in Jesus' specific announcements "I am going to him who sent me" (John 7:33; 16:5) and "I am ascending to my Father" (John 20:17). The description of the angel's departure, particularly the details that they "could see him no more" and that they "kept blessing God and singing his praises" (Tob. 12:21–22), may have provided a model for expressing the events in Luke 24:51–53 and Acts 1:9.

The angelology reflected in Tobit continues to be manifested, in even more developed form, throughout the New Testament. Demons are the source of the affliction of individuals throughout the Gospels and Acts, and exorcism is the vehicle for relief. Angels act on behalf of individuals, even to the point that each person is presumed to have his or her own angelic protector or representative in God's court (Matt. 18:10; Acts 12:15). Demonic forces must be bound

18. Zimmermann believes that Jesus uttered the saying in its negative form but Luke inverted it to the positive form as more congenial to his own Gentile heritage (an assumption about Luke) and readership. In so doing, however, Zimmermann completely passes over the evidence of Matthew, perhaps the most Jewish of the Gospels, where Jesus also articulates the positive form of the saying. It is unlikely that the church would have assimilated Matt. 7:12 to Luke 6:31, since the tendency is to assimilate Mark and Luke to Matthew. It remains most likely that Jesus gave the positive turn to the saying he had learned from his Jewish heritage. Zimmermann also uses a quaint version of Acts that still has the negative version of the Golden Rule in 15:29 (now clearly recognized as an early expansion of the requirements laid on Gentiles).

in order to be rendered ineffective (Tob. 8:3; cf. Rev. 20:2). The second-century Christian text *Testament of Solomon* shows clear signs of direct dependence on Tobit in the interview of Solomon with the demon Asmodeus, who plots against newlyweds and is defeated by precisely the same means as in Tobit (*Testament of Solomon* 5.1–13).

As with most books of the Apocrypha, Tobit's status was disputed. Clement of Alexandria quotes Tob. 4:16 as "the scripture" (*Stromata* 2.23.139; see also the references at 1.21.123 and 6.12.102), but he is followed by few other noteworthy fathers in the East except John Chrysostom. In the West, the book tended to be regarded as canonical, with Augustine's judgment being preferred over Jerome's (see Moore 1996: 52–53). Of all the Apocrypha except Ben Sira, however, Tobit has enjoyed the most positive assessment and use even in Protestant circles. Luther commended it in the preface to Tobit in his German Bible as an edifying story profitable for Christians to read (Metzger 1957: 37). The Anglican and United Methodist Churches include Tob. 8:5–8 as a possible Old Testament reading for marriage services. The story was woven into a collect (prayer) in the marriage service of the 1549 *Book of Common Prayer* and is promoted as the basis for a marriage service homily in the Old Order Amish *Minister's Manual* (Metzger 1957: 40–41).

Judith

"Hear Me Also, a Widow"

The Book of Judith tells the story of a contest between the dominant Gentiles, with their claims about the gods, and the God of Israel—a prominent dynamic that runs throughout the history of Israel from the exodus through the Second Temple period. God gains victory in this story through a pious widow, Judith, who uses her wiles to save her people and the temple of her God from a hostile Assyrian invader, Holofernes, and his vast army. A Delilah for the cause of God, Judith uses the commander's lack of mastery of his own passions to lure him into a position of weakness and then beheads him. Despite modern criticisms of Judith's strategy, the Book of Judith is, from beginning to end, a moral tale, reinforcing for its hearers the basic theology of the Deuteronomistic History, presenting in Judith a model of piety and rigorous observance of God's covenant, affirming the efficacy of prayer coupled with faithful action, and encouraging confidence in the God of Israel and in the ability of the Torah-observant Jew to become a vehicle through which God may benefit God's people.

Structure and Contents

The tale opens with a fictionalized Nebuchadnezzar making war on a fictitious Arphaxad, king of the Medes. Nebuchadnezzar calls upon all his vassal peoples to aid him in this endeavor. The eastern vassals rally to his cause, but the western nations ignore his summons out of disregard for Nebuchadnezzar, who vows revenge against them (1:1–16). After defeating Arphaxad, Nebuchadnezzar commissions Holofernes, commander-in-chief of his armies, to subdue the western nations. Those that surrender will not be destroyed but reserved for some unspecified punitive actions; those who resist are to be slaughtered and plundered (2:1–13). Holofernes ravages Persia, Cilicia, Libya, and the Midianites, with the result that most of the remaining peoples surrender peacefully (2:14–3:4). Holofernes accepts their

85

surrender, destroying local sacred shrines in favor of an empire-wide cult of Nebuchadnezzar, and selects men from those nations to join his army as auxiliaries (3:5–9).

The scene shifts to the "children of Israel living in Judea," recently returned from exile and terrified at the approach of Holofernes. They are particularly concerned about the welfare of the temple, which had only recently been consecrated after its profanation (4:1–3). Under the high priest Joakim's directions, the people seize every strategic place within Judea and Samaria in preparation. Their corporate repentance and prayer in sackcloth and ashes come to God's attention, whose intervention is now anticipated (4:4–15).

Back in Holofernes' camp, the commander hears reports of Israel's mobilization. Astounded that they would resist while all their neighbors surrendered, he summons the Ammonite and Moabite leaders to inquire about the military strength of this people (5:1–4). Achior, the Ammonite leader, provides a faithful summary of the history of the Israelites from Abraham's expulsion from Chaldea through the return from the Babylonian exile, underscoring the basic Deuteronomic principle that, as long as the Israelites are faithful to the law of God, they are invincible. Only if the Israelites have sinned against God can Holofernes hope to vanquish them (5:5–21). Holofernes and the other Canaanite auxiliaries are incensed at Achior. Holofernes exclaims, "What god is there except Nebuchadnezzar?" (6:2), thus making the ensuing conflict a contest in which the honor of God is invested and thus one that Holofernes cannot win. Achior is banished from the camp and sent to die with the residents of Bethulia, the town that Holofernes must overtake first (5:22–6:13). After hearing his story, the Israelites in Bethulia receive Achior amicably (6:14–21).

The Edomites among Holofernes' retinue advise him to capture Bethulia's water supply and to wait until the drought causes the residents to grow desperate and surrender. That way, Holofernes would achieve his objective without losing a single soldier. Holofernes is pleased with this plan and deploys his troops to surround the town, so as to allow none to escape (7:1–18). After thirty-four days, the residents of Bethulia cry out against their leadership, preferring surrender and slavery with life to watching their children die. Uzziah agrees to yield to their demand if God has not delivered them in five more days (7:19–32).

Only now do we meet the champion, Judith, a beautiful woman widowed three years and four months prior to the siege. She lives a life of self-discipline and rigorous piety, fasting continuously and living in a tent on her roof except on Sabbaths and festivals and their eves, maintaining her deceased husband's estate with the help of her faithful maidservant (8:1–7). "No one spoke ill of her, for she feared God with great devotion" (8:8). She summons the town elders before her and chides them for creating a situation that puts God to the test. They should rather wait on the Lord and remain steadfast. She reminds them that their resistance there is not for their sakes alone but for the temple itself. They owe it to God to defend God's honor to the death, and their surrender will mean only dishonor for God, who will exact it from their own hides. She encourages them, rather than testing God, to prove their loyalty and steadfastness in the test that God has set for them (8:9–27). Uzziah cannot disagree, but since he has given his oath to the people, he cannot now change his course. Judith therefore announces that the Lord will deliver them by her hand, and so plans to leave the camp with her servant that night (8:28–36).

She prays at the hour of the evening incense offering, invoking the zeal of her ancestor Simeon, who was empowered by God to kill and plunder those who had defiled his sister Dinah, as the paradigm for what she now sets out to do. The temple, rather than an individual Jewish woman, is now at risk of defilement and dishonor, and Judith presents herself as the instrument of God's indignation. She emphasizes her weakness and vulnerability but also expresses confidence in the God who is "God of the lowly, helper of the oppressed, upholder of the weak" (9:11). She concludes her prayer by bringing back to expression the main issue: the manifestation of who truly is God in this world (9:14).

Judith adorns herself with the choicest clothes, jewelry, and perfumes and prepares the food and dishes she will use during her stay among the Gentiles (10:1–5). Dressed to kill, she leaves Bethulia and is arrested by an Assyrian patrol. Presenting herself as a refugee from the doomed Bethulia, she is escorted to Holofernes' tent (10:6–23). Holofernes greets her with amnesty. After flattering Holofernes and speaking ironically about how God was about to accomplish something marvelous through him, Judith tells him that Achior's speech was essentially correct. However, Judith has learned that her people are about to sin against God by consuming the tithes and firstfruits of grain, oil, and wine, things holy to God and not for consumption by non-priests.[1] She has therefore fled to Holofernes to save her life and will betray the people who have betrayed her God. She proposes that she be allowed to leave the camp each night to pray to God so that God may reveal to her when the people have committed this sin. Then she promises to lead Holofernes to Jerusalem in triumph (11:1–19).

Holofernes is pleased by her words, gives her leave to come and go as she pleases (thus preparing the way for her escape), and invites her to dine with him each evening. She scrupulously avoids eating or drinking the Gentiles' food, using instead her own wine, food, and plates. Each night she immerses herself in a spring of water, prays to God, and returns purified (11:20–12:9).

---

1. They are also said to be about to "kill their livestock and . . . use all that God by his laws has forbidden them to eat" (11:12). This may refer to the prohibition against drinking blood, something that the Israelites, in desperate thirst, perhaps are considering. Latin versions include this detail explicitly and may in fact represent something in the original text that was lost in the Septuagint, since without this the killing of livestock does not seem irreligious in the least (Moore 1985: 210).

On the fourth evening, Holofernes determines that he will seduce this beautiful woman. At the banquet, his passions are deeply aroused, and he consumes far too much wine. When his attendants excuse themselves to give Holofernes and Judith some privacy, he falls asleep on his bed, overcome by drink (12:10–13:2). Judith prays to God as she takes Holofernes' sword and severs his head with two strokes. She puts the head in her food bag and leaves the camp with her servant, ostensibly for her nightly ablutions and prayer (13:3–10). Instead, they run to Bethulia and show their prize, as Judith also affirms that Holofernes did not defile her body. The whole town, led by Uzziah, praises her for "walking in the straight path before our God" (13:11–20).

After Achior identifies the severed head as indeed that of Holofernes and converts to Judaism, Judith gives orders for the armed men of Bethulia to descend upon the Assyrian camp. The Assyrians are amazed at the boldness of these Israelites and send Bagoas, Holofernes' attendant, to wake up the commander. Finding only his decapitated body, Bagoas exclaims, "One Hebrew woman has brought disgrace on the house of King Nebuchadnezzar" (14:18). The Assyrian army flees, being pursued by Israelites from every town, as the Assyrian camp is plundered for an entire month (14:1–15:7). Joakim blesses Judith, who leads the women of Israel, followed by the men, in a festal dance and psalm of deliverance (15:8–16:17). Judith dedicates her share of the spoils to the temple as an offering and returns to her private affairs, never to remarry. Before dying at the age of 105, she frees her servant and distributes her estate amongst her husband's and her relatives (16:18–25).

The careful structuring of this balanced work attests to the literary artistry of the author. Toni Craven (1983: 60, 62–63; cf. Moore 1985: 57–59) proposes an outline of the book in two parts (1:1–7:32; 8:1–16:25), each of which is dominated by a concentric structure:

Part I
  Section 1: Nebuchadnezzar's campaigns against Arphaxad (1:1–16)
  Section 2: Nebuchadnezzar sends Holofernes to punish the disobedient vassal nations (2:1–13)
  Section 3: 2:14–7:32
    A   Campaign against the western nations; the people surrender (2:14–3:10)
      B   Israel hears about Holofernes' advance and is "greatly terrified"; Joakim orders preparations for war (4:1–15)
        C   Holofernes confers with Achior and expels him (5:1–6:11)
        C′ Achior is welcomed into Bethulia and confers with the assembly (6:12–21)
      B′ Holofernes orders preparations for war; Israel sees and is "greatly terrified" (7:1–5)
    A′ Campaign against Bethulia; the people want to surrender (7:6–32)

Part II
A   Judith introduced (8:1–8)
   B   Judith plans to deliver Israel (8:9–10:9a)
      C   Judith and her maid leave Bethulia (10:9b–10)
         D   Judith overcomes Holofernes (10:11–13:10a)
      C′ Judith and her maid return to Bethulia (13:10b–11)
   B′ Judith plans (and the Israelites execute) the destruction of the
         enemy (13:12–16:20)
A′ Conclusion about Judith (16:21–25)

Attempts to discern concentric outlines for entire books often appear forced, with scholars merely underscoring that small part of each section that makes the outline work. Craven's analysis, however, would withstand such criticism.

   The literary crafting of the story also appears in the ways in which Achior's story parallels Judith's story (Roitman 1992). Each character goes through four stages. In stage one, they are in opposite locations and roles (Achior is a pagan, enemy soldier in the Assyrian camp, Judith a devout, secluded widow in Bethulia). In stage two, each delivers a speech drawing a lesson from the history of Israel, provoking a reaction (anger against Achior, wonder at Judith) that transforms them (Achior into an enemy of Holofernes, Judith into a champion for her people). In stage three, they exchange locations. In stage four, they have exchanged roles (Achior now acts as a friend to the Jews, Judith as the betrayer of her people) and are both welcomed into and praised by their new circles of comrades. In a fifth stage, only after the denouement of the story, the two characters meet for the first time and enter into their final states (Achior a converted Jew and civilian, Judith once again a secluded widow) (Roitman 1992: 37–38).

   Another marker of the author's literary skill is the extensive use of irony, the recognition of which is essential to understanding the book (Moore 1985: 78).[2] Irony, itself a pleasing device for readers, is also a measure of literary craft, since irony is revealed to be such only in light of the larger movement of the whole work. Among the more striking examples of irony in Judith are Achior's expulsion to the Bethulian camp, ostensibly for his death but really for his deliverance (6:5–8), and the Assyrian soldiers' reaction to seeing Judith's beauty: "It is not wise to leave one of [the Israelite] men alive, for if we let them go they will be able to beguile the whole world!" (10:19). This single Hebrew woman, of course, will indeed beguile the Assyrian commander and bring defeat to the whole army.

   Irony is concentrated in the episodes depicting the encounter between Judith and Holofernes. Judith's prediction "If you follow out the words of your servant, God will accomplish something through you, and my lord will not fail to achieve his purposes" (11:6) teems with ambiguity, since God is indeed

2. See Moore 1985: 78–84 for an excellent catalogue of ironic moments in Judith.

about to "accomplish with [Holofernes] things that will astonish the whole world" (11:16). Moreover, "my lord" is understood by Holofernes to refer to himself, but Judith may well be thinking about her only Lord, whose purposes are about to be fulfilled. A close examination of 12:4, 14, 18 reveals further intentional ambiguities and double entendres.

Textual Transmission

The text of Judith survives chiefly in the Septuagint tradition, in three distinct editions: (1) Sinaiticus (which shows a greater degree of scribal corruption than the other major codices [Moore 1985: 91–92]),[3] Alexandrinus, and Vaticanus; (2) Codices 19, 108; (3) Codex 58, represented also in the Old Latin and Syriac. The differences, which tend to be minor, are not due to new examinations of the Hebrew or to different underlying Hebrew manuscripts (Cowley 1913: 243). Jerome created his Vulgate version by emending the Old Latin in light of an Aramaic version known to him (but evidently itself not a direct witness to the original) (Moore 1985: 94–101; Enslin and Zeitlin 1972: 44). Jerome himself does not pretend to give a precise or careful translation; his goal is to give "sense for sense, more than word for word" (see Cowley 1913: 244). The Sahidic (Coptic), Syriac, and Ethiopic are translations of the Septuagint, and the Hebrew versions are later compositions based on Greek or Latin translations or are completely free paraphrases, rather than independent witnesses to the original Hebrew (Moore 1985: 108; Moore 1992e: 1124). The result is that, ultimately, our only reliable access to the original text of Judith is through the Septuagint tradition.

Given the many Hebraisms found in the Greek, it is most likely that the original language of Judith was Hebrew.[4] The translator nevertheless did not lack fluency in Greek, given the rich vocabulary. For example, the translator chooses synonyms or creates prepositional compounds to avoid repetition of the same translational equivalents (Enslin and Zeitlin 1972: 40–41). There is general agreement that the translation into Greek was completed before the late part of the first century C.E., when Clement of Rome refers to the story (presupposing his readers' familiarity with it as well).

Author, Date, and Setting

The anonymous author probably was a Palestinian Jew (Bissell 1899: 164; Moore 1985: 70; Metzger 1957: 42). The improvement in the author's geog-

---

3. The preferred critical edition is Hanhart 1979a.
4. Discussions of the linguistic evidence appear in Bissell 1899: 164; Pfeiffer 1949: 298; Moore 1985: 66–67, 92–93; Enslin and Zeitlin 1972: 40–41; Cowley 1913: 244.

raphy once Holofernes reaches Palestine, the quality of piety reflected in Judith's actions, and the probability of a Hebrew original all point in this direction.[5] The question of when the author wrote and under what circumstances has incurred far more discussion. Several urge that the author wrote "at a time of national emergency when the Jewish religion and independence were at stake" or "in a time of war" (Metzger 1957: 42, 52; also Pfeiffer 1949: 301). This represents a misuse of mirror-reading—the attempt to discern the circumstances of the author from clues in the text, a process that requires special care when the text is a narrative. The author need not be living in a time of crisis in order to write about a crisis. While details of the narrative may help tell us something of the author's time and setting, the "crisis" belongs to the literary plot of the story.

A postexilic date is necessitated by Achior's discourse (5:17–19; cf. 4:3). The names Holofernes and Bagoas, moreover, are otherwise attested only in the Persian period, as are the loan words "satrap" (5:2), "turban" (4:15), and "sword" (*akinakēs*, 13:6), as well as the practice of "preparing earth and water" (2:7). Together, these clues point to the influence of knowledge that entered Israel during the Persian period (Moore 1985: 50). Moreover, it is highly probable that the book came into being after the Maccabean Revolt. Holofernes' plan to destroy native sanctuaries and religions in favor of the worship of the Gentile king Neduchadnezzar (3:8) resembles the depiction of Antiochus IV's unprecedented imposition of a foreign cult on the people of Judea (especially in 1 Maccabees). The description of the threat to the temple as profanation and of the desecration of the temple "to the malicious joy of the Gentiles" also reflects the events of 167–165 B.C.E. (4:12). That the temple, altar, and vessels are remembered as having recently been polluted and reconsecrated (4:1–3), rather than destroyed and rebuilt, also suggests that the events of 164 B.C.E. are more firmly inscribed on the author's mind than those of the postexilic period. In addition, the power of the high priest as military commander and the prominence of the senate (*gerousia*) reflects a Hasmonean date, since this body, though perhaps constituted already under Antiochus III (Josephus, *Jewish Antiquities* 12.119–124), rises to prominence during the period of Judas and his brothers (Pfeiffer 1949: 295; Moore 1985: 50). Finally, the denouement of the tale is full of reminiscences of the rout of Nicanor's army after the death of their commander (see 1 Macc. 7:43–50),

5. Zeitlin (Enslin and Zeitlin 1972: 31–32) is confident that the author cannot have been a Palestinian Jew, since the author refers to the "children of Israel living in Judea," whereas the normal self-designation of such people is "Judeans." Outside Judea, Jews called themselves "Israelites" or "Hebrews." Zeitlin's argument has failed to sway scholarly opinion. The author, in fact, uses neither "Israelites" nor "Hebrews" (titles such as are employed by Paul in 2 Cor. 11:22) but "children of Israel," a designation for the Jews shaped by the Hebrew Scriptures and chosen, no doubt, to highlight the fact that Jewish identity is determined mainly by genealogy, not geography. All that the appellation tells us is that the author was aware that many "children of Israel" also resided outside of Judea.

including the hanging of the enemy commander's head on the wall (Jdt. 14:11), the flight of the enemy in terror (15:1–3), the outpouring of Jewish soldiers from the surrounding area to join the pursuit and outflanking of the enemy (15:4–5), and the plunder of the enemy camp (15:6–7) (Moore 1985: 50–51).

These clues combine to form a strong impression that Judith was composed sometime during the Hasmonean period. Can further specificity be achieved? Moore (1985: 69) posits that the setting of the story in Samaria (Bethulia may be a literary reflection of the city of Shechem) (see Cowley 1913: 246) and the sense of cooperation between Samaria and Jerusalem reflect a date after the incorporation of Samaria into the Hasmonean state by John Hyrcanus in 107 B.C.E. This is certainly possible, although the author may also merely be reflecting the ideal of Israel from Davidic and Solomonic times. Given the mélange of historical conditions in this single story, I would not rule this out. Moore (1985: 70) further suggests that the lack of virulent sectarianism shows that the book was written before the reign of Alexander Janneus, in which partisanship between Pharisees and Sadducees became rather bitter, had progressed too far. Again, the usefulness of these historical conditions for dating the book depends greatly on how much one is convinced that any author will reflect precisely those things that are known to history from his or her general period. The author of Judith's own disposition, removal from the hotbeds of sectarian conflict, or even desire to counter the rampant sectarianism with a tale that portrays a unified Jewry might also account for this "irenic" approach to other Jews.

J. W. van Henten (1995: 244) regards the Book of Judith as "a way of releasing criticism against the new Hasmonean dynasty." How Judith presents such a criticism is difficult to determine, unless it is in the fact that Judith retired to private life when the Lord's work in and through her for the people had been achieved, rather than consolidating power and forming a dynasty. It might, however, have served to provide legitimation for the policies of Jonathan, Simon, and Hyrcanus I, which often involved duplicitous treaties, playing one rival Syrian king off another, "getting into bed" with the enemy, as it were, to win political freedom for Judea. These Hasmoneans were not nearly so direct and "manly" in their dealings with the Syrian dynasts as were Mattathias and Judas, but the story of Judith might have shed a new and more positive light on their use of deceit in foreign affairs and their shifting of allegiances so as to benefit their people.

Genre and Purpose

Determining the genre of Judith centers on the basic question of whether the author presumed to be writing an actual history or a fictional tale. Although the story gives the impression of historiography (an attempt to re-count events that really happened), taking well-known names and kingdoms into its scope, those who would uphold the claim that Judith is a specimen of historiography have to face the many historical and geographical errors of the book. Most obviously, Nebuchadnezzar was the Babylonian king, not the As-syrian king, and reigned from Babylon, not Nineveh (which had been de-stroyed some seven years before Nebuchadnezzar came to the throne) (Metzger 1957: 51; Harrington 1999: 28). He never waged war against Media or laid siege to Ecbatana. No Median Arphaxad is otherwise known, so his enemy appears to be fictitious as well (Moore 1985: 46–47). The story speaks of the twelfth, seventeenth, and eighteenth years of the reign of Nebuchadnezzar (1:1; 1:13; 2:1). The temple would only be destroyed in the nineteenth year of his reign (2 Kings 25:8–9), not rebuilt before or during his reign, as is clearly the situation presupposed in Jdt. 4:3. The destruction of the temple and the exile and return are also portrayed in Achior's speech as past events (5:17–19). This is perhaps the most glaring anachronism: surely the Jewish author would have learned (together with his audience) from his own Scrip-tures the correlation of the nineteenth year of Nebuchadnezzar's reign with the destruction of the Jerusalem temple, with the return from exile not to come for seventy years after that.

Other details of the book speak against Judith being a work of historiogra-phy. Holofernes moves a huge army an impossible three hundred miles in three days (Metzger 1957: 50). Holofernes' itinerary is also confused: he marches through Put (Libya) and then *westward* across Mesopotamia. Be-thulia is not mentioned outside Judith, and, despite the rather numerous geo-graphical clues given by the author, defies identification. Moreover, Jerusalem stands very much open to invasion, the preferred route being to come around and attack the city from the west. Holofernes has no need to attack from the north, and there is no narrow pass that *must* be crossed in the north for for-eign invaders to gain access to Jerusalem. This is a detail borrowed from the story of the battle of Thermopylae (Momigliano 1982: 226–27).

Granted, then, that Judith is not a history about Nebuchadnezzar, some have ventured to suggest that it represents a history of a later time with char-acters whose names have been disguised. Some have seen in Nebuchadnez-zar's campaigns in Judith 1–3 a reflection of the earlier campaigns of Ashur-banipal, king of the Assyrians until 625 B.C.E.,[6] or that the book as a whole reflects the campaign of the Persian king Artaxerxes III Ochus against Pales-tine and Egypt. The latter, in fact, had generals named Holofernes and Bagoas, who was even a eunuch (Pfeiffer 1949: 294; Moore 1985: 55).[7] Of course, Antiochus IV is also a popular candidate, since he is remembered in Jewish history as the first real threat to the worship of the God of Israel in

---

6. The correlations are summarized in Pfeiffer 1949: 293; Moore 1985: 54.
7. These names are well documented in ancient historians.

Judea.[8] Judith, in each case, becomes the personification of the pious Jews, bravely and successfully resisting the foreign invader.

The attempt to defend the historicity of Judith, either at face value or in terms of a veiled history of a later period, presents insurmountable obstacles because, in fact, the book combines allusions to events that transpire over five centuries of "real life" history (Pfeiffer 1949: 293–97). No single period could possibly contain all the people, movements, and events. The work is better read as a piece of historical fiction—an attempt to write a nonhistorical story set in the midst of known historical personages and dynamics. The many historical allusions and reminiscences should be seen as bits and pieces of the author's inspiration, one aspect of the formative influences that have shaped his creative endeavors. "Details of history provide the raw materials for a fictional story" (Cowley 1913: 246).[9]

The author may in fact give the audience sufficient clues as early as 1:1 that the work is to be heard as fiction, since Nebuchadnezzar's actual exploits would be well known from their sacred history (Moore 1985: 79).[10] Martin Luther had already recognized its ahistorical character, calling it a "religious fable," interpreting it allegorically (see Metzger 1957: 51). Judith's name (meaning "Jewess") and the name of the unidentifiable town Bethulia (resembling the Hebrew word *bethulah*, "virgin") certainly encourage symbolic or allegorical readings or at least point away from a historicizing reading.

For what ends, then, did the author write this piece of historical fiction? Some read it as resistance literature, "written in a time of war to inspire a people who were fighting desperately for their religion as well as for their independence" (Metzger 1957: 52; Cowley 1913: 245), but this results from excessive mirror-reading. If we accept a Hasmonean period date (under John Hyrcanus or Alexander Janneus), then Israel is ascendant, while it is their neighbors who are fighting (unsuccessfully) against Israel for their independence.

More likely the product of a time of Israel's renewed independence and prosperity, the Book of Judith was written first to entertain. Particularly with Tobit and Judith, both of which show an elevated interest in literary crafting, we should not overlook the likelihood that the authors set out to tell a good

8. Ball (1888) read the book as an allegory of the history of 167–161 B.C.E.

9. Skehan (1962: 151) also comes to this conclusion as he wrestles with the tendency, especially within earlier Catholic scholarship, both to historicize Judith and to critique Judith as a work of historiography. It would be unnecessary, then, to "posit two stages of composition," one in the Persian period and one, a revision, in the Hasmonean period (Nickelsburg 1984: 51), since the imprecise reflections of historical detail in the work indicate the imaginative art of the author, not the period of composition.

10. Moore characterizes Judith as a folktale, combining the motifs of the "Faithful Wife" and "Female Deliverer" tales (Moore 1985: 72). But calling Judith a folktale seems inappropriate, given the trappings of historiography and the interest in public matters (the stuff of history, real or fictive) rather than the events of private life, which are more customary for folktales.

story and to tell it well. Nevertheless, that which entertains can also instruct. Judith's didactic value has been widely noted, particularly the way in which the story reinforces the basic premises of Deuteronomy's philosophy of history. Whether its instruction should be seen as the promotion of a particular sectarian interpretation of the keeping of covenant (Pharisaism) (Ball 1888: 246) or the more general provision of an "inspirational example" of piety, dedication to God, and courage (Moore 1985: 62; Enslin and Zeitlin 1972: 14), the author clearly sought to present his audience with a model of the kind of piety that can achieve great things for God and God's people. Judith's triumph and the honor that her people heap upon her will rouse emulation in the hearts of the readers, with the result that their own commitment to such piety will be confirmed and energized.

Formative Influences

The new tale of Judith was inspired by the stories that the author learned from Israel's sacred Scriptures. Perhaps the most immediately obvious inspiration is the story of Jael and Sisera in Judges 4–5. The two stories have a similar structure: in both, the action moves from a public, political, and military struggle, to a climax in a private scene between champion and enemy commander, to a triumphant victory song (White 1992: 6). The routing of the enemy forces has been transposed from a place prior to the killing of the enemy commander in the Jael story to a place subsequent to his death in the Judith story, perhaps under the influence of the story of Nicanor in 1 Maccabees 7. In both, the enemy commander is acting out the orders of an absent king (White 1992: 13). Deborah prophesies that God will deliver Sisera "into the hand of a woman" (Judg. 4:9; see 4:21; 5:26) (White 1992: 7–8; van Henten 1995: 242)—a motif that becomes even more prominent in the story of Judith (Jdt. 8:33; 9:10; 12:4; 13:14; 15:10; 16:5).

Deceit and the violation of hospitality also play a crucial role in both. Jael lulls Sisera into a false sense of security by offering him hospitality, and he trusts her commitment to that code. Nevertheless, Jael violates this code and his trust in order to kill him. Similarly, Judith, a guest in Holofernes' tent, uses deceit in order to lull Holofernes into the same sense of security. In both, a drink plays an important part, milk and wine bringing sleep upon the commanders (White 1992: 8). Both women attack the head of the commanders in order to kill them (White 1992: 9). Finally, the Song of Deborah, which concludes the episode in Judges 5, has influenced the song that concludes Judith (as has Exodus 15). Both songs conclude by invoking a woe or curse upon the enemies of God and God's people (Judg. 5:31; Jdt. 16:17) (White 1992: 11). Also noteworthy are the shared motif of the earth and mountains shaking in response to God's acts (Judg. 5:4–5; Jdt. 16:15) and the celebra-

tion specifically of the deceitful means by which the heroine lulled the enemy
into a place of weakness and then struck with her hand (Judg. 5:24–27; Jdt.
16:5–9).

Another important character type that the author used to shape one of the
characters is that of Abraham, who becomes a model for Achior. Both "believe
God" (Gen. 15:6; Jdt. 14:10) at a crucial juncture in their stories. Just as
Abraham's testimony to the One God led him to be expelled from Ur (Jdt.
5:6–8), so Achior is expelled from Holofernes' camp for his testimony to that
God (Jdt. 6:5–7) (Roitman 1992: 39–40). The author evidently knew of an
expanded tradition concerning Abraham, adding the detail that Abraham's
family was expelled from Chaldea on account of their departure from the
idolatrous worship of the region in favor of worship of the "God of heaven"
(5:8). Speculation during this period on why Abraham left Ur often focused
on the dangers of worshiping the One God and abstaining from the worship
of local deities on account of the hostility of the local polytheists.[11]

Judith specifically invokes the episode of Simeon and Levi's vengeance
upon Shechem in Genesis 34 in her prayer (Jdt. 9:2–4) as models for active,
and even violent, expressions of faith—a pattern that she intends to reenact.
Bissell (1899: 163) criticizes the author for reversing Jacob's own judgment
that Simeon and Levi's act of anger is to be "cursed" rather than emulated
(Gen. 49:6–7; cf. 4 Macc. 2:18–20). Judith is not alone in her exoneration of
Simeon and Levi. *Testament of Levi* also overturns Jacob's verdict, in no less a
court than God's own. God personally orders Levi to take vengeance on
Shechem: while it costs Levi his father's blessing, God awards Levi with the
honor of a perpetual priesthood for his zeal to keep Israel pure (*Testament of
Levi* 5–8). Together, these texts evidence a reading of Genesis 34 in which it
is Jacob, not Levi and Simeon, who is out of touch with God's values.

The song of deliverance in Judith 16 shows signs of dependence not only
on the Song of Deborah in Judges 5 but also the Song of Moses in Exodus 15
(Skehan 1963a: 96–98). Both songs declare that "the Lord is a God who
crushes wars" (LXX Exod. 15:3; Jdt. 16:2; cf. 9:7), provide a summary of the
boast of the enemy, which has turned out to be an empty boast (Exod. 15:9;
Jdt. 16:4), and claim that other Gentile nations are filled with fear and awe
on account of God's deliverance of God's people and unexpected destruction
of the enemy (Exod. 15:14–16; Jdt. 16:10).[12]

11. In *Jubilees* 12.1–7, Abraham chides his father, Terah, for worshiping idols, and Terah
admits that he does it only out of fear of what his neighbors will do to him and his family if he
abandons the religious practices of the region. Josephus (*Jewish Antiquities* 1.154–157) follows
the tradition attested in Judith. See deSilva 2000c: 16–21, 42–44.

12. Jansen (1937: 63–71) and Moore (1985: 254–57) argue that an earlier deliverance
song has been adapted in Jdt. 16:1–17, with the middle section (16:5–10) being composed
anew by the author to replace the description of some other act of God's deliverance. If this is
the case, then the original psalm was already patterned after Exodus 15 (Moore 1985: 256).

The incidents at Massah and Meribah (Exod. 17:1–7; Num. 20:2–13) provide an important and meaningful layer of intertexture for reading Judith, particularly when combined with the experience of the bitter water made sweet, which was a test from God (Exod. 15:25), and the provision of manna as a test from God, to see if the Hebrews would follow his instructions or not (Exod. 16:4) (van Henten 1995: 234–36). The residents of Bethulia are stricken with thirst, convinced that God has given them over to death, and prefer surrender to and enslavement by the enemy to seeing their children dying before their eyes, and so they complain against their leaders (Jdt. 7:23–28). The elders' response of giving God five days to deliver them is interpreted by Judith as testing God (8:11–13) and failing the test that God has set for God's people (8:25). This story reconfigures the earlier testing of God in response to hunger and thirst prior to, and at, Massah in particular. Hunger and thirst lead the people to complain against Moses' leadership and to prefer slavery with food (Exod. 16:2–3; 17:1–4). The people are rebuked for putting God to the test (17:2), when in fact it is God who is testing their obedience (16:4).

Additionally, Judith's striking of Holofernes re-creates Moses' striking of the rock (Jdt. 13:8; Exod. 17:6) (van Henten 1995: 236, 240). In this regard, Judith appears to be seen even more favorably than Moses. In the incident at Meribah, Moses strikes the rock twice as he cries out to the Israelites, "Shall we bring water for you out of this rock?" (Num. 20:10). This was a costly act of disobedience on Moses' part, whose anger at the people overrode his knowledge of his dependence upon God. Judith, however, prays to God and acknowledges the necessity for God's hand to be at work as she too strikes her mark two times.

The author recontextualizes Num. 23:19, where it is said that "God is not a human being, that he should lie, or a mortal, that he should change his mind," in Judith's censure of the elders (Jdt. 8:16). The broad sweep of the history of Israel, along with the principal theological lesson conveyed by the Deuteronomistic History, are reflected in Achior's speech (Jdt. 5:5–21; cf. 8:18–20). The strange detail that the Israelites clothed not only themselves but also their cattle with sackcloth in their corporate act of repentance (Jdt. 4:10–11) may have been suggested by Jon. 3:8. Finally, Holofernes' attempts to cause "all their dialects and tribes" to "call upon [Nebuchadnezzar] as a god" (Jdt. 3:8) recalls the imposed cult in Dan. 3:5–7, where "all the peoples, nations, and languages fell down and worshiped the golden statue that King Nebuchadnezzar had set up" (note Dan. 3:7 Θ, which uses "all the peoples, tribes, tongues").

The author's work is deeply enriched by allusions to the Jewish Scriptures, but one can also detect extrabiblical influences. One noteworthy influence is the work of Herodotus, particularly the story of Xerxes' campaign against Greece and his defeat at Salamis (Hadas 1959: 165–69; Momigliano 1982: 227–28).[13] For example, the "preparation of earth and water" (see Jdt. 2:7) is

---

13. The most comprehensive study of Herodotean influence is Caponigro 1992.

well known from Herodotus as a sign of surrender demanded by Persian kings (*Historiae* 6.48, 94; 7.131–133) (Caponigro 1992: 49). The use of this sign in Judith is admittedly somewhat strange, since it does not free the surrendered cities completely from punishment as in Herodotus (Caponigro 1992: 49); but it does save them, at least, from being pillaged and leveled. Whatever punishment they might face at Nebuchadnezzar's hands, it likely would be more lenient than their fate at Holofernes' hands (the result of not preparing earth and water). In Bethulia, reduction to slavery seems to be the result of surrender (but this may mean no more than absolute subjection to the foreign monarch as opposed to independence, as in ancient Egypt all residents were, technically, the pharaoh's slaves). The author's imprecise inclusion of such details renders the work "learned and allusive, and also what we might call impressionistic" (Caponigro 1992: 51).

Nebuchadnezzar's campaign shows signs of being patterned after Xerxes' campaign against Greece. Despite having previously resolved upon revenge, Nebuchadnezzar holds a war conference in Jdt. 2:1–3 after the pattern of Xerxes (Herodotus, *Historiae* 7.5–11). A speech against war with Athens delivered by Artabanus, to the chagrin of Xerxes, is deferred until later in Judith, appearing as Achior's speech in chapter 5 (Caponigro 1992: 51–52).

Bethulia's strategic importance for the capture of Jerusalem—whatever Bethulia's location, if it existed at all, it had no such significance in "real life"—results from the influence of the stirring tale of the battle of Thermopylae (Herodotus, *Historiae* 7.176, 201–233), where a brave band of Spartan soldiers held off Xerxes' army long enough for the Athenians to mobilize and defeat them. Here the "set up" is undertaken to highlight Judith's heroism and not that of the whole town or its armed men (Momigliano 1982: 226–27; Caponigro 1992: 54–55). Judith also resembles Themistocles, the Athenian naval commander who sends word to the Persian fleet commanders that he is favorable to their cause, luring them to the battle of Salamis, where the Persians were defeated (Herodotus, *Historiae* 8.75–90) (Caponigro 1992:55–56). This also attests incidentally to the acceptable use of deceit to defeat one's enemies and to lure them into a position of weakness.

Caponigro's presentation of Herodotean influence is all the more credible insofar as the allusions or inspiration all come from a self-contained portion of the book (*Historiae* 7.1–8.90). The author of Judith need only have read—or heard in some oral form—this most famous segment of the story to be supplied with all the material needed to substantiate Caponigro's claims. Such a clustered borrowing of motifs from a Greek historical source, even if that source has been mediated to the author of Judith through the oral telling of the tale in the Hebrew language, reminds us of the potential for people of one culture to gain a certain level of "cultural literacy" with regard to another culture in the Hellenistic age.

Lies, Seduction, and Murder: A Cultural Perspective

Modern readers seldom express the same appreciation and admiration of Judith's strategy that one sees in the response of her fellow residents in Bethulia. In the view of Bissell (1899: 163), her use of deception and violence against her host makes her "even more reprehensible" than Jael, and the invocation of God's blessing over deception and premeditated assassination is especially censured. Bissell is especially concerned that Judith exposed herself to sexual impurity, and, in fact, speculates that she would have had intercourse with Holofernes if that had been needed to serve her ends. Finally, Bissell (1899: 163) goes on to condemn, in a manner rather typical of the nineteenth century, the whole religious stream represented by the author because of the author's willingness to overlook—even commend—"dissimulation, revenge, and indecent coquetry, an abuse of prayer and the divine Providence" while being concerned about offending "the ceremonial law in the least particular." More recent authors also leave us merely to wonder at the moral integrity of Judith's strategy (Harrington 1999: 42) or offer explanations based on the maxims "All's fair in love and war" and "The end justifies the means," excusing her on account of the dire circumstances faced by her people (Enslin and Zeitlin 1972: 14; Harrington 1999: 42; Pfeiffer 1949: 300).

The impasse in coming to terms with Judith's conduct—and, more to the point, the author's commendation of her conduct—may be crossed by a more culturally attuned reading of the book. This involves looking at the story in terms of honor and shame and especially the dynamics of challenges to honor, contests for honor, and the role of deception and lying in strategies for preserving honor.[14] In a culture in which one party will use knowledge about another party in order to augment one's own honor at the expense of the other, deception, withholding information, and projecting false appearances become accepted means of preserving the honor of oneself and one's primary group (Pilch 1992: 128; du Boylay 1976). Not everyone is privileged to know the "truth" about oneself and one's group; that is reserved for members of the group who will not use the information against the group. When a group's honor or safety is threatened by outsiders, then deceit emerges as one of a number of strategies by which to minimize any potential harm (Pilch 1992: 130). The observation of Jerome Neyrey (1993: 42), "Those who deceive are cheered by the crowd, even as those who have been 'taken in' smart from the shame,"[15] would serve as an apt summary of Judith.

14. On honor and shame in the Hellenistic and Greco-Roman periods, see deSilva 2000b, chapters 1 and 2 and the bibliography.

15. We should recall at this point the example of Themistocles, the Athenian who lures the Persian fleet commanders to their defeat through feigning alliance and deceitful reports (Herodotus, *Historiae* 8.75–90). His success, and the honors that came to him, attest to the acceptance of deceit as a means by which to defeat one's enemies.

The author of Judith spins a complex web of challenges to, and defenses of, honor as the framework for the plot. The main action of the book is initiated by a challenge to Nebuchadnezzar's honor by the western territories (1:11), who disregard him and dismiss his representatives in disgrace, and Nebuchadnezzar's response to this challenge (1:12). Holofernes' campaign is motivated chiefly by Nebuchadnezzar's desire to vindicate his honor against the slight he has suffered (2:1), and the general has great success vindicating his lord's honor (2:28). The fear and dread of Holofernes is but a sign of the fear and dread that Nebuchadnezzar now enjoys, such as was absent in 1:11 when the western territories esteemed his power only lightly.

In the midst of this honor contest, a second and more sweeping one emerges. Holofernes makes a claim to divinity on Nebuchadnezzar's behalf, challenging the honor of every local deity in the west by suppressing their worship in favor of ruler cult (3:8) (Moore 1985: 142–43). The Jewish reader is not surprised to find that none of these gods defends his or her honor, but the challenge put out by Holofernes in 6:2, "What god is there except Nebuchadnezzar?" demands an answer from the One God, and the remainder of the story focuses on this contest between God and the forces of Nebuchadnezzar. If the latter succeed, God's honor will be grossly diminished. When Achior reports Holofernes' words to the Bethulians, they immediately perceive and highlight the "arrogance" (*hyperēphania*, 6:19), the impudent encroachment upon the honor of God, in the general's words, and call upon God to defend God's honor as embodied in the people who huddle under God for protection.

Judith understands that the honor of God is at stake. The conclusion of her prayer, that "every tribe know and understand that you are God . . . and that there is no other" (9:14), is the counterchallenge to Holofernes' challenge (6:2). She also understands that the people of God have an obligation to defend God's honor with their lives. She ultimately rebukes the town rulers for their plan to surrender, because such surrender would leave God's temple in Jerusalem vulnerable to defilement. God would hold God's clients accountable for not protecting God's honor as embodied in the temple (8:21–25; cf. 9:7–8, 13–14). She gives herself wholly over to the defense of her God's honor and plans to uncover the emptiness of the enemy's boasts by allowing God to defeat their vast host with that which is thought weakest—the hand of a woman (9:9–14; 16:5–6).

At this point, Judith turns to the defensive strategies of deception discussed above. She is so adept that she can even employ oaths, normally introduced to ensure that speech would be truthful rather than deceptive, to further deceive her enemy. Swearing "by the life of Nebuchadnezzar" would mean nothing to her (11:7), since he was but a mere man in her opinion. The third commandment sought to safeguard only the oath taken in the name of God. She hides the true information about what is happening inside her primary reference group (the revelation of which would be damning to her cause), instead creating an appearance for them that will lure Holofernes into biding his time and giving her time to make her move. She also projects a false appearance for herself, posing as a prophet to whom God has revealed and will reveal secrets about Holofernes' enemy, her own people (11:17–19). In the eyes of the audience, however, Holofernes will be seen as a fool. He ought at least to have kept a healthy level of suspicion toward an outsider who claimed to be about to betray her group to those who were outsiders to her. For the remainder, Judith tends to abstain from outright deceit, relying instead on ambiguity (hence the wealth of irony in this episode). It would again be a mark against Holofernes that he was unable to discern potential double meanings and uncover her deception.

At the critical moment, a third honor contest is joined, this time directly between Holofernes and Judith. He thinks it will be a disgrace to himself and his army to let Judith go without taking her sexually (12:12) and so tries to seduce Judith as a means of enhancing or preserving his reputation as a virile male (and the reputation of his camp) (Levine 1992: 20). Indeed, he thinks that *she* will scorn him if he does not behave in this way and succeed in taking her. Judith is able to defend her own honor at the same time as she defends the honor of her God and the safety of her people, although she puts her own honor at great risk (left alone with a drunken soldier) in the service of God's honor.

In the end, she defeats Holofernes because he does not remain in control of himself, acting with neither prudence (she is, after all, one of the enemy) nor temperance. Excessive drinking and his own sexual desire rob him of the ability to defend himself like a man, leading him to disgrace at the hands of a woman. This also means "disgrace on the house of King Nebuchadnezzar" (14:18; cf. 13:17). The first honor contest, which Nebuchadnezzar had been winning, is now lost to the Israelites, who come out on top thanks to Judith. Her victory in this honor contest is celebrated in 15:9: she is their "exaltation" (specifically, the one who elevated Israel by getting "one up" on Nebuchadnezzar in the person of Holofernes), their "pride," and their "boast" (their claim to honor, won at the expense of Nebuchadnezzar). God's honor is, of course, publicly demonstrated (16:4–5). In keeping with the definition of female honor as sexual exclusivity (Pitt-Rivers 1966: 42), Judith must, in the end, solemnly affirm that her own sexual exclusivity was preserved intact—she had successfully defended herself in the third contest. To have lost this would have been to have lost her own honor in this contest (13:16; contra Bissell 1899, not an acceptable loss).

Did Judith indeed violate "the basic moral laws in the interest of her people"? Did she "break the law in order to maintain the greater principle for which it stands" (Pfeiffer 1949: 302; Craven 1983: 115)? I assume that these authors have in mind the Ten Commandments, particularly those proscribing false witness and murder. I suggest that Judith's actions, lauded by the author (and, presumably, the audience), rather demand that we reexamine our presuppositions about how those commandments were interpreted and applied by the covenant people of the Second Temple period. While this would not answer the ultimate moral questions about how we are to fulfill those commandments, it would open up an insider's perspective on Judith as a moral character, exhibiting integrity between her piety practiced in her rooftop tent and her words and actions in Holofernes' tent.

Theology and Piety: A Window into Late–Second–Century Judaism

The author of Judith provides much grist for the mills of theology. The God of Israel is the "God of heaven" (6:19). God has personally created and formed all things through word and spirit, with the result that all creatures owe God proper service (16:14). On this basis, the Gentiles' worship of other gods continues to be seen as ignorance about the nature of God and a failure to serve God as God merits. God stands ready to receive the Gentile who turns from false gods to acknowledge and serve the Living God, as Achior does. God's power is irresistible (16:14). The elements themselves shake and melt before God's glance—how much more so will recalcitrant human beings of mere flesh, who set themselves against God and God's people (16:15, 17)! Nevertheless, God is remembered as merciful and kind toward those who revere God by doing what pleases God (16:15b–16).

God's foreknowledge is absolute (9:5–6), but since God's ways and values have been shown, in part, in those things that have come to pass, mortals (like Judith) can hope to perceive and fall in line with what God will do in the forthcoming future (9:2–4, 7–14). God's purposes are sovereign, and mortals do best to yield themselves to God's providence, whether that be for their destruction or deliverance (8:15–17), though for the faithful there is the strong hope of deliverance (8:17). Suffering and hardship are presented as an opportunity to prove one's fidelity and devotion to God (8:25) and might also be embraced as educative discipline (8:27) (Harrington 1999: 41).

God's help is greater than the help of armies, and those who trust in God rather than in visible signs of power will not come to disgrace (see Ps. 20:7; Isa. 31:1; 2 Macc. 8:18). God's special commitment to, and connection with, the lowly, oppressed, and weak (Jdt. 9:11) is a recurring theme of Scripture (1 Sam. 2:8; Ps. 9:9; 10:17–18; 35:10; 82:1–4; Isa. 25:4; Sir. 4:1–5). "God uses the weak things to confound the strong" (Cowley 1913: 247), as Jdt. 9:10–14 and 16:4–5 especially suggest, and there is thematic consistency between these passages and certain New Testament passages (see especially Luke 1:46–55; 1 Cor. 1:26–31).

In concert with several others of the Apocrypha, Judith reaffirms Deuteronomy's basic viewpoint that Israel's fidelity to God's commandments results in divine favor and protection against all adversaries, whereas Israel's transgression of Torah (particularly idolatry) exposes them to the ravages of conquest and the like (5:17–21; 8:18–20; 11:10–15). God remains faithful to hear the cry of God's people (4:13) and to deliver them. While Judith formulates and executes her plan, victory is correctly ascribed to God (12:4; 13:14; 16:5), just as in 1 Maccabees the victory over the Syrian forces is executed by Judas and his armies but effected by God. God is seen at work in and through the courageous actions of God's people, particularly those who are rigorously committed to the covenant and the exclusive worship of the One God. There is an absence of "miracle" (so Enslin and Zeitlin 1972: 42) in the sense of miracle as atypical suspension of natural laws but not in the sense of perceiving God's hand at work bringing about God's surprising ends in history.

In addition to offering rich theological content, the author of Judith also seeks to inculcate or reinforce commitment to particular aspects of Jewish piety. As in Ben Sira and Tobit, "fearing God" is the basic mark of a person's value and the essential requirement for a good reputation (8:8; 16:16). The person who fears God prays. Judith prays at the time of the evening incense offering (9:1), which accords well with what is known of later Jewish practice. In Luke 1:10, for example, this is a time for corporate prayer as a people of God in the temple, an act perhaps suggested by Ps. 141:2. Prayer is not, however, limited to certain times and places but fills the life of the pious person. National, corporate prayer is heard by God (Jdt. 4:8–13; cf. 2 Macc. 3:15–24; 3 Macc. 1:16–2:20), with the result that God will be attentive to the petitioners' plight and will effect their deliverance. Prayer is also the manner in which the individual can tap into God's strength for perilous but essential endeavors, as Judith's prayers for strength mark the beginning of her journey in chapter 9 and the final stroke of the sword in 13:7–8. Judith's prayer also reveals an understanding of Scripture as the sourcebook of paradigms that reveal how God would have people act in new generations. Judith reaches into the zeal of her ancestor Simeon and the manner in which he defended the honor and purity of God's people for the inspiration of her own act of subterfuge and violence.

Even the most casual readers cannot fail to notice Judith's strict observance of dietary laws, which involves eating clean food from clean plates (10:5; 11:13; 12:2, 9, 19). She prepares for her stay in the Gentile tents by packing her own food and dishes and makes a point of eating and drinking only what she herself has brought, from her own utensils, at the table of Holofernes. Thus, while we catch a glimpse of the way in which a Jew and a Gentile might have table fellowship, it is still in such a manner as allows the Jew to maintain his or her social distinctiveness from the Gentile(s) at the table. A concern for maintaining purity is also evidenced in the ritual ablutions performed by Judith before entering God's presence in prayer (12:7–8).

Judith models rigorous self-discipline. As a widow, she continues in mourning, girded with sackcloth under her widow's garb. She fasts continuously and dwells in a rooftop tent, coming down into her house and enjoying food only on the Sabbaths and festivals and their eves (8:4–6). These practices may be related more closely to her perpetual mourning for her husband than part of a regimen of religious asceticism.

Although intensely interested in the tithes and firstfruits due the priestly staff (11:11–13) and the correlation of prayer with incense offering (9:1), the author also includes a statement that relativizes the value of sacrifices and offerings in regard to a heart that fears God (16:16). This should not be read as a necessarily anticultic verse and thus out of place in a story that gives central importance to the temple. Many psalms (see Ps. 40:6–8; 51:16–17) speak of inward piety and Torah obedience having greater value than sacrifices and would have been sung in the very courts of the temple where sacrifices were being offered.

The majority of scholars regard Judith as an example of early Pharisaic piety. One scholar, Hugo Mantel (1976), argues that the author had a Sadducean orientation.[16] His arguments do not, however, point convincingly and exclusively to Sadducean concerns. For example, Judith abstains from eating the food of Gentiles, as would the Sadducees (Mantel 1976: 75), but the Pharisees and Essenes would do so as well. After leaving the camp of Holofernes, Judith bathes before praying (Mantel 1976: 72), but the connection between washing and prayer is not exclusively Sadducean. Essene practice highlights the importance of ablutions as preparation for entering into prayer and worship (at Qumran, at least). The fact that Judith prays at the same time as the evening offering of incense certainly reveals an interest in connecting with the rhythms of the temple worship (Mantel 1976: 7), but this was also valued beyond Sadducean circles. That Judith should propose to act as a prophet in informing Holofernes of the exact time when the people sin against God does not suggest the Sadducean conviction that prophecy continued after Malachi (Mantel 1976: 80), only that Judith pretended to use divination as part of her ruse. The definition of sin in Judith does not merely revolve around idolatry (which Mantel takes to be the definition most appropriate to priests—itself a questionable assumption since idolatry would have been regarded as a cardinal sin in the eyes of all the Jewish sects) (Mantel 1976: 75), for the author also refers to fornication as sin (13:16) and, indeed, presents the eating of the consecrated tithes as a damning offense (11:11).

What we can learn from the more positive points in Mantel's article, however, is that the piety of Judith should not be too quickly or too exclusively aligned with Pharisaic piety either. While containing many features that clearly overlap with Pharisaic piety, Judith's piety is at many points characteristic of more than one sect and is probably also informed by other streams of piety. Without being strictly sectarian or partisan, then, Judith remains an

---

16. Conveniently summarized in English in Craven 1983: 118-20.

"inspirational example" for the readers, in her piety, courage, nationalism, and faith (Moore 1985: 62).

Judith and the Place of Women in the Intertestamental Period

The Book of Judith has deservedly attracted the attention of scholars interested in the roles, limitations, and ideology of women in the Second Temple period. Judith's behavior contravenes convention at a number of points, while also reinforcing those conventions along the way. She is not the stereotypical widow, weak and in need of protection (Levine 1992: 19). Rather, she stands as the head of her household in the absence of Manasseh, her departed husband, and is introduced with her own genealogy (8:1); and indeed, it is her achievement that secures a memory for her ancestors and reestablishes the memory of the line of Simeon (Levine 1992: 21).[17] She summons the elders to her home and censures them for their conduct, which is certainly not in keeping with the feminine ideals of silence and submissiveness. Nevertheless, she does remain in a private space to do this, which accords with convention. She is entrusted with the deliverance of the town, which certainly runs counter to the normal expectations of what women can accomplish. While Judith "rises above the sexism of her author's culture" (Montley 1978: 40), she also uses that sexism to her advantage in Holofernes' tent. His lack of suspicion that a woman can do him any harm or take him by craft and his objectification of Judith as an object of sexual conquest for the confirmation of manly power and virility make Judith's plan work. Perhaps the most striking reversal appears in 14:1–5, where Judith replaces Joakim as the military strategist and commander, giving the orders for the counterattack (van Henten 1995: 251).

Judith, who has contravened so many conventions of behavior appropriate for women, is indeed domesticated again at the end of the story (Levine 1992: 17). After her victory over Holofernes, Judith retires from the public scene, and the women who led her celebration also disappear from view (Levine 1992: 24, 27). The insight that Judith fits the pattern of a judge who appears on the scene to accomplish some deed for the Lord and then retires from the scene is quite apt (White 1992: 12; van Henten 1995: 242), but it also may underscore the limitations on Judith's ability to break with conventional gender roles. There simply is no place for her in society, no institution that can accept her continued presence as a leading figure (not priest, not king, not senator).

17. Simeon is omitted from the genealogy of 8:1, but as the father of Sarasadai and grandfather of Salamiel, as in Num. 1:6, he is surely intended (as the Old Latin, Syriac, and Vulgate make explicit) (Moore 1985: 179). See also Jdt. 9:2, where Simeon is named by Judith as her ancestor.

Despite the domestication of Judith at the end of her story, the author has made some important claims about a woman's potential in an environment in which the opposite claims had already been made (especially by Ben Sira). The author of Judith may have "intended to challenge, among other things, many of Ben Sira's sexist biases against women" (Di Lella 1995: 51). Judith proves, against Ben Sira's regrettable statement, that the birth of a daughter is not "a loss" (Sir. 22:3), since her courage and virtue put her father, Merari, on the map of national memory. Her celibacy after marriage and her rigorous self-discipline are the polar opposite of Ben Sira's woman, who is always in danger of yielding her sexuality to any man who comes along. She uses her powers of seduction not to lead any Israelite male astray but to entrap a male Assyrian who is slave to his own passions and thus to become the agent of God's deliverance for the whole nation (Di Lella 1995: 46–47). Whereas Ben Sira considered the (male) elders of the people to drip wisdom from their lips, the author of Judith portrays these elders as vacillating and weak, unable to lead the people effectively. Rather, it is a woman who will speak wisdom and give leadership in this story (Di Lella 1995: 48–49). While the Book of Judith does not, then, carve out for women a permanent role in the public sphere, it does represent an attempt to promote a greater appreciation for their value and potential as members of the people of God, while also calling into question the assumptions about the "naturally superior" contributions of males to that people.

Influence

The failure of Judith to achieve canonical status, despite the deep presence of God and piety in the book, is all the more surprising when one considers that Esther—in its Hebrew form, which lacks any reference to God or the distinctive customs of Judaism—did attain that status.[18] Many explanations for the omission of Judith from the Hebrew canon have been offered. Craven (1983: 117–18) suggests that it was excluded because it would have been dangerous to the normal division of roles and behaviors between genders to confer authoritative status to this text. Given the taming of Judith at the conclusion of the book and the precedents of Deborah and Jael, this seems unlikely to have caused Judith to fall short of the canonical mark.

Others have suggested that the conversion of Achior conflicted with the prohibition of allowing Ammonites to convert (Deut. 23:3) (Steinmann 1953: 61–62; Enslin and Zeitlin 1972: 24). This is a complicated question,

18. Zeitlin (Enslin and Zeitlin 1972: 13–14) goes so far as to suggest that Judith represents an intentional attempt to "neutralize the book of Esther" by presenting a heroine who was scrupulous in her observance of Jewish law (rather than a diner at the table of Xerxes and a frequenter of his bed) and courageous in her defense of the people (rather than a reluctant heroine).

not least because the provision that the Edomites and Egyptians should be allowed to convert after the third generation from the exodus (Deut. 23:7–8) suggests that the exclusion of Moabites and Ammonites should be lifted after the tenth generation (see *m. Yadayim* 4.4). The author of Ezra 9:1, however, does not regard the conversion of any Gentile—Ammonite, Moabite, or Egyptian—to be a possible solution to the dilemma of mixed marriages in Israel (Nickelsburg 1984: 49), and many rabbis followed the practice of excluding Ammonite and Moabite males, at least, from the congregation well into the rabbinic era (*b. Yebamot* 76b; *m. Yebamot* 8.3).[19] Some rabbis would have had serious misgivings about a book that, once granted canonical status, could displace their interpretation of Deut. 23:3. A related hypothesis claims that rabbinic practice required converts to be baptized as well as circumcised. The omission of this in the case of Achior would have been seen as a threat to their halakhah were the book admitted to canonical status (Orlinsky 1974: 218; Enslin and Zeitlin 1972: 25). We do not know enough about conversion practices in the intertestamental period to substantiate that claim, however. "There are no second temple texts attesting to immersion and sacrifice as required rituals of conversion" (Moore 1992a: 64).

Perhaps the best suggestion is that the book was written too late and was known to come from the Hasmonean period, the fictitious setting in Nebuchadnezzar's reign being recognized as such by its readers.[20] It is probably more correct to say that Judith was never included rather than to say that it was intentionally excluded. The book is never mentioned by name in any record of debates concerning canonicity, unlike Esther, Ecclesiastes, and Ben Sira (Moore 1992a: 64). Judith grew in popularity in the post-talmudic age as the story came to be closely associated with Hanukkah and thus the subject of several different midrashim connected with that festival.[21] Her story was told in tandem with the victories of Judah, her male namesake. Jewish art also attests to her growing popularity during the medieval period.

The influence of Judith on the authors of the New Testament is difficult to document. Most verbal parallels listed in the marginal notes in the Nestle-Aland *Novum Testamentum Graece* are better explained as common dependence on Old Testament texts (e.g., both Matt. 9:36 and Jdt. 11:19 reflect the depiction of the people as "sheep that have no shepherd" in 1 Kings

19. Rabbinic references are from Moore 1985: 235.

20. Zeitlin (Enslin and Zeitlin 1972: 25–26) correctly suggests this hypothesis but for the wrong reason. Judith was not omitted from the canon because "the story of Judith was placed after the time of Antiochus Epiphanes" while "Esther's story was placed in the time of Ahasuerus." If anything, Judith is "placed" earlier than Esther. Additionally, Zeitlin's theory that Judith was "compiled in the diaspora," and therefore was never a serious contender for canonicity (1972: 26), has not withstood scrutiny (see Moore 1992a: 63).

21. See Moore 1985: 103–7 for the full texts of two of these. Dubarle (1966: 1.80–1.104; 1.105–9) provides access to thirteen known midrashim and documents rabbinic references as well.

22:17) or shared use of liturgical, stereotyped, or everyday expressions. The most impressive of these parallels is the description of God's vengeance on the oppressors of God's people in Jdt. 16:17, which includes fire and flesh-eating worms (influenced perhaps by Sir. 7:17) and endless weeping in the day of judgment, images that also figure prominently in New Testament portrayals of the day of judgment (see Matt. 24:51; Mark 9:48; James 5:3). But even this would not be sufficient evidence for direct influence.

Rendel Harris (1915–16) has noted the strongest example of direct influence of Judith on a New Testament author:

> You cannot plumb the depths of the human heart or understand the workings of the human mind: how do you expect to search out God; who made all these things, and find out his mind or comprehend his thought? (Jdt. 8:14)

> The Spirit searches out all things, even the depths of God. For who among human beings knows the things of a human being except the spirit of the human being that is inside him? And in this manner no one has known the things of God except the spirit of God. . . . For "who has known the mind of the Lord, who will advise him?" (1 Cor. 2:10–11, 16; translation mine)

Both contrast the "depths" (a word for "inner designs, thoughts," and the like) of a person with the "depths" of God and reason by analogy (Paul) or by lesser to greater (Judith) that just as one cannot know another human being's depths, so one cannot (on one's own, at least) know the mind of God. Both also use peculiar terminology (*eraunaō*, "search out"; *bathos*, "depth, deep things"). The case is indeed strong that Paul has been influenced in his thinking by Jdt. 8:14 (directly, or indirectly by someone who had read and meditated upon the verse).

Judith's influence upon early Christian writers, on the other hand, is abundantly attested.[22] Clement of Rome cites Judith, together with Esther, as an example of a woman receiving power "by the favor of God" to do "manly things" (= "courageous things"; the Greek etymology of *andreia*, "courage," is noteworthy), praising her for embracing personal danger for the love of her people (*1 Clement* 55.4–5). Judith's prayer addresses God as "God of the lowly, help of the oppressed, upholder of the weak" (9:11), a phrase that Origen recontextualizes in *Commentarii in evangelium Joannis* 2.22.16. Origen further regards Judith's necessary use of falsehood as a model for those who are pressed of necessity into dissimulation (*Stromata* 6; quoted in Jerome, *Adversus Rufinum libri III* 1.474). Clement of Alexandria derives the proverb "Whoever is near the Lord is full of stripes" (*Stromata* 2.7) from Jdt. 8:27, "The Lord scourges those who are close to him" (Enslin and Zeitlin 1972: 48).

---

22. See Dubarle 1969: 1.110–25 for an inventory of patristic witnesses to Judith.

One particular thread binding together several patristic references to Judith is her exemplification of celibacy and the ideal of the "wife of one man" (Tertullian, *De monogamia* 17; Methodius, *Symposium [Convivium decem virginum]*, Oration 11.2; Ambrose, *De virginibus* 1.2.4) (Moore 1985: 64). It is likely that Jerome himself added a brief promotion of Judith's celibacy in his rendition of 15:9–10, which adds, "For you have done manfully, and your heart has been strengthened, because you have loved chastity, and after your husband has not known another man." With the exception of Jerome, most Western church fathers treat the book as canonical Scripture; in the East, it was seen as noncanonical by Melito of Sardis, Origen, Athanasius, and Cyril of Jerusalem (Moore 1985: 90; Enslin and Zeitlin 1972: 50).

Its canonical ambiguity notwithstanding, the Book of Judith has been given a prominent place by European artists and writers in their creative endeavors. Judith, holding Holofernes' head, has been the subject of many paintings and other visual representations,[23] and the story has been a recurring theme of plays, oratorios, and operas (Enslin and Zeitlin 1972: 54; Purdie 1927).

23. See Stone 1992 for a fine interpretation of changing trends in the depiction of this subject; also Montley 1978.

Additions to Esther

"The Aid of the All-Seeing God and Savior"

The Greek version of Esther contains six blocks of material not contained in the Masoretic Text. These major "Additions to Esther" stand alongside smaller but significant modifications of Hebrew Esther, both in terms of added phrases or verses that introduce the overt acts and oversight of God into the story and in terms of omissions of details and redundancies considered superfluous by the translator. The cumulative effect of these alterations is to make Esther an overtly religious tale in which the main characters embody the distinctive marks of Judaism (dedication to the One God, the observance of Torah in all its particulars as a way of life, and the practice of pious acts of prayer, fasting, and almsgiving). A second effect is to enhance the impression of historiography as the major genre of the book through the reproduction of the full texts of official edicts, a common feature of that genre. A third effect is to heighten the reader's awareness of the tension and animosity between Jew and Gentile, at the same time introducing alternative models for Jewish-Gentile relations in which the symbiosis is mutually beneficial. The century-old judgment of Gregg (1913: 665) thus remains essentially intact: the value of these modifications "lies not in their power to enlarge our knowledge of the story of Esther, but in the reflection they offer of the religious development [and social dynamics] of the circle[s] in which they originated."

The six major additions were removed by Jerome and relocated to the end of his translation of Esther, the last of them now coming first. These additions came, therefore, to be enumerated as 10:4–16:24 and appear as such in the KJV Apocrypha and its derivatives. Read in this order, of course, the book makes no sense. The RSV and NRSV, along with most other recent translations that include the Apocrypha, have remedied this deficiency by restoring the additions to their proper order within complete translations of Greek Esther.

Structure and Contents

Addition A (11:2–12:6) introduces Mordecai under the impossible terms of being a courtier at the time of Artaxerxes *and* one of the captives brought

110

from Jerusalem by Nebuchadnezzar some 112 years prior, and relates a dream that he had. In this dream, two dragons come forward to fight amidst the typical disturbances of apocalyptic visions (voices, thunders, earthquakes). In response to their roaring, every nation prepares to fight against "the righteous nation." On a "day of darkness and gloom," they cry out to God and are delivered: from a tiny spring comes a great river, the light returns, and the "lowly were exalted and devoured those held in honor" (11:11). Mordecai understands this to be a revelation about "what God had determined to do" (11:12). In a second part of this addition, Mordecai uncovers a plot against the king's life and is rewarded by Artaxerxes. Haman, however, who favored the conspirators, determines to injure Mordecai and his people (12:6).

Addition B (13:1–7, added after Esth. 3:13) provides the "actual text" of the edict dictated by Haman. Written in the king's name, the edict speaks of Artaxerxes' benevolent desires to unify his kingdom, the Jews' commitment to a different way of life as an impediment to that end, and the king's resolution that this contrary and subversive element be eliminated. One man's vendetta is thus effectively disguised as a "benevolent policy" undertaken to unify and strengthen the kingdom.

Addition C (13:8–14:19, added after Esth. 4:17) introduces two prayers, one by Mordecai (13:8–17) and one by Esther (14:3–19), prior to Esther's going before the king unbidden, an act of some potential danger. Mordecai acknowledges God as the irresistible sovereign of the universe and explains that it was not out of arrogance or pride that he refused to bow down to Haman and thus brought Israel into danger but out of a desire to revere only the One God with such gestures as bowing. Mordecai goes on to beg God to save Israel, identified as God's own portion among the nations, redeemed for God's Self. The prayer is replete with the themes of God's universal sovereignty and God's unique attachment to Israel.

Esther's prayer begins with the theme of God's election of Israel, acknowledging God's justice in handing a disobedient Israel over to foreign domination (affirming Deuteronomy's theology of history). She sees, however, in the conflict between non-Jews and the Jewish people the contest for honor between the one true God and the lifeless idols adored by the Gentiles. God is urged to deliver Israel so that God's glory may be undiminished and God's empty rivals not be praised. She acknowledges that God alone will be at work saving God's people, emboldening Esther, turning the heart of the king, and bringing about a good end. She expresses here her loathing for sharing her bed with an uncircumcised Gentile and avers that she has kept kosher and avoided all semblances of participation in idolatry (e.g., drinking libations, 14:17).

Addition D (15:1–16) replaces two verses in the Hebrew (Esth. 5:1–2) with a greatly extended and dramatically enhanced scene of the queen's intrusion into Artaxerxes' throne room. In the new scene, it is God who saves the day, turning the king's heart from anger at the intrusion to softness and concern for his wife.

Addition E (16:1–24, added after Esth. 8:12) provides the text of the edict of the king rescinding his previous order (Addition B). Haman is censured as an ungrateful recipient of the king's favors, treacherously plotting against his benefactor. Haman is in fact called a Macedonian who is trying to weaken Artaxerxes' rule from inside so that the Persian Empire could be transferred to the Macedonians (as one day would happen). The well-being of the Jewish subjects is thus seen to be intimately connected with the stability of the Gentile kingdom in which they live. The king admits responsibility for not weighing Haman's advice more carefully (16:8–9) and announces that he will be more alert to such treachery in the future. The king exonerates the Jews of all charges and instructs his subjects not to act on his prior edict. His loyal subjects are to arm and assist the Jews, should any others be resolved to act out their anti-Jewish sentiments on Haman's orders. The king even orders his Persian subjects to celebrate the deliverance of the Jews (a sort of Gentile counterpart to Purim).

Greek Esther closes with the Addition F (10:4–11:1), which returns to Mordecai's dream (Addition A), and thus is clearly dependent upon and linked to Addition A. Mordecai now interprets his dream: he and Haman were the two dragons, ready to fight; the nations were all the subjects of Artaxerxes poised to attack the Jews; Esther was the stream of water through which help came from God. Mordecai goes on to focus on two very different lots from the ones that originally gave rise to the name of the festival authorized by this book (i.e., Purim, "lots" such as were cast by Haman to determine the date of the massacre). Now, these lots are the fates or destinies apportioned by God to the non-Jewish nations and to the Jewish people, which, when they came together, resulted in God's vindicating God's chosen people. The Purim festival is thus presented in such a way as emphasizes not only timely deliverance from disaster but also the fundamental difference between, and separation of, Jew and Gentile in the plan of God. Esther 11:1 provides a colophon, a brief note recorded by the librarian who received the text concerning its pedigree.

The additions enhance the literary structure of Esther in two ways. First, and most prominently, Additions A and F provide a framing narrative for the whole story, setting the court intrigue between Haman and Mordecai and then the pogroms between Jews and Gentiles in the interpretative framework of an apocalyptic vision and its interpretation. The interpretative power of this framework is not to be underestimated. The reader of Greek Esther knows from the beginning that God has determined in advance the outcome of this story and will be at work to bring about the end that God has chosen.

In a similar way, Additions B and E heighten the sense of a concentric structure for the work. While Hebrew Esther mentions these two edicts, actually "quoting" them now increases their potential to act as a second layer of a narrative frame, as well as to heighten the dramatic movement of the story. To borrow from Aristotle's *Poetics* 18, the first edict announces the complication (*desis*) that must be undone, the second announces the successful resolution (*lysis*) of that crisis.

Additions C and D alter the original story's structure by displacing its climax. Addition C highlights the importance of Esther's uninvited entrance into the king's presence by drawing out its preparations, and Addition D, which replaces two verses in the original with fifteen, greatly expands and renders more dramatically the episode of Esther's appearing before Artaxerxes (Moore 1992b: 629). This, then, becomes the new centerpiece of the narrative.

Although the six additions outlined above constitute the main focus of discussions of the Additions to Esther, there are actually numerous other additions and omissions to be noted when one sets the Septuagint side by side with the Masoretic Text. Some of these additions pertain to small matters of detail. The Greek mentions a miniature cup made of ruby (1:7), absent from the Hebrew. Haman is present and mentioned by name at the summoning of Vashti (1:10). The Greek names three counselors by name in 1:14, where the Hebrew names seven. Mordecai merely laments in the Hebrew, but the content of his cry is given in the Greek version of 4:1: "An innocent nation is being destroyed!" Similarly, a direct recitation of Mordecai's speech occurs in 4:8 in the Greek (but not in the Hebrew), as he advises Esther, "Call upon the Lord; then speak to the king in our behalf, and save us from death." Haman the Amalekite becomes Haman the Macedonian in Greek Esther 9:24. At two places, the Greek supplies a lacking, or improves an embarrassing, motive: Artaxerxes does not merely summon Vashti to display her as another of his treasures or trophies but to crown her queen at the climax of the festival (1:11); the eunuchs who plot against the king in chapter 2 do so, in the Greek, because they were "angry because of Mordecai's advancement" (2:21).

In keeping with a major theme of the larger additions, several of these minor additions introduce religious topics or concerns. In the Greek version, Esther is instructed by Mordecai to "fear God and keep his laws," and the audience is told that, after her introduction to the king's harem, she "did not change her mode of life" (2:20), remaining a Torah-observant Jew. Esther is enjoined to pray before her audience with the king (4:8). At 6:1, the Hebrew merely says that the king could not sleep; the Greek attributes this sleeplessness to God's act. In both versions, Haman's wife and friends warn him against the dangers of going up against the Jewish nation, but in the Greek they attribute this directly to divine agency: "because the living God is with them" (6:13). Finally, the Greek adds to Artaxerxes' second edict an extra stipulation: in addition to being authorized to defend themselves on the thirteenth day of Adar, the Jews are "to observe their own laws" (8:11).

While making numerous additions, small and extensive, the Greek version also strives to condense the Hebrew, eliminating redundancies and seeking more concise ways to deliver the same basic details. A casual comparison of the Greek and Hebrew versions of 3:1–13, 5:1–10, or 9:1–2 (the NRSV makes this easy by providing a complete translation of both versions of Esther) would introduce the interested reader to the kinds of omissions routinely made.

Textual Transmission

The textual history of Esther is complicated by the existence of two major families of Greek texts. The better-attested version, called the B-Text, is represented in the major Septuagint codices and manuscripts (notably Vaticanus, Sinaiticus, and Alexandrinus) and undergirds modern English translations of Greek Esther. The Greek translator did not mechanically reproduce the Hebrew but performed a freer, more literary translation (Moore 1982: lxiii; 1977: 162).[1] The second Greek edition, labeled the A-Text, was formerly identified with the second-century-C.E. edition of Lucian but is now held to date from before Lucian's lifetime. It appears to be a translation from a Semitic text of a different type from that underlying the Septuagint (B-Text) (Moore 1967; 1977: 164; Cook 1969) and is shorter than the Septuagint version, offering a more concise reporting of the story (Moore 1977: 163). The closer verbal correspondence between the A-Text and the Septuagint in the Additions suggests that the translator of the A-Text imported the additions from the Septuagint version (Moore 1977: 165, 194; Clines 1984: 72–92).[2] The Old Latin version is valuable as a second-century witness to the Greek B-Text (Oesterley 1935: 194). The Sahidic and Ethiopic books of Esther are based on the Septuagint, while the Syriac and Vulgate are based on the Hebrew text (Moore 1977: 167).

What was the original form of Esther? We are accustomed to speaking of the Masoretic Text as representing, in effect, the original form, and the Greek version as containing additions and other changes, but this model has not gone unchallenged in scholarship. C. C. Torrey championed the idea that the original Esther contained Additions C and D, as well as more frequent mention of God throughout, which were later expurgated as a safeguard against blasphemy (the book being read at Purim, a festival at which it was considered an obligation, according to *b. Megillah* 7b, to get so drunk as to be unable to distinguish between "Cursed be Haman" and "Blessed be Mordecai"). Torrey believed that the Greek versions are substantially closer to the original Hebrew version than is the Masoretic Text (and our present Old Testament) (Torrey 1945: 58–59).[3] One must concede that Additions C and D are quite at home in the world of Palestinian Jewish literature such as Daniel (with

1. A critical edition of Greek Esther in the Septuagint is available in Hanhart 1966.
2. Clines (1984: 217–48) provides an English translation of the A-Text.
3. See also Pfeiffer 1949: 309–10. The argument is developed at length in Torrey 1944.

Daniel's prayer of confession in chapter 9) and Judith (with Judith's impassioned prayer before a courageous attempt to save Israel and her commitment to *kashrut*). Francis Roiron (1916) presses this theory further to include Additions A and F, which are also quite consistent with Palestinian Jewish apocalyptic literature. The consonance of Additions A, C, D, and F with second-century Jewish literature written in Hebrew does have important bearing on the origins of the Additions but ultimately cannot demonstrate that these additions were part of the "original" Book of Esther.

While it may be true that the original form of Esther did make explicit references to God, which later were excised, it is unlikely that the larger Additions formed a part of that original. The most important indicator in this regard is the secondary character of the Additions: without them, the story is a coherent whole; with them, contradictions are unnecessarily introduced into a formerly consistent narrative (especially in the cases of Additions A, E, and F).

First, there are numerous contradictions between Addition A 12:1–6 and the older report of a foiled assassination attempt on the king by two eunuchs in 2:21–23, if these are taken to be doublets of the same event. Even if they are taken as different plots thwarted by Mordecai five years apart, at least one contradiction remains: Haman's motive for destroying Mordecai along with his people. In Addition A 12:6, Haman looms behind the assassination attempt on Artaxerxes that Mordecai thwarted and seeks vengeance on Mordecai for spoiling his plans, whereas in Hebrew Esth. 3:5–6, Haman is motivated by Mordecai's refusal to do him obeisance (a motive also assumed, however, in Addition C 13:12–15). Addition E 16:10–14 ascribes still another motivation to Haman for assaulting the Jews: undermining the king's support base so that the Macedonians could take over the Persian Empire.

There is also a contradiction in the descriptions of the fate of Haman and his sons. In Esth. 7:9–10; 9:6–19, Haman is hanged on a gallows in his own house and his ten sons killed in the riots on the thirteenth of Adar; in Addition E 16:17–18, Haman and his sons are all hanged on the city gate prior to the thirteenth of Adar (Moore 1992b: 630).

In a way, the marginal status of Esther within the body of "canonical" literature was what caused attempts to emend the book to make it more religious and thus more worthy of sacred status and also what allowed translators and authors to dare to alter the text in a manner, and to an extent, that they did not do with any other book that came to be canonical within Judaism (Bickerman 1950: 113–14; Moore 1977: 160).

The original language of all six Additions was once thought to have been Greek (Gregg 1913: 665; Oesterley 1935: 191), composed perhaps at the time of the translation of Esther. Now, scholars seek a more precise estimation of the original language of each addition on its own. Many scholars have come to regard the numerous Semitisms in Additions A, C, D, and F as a sign of their having been written in Hebrew or Aramaic and the lofty, fluid Greek style of Additions B and E as a sign of their having been composed in Greek for inclusion in Esther (Torrey 1944: 2; Pfeiffer 1949: 308; Enslin and Zeitlin 1972: 20).[4]

Moore adds an important refinement at this point, calling students to consider the possibility that each addition itself took shape over time. Addition A, for example, appears to have been compiled in two stages. The earlier, 11:1–11, was originally written in Hebrew, while a secondary addition, 11:12–12:6, was made (possibly in Greek) after Addition A was joined to Esther.[5] Similarly with Addition C, the bulk was originally written in Hebrew, with 14:6–12 added (again, possibly in Greek) at a later time. The absence of 11:12–12:6 and 14:6–12 in the Old Latin, a second-century version, as well as Josephus's retelling of Esther, strongly suggest that these are later additions to the book (Moore 1973: 387).

With regard to Additions B and E, composition in Greek is now universally recognized. The literary—indeed, the rhetorically florid—character of the Greek in these additions rules out the possibility of a Semitic *Vorlage* (Moore 1977: 193).[6] The similarity of form and content between Addition B and 3 Macc. 3:11–29 also argues for an Alexandrian provenance and composition in Greek (Moore 1973: 384).[7]

Author, Date, and Setting

The evolution of Esther from its original Hebrew form to the text as it stands in the Septuagint took place over a considerable span of time. Josephus's paraphrase of Esther includes Additions B through E, giving a firm *terminus ad quem* of 90 C.E. for those additions. The lack of mention of Additions A and F may be attributed to Josephus's choice rather than to their absence from his text (Moore 1992b: 632). The colophon to Greek Esther (11:1), however, most likely provides authentic and reliable information and so yields a more precise *terminus ad quem:*

4. Moore (1973: 393) favors a Greek origin for Addition D but offers no argumentation on this point.

5. Cook (1969) opposes Moore on this point: 11:12–12:6 is seen as translated from a Hebrew *Vorlage*, while the earlier section could represent Septuagint-style Greek.

6. Martin (1975) offers a rigorous and sound approach to this question, looking to the analysis and enumeration of specific syntactical features of compositional Greek and translation Greek for an answer to the question of original language. His findings largely confirm the majority report: B and E were definitely composed in Greek; A, C, and D are translations of a Semitic *Vorlage;* and F is inconclusive (1975: 65).

7. Moore thinks it unlikely that Lysimachus himself added these edicts, since the sumptuous rhetorical style is not to be found elsewhere in the book (1973: 385), although an individual's free compositions might be significantly different from his or her translations in terms of style (not to mention the likelihood that ornate style was deemed appropriate for official edicts but perhaps not for visions, prayers, and the like). Bickerman (1950: 126) regards Lysimachus as the source for Additions B and E.

> In the fourth year of the reign of Ptolemy and Cleopatra, Dositheus, who said that he was a priest and a Levite, and his son Ptolemy brought to Egypt the preceding Letter about Purim, which they said was authentic and had been translated by Lysimachus son of Ptolemy, one of the residents of Jerusalem.

The librarian who received the original added this colophon, giving information about its immediate source (Dositheus and his son) and recording for posterity their report about its actual origin (Lysimachus's translation efforts). The author of the colophon expresses a certain reserve about affirming the claims made by Dositheus, who "said" that he was a priest and a Levite[8] and who "said" that the book of Esther they brought was genuine and had been translated by Lysimachus. On the one hand, the word "said" might simply be a means by which to record the testimony of Dositheus and his son Ptolemy without the colophonist having gone to the trouble of authenticating their story. It might, however, express doubt about their story, perhaps inspired by the colophonist's knowledge of other editions of Esther (Moore 1977: 250–51).

The date, however, helpfully records the year in which Dositheus brought the scroll to Alexandria. Unfortunately, every successor of Ptolemy I took the name Ptolemy, and several were married to a Cleopatra. Bickerman (1944: 346–47) determined that the translation was accomplished in 78–77 B.C.E., the fourth year of the reign of Ptolemy XII Auletes and Cleopatra V.[9] The other popular date is 114–113 B.C.E., the fourth year of the reign of Ptolemy VIII Soter II and an earlier Cleopatra (Moore 1977: 250; Jacob 1890: 279–80). Bickerman rejects this possibility—as well as a third, Ptolemy XIII, the brother and husband of the famous Cleopatra—since the queen was acting in both cases as a regent for a younger Ptolemy in the fourth years of those reigns, and official documents listed Cleopatra first in those cases, unlike the colophon of Esther. In addition to two lively possibilities for the date of the translation, the colophon also preserves a name, Lysimachus—a resident of Jerusalem, probably with an Egyptian Jewish background (his father's name, Ptolemy, suggests this), thus perhaps explaining why the book should speak so well to the Egyptian Jewish situation, whither it was sent (Pfeiffer 1949: 311).

How are these data relevant for reconstructing the history of the development of the Additions? First, the colophon's position, following Addition F, strongly suggests that Addition F, and therefore of necessity Addition A, were already part of Esther at the time of its translation (Moore 1973: 382, 387). Moreover, it is likely that Additions C and D, which give strong evidence for having been translated from a Semitic *Vorlage* and which resonate so well with

---

8. Bickerman's suggestion (1944: 348) that Levitas was a personal name is now widely rejected.

9. Collins (2000: 110–11) regards Bickerman's arguments to be decisive.

Judith and the court tales of Daniel, also taking shape in the second century B.C.E., were part of Esther at this time as well.[10] All of these additions would come from Palestine. Sometime after Lysimachus translated Esther, another hand added Additions B and E, composed originally in Greek and not translations of Hebrew or Aramaic. These additions may well have originated in the Jewish community in Egypt, all the more so as Addition B shows a striking similarity to 3 Macc. 3:12–29, a work of Egyptian (Alexandrian) Jewish origin.

Genres, Purpose, and Formative Influences

Additions A and F developed, in large measure, as an adaptation of a brief apocalyptic dream vision to the story of Esther. Moore correctly shows that Addition A does not precisely fit the story of Esther. The dragon, a typical symbol of an evil power, is hardly a suitable symbol for Mordecai (although it works for Haman). Moreover, the Septuagint and the A-Text have differing interpretations of this dream in Addition F, revealing disagreement as to how the dream fits the Esther story. In the A-Text, the river represents the nations gathered against the Jews and not Esther as the vehicle for divine deliverance. The dream vision, then, was composed independently of Esther and only later brought in because, in broad terms, it could be serviceable (Moore 1977: 180–81, 248–49).

Addition A, therefore, contains a text originally composed to speak to a specific scenario other than the narrative of Esther. Gardner persuasively suggests that the dream vision dates from the Hellenization crisis (as does Daniel 7–12). The two dragons represent the Ptolemaic and Seleucid empires. That the "kings of the north" and "kings of the south" figure prominently in Daniel lends credence to the view that the contest of these two kingdoms for control of Palestine could be in the forefront of another apocalypticist's mind. The nations gather against the Jews; the Jews are troubled and in dread on account of the edicts proscribing Torah; the stream that becomes a river could represent the growing success of the Maccabean Revolt (Gardner 1984: 7–8).

The dream vision now becomes a revelation of God to Mordecai concerning the future intervention of God in Jewish history and thus opens Esther on a strongly theological note with the topics of God's providence, foreknowledge, and close interaction with God's people. The plot of the eunuchs against Artaxerxes in 2:21–23 is reduplicated so as to present at the outset the two major antagonists (Mordecai and Haman) and to color each in a particular light (the first is loyal and beneficial to the king, the latter is a treasonous

10. "The rigid division between Israel and the nations and the exaggerated emphasis on the separatist piety of Esther may be taken to reflect the Hasmonean milieu in which the translation was made" (Collins 2000: 111–12).

villain). Addition F returns explicitly to the content of Addition A, presenting an interpretation in a manner suited to the Esther story (rather than second-century Palestinian history). The apocalyptic tenor of the original dream is not lost, however, as Addition F closes the book with theological musings about God's predetermination of history and God's special election of the Jewish people, expanding the nature of the festival of Purim (10:13) from a festival of deliverance only to a commemoration of Israel's separateness from the hostile Gentiles and its privileged position in God's plan.

Additions B and E are in the form of royal edicts, and their insertion into Esther brings the whole book more in line with the genre of historiography, which included the texts of official documents wherever possible. The effect of these additions would be to lend greater credibility to the historicity of the story (Moore 1973: 383). Addition B bears a striking similarity to another edict against Judaism in 3 Macc. 3:12–29 in terms of content, form, and structure, down to the order of topics (Moore 1977: 197–99). Both include a statement of the king's interest in general benevolence as the driving motive for the decree, including an explicit rejection of a base motive in favor of the noble one (3 Macc. 3:15; Add. Esth. 13:2); similar charges of antisocial and subversive behavior leveled against the Jews (3 Macc. 3:19–24; Add. Esth. 13:4–5); the order for the termination of the antisocial element (3 Macc. 3:25; Add. Esth. 13:6); and finally, the same projected results of this order, namely, the stability and peace of the kingdom (3 Macc. 3:26; Add. Esth. 13:7). Even though 3 Maccabees was written after the translation of Esther into Greek, it might still have been in a position to exercise a direct influence on a later addition such as Addition B (Moore 1977: 199).

Bickerman (1950: 129–30) considers the strife within the Ptolemaic dynasty to provide a suitable background for the composition of Additions B and E, in which Haman and Mordecai, in effect, each persuade the king that the other is a traitor. The Jews were supportive of one claimant against another in these dynastic feuds—for example, supportive of Cleopatra II against Ptolemy VIII, who unfortunately gained the upper hand and punished Cleopatra's supporters. Similarly, the Jews sided with Ptolemy X while many Alexandrians opposed him, with the result that the latter rioted also against the Jews as enemies of the state (Bickerman 1950: 131).

Although texts in which a ruler is first persuaded that Jews are a threat to the government and then comes to see that the Jews are in fact a loyal and order-sustaining element are especially suited to the political climate in Egypt—and thus the likelihood of their being composed there increases—Additions B and E are wholly and consistently directed toward the situation described in Esther. They do not, that is, take their shape primarily because of the situation of the author but because they flesh out specifically what the king's edicts were supposed to express within the plot of Esther as expansions of Esth. 3:8–9, 13–14; 8:5–12.

Additions C and D show clear signs of dependence on the Jewish Scriptures, the source of many of the specific petitions or exclamations in the prayers. Esther's prayer in particular also bears a marked resemblance to the prayers in Daniel 9 and Judith 9. Nevertheless, both prayers were composed specifically for their incorporation into the Esther story (rather than representing independent prayers that were awkwardly fitted into the narrative). Brownlee (1966:177–78) suggests that these additions especially reflect the crisis under Antiochus IV and represent an agenda for motivating some high-positioned Jew to intercede on behalf of the Jewish people, to show Antiochus IV how he is being misled by some wicked counselors, and thus to revoke his proscription of Torah observance. This would make the author unique in the surviving Jewish literature in giving Antiochus IV such a generous benefit of the doubt. Moreover, the main point of emulation—a person rising to high position through God's providence so as to intercede for God's people—is not an invention of the Additions but a feature of the original Esther. Rather than serving such a specific purpose, then, it is more likely that a Jew composed these prayers so as to underscore the importance and efficacy of prayer and the reality of divine help in the timely reversals of Israel's misfortunes.[11]

In sum, if the various editors' purposes in developing and including these additions can be read from their effects, one could point to a threefold agenda. First, the Book of Esther is made explicitly to reflect and articulate important aspects of the theology of second- and early-first-century-B.C.E. Judaism and to present Esther and Mordecai as role models for Jews living under foreign domination. Second, the historiographic quality of the book, and hence its impression of recording actual events, is enhanced by the addition of the texts of the edicts. Third, the Additions serve a group-maintenance function both by increasing the sense of separation of Jew and Gentile in the divine plan, as well as the mutual antagonism and hostility between Jew and Gentile,[12] and also by assisting Jews to persevere in the face of growing anti-Judaism through attributing anti-Judaism to the baser sort of Gentiles, whereas the noble Gentiles must acknowledge the Jews' contribution to the stability and well-being of the government.

Theological Contributions

Why the Hebrew version of Esther fails to mention God directly and explicitly even once remains a mystery. Even though the author clearly believes in God's

11. That is, if Torrey was incorrect to argue that Additions C and D were actually a part of the original Hebrew Esther. These Additions are free of contradiction with the main text.

12. Bickerman (1944: 362) regards the colophon as evidence of the fostering and intentional dissemination of the mutual dislike of Jew and Gentile, spread from Palestine "by such missionaries of exclusiveness as Dositheus and his companions."

providential guiding of events and in particular God's commitment to ensure the survival of Israel (4:14), God does not enter the story as a personal character in any sense. God's sovereignty is unseen, active only from behind a thick curtain. Metzger (1957: 62) suggests that the author wrote at a time when it was dangerous to mention the God of Israel, but this is mere speculation—all the more so as Jewish authors often show themselves most vigorous in their declarations about God when it is dangerous so to do. Another explanation posits that Hebrew Esther, being associated with and publicly read at a festival marked by drinking to the point of being unable to distinguish between "Cursed be Haman" and "Blessed be Mordecai," omits mention of God so as to reduce the chance of blasphemy (Moore 1977: 157; Torrey 1945: 58–59; see *b. Megillah* 7b).[13] It is, however, this silence about God and distinctive marks of Jewish piety and lifestyle that eroded respect for Esther in the debates about its canonicity (or better, sanctity—whether or not it contaminated the hands with holiness).

Greek Esther breaks the silence about God and Jewish affiliation with this God through prayer and Torah observance, remaking the story after the fashion of the court tales of Daniel, or Judith, or 2 Maccabees, in which God appears explicitly as a major player and the principal characters live as models of covenant faithfulness. The Additions to Esther present God as the creator of all things (13:10) but are more interested in God's providential ordering of history and government, with a special emphasis on God's closeness to, and special choice of, Israel. In Addition C, Mordecai affirms that God rules with no one to oppose God's will (13:9, 11). This affirmation of the absolute control of the One God is also attributed to King Artaxerxes in Addition E: God "has directed the kingdom both for us and for our ancestors in excellent order" (16:16)—a conviction reminiscent of the theology of Daniel, which stresses God's ordering of kingdoms and allotment of their times. Providence and control are also presupposed in Addition A, where God can and does reveal to God's people what God has determined to do (11:12).

God's providence is stacked in favor of the Jews. The lots that gave Purim its name are reinterpreted in Addition F in this direction: "For this purpose God made two lots, one for the people of God and one for all the nations, and these two lots came to the hour and moment and day of decision before God and among all the nations. And God remembered his people and vindicated his inheritance" (10:10–12). Purim is reinterpreted as a celebration of the separate and different lots or destinies that God had ordered long ago for the Jews, on the one hand, and everyone else, on the other hand. These two groups are pitted against one another in this scheme, and God has ordered history so as to deliver and benefit God's special people.

13. Torrey, who thought that the original version of Hebrew Esther already contained Additions A, C, D, and F as well as made mention of God, as in the Greek, thought that these were expurgated from the edition that came to be regarded as canonical by the Jews (1945: 58–59).

Deuteronomistic theodicy plays a role in this view of God's providential ordering of history, specifically in 14:6–7, where Esther's prayer is reminiscent of Daniel 9 and Baruch 1–2 both in the acknowledgment of idolatry as the primary cause of national misfortune and in the acknowledgment that the devastating events of Israel's history have shown God to be just, rather than unjust or weak.

Nevertheless, Israel is "the righteous nation" (11:7, 9) even in exile. They remain God's particular inheritance, portion, and purchase (13:15–17) among all the nations, the rest of whom do not seem to figure in God's salvific plan. The Jews are the "children of the living God" (16:16) and God's "chosen people" (16:21), set apart from the ordinary nations. The contest between Gentiles and Jews is interpreted as a contest between God and the idols, the false and empty rivals for worship (14:9–11). Israel's destruction would amount to God's abdication of the throne of the universe, so closely tied to Israel is God's own presence and testimony in the world. The destruction of the Jewish people would amount to the erasure of God's honor and the witness to God's power in the world (13:17; 14:9) and the victory of the false gods in the ongoing contest of this aeon concerning who is God. This fact necessitates the deliverance, even the triumph, of the Jewish people. Addition A affirms the pattern of reversal familiar from 1 Sam. 2:4–5, 7–8: the lowly (Jews) are exalted while those "held in honor" (the inimical Gentiles) are devoured. More noteworthy, however, is the active participation of the "lowly" in devouring their enemies, a detail reminiscent of the pattern of Judith as well as the proto-Zealot philosophy of the Maccabees.

With regard to personal piety, the Additions are equally rich. The prayers of Mordecai and Esther, with the consequences recorded in the story (beginning with Addition D, where God changes the king's heart toward Esther), become an affirmation of the efficacy of the prayer of the obedient Jew. Addition C also affords a view into the trappings of heartfelt prayer—the change of garments, specifically the use of rougher garb deemed suitable for supplication together with other signs of self-abasement (ashes and dung in the hair), both of which practices are also reflected in Dan. 9:3. Greek Esther lays special stress on Esther's commitment to a Torah-observant, Jewish way of life even while at court (LXX 2:20; 14:15, 17–18). Despite being married to a Gentile king, she becomes another testimony to the value of endogamy ("I . . . abhor the bed of the uncircumcised and of any alien" [14:15]).

Finally, Mordecai's prayer promotes the responsibility of the Jew to honor God alone with forms of reverence expressive of subjection and obeisance. Mordecai explains his dangerous behavior vis-à-vis Haman as springing not from pride or arrogance but from Mordecai's desire to distinguish carefully between forms of honor appropriate for other human beings and forms of honor appropriate only for the sovereign Lord (13:12–14). Esther's abstinence from drinking "the wine of libations" (14:17) also bears witness to the Jew's complete self-separation from any act that might seem to compromise her or his devotion to one, and only one, God.

The Additions as a Window into Jewish–Gentile Relations

Anti-Gentile and anti-Jewish sentiments are already present in Hebrew Esther. For example, both versions end with a fantasy of reversal in which Jews are authorized by the Gentile king to kill the Gentiles who wish to do them harm before the latter have a chance (the darker side of ethnic separatism that comes to bloody expression in the Diaspora Jewish revolts in 115–117 C.E.). Four of the six major additions underscore this antagonism, making Greek Esther an extended expression of the theme of ethnic hostility legitimated by religious claims.

To begin with the Gentile side of this antagonism, Addition B expands on the complaint against the Jews leveled by Haman in Esth. 3:8: "Their laws are different from those of every other people, and they do not keep the king's laws, so that it is not appropriate for the king to tolerate them." This brief sentence raises the issues of the distinctive laws (and thus the distinctive way of life) of the Jewish people, wherever they appear, and the suggestion that this people so dedicated to their way of life cannot also keep the king's laws. The edict plays expansive variations on this theme:

> . . . among all the nations in the world there is scattered a certain hostile people, who have laws contrary to those of every nation and continually disregard the ordinances of kings, so that the unifying of the kingdom that we honorably intend cannot be brought about. We understand that this people, and it alone, stands constantly in opposition to every nation, perversely following a strange manner of life and laws, and is ill-disposed to our government, doing all the harm they can so that our kingdom may not attain stability. (13:4–5)

The image of Jews inscribed in this text is that of a people who rigidly keep to their own ethnic way of life, one that defies logic and explanation in the eyes of Gentile detractors, and who refuse to cooperate with their non-Jewish neighbors, with the result that the places in which they live can never become strong, unified communities.

The Jewish author of Addition B very succinctly captures a broadly attested Gentile critique of Jews.[14] Here we see both the genius and the liability of the Torah as the force that sustained the Jewish people through centuries of foreign domination; on the one hand, the boundaries that observance of Torah created around the Jewish group (through purity and dietary regula-

---

14. See, for example, the comments made by Tacitus (*Historiae* 5.5), Juvenal (*Satirae* 14.100–104), Diodorus of Sicily (*Historical Library* 34.1–4; 40.3.4), Apollonius Molon of Rhodes (preserved in Josephus, *Against Apion* 2.258), and Apion (preserved in Josephus, *Against Apion* 2.121). These authors all speak of Jews' perceived avoidance of non-Jews, their refusal to mix in with the general population and support all their neighbors as part of one larger whole. This was exacerbated by the fact that Gentiles put a negative spin on the most distinctive markers of Jewish identity, calling their devotion to only One God "atheism" (i.e., negating the reality of the many gods), circumcision a barbaric mutilation of the body, Sabbath observance a sign of laziness, and avoidance of pork an irrational superstition.

tions and through insistence on the absolute avoidance of idolatry) were an effective means of preserving the distinctive identity and culture of the Jewish people. On the other hand, these very mechanisms that preserved the distinctiveness of the Jewish ethnic group also led to serious misunderstandings about the Jewish people.

Prominent in Addition B is the "scapegoat mechanism" (Moore 1977: 194) that majority cultures frequently employ when their members have a sense that all is not right in the world. "Everything would be going smoothly for us if it weren't for those people" becomes the battle cry, and the elimination of a particular segment of society is identified as the path to achieve the society's greater goals. The recent past has shown the devastating horrors of that kind of thinking, but we can be sure that Adolf Hitler was not the first to subscribe to it. The history of the Hellenistic and Roman periods is marred with frequent anti-Jewish riots, such that the "logic" of Addition B can be taken to reflect the thinking of at least a segment of Gentile society that would bide its time and take advantage of a lapse in vigilance on the part of those in authority to wreak havoc on the local Jewish population.

On the other side of the minefield stand Additions A, C, and F. In Addition C, Esther is made to give voice to her displeasure at having to associate so closely with a Gentile (her husband, Artaxerxes):

> You know that I hate the splendor of the wicked and abhor the bed of the uncircumcised and of any alien. . . . And your servant has not eaten at Haman's table, and I have not honored the king's feast or drunk the wine of the libations. (14:15, 17)

The author of this addition wants the readers to be sure that Esther, being a good Jew, would have far preferred to have been far removed from the haunts of the Gentiles. Marriage with a Gentile, irrespective of any positive virtues or graces he might have, was in principle odious to her. The affirmation of her abstinence from the table of any Gentile is another testimony to how the Torah's dietary regulations (and proscription of all hints of idolatry, hence the abstinence from drinking wine at a table where the host had offered a splash from his cup in honor of a deity) maintained the awareness of separateness.

Additions A and F transform a court intrigue between Haman and Mordecai into absolute enmity and contention between the Jews ("the righteous nation"), on the one hand, and "all the nations," on the other hand (Moore 1973: 390). The editor has historicized the apocalyptic dream vision, reading it in light of the "events" of Artaxerxes' reign instead of the present or imminent future, but has retained the stark dualism of apocalyptic thinking in which Jew and non-Jew are pitted against one another in mutual antagonism and hostility. Perhaps the most virulent expression of this anti-Gentilism is the active participation of the Jews in the destruction of their enemies, something highlighted in Addition A (11:11).

The Additions do not speak only of irreconcilable differences, however. Addition E, the edict of reversal, presents a different model for Jewish-Gentile relations in which the Gentile authorities acknowledge the positive contributions that Jews make to the stability and prosperity of their governments (see 16:15–16). This Addition gives voice to the hope of the Diaspora Jew that the blamelessness of their conduct, and indeed their willingness to defend the beneficent king's interests against all adversaries, would be recognized and valued, rather than that their differentness in matters of food and Sabbath and the like should become a source of suspicion and slander. The simple hope of the author, like that of many Jews, was that their neighbors would "permit the Jews to live under their own laws" (16:19; cf. LXX 8:11) without let or hindrance.

Influence

The influence of Greek Esther is rather limited, a fact that is compounded by the lack of consensus among early Jews and Christians concerning the canonical value of Esther in any form. No copies of Hebrew Esther were found at Qumran nor is Purim featured in the community's liturgical calendars (Moore 1977: 156), strongly suggesting that it lay outside their canon. The story of Esther was sufficiently popular, thanks to its connection with Purim, that the doubts of a few rabbis could not halt its procession to canonicity (Enslin and Zeitlin 1972: 23). As Purim continued to be celebrated, the story continued to be told and embellished, as the medieval legends and expansions in the Targumim and other midrashim attest.[15] Josephus incorporated a paraphrase of a version of Greek Esther in his *Jewish Antiquities* (11.184–296), taking Esther to represent a true chronicle of the Jews' fortunes under Persian rule. His paraphrase shows knowledge of Additions B through E.

Esther's canonical status in the church was no more secure during the first four centuries, during which the status of the whole was debated along with the status of the additions. Origen, for example, clearly noted the absence of Additions B, C, and E from the Hebrew version (*Epistula ad Africanum* 3) but did not regard the mere fact that Hebrew Esther lacked these texts as a sign that the Christian church's text was defective. He writes with biting sarcasm concerning the suggestion that the Christians "reject as spurious the copies in use in our Churches" and replace their text with the Hebrew text:

Are we to suppose that the Providence that in the sacred Scriptures has ministered to the edification of all the Churches of Christ, had no thought for those bought with a price, for whom Christ died; whom, although His Son, God who

15. These are listed in Oesterley 1935: 188–90. See also the excerpts in Moore 1977: 195, 205–6, 215; Paton 1908: 101–4.

is love spared not, but gave Him up for us all, that with Him He might freely give us all things? (*Epistula ad Africanum* 4)

Even where its canonicity was affirmed, however, the story did not make a huge impact. Addition C made an impression on the early church fathers, turning Esther into a model of effective prayer. Clement of Rome knows of the prayer of Esther (*1 Clement* 55.6) and holds her up as evidence that God is able to empower even the weak to perform great feats for God's people. Clement of Alexandria also speaks of Esther's "perfect prayer to God" (*Stromata* 4.19), holding her up as a model of the perfection of faith and service that women can attain as well as men.

Wisdom of Solomon 6

"The Righteous Live Forever"

Wisdom of Solomon, a product of Alexandrian Judaism from the turn of the era, promotes the wholehearted pursuit of that wisdom which begins with the reverence for God and for God's law, to which all are accountable. The unknown author focuses the hearers on the judgment of God in order to demonstrate that forsaking the path of God-fearing and lawful conduct that leads to immortality means utter folly and loss. Before this same court, however, the honor and right choices of the righteous will be made clear to all the world. Despite universalistic principles, the author understands God to have a special relationship with the Jewish people (or better, the righteous among the Jews) and encourages Jews to persist in their distinctive way of life by recalling God's care for and presence with them throughout history, especially in the exodus, and by showing the ignorance of the Gentiles who have been duped into idolatry. Wisdom is perhaps the most important of the Apocrypha in terms of impact upon the early church during the most formative centuries of Christian theology.

Structure and Contents

In the address (1:1–15), the author invites the "rulers of the earth" to pursue justice in a spirit of reverence for God (1:1). The heart of the first section (1:16–5:23) contrasts vividly the fate of "the ungodly," who "made a covenant with death" by their unsound reasoning (1:16–2:1), with that of "the righteous," who remain faithful to their training in the law and live for God's approval. The ungodly live for the enjoyment of this life only, with no thought of the life to come, whereas the righteous approach this life as the arena in which to gain immortality. Even though the ungodly may oppress the righteous in this life and strip them of all honor, God will vindicate and exalt the righteous at the judgment, while punishing the ungodly and putting them to shame.

In a second section, the author presents the origin, character, deeds, and rewards of Wisdom. The author takes on the persona of Solomon (without actually mentioning the name), providing a first-person autobiographical expansion of Solomon's prayer for wisdom and God's response in 1 Kings 3:5–15, filling in many details concerning the joy and benefits that came to Solomon from receiving Wisdom. The conclusion of Solomon's prayer (Wis. 9:18) becomes the theme demonstrated by the narrative of Wisdom's saving acts in chapter 10, which takes the audience to the narratives of Adam, Cain, Noah, Babel, Abraham, Isaac, Lot, Jacob, Joseph, and finally Moses and the exodus generation.

This third section develops a series of antitheses, contrasting God's punishment of the Egyptians with God's provision for the Israelites (11:1–14; 11:15–16 + 16:1–4;[1] 16:5–14; 16:15–29; 17:1–18:4; 18:5–25; 19:1–21). These contrasts between the fates of the ungodly and the righteous demonstrate the theses found in 11:5 ("through the very things by which their enemies were punished, [the Israelites] themselves received benefit in their need," though this will often be tempered to showing how God acts in similar ways to bring benefit to God's people but punishment to the ungodly) and 11:16 ("one is punished by the very things by which one sins," though this also will be tempered into a more general sense of the punishment fitting the crime).

First, the Nile is turned to blood as a punishment for the Egyptians' massacre of the Israelite infants (11:6–7). Where the Egyptians are made to thirst despite the abundance of the Nile, the Israelites' thirst is quenched by water from a rock in the desert. The author introduces a subtheme here at 11:9: the people of God are tried in small amounts, "being disciplined in mercy," while the ungodly are "judged in wrath." At the beginning of the second antithesis, Egyptians worship animals, with the result that God uses animals to plague them (11:15–16). The fact that God uses creatures such as frogs and insects to plague the ungodly rather than summoning the fiercer beasts or even creating new monstrous animals for the task invites the author to ponder God's mercy in the midst of judgment, the topic of the first excursus in 11:21–12:22, in which the author struggles with the place of the Gentiles in God's creation and God's acts of redemption.

The author returns briefly to the topic of the Egyptians being plagued by animals on account of their worship of animals, ending in a contrast between those "thought to be gods" and the perception of the "true God" (12:27). This leads into a second excursus, expatiating on the folly of Gentile religion (13:1–15:17). Discussing first the least culpable form of idolatry, namely, worship of the astral bodies (13:1–9) and then the baser worship of carved im-

---

1. Wright (1965: 30–31) correctly observes that the second antithesis begins at 11:15–16 before the two digressions (and not at 16:1, as most others posit: Reese 1965: 398; Barclay 1996: 189 n. 14; Gilbert 1984: 305; Harrington 1999: 68, 71), with 12:23–27 resuming the thought that is not finally completed until 15:18–16:4.

ages of human forms (13:10–15:17), the author effects a transition back to the main stream of the discussion with mention of the most debased practice of animal worship (15:18–19). In a contrast that develops the theme of 11:5, God gave quails to God's people, who had suffered want so long, but the vermin that plagued the Egyptians caused them to lose their appetites (16:1–4). Moreover, in a contrast that develops the subtheme of 11:9, the Israelites were punished for a brief time by snakes in the desert on account of their sin but were saved as they looked to the "symbol of deliverance," the bronze serpent, while the Egyptians were hounded to death by the stings of the insects God sent upon them (16:5–14).

As another example of the principle in 11:5, the author considers how God rained down fiery hail upon the Egyptians, destroying their crops, but rained down manna from heaven to feed God's people (16:15–29). Because the Egyptians had kept the Israelites imprisoned in slavery, God imprisoned them in a prison of darkness while giving the Israelites a pillar of fire to light their way through the night in the exodus (17:1–18:4). Here, the Egyptians were not punished "by the very things by which one sins" (11:16) but in a manner that presents the punishment as fitting the crime.

The final antithesis demonstrates the topic of 11:5 in a precise manner (see 18:8). The slaughter of the Egyptian firstborn is at once seen as the suitable punishment for their resolve to kill the Hebrew firstborn (18:5) but also as the precise means by which God ended the Hebrews' bondage and brought the Egyptians to recognize God's connection with the Hebrews (18:13). The subtheme of 11:9 emerges in 18:20–25 as the author recalls the plague that broke out among the Israelites in Num. 16:41–50, but this brief outbreak is contrasted with the way in which "the ungodly were assailed to the end by pitiless anger" (19:1). The final contrast (19:1–9) also demonstrates the thesis of 11:5: the Red Sea incident was at once the deliverance of the Hebrews and the destruction of the Egyptian armies.[2] Wisdom 19:10–22 presents a rhapsodic résumé of the whole story (see especially 19:10–12), a final affirmation of the guilt incurred by the Egyptians for their practice of *misoxenia* ("hatred of strangers") and violation of the code of hospitality (19:13–17) and a prescientific explanation of the marvelous transmutations of nature by means of which God worked out God's purpose to help, glorify, and exalt God's people (19:22).

The author's literary skill in weaving together this organic whole is evident in the difficulties scholars have had in agreeing on the outline of its parts. Virtually all agree that Wisdom subdivides into three major sections: the "book of eschatology," the "panegyric on Wisdom," and the "historical retrospect" (Reider 1957: 2). There is little agreement, however, concerning where one section ends and the next begins, where one finds the "seams," as it were. The

2. Wright (1965: 30) notes the confusion among scholars concerning where the seventh antithesis ends and the conclusion begins. Here, I follow Pfeiffer 1949: 318.

first section has been seen to end variously at 5:23, 6:8, 6:11, 6:21, and 6:25 and the second section at 9:18, 10:21, and 11:1.[3] With regard to the first part of the book, the most persuasive analysis is offered by Gilbert (1984: 302 [somewhat modified here]), who suggests a concentric pattern that would require chapter 6 to belong to this first part:

1:1–15: Address to rulers, enjoining pursuit of wisdom
1:16–2:24: Speech of the ungodly (with introduction and conclusion)
3:1–4:19: Contrasts between the just and the impious
4:20–5:23: Speech of the ungodly (with introduction and conclusion)
6:1–25: Address to rulers, enjoining pursuit of wisdom

Even this outline, however, fails to take into account the complexities of the author's crafting, whereby the first two parts exhibit an interlocking structure. Wisdom 6:1–11 returns to the themes of 1:1–11 (an inclusio) with the address to the "rulers of the world" (1:1) and the assurance of God's inquiry into human ways.[4] Wisdom 6:12–25, however, introduces the themes of section two, namely, the nature, works, and rewards of Wisdom (foreshadowed in 6:12–20) and the narrative of Solomon's acquisition of Wisdom, which will be presented as a model for imitation (introduced by the shift to autobiographical narration in 6:22–25). Nevertheless, even within 6:1–11, 6:9–11 looks ahead to the first-person address of "Solomon" in the second part as well as his self-presentation as a model for how the kings of the world should proceed. Likewise, within 6:12–25, 6:21 deliberately echoes 1:1 and 6:1 and so hearkens back to the first section.

Marking a clear break between the second and third sections also is a rather arbitrary matter. Wisdom 10:1 begins to elaborate on 9:18, where Wisdom is credited with saving the people who received her, and thus continues the discussion of Wisdom's works that had occupied a major portion of the second part. Between 11:1 and 11:4, the author has moved from speaking about Wisdom's acts in the third person to adopting the form of a confession of God's works in the second person, done without ever breaking the narrative thread—a shift, however, prepared by 10:20. The author thus obscures the seam in this smooth transition from the praise of Wisdom's character and works, Wisdom's saving activity, and God's saving activity.[5]

3. See Pfeiffer 1949: 321–22 for a review of fourteen different positions; also Winston 1979: 4–9.
4. The "inclusio" is a literary-rhetorical device by means of which a speaker or author marks off a section of a speech by using similar words, phrases, or cadences at the beginning and ending of that section.
5. Reese (1965) and Wright (1967) focus on inclusions and concentric patterns as clues to structure and outline. This methodologically sound procedure (inclusio being a conscious structuring device in Greco-Roman composition and oratory) has left its mark on Winston's outline (1979: 9–12).

Textual Transmission

Wisdom of Solomon is found in Greek in Codices Sinaiticus, Alexandrinus, and Vaticanus, as well as the majority of later Septuagint manuscripts.[6] Of the ancient translations (or versions), the Old Latin, which closely follows the Greek, is the most valuable for textual criticism. It offers some variants that are preferred in critical editions, as well as a variety of glosses that witness to early interpretation of and reflection on the book (Holmes 1913: 520). The Syriac Peshitta follows the Septuagint but shows a curious relationship with the Old Latin as well, suggesting that one has been influenced by the other at some stage, while the Syro-Hexaplar is a wooden rendering from the Septuagint (Reider 1957: 7). Wisdom is also found in two Sahidic manuscripts from the sixth and seventh centuries, as well as Ethiopic, Arabic, and Armenian translations, all less useful for textual criticism than as a witness to the widespread popularity of this book throughout the Christian churches (Winston 1979: 64–66).

Arguments for a Hebrew original of Wisdom have given way to a general consensus that the book was written in Greek.[7] The large number of Hebraisms does not argue against this, since these are all of a sort common to Hellenistic Jewish authors.[8] The use of the Septuagint, especially the quotations of Isa. 44:20 at Wis. 15:10 and Isa. 3:10 at Wis. 2:12, where one finds dependence on the Septuagint tradition over against the Hebrew precursors to the Masoretic Text tradition, almost necessitates a Greek original.[9] Finally, the author's familiarity with Greek rhetorical devices (such as *sorites, accumulatio,* alliteration, and assonance),[10] the affinity for compound words (common in Alexandrian Greek), knowledge of Greek words found only in the Greek poets, and use of technical Greek philosophical terminology are strong arguments for composition in Greek.[11]

Author, Date, and Setting

The anonymous author speaks in the voice of Solomon, Israel's sage par excellence. Although attempts have been made to defend Solomonic author-

6. The preferred critical edition is Ziegler 1980.

7. Torrey (1945: 101) was quite convinced by Speiser (1923–24) and Purinton (1928) concerning the existence of a Hebrew original for 1:1–10:21. See Reider 1957: 22–29 for a fine summary of the arguments for and against.

8. See Reider 1957: 24 n. 118 for a lengthy list of Hebraisms.

9. See the longer lists of Septuagint quotations in Holmes 1913: 524–25; Reider 1957: 14 nn. 61, 62.

10. Winston (1979: 15–16 and nn. 5–14) provides an impressive catalog of these ornaments.

11. Reese (1970: 3–31) offers a fine discussion of distinctive vocabulary and Hellenistic influence on the author's style.

ship (thus necessitating a Hebrew original), readers recognized as early as the second century the pseudepigraphic nature of the work. The Muratorian Fragment, a late-second-century canonical list of the New Testament books, lists Wisdom as having been "written by Solomon's friends in his honor." Augustine and Jerome also both affirmed the non-Solomonic authorship of Wisdom (Pfeiffer 1949: 320). The author was a pious Jew living in Alexandria, the famous center of learning and Hellenistic culture. The marked hostility against the native Egyptians in the third part of the work (see 19:13–17) and the fact that the author dwells on cult practices peculiar to Egypt, such as the worship of animals or gods depicted with animal features, support the general consensus on this point (Winston 1979: 25; Collins 1997b: 178), as does the strong reception of Wisdom among Alexandrian Christians. The author displays a fine grasp of rhetorical ornament and style, as well as a wide variety of literary forms, including speech-in-character, *sorites* or climax (6:17–20), prayers, lists, and comparison (*synkrisis*).

Theories of multiple authorship abounded in the eighteenth through early twentieth centuries.[12] Supporters of this view noted that Wisdom 1–11 and 12–19 express different conceptions of God's dealing with the world (mediated through Wisdom versus direct) and alleged the different use of certain terms, particles, and types of compound words. The similarities between the two parts, however, have always necessitated some kind of connection to be made between these authors—for example, the author of the second part studied or perhaps even translated the first part and made a contribution of material as a self-conscious continuation of the older text. More recently, however, scholars have returned to a view of single authorship (beginning with Grimm 1860: 9–15; see also Winston 1979: 12–14), particularly because of the consistent use of "unusual words and expressions throughout" (Reider 1957: 21 and n. 105), the echoes of the first part in the second half (Reese 1970: 122–45), and the tight structural interweaving of the main parts of the discourse.

There is wider debate concerning the date of Wisdom, which has been placed anywhere between 220 B.C.E. and 100 C.E. The *terminus a quo* is set by the author's use of the Greek translation of Isaiah, Job, and Proverbs, the first of which was probably available by 200 B.C.E. (Reider 1957: 14; Holmes 1913: 520). The *terminus ad quem* is set by the evident use of the work by several New Testament authors (Holmes 1913: 521; Reider 1957: 14).[13] A date within the early period of Roman domination of Egypt, especially the early Roman Principate (or Empire), seems most likely. First, the description of the development of the ruler cult in 14:16–20 best describes not the cult

---

12. See Holmes 1913: 521–24 for a fine review of the cases for single and for composite authorship.

13. Gilbert (1984: 312) and Grant (1967: 70), however, express reservations concerning demonstrable dependence.

of the Ptolemaic kings of Egypt, a cult that was organized and promoted from the center, but the spontaneous, decentralized development of the imperial cult under Augustus, who was also Egypt's first "remote" ruler since Alexander (Holmes 1913: 521; Oesterley 1935: 207; Winston 1979: 21–22; Collins 2000: 195). Second, the author uses some thirty-five terms or phrases unattested in secular Greek before the first century C.E. (Winston 1979: 22–23 and n. 33). Further, Gilbert (1984: 312; 1973: 172) has detected a critique of the *pax Romana* in 14:22, "though living in great strife due to ignorance, they call such great evils peace" (cf. Tacitus *Agricola* 30), and considers the author's address in 6:1–2 to the "judges of the ends of the earth" who "rule over multitudes, and boast of many nations" to fit the Roman imperial period better than its predecessors.

Scholars often insist that Wisdom of Solomon arose during a known period of persecution, whether under the Ptolemies or under Roman rule. Ruling out a Ptolemaic date on strong grounds, Winston (1979: 23–24) revives the theory that the work comes specifically from the reign of Gaius, responding to the "desperate historical situation" of the Jews under Flaccus.[14] While this allows for a very precise dating and assessment of the rhetorical situation being addressed, it considerably exceeds the evidence. A situation of open persecution is not required in order to understand the "ferocious passion" with which the author narrates "the annihilation of the wicked" in 5:16–23 as well as the particularly intense anti-Egyptian sentiments of the work.[15]

For centuries, the Jews under the cultural hegemony of Hellenism had been struggling to find ways to reaffirm their ancestral heritage in the face of a dominant majority that devalued that heritage. Such rhetoric as we find in Wisdom would have been a welcome reinforcement for Jewish commitment at any period, and the tone of hostility within the document may be intended more to promote a "we versus they" mentality in order to guard against assimilation. Winston's argument rests on the assumption that the apocalyptic dualism marking Wisdom 1–5 must *reflect* a situation of high tension; however, apocalyptic literature and topics may equally seek to be *productive* of high tension, high boundaries, and mutual antagonism and rejection between groups.[16] Thus, while the reign of Caligula brought the most open and dramatic pressures to bear on the Jewish community in Alexandria, at any point since the accession of Augustus they would have welcomed the word of Wisdom of Solomon as a means by which to enhance commitment to their ancestral traditions and their sense of self-esteem in an often unsupportive environment.[17]

14. See also Oesterley 1935: 208–9.

15. Collins (2000: 195) agrees that the book reflects "a philosophical and religious debate that does not require a context of actual persecution"; so also Pfeiffer 1949: 327.

16. See, for example, the discussion of the social setting of Revelation in deSilva 1992 and 1993 and the literature therein cited.

17. See further the chapter on 3 Maccabees in the present volume; Collins 1997b: 136–57.

Genre and Purpose

The discussion of the genre of Wisdom of Solomon has been dominated by two cogent proposals. Gilbert (1984: 307–8) understands Wisdom to reflect the form of the encomium, a speech in praise of some figure or virtue. This would make Wisdom an example of epideictic or demonstrative oratory, a work the goal of which was to win the assent of the hearers to a particular set of values or a proposition. According to Gilbert, Wisdom 1–5 briefly presents the theme, criticizes those who neglect Wisdom, and posits the harmful results of failing to pursue Wisdom as well as the lasting benefits of attending to that virtue with a whole heart. Wisdom 6–10, which has often been labeled a panegyric in its own right, then discourses on the origin, nature, and deeds of Wisdom. Wisdom 11–19 demonstrates the benefits of pursuing this virtue through historical examples and especially through *synkrisis,* or the comparison of the fate of Wisdom's devotees and the strangers to Wisdom. Within this section of the encomium, there is room for digressions, "to fortify the resolution of the reader."

Reese (1970: 117–21), followed by Winston (1979: 18–20), regards the work as a "protreptic" discourse—an exhortation to take up a particular course of action. Winston insightfully connects numerous claims made by the author concerning the pursuit of Wisdom with the criteria listed in *Rhetorica ad Alexandrum* 1421.b21 as requirements for the successful exhortation: a speaker should show the preferred course of action to be "just, lawful, expedient, honorable, pleasant, and easily practicable" (cf. Wis. 6:12–14; 8:7, 10, 16, 18). The presence of deliberative topics in Wisdom, then, also cannot be denied.

At this point some clarification of terminology is in order, a clarification that might go far to resolve the debate within scholarship concerning the genre of this book. The author of *Rhetorica ad Alexandrum* uses the term "protreptic" to refer to the whole range of deliberative rhetoric pitched toward exhortation as opposed to dissuasion ("apotreptic"). The protreptic discourse, for that author, urges the audience to decide in favor of a particular course of action in a particular situation. Reese, however, has in mind a specific type of "proptreptic" speech, the prototype for which is the lost *Protrepticus* of Aristotle, an exhortation to take up the life of virtue and philosophy.[18] This kind of *logos protreptikos* invites the hearers to decide in favor of a general course of action or in favor of certain key goals and values that are to guide them in their day-to-day pursuits and decisions. These, however, tend to be the goals of epideictic oratory. Another difficulty in determining the genre of Wisdom is the fact that different genres dominate the different sections. The hortatory aspect dominates part one (chapters 1–6), and the epideictic aspect dominates

18. Chroust (1964) offers a reconstruction of the *Protrepticus* from Cicero's paraphrase in the *Hortensius.*

parts two and three (Collins 2000: 196; 1997b: 182). Aristotle and other classical rhetorical theorists expect to find different rhetorical genres side by side in a single discourse, all serving the goals of the macrogenre. In Wisdom, the elevation of the value of the goal being promoted (chapters 7–9) and the narrative demonstration of the greater expediency and pleasantness of pursuing Wisdom and remaining a loyal client of God (chapters 10–19) rather than joining oneself to the Gentiles in their folly make the pursuit of Wisdom through piety and righteous living all the more attractive, confirming the hearers in that set of values or calling them powerfully back to their ancestral way of life if they are on the verge of abandoning it.

Questions of the purpose of the book are connected not only with the determination of the genre but also with whom one understands to constitute the audience. There is a marked tendency to delineate a threefold audience and thus a threefold purpose (see Oesterley 1935: 212–13; Clarke 1973: 5; Pfeiffer 1949: 334). According to Metzger (1957: 68), Wisdom of Solomon (1) attempts to rekindle in apostate Jews a "genuine zeal for God and his law" (so Clarke 1973: 4; Winston 1979: 63–64; Reider 1957: 10; Pfeiffer 1949: 325); (2) provides for faithful Jews facing disappointment or persecution an "apologia that was calculated to encourage and fortify their faith and practice"; and (3) possibly addresses "thoughtful pagans" in chapters 6–9 and 13–15 on the truth of Judaism and folly of idolatry (so Clarke 1973: 5; Pfeiffer 1949: 325; Reider 1957: 11).[19]

While one should not be dogmatic about the audience envisioned by the author, one can begin to assess the effectiveness of the work for the various proposals. Although the only explicit addressees in the work are Gentile rulers (1:1; 6:1, 9, 21) and God (10:20; 11:4; 15:1), it is unlikely that the work would have been received kindly by either a local ruler or the emperor, given the explicit announcements of the rulers' wickedness and impending judgment. The author's deconstruction of the imperial cult would also have made the work more suspect than persuasive. To the author's critique of idolatry, "thoughtful pagans" would have said about idols the same thing Wisdom says about the bronze serpent (16:7): they certainly did not worship stone and metal but by means of such could revere the invisible deity (see below under "Critique of Gentile Society"). Also relevant here is Metzger's (1957: 71) correct observation, which he did not, however, integrate into his theory concerning the audience, that the author was writing in a context-rich environment. The readers of Wisdom were expected to be able to supply much missing information, particularly to make the connections with the Solomonic narrative in 1 Kings 3 in Wisdom 7–9, to infer the names and episodes from the Pentateuchal narratives for the highly allusive Wisdom 10, and to hold in mind the order of the exodus and wilderness events sufficiently well to navigate the author's disjunctive treatment of these stories in part three. If

19. Reider claims this "missionary" purpose for "Alexandrine-Jewish literature generally."

writing to persuade Gentiles to become Jewish, the author wrote most inef-
fectively. It is more likely that, aside from God-fearers and proselytes, Gentiles were not part of the author's real audience.

Much more can be said for a Jewish audience, beginning with the Jews who
had discarded their heritage. The existence of lapsed Jews in Alexandrian
Egypt and the scandal they represented to the faithful Jew's mind are attested
in Philo, *De vita Mosis* 1.31: Those whom fortune exalts to wealth

> overlook their friends and relations, transgress the laws according to which they
> were born and brought up; and they overturn their national hereditary customs
> to which no just blame whatever is attached, dwelling in a foreign land, and by
> reason of their cordial reception of the customs among which they are living,
> no longer remember a single one of their ancient usages.

Such apostates distanced themselves from the Jewish way of life to attain acceptance into the dominant, majority culture and all of the benefits that acceptance could bring (such as enhanced networks of patrons and friends, full
citizenship, advancement in the chain of offices, attainment of prestigious offices, and the like). Leaving behind the "closed-minded" avoidance of Gentile
forms of piety would be among the first requirements for the Jew who would
wish to be a fully accepted player in the dominant culture. Wisdom might indeed open up the possibility of a return for apostates, if there remained some
doubt in their minds about their choice and if they cared to read the work.

Wisdom would be most effective, however, for an audience of faithful
Jews. Part one assures them, in the manner of Psalms 37, 49, and 73 (Holmes
1913: 519), that the apostate Jews are the ones who have departed from the
truth. Even if the apostates' temporal enjoyments have increased and even if
they have gained the upper hand over the loyal Jews, God's court will reveal
their folly and the honor of the righteous. Parts two and three encourage loyal
Jews to persist in their way of life by reminding the hearers of God's protection of and commitment to bring benefit to God's own people throughout
history. The polemic against idolatry assures the Jews that their way of life is
the truly enlightened one, while the Gentiles and apostates, despite their pre-
tensions, grope in darkness. The use of Greek philosophical terminology enhances the author's claim that "Judaism need not take second place to anything in Hellenism" (Clarke 1973: 5). Reese (1970: 146–51) in particular
thinks that Wisdom would address the circles of educated Jewish youth,
trained in their own religious heritage and culturally literate in terms of Greek
and Roman philosophy, religion, and rhetoric; the literary artistry and "arti-
ficiality" of the presentation would find a better reception among the learned.
Thus, Wisdom is chiefly written to encourage *continued* adherence to the
Jewish way of life in a setting where the enticements of Hellenization and the
ability of apostates to reject their heritage as of little value weigh heavily upon
Jewish consciousness. For a text that explicitly encourages one way of life over

alternatives, the protreptic discourses of the philosophers provide the closest generic equivalents.

While not written necessarily during a time of persecution, Wisdom does reflect a high degree of tension between Gentile and Jewish groups. Barclay's (1996: 183, 191) perception that Wisdom would promote cultural antagonism rather than rapprochement seems to be very apt. The author, although highly acculturated—that is, imbued with the Greek language, philosophy, and rhetorical art—seeks not to assimilate into the dominant culture but rather uses that learning to reinforce strong group boundaries and commitment to the Jewish way of life. Collins (2000: 201) is correct to observe that several Greco-Roman philosophers would agree with the author of Wisdom on several points of his critique of Gentile culture (specifically, idolatry and animal worship); but if the author of Wisdom seeks "rapprochement," as Collins suggests, it would be on the very hard terms of Gentiles in effect converting to the worship of the One God to the exclusion of all other cults.

Formative Influences

The author drew extensively upon the Jewish Scriptures to fashion the text, such that only the major sources of influence can be considered here.[20] In many cases, the author recontextualizes whole phrases from the Scriptures into the text, suggesting a conscious attempt to create a conversation between the older text and the new work. Many of these recontextualizations, and even more especially the reconfigurations of Old Testament texts and patterns, may reveal something of the deep structures of the author's mind—the dynamics of the world-construct into which the author had been inducted since birth and throughout life—rather than conscious attempts at borrowing and patterning.[21] As we consider formative influences, then, we are not assuming the model of a scholar surrounded by notes of material she wishes to use in her new book but the model of a sage or pastor whose words are shaped by and imprinted with the stamp of the texts and hopes and expectations that have formed his own consciousness.

The first part of Wisdom reflects an apocalyptic reconfiguration of the court tale, familiar from Daniel 1–6 or Esther, in which a wise man in the king's court is falsely accused or caught in a trap and sentenced to death and then is rescued, vindicated, and exalted while his adversaries succumb to the

20. See Larcher 1969: 85–178 for an extensive survey of potential sources for Wisdom and of points of contact and disagreement between Wisdom and pseudo-Solomon's near contemporaries.

21. "Recontextualization" refers to the taking of words or phrases from an older text and weaving them into a newer text without drawing explicit attention to the fact that some work outside the text is being quoted (which would be called a recitation or quotation).

king's vengeance (Nickelsburg 1972: 170). The language of the new tale, particularly the chapters that depict the postmortem vindication scene, reflects the diction and conceptual inventory of Daniel and, to a surprising extent, *1 Enoch*.[22] The acknowledgment that it is God who apportions to kings and rulers their seasons of rule (Wis. 6:3) is consonant with, and quite possibly learned from, Daniel as well (see Dan. 2:21; 4:16–17, 26, 32; 5:18–23) (Schaberg 1982: 77–78).

This apocalyptic court tale, moreover, reconfigures the fourth Servant Song of Isaiah (Isa. 52:13–53:12) (Suggs 1957: 28–30; Nickelsburg 1972: 61–65). In both, the righteous protagonist is depicted as a child of God (Wis. 2:13, 16, 18; Isa. 53:2) who bears himself gently in the face of marginalization and death (Wis. 2:19–20; Isa. 53:7–9). That death is viewed as a loss and as injury in both, an interpretation that the unrighteous "we" in Wisdom and the spectator "we" in Isaiah must reverse (Wis. 3:2–3; 5:1–2; Isa. 53:4, 11–12; 52:13–15). The onlookers must confess at the end that it was "we" who went astray from the truth or went astray like sheep (Wis. 5:4–6; Isa. 53:6). Additionally, Wis. 3:13 speaks of the blessedness of the barren woman who is undefiled, a theme that immediately follows the Servant Song in Isa. 54:1, and Wis. 3:14 speaks of the favored status of the righteous eunuch in terms reminiscent of Isa. 56:4–5, topics that are then expounded in 3:14–4:15. One critical topic in Isaiah is notably lacking in Wisdom: the death of the righteous child of God effecting atonement for and bringing benefit to the sinners.

The Psalms, so important and prominent in the worship life of the pious Jew, have also made a deep and pervasive impact on the diction and thought of the author. Psalm 2, for example, has contributed to Wisdom 1–5 the addresses to the rulers of the earth (Wis. 1:1; Ps. 2:2), the expectation that God would laugh at and dash to the ground those who set themselves against God and God's standards (Wis. 4:18–19; Ps. 2:4, 9), and the admonition to the rulers to understand and be instructed (Wis. 6:1; Ps. 2:10) (Skehan 1971: 149, 152; Schaberg 1982: 76).[23]

Jewish wisdom literature also exercises an important influence, as would be expected. The correspondences between the speech of the ungodly in Wis. 2:1–20 and numerous expressions in Ecclesiastes have led some to conclude that the author combats a form of thinking derived from (but not necessarily the same as) the view of life articulated in Ecclesiastes (Holmes 1913: 525–26; Reider 1957: 9–10; Oesterley 1935: 214–17). Readers of Ecclesiastes disheartened by its musings on the shortness of life, the same end that comes to

22. Compare, for example, the vindication of the righteous in Dan. 12:1–3 and Wis. 3:7–9; see Holmes 1913: 526, 529–30 on *1 Enoch*.

23. See Skehan 1971: 149–62 for an extensive examination of psalmic influence on Wisdom's language and thought.

the wicked and righteous, and the enjoyment of this world's goods as one's only reward, might sympathize with this position.[24]

The second section draws even more heavily on the wisdom traditions of Israel, starting with Solomon's prayer for wisdom in 1 Kings 3:5–9, greatly expanded into the prayer of Wisdom 9. Wisdom 7:7–11 also refers to the content of Solomon's prayer in 1 Kings, in which he preferred wisdom to wealth, power, and long life and yet received these as blessings along with wisdom from God's hands. Proverbs has left its imprint on the poetic form of the first and second parts of Wisdom in the form of the synonymous and antithetical parallelism, the traditional form of Jewish wisdom texts. The portrait of Wisdom as God's artisan and coworker in creation, as well as the promised benefits that Wisdom brings to her devotees, draw their inspiration from the portrait of Lady Wisdom in Proverbs 8 (and other parts of Proverbs 1–9).[25]

Genesis, Exodus, and Numbers are major resources throughout the Wisdom of Solomon. In part one, the author offers a theological interpretation of key aspects of the creation story. Reflecting on Genesis 2–3, the author concludes, "God created us for incorruption, and made us in the image of his own eternity ['nature,' in some manuscripts], but through the devil's envy death entered the world" (2:23–24). Based on his reading of the creation account, the author finds that death was not part of God's original intent for humankind but rather is a consequence that came about through the conjunction of Satan's mischief and the decision of humankind to "make a covenant with death" (1:16; cf. Isa. 28:15) through disobedience.[26] Contrasting the premature death of the righteous with the long life of the wicked, the author refers allusively to the story of Enoch (4:10–13), whose case demonstrates that God removes early from this world those who most please God.

The whole of part three offers a midrash on the majority of the stories of the patriarchal period (chapter 10, which covers Genesis and ends with the presentation of Moses and the exodus generation) and focuses especially on the plagues sent upon the Egyptians and the corresponding mercies shown to Israel in the exodus experience as well as in the wilderness wanderings (Siebeneck 1960; Cheon 1997; Enns 1997). The author, reflecting on the plagues of Egypt, which become a type of God's present and future judgments of the world as well, has learned that creation itself acts as God's agent in punishing

---

24. Skehan (1971: 191–94, 213–36), however, vehemently opposes the view that in Wis. 2:1–20 the author of Wisdom identifies the logic and ethos of Ecclesiastes as his target, noting instead the verbal correspondences between the speech of the wicked in Wis. 2:1–9 and the diction (though not the position) of Job.

25. There are also examples of specific recontextualizations, as the use of Prov. 1:7 in Wis. 3:11 or Prov. 8:17 in Wis. 6:12 (Skehan 1971: 181, which he perhaps too quickly dismisses as coincidental). The same is the case with Job, seen from the comparison of Wis. 12:12 with LXX Job 9:12, 19 (Skehan 1971: 200), for example.

26. Collins (1997b: 187–88) rightly observes the contrast here with Palestinian Jewish thought as seen in Sir. 17:1; 41:4.

the wicked and helping the righteous (5:20–23; 12:27; 15:17). This is an important topic in apocalyptic literature, both Jewish (as in *Testament of Levi* 2–5, where the lower heavens contain hail, fire, and other elements of judgment) and Jewish Christian (as in Revelation, where virtually all of God's judgments involve natural elements divinely directed).

When reading and interpreting the Scriptures, the author rarely engages in allegorical or moralizing interpretations, such as one finds in the Stoic treatment of the Homeric myths or Philo's handling of Torah. The most notable example in the book concerns the miracle of manna in the wilderness and the dissolution of the leftover portion, which teaches, addressing God, that "one must rise before the sun to give you thanks, and must pray to you at the dawning of the light; for the hope of an ungrateful person will melt like wintry frost" (16:28–29).

One vital component of Wisdom of Solomon's attempts to promote loyalty to the Jewish worship of the One God is the way the author articulates and supports the appeal with concepts learned from Greek philosophy (see Reese 1970: 32–89; Larcher 1969: 179–327). When borrowing from Greek philosophy, the author has not acted in a random, haphazard manner but rather reflects the tendencies of Middle Platonism to create a viable synthesis drawn from Stoic and Platonic thought (Collins 1997b: 200–201; Winston 1979: 33).[27] Part of the author's appeal to the readers, no doubt, was this incipient synthesis of the best of the Greek tradition with the Jewish tradition. The pursuit of God-given Wisdom trains the devotee in the four cardinal virtues prized by Stoics and Platonists (Wis. 8:7; cf. 4 Macc. 1:16–18; 5:22–24). Solomon's choice of Wisdom (Wis. 8:2–18) mirrors Xenophon's account of the similarly noble choice of Heracles (*Memorabilia* 2.1) (Holmes 1913: 532). The author thus claims that the Jewish way of life produces the same noble virtues prized by Hellenic culture.

The author incorporates the Platonic view that God created the cosmos out of "formless matter" (Wis. 11:17).[28] The author of Wisdom has often been thought to depart from "orthodox" Jewish teaching about creation ex nihilo, as seems to be the position in 2 Macc. 7:28. Winston (1971–72: 186–87) has shown, however, that both 2 Maccabees and *Letter of Aristeas*, which are often assumed to articulate a doctrine of creation ex nihilo, are really only expressing a commonplace that distinguished God, who creates things out of unformed matter, from human beings, who can only create new things from previously formed things (e.g., a table out of wood).[29] Within this creation, Wisdom herself takes on the roles of the Stoic *Logos*, as mediator between

27. This is the same background as Renehan 1972 has shown to be the case for 4 Maccabees.

28. Plato (*Timaeus* 31–37) describes the creation of the heaven and earth out of the four primeval elements, into which God then infused a soul to animate the whole. Philo follows Plato on this point (see Winston 1979: 60).

29. See further the ongoing debate in Goldstein 1984; Winston 1986; Goldstein 1987.

God and creation in all things, and the Stoic *Pneuma*, the all-pervading force that animates all things (cf. Wis. 1:7; 7:24; 8:1) (Gilbert 1984: 311; Collins 1997b: 197–98; Diogenes Laertius, *Lives of the Philosophers* 2.439). The omnipresence of divine Wisdom also signifies human accountability before God, for all human acts and words are exposed to Wisdom's all-pervading gaze (1:7–11). The author also uses the Stoic term *pronoia* ("providence," 6:7; 14:3; 17:2) to express God's oversight and care for God's creation.

Wisdom of Solomon's anthropology also connects with Platonic thought, beginning with the doctrine of the preexistence of souls, attested here for the first time in Jewish writing (8:19–20).[30] The soul enters a body, which is conceived of as a "burden" to the soul, an "earthly tent" that weighs down the mind (9:15). Only God's gift of the Holy Spirit can assist the human mind in the quest for spiritual truths. The author's dependence on Plato at this point comes close to direct borrowing, a remarkable similarity of word choice being observable when one sets Wis. 9:15 side by side with Plato, *Phaedo* 81C: "The body is a heavy load, my friend, weighty and earthly and visible. Such a soul lugging around this load is weighed down and led back to the visible realm by fear of the invisible."[31] The author does not regard the body as evil in and of itself. The body is neutral and a suitable receptacle for Wisdom as long as the person's soul is not enslaved to sin. Wisdom can dwell in the noble soul and in the body that is not an instrument of unrighteousness.

Finally, the author shares the Platonic idea of the immortality of the soul, stressing that one's moral character determines one's place in the afterlife. Many Jewish writers expressed views of an afterlife very much compatible with the Platonic position (see *1 Enoch* 102.5; 103.3–4; 104.6; *Jubilees* 23.31; *Testament of Asher* 6.5; and 4 Macc. 7:19; 13:17; 16:25), with the result that the popular distinction between resurrection as a Jewish concept and immortality of the soul as a Greek concept is simplistic at best (Winston 1979: 25–32; Collins 1997b: 185–87). The fate of the wicked in Wisdom of Solomon is difficult to untangle. On the one hand, immortality is the reward of righteousness (see 2:22–23; 3:4–5; 4:1; 6:18; 8:13, 17; 15:3) (Grabbe 1997: 55) and not something inherent (any more, at least) in human nature. On the other hand, the impious seem to experience a postmortem judgment in which they view the godly and realize their mistake. Collins (1997b: 185) aptly points out, however, that this may be merely a dramatic way of expressing the

30. This concept will appear in Philo, as might be expected, but also in talmudic texts; see Winston 1979: 28; Collins (1997b: 185) points to Plato, *Respublica* 617E, as the classic text on the soul's existence prior to entering a body.

31. Plato, however, actually speaks of the fate of the soul that has allowed its union with a body to corrupt and defile it, with the result that it cannot pass on after death to the realms of invisible light but rather wanders around the haunts of the visible realm with which it has become too closely attached. Plato (*Phaedo* 66B) reflects the thought more closely but not the diction. Philo also incorporates this Platonic teaching (Collins 1997b: 185–86).

vindication of the righteous after death rather than an expression of a belief that the ungodly will also survive their own death in some form.

Reinforcing Group Commitment amidst the Tensions of Diaspora Life

The first part of Wisdom of Solomon seeks to prove the reasoning that guides the "ungodly" (2:1–20) unsound and unreliable. The emphasis throughout this section falls on the vindication of the honor of the righteous in the presence of those who have held the righteous in contempt and assaulted their honor. This suggests a situation of high social tension between these groups, highlighting the author's desire to insulate the "righteous" from the negative opinion and shaming efforts of those designated as "ungodly," so that the righteous may be enabled to persevere in their way of life in the face of the strong currents washing against them.

The position of the ungodly is developed at great length in a manner reminiscent both of Ecclesiastes' emphasis on securing enjoyment in this life (cf. Eccl. 3:22; 5:18; 9:9) (Holmes 1913: 525–26; Reider 1957: 9–10; Oesterley 1935: 214–17) and of Epicurean denial of judgment, afterlife, and the involvement of God in human affairs. The ungodly take this in a direction that neither Epicurus nor the author of Ecclesiastes would ever have endorsed. The ungodly here include apostate Jews (Reider 1957: 12; Gilbert 1984: 309; Collins 1997b: 193–95; see also Weisengoff 1949; Dupont-Sommer 1935), since they are said to have gone against their training, sinned against the law, and fallen away from God (Wis. 2:12; 3:10). The opening motif of making a "covenant with death" (Wis. 1:16) recontextualizes Isaiah's description of the activity and lifestyle of the apostate rulers of Jerusalem, who had abandoned their ancestral ways (Isa. 28:15).

Like the author, the ungodly have witnessed the failure of this life to ascribe wealth, power, and security to the Torah-observant and poverty, premature death, and misery to those who take no thought of God. The traditional theodicies found in Deuteronomy and the Israelite wisdom tradition having failed, the ungodly have lost their moorings. Seeking to do whatever it takes to acquire the good things of this life, they have abandoned the path of righteousness and piety that their tradition had promoted as the way to acquire those good things. Indeed, they now regard those who continue to live out the values they have rejected as their enemies, a needling prick to their consciences. By attacking the righteous and exposing the folly of their claims to enjoy God's favor and personal patronage, the ungodly seek to reassure themselves about the wisdom of their own decision to leave God and God's impractical law behind.

Wisdom of Solomon answers that challenge, demonstrating that investment in piety, even where quite costly in this life, proves still to be advantageous and wise. One major topic of this first section is the redefinition of what constitutes a "happy life," negating the value of this-worldly components such as long life and many children (markers suggested by Deuteronomy and the Jewish wisdom tradition itself but also shared with the dominant culture, as in Aristotle, *Rhetorica* 1.5) and replacing this with the elevation of virtue and pious obedience to God as the single, lasting source of happiness and honor.[32]

Despite the apparent success of apostates in this life and despite the insult and abuse that they might heap on the righteous, Wisdom of Solomon assures the audience that God will honor the righteous with the prize of immortality (2:21–3:9) while showering disgrace and punishment on those who have not kept to God's ways (3:10; 4:17–19). The vivid description of the scenes beyond death, in which the apostates and all the Gentiles will confess their error and acknowledge the lasting honor of the loyal Jew, helps the audience grasp anew the reality of those eschatological events and live with them in view as a primary compass point in their lives. The vindication of the righteous in the sight of the ungodly, who have scorned them and even openly affronted them, is prominent in these postmortem scenes. This reversal is highlighted structurally by a second speech-in-character (5:3–13), in which the ungodly admit the error and folly of their earlier speech (2:1–20), admitting themselves to be the deviants and the godly to be in the right. A firm belief in a judgment and reward beyond this life becomes in this period an essential part of sustaining commitment to the values of the Jewish minority culture, neutralizing the attractiveness of succumbing to the pressures of non-Jews and lapsed Jews to join in the way of life that characterizes the dominant culture.

The author also reinterprets the suffering that befalls the righteous—particularly the misfortunes that befall them at the hands of the ungodly—in a positive way, a way productive of honor. In 3:1–9, the trials of the righteous constitute the divine discipline that trains them for their eternal destiny; they are the fire and crucible that manifest the genuineness and value of their virtuous character. Far from being signs of defeat or dishonor (or signs of the irrelevance of virtue in the sight of a God who allows calamity to befall the virtuous and good fortune to visit the wicked), these trials become opportunities for eternal honor and advantage.

The rest of the book offers support for this primary goal. Attaining Wisdom is presented as the path to lasting honor, a praiseworthy remembrance, and immortality beyond death (8:10, 13); Wisdom is found where individuals act in accordance with God's commandments, with what is pleasing in

32. Failure of the good to attain what are commonly held to be good things in this life (old age, wealth, etc.) was dealt with in a similar manner by Greco-Roman philosophers: those who are quickly perfected are more quickly removed to a place of safety (see Seneca, *Ad Marciam de consolatione* 22–23; Collins 1997b: 191).

God's sight (9:9), thus showing them to be the honorable elements in society, whatever the ungodly might think of them. Part three, moreover, provides a historical demonstration of the affirmations and themes of part one, especially the vivid contrast between the fate of the ungodly and of God's chosen people and in the denunciation of foolish ways of thinking (from which the audience is therefore to distance itself). The language of 11:13–14; 15:10–12; 18:13 is especially reminiscent of the topics introduced in part one. The exodus story, so central to Jewish identity, thus becomes a resource for the preservation of that identity in a new way, in a new setting.

Critique of Gentile Society

In a fictive address to the "monarchs of the earth," the author of Wisdom expresses a criticism of Gentile rulers shared by many Jews. The author upbraids them because, although they had received their authority from God, they failed to honor God, disregarded the law (the Torah; Wis. 18:4), and neglected to rule rightly and serve God's purposes (Wis. 6:1–8). Gentile kings are indicted as ignoble clients of the One God and are called either to repent or face the wrath of the God whom they have disregarded. Such a critique encouraged loyal Jews who felt the sting of injustice and saw the preferential treatment awarded the apostates. The Torah-observant Jews' loyalty to the One God would assure them of vindication against their enemies when God searched out iniquity.

Near the close of the book, the author indicts the Egyptians for showing a "more bitter hatred of strangers [*misoxenia*]" than seen in Sodom (19:13–16)—quite a stunning charge to make, seeing that the Jews were frequently accused of this very trait on account of their tendency to live, eat, and pull together as a community distinct and separate from their non-Jewish neighbors.[33] The author avers, however, that it was the non-Jews in Egypt who had originated and perfected that vice, enslaving their "guests who were their benefactors" (a reference to the Joseph story). When the author speaks of their afflicting "those who had already shared the same rights," one may be hearing an echo of the persistent debate over the civic status of Jews in Alexandria (whether the Jews were equal citizens or resident aliens), as in many other Greek cities.

The author presents a lengthy argument against the legitimacy of Gentile religion (13:1–15:19), including traditional criticisms (e.g., Isa. 44:9–20, the source of Wis. 13:11–19; and Ps. 115:4–8, used in Wis. 15:15–16) but also taking the polemic to a new level of sophistication. The parallels with the

33. See, for example, Diodorus of Sicily, *Historical Library* 34.1–4; 40.3.4; Tacitus, *Historiae* 5.5; Juvenal, *Satirae* 14.100–104; the charge of showing ill-will toward non-Jews is also reflected in Josephus, *Against Apion* 2.121; 2.258; 3 Macc. 3:4, 7.

much longer treatment of this theme in Philo, *De decaloga* 52–81, are note-worthy, suggesting that these topics were already, or quickly became, com-monplaces in Jewish critiques of Gentile religion.[34] Letter of Jeremiah and Bel and the Dragon offer other virulent polemics against, or parodies of, idol wor-ship, although neither reaches the sophistication found here.

The author first reprimands those who worship natural objects such as the sun, moon, and stars. While they are less blameworthy, they are still faulted for not pushing beyond fascination with created things to the adoration of the Creator (13:1–9; cf. Rom. 1:19–21, 25). The author's conviction that obser-vation of these marvels of creation should lead to the perception of the Cre-ator was shared by Gentile philosophers such as Cleanthes (see Cicero, *De natura deorum* 2.12–15) (Collins 1997b: 207). More reprehensible are those who worship lifeless objects—the idols that abounded in Gentile religions. The author begins with the reductio ad absurdum drawn from Isa. 44:12–20: a skilled woodcutter makes some fine utensil, uses some of the cast-off wood for a fire that heats his food, and uses another scrap to fashion an idol (Wis. 13:10–16; the theme returns in 15:7–17). The author expands on this with a series of paradoxes to show the folly of such religion: the idolater prays about an upcoming voyage to a thing that cannot move, about matters of life to a lifeless piece of wood (13:17–14:2).

In a manner typical of Jewish anti-idolatry satires and polemics, however, the author of Wisdom does not try to present an insider's understanding of the role of idols in worship, that they are representations of the deity and not the deity itself. Authors as early as Plato wrote that, as the pious worshiped before the idols, "although these are lifeless, the living gods beyond feel well disposed and favorable toward us" (*Leges* 931A).[35] What the author says about the bronze serpent in the wilderness (16:6–7), Plato would have said also about the intervention of the gods on behalf of the suppliants in the idol tem-ples. Moreover, Greco-Roman authors were often critical of the place of idols in enlightened religion. Horace (*Satirae* 1.8), for example, also mocks the use of visual representations of divinities, bearing witness to the fact that thought-ful pagans could have shared Wisdom's contempt for the superstitious vener-ation of idols:

> A long time ago, I was the trunk of a fig tree.
> The wood was not fine, so the carpenter contemplated
> Whether it would be better to turn me into a stool
> Or into a Priapus, and he decided on the latter.
> So now I'm a god,
> And I scare the wits out of thieves and birds.

34. See also *Sibylline Oracle* 3, although there, references to Gentile worship of nature, idols, and animals are spread throughout the whole rather than concentrated in a single, unified section, as in Philo or Wisdom.

35. Translation mine; reference in Winston 1979: 262.

It is curious that the author suppresses these points of contact with the more philosophically minded or sophisticated non-Jews; either the author was not aware of those currents or was intentionally depicting Gentiles as uniformly bemired in darkness and ignorance, so as to better reinforce the social and intellectual boundaries around the Jewish culture.

The author makes a strong advance on previous anti-idolatry polemic by presenting a theory of the origins of idolatrous cults (14:12–16; strikingly similar to Euhemerus's explanation of the origin of the pagan gods in the divinization of deceased kings) (Collins 2000: 200). By demystifying and rationalizing the process by which the pagan gods developed—the understandable longing to hold on to one's dearly departed and to maintain a connection beyond death and the accretion of rites, customs, and superstitions over time—the author is able to uncover its human origins and, indeed, fabrication. Equally insightful is the author's explanation of the origins of ruler cult in the desire on the part of subject peoples to demonstrate their loyalty and gratitude to the distant ruler. The imperial cult represents their attempt to establish a language of diplomacy and a favorable relationship with the center of power, but the author goes on to suggest that the paraphernalia of the cult made the human origins of the king dangerously obscure.[36]

Wisdom 14:11 makes an original contribution to reflection on why idol worship should be so hateful to the God of Israel. Idolaters use the material of God's own creation to promote a cult that dishonors the Creator, thus misusing the gifts of God's creation, which should have aroused gratitude and reverence for the true Giver. This suggests a theology of creation that could speak poignantly to our ecologically challenged times. Any use of the elements of creation that does not honor God but instead promotes the modern iterations of idolatry is an affront to the Creator. Idolatry is blameworthy not only as an affront to the One Creator God (14:21b) but also as the "beginning of fornication" and "corruption of life" (14:12); it is the "beginning and cause and the end of every evil," including murder, violation of marriage, theft, deceit, perjury, disloyalty, ingratitude, and sexual perversion (14:22–31; cf. Rom. 1:22–32). The association of Gentile religion with all things base, a connection asserted rather than argued, helps the audience to remain steadfast in their commitment to true religion (15:1–6).

While such a polemic would serve to reinforce the lines drawn between Jewish culture and the unenlightened Gentile masses, the points of contact with Greco-Roman philosophical texts suggest that the author sought to present Jewish piety as a comparable manifestation of that pure piety taught by the universal law of the philosophers. Contrary to typical anti-Jewish satire and polemics, the Jewish way of life taught a form of piety that was on a par with the tenets of the most enlightened Greco-Roman intellectuals. It was not

---

36. Winston (1979: 64) insightfully suggests that Wis. 7:1–7 and 9:5 combat this tendency, portraying a king emphasizing his own humble and mortal origins.

the Jews who were "superstitious" or "backwards" in their religious obser-vances, and the most sophisticated Gentiles should recognize this. This might even have social implications, with the author of Wisdom "attempting to make common cause with enlightened Greeks" against the superstitious and debased Egyptians (Collins 1997b: 212–13).[37]

Universalism versus Particularism

The author wrestles at some length with the relationship of the One God to all the peoples of the earth in the first excursus in part three. As Paul would frame the question, "Is God the God of the Jews only? Is he not the God of the Gentiles also. . . . since God is One?" (Rom. 3:29–30). On the one hand, students of Wisdom have found "an arrogant and undisguised particularism" in the book in which "God appears as a tribal god who is partial to the Jews and inimical to their enemies" (Reider 1957: 41). On the other hand, the au-thor shows considerable leanings toward universalism. It is not simply that "sinning Jews are freed from punishment, but God hates the sinning Canaan-ites and exterminates them for their sins" (Reider 1957: 41). Rather, the au-thor argues that God in fact loves all that God has created and detests none of God's works, infused with God's "immortal spirit" as they are (Wis. 11:23–12:1). Moreover, the spirit of Wisdom herself is *philanthrōpon*, "be-nevolent, humane" toward all humanity (1:6; 7:23), as is God, whose univer-sal mercy sets an example for God's people to follow (12:19). Thus, even if Gentiles should persist in disregarding the righteous and rebelling against God (3:10), the righteous are called to be imitators of God's benevolence rather than their neighbors' hostility.

The author seeks an explanation of God's destruction of the Canaanites and punishment of the Egyptians beyond an appeal to God's election of Is-rael. He focuses on the blatant wickedness of the Canaanites: they had done so much evil in God's sight, that the conquest of Canaan was intended as much to punish them as to benefit the Hebrews (compare Wis. 12:3–7 with Lev. 18:24–30; 20:2–5). The author of Wisdom does not condemn the Gen-tiles for failing to observe those customs that are normally associated with marks of Jewish identity but only for what would be recognized commonly as vices (save for idolatry, since this was regarded as piety). The law of Wisdom is seen thus to be the universal law of the philosophers, which Philo, for ex-ample, held to be the main object of Torah (Collins 1997b: 220–22).

The author also gives a striking new interpretation to the detail in Exod. 23:29–30 that God would drive out the Canaanites "little by little." In Exo-

37. See also texts from Cicero, *De natura deorum* 1.29, 82; 3.15, 39; Juvenal, *Satirae* 15.1–13, on Roman scorn for Egyptian animal worship (cited in Pfeiffer 1949: 349), a scorn referred to by the author in Wis. 12:24.

dus, this happens so that the land does not become desolate and overrun with wild animals. In Wisdom, however, it is a sign of God's desire to give the Canaanites "an opportunity to repent" (12:8–10; 12:20, 26). The author of 2 Maccabees could write that God corrects the people of Israel little by little so as to discipline and restore them but saves up punishment against the Gentiles to destroy them all at once (2 Macc. 6:13–16), but the author of Wisdom applies the idea of God's corrective discipline to Gentiles as well. Only when this fails due to the depth to which wickedness has taken root in the Gentiles does God finally destroy them.

Although the author has made impressive strides in the direction of affirming God's love and salvific designs for all people, the tension between universalism and particularism remains because of the author's view of the Canaanites being so steeped in evil that their very nature is perverse and incorrigible. In effect, universalism founders on the related question of free will and determinism.[38] Are the Gentiles actually free to choose Wisdom, or is their will itself perverted, such that no warning or correction from God can break their commitment to impiety? Reflecting on the destruction of the Egyptians at the Red Sea, the author writes, "The fate they deserved drew them on to this end . . . in order that they might fill up the punishment that their torments still lacked" (19:4).[39] The Egyptians appear to have been destined for destruction and led on to that end by a force beyond their own choosing. The limitations that the author places on the Gentiles' ability to respond positively to God's corrective discipline thus severely undermine the author's overtures to universalism.

The Personification of Wisdom

Key attributes of deities were often separated and personified in Egyptian and Akkadian religion. Abstract qualities like wisdom and justice could thus become intermediate objects of veneration or at least come to be seen as special parts of the "entourage" of a primary deity (see Ringgren 1947: 27, 49–58). This tendency provides the primary background for the development of the figure of Wisdom first in Proverbs (1:20–33; 8:22–31) and thence to Wisdom 6–9, where she achieves new heights of personification, even hypostatization. Like Philo, the author speaks of Wisdom as an emanation of God rather than a created being: "She is a breath of the power of God, and a pure emanation of the glory of the Almighty; . . . a reflection of eternal light, a spotless mirror of the working of God, and an image of his good-

38. See Winston 1979: 46–58 for a lengthy examination of this question.
39. This is a similar tension to the one observed in Josephus's (*Jewish War* 2.162–163) description of the Pharisaic doctrine: "The Pharisees . . . attribute everything to Fate and to God; they hold that to act rightly or otherwise rests, indeed, for the most part with people, but that in each action Fate cooperates" (Grabbe 1997: 62).

ness" (Wis. 7:25–26). Wisdom is God's companion and agent in the creation and ongoing governance of the world (8:1; 9:9). While Reider (1957: 36) goes too far to find in Wisdom a "throne partner" for God in 6:14 and 9:4, she nevertheless affords the most intimate fellowship between God and human beings. She participates in God and, entering human souls, makes them friends of God (7:27–28). Since Wisdom remains "intact" as she emanates from God and enters holy souls, she becomes the bridge by which human beings become connected to the Divine, the mediator between God and humanity. This Wisdom can be attained only through prayer (7:7; 8:21–9:18); and while she is not here identified with the Torah as in Ben Sira, she does teach what pleases God, and this involves keeping the commandments (Wis. 6:18; 9:9).

Unlike Ben Sira, who sought to make of Wisdom a cipher for Torah observance, the author of Wisdom of Solomon defines Wisdom broadly enough to encompass also the whole realm of learning (7:17–22). God's gift of Wisdom also grants facility in all the subjects comprehended within "the curriculum in a Greek school: philosophy, physics, history, astronomy, zoology, religion, botany, medicine" (Crenshaw 1981: 177). Thus, training in Jewish Wisdom would afford one all the benefits of Greek education, which made her "the perfect bridge between the exclusive nationalist tradition of Israel and the universalist philosophical tradition which appealed so strongly to the youth of Roman Alexandria" (Winston 1979: 37).

Mack (1973: 63–107) has also shown how the author adapts the aretalogies (lists of virtues) of the popular Egyptian goddess Isis to promote the figure of Wisdom. Isis was a revealer, a savior figure,[40] and, when identified with Ma'at, the Egyptian goddess of wisdom, an associate of the chief deity who knows all his works.[41] The advances made by the author concerning the figure of Wisdom as mediator between God and creation would prove helpful for the early church as it wrestled with the person of the Son.

Influence

Wisdom of Solomon does not appear to have left an enduring mark on Jewish literature, although certain elements of its midrash on Exodus appear also in rabbinic literature. For example, in a manner reminiscent of Wis. 16:25–26, *b. Yoma* 75a states that the manna changed its taste so as to

40. The self-revelation discourse in Apuleius, *Metamorphoses* 12, is a readily accessible resource for glimpsing the significance of Isis at the turn of the era; see also Kloppenberg 1982: 68–71; Collins 1997b: 203–4.

41. See Grabbe 1997: 75–76 for connections between Ma'at and Wisdom in the Wisdom of Solomon.

provide the Israelites with variety.[42] Direct dependence, however, cannot be demonstrated.

The early church, however, made extensive use of the Wisdom of Solomon.[43] Wisdom's portrait of the persecution of the righteous person (Wis. 2:12–20) was read as a prediction of Christ's passion (see Augustine, *De civitate Dei* 17.20). As early as Matthew one finds hints that the passage is being read in this way, for the evangelist adds to the taunt of Ps. 22:8 the rationale "For he said, 'I am the Son of God'" (Matt. 27:43), the very claim that the ungodly seek to test in Wis. 2:17–20.

The author of Hebrews presents not Wisdom but the Son, as the "reflection of God's glory and the exact imprint of God's very being" (Heb. 1:3), thus understanding Christ's relationship to God in terms very similar to those used to describe Wisdom's relationship to God (Wis. 7:26). Colossians 1:15 also moves in this direction, speaking of Jesus as the "image of the invisible God." Wisdom of Solomon's lavish expansions on the personified Wisdom's relationship to God thus provided important raw material for Christology in the early church.

The most pervasive influence of Wisdom surfaces in the writings of Paul.[44] First, Paul's statement on the depravity of humanity on account of idolatry in Rom. 1:19–32 shows strong signs of Wisdom's influence (Wis. 13:1–9; 14:22–27). Both move through the same progression of thought: Gentiles ought to have been able to perceive the One God through observation of creation and so are "without excuse" (Wis. 13:1–9; Rom. 1:19–20); Gentiles instead turned to the worship of created things (Wis. 13:2, 7; Rom. 1:22–23, 25); this ignorance of God (Wis. 14:22; Rom. 1:21) produced all manner of wickedness, including murder, theft, deceit, and sexual perversion (Wis. 14:22–27; Rom. 1:24, 26–31); God's just sentence remains on those who practice such deeds (Wis. 14:30–31; Rom. 1:32).

Second, when Paul, in Rom. 9:21, affirms God's absolute sovereignty over the human being as God's creation in terms similar to Sir. 33:10–13 (all are as clay in the hands of the potter, "to be given whatever he decides"), he adds a detail from Wis. 15:7, where the potter makes "out of the same clay both the vessels that serve clean uses and those for contrary uses." Paul now takes this distinction out of the context of the anti-idolatry polemic and applies it to the various destinies of the wicked and the godly in God's plan. Paul also

42. See Reider 1957: 41, who takes this as a "source" for the idea in Wisdom even though the written form of the tradition is much later than Wisdom.

43. Larcher (1969: 11–84) provides an extensive and cautious treatment of New Testament texts showing possible points of influence from Wisdom and the ongoing influence of Wisdom on the literature of the early church and the church of the Medieval, Reformation, and post-Reformation periods.

44. The judgment of Grant (1967: 70) that "Paul, like John, knew ideas related to Wisdom but not the book itself" is highly suspect given the numerous and impressive points of contact between Paul and Wisdom.

shares with Wisdom the view that the judgment of God is beyond criticism and the will of God irresistible (Rom. 9:19; Wis. 12:12; cf. *1 Clement* 27.5–6) but also stresses that God is patient, allowing opportunity for repentance (Rom. 2:4; Wis. 11:23; 12:19–20; cf. Acts 17:30).

Augustine had already implicitly noted the connection between 2 Cor. 5:1–4 and Wis. 9:15 when he blended the two passages together in a paraphrase. Paul views life in the body as the soul's sojourn in an "earthly tent," a "burden" that makes us "groan" (2 Cor. 5:1, 4). Although Paul expects a resurrected body, his description of the mortal body is remarkably similar to Wis. 9:15. The larger context of this verse appears also to have left its mark on 1 Cor. 2:7–12, which, together with Wis. 9:13, 17, announces the impossibility of the earthly mind comprehending spiritual truths or the mind of God apart from receiving the Spirit from God.

A number of other New Testament texts resonate with Wisdom. The description of the "armor of God" in Eph. 6:11–17 is more closely related to Wis. 5:17–20 than to Isa. 59:17. Both Wisdom and Ephesians speak of God's *panoplia* ("whole armor") and add references to a shield and sword beyond the helmet and breastplate. While Ephesians is clearly aware of Isaiah's description of God's armor, it thus also shows signs of direct awareness of Wisdom's earlier expansion of that image. Wisdom's interpretation of the trials endured by the righteous at the hands of the ungodly as God's refining of the individual for the reward of the righteous (Wis. 3:5–6) appears again in 1 Pet. 1:6–7. Hebrews 8:2–5 and Wis. 9:8 move in a similar direction in their exegesis of Exod. 25:40, both stressing that the earthly temple was but a copy of the abiding tabernacle that God "prepared from the beginning." Given other connections between Hebrews and Wisdom (cf. the use of Wis. 7:25–26 in Heb. 1:1–3), it is likely that Hebrews learned this from Wisdom as well.

Johannine echoes of Wisdom are less evident, although Wisdom's equation of knowledge of God with "complete righteousness" and "immortality" (Wis. 15:3) is similar to Jesus' definition of eternal life in John 17:3. Similarly, Jesus' equation of love of him with obedience to his commandments may recall Wis. 6:18: "love of Wisdom is the keeping of her laws." John also depicts the helplessness of the unaided, earthly mind in the face of spiritual revelation, also in the context of receiving God's Spirit (John 3:10–12; cf. Wis. 9:14, 16–17). Finally, just as all who receive Wisdom are made "friends of God" (Wis. 7:27), so all who receive the Son are made "children of God" (John 1:12). Such similarities suggest that John was indeed familiar with the ideas one finds in Wisdom, though not necessarily directly indebted. Revelation also shares a number of concepts with Wisdom. Signs precede judgment (Wis. 19:13; Rev. 6:12–15; 8:7–9:21; 16:1–20); God seeks to stimulate repentance before visiting destruction upon the ungodly (Wis. 12:2, 10, 20; Rev. 14:6–7); the ungodly refuse to repent (Wis. 12:10–11; Rev. 9:20–21; 16:8–11); natural elements play a role in helping the righteous and punishing the wicked (Wis. 5:17, 20–23; 16:17; Rev. 8:1–9:21; 12:16; 16:1–9, 18–21).

The evidence points again not to direct dependence but to the possibility that Revelation plays out in visionary form a number of concepts already present in the Jewish wisdom traditions.

Despite disagreement concerning its status as Scripture, Wisdom continued to exert a pervasive influence on the early church, seen conspicuously in the Muratorian Canon listing of the book as acceptable for liturgical use (although, oddly, as a book of the New Testament). Wisdom's teaching that death entered the world because of the devil's envy (Wis. 2:24) appears frequently (*1 Clement* 3.4; Augustine, *De trinitate* 4.12.15; *In Evangelium Johannis tractatus* 12.10). Augustine made much use of Wis. 9:15, frequently interrupting his argument to reflect on the difficulty of pursuing theological reflection because this "body, which is corrupt, weighs down the soul; and the earthly dwelling depresses the mind as it meditates on many things" (cf. *In Evangelium Johannis tractatus* 21.1; 23.5; 35.9; 69.2; 96.4; 124.5; *De trinitate* 4.5, 10; 8.2; 17.28; 24.44). This feeds quite naturally into his rather negative anthropology. This human state, in which the corrupt body weighs down the soul, also explains the impossibility of coming to faith through reason alone (cf. Rom. 1:20 and Wis. 13:1–5, which Augustine quotes side by side in *De trinitate* 15.2.3). As Wis. 9:17 asserts, only the gift of the Spirit allows the human mind to arrive at spiritual truths (*De trinitate* 3.21).

Wisdom's deconstruction of the validity of Greco-Roman religion as the development of the desire to memorialize and immortalize the dearly departed or to honor kings is taken over in early Christian apologetics, as in Minucius Felix, *Octavius* 20.5, and Lactantius, *Divinarum institutionum libri VII* 2.2–3 (Pfeiffer 1949: 348). That they learned this directly from Wisdom is difficult to prove, but the widely read text would have provided a most immediate and accessible venue.

Finally, Wisdom continued to have a strong impact on the church's reflection on the person of Jesus and on the doctrine of the Trinity. Ignatius weaves phrases from Wis. 7:29–30 and 18:14–15 into his treatments of Christ's appearing (Ignatius, *To the Ephesians* 19.2–3; Ignatius, *To the Magnesians* 8.2). Athenagoras applies Wis. 7:25 to the Holy Spirit (*Legatio pro Christianis* 10.4), while later Alexandrian teachers apply Wis. 7:24–8:1 to the work of the Son, the "eternal generation" of the Son by the Father, and the sharing of the Father and the Son in the same essence (*homoousios*; Origen, *De principiis* 1.2.9; also *Contra Celsum* 3.62; 5.10; 6.63; 8.14) (Grant 1967: 74–77).[45] While Origen takes this discussion in a subordinationist direction, Augustine would use the same texts to support the complete equality of persons in the Trinity (most forcefully in *In Evangelium Johannis tractatus* 21.2; 22.10; 111.2; *De trinitate* 2.5.6; 2.8.14; 3.3; 4.20.27).

45. See also the use of this passage by Dionysius and Theognostus, documented in Grant 1967: 77–80.

Wisdom of Ben Sira

"In All Wisdom There Is the Doing of Torah"

Yeshua Ben Sira, a scribe living and teaching in Jerusalem, brought the wisdom tradition of Israel squarely in line with the core value of Torah observance. Unlike Proverbs Job, and Ecclesiastes, from which he learned much and which he also rebutted on certain points, Ben Sira places the pursuit of piety and obedience to the ancestral Jewish law at the center of the pursuit of Wisdom—and this at a time when tensions concerning assimilation to the dominant culture of Hellenism were mounting and about to reach a fevered pitch in the crisis of 175–164 B.C.E. Ben Sira was no reactionary, but he was definitely a conservative voice in the first decades of the second century B.C.E., calling his pupils to seek their fortune, their honor, and their good name through diligent observance of the demands of the God of Israel first and foremost. The path to Wisdom, and to a successful and secure life, was first of all the way of Torah, supplemented (but never displaced or replaced) by the worldly wisdom learned from many different cultures.

Structure and Contents

Although Ben Sira has organized his material far better than the compilers of Proverbs did theirs, where it is rare to find two topical sayings side by side, his work still does not readily lend itself to outlines. In its Greek form, the book begins with a prologue written by Ben Sira's grandson, who translated the work from Hebrew into Greek for the benefit of Greek-speaking Jews living outside of Palestine. The first two chapters of Ben Sira's own work set forth the benefits of wisdom, establish its connectedness with the "fear of the Lord," and prepare the student for endurance in the pursuit of wisdom through fearing the Lord.

The next section, about forty chapters (3:1–42:14), consists of a series of instructions on a wide range of topics.[1] Some of these instructions are given a

---

1. Alternative analyses of the content of this section can be found in Skehan and Di Lella 1987: 4–5; Harrington 1999: 80–82.

section heading in the Greek text to mark them off: "Self Control" as a heading for 18:30–19:3, "Proverbial Sayings" at 20:27 (it is not clear how much of what follows would have been included under this general heading), "Discipline of the Tongue" for 23:7–15, and "The Praise of Wisdom" for 24:1–29. It is strange that just these few section headings should be found in the text, rather than a more comprehensive attempt to indicate the beginning of new topics or a complete lack of such headings.

Within the body of the work are to be found well-developed instructions on Wisdom and the pursuit of Wisdom (interwoven with "fear of the Lord" and keeping of the "commandments"; 4:11–19; 6:18–37; 14:20–15:10; 19:20–24; 21:11; 24:1–29; 32:14–17; 32:24–33:3); education (21:12–21; 22:9–18); the contributions of travel to sagacity (34:9–13); and the preparation and profession of the scribe (38:24–39:11). Ben Sira devotes much attention to topics that, one might surmise, were essential to making one's way in the world. Thus, we find extensive instructions on speech (including the dangers of slander, gossip, and the "double-tongue"; 4:23–26, 29; 5:9–6:1; 7:11–14; 9:17–18; 11:7–9, 20; 19:4–17; 20:1–8, 18–20, 24–31; 21:25–28; 23:7–15; 27:4–7, 16–21; 28:13–26); friendship and enmity (6:5–17; 7:18; 9:10; 11:29–34; 12:8–18; 19:4, 13–17, 25–30; 22:19–26; 27:22–29; 37:1–6; 40:20); the importance of choosing one's associates correctly (namely, Torah-observant people; 6:32–36; 9:14–16; 27:11–15) and insulating oneself against sinners and their values (9:11–12; 11:21–22; 21:9–10); proper conduct for visiting and for eating at another's table (including very practical advice about moderation in drinking and eating and how to behave appropriately at symposia and banquets; 21:22–24; 31:12–32:13; 37:27–31); the core value of reciprocity (3:31; 18:15–18; 20:9–17); discerning reliable advice (37:7–15); and the importance of forgiving offenses rather than harboring wrath (27:30–28:7). Moving away from a practical to a more reflective vein, Ben Sira also offers observations about government (10:1–5); the social tensions between rich and poor (13:1–7, 15–24); the difficulties of being a stranger and guest (29:21–28); the universal human condition (40:1–11); and death and the importance of leaving a good name (41:1–13).

The sage offers what he considers to be much-needed advice for those young men going out into society: cautions concerning consorting with the great or aspiring to visible greatness (7:4–7; 8:1–2, 12, 14; 9:13; 13:1–13); cautions against indulging one's passions (6:2–4; 18:30–19:3); cautions for dealing with various kinds of people (8:3–19); and a sort of preventative wisdom that, essentially, guards against loss through foresight (18:19–29; 32:18–23). His practical advice extends to money matters, including the anxiety that wealth brings (31:1–4); the need to be cautious in lending and taking loans (21:8; 29:1–7); the economic dangers of going as surety for another person (29:14–20); and maintaining integrity in business and virtue when wealthy (26:29–27:3; 31:5–11). His pupils are taught to avoid idleness and pursue industry (22:1–2; 40:28–30) while also seeking moderation in their pursuits, not taking on so much that they fail to enjoy life along the road (11:10–19; 14:3–19). Ben Sira also teaches his students about household management, including the proper treatment of slaves (7:21; 33:25–33); duties toward parents (3:1–16; 7:27–28); raising children (7:23; 16:1–4; 22:3–6; 30:1–13; 41:5–9); the special challenges of having daughters (7:24–25; 26:10–12; 42:9–14); looking after and keeping control over one's property (7:22; 33:20–24); the benefits and dangers of adult women (7:19, 26; 9:1–9; 25:13–26:27; 36:26–31; 40:19b; 42:14); and the necessity of avoiding sexual promiscuity (23:16–27; 26:19–20). Ben Sira's observations concerning women are, to be sure, among the most objectionable in the book. Ben Sira is acutely aware of the importance of looking after one's health and making use of both religious and medical venues of healing when ill (30:14–17; 38:1–15); his advice on how to mourn the dead is also marked by a consideration for not allowing grief to compromise health (38:16–23).

This sage is concerned not only with imparting practical wisdom but even more with grounding his students in virtue and, most especially, in the piety that is characteristic of the Jewish tradition. Thus, he teaches the expedience of virtue and of avoiding vice (7:1–3; 27:8–10), particularly the value of humility (3:17–29; 7:15–17; 10:28–31; 11:1–6) and the dangers of arrogance and presumption (5:1–8; 7:8–11; 10:6–18; 11:23–28; 21:4). He is concerned to implant a clear sense that honor comes only through, and along with, Torah observance, irrespective of whether or not one is wealthy or influential or powerful (10:19–24). He also composes lengthy instructions on proper and improper "shame" (i.e., regard for the opinion of others; 4:20–28; 20:21–23; 41:14–42:8), thus using the two most basic coordinating values of his culture (honor and shame) to reinforce the behaviors and attitudes he wants his pupils to embody.

Ben Sira's wisdom is by no means as strictly "secular" or "worldly" as that of Proverbs or Ecclesiastes. A large amount of his instruction is given over to promoting Jewish piety as an essential component of the life of the wise person (37:7–15; 39:5–8). In these sections his debt to the Hebrew prophets is unmistakable, as he teaches on acceptable sacrifices, the importance of doing Torah (which is equated with sacrificial offerings), and social justice (7:29–31; 34:21–35:26). Especially noteworthy is the attention Ben Sira gives to almsgiving, acts of mercy, and social justice (3:30; 4:1–10, 31; 7:10, 32–36; 12:1–7; 29:8–13; 34:21–27; 35:15b–26; 40:16–17). While he wants his pupils to be religious, he does not want them involved in the more flighty aspects of the otherworldly, such as becoming involved with divination, omens, and the interpretation of dreams (34:1–8).

As Ben Sira could move into a more reflective mode where the practical aspects of life were concerned, he could also do this with regard to theological realities. Thus, we find extended reflections on the source and consequences of sin (15:11–20; 16:6–14; 21:1–3) and meditations on God's created order, serving either to motivate repentance from sin (breaches of that order) or to affirm God's provision for care of the righteous and punishment of the wicked in the created order (16:24–18:14; 33:7–15; 39:16–35).

The last major part of the work consists of an encomium (a celebratory speech) in praise of the works of God (42:15–43:33) followed by an encomium of the illustrious people of Israel's sacred history from Enoch through Simon II (44:1–50:29), whose high priesthood Ben Sira had personally experienced (219–196 B.C.E.). These form a sort of diptych praising the God of Israel and the people who have built up Israel by their commitment to God:

> I will now call to mind the works of the Lord . . . (42:15)
> Let us now praise famous persons . . . (44:1)

Only the latter encomium, however, is given special notice by a section heading, "Hymn in Honor of Our Ancestors," in the Greek text. The book concludes with the author's autobiographical note (50:27–29), a thanksgiving psalm by Ben Sira showing the way in which canonical Psalms influenced and facilitated personal prayer (51:1–12; introduced as "Prayer of Jesus Son of Sirach" in the Greek text), a second thanksgiving psalm patterned after Psalm 136,[2] and an acrostic poem about Ben Sira's search for Wisdom and his invitation to others to come learn of Wisdom at his school (51:13–30)[3]—a school that now exists only where his words are read.

Textual Transmission

For nearly eighteen centuries, the Wisdom of Ben Sira had been known and read primarily from the Greek version preserved in the Septuagint and translations based upon that version. Ben Sira, however, originally wrote his work in Hebrew. It was his grandson who translated the book into Greek for the benefit of the Jewish community in Egypt sometime after he had moved there in 132 B.C.E. As Ben Sira had written his book in order that "those who love learning might make even greater progress in living according to the law," so his grandson published a Greek translation for the sake of Egyptian Jews who "are disposed to live according to the law" (Prologue 12–14, 34–

---

2. This appears only in one Hebrew manuscript and may well be an interpolation (part of the HTII expansions). See Skehan and Di Lella 1987: 569.

3. Part of this was found included in the Qumran Psalms Scroll, leading to the suggestion that it was not original to Ben Sira. On the other hand, the fact that Christians later could cull their sacred literature for additional hymns (which would be grouped together as the Odes in Septuagint manuscripts) suggests that it is not impossible that the Qumran covenanters did the same centuries before. Moreover, the material seems out of place in a psalms scroll but agrees beautifully with the rest of Ben Sira in terms of content (and even context, as the close of Ben Sira turns to more autobiographical material).

36), making his grandfather's promotion of a conservative ideology available to a major center of Diaspora Judaism.

Since the late nineteenth century, however, extensive portions of Hebrew versions have been discovered: medieval manuscripts found in the storage room of a synagogue in Cairo and first-century-B.C.E. or -C.E. manuscripts discovered at Qumran and Masada. The latter texts have a shorter version (called HTI), while the Cairo finds are of two types: the shorter version and a more expansive version (HTII).[4] These two families of Hebrew texts correspond to the two families of Greek texts (GI and GII), the shorter being considered more original. GII contains over three hundred lines not found in GI, but this expanded form became the basis for the Old Latin and the Vulgate and hence became the form of Ben Sira used by the churches as a whole through the Reformation.[5]

A little more than two-thirds of Ben Sira is now available in Hebrew, a fact that has opened up important new avenues for text critics to work toward establishing Ben Sira's original Hebrew text (Skehan and Di Lella 1987: 51–62; Di Lella 1966a). In his prologue, the grandson admits that neither the Septuagint as a whole nor his own work preserves the original Hebrew perfectly (Prologue 21–26). Indeed, he has been shown to have been more concerned with conveying the sense of Ben Sira's wisdom than with making a "mechanical *reproduction* of his grandfather's Hebrew" (Wright 1989: 249). While the grandson's Greek version remains the most important witness to Ben Sira's work, it is especially important to consult both Hebrew and Greek texts in the study of Ben Sira, particularly if one's goal is to get at Yeshua Ben Sira's words and goals, beyond the goals and interpretative moves of the grandson.

The Author and His Setting

The Wisdom of Ben Sira is the only book among the Apocrypha whose author identifies himself (50:27), an identity confirmed in the grandson's prologue. Ben Sira was a scribe by profession, and his work included the training of the sons of the more affluent Jews in his "house of instruction," a school, in Jerusalem (51:23).[6]

The date of the work can also be determined with certainty within a narrow range. Ben Sira experienced the high priesthood of Simon II, who officiated from 219 to 196 B.C.E. Ben Sira speaks of Simon's leadership and priestly ministrations in the eulogy of Sir. 50:1–21 as something belonging to the

4. See Beentjes 1997 for the complete Hebrew texts (in translation, Abegg, Flint, and Ulrich 1999: 597–606; Yadin 1965 for the Masada Scroll).

5. See further Coggins 1998: 37; Skehan and Di Lella 1987: 51–62; Box and Oesterley 1913: 271–91.

6. On schools in this period, and Ben Sira's school in particular, see Collins 1997b: 35–39.

(still recent) past. However, the lack of any comment on the subversion of the high priesthood by Jason, the younger son of Simon II who initiated the radical Hellenization of Jerusalem, or the persecution of faithful Jews that followed that initiative, indicates that Ben Sira's work, and probably his life, were finished before those dark times. We can thus place the original Hebrew text with confidence between 196 and 175 B.C.E., which also allows enough time, but not too much time, to pass before a grandson would translate the Hebrew into Greek sometime after 132 B.C.E. (the year the translator arrived in Egypt).[7]

Ben Sira's personality peers through his literary work rather directly at several places (see 16:24–25; 24:30–34; 33:16–18; 34:12–13; 38:34b–39:5; 50:27–51:30), affording us a number of windows into the life of this ancient author.[8] Ben Sira's description of the sage's activity (38:34b–39:5) might naturally be supposed to reflect the author's own course of study. Ben Sira studied the Hebrew Scriptures as well as the wisdom traditions of Egypt and Greece as he sought wisdom first for himself and then for all who would come to study under him. He also traveled extensively, and he claims that his study prepared him for navigating the dangers and challenges of travel through foreign lands (34:12–13; cf. 39:4b). He apparently also served "among the great" and appeared "before rulers" (39:4a). In the psalm of thanksgiving appended to the work (51:1–12), Ben Sira uses the language of the biblical psalms to speak about being delivered from the dangers brought upon him by someone who slandered him before a high official, giving a special poignancy to his own cautions against slander and the dangers of the slanderer. Being close to high places, Ben Sira learned, increased the likelihood of a bad fall.

Having set out to find the wise and secure path through life, Ben Sira was surprised at where his quest led him. He discovered far more than he had bargained for and now looks back at his earlier years of study with an understanding that all his research, travels, and experience have had a larger, beneficent purpose after all: the passing on of wisdom to the newer generations (24:30–34; 33:16–18). When he speaks of his little canal (i.e., of wisdom) becoming

7. This is the thirty-eighth year of the reign of Ptolemy Euergetes, the date given in the Prologue. Williams (1994: 563–65) argues that the date for the composition of the Hebrew original should be placed closer to 175 B.C.E., based on his estimation of the age of the grandson when he came to Egypt in 132 B.C.E., his estimation of Ben Sira's age when the book was written, the likelihood that the grandson's work was not executed until about 116–115 B.C.E., and the allowance of thirty years for each of the two generations between Ben Sira and the translator. It is a clever approach to the problem of dating the original work but not convincing. The approach does not take into account the factor of multiple childbirths for each generation. If the grandson were one of the younger children of one of Ben Sira's younger children, the generational spread could easily be eighty years instead of the sixty-year gap that Williams works with. Hence, the 175-B.C.E. end of the spectrum of possible dates remains no more likely than the 195-B.C.E. end.

8. Excellent insights into the autobiographical passages of Ben Sira and the training of the sage can be found in Roth 1980.

a river or compares himself to a person who thought he would merely be gleaning the grapes of the field but instead filled his winepress, he is not expressing arrogance or shameless self-promotion, as one might suppose at first glance; rather, he is acknowledging that the scribe's prayer for wisdom had in fact been answered by God, the giver of wisdom (39:5–9). Unlike the author of Ecclesiastes, whose quest for wisdom left him listless and empty, Ben Sira has found deep pools that, despite life's difficult times, filled his soul and that he hopes his students—both those he has taught personally and those he still teaches through his written legacy—will discover as well.

The political situation within which Ben Sira lived and carried on his work was marked by instability due to the frequent contests between the reigning Ptolemy and reigning Seleucid over who would control Palestine. While the Jewish farmer or laborer might not have been much concerned with such political struggles, Ben Sira was in a position to witness, and perhaps even get caught up in, the jockeying of pro-Ptolemaic Jewish aristocrats against pro-Seleucid ones. He was also in a position to see the effects of rubbing shoulders too closely with the foreign overlords, as is documented in the family history of the Tobiads (Josephus, *Jewish Antiquities* 12.154–236), a family that grew to immense influence and wealth by being more interested in cementing alliances with Gentile leaders and gaining their trust and respect than in maintaining a strict observance of Torah.

While Hellenization of Palestine may have been slow in the third century,[9] it increased rapidly in the early part of the second century in preparation for Jason's coup d'état. The radical moves toward the adoption of a Greek constitution were not imposed by Jason on an unwilling aristocracy but appear to have had the support of a substantial faction among the elites,[10] such as would have taken decades to simmer and come to a boil. Ben Sira lived and taught in a time of cultural tension, at least for the last decades of his career. Some of his own pupils, perhaps following the lead of their own fathers or other notable figures, were increasingly attracted to the Greek way of life, even while others were concerned to preserve the Jewish way of life or discover some viable synthesis between the two.

In these circumstances, Ben Sira can be seen to have had a number of goals for his students and his writing. Fundamentally, of course, his primary goal was the same as that of his predecessors in the wisdom traditions of Israel, Egypt, and Greece: teaching young men how to make their way in the world advantageously, how to gain honor and negotiate the challenges of politics and business, and how to secure happiness and contentment in the domestic

9. For corrections of the picture in Hengel 1974, see Feldman 1986 and Harrison 1994 (which, remarkably, shows no interest in Feldman 1986). Though less celebrated, Hengel 1980 is far more cautious and reliable.

10. See 1 Macc. 1:11–12; 2 Macc. 4:7–15. The fact that Jason was able to raise a tremendous sum of money for his purchase and annual maintenance of the high priesthood suggests many families contributing to the common pot.

sphere. Ben Sira, however, is also particularly interested in convincing his pupils that these goals are attainable only within the context of keeping covenant with the God of Israel. Ben Sira was not closed-minded about the contributions that other cultures had to make to the pursuit of Wisdom. All this, however, was supplemental to the way of life prescribed in the Scriptures.

Ben Sira was not working in a neutral environment. There were definite tendencies toward assimilation with the Greek way of life, toward relaxing Torah's demands where these inhibited forming relations with Gentile associates and profiting from their partnership. His intensification of the value of "the fear of the Lord" promoted in Proverbs, and above all his identification of the way of life laid out in the Torah with the way to attain Wisdom,[11] show that he, too, has an ideological agenda to advance: "the whole of wisdom is fear of the Lord, and in all wisdom there is the fulfillment of the law" (19:20). His most extended reflection on Wisdom (24:1–29) likewise climaxes in the assertion "All this is the book of the covenant of the Most High God, the law that Moses commanded us" (24:23). It is in the study and doing of the Torah that one can gain access to Wisdom, whom God has made to dwell with God's chosen people.

Rather than simply preparing his students to be wise and reputable in the world's eyes, Ben Sira seeks to make them wise and honorable in God's eyes as well. He does this by focusing youth on commitment to their ancestral heritage as the true path to honor:

> Whose offspring are worthy of honor?
>   Human offspring.
> Whose offspring are worthy of honor?
>   Those who fear the Lord.
> Whose offspring are unworthy of honor?
>   Human offspring.
> Whose offspring are unworthy of honor?
>   Those who break the commandments. . . .
> The rich, and the eminent, and the poor—
>   their glory is the fear of the Lord.
> It is not right to despise one who is intelligent but poor,
>   and it is not proper to honor one who is sinful.
> The prince and the judge and the ruler are honored,
>   but none of them is greater than the one who fears the Lord. (10:19, 22–24)

With instructions such as these, Ben Sira hopes to instill in his students the sense that honor and security can never be gained apart from remaining faith-

---

11. Although many claim that Ben Sira identifies Wisdom with Torah (Hengel 1974: 1.139; Di Lella 1992: 940; Duesberg and Auvray 1958:14), Boccaccini (1991: 77–125) argues that Wisdom remains greater than Torah, despite the apparent climax of the conclusion of the poem in chapter 24. Following Torah is the irreplaceable path to attaining Wisdom, the training in Wisdom without which one can never be wise (see especially Boccaccini 1991: 81–99).

ful to the Jewish tradition and that any precedence or material gain acquired through alienating God will, in the end, prove vapid and worthless.[12]

Ben Sira knows that total commitment to Torah observance as the path to Wisdom may bring tension, fear, and distress before it brings reward, and the devotee of Wisdom must be prepared for this in advance (2:1–17; 4:11–19; 6:22–31). He therefore lays a special emphasis on the disciplinary stage of pursuing Wisdom, using the imagery of a slave's lot (fetters, collar, and other bonds; bearing the weight of Wisdom like a litter bearer) to speak of the beginning stages of learning wisdom. These signs of humiliation, however, become the very symbols of honor in the end. These passages definitely reflect the commonplace that "the roots of education are bitter, but the fruits sweet"[13] but also reveal the difficulties and disadvantages that the Torah-observant devotee of Wisdom will encounter in the midst of a rapidly Hellenizing Jerusalem. Their commitment will be tested as they see their peers grow lax and seem to be rewarded for it, as their own practice is questioned and criticized. They are guided by their teacher, however, to form for themselves a suitable circle of associates and patrons—those who share the commitment to doing Torah—and to insulate themselves against the company and opinion of those who neglect Torah. In such a way, the company they keep will confirm them in their pursuit of the Wisdom that comes from God.[14]

Formative Influences

Ben Sira's description of the scribe's training and occupation guides us in the quest for formative influences on his thinking: "He seeks out the wisdom of all the ancients, and is concerned with prophecies; he preserves the sayings of the famous and penetrates the subtleties of parables. . . . He travels in foreign lands and learns what is good and evil in the human lot" (39:1–2, 4b). The main source for Ben Sira's study was the Hebrew Scriptures. His instructions evidence reflection not only on the wisdom tradition (with a special indebtedness to Proverbs) but also on the Torah, the prophets, and the psalms of Israel. A complete study of Ben Sira's use of the Old Testament is impossible here, since the diction is imbued throughout with recontextualizations and echoes of the Old Tes-

12. See also 25:7–11 (where the numerical sayings serve to elevate "fear of the Lord"); 40:18–27 (where a series of "better than" sayings climaxes in "fear of the Lord"); 9:16; 19:20–24; 32:24–33:3. Ben Sira's grandson well understood the sage's purpose: he wrote to aid people seeking to "make even greater progress in living according to the law."

13. Mack (1989: 84) points out that Ben Sira's conceptualization of education as "first discipline, then reward" corresponds to the Greek view of *paideia*.

14. See further deSilva 1996.

tament.[15] The encomium on the Jewish heroes (44:1–50:29), by itself, shows Ben Sira's familiarity with the bulk of what we now call the Hebrew Scriptures: the Pentateuch and all the Former and Latter Prophets are attested down to the mention of "the Twelve Prophets" (49:10), showing that the Minor Prophets had already begun to be conceived of as a single group. The only Writings alluded to in the whole are Job, Proverbs, and Psalms. Daniel is not mentioned, nor the book alluded to, anywhere in Ben Sira, as is also the case with Ruth, Esther, and Ezra.

Several of Ben Sira's instructions may be read as extended reflections on the precepts of Torah (explicitly referred to at 24:23). For example, 3:1–16 is an extended instruction based on the commandment to honor one's father and mother (Exod. 20:12; Deut. 5:16), including the rationale offered in the commandment: the promise of long life to those who so act. Ben Sira's emphasis on care for the poor, avoidance of adultery, and truthfulness in speech also has a basis in the Deuteronomic law code (although these have become traditional topics of wisdom literature as well, as seen in Proverbs). When Ben Sira declares that "fire and water" and "life and death" have been set before his pupils and when he urges them to choose to keep Torah (15:15–17), he echoes the similar choice set before the Hebrews in Deut. 30:19. Wisdom, for him, means making the right choice in the ancient, Deuteronomic set of alternatives. Torah also provides images that Ben Sira uses to develop instructions quite unrelated to the original context of the images. For example, the rivers of Gen. 2:10–14 are used to speak of the abundant, overflowing character of Wisdom.

The narrative parts of the Pentateuch also left their mark on Ben Sira. Genesis 1–3 is the basis for Ben Sira's reflection on God's Wisdom at work in the order of creation—the orderliness of the natural world, the authority of people over animals and God over people, and similar topics. It is possible, though contested, that 25:24 uses the sin of Eve and its consequences for the human race as a rationale for being wary of a bad wife. The encomium on the heroes of the Jewish people (44:1–50:29) is in many ways simply a laudatory summary of the stories of Noah, Abraham, Isaac, Moses, Aaron, and other patriarchs well known from the Hebrew Scriptures.

Ben Sira also occupied himself with "prophecies" (39:1). We must remember that for Ben Sira, the "prophets" included what Christians would call the Historical Books of Joshua through 2 Kings (the Former Prophets) as well as the books of Isaiah, Jeremiah, Ezekiel, and the twelve Minor Prophets (the Latter Prophets). Thus, the encomium on the Jewish heroes continues to

---

15. The study of these is somewhat complicated by the textual situation of Ben Sira. Ideally, one might read the Hebrew and search for recontextualizations of phrases or lines from the Hebrew Scriptures, but one frequently must rely on the Greek version and search out echoes in the Septuagint or in the Hebrew Scriptures on the basis of a "retroversion" of the Greek back into Hebrew.

summarize the principal actors in the Former Prophets, referring also to the ministries and contents of the Latter Prophets. Just a few examples of how Ben Sira interacts with these texts in his encomium are possible here. Sirach 48:1–11 provides an abridgement of 1 Kings 17–19, joining this Elijah tradition of the Deuteronomistic History with the tradition of Elijah's return expressed in Mal. 4:5–6. Sirach 48:10, in fact, draws attention to the fact that "it is written" that Elijah shall have a future role in sparing Israel from God's wrath by turning the hearts of children back to their parents. Sirach 49:4–7 refers to Israel's departure from God's way, with the result that they were overthrown by a foreign power. Here, Ben Sira gives a summary of Jeremiah's contribution:

> They gave their power to others,
>   and their glory to a foreign nation,
> who set fire to the chosen city of the sanctuary,
>   and made its streets desolate,
>   as Jeremiah had foretold.
> For they had mistreated him,
>   who even in the womb had been consecrated a prophet,
> to pluck up and ruin and destroy,
>   and likewise to build and to plant. (49:5–7)

In such brief compass, Ben Sira has brought together a summary of Jeremiah's message about Jerusalem's fate (Sir. 49:6; see Jer. 36:2–4, 29–32; 37:8–10; 38:3), the Jerusalem leaders' opposition to, and mistreatment of, Jeremiah (see Jer. 20:7–10; 37:13–16; 38:4–6), and Jeremiah's significance as expressed in his call narrative (introduced through the restatement of Jer 1:5 and recontextualization of Jer. 1:10 in Sir. 49:7) (Skehan and Di Lella 1987: 543).

The Latter Prophets infused Ben Sira with their passion for justice and care of the weak (see Hos. 6:6; Amos 5:21–24; Isa. 1:11–18; Mic. 6:6–8). His passion for the poor, the widow, and the orphan coupled with his declaration of God's visitation upon those who oppress such people (35:17–26) brings the proclamation of the Hebrew prophets into the wisdom tradition in a way that surpasses Proverbs. Similarly, Ben Sira's awareness of God's sovereignty over nations and the succession of nations (10:4–5, 8) has its roots in his reflection upon the scriptural history of Israel and the prophetic literature, in which the rise and fall of Israel's fortunes as well as the fortunes of the Gentile nations are attributed to God's disposition. This is a point of contact between Ben Sira and apocalypticism.

Ben Sira appears to have reflected on the narratives and speeches of the Hebrew Scriptures as a source for wisdom sayings, creating maxims from situation-specific judgments. David, for example, having offended God by taking a census of the people, is given the choice of being punished by seeing Israel overtaken by famine, pestilence, or foreign armies. He replies, "Let us fall into the hands of the Lord, for his mercy is great; but let me not fall into human hands" (2 Sam. 24:14). Ben Sira rephrases and expands this as a general saying: "Let us fall into the hands of the Lord, but not into the hands of mortals; for equal to his majesty is his mercy, and equal to his name are his works" (2:17).

Ben Sira reflected also on the psalms in worship and in study. Not only does he imitate their form (the corporate lament in Sir. 36:1–22 and the individual thanksgiving in Sir. 51:1–12, which draw heavily on the canonical psalms), but he also incorporates their content and spirituality, as, for example, their reflection on God's majesty and sovereignty as revealed in the wonders of creation (Sir. 42:15–43:33) and their celebration of Torah as the path for instruction and for living wisely (Psalms 1; 19; 119; cf. Sir. 6:37; 15:1).

A major source for Ben Sira remains, of course, the wisdom tradition of Israel (Sir. 8:8–9; 39:1–3), especially Proverbs (see Sanders 1983: 3–22; Skehan and Di Lella 1987: 42–45; deSilva 1996: 438–43). Both, of course, share the same literary forms, including the numerical saying, the instruction, the "better than" saying, and poetical devices (synonymous and antithetical parallelism being prominent in both). A good many of Ben Sira's proverbs are paraphrases of sayings from the canonical book of Proverbs.[16] The form may be changed (e.g., an observation may become an injunction), the content expanded, or scattered sayings on the same topic collected into one place. Shared topics include women (the good wife and her opposite, the adulteress); friendship; money and giving; wine; the inexpedience of violence, anger, and lying; the expedience of virtue; the necessity of parental discipline; the importance of marital fidelity; the dangers of the table of the rich and powerful; tensions between rich and poor; and the benefits of the pursuit of Wisdom. Both warn against arrogance, impropriety of speech, and dishonesty in business dealings.

Ben Sira often intensifies claims made in Proverbs so as to support his major goal of promoting complete dedication to God's law as a way of life. "Fear of the Lord," that is, caution with regard to provoking God by showing disregard for God, is no longer simply the beginning of wisdom (Prov. 1:7; Sir. 1:14) but also its fullness (Sir. 1:16), its crown (1:18), and its root (1:20). "Fear of the Lord" and "doing of the law" are emphasized by Ben Sira as part of his agenda to bring commitment to a particular ethnic tradition together with the more universalistic wisdom traditions at a time when the latter, taken alone, could facilitate assimilation and apostasy.

Formative influences are not always positive. Ben Sira is shaped not only by the traditions with which he agrees but also by those with which he takes issue. This seems to be the case in Ben Sira's argument against Job and Ecclesiastes with regard to the reliability of the basic convenantal principle

16. Skehan and Di Lella (1987: 43–44) provide tables of parallels.

that righteousness results in reward and transgression results in punishment (Boccaccini 1991: 114–19). In addition, Ben Sira appears to be correcting certain features of the apocalyptic writers, who, though not part of Ben Sira's scriptural tradition (Daniel's stories would be compiled and its visions composed in the decades after Ben Sira), were becoming important influences within Israel. Rather than locate human evil in any force outside of a person, as apocalyptists were doing by developing the story of the Watchers (cf. Gen. 6:1–4 with *1 Enoch* 6–36!) and the birth of demons who lead human beings astray or by overemphasizing divine determinism, Ben Sira places full responsibility squarely with people (15:11–20) (Boccaccini 1991: 105–7).[17] Ben Sira thus again reaffirms the Deuteronomistic tradition and its answers to life's questions.

While the Hebrew Scriptures permeate Ben Sira's thinking, he did not insulate himself from non-Jewish sources, for it is the responsibility of the sage also to travel "among the peoples of foreign lands to test what is good and evil among people" (39:4).[18] The advent of Greek rule and the cosmopolitan spirit of the age allowed for a freer flowing of ideas between cultures, and Ben Sira certainly took advantage of these developments in his proactive study of the wisdom of other cultures. In this regard, Ben Sira carries on in line with his own Jewish wisdom tradition, which had always been open to the ethical and practical teachings of other races in its quest for wisdom.[19]

Ben Sira studied the wisdom of the Greeks, particularly their practical wisdom such as is preserved in collections of advice, and incorporated several tenets of these traditions into his teaching. Carl Semler (1943) displayed the correlation between the "Sayings of the Seven Sages" compiled by Demetrius Phalerus (345–283 B.C.E.) and the contents of Ben Sira:

1. Keep secrets [of friends] hidden.
2. Speak little.
3. Be truthful.
4. Be not quick to speak.
5. Avoid wrath.
6. Give ground in a controversy.
7. Belittle no one.
8. Beware of wine.
9. Keep in mind that you will die.
10. Do not associate with persons unknown to you.
11. Do not too quickly believe what is said.

17. Although, Boccaccini's reading of Sir. 21:27 as a reference to Satan rather than merely to a human opponent whom one might curse because he or she opposes one's desires is unconvincing; see, better, Skehan and Di Lella 1987: 311–12.

18. Translation from Skehan and Di Lella 1987: 447.

19. "Ben Sira . . . is entirely open to hellenic thought *as long as it can be Judaized*" (Sanders 1983: 58); also Crenshaw 1981: 159.

12. Do not trust a conciliatory enemy.
13. Do not grieve over an irrecoverable loss.
14. Do not rejoice in the adversity of your neighbors.
15. Do not contend with one more powerful than yourself.
16. Should it be necessary, hand over your secrets to one most carefully chosen. (author's translation)

The correspondence with Ben Sira on each point is indeed remarkable. Semler refers the reader to the following passages, numbered respectively (his versification is emended to correspond with the NRSV): (1) 27:16–21; (2) 20:5–8; (3) 7:12–13; (4) 5:11–6:1; (5) and (6) 28:8–12; (7) 28:13–26; (8) 31:25–31; (9) 41:1–4; (10) 11:29–34; (11) 19:4, 15–17; (12) 12:8–12; (13) 38:16–23; (14) 8:6–7; (15) 8:1–3, 12, 14; (16) 8:18–19. The majority of these references elaborate at greater length what the Greek maxim briefly encapsulates, suggesting that Ben Sira was influenced by this, or a similar, Greek collection at an early stage in his research and incorporated its advice into his own curriculum.[20]

One especially important Greek resource for Ben Sira was Theognis's *Elegies*. The parallels between Ben Sira and the sixth-century-B.C.E. Greek author are sufficiently impressive to suggest that Ben Sira had probably read at least the first book of Theognis and found much material there to expand particularly the Jewish wisdom tradition's reflections on friendship and enmity (Sanders 1983: 29–38).[21] Theognis's elegies largely offer practical advice addressed to younger aristocrats, although they occasionally offer observations or complaints about particular female or male relationships he is enjoying— an aspect that would have met with a lack of sympathy on Ben Sira's part (Sanders 1983: 29–30). Nevertheless, Ben Sira sorted out the useful from the useless. Theognis advises caution about the company one keeps, avoiding the ill-bred, who would corrupt, and spending all one's time with the more noble, from whom one learns excellence while increasing one's network of friends and patrons (*Elegies* 29–38; 563–566). He praises the value of the faithful friend as being "worth his weight in silver, and in gold" (77–78)[22] and warns against leaving old friends for the sake of new ones (1151–1152). Theognis

---

20. Many of these maxims would have been reinforced by, or would have reinforced, precepts that Ben Sira would have also encountered elsewhere. *Instruction of Ani*, for example, also cautions against talking a lot or revealing one's plans or heart to strangers, who might use one's words to one's disadvantage, as well as instructs the pupil to prepare for death so as to be ready whenever the day comes (here, by preparing one's tomb while one is still young). What is remarkable about the "Sayings of the Seven Sages" is that Ben Sira's text resonates at some point with all the maxims therein collected.

21. See Middendorp 1973: 8–24 for an extensive list of alleged allusions to Greek literature in Ben Sira but also the critique of that list found in chapter 2 of Sanders 1983.

22. Translations from Theognis are taken from Dorothea Wender, *Hesiod and Theognis* (Harmondsworth and New York: Penguin, 1973).

counsels that, while one may have many comrades, one should choose only a few as confidants (115–116). He often speaks of the fair-weather friend, the one who stands by you while you are rich or fortunate but deserts you if your good fortune changes (79–82; 643–644; 697–698). Finally, he warns against getting angry with a friend or comrade over every injury, urging patience instead (325–328). Ben Sira incorporates all of this into his own curriculum (see Sir. 6:6–12, 14–15; 9:10, 15–16; 10:6; 12:8–9; 13:1; 37:12), and a perusal of these passages shows his agreement with Theognis on these points to be quite impressive.

Also noteworthy is the advice Theognis provides about speech and especially insulating oneself against folly where words are concerned. He advises his young friend to select only a few among his friends with whom to share his thoughts, since many people prove untrustworthy and will use the information you give them to your hurt (*Elegies* 73–76; cf. Sir. 8:17–19; 13:12–13). He also advises him not to be quick to believe slander against a friend (323–324; cf. Sir. 19:13–17). Another area of extensive overlap is the use of wine and care for one's behavior "under the influence." Wine should not lead a person to speak ill of a friend, and it is advisable not to engage in an argument where wine is poured (413–414; 493–496; cf. Sir. 31:31). Wine shows the character of a person just as fire shows the quality of gold and silver (499–500; cf. Sir. 31:26). Moderation in wine drinking is commended and overindulgence censured (509–510; cf. Sir. 31:27). Finally, both authors give advice about discerning the character of the person to whom one is considering to give a gift or show beneficence (105–112; cf. Sir. 12:1–7), urging that the good be sought out as recipients of one's favors and the bad, or "sinner," excluded, since one will never have a good return from that person. From these examples it becomes clear that Theognis's collection of (mostly) ethical and practical instructions served as an important resource for Ben Sira in his own study.

Most other influences from Greek literature require not literary awareness but only an attentive ear on the part of Ben Sira. In 14:18, for example, he uses the image of humanity as a tree that is always losing leaves (i.e., to individual deaths) to make room for new leaves found in Homer, *Iliad* 6.146–149 (Collins 1997b: 40). Ben Sira certainly would not have to have read the *Iliad* to learn of this image, for it would have been easy enough for him to learn this simile from common parlance, like so many today may quote a line from Shakespeare without ever having read him. Two other places where Greek ideas penetrate Ben Sira merit attention. The first is Ben Sira's description of the friend as a "second self" in 6:11, which is Aristotle's definition of a friend (*Ethica nichomachea* 9.4.1166.a30–31), even though Ben Sira uses it to describe the hypocritical behavior of a false friend (acting as a second self, that is, as a true friend). The second is Ben Sira's caution in 11:28, "Call no one happy before his death," which recalls the conclusion from Sophocles' *Oedipus the King*, where the chorus solemnly intones the moral "Count no person happy until he is dead." Again, both of these concepts could easily have come to Ben Sira through common parlance.

Ben Sira looked not only to the Greeks but also to the Egyptians for wisdom. Proverbs has given Ben Sira a good precedent here, as scholars have shown the degree of indebtedness of Proverbs to Egyptian wisdom sources. *Satire on the Trades,* earlier attributed to Duauf but more recently ascribed to Kheti (Pritchard, ed., 1950: 432), was probably used in some form (or, at least, a work that included essentially the same content) by Ben Sira as a resource for 38:24–39:11.[23] Both speak of the importance of leisure for learning the scribal arts, the arduousness of a variety of occupations involving manual labor, and the greater honor that comes to the scribe. Ben Sira's descriptions of the crafts of the farmer, smith, and potter include many specifics found in the older, Egyptian text, which, however, includes many more occupations in its litany and is much more negative about the value of these people and the quality of their life. Ben Sira exhibits here a considerably greater degree of respect for manual laborers and artisans than does his source (see 38:32, 34).

Sanders (1983: 64–103) has demonstrated the importance of the *Instruction of Phibis* (also known as Papyrus Insinger) as a resource for Ben Sira. *Phibis* is imbued with the same spirit of an "ethic of caution" that one finds in Ben Sira—caution in selecting and proving one's friends, caution in one's dealings with those in power, caution in table manners and eating, caution against being slandered or speaking slander. Ben Sira appears to have learned this mainly from *Phibis,* as well as to have incorporated several concepts that he found especially congenial to his own interests (such as material on filial duty as part of his expansion on the commandment "Honor your father and mother") or simply discerned to be true and worth passing on. This would include the advice in *Phibis* against being an overindulgent parent, warnings about the dangers of gluttony (and this specifically as a risk to health) and lust, praises of the merits of frugality, and cautions concerning the need for moderation in mourning.

Ben Sira's use of non-Jewish materials reveals his interest in carrying on in the tradition of his predecessors in the Jewish wisdom tradition, who had always been far-ranging in their quest for wisdom (again, see 39:4). His guiding principle in using foreign wisdom remains, however, its compatibility with the ultimate repository of wisdom: "the Book of the Law of the Most High." It is possible that, by drawing so heavily on the "best" of Gentile wisdom, Ben Sira hopes to show that "the best of Gentile thought is no danger to the faith but could even be incorporated into an authentically Jewish work, the purpose of which was to encourage fidelity to their ancestral practices" (Skehan and Di Lella 1987: 50).

---

23. Several works of this kind, particularly from the Nineteenth Dynasty (1350–1200 B.C.E.), are attested. The text of the *Satire on the Trades* can be found in Hallo, ed., 1997: 122–25 and Pritchard, ed., 1950: 432–34.

It would be a mistake, however, to end the discussion of formative influences on Ben Sira with the conclusion of the list of textual and other human influences. Describing the business of the sage, Ben Sira writes, "He sets his heart to rise early to seek the Lord who made him, and to petition the Most High; he opens his mouth in prayer and asks pardon for his sins. If the great Lord is willing, he will be filled with the spirit of understanding" (39:5–6a). From his personal testimonies, we know that Ben Sira followed this practice himself in his search for Wisdom: "While I was still young, before I went on my travels, I sought wisdom openly in my prayer. Before the temple I asked for her" (51:13–14a). This practice continued long into his search (51:19). We have also seen the impact of praying the canonical psalms on Ben Sira as he imitated their form and syntax in his own prayers. The description of the morning whole-burnt offering in 50:5–21 is the description of an eyewitness who, we can be sure, was no stranger to the temple. Ben Sira's wisdom was not merely the result of the study of texts, whether scriptural or otherwise, but also the result of a life lived piously in the presence of God. Liturgy, personal prayer, and seeking God were all potent influences on this sage as well, so much so that he held out no hope for the person who neglected these things ever to attain wisdom (15:7; 19:20–24).

Literary Forms and Argumentation

Ben Sira uses a wide array of literary forms in his collection as vehicles for the advice he wishes to transmit. Not only does one find the maxims and proverbs (usually comprised of two-line sayings), the instructions (the elaboration of a maxim or topic), and the observations typical of Jewish wisdom literature but also the disputation form, best attested in Egyptian wisdom literature (the form is found in *Instruction of Ani* and *Instruction of Amenemope*),[24] though not completely unknown to Israelite wisdom (see Prov. 20:22; 24:29; Eccl. 7:10).[25] This form begins with "Do not say," followed by the forbidden quotation or opinion, followed by a rationale for why that position ought not to be held or expressed (see Sir. 5:1–6; 11:23–24; 15:11–12; 16:17). Ben Sira also includes a psalm of lament (36:1–22), a psalm of deliverance (51:1–12), wisdom psalms (14:20–15:10; 34:14–20), an autobiographical poem (51:13–30), a prayer for a disciplined tongue and mind (22:27–23:6), and an encomiastic reflection on prominent figures of Israel's sacred history (44:1–50:24). He thus combines liturgical and laudatory literary forms with the forms more at home in wisdom literature.

24. *Instruction of Ani* and *Instruction of Amenemope* can be found in Hallo, ed., 1997: 110–22 and Pritchard, ed., 1950: 420–24.

25. Crenshaw (1975: 48–49) points out that the form is not complete in the two examples from Proverbs, since the rationale is not present.

Aristotle recognized the importance of maxims as argumentative tools, and wisdom collections may be regarded in one respect as a treasure trove of maxims that can serve as support for a great variety of arguments (*Rhetorica* 2.21). However, the composers of wisdom sayings, and especially the composers of the lengthier wisdom form called the "instruction," themselves display an attentiveness to argumentative strategies. Proverbs tends to be the simplest with regard to inner argumentation. Advice is often given without any supporting rationale. When a rationale is offered for a piece of advice or an exhortation (a thesis in the form of a proposed course of action or claim about value), it is usually drawn from the consequences, that is, by positing a result of heeding or ignoring that piece of advice (see, e.g., Prov. 22:22–23, 24–25; 23:10–11, 20–21; 24:15–16). A survey of Proverbs 10–11 reveals the following argumentative strategies:

1. The rhetorical device of antithesis ("antithetical parallelism")— 10:1–17, 19–21, 23–25, 27–32; 11:1–6, 8–9, 11–21, 23–24, 26–28
2. The rhetorical device of reinforcement ("synonymous parallelism")—10:18, 22; 11:7, 10, 25
3. Analogy or comparison—10:26; 11:22 (see also 25:11–14, 18–20, 25–26, 28)
4. Lesser-to-greater argument—11:31

Elsewhere in Proverbs one can find the use of characterization (the "scoundrel" in 6:12–15), often in conjunction with speech-in-character (*prosopopoiia*), as in the presentation of the adulteress in 7:10–20 or the sinner in 1:11–14.[26] These devices serve to hold up what is censurable or praiseworthy and help the pupil identify a dangerous influence quickly. A proverb can even be used as a maxim to conclude a short instruction, as in 24:30–34, which reuses 6:10–11 as the concluding maxim at 24:33–34. Claims to relative value are made using the "better than" sayings (see 17:1, 12; 19:1; 25:24).

Argumentation thus tends to be simple and undeveloped in Proverbs, advice or values being proposed rather than argued. This is somewhat surprising given the fact that the Egyptian literature that served as a source for some of the sages represented in Proverbs shows a more highly developed sense of argumentation and elaboration. The sixth chapter of *Instruction of Amenemope* (about seven centuries earlier than Proverbs) offers a well-developed example. The thesis of this chapter is presented in the form of a proposed course of action, urging the student not to move boundary markers of fields or other property. The argument develops thus:

---

26. In the latter passage, the teacher/father advises his pupil/son not to heed the enticing speech of sinners and then provides an example of that speech (*prosopopoiia*) followed by a characterization of how the sinner acts.

Thesis: Do not move boundary markers;

Rationale (from the consequences): The Moon-goddess will catch such a person;

Characterization of the boundary mover;

Restatement of thesis with rationale drawn from negative consequences: Do not move boundaries, "lest a terror carry you away";

Argument from the contrary: "The one who observes boundaries pleases god";

Argument from the expedient: Keeping a boundary sound makes for a sound being; it is profitable; one will find sufficiency from one's own field;

Conclusion in the form of several "better than" sayings, the first with a rationale drawn from the consequences (ill-gotten gains do not last).

This single example from *Instruction of Amenemope* brings together a number of important building blocks of an argument (thesis with rationale, restatement of the thesis) as well as argumentative topics (consideration of the contrary course of action, prediction of the consequences, consideration of the expedient) and forms (characterization), all in the service of promoting a particular kind of behavior. This is much more in keeping with Ben Sira's pedagogical strategy.

"When an intelligent person hears a wise saying, he praises it and adds to it" (21:15a). Attention to the rhetorical and poetical textures of the Wisdom of Ben Sira reveals something of how Ben Sira, having approved a saying ("praises it"), goes on and "adds to it." Ben Sira's textbook has much more in common with the instruction genre. Ben Sira's argumentation is influenced by the Egyptian literature and by Greek rhetoric at the level of the "elementary exercises." It would be foolhardy to suggest that Ben Sira had anything like a Greek education, but it is likely that in his travels and study he learned inductively much of what would be learned deductively by Greek students working through the *Progymnasmata*, or "elementary exercises" in rhetorical composition. The *Progymnasmata*, a curriculum preparing students for advanced training in rhetoric, already provides an impressive arsenal of arguments to use in support of a thesis or of a proposal, including the use of rationales, restatements, considerations of the contrary course of action or principle, analogies, arguments from historical precedents or examples, and appeals to maxims or other authoritative sayings or texts. Many of these were at work long before there was a tradition of Greek rhetoric, as in *Instruction of Amenemope,* but the Greek age brought a systematization to the art of argumentation that had been practiced for centuries, as well as to the kinds of rhetorical devices that could be used to embellish, support, and beautify an argument.

Like Proverbs, Ben Sira often provides rationales or arguments drawn from the consequences, which is appropriate for works seeking to give advice about how to behave. These rationales often employ topics of honor (1:13, 24; 3:10–11; 5:13–6:1; 6:29–31), promising that following the advice leads to a good name or the avoidance of disgrace, and expedience (see 2:6a; 3:5, 6a, 14–15, 28; 4:14, 28; 5:4–7; 7:1–3; 8:8–9). One argues from the expedient by showing that the behavior one proposes preserves the goods one currently has, opens the door to attaining more goods, and avoids harm or loss in the present or the future. The topic of the inexpedient is precisely the reverse. Here, goods are to be understood as the components of a happy life, such as long life, joy in one's children, preservation of property, and the like. Ben Sira also uses the topics of the right, the just, and the lawful, as when he urges reverence and care for one's parents (3:6b; 7:27–28) or avoidance of arrogance as an overstepping of what is proper for mortals to claim for themselves (10:6–7).

Ben Sira also employs the argument from the lesser to the greater (28:3–5), topics of refutation (15:11–20; 23:18–21), historical precedents (16:6–10; used here as proof of the reality of God's punishment of the wicked and hence of the inexpediency of sin), analogies (3:25, 30; 22:9), and comparison (22:11–12). The last passage merits special attention:

> Weep for the dead, for he lacks the light;
> and weep for the fool, for he lacks intelligence;
> weep less bitterly for the dead, for he has attained rest;
> but the life of the fool is worse than death.
> Mourning for the dead lasts seven days,
> but for a fool or an ungodly man it lasts all his life. (RSV)

Verse 11a posits the similarity between the fool and the dead person; vv. 11b–12 develop the dissimilarity, showing the state of the fool to be worse than that of the corpse.

In addition to these argumentative strategies, Ben Sira utilizes several rhetorical devices. Like Proverbs, but more extensively, he uses characterization (the one who fears God, 2:15–17; the enemy, 12:15–18; the rich person, 13:3–7; the miser, 14:3–10; the ungracious giver, 20:14–17; the husband of an evil woman, 25:16–18) and speech-in-character (*prosopopoiia:* the misguided person in 16:17–22; Wisdom in 24:3–22; the ungracious giver in 20:16). He makes frequent use of simile and metaphor (see, e.g., 21:8–10, 13–14, 16, 19, 21; 22:1–2, 6, 9; 25:20) and antithesis (sometimes crafted with repetitions or chiasm; see 21:15–16, 22–23, 25–26; 26:23–26). Within his lengthy encomium on Jewish heroes, Ben Sira even employs apostrophe, or a direct address to some character, at 47:14–21 (directed to Solomon, a lament for the patron saint of sages and scribes).

Ben Sira attends to the art of persuasion not only through logical argument and other rhetorical devices but also through decorating his carefully crafted instructions with appropriate ornamentation, especially through the use of alliteration and assonance, inclusio, and chiasm (see Skehan and Di Lella 1987: 63–74). In addition, repetition of key phrases or whole sayings provides a kind of poetic reinforcement of the argument. In 7:29–31, for example, the repetition itself carries the persuasion:

> With all your soul fear the Lord,
>   and revere his priests.
> With all your might love your Maker,
>   and do not neglect his ministers.
> Fear the Lord and honor the priest,
>   and give him his portion, as you have been commanded.

The first two verses set reverence for the temple staff in close connection with fear of the Lord and fulfillment of the core injunction of Deuteronomy (6:5), "You shall love the Lord your God with all your heart, and with all your soul, and with all your might"—an association made even stronger in the first half of the third couplet through abbreviation. The obligation to support the temple personnel, itself prescribed by Torah, is reinforced through association with another, more central prescription of Torah. Repetition also aids Ben Sira's promotion of particular values or behaviors in 12:1–7 (cf. 12:4, 7) and 22:27–23:6, where parallelism and repetition in 22:27 and 23:2, as well as 23:1 and 23:4, underscore the progression being made from discipline of the tongue to discipline of the mind, the source of speech; and 39:16–35, where repetition of two different refrains in 39:16–17, 21, 23–24 drives home Ben Sira's answers to the question of the rightness of God's created order. Repetition and parallelism are also used to reinforce a contrast being developed, as in 21:19, 21 and in 41:1–2.

An analysis of Ben Sira's instruction on Wisdom and the fear of the Lord (1:1–2:17) well displays the art of argumentation at work in this book. The opening poem on Wisdom (1:1–10) intimates the themes that will be developed in 1:11–2:17. The question of 1:6, "The root of wisdom—to whom has it been revealed?" is answered in 1:8–10. God is the one who is "greatly to be feared," and God gives wisdom to "those who love him" (1:8, 10). Thus, the question of 1:6 is answered at the same time that Ben Sira introduces the twin motifs that run throughout 1:11–2:17, namely, the fear of the Lord and the love of the Lord.

Ben Sira elevates the "fear of the Lord" throughout 1:11–2:17 as the core value to guide his students.[27] The repetition of this phrase is thick indeed

---

27. The expression comes from Proverbs and ultimately from Deuteronomy (see Deut. 10:12; also 4:9–10; 8:5–6).

throughout this section (1:11, 12, 13, 14, 16, 18, 20, 27, 28, 30; 2:7, 8, 9, 10, 15, 16, 17), showing how Ben Sira is drumming into his students' ears and minds this primary value as the epitome of their way of life, the motto they are to carry within them to their graves. In 1:11–13, he asserts the positive, honorable consequences that attend the fear of the Lord. In 1:14–20, he creates a beautifully balanced poem on the relationship of the fear of the Lord to Wisdom:

> To fear the Lord is the beginning of wisdom. . . .
> To fear the Lord is the fullness of wisdom. . . .
> The fear of the Lord is the crown of wisdom. . . .
> To fear the Lord is the root of wisdom. . . . (1:14, 16, 18, 20)

Interspersed between these lines, which fall upon the ear like a refrain, are assertions about the character and activity of Wisdom. Indeed, it is almost as if Ben Sira took a paragraph about Wisdom and inserted the fourfold emphasis on the fear of the Lord as the first and last ingredients of Wisdom.

Sirach 1:22–24 moves away from celebration of the fear of the Lord to more practical advice about patience versus hotheadedness, but the theme returns in 1:25–27, where Wisdom is linked closely with keeping the commandments (a theme that Ben Sira develops at considerable length), and in 1:28–30, where the author turns from positive exhortation to fear the Lord to dissuasion against acting contrary to the fear of the Lord. He supports this proposal with rationales drawn from the consequences (the threat of dishonor).

An exhortation to persevere courageously in the fear of the Lord in times of distress follows. Ben Sira taught in times when advantage might seem to come to those who grew lax about the fear of the Lord and disadvantage befall those who were strict in their observance. Indeed, this encouragement might well have seemed prophetic to those who remembered or read it just a decade following Ben Sira's death. Sirach 2:1–6 announces this proposition (i.e., remain steadfast in trust in times of trial) and already includes several rationales in support of it. First, he asserts that the consequences of steadfastness are positive, including topics of expediency (2:3a) and security (2:6a); second, he uses the analogy of gold being tried in the furnace as a means of affirming the value of testing (since it proves and makes manifest one's worth or honor) (2:5).

This is followed by a threefold repetitive series of declarations to "you who fear the Lord" (2:7, 8, 9), each one of which restates the thesis (i.e., the proposed course of action), the first two of which append rationales from the consequences of accepting or not accepting this proposition. Ben Sira now moves into a new argumentative strategy: appeal to historical precedent—in this case, more precisely, the lack of historical precedent. He invites the hearer to supply a single example where someone has persevered in trust and hope toward God and failed to come to a happy end (2:10).[28] He then uses an appeal to ancient authority by means of a recontextualization of key phrases from Exod. 34:6–7 and Ps. 103:8–9 (that God is "compassionate and merciful") as a confirmation of his thesis. The lack of historical precedents confirms the trustworthiness of this ancient testimony about God's character, which in turn confirms Ben Sira's proposal (2:1–6).

Ben Sira then considers the contrary course of action, which he has cast again as a threefold repetitive series of woes (2:12, 13, 14). Those who exhibit timidity, faintheartedness, and doublemindedness in times of adversity will come to grief. Topics of security (the lack of safety) and inexpedience (loss at the time of God's reckoning) are embedded in this censure of the contrary course. This is immediately followed by another restatement of the thesis, again in the form of a threefold repetitive series:

> Those who fear the Lord . . .
> and those who love him . . .
> Those who fear the Lord . . .
> and those who love him . . .
> Those who fear the Lord . . . (2:15, 16, 17)

The first two verses in this series speak in general terms about the characteristics of this kind of person, but the third verse, the climax, returns specifically to the topic of preparing one's heart and humbling oneself before God (terms forming an inclusio with 2:1–6; see especially "prepare" in 2:1 and "humiliation" in 2:4–5). The instruction concludes with an exhortation, the speaker now including himself, to "fall into the hands of the Lord, but not into the hands of mortals," employing thus another recontextualization of an ancient authority, this time 2 Sam. 24:14, with an expansion of David's rationale ("for [the Lord's] mercy is great").

This is a highly developed and ornamented argument, going well beyond anything previously encountered in the instruction genre, and one that shows many parallels with the argumentative strategies learned in the elementary Greek rhetorical exercises. This is not to claim that Ben Sira has learned from the latter directly but to highlight the complexity found in his instruction next to earlier examples of wisdom literature. Indeed, one can observe a noticeable confluence between the Near Eastern instruction and the Greek elaboration of a thesis that will make it increasingly suitable and natural for those students of the former also to use the tools provided by the latter.

28. This is not to say that the problem of theodicy does not concern Ben Sira. He knows that circumstances do not in fact always support the assertion that those who are faithful to God are never in dire straits or "forsaken," in appearances at least. In the context of this argument, however, he invites the hearers to draw on the testimony of their shared scriptural heritage—the record of those "generations of old" that do tend to bear out his assertion (cf. Ps. 37:25).

Ben Sira's Curriculum

Several aspects of Ben Sira's instruction merit special attention beyond the summary of contents given above. What follows cannot replace a thorough reading of Ben Sira but can serve to create a series of mental hooks on which to hang the material found therein, as well as to bring the reader into contact with some of the points of scholarly debate concerning this text.

Wisdom and Piety

Ben Sira was heir to the figure of Lady Wisdom in her personified form (24:1–22; 1:4–20), celebrating her as the first of God's creation (1:4; 24:3) and God's special gift for those who fear God (1:10, 26). Ben Sira was also heir to the tradition of the "fear of the Lord" as the starting point of one's journey toward Wisdom. He is not, however, content to limit its role to the foundational stage, presenting the fear of the Lord as "beginning, fullness, crown, and root" of wisdom (1:14–20) and the "whole of wisdom" as well (19:20). He also brings specificity to the fear of the Lord in a way not previously encountered in the Jewish wisdom tradition: it involves keeping the commandments (1:26; 2:15; 10:19) and honoring the Jerusalem priesthood through participation in the cultic system (7:29–31).

Ben Sira presses further, joining Wisdom and Torah observance with adamantine bands: "If you desire wisdom, keep the commandments, and the Lord will lavish her upon you" (1:26); "In all wisdom there is the fulfillment of the law" (19:20). Wisdom has lost her universalistic trappings and now resides in Jerusalem (24:8–12), living in the midst of the people God chose (24:12). Election theology and the (formerly) universalistic tradition of Wisdom are here joined. The hymn in praise of Wisdom in Wisdom of Ben Sira 24 closes with a demythologization of Lady Wisdom: she is none other than Torah (24:23) (Blenkinsopp 1995: 166).[29] This point of identification must not overshadow, however, the counterpoint between Wisdom and Torah elsewhere in Ben Sira. Torah is not the sum of Wisdom, though Wisdom resides in it and is found and known in the doing of Torah. Torah is also the educative discipline by which one lives wisely and arrives at Wisdom (6:18–37), the gift of God for Torah-observant people (Boccaccini 1991: 88–89, 94–99).

Wisdom teachers from antiquity frequently promoted their instruction by invoking the sanctions of honor and dishonor: following the path they advised was the way to honor, wealth, influence, and a noble end, while ignoring their precepts was sure to result in disgrace. Ben Sira also makes extensive use of this strategy, countering the tendency to view observance of Torah as an obstacle to

---

29. It would appear that this identification has survivals in later Jewish (rabbinic) reflection on the eternity of Torah and on Torah as the first creation of God—identification that loses, however, the asymmetrical relationship between Wisdom and Torah in Ben Sira (Boccaccini 1991: 88).

individual and national honor in the international scene. Thus, Ben Sira elevates the keeping of Torah as the sole determinative criterion for a person's honor, independent of social standing, wealth, and other markers of status (9:16; 10:19–24) (deSilva 1996: 443–49). Wealth gained through transgression of Torah becomes a source of dishonor (11:4–6; 13:24), but fidelity to the Mosaic law remained a source of honor even in poverty (25:10–11).

For Ben Sira, the path of Wisdom was the path of piety, and so he devotes a large portion of his book to instruction about pious living. Fear of the Lord entails a high regard for God's honor and caution about behaving toward God in a way that undervalues God. Hence, he advises that those who hope to be forgiven by God must forgive their fellow mortals (28:1–7). One must also not presume upon God's mercy by careless or willful sin (5:1–7; 21:1–2) but rather repent quickly and turn to obedience with redoubled effort (18:21; 21:1). The slowness of divine punishment does not mean that sin is without consequences, so one must repent swiftly and not turn again to the same sins (34:28–31). Righteous living, in fact, is seen as a way in which one can atone for sins (see, e.g., 3:14–15, 30)—a sentiment that may have aroused suspicion against this work among early Protestants. There is in Ben Sira, however, a balance between awareness of God's mercy and wrath, of the possibilities of forgiveness and judgment, that we might do well to recapture (5:5–6; 16:11–12). Jesus, Paul, and the author of Hebrews understood this balance, but it often disappears from the dynamic of discipleship taught in Christian churches and appears at its worst when a particular church's members are taught to assume mercy and forgiveness for themselves and wrath and judgment for nonmembers.

Ben Sira made wide room in his curriculum for the appreciation of the beauty and marvel of liturgy (see, e.g., 50:5–21). Fear of the Lord manifests itself not just in heeding the "ethical" but also the "cultic" law, particularly in giving tithes to God's priests (7:29–31) and making generous offerings to God (35:6–13). The teaching of the prophets undergirds Ben Sira's warning that God will not accept tithes from ill-gotten gains (34:21–24). Cheating one's fellow human being in business defiles wealth with its tithe. God cannot be bought off with such gifts and will not overlook the injustices that the gifts seek to hide or ignore (35:14–15). Just as ethics cannot be divorced from piety in Ben Sira's delineation of wisdom, so piety cannot be divorced from ethics. He commends moral conduct, returning a kindness, giving aid to those in need, turning a neighbor from sin, and doing the commandments in cultic terms as the sacrifices and offerings that please God (35:1–5); but such "rational and bloodless" oblations do not replace, but only complement, participation in the temple cult.

Like Tobit, Ben Sira elevates the importance of almsgiving, of showing concern for the poor and marginalized through the sharing of possessions and other works of mercy, which are to characterize the lives of the wise (3:30–4:10; 7:10, 32–36; 12:1–7; 29:8–13; 35:17–26). The cry of the poor is dangerous to the comfortable, since God stands ready to avenge those who are left without aid and oppressed. This danger looms not merely over the heads of those who actively oppress the poor (4:1–2; cf. 35:17–26) but also to those who fail to act to relieve them (4:3–5). Sins of omission are every bit as grave as sins of commission. Positively, those who are generous toward, and advocates for, the poor reflect God's character and are shown to be "like children of the Most High," enjoying the favor of the heavenly Father (4:10). Almsgiving becomes one's best defense against the unforeseen troubles awaiting one in the future, a veritable treasure against future need (29:8–13).

Ben Sira, as we have already seen, carves out an important place for prayer in the life of the wise person. It is through prayer, and not only study, that the sage attains intelligence and understanding (39:5–7). While it is important to seek the counsel of reliable people, the most reliable source of good counsel is prayer: "But above all pray to the Most High that he may direct your way in truth" (37:15; the climax to a section on discerning reliable advice). Prayer is the source of spiritual counsel here and not dreams, divination, and omens (34:1–8). As prayer has an important place in the life of the wise person (7:10), so prayers and personal expressions of his own piety are given a place in Ben Sira's writing. The psalm of deliverance in 51:1–12 especially bears witness to Ben Sira's reliance on God's help, and not merely his own wisdom, to rescue him from difficult situations. Ultimately, it is God, not one's personal savvy, who is one's surest defense.

Ben Sira's emphasis on piety, and especially the attention given to the cultivation of virtue and the rooting out of vice that is so important a part of the fear of the Lord, secured its place in the church, making it a resource particularly recommended to initiates in the faith. Ben Sira seeks to steer pupils away from damaging vices such as arrogance (10:6–18), stubbornness (3:25–29), slander (27:22–28:26), and self-indulgence (18:30–19:3), and point them toward the goal of prudence (8:1–19), humility (3:17–24; 7:16–17; 11:1–6), truthfulness (20:24–26), and mastery of the passions (6:2–4; 18:30–19:3), so that they may enjoy the good things life has to offer and avoid the grosser pitfalls. Undoubtedly, the center of Ben Sira's curriculum—the prerequisite for all other training—is instilling an understanding of the fear of the Lord and all its manifestations in the sagacious life.

Surviving in Society

As with Proverbs, Egyptian wisdom collections, and Greek advice collections, a principal component of Ben Sira's curriculum concerns negotiating life in the household and in the larger society to advantage. Because of this, Ben Sira's text can enrich the reader in two ways. First, he provides important windows into the social customs and realities of second-century-B.C.E. Jerusalem. Second, he has much sound advice for people in the twenty-first century, who still wrestle with being wise in their friendships and in money matters, being careful in speaking and weighing what is heard, and finding the balance between industry and leisure.

One area of life in which Ben Sira offers much advice is the realm of bene-faction and reciprocity, which is a prominent feature of the cultural and social landscape. Access to goods, relief, advancement, and social contacts came chiefly through a friend's or a patron's willingness to do a favor for someone. The favor was done freely and graciously, but the recipient was nonetheless placed in the debt of the giver. A person of virtue would seek to show gratitude for the favor and also to return the favor at some later date (even if that was only through public testimony or personal services).[30] Ben Sira advises his students to seek out people of good character for their gifts, and for him, one's character is revealed in one's commitment to the devout life (12:1–7). Those who do not hold to the covenant are to be excluded from one's benefactions, since they might well use them to hurt the giver. From those who share in the fear of the Lord, however, one can expect thanks, fidelity, and even the requital of favors—from God, if the human recipient is unable. He commends generosity, partic-ularly in public benefactions such as distributions of food, as the path to good repute (31:23–24) and upholds gratitude as the necessary response to those who have been generous and supportive (29:15–17). Bonds of reciprocity are inter-generational: children are to continue to "repay the kindness" of their parents' friends (30:6), such that gratitude does not die with the parents. Ben Sira in-structs his pupils not to sour generous acts by mingling them with reproach but rather to add kind words to kind acts (18:15–18). He warns them against ac-cepting favors from ill-bred people who give gifts only in order to get better ones in return (20:14–17)—the sort of person whom Seneca (*De beneficiis* 3.15.4) would censure centuries later as being an investor, not a generous giver. He is also aware of the darker side of patronage and reciprocity, as when people call in favors to subvert justice in the courts (19:25; i.e., having a judge render a fa-vorable verdict for one's clients or friends). The ultimate benefactor of all is God, and so one must be faithful in returning to God all the honor and service one can (35:12–13); in this way, one keeps the circle of favor alive with the most important Patron of all.

Another social institution that Ben Sira considers is the symposium, the banquet that consists of food, abundant wine, music or other entertainment, and cultivated conversation (31:12–32:13). Although the symposium would come to be most popularly associated with the Greeks, symposia are attested in Persian culture and its antecedents (as in Esth. 1:5–12; 5:4–8; 6:14–7:2; Dan. 5:1–4), Egyptian culture (3 Macc. 4:16–5:22; *Letter of Aristeas*), and Is-raelite culture (e.g., feasts such as Ben Sira envisions; see also Isa. 5:11–12; 1 Macc. 16:15–16; Mark 6:21–22). The social setting, then, should not be considered a Greek innovation, although it would be fair to say that as Pales-tine became increasingly Hellenized in the second-century B.C.E. on into the Roman period, its symposia took on more of a Greek hue.

---

30. For a fuller introduction to this facet of the Greco-Roman, including the Palestinian, environment, see deSilva 2000b: chs. 3–4.

Ben Sira advises moderation in eating and drinking, never allowing one's desire for the delicacies to interfere with social good feeling or with others' view of one as a moderate, well-bred individual. The most important thing at a banquet is not what one eats or drinks but how well one preserves one's image and manifests self-control. Ben Sira also cautions his students to be aware of the proper timing at a party. After the wine has freely flowed, one should not engage in a serious argument nor should one censure one's fellow in the midst of merrymaking; the time for the musicians is not the time for one to spout off one's "wisdom" so as to distract from the entertainment and others' enjoyment of it. Practical tips, such as being the first to finish eating, not being the last to go home, and not "crowding your neighbor at the dish" (31:14), help one avoid putting the belly and oneself ahead of good manners: "Judge your neighbor's feelings by your own, and in every matter be thoughtful" (31:15).

Ben Sira advises being a reliable friend and being on guard against fair-weather friends who might easily use one's trust and confidences to one's harm down the road. Equally useful are his cautions against believing slander against a friend or neighbor without checking out the facts (preferably by going to the person slandered; 19:13–17), his instructions not to reveal a friend's secrets or betray confidences (19:7–9), and his warnings against gossip (19:4–12). "Who has not sinned with his tongue?" (19:16). All those who cannot answer "I have not" would profit from pondering and frequently reviewing Ben Sira's advice. Since the topics of friendship and navigating through the turbulent waters of speech appear frequently in most wisdom and advice literature, they have already been discussed in the section "Formative Influences."

A noteworthy feature of Ben Sira's practical advice is his "ethics of caution" (see Sanders 1979)—an ethic shared by Egyptian and Greek advice collections (see "Formative Influences") but not meant to deter people from seeking honor and greatness so much as to help them achieve it without falling along the way. Ben Sira wants to show his students the "safe" and "smart" way to success, which naturally involves being cautious when rubbing shoulders with the great (who can make or break the upward climber; 9:13; 13:8–13), preventing disgrace or loss through forethought as far as possible (18:19–29; 38:18–23), and avoiding battles one cannot win (8:1–2, 12, 14).

Since one's household is the most important sphere of life, Ben Sira does not neglect to teach economics—the art of managing the household. He advises a posture of financial independence; one should not give others control over one's estate or oneself until after death (33:20–24)—a lesson King Lear learned to his harm—and should avoid relying on loans: "Whoever builds his house with other people's money is like one who gathers stones for his burial mound" (21:8). Many families have come to discover their mortgage and other payments to be nothing less than debt slavery, and so one should at least hear Ben Sira's caution and seek to minimize rather than build up debt. Another timely lesson from the ancient sage is his instruction about striking a balance between, on the one hand, conducting business endeavors and establishing a secure financial base and, on the other hand, not letting life pass one by in the process (11:10–19; 14:3–19; 22:1–2; 40:28–30). Such a word is almost prophetic to the increasingly frenetic, work-bound culture that corporate America, for example, has become.

With regard to household relationships, some of Ben Sira's advice has become passé. He attests to the continued institution of slavery in second-century-B.C.E. Palestine and urges both moderation in treatment of slaves (since they represent a substantial investment) and stern discipline for the disobedient slave (7:21; 33:25–33). His observations and advice concerning daughters poses its own problems (see "The Special Case of Women"), although it should remain a parent's concern to safeguard the chastity of *both* sons and daughters prior to marriage. He teaches the importance of bringing up well-disciplined children, warning his students of the heartaches that come from children who grow up without internalizing the core values that make for an honorable and happy life (7:23; 16:1–4; 22:3–6; 30:1–13; 41:5–9). Additionally, one of his first instructions concerns honoring one's parents especially through care and patience in their old age (3:1–16). With regard to both of these topics, Ben Sira also speaks prophetically to modern Western cultures, where intergenerational responsibility is deteriorating, both in the lack of personally involved training of children by parents and in the relegation of the aged to the margins of society. Ben Sira teaches an ethics of responsibility both toward parents and children that is increasingly a rare commodity.

The Special Case of Women

Ben Sira wrote many things that are good, noble, and edifying, but his disparaging remarks about women are not among them. Two of his most regrettable sayings are "The birth of a daughter is a loss" (22:3) and "Better is the wickedness of a man than a woman who does good" (42:14). Our purpose in this section is not to excuse Ben Sira but rather to understand him and his value judgments about women. Ultimately, Ben Sira is in many ways merely a spokesperson for widely held social mores concerning women. He is no reformer, no visionary, where gender roles are concerned, but neither is he an isolated misogynist. Rather, he is a mirror of the values he has observed at work and heard praised or censured around him.

Women are discussed only in relation to men (Bailey 1972: 56–58). Those qualities for which Ben Sira praises the "good" woman—such as silence, obedience, and modesty—are traits that also exhibit her subordination to a male's authority and the absence of a threat to male honor through a female's promiscuity (Bailey 1972: 60), which were quite pressing for males in these Mediterranean cultures. This helpful analysis invites further explanation. First, women were not viewed as independent entities but as in some sense "embedded" in a male. Men were the "actors," and women had a role and place only insofar as they were embedded in such an agent, whether a father or a husband. That Ben Sira speaks of women (good or bad) only as they relate to men reflects this cultural situation. Second, the female virtues promoted in Ben Sira—silence, obedience, and modesty (chastity)—are also the three central components of the model wife according to virtually all Greco-Roman era ethicists from Aristotle through Plutarch (see deSilva 2000b: 183–85).

Warren Trenchard's work (1982) merits special discussion here. Trenchard concludes that Ben Sira has a distinctly and personally negative view of women. He comes to this conclusion from his analysis not only of the obviously negative portraits of women (the adulteress, the bad wife, and the wayward daughter) but also of those portraits often taken to be positive and to provide balance to Ben Sira's negative portraits (the good wife, the mother). Especially cogent is Trenchard's analysis of how Ben Sira alters his source material (e.g., Proverbs) on the topic of women, showing how Ben Sira omits positive lines that might balance negative lines in the source, how he takes what was positive or neutral in the source and turns it into a negative saying. Trenchard is attentive both to what Ben Sira says and what he omits saying. Even at his most affirming, then, Ben Sira is still read as negative in his view of women. The good wife is "good" as long as she is useful and desirable to her husband, as long as she remains silent and submissive. Both as wife and mother, the woman is strictly the second in a pair with a male, embedded in and passive toward the husband and father. Fathers receive extended discussion, while mothers are mentioned only as the second line in a couplet exhibiting synonymous parallelism.

When speaking of the bad wife, Trenchard finds Ben Sira going well beyond his sources, using negative metaphors from the Old Testament that were not originally applied to wives. He is the first known author to lay the blame for the fall at Eve's feet (25:24), whereas Paul and the author of 4 Ezra (= 2 Esdras 3–14) still lay the blame on Adam's shoulders.[31] He gives more attention to amplifying the crime of, and proper punishment for, the adulter-

---

31. Levison (1985) contests the reading of Sir. 25:24 as an interpretation of Genesis 3, since this would conflict with Ben Sira's convictions expressed elsewhere about the origins of death as well as interrupt the flow of the passage. He reads it, rather, as a statement about any bad wife (Levison 1985: 621–22), adducing a parallel from 4Q184 to support his reading. The tense one gives to the sentence "From a woman is/was sin's beginning"—the verb "is" or "was" is lacking in the Greek but supplied by the translator—both determines and is determined by one's choice of Eve or the bad wife as the topic. Boccaccini (1991: 111) and Collins (1997b: 59) supply "was" and thus read 25:24 as a statement about Eve. Collins (1997b: 67) rightly points out, moreover, that Ben Sira speaks not of the fate of the unfortunate husband but of the fate of all. Since this verse explains why "all" die, it must be a statement about Eve (all the more as Ben Sira does not believe that "all" men have unhappy marriages). Camp (1991: 29) tries to allow both readings to stand side by side, and I believe this is wisest given not only the ambiguity of the verse but also the rhetorical contribution such an ambiguity would make. Ben Sira invites husbands not to repeat Adam's failure, not to allow their wives to reject their authority and lead them into dangerous places. The rather uncharitable conclusion to the section, "If she does not go as you direct, separate her from yourself" (literally, "cut her off from your flesh,") (25:26), is precisely what Adam did not do, to the detriment of all. He places every disobedient (or even displeasing) wife in the role of Eve and every husband in the role of Adam, giving such husbands the chance—and the ideological armament—to assert themselves over such wives.

ess than the adulterer (9:8–9). Daughters—and we can only hope that Ben Sira had none—are presented only as a source of anxiety and fear on account of their (perceived) brazen sexuality (26:10–12; 42:9–12). Proverbs says nothing of daughters (which may bespeak its own kind of misogyny), but Ben Sira emphasizes the need to watch over daughters and safeguard their virginity. One finds nothing in the Old Testament or other available wisdom texts to match the contempt for a daughter's lack of sexual modesty and self-control as one finds in Sir. 26:10–12.

Trenchard has been criticized for being personally biased against Ben Sira (Skehan and Di Lella 1987: 90–92), with the result that his major thesis concerning Ben Sira's *personal* negativity toward women has not won broad assent. Di Lella is able to adduce Greek and Latin literature that is equally if not far more negative and cynical in its evaluation of women than anything one finds in Ben Sira (save for the infamous "Better is the wickedness of a man than a woman who does good" [42:14]). As stated at the outset of this section, then, Ben Sira's words on women, which one must grant are more negative than Old Testament sources, still provide more of a window into the patriarchal dynamics of the intertestamental period than into the mind of an idiosyncratic misogynist. Trenchard's study cautions us not to take Ben Sira as a spokesperson for everyone living in his time, but one might find both those men who are more positively disposed toward women (reading Proverbs more positively) *and* those who are even less well disposed toward them.

It is perhaps in Ben Sira's attention to the sexuality of women that we may penetrate further into the inner "logic" of patriarchal fears about women. Mediterranean and Near Eastern cultures certainly viewed sexuality as an expression of intimacy between two people, but there was another important dynamic overlaying sexuality: honor and disgrace. A man's honor was not just a matter of his individual achievements or merits but also involved the behavior of the members of his household, those "embedded" in the male head of the household—wife, minor children, and other dependents. If his wife or daughter compromised her chastity through extramarital intercourse, then the male head of the household lost face—he was made, in Ben Sira's words, "a laughingstock to [his] enemies, a byword in the city and the assembly" and was "put to shame in public gatherings" (42:11).[32] Ben Sira's rather rude depiction of the daughter's openness is a natural result of the cultural fixation upon female sexuality as a point of vulnerability for the male in whom the female is conceptually embedded. In such a world, a daughter was, in theory at least, a potential liability to a father's honor. In reality, however, the personal

32. It is often taken for granted that the male, on the other hand, would win honor by sexual conquest outside the bounds of marriage. While this perhaps may be true for the modern Mediterranean cultures studied by cultural anthropologists, we must not forget the central sanctions against adultery and premarital intercourse in the Jewish tradition nor assume that these could be violated lightly.

virtue of the daughter would determine whether or not her birth was a favor
from God or a loss, and Ben Sira's blanket consignment of all daughters to
the debit column is at best an unhelpful hyperbole and at worst an unmerited
vote of no confidence in women's commitment to virtue. In light of 26:10–
12, it is, sadly, likely to be the latter.

Several other useful contributions to this conversation have been made
more recently by two scholars. Lewis Eron (1991) suggests that the negative
view of women demonstrated in Ben Sira and near-contemporary literature
(1 Esdras and *Testament of Judah*) derives from the threat of the passions to a
male person's mastery of himself. Greed, alcohol, and sexual passion were
three great threats to a male's self-control, and so money, wine, and women
were regarded as negative influences. In the case of the last, the desire to avoid
the domination of the passions "provided a psychological and philosophical
justification for the exclusion of women from positions of power and influence in public and private life" (Eron 1991: 46). A woman in charge of males
would be symbolic of the passions in charge of reason. This insight helps to
connect Ben Sira's warnings against giving oneself over to lust and other passions with his view of women as ever-available agents for passion's dominance
and may be regarded as an ancillary factor in Ben Sira's thinking. Claudia
Camp (1991) has added to this discussion by connecting Ben Sira's increased
anxiety about the sexuality of wives and daughters with the loss of control that
males were coming to experience in the public sphere, a sphere that was rapidly changing and expanding with the opening up of Judea to Greek culture
and politics. This made a man's control over his household and possessions
all the more crucial to the preservation of his sense of manliness and honor
and hence the threat of female sexuality all the more grave.

Ben Sira's remarks about women, then, are to be understood as a reflection
of the social and cultural world in which the sage lived. For better or for
worse, he accurately identifies the components of the contemporary ideal for
the good woman and the ways in which women could become detriments to
a man's honor and the honor of his household. Ben Sira's observations and
evaluations are thus best understood as functions of the way in which honor
and sexuality were linked in the ancient world and the way in which control,
authority, and manliness were conceptualized and symbolized in that world.
It is, however, Ben Sira's absolute lack of visionary critique of that world in
regard to women and their worth that led the rabbis and early Christians to
seek his worth in other parts of his book.

The Encomium on Jewish Heroes

The last major section of Ben Sira's work is the famous hymn in praise of
the illustrious figures of Israel's history, from the earliest heroes of Genesis
through the recently deceased high priest, Simon II (219–196 B.C.E.). Ben
Sira's work is unique among other surviving collections of Jewish wisdom in-

sofar as it includes a hymn celebrating the deeds not of God but of human heroes of the past (Lee 1986). Lee (1986) has argued that the whole of Sir. 44:1–50:24 should be understood as an encomium celebrating the high priest Simon II, with the praise of the heroes from Noah through the prophets serving merely as the introductory praise of Simon's ancestors. While it is true that the Greek encomium included the praise of the subject's parents and family line as an aspect of the honor and excellence that the subject enjoyed by virtue of his or her birth, it is more than a little forced to argue that 80 percent of an encomium would be devoted to that topic. Additionally, the fact that *synkrisis*—the explicit comparison of the subject of an encomium to figures of the past to demonstrate his or her equality or superiority—is entirely absent tells against seeing this passage as an encomium on Simon per se. As Collins (1997b: 99) observes, "The fathers are praised in their own right, and not merely as a buildup for Simon."

The lengthy passage is a specimen of epideictic rhetoric, which is primarily concerned with strengthening the audience's commitment to certain values of particular importance for the culture (deSilva 1996: 450–53). The genre of the encomium was used to rouse the hearers to emulation of the person or people praised in the speech, since hearing others praised would lead them to seek to embody that which was praiseworthy. Ben Sira's goal is not merely to celebrate Israel's heritage, although promoting ethnic and national pride in the shadow of the dominant Greek culture would certainly help his goal of building commitment to that heritage and its customs.[33] More specifically, however, this encomium reinforces the values promoted throughout the work, especially loyalty to the Mosaic covenant. In 44:1, the "famous men" (Greek) are really the "men of *hesed*, of covenant loyalty" (Hebrew) (Siebeneck 1959: 417; Skehan and Di Lella 1987: 500; MacKenzie 1983: 168). Ben Sira aims at "motivating his young hearers to similar loyalty" as was found in these persons who achieved an honorable and lasting name and remembrance (Mackenzie 1983: 168).

Ben Sira chooses the exemplary figures and enumerates their praiseworthy (or, in a few cases, censurable) acts so as to highlight Torah obedience as the path to honor and lasting distinction. Abraham enjoys incomparable honor (44:19) because "He kept the law of the Most High, and entered into a covenant with him; he certified the covenant in his flesh, and when he was tested he was proved faithful" (44:20). Fidelity to God and perseverance in the covenant (see 2:10; 41:19), including such ethnically defining marks as circumcision, which would come under serious question in the decades to follow, are here shown to lead to a praiseworthy remembrance. Phinehas distinguishes himself through "being zealous in the fear of the Lord" (45:23). The source of his honor is his commitment to the exclusive worship of the God of Israel and his maintenance of strict boundaries between the people of God and the

---

33. This purpose is advanced in Mack 1985.

Gentiles (see Num. 25:1–9). Caleb is held in high repute for his steadfastness before God's command even when the opposition seemed overwhelming. God's elevation of Caleb and Joshua above their whole generation shows "how good it is to follow the Lord" (46:10). Ben Sira hopes that his teaching will lead to the fulfillment of his prayer "May the names of those who have been honored live again in their children" (46:12). He fervently hopes that his pupils, the children of such committed ancestors, will continue in their ancestral ways, embodying the values, behaviors, and commitments that marked the distinguished people of Israel's past.

Ben Sira's praiseworthy models are reinforced by brief considerations of their negative counterparts. Solomon, whose youth is marked by all the fine virtues that would make for eternal fame, mars his honor through the indiscretions of his old age. Dishonor comes from transgressing the boundaries between the chosen people and the Gentiles (47:19–21), even as maintaining these boundaries brought honor to Phinehas. Among the kings of Judah and Israel, only David, Hezekiah, and Josiah receive high praise. All the others receive lasting disgrace and are passed over with the notice "They abandoned the law of the Most High. . . . They gave their power to others, and their glory to a foreign nation" (49:4–5). Forsaking Torah, they lost their sole claim to honor. This sounded a timely warning for the inhabitants of Jerusalem flirting with radical Hellenization.

This encomium also enacts and elevates the "collective memory of Israel" (Boccaccini 1991: 122–23). Ben Sira does not leave room for compensation in a life after death. Rather, righteousness and ungodliness meet their respective rewards and punishments within this life and in the memory that the person leaves behind. Boccaccini's observation is therefore quite apt: in a book in which one's memory, or the name and reputation one leaves behind, becomes a major motivation for choosing covenant loyalty and integrity rather than more shady paths to wealth, enjoyment, and power, it is strategic to display that collective memory at work. The hearers can choose, therefore, to "be in that number" or to be excluded and forgotten—to die a sort of second death—on account of their failure to distinguish themselves among the righteous.

The theme of priesthood also lends consistency to this encomium. The praise of Aaron and Simon, the first and the most recent of the high priests, receives the most space, and the enumeration of Aaron and Phinehas as second and third in "glory" (45:20, 23; next to Moses, 45:2) gives to priests a prominent place in the roster of honor. Ben Sira is especially impressed by the cultic performances of these priests—Aaron's vestments and ministrations being available only though the study of the Torah but Simon's being available for Ben Sira to witness as a worshiper at the temple. Simon II is praised first for his architectural improvements to Jerusalem—fortification of the walls and provision of a water supply (50:1–4)—the sorts of accomplishments for which leaders most often receive praise in the Greco-Roman period. Ben

Sira quickly segues, however, to Simon's liturgical panache and devotes most of this section to a description of an actual temple service (50:5–21). Most scholars have assumed that the liturgy described here is the Day of Atonement sacrifices, based on the heightened tone of solemnity evoked by Ben Sira's description, the reference to the high priest coming "out of the house of the curtain" (50:5), and the reference to the pronunciation of the Divine Name in the priestly blessing (50:20–21) (Box and Oesterley 1913: 293; Lehmann 1961: 117). Fearghas O'Fearghail (1978), however, put forward a strong case for viewing this passage as a description of the morning *tamid* or whole-burnt offering.[34] This liturgy, described in great detail in the Mishnah (in the tractate *Yoma*), features an incense offering (which involved the officiating priest's entry into the Holy Place, part of the "house of the curtain" but not behind the inner curtain), the burnt offering, and then the drink offering. The order of service in Sir. 50:5–21 follows this procedure perfectly, beginning with the priest's return from behind the first curtain after the incense offering is completed, and does not match any part of the rituals specifically connected with the Day of Atonement. The high priest did not ordinarily (but on special occasions would) perform the daily whole-burnt offering, which is perhaps why Ben Sira's description of this *tamid* is all the more solemn and striking.

The encomium on the Jewish heroes, then, serves to focus the hearers on their particular Jewish heritage, encouraging them to take pride in their ancestors, to stand in awe of their own traditions of liturgy and worship, and to see the loyalty to the ancient covenant as the path to their own honorable remembrance in the future. In all its particulars, it points the students to see the Jewish way of life as a thing of great value and as the way to establish their own value in the eyes of the present generation and the generations yet to come.

Theological Questions of the Day

Wisdom literature had already moved from the practical, with Proverbs, to the philosophical, with Job and Ecclesiastes, and Ben Sira gives attention to both aspects of the expanding purview of the sage. He wrestles with the questions of sin and human responsibility, on the one hand, and God's omnipotence and sovereignty, on the other. He seeks also to discover the signs of God's justice at work in the human sphere, rewarding those who are faithful to the covenant and punishing those who neglect God's law and justice. If the prayer of Wisdom of Ben Sira 36 derives from Ben Sira's own hand, this would show that his interest in this second question pertains not only to the case of individuals but also to the case of the nation of Israel.

Ben Sira believes human beings to be capable of doing what is righteous or doing what is wicked: God "created humankind in the beginning, and he left

---

34. Accepted by Skehan and Di Lella (1987: 550–51) against the majority view.

them in the power of their own free choice" (15:14). The echo of Gen. 1:1 ("in the beginning") may be meant to call the hearers' minds to the story of Gen. 3:1–8, humankind's first exercise of their will in the direction of sin. This same choice, however, remains available to every person: "If you choose, you can keep the commandments, and to act faithfully is a matter of your own choice" (15:15). Ben Sira thus categorically denies that God's sovereignty is somehow an excuse for sin (15:11–13) and reaffirms the basic principle of Deuteronomy: life and death are placed in front of each person, who has the power to choose and thus the responsibility for his or her actions (15:16–17; cf. Deut. 30:19).

Another passage in Ben Sira, however, stands in apparent contradiction with this one and in agreement with the opponents whom he refutes in 15:11–12 (Collins 1997b: 81, 83).

> In the fullness of his knowledge the Lord distinguished them
>   and appointed their different ways.
> Some he blessed and exalted,
>   and some he made holy and brought near to himself;
> but some he cursed and brought low,
>   and turned them out of their place.
> Like clay in the hand of the potter,
>   to be molded as he pleases,
> so are all in the hand of their Maker,
>   to be given whatever he decides. (33:11–13)

Paul's use of the potter image in Rom. 9:11–24 does in fact ascribe to God the initiative of making certain individuals receptive to mercy while hardening others against obedience, with the result that some are blessed and others destroyed. One must guard against reading Ben Sira through a Pauline lens, however, and drawing from that the conclusion that he contradicts himself.

The intertexture of this passage calls to mind Abraham (who is blessed and made great), the priests (who are made holy and allowed to draw near to God), and the Gentiles, especially the Canaanites, who indeed are turned out of their place (Skehan and Di Lella 1987: 400–401). "Ways," in this instance, would refer to destinies rather than ethical choices, and the passage would serve to affirm God's sovereign rights as these pertain to election theology. As the author of the Wisdom of Solomon later would explain, it was still within the Canaanites' power to find and obey God, such that their eventual destiny did not determine their choices or remove their responsibility (Wis. 12:3–13:9). Ben Sira's apparent contradiction is part and parcel, then, of a Judaism that affirms election theology in God's choice of Abraham and Israel while at the same time affirming covenant theology within Israel, such that obedience and transgression are both within the Israelite's grasp.

How, then, do God's promises to reward the godly and punish the impious manifest themselves? Two noteworthy passages that contribute to Ben Sira's answer are 40:1–11 and 41:1–13. Both sections speak of the lot of all human beings under the primal curse that befell Adam: hard labor and death (40:1, 11; 41:4, 10; cf. Gen. 3:17–19). Indeed, both sections uphold the affirmation that "whatever comes from earth returns to earth," a clear allusion to Gen. 3:19. Within this scenario common to all people, however, God finds ways to distinguish between the godly and ungodly, to make the righteous fare better than the sinful. The first, which is far less convincing, is that all of life's ills strike the sinner "seven times more" than they strike the pious (40:8–10). Bad things may happen to good people, but they happen far more frequently and far worse to bad people. More solid is Ben Sira's second claim: the righteous enjoys an honored reputation, a "virtuous name" that "will never be blotted out," whereas the sinner's memory will be cursed and his or her children amount to nothing (41:5–13). This sounds a very important theme in Ben Sira, for whom there is postmortem justice only in the lasting good name of the righteous and the oblivion or infamy that befalls the sinner.

In general, Ben Sira, like Proverbs, affirms that the virtuous and God-fearing life is accompanied by the good things that make life enjoyable for its duration (e.g., 30:21–25; 40:26–27), whereas neglect of God and the behaviors that please God result in failure to attain the components of a happy life. Ben Sira is aware, though, that many sinners enjoy life all too well, and so he suggests that God brings on the wicked such anxiety and wretchedness at death as obliterates all memory of happiness for them (11:21, 25–28) (Crenshaw 1975: 54). This has the advantage of not being readily open to disconfirmation but is still a counsel of despair. Ben Sira also knows that bad things happen to the godly. For such situations, Ben Sira can only counsel perseverance—primarily because God's good purposes must eventually be revealed at "the appointed time" (39:17, 34) when "all such questions will be answered" (39:17). This calls for trust in the goodness of God, even when that goodness is obscured (2:1–17, especially 2:17). In this regard, he has learned something from Job, who, though he basically accused God of making a terrible mistake in his case, was still committed to a belief that God was just and that everything would be straightened out in the end. He also prepares his students to regard suffering as probative and formative for the seeker of Wisdom (2:1–6; 4:15–19; 6:22–31) (Boccaccini 1991: 118–19; Crenshaw 1975: 55). The endurance of distress thus becomes not a matter of punishment for sin, or a lapse in God's justice, but an opportunity for character formation and for proving oneself committed to God and worthy of God's mysteries.

At a grander level, Ben Sira sees in God's creation a certain mysterious order and balance that all works together to accomplish God's just and good purposes. The teaching of the "opposite pairs" in creation, including good and bad, is a part of this exploration (33:14–15; 42:24–25)—perhaps an echo of the stoic teaching that one member of a pair of opposites, like justice, cannot exist without the other member of the pair, injustice (Collins 1997b: 85). Ben Sira sings of all aspects of God's creation serving God's purposes, both to benefit the godly and to punish the wicked (39:25–31; 40:8–10). God's ways remain, to the human mind, mysterious and inscrutable, but the final posture of the human being as creature must be awe and praise for God in God's works and a yielding of one's own questioning and doubting to confidence in the greater wisdom and authority of the Creator (39:16–35).

Ben Sira does not leave room for God's justice to work itself out in the postmortem punishment of the wicked or reward of the righteous. Several scholars have tried to make a place for these beliefs in Ben Sira's text. Francesco Saracino (1982), for example, argues that Ben Sira's encomium on the ancestors gives evidence of a belief in the resurrection. He looks particularly at the expression "may their bones send forth new life" (or, "may their bones flourish") at 46:12 and 49:10, noting how the vegetative metaphor of flowering is also used in Isa. 66:14 and *Testament of Simeon* 6.2 and would come to be a metaphor for resurrection in rabbinic texts. He suggests that this expression denotes the resurrection of the people named (i.e., the judges and the prophets). He looks also to the passage on Elijah, who was expected to return to restore Israel (48:10; Ben Sira weaves Mal. 4:1–6 into the "history" of Elijah's accomplishments, past and future), and the notice that Elisha's corpse "prophesied" (48:13) as indications of resurrection.

In all these passages, however, Saracino is forcing the notion of resurrection where other interpretations are far more natural. Ben Sira prays that the prophets and judges will be a source of strength for the new generation of Israelites and nothing more. This is most apparent in the way 46:12b limits and interprets 46:12a: the life Ben Sira hopes the judges will have is in the present and future generations of their children, the Jews. It is their "name," their honor, their reputation, their character that will be reincarnated in each successive generation of courageous, Torah-observant, God-fearing Jews. The "new life" does not come to their bones but derives from their bones as a sort of spiritual nutrient for the new generations growing from the holy soil of the land of Israel. In *Testament of Simeon* 6.2, moreover, the hoped-for flourishing of Simeon's bones also refers to the multiplication of descendants rather than a personal afterlife for Simeon; and it is not at all clear that resurrection is meant in Isa. 66:14, which simply could refer to the restoration of Israel as God drives back their enemies. Wisdom of Ben Sira 48:11 is far too textually uncertain and obscure to be used as evidence of Ben Sira's expectation of a resurrection. The Elisha story refers, however, to the resuscitation of a corpse that fell upon Elisha's grave. Even if the Hebrew text reads "his flesh was created anew" rather than "his flesh prophesied," this probably would have resulted from a scribal confusion about the revivification of the corpse that fell on Elisha's grave rather than an alleged belief in a general resurrection to everlasting life on Ben Sira's part.

To be sure, Ben Sira's theodicy was not sufficient to meet the demands of the decades that would follow. When torture and death were specifically the result of covenant loyalty, the belief that God would indeed provide a life of blessedness beyond death for the loyal rose to prominence (as in 2 Maccabees 7 and Daniel 12). It would finally fall to the Wisdom of Solomon to bring personal eschatology and wisdom traditions into one stream. It is noteworthy that both the first translator and the later copyists were as uncomfortable with Ben Sira's silence about resurrection as are some modern scholars. Ben Sira's own grandson appears to have brought the hope of the resurrection into his grandfather's work at 7:17b and 48:11b. The longer GII recension expands this tendency at 2:9c; 16:22c; 19:19 (Collins 1987: 95). Comparison with HTI shows these to be secondary additions and no part of Ben Sira's thought or original work.

The manifestations of divine justice—rewards and punishments—belong first to this life, if only in the psychological realm (nightmares and anxiety multiplied for the wicked) (Crenshaw 1975: 57, 59–60,) and after death in the name one leaves behind, which can be an honorable reward or a second death (Boccaccini 1991: 119–24). Nevertheless, it remains better to continue to resist the domination of the passions (18:30–31), to struggle to find mastery, with God's help, over the lips and the thoughts (22:27–23:6), to guard oneself from bad influences (12:13–14; 13:1; 22:13), to walk in moderation and justice with regard to wine, women, and wealth, to live the life of piety and covenant loyalty (Boccaccini 1991: 109–13). Such a way of life will result in happier circumstances in this life and the gift of a good name remembered forever in the congregation.

Ben Sira looks forward not only to the demonstration of God's justice toward each individual and in every circumstance "at the appointed time" (39:16–35) but also to the vindication of Israel's nationalistic hope. This is expressed mainly in 36:1–22, a prayer for God's intervention on Israel's behalf. The election theology that lies behind 33:7–13 also emerges forcefully here, as Ben Sira cries out for the vindication of the Israelite worldview in the eyes of the Gentiles, mainly through God's holding the latter also accountable to God's laws and standards. Ben Sira wants to see the truths he holds dear active in his situation, to see the tradition he affirms vindicated in practice (note especially 36:21). Benjamin Wright (1999: 90) correctly observes, "Ben Sira has a fundamental difficulty with foreigners ruling over God's people at any time," which is contrary to his conviction that Israel was chosen as "the Lord's own portion" (17:17), under God's direct sway. Events after the time of the high priest Simon II might have increased Ben Sira's dissatisfaction. During the first decade of its control of Judea (198–188 B.C.E.), the Seleucid government provided some tax relief, a welcome change from the more burdensome taxes imposed by the Ptolemies. When Rome imposed a heavy tribute on Antiochus III, however, these financial burdens were passed on to the Seleucid client states and taxation again became onerous (Wright 1992: 92).

Whether or not the domination of the Gentiles was light or burdensome, however, it would still fundamentally be viewed by Ben Sira as "out of order"—a view that would only increase exponentially in the decades and centuries to come.

Influence

Judaism

Despite the fact that the Wisdom of Ben Sira remained a book that did not "defile the hands," that is, was not considered sacred Scripture, it continued to be a respected and weighty resource for the leaders of rabbinic Judaism. Ben Sira is frequently quoted in the Babylonian and Jerusalem Talmuds, the midrashim, and later rabbinic literature.[35] Often he is quoted by name with a passage that comes from his actual work, which shows that the rabbis continued to read Ben Sira. Sometimes the saying is attributed to a later rabbi, but the quotation is clearly recognizable as something from his book. In this case, Ben Sira can be seen to have influenced the named rabbi, but the distant source is no longer remembered. Occasionally, he is quoted by name, but the saying attributed to him is not to be found in the Wisdom of Ben Sira. One rabbi even quotes a line from Ben Sira as contained in "the Writings" (*Kethubim*),[36] the third part of the Jewish canon, and this has been taken as evidence that at some point Ben Sira was contained in the canon and afterwards excluded. It is more likely, however, that the rabbi thought he was quoting from Proverbs.

From these quotations, we also find some hints as to why Ben Sira would be read and respected but not regarded as sacred and thus fit for reading and exposition in worship. One rabbi laments that, were Ben Sira's book not excluded from the canon, he and his colleagues could expound upon the many "good things which are in it," giving a string of quotations from Ben Sira's advice against lust, having strangers in the house, and revealing secrets too freely. It would appear that Ben Sira's disparaging words against daughters weighed heavily against him as the sacredness of his work was evaluated.[37] Neither the rabbis nor the early church would sanction his devaluing of daughters.

Ben Sira appears also to have left a mark on the Day of Atonement liturgy as celebrated in synagogues (the *Avodah*), an important part of which involved a description of the temple liturgy conducted on the Day of Atonement (a way in which Jews remained connected with that critically important

---

35. An excellent collection of these quotations, with notes, can be found in Schechter 1891.
36. *b. Babba Qamma* 92b (see Schechter 1891: 690).
37. Both found in *b. Sanhedrin* 100b (see Schechter 1891: 691–92).

ritual long after the temple was destroyed and sacrifices there ceased). The opening sections of Ben Sira's praise of the ancestors (44:1–45:26)—the recitation of sacred history from Adam through Aaron—appear to have provided the model for the opening recitation of this same history in the *Avodah*, which preceded the description of the Day of Atonement liturgy (taken from the Mishnah). Ben Sira's description of Simon the high priest emerging from behind the curtain and giving the benediction (though reflective of the daily burnt-offering liturgy rather than the Yom Kippur ritual) appears to have left its mark on the effusive description of the high priest emerging from the Holy of Holies in the *Avodah*. Thus, Ben Sira's encomium on the ancestors made a lasting impression on the most solemn liturgy of the Jewish calendar.[38]

Early Christianity

Ben Sira had a thorough and profound impact on the authors of the New Testament. As a wisdom teacher lodged in Jerusalem, Ben Sira was well placed to leave his mark on the soil in which the church would take root two centuries later. We are concerned here not so much with literary dependence as with influence. None of the New Testament authors actually quotes Ben Sira, but several of the more prominent among them (Matthew, Luke, Paul, James) weave into their own teaching lessons already attested in the writings of the Jerusalem sage. It is likely that Ben Sira's material was studied by the religious leaders and teachers, who in turn wove the more beneficial aspects of his teaching into their own synagogue homilies (perhaps without even attributing them to Ben Sira),[39] and thus made them available for the Jewish leaders of the early church to weigh and use in their own reformulation of the way of life that honored God.

The parallels between Ben Sira and the sayings of Jesus preserved in Matthew and Luke are so striking and numerous as to render it certain that Jesus Ben Joseph knew and valued some of the sayings of Jesus Ben Sira (though again, one need not go so far as to claim that Jesus had read and studied Ben Sira's writings directly). The sayings and instructions compiled by Matthew in the Sermon on the Mount contain numerous points of connection with Ben Sira. Jesus' method of expounding on the law by extending the range of the commandments (e.g., extending the prohibition of murder to include anger and demeaning speech) appears already in Ben Sira, for whom economic oppression is prohibited by the commandment against murder (34:25–27). Additionally, Ben Sira had already linked setting aside anger against a neighbor with obedience to the commandments of God (Sir. 28:7; cf. Matt.

38. This is developed at length in Roth 1952; see also the note in Box and Oesterley 1913: 298.

39. The ongoing influence of Ben Sira even after Rabbi Akiba's criticism of his work makes it highly likely that he enjoyed an even greater influence before leading rabbis tried to discourage the overuse of this book.

5:21–22). Both Ben Sira and Jesus urge giving to the one who asks (Sir. 4:4; Matt. 5:42) and claim that mirroring God's generous love makes one like a child of God (Sir. 4:10; Matt. 5:45). Both warn against vain repetition in prayer (Sir. 7:14; Matt. 6:7); both address God as Father in prayer (Sir. 23:1, 4; Matt. 6:9; cf. James 3:9). One development in Ben Sira is especially arresting. The Jerusalem sage had taught that those who hope for forgiveness from God must not harbor unforgiveness against mortals like themselves. If humans expect God, whose honor is incomparably greater than theirs, to forgive offenses against God's Self, then they must not presume to cherish grudges or else they will "face the Lord's vengeance" (Sir. 28:1–5; cf. Matt. 6:12, 14–15; 18:23–35).

Torah itself, of course, already commands almsgiving as an essential aspect of piety and covenant loyalty, and other intertestamental writings, such as Tobit, keep this value in the public consciousness, but Ben Sira promotes the giving away of money to the needy, somewhat ironically, as "laying up a treasure" for oneself:

> Help the poor for the commandment's sake, and in their need do not send them away empty-handed. Lose your silver for the sake of a brother or a friend, and do not let it rust under a stone and be lost. Lay up your treasure according to the commandments of the Most High, and it will profit you more than gold. Store up almsgiving in your treasury, and it will rescue you from every disaster. (29:9–12)

This instruction is remarkably close to Jesus' teaching that giving away one's possessions to those in need results in laying up a treasure (Luke 12:33; 18:22; Matt. 19:21), whereas the stash of money that sits idle rather than being spent in works of mercy ends up being lost to rust, worms, moths, or thieves (a natural expansion of Ben Sira's "rust"; Matt. 6:19–21; Luke 12:33). The most noticeable difference is that Ben Sira sees this treasure as a source of help against future times of adversity in this life (whether through divine aid as recompense or through the rallying of one's neighbors to aid so generous a soul), whereas Jesus regards this treasure as one's reward in heaven, a sort of eschatological "individual retirement account." This is due, of course, to the fact that Ben Sira holds no view of postmortem rewards and punishments, whereas Jesus is fully committed to the belief in an afterlife where God's perfect justice is manifested.

Two other points of contact are worth pondering. First, Jesus' parable of the Pharisee and the tax collector (Luke 18:10–14) may have grown out of Jesus' reflection on Sir 7:8–9: "Do not commit a sin twice; not even for one will you go unpunished. Do not say, 'He will consider the great number of my gifts, and when I make an offering to the Most High God, he will accept it.'" This is precisely the reasoning of the Pharisee in the parable, who stands before God with head erect and declares, "I fast twice a week; I give a tenth of all my income" (Luke 18:12), thinking himself to stand in a special place in God's favor far above other people (Luke 18:11). Jesus declares, however, that the tax collector, who merely lamented his sinfulness and asked for God's mercy, is the one who received forgiveness and not the Pharisee, who thought that his laurels assured him of God's favor. Luke's introductory interpretation of the parable (Luke 18:9) brings out two important aspects of the parable: the negative value of despising one's fellow Jew and of being complacent in regard to one's righteousness before God. It does not highlight, however, the third and perhaps, in Jesus' setting, most central aspect: the question of who receives forgiveness for his or her sins. The Pharisee never asked for forgiveness but assumed it on the basis of his works of piety, which is exactly what Ben Sira said one must not do.

Finally, Jesus' invitation to all to come to him, take up his yoke of instruction, and find rest with little labor (Matt. 11:28–30) brings together elements from Wisdom's invitations to do the same (Sir. 6:24–28; 24:19; 51:23–27). Such an invitation, combined with Jesus' frequent use of maxims, sayings, and instructions in his own teaching, may suggest that one important category Jesus gave his contemporaries for understanding his ministry was that of a wisdom teacher or sage, one who showed the way to live well pleasing to God and advantageously among people. All these parallels taken together strongly suggest that Jesus took up the best of the Jewish wisdom tradition into his proclamation of the life that pleased God and that Ben Sira contributed much that was good to this proclamation.

The connections between Ben Sira and the Epistle of James also command attention, which is not at all surprising given James's placement within Palestinian Jewish Christianity, indeed, in Jerusalem itself for the duration of his ministry as leader of Jewish Christianity. His location at the hub of Judaism, the respect he commanded from many non-Christian Jews on account of his piety, and his own identity as, in effect, the leader of a school within Judaism make him a good candidate for studying or conversing with others about the Jewish ethical tradition and hence learning more about Ben Sira than he might have gleaned from his brother's preaching. James's instructions concerning the dangers of the tongue build on the foundation laid by Ben Sira, who also noted that the unbridled tongue was a source of ruin (Sir. 22:27; cf. James 3:6). Ben Sira marveled that from one source, the mouth, could come both wind to fan a fire and spit to extinguish a flame (Sir. 28:12) and proceeded to urge putting a fence around one's tongue so as not to sin or err with it. James also is struck by the anomaly that one source should put forth blessing and cursing and urges that the tongue be reserved for the former (James 3:9–12). James even recontextualizes (i.e., incorporates without citing) Ben Sira's proverb "Be quick to hear, but deliberate in answering" (Sir. 5:11), acting as a wise man who "approves a proverb and adds to it": "Let everyone be quick to listen, slow to speak, slow to anger" (James 1:19). The two authors share other concerns as well. Both point out that God is not the cause of sin or enticements to sin, which rather are lodged in human choice (compare Sir. 15:11–20 with the abridgment of this teaching in James 1:13–14). Both regard testing as the natural outcome of walking in God's ways and urge the acceptance of testing as an opportunity for the cultivation of steadfastness and for being proven acceptable (Sir. 2:1–6; James 1:2–4; also compare Sir. 2:5 with 1 Pet. 1:7).

Other voices appear to have been less profoundly shaped by Ben Sira, although occasional correspondences do appear. John, for example, may have learned about the benefits of a clear conscience from Ben Sira:

> Happy [favored, honored] are those whose hearts do not condemn them, and who have not given up their hope. (Sir. 14:2)

> Beloved, if our hearts do not condemn us, we have boldness before God; and we receive from him whatever we ask. (1 John 3:21–22)

Noteworthy here is the specific linkage of hope, or confidence in God's help, with the conscience that is aware of not having offended God.

Paul, likewise, echoes Ben Sira from time to time, as in his exhortation "Rejoice with those who rejoice, weep with those who weep" (Rom. 12:15), which recontextualizes Ben Sira's advice to "mourn with those who mourn" (Sir. 7:34) and amplifies it by including the positive counterpart. Paul also uses the image of the potter and the potter's right to work the clay any way he or she pleases as an image for God's sovereignty over human beings and their destinies:

> Will what is molded say to the one who molds it, "Why have you made me like this?" Has the potter no right over the clay, to make out of the same lump one object for special use and another for ordinary use? (Rom. 9:20–21)

The image was used in precisely that way by the Jerusalem sage:

> Some [human beings] he blessed and exalted, and some he made holy and brought near to himself; but some he cursed and brought low, and turned them out of their place. Like clay in the hand of the potter, to be molded as he pleases, so all are in the hand of their Maker, to be given whatever he decides. (Sir. 33:12–13)

It is difficult to avoid the impression that Paul learned this from Ben Sira, especially given Paul's acquaintance with the other apocryphal wisdom text, Wisdom of Solomon. Both may well have been on Paul's reading list during his days as a student in Tarsus and Jerusalem.

One final text to consider here is the *Didache*, the first Christian manual on ethical conduct, worship, and church life (ca. 100–125). The compiler(s) of this manual clearly valued Ben Sira's instructions about almsgiving. *Di-*

dache 4.5 incorporates Ben Sira's admonition "Do not let your hand be stretched out to receive and closed when it is time to give" (Sir. 4:31) and promotes almsgiving as a "ransom for sins" (*Didache* 4.6; cf. Sir. 3:30). *Didache* 1.6 also cites a proverb, the second half of which preserves an admonition from Ben Sira: "Know to whom you are giving" (Sir. 12:1)—so as to be a good steward of charity, bestowing it on the needy and virtuous rather than allowing oneself to be taken advantage of (Skehan 1963b). The formative influence of Ben Sira on Christian ethics was thus very strong from the beginning, and he continued to enjoy a strong influence in the centuries that followed (see Schürer 1986: 3.1.207–8; Box and Oesterley 1913: 298–303).

Baruch

8

"Return with Tenfold Zeal to Seek God"

The Book of Baruch, sometimes referred to as 1 Baruch to distinguish it from a number of other pseudepigrapha ascribed to Jeremiah's secretary, is a combination of three distinct literary forms: a prayer of confession and plea for help, a sapiential poem, and a prophetic poem written as Zion's lament and a corresponding encouragement addressed to Zion. United into a single work, these different parts reenact the process of sin, punishment, repentance, renewed obedience, and restoration articulated in Deuteronomy 28–30, exemplified throughout the Deuteronomistic History (Joshua through 2 Kings), and embraced by prophets such as Jeremiah. Dependent on Old Testament texts in nearly every verse, Baruch presents a summary statement of the entire Hebrew scriptural tradition, focusing its readers on those aspects of the tradition that the authors and final redactor considered most salient and helpful for the survival of Jewish identity and culture in a situation of Gentile domination.

Structure and Contents

Baruch opens with a narrative resembling Israelite historiography, recalling a public reading of the law followed by a response of penitence (Bar. 1:1–14; cf. 2 Kings 22:8–13; Nehemiah 8–9). This narrative creates the fictive setting for the whole, presenting Baruch, as its author, reading it to the exiles in Babylon five years after the destruction of the temple (i.e., 582 B.C.E.). The exiles send the book, along with a collection, to the priests and people in Jerusalem, requesting that sacrifices and prayers be made on their behalf. The first major section (1:15–3:8) contains the prayer of confession that the priests and the remnant in Judea are to use to entreat the Lord's favor for the scattered nation. In the prayer, God is exonerated as just in all that has happened to Israel, which claims full responsibility for breaking the covenant and inviting all its curses upon its head, which are recalled in detail. The suppliants beg God's help for the sake of God's reputation among the nations, as this is tied to the fate of the people called by God's name, and on account of God's compassion and promise to hear God's people when they "come to themselves" in exile and turn to God with a humble and obedient heart.

The prayer itself is well structured. The repetition of 1:15 at 2:6 is often taken to divide the prayer into two halves, the first being appropriate for the Jews in Judea, the second being appropriate for the exiles. Such a division is, however, unsatisfactory, leaving 1:15–2:5 with no supplication at all. Rather, 2:6 is a resumption that signals the closure of the confession prior to the petition, which is found in 2:11–18. In 2:19–35, the motivation for the prayer is clarified by disallowing any claim to merit on Israel's part, which claims only God's own compassion and desire to rehabilitate God's people. The prayer is closed in 3:1–8, not so much by resuming the petition as by affirming that the preparation of the people's hearts that God set as prerequisite to restoration (2:31–34) has been accomplished (3:7).

Baruch 3:9–4:4 is a self-contained sapiential poem, similar to Proverbs 8, Job 28, and Wisdom of Ben Sira 24. Its purpose, in and of itself, is to focus the hearers on the distinctive heritage of Israel as the place where Wisdom is to be sought and found and explicitly to deny that other nations have found the key to Wisdom. In effect, it reproduces Deut. 30:11–20 in a wisdom discourse mode, containing the same topics of a happy life following upon obedience to the commandments of God and disaster following upon disobedience, as well as the proximity and availability of sound instruction in the law of Moses (Bar. 3:29; Deut. 30:12–13). In its present context, it functions as an affirmation of, and encouragement to pursue, the sole path to national recovery: wholehearted pursuit of the doing of God's law, which is identified with Wisdom.

In the final section (4:5–5:9), a personified Jerusalem gives expression to her grief at seeing her children taken off into exile and encourages them to return to God's ways, assured that God will deliver them (4:5–29). After Zion's speech, the voice of the prophet delivers oracles of consolation in the form of an apostrophe (a direct address to an impersonal object) to Jerusalem (4:30–5:9), assuring her that Israel's oppressors will themselves be judged by God with fire and desolation, while all the scattered Jews are gathered together into Jerusalem, whose glory and splendor will be fully restored. The consolation of Jerusalem shows signs of conscious structuring, chiefly through the repeated exhortations (an imperative with a vocative, as in "Take courage, O Jerusalem"), the first three encouraging the scattered "children" of Jerusalem (4:5, 21, 27), the last encouraging Jerusalem in the light of the return of her children (4:30, 36; 5:1, 7) (Moore 1977: 313; Harrington 1999: 98–99). Additional signs of literary crafting are found in the reversal of events in 4:11 and 4:23: "With joy I nurtured them, but I sent them away with weeping and sorrow" (4:11); "For I sent you out with sorrow and weeping, but God will give you back to me with joy and gladness forever" (4:23). Also, the motif of the change of garments reveals the author's attempt to weave together the lament and the consolation: "I have taken off the robe of peace and put on sackcloth for my supplication" (4:20); "Take off the garment of your sorrow and affliction, O Jerusalem. . . . Put on the robe of the righteousness from God" (5:1–2).

Baruch is generally regarded as a composite work, a main break being easily identified by the shift from prose to poetry at 3:9, from prayer to didactic wisdom speech (Moore 1977: 303).[1] The first half is dominated by the prayer of confession, and the second half further subdivides into the Wisdom poem and the consolation of Jerusalem (Pfeiffer 1949: 413; Schürer 1986: 3.2.734). The sections also draw upon very different pools of primary resources: Deuteronomy, Jeremiah, and Daniel for 1:1–3:8, wisdom literature for 3:9–4:4, and Second and Third Isaiah for the lament and consolation of Jerusalem (Whitehouse 1913: 570; Oesterley 1935: 262). An additional indicator of composite authorship is found in the different attitudes toward the dominant Gentile power: in the opening prologue, the readers are enjoined to pray for the longevity of Nebuchadnezzar and his son; in the consolation of Jerusalem, God's decree is not longevity but deserved destruction for the oppressive overlords (Whitehouse 1913: 570; Oesterley 1935: 261).[2]

Baruch is one book where a theory of literary partition has the advantage of a strong explanation for the editor's strategy and rationale. The movement of the whole book was noted as early as Theodoret in the first half of the fifth century C.E.: "The admirable Baruch, having inserted this prayer of the people into the book, put [there] also the divine answer" (Pfeiffer 1949: 412). Baruch opens with a narrative description of the situation to be remedied: the scattering of Israel and the loss of national independence. The confession interprets that state of affairs in the terms familiar from Deuteronomy 28–29, representing in itself the kind of act of repentance that would begin to effect reversal. The change in attitude from 1:15–2:26, an outright confession of sinfulness, to 3:1–8, in which the speakers begin to distance themselves from their ancestors' sin, reflects a further step in this movement through the stages of punishment and reversal laid out in Deuteronomy 30. Far from being "self-righteous" (Moore 1977: 293), Bar. 3:7–8 rather is reflective of God's accom-

---

1. I do not regard 1:15–3:8, however, as "prophetic," although the prayer is rich in intertexture with the prophetic books. Baruch 4:5–5:9 does reflect both the form and content of Hebrew scriptural prophetic discourse.

2. Both scholars also suggest that the first and second sections identify the cause for disaster and the path to restoration in different and irreconcilable manners, 1:15–3:8 stressing sin against God as the cause for misfortune, 3:9–4:4 emphasizing the forsaking of the path of Wisdom as the way to misery. When it is recognized, however, that for the poet of 3:9–4:4, forsaking Wisdom is synonymous with not following Torah, this alleged inconsistency disappears. Both sections share the viewpoint of Deuteronomy, the former expressing it quite overtly with extensive intertexture from Deuteronomy, Jeremiah, and Daniel 9 (the latter two texts themselves infused with Deuteronomy's model of cause and effect), the latter playing a variation on that particular theodicy in the key of Wisdom.

plishment of God's promise to change the hearts of the exiled community and restore it to obedience in the fear of the Lord (Deut. 30:2, 6, 8). The central section of Baruch holds up Torah, which is near to every Jew to take up and practice, as the solution for the plight of domination and dispersion. It is by turning to Torah that the prayer of 1:15–3:8 will come to be answered and that the courage and confidence offered in 4:5–5:9 seized upon. Internalizing the solution presented in 3:9–4:4—commitment to follow Torah as the path to life, the path of Wisdom—is the means by which the children of Jerusalem can receive the encouragement of Zion herself in 4:5–29, as well as the grounds for confidence that the promises of 4:30–5:9 will indeed come to pass.

Textual Transmission

Baruch is preserved chiefly in the Septuagint tradition (Codices Vaticanus, Alexandrinus, Venetus; Sinaiticus is defective) (see Ziegler 1957). Impressive arguments have been put forward suggesting that the second half of Baruch (3:9–5:9) was translated by a translator other than the one responsible for Bar. 1:1–3:8, who frequently is identified with the translator responsible for the second half of Jeremiah (Thackeray 1903; Tov 1976). If this is true, it has important implications for the history of the composition of Baruch, suggesting that 3:9–5:9 was added to 1:1–3:8 after a "book of Baruch" became known, and for the history of Baruch's reception, since its close connection with Jeremiah helped its acceptance as Scripture in the early church. All the known versions, from the Syriac and the Syro-Hexaplar (the work of Paul of Tella, ca. 617 C.E.) (Whitehouse 1913: 577), to the Old Latin, to the Arabic, Ethiopic, Coptic, and Armenian, depend on the Greek. Only the Syriac version has been viewed by some scholars as a possible window into the hypothetical Semitic original (Whitehouse 1913: 577–79; Burke 1982: 12–14).

Although no ancient Hebrew manuscript of any part of Baruch has surfaced, scholars are agreed that at least 1:1–3:8 was composed originally in Hebrew (Whitehouse 1913: 571–72; Tov 1975: 3–7; Moore 1977: 257–58; Schürer 1986: 3.2.735). This part is easily retroverted into Hebrew, the Greek giving every impression of being a wooden translation of a Semitic original. Moreover, out of place words or odd phrases in the Greek can be clarified by positing a mistranslation from a Hebrew original. Some examples: The Greek reads *manna* in 1:10, where *minchah*, or "grain offering," would have been more appropriate. The word "desert" or "desolation" in 2:4 might represent an original Hebrew *shammah*, which could be translated either "desert" or "horror," the second perhaps being more appropriate in this context. The "prayer of the dead of Israel" in the Greek of 3:4 is most likely a misreading of an original Hebrew "prayer of the men of Israel," the words for "dead" and "men" being differentiated merely by vowel pointing (Pfeiffer 1949: 416–17).

Several scholars argue that 3:9–5:9 was also composed in Hebrew (Torrey 1945: 62–63; Harwell 1915; Pfeiffer 1949: 416–17), but here there is greater debate. The Greek of this section is more idiomatic, with fewer obvious, wooden translations of Hebrew idioms (Pfeiffer 1949: 419). There are also a number of places where the author seems to follow the Septuagint readings of the Old Testament passages being recontextualized, over against the Masoretic Text (Whitehouse 1913: 573; Tov 1975: 7 and n. 5). This could also be due, however, to a Greek translator who, recognizing the scriptural allusions and being familiar with their equivalents in the Greek Scriptures, was influenced by the latter when translating. The close correspondence between the Greek versions of Bar. 4:37–5:8 and *Psalms of Solomon* 11.3–8 struck Whitehouse (1913: 572–73) as the strongest proof for the Greek origins of the last part of Baruch.

In favor of a Hebrew original for 3:9–4:4, scholars point to the likelihood of a Palestinian provenance of this part. When 3:22–23 claims that Wisdom has not surfaced in Canaan, Teman (in Edom), Merran (Midian?), or any of the descendants of Hagar, the author is identifying the neighbors of Palestine as the foil for the Jews, who did receive Wisdom in Torah (Pfeiffer 1949: 420). As with 1:1–3:8, although to a lesser extent, retroversion into Hebrew and contemplation of some alternative vocalizations of certain words lead to the solution of some oddities in the Greek, which is another strong indication of translation (Pfeiffer 1949: 420–21). Finally, the ability of scholars to translate these chapters back into Hebrew with some form of poetic meter strengthens the suggestion of a Hebrew original (Harwell 1915).[3] The absence of a Hebrew manuscript may indicate merely the neglect into which the book fell in Palestinian Jewish circles.

Author, Date, and Setting

The composite nature of the book makes discussions of authorship and date rather complex. The book's claim to be authored by Baruch, the companion of the prophet Jeremiah, is a literary fiction. There is no reliable evidence that Baruch ever went to Babylon; more likely, he remained in Egypt with Jeremiah and the Jewish community there. No temple vessels (a replacement set made by Zedekiah after the initial raid of the temple but before its final destruction) are likely to have been returned five years after the temple's destruction but only following Cyrus's edict allowing Jews to return to Judea and to rebuild their temple. Finally, it is difficult to believe that a contemporary of Nebuchadnezzar would mistake Belshazzar for his son and immediate successor (1:11).

---

3. Burke's (1982) less rigid metrical translation being preferred to Harwell's (1915) more forced meter; see Moore 1992c: 700–701.

Scholars therefore have searched for other clues to dating the book (and its component parts), but the lack of historical reflections of the authors' circumstances makes this difficult. Sending money to Palestine for sacrifices (1:10) presupposes a functioning cult in Jerusalem (Bissell 1899: 414), but Jer. 41:5 provides evidence that sacrifices and cult continued in some form on the site of the ruined temple (Whitehouse 1913: 570). Beyond this, the only setting that is presumed is the Jewish Diaspora and the Gentile domination of the homeland, circumstances that characterized most of the period from 587 B.C.E. to 1948 C.E., with the exception of the revival of a native dynasty under the Hasmonean household from about 141–63 B.C.E. An absolute *terminus ad quem* for the work is fixed by the quotation of Bar. 3:35 in Athenagoras's *Plea on Behalf of the Christians,* a work dated to 177 C.E. (Moore 1977: 260).

Scholars therefore turn to signs of literary dependence for clues to dating the book. Baruch and Daniel share the historical error of thinking Belshazzar to be Nebuchadnezzar's son (Dan. 5:2, 11, 13, 18, 22; Bar. 1:11), as well as the greater part of the content of the prayer preserved in Dan. 9:4–19 (cf. Bar. 1:15–3:8). The prayer in Baruch is probably based on the prayer found in Daniel 9 and not vice versa, since the author of Baruch expands the material known from Daniel 9 with material drawn from Jeremiah and Deuteronomy. Thus, at Bar. 1:21–22 and 2:3–4 the author suddenly departs from recontextualizing Daniel material in favor of Jeremiah material, with the latter taking over completely in Bar. 2:20, after the Danielic prayer has been exhausted.

This dependence could suggest a date after 164 B.C.E. (the date for the redaction of Daniel) for Bar. 1:1–3:8 (Torrey 1945: 63; Oesterley 1935: 259). The situation is considerably more complex, however, since Daniel 9 may actually contain a prayer that predates the final redaction of Daniel by several centuries, with the result that Bar. 1:15–3:8 could be dependent on the prayer now found in Daniel 9 and nevertheless originate in the fourth or third century B.C.E. (Pfeiffer 1949: 415; Moore 1977: 291–93). Bernard Wambacq (1959: 475) has shown that the prayer in Baruch has edited out all the references in Dan. 9:17–18 to the ruined state of the city of Jerusalem and its temple, with the result that Baruch would contain the later form of the prayer and would have been edited in a time when the city was inhabited and the temple standing and in operation. This would at least establish a postexilic date for the first half of Baruch (Whitehouse 1913: 574).

A less fruitful venue of investigation has proceeded on the assumption that the conditions of exile and dispersion reflected in Baruch must reflect some recent disaster or significant displacement in the life of Israel. Thus, Nickelsburg (1984: 145) suggests that Nebuchadnezzar and Belshazzar are "stand-ins" for Antiochus IV and his son Antiochus V, in which case the book urges quiet acceptance of, rather than provocation of, Antiochus V's governance. Wambacq (1966) argues that the siege of Jerusalem by Pompey, with the deportation of dissidents and invasion of the temple precincts effected by him, would have been the most likely background for the redaction and unifying of Baruch, the prayer needing no updating, the Wisdom poem requiring only the insertion of 3:10–13 to connect it with an event of defeat and exile. Others regard a date after 70 C.E. as the most natural for, at least, the final redaction of Baruch, with Vespasian and Titus being thinly veiled by Nebuchadnezzar and Belshazzar (Whitehouse 1913: 569, 574–75; Oesterley 1935: 263–65). Stories about the consumption of a child by its mother during the siege of Jerusalem in 70 C.E. are told by Josephus (*Jewish War* 6.201–213), but since both Deuteronomy and Jeremiah speak of this in connection with the consequences of breaking the covenant, the author of Baruch need only be acquainted with those texts and not an actual siege. It is certainly true that the first destruction of the temple provided "a thin historic drapery which invests the greater tragedy of the Jewish race in A.D. 70" (Whitehouse 1913: 569) in the apocalypse *2 Baruch*, but this assertion is far from convincing with regard to Baruch. The main problem with this line of investigation is that exile and dispersion are facts of Jewish existence that could be lamented anytime from 587 B.C.E. on, irrespective of new deportations (all of which pale in comparison anyway with the events of 597–587 B.C.E., even the events of 70 C.E.). At any point during the Second Temple period, and not just at a time of special disaster, the fall of the kingdom of Judah to Nebuchadnezzar would constitute a natural point of reference for dealing with the circumstances of Gentile domination and Jewish dispersion.

Dating the second half of Baruch (3:9–5:9) presents similar challenges, all the more as 3:9–4:4 and 4:5–5:9 may have originated as independent compositions. The fact that 3:9–4:4 (particularly 3:36–4:1) shares with Sir. 24:8 and 23 the limitation of Wisdom to Israel and the identification of Wisdom and Torah has suggested a date later than 180 B.C.E. (the latest date for the Hebrew Ben Sira) for that section (Oesterley 1935: 264); if the poem was in fact composed in Greek, that date could be moved forward to about 120–110 B.C.E., after the translation of Ben Sira into Greek. Is it certain, however, that Ben Sira did not learn from Baruch? The opening of the Wisdom poem speaks of the exile as a long-established reality rather than a recent development—"Why are you growing old in a foreign land?" (3:10)—but even a date in the early third century B.C.E. would accord well with this query.[4]

The relationship between Bar. 5:5–9 and *Psalms of Solomon* 11.3–7 has also been rightly regarded as relevant for the dating of Baruch. It is likely that Bar. 5:5–9 is dependent on *Psalms of Solomon* 11.3–7 and not vice versa (Wright 1985: 647–48); the latter is more tightly ordered and concise, whereas the author of Bar. 5:5–9 appears to have embellished *Psalms of Solomon* 11 with language drawn from Second and Third Isaiah,[5] much as the author of Bar. 1:15–3:8 expanded the prayer known from Daniel 9. But although the more cele-

---

4. Torrey (1945: 64) dates 3:9–5:9 to the third century B.C.E.
5. For example, the author of Baruch fills out the resonances of Isa. 40:4 in Bar. 5:7, speaking both of the elevation of valleys and leveling of hills, whereas *Psalms of Solomon* 11.4 only speaks of the latter. Baruch also introduces the thought of Isa. 66:20 at Bar. 5:6, breaking up his recontextualizations of *Psalms of Solomon* 11.

brated of the *Psalms of Solomon* reflect the events of 63–48 B.C.E. (the intrusion of Pompey into Judean affairs and his fate in Egypt), *Psalms of Solomon* 11 may have had a much longer history before finally coming to be included in that collection. Additionally, Moore (1977: 315–16) has suggested that Bar. 5:5–9 is an addition, composed in Greek, and that this is the only part that need be dependent upon *Psalms of Solomon* 11; the remainder of the book may, in all its various parts, date from the fourth through the second centuries B.C.E.

As with several other texts of the Apocrypha, we cannot be precise about the date of Baruch nor about the history of its compilation. If originally written in Hebrew, most of its constituent parts could easily predate the Hellenization crisis of 175–166 B.C.E. and would derive from Palestine or perhaps a Jewish community in the eastern Diaspora. If 1:1–14 was written as an introduction to an earlier prayer (1:15–3:8), the historical error of 1:11 probably would best be explained as a datum learned from Daniel, thus dating that introduction to a time after 164 B.C.E. If 1:1–3:8 was all part of a single work, then the whole would then postdate Daniel. The different hands responsible for the Greek translation of Baruch between 1:1–3:8 and 3:9–5:9 suggest that, whatever the origin of 3:9–5:9, it was not actually added to Baruch until the late second century or early first century B.C.E.

Genre and Purpose

It is tempting to classify Baruch as "the last dying flame of typical Hebrew prophecy" (Torrey 1945: 62), all the more as the opening verses of the book use the form typical of the introductions to Hebrew prophecy. Within this macrogenre, however, Baruch brings together several distinct genres into a single work. It begins with a historical narrative, moves into a prayer, then a Wisdom poem, and finally a lament and oracle of consolation reminiscent of exilic prophecy. The purpose (or, perhaps better, effect) of each of its constituent parts is easy enough to discern. The contribution of the redactor to the book's effect, however, is far greater than the sum of its parts.

Although the book is often criticized as unoriginal, the redactor, by assembling the independent materials into a single text, has created a movement and a process that constitute a potentially profound therapeutic response to the challenge of displacement, domination, and dispersion experienced by the Jewish people. Using the resources of Deuteronomy, Jeremiah, and the prayer known from Daniel 9, the redactor first makes these conditions, which could completely destroy the meaningfulness of the Jewish worldview for its adherents, manageable. Displacement, domination, and dispersion are not circumstances beyond the control of the Jew to help or ameliorate; they are not the result of Jews being wrong about their God and their place in an ordered universe. Instead, they are shown to be the result of not being sufficiently Jewish—that is, not being sufficiently committed to living out the vision articulated in the Jewish Scriptures. Deuteronomy supplied the basic program for dealing with these threatening circumstances, and the redactor of Baruch constructs a liturgical and poetic experience by which the Jew can take control of circumstances beyond his or her control and come to a place of hope again.

The confession of the Judean remnant and the exiles allows the participant to remove from himself or herself the cause of displacement and thus remove the obstacle to the hoped-for future. By naming the cause of the disruptive circumstances "sin," the circumstances are tamed, in effect, since individual Jews (and their community) have the resources to deal with "sin," even if they do not have the resources to fight for political liberation for all their coreligionists. The confession is a cathartic experience, designed at once to affirm the justness of their current situation (its appropriateness in light of their traditional worldview, which displacement does not now call into question but rather confirms!) and purge the reader of the sin, the breach in the covenant relationship, that is the "real" reason for the Jewish condition. At the conclusion of this prayer, the Wisdom poem invites the reader to rededicate himself or herself to the distinctive lifestyle of the Torah-observant Jew that will result in the overcoming of the disturbing and threatening circumstances.

Thus purged and rehabilitated, the reader is in a position to hear the lament and encouragement of his or her native land in 4:5–29, perhaps the most important effect of which is the affirmation that the ancestral land, personalized and crystalized in the figure of Zion, longs for the individual Jew as much as the Jew longs for the restoration of his or her people. The lament and the encouragement renew the connection between the Jew suffering cognitive dissonance and the land itself, suffering the same tensions on behalf of its people. This effect of constructing a mutual affective attachment is intensified all the more by the use of the image of "mother" for Jerusalem, who longs for all her children. Finally, the reader, aware that the land and the people are united in this mutual longing and thus still connected at the heart despite signs of displacement (whether the reader is in Palestine or outside the land), can hear again the promise of God's restoration of both to the state God intends (4:30–5:9).

The potentially erosive effects of Jews being dominated by non-Jewish peoples and their cultures and of being displaced from their land (or, for the Palestinian residents, seeing their land owned and ruled by outsiders to the covenant) are thus neutralized. The victims of history are given a framework and a means by which to take charge of their situation (through isolation of sin and its purgation in confession). Most vitally, the readers are impelled again to grasp that which lies at the heart of Jewish identity and culture—the Torah and its way of life—as the road to reversal of misfortunes. However "unoriginal," Baruch nevertheless contributes to one of the most astounding data of history: the ability of the Jewish people to maintain their distinctive culture and way of life despite millennia of political domination by non-Jews.

Formative Influences

The primary influence upon Baruch is the Hebrew Scriptures, an influence seen in the majority of the verses of Baruch. While Baruch especially invites the study of its rich intertextural conversations, only a partial study can be attempted here as a means of introducing the reader to the ways in which the older traditions are being woven together into this new text.

Intertexture is thickest in Baruch's penitential liturgy, or prayer of confession.[6] The primary resource used here is the prayer found in Dan. 9:4–19, which in turn is deeply informed by the basic theodicy of Deuteronomy. Their parallel content and structure may be outlined as follows:

1. Acknowledgment of God's justice in dealing with Israel by bringing calamity upon it (Dan. 9:7, 14; Bar. 1:15; 2:6)
2. Acknowledgment of the shame that has befallen Israel (Dan. 9:7–8; Bar. 1:15; 2:6)
3. Acknowledgment of Israel's sin as the cause of present sufferings (Dan. 9:8–11, 14b [also 9:5–6]; Bar. 1:17–18, 21)
4. Affirmation of the principle that sinning against God's law leads to God's giving Israel over "into the hands of their enemies," citing the law of Moses as the place where these terms are spelled out in detail (Dan. 9:11–13; Bar. 1:20; 2:2)
5. Incentive offered to God to preserve and restore Israel: to maintain God's own reputation, which became great and feared among the nations by means of the exodus and conquest (Dan. 9:15, 17–19; Bar. 2:11, 14–15)

The only significant omissions Baruch has made involve the ruined state of the temple and Jerusalem in Dan. 9:17–18, thus making Baruch's prayer more at home in a period in which the temple has been restored and the city inhabited once more.

Beyond the Deuteronomistic pattern of sin leading to punishment and exile and repentance leading to restoration, a number of other details from Deuteronomy's descriptions of the punishments that would befall an unfaithful Israel are brought in directly by the author. What were threats in Deuteronomy are narrated as accomplished facts in Baruch. Thus, for example, the residents of Jerusalem were reduced to consuming their young during the siege (Bar. 2:3; Deut. 28:53),[7] and the people of Israel were radically dimin-

---

6. Tov 1975: 12–27 is a most valuable resource, providing the text of all relevant parallels from the Hebrew Bible. See also Moore 1977: 267–94.

7. Alternatively, this detail might have been taken directly from Jer. 19:9. The consumption of one's offspring is presented in the source texts and in Baruch as the pinnacle of the horrors that would befall Israel as a result of Israel's sin and not, as Harrington (1999: 95) states, as "the culmination of Israel's sinfulness" that brings about punishment.

ished in number (Bar. 2:29; Deut. 28:62). The promise of the hope of reversal and restoration following wholehearted repentance in Deut. 30:1–6 provides the primary resource for Bar. 2:30–35.

The third principal resource for the first half of Baruch is, of course, Jeremiah. In the historical introduction, Bar. 1:11–12 reflects Jeremiah's command to "pray to the Lord on [Babylon's] behalf, for in its welfare you will find your welfare" (Jer. 29:7). Jeremiah's instructions concerning subservience to Nebuchadnezzar and acceptance of the Lord's discipline (Jer. 27:11–12), which were ignored by Judea's rulers to their own demise, are explicitly recalled at Bar. 2:21–23. In addition, two passages in Bar. 1:15–2:15 interrupt their recontextualizing of the Danielic prayer to include details from Jeremiah's prophecies, once again transforming the prediction into past-tense narration (compare Jer. 7:25–26; 26:5; 32:30 with Bar. 1:21–22; Jer. 19:9; 26:18 with Bar. 2:3–4; Jer. 7:34 with Bar. 2:23). All in all, the author of Bar. 1:1–3:8 has provided a thoughtful consolidation of Jeremiah's message within the basic framework of the Danielic prayer.

The Wisdom poem, perhaps the most original part of Baruch, was clearly inspired by Job 28:12–13, 23–28. Baruch 3:15–31 descants on the theme of Job 28:12–13: "But where shall wisdom be found? And where is the place of understanding? Mortals do not know the way to it, and it is not found in the land of the living." Where Job goes on to assert that no wealth can purchase wisdom, the Wisdom poem speaks of the failure of human beings (the rich and the overlords and especially the inhabitants of the neighboring non-Jewish lands) to attain Wisdom. The positive counterpart in Bar. 3:32–4:4, again, takes its starting point from Job 28:23, 27—"God understands the way to it, and he knows its place. . . . He established it, and searched it out"—but goes on to develop it in the particularistic way found also in Sir. 24:23: Wisdom is found in Torah. Here, appropriately, the author draws on Deuteronomy, Bar. 4:1 recalling the antitheses of Deut. 30:15–19: life and death stand before the hearer, the former being the result of obeying Torah, the latter the result of forsaking it. Baruch 4:3 offers a particularly interesting reconfiguration of an Old Testament resource. God's refusal to give God's glory to another (an idol or rival god; Isa. 48:11) becomes an injunction to Israel not to yield its glory to another (a foreign nation) by abandoning the distinctive way of life by which it shows absolute allegiance to and reverence for the One God. As Israel honors God as God deserves, refusing to provoke God by worshiping idols, Israel will retain its own honor and status among the nations as well, rather than succumb to foreign domination and national disgrace (Bar. 1:15; 2:6).

The final section, the consolation of Jerusalem, reflects the forms of a lament by Zion followed by an oracle of consolation seen already in Isa. 49:14–21, 22–26 (see also the oracles of consolation in Isa. 52:1–12; 54:1–17; 60:1–22; 62:1–12). In addition to providing the model for the section as a whole, Second and Third Isaiah also provide many specific details or images. For example, Isa. 61:10 suggests the change of garments as an image for deliverance (cf. Bar. 5:2); Bar. 5:5 recontextualizes the command to Jerusalem in Isa. 60:4 to stand up and observe the ingathering of her children; the vision in Isa. 49:22 of the return of the exiles on the shoulders of, or somehow carried by, their erstwhile Gentile overlords is taken up in Bar. 5:6.

Not surprisingly, Deuteronomy continues to contribute details to this book that, in all its parts, breathes the theodicy of Deuteronomy. Thus, in Bar. 4:7 Jerusalem uses the words of Deut. 32:16–17 (concerning the provocation of God's wrath by sacrificing "to demons and not to God") to indict her exiled children. Similarly, Bar. 4:15 recontextualizes another detail of the curses of Deuteronomy as a *fait accompli:* "The Lord will bring a nation from far away, from the end of the earth, to swoop down on you like an eagle, a nation whose language you do not understand, a grim-faced nation showing no respect to the old or favor to the young" (Deut. 28:49–50).

As previously mentioned, Bar. 5:5–9 (and possibly all of chapter 5) follows closely, and at some points recontextualizes verbatim, *Psalms of Solomon* 11, with the latter more likely being the earlier text:

> Stand on a high place, Jerusalem, and look at your children, from the east and the west assembled together by the Lord. (*Psalms of Solomon* 11.2)
> Arise, O Jerusalem, stand upon the height; look toward the east, and see your children gathered from west and east at the word of the Holy One. (Bar. 5:5)

> He flattened high mountains into level ground for them; the hills fled at their coming. (*Psalms of Solomon* 11.4)
> For God has ordered that every high mountain and the everlasting hills be made low and the valleys filled up, to make level ground, so that Israel may walk safely in the glory of God. (Bar. 5:7)

> The forests shaded them as they passed by; God made every fragrant tree to grow for them. So that Israel might proceed under the supervision of the glory of their God. (*Psalms of Solomon* 11.5–6)
> The woods and every fragrant tree have shaded Israel at God's command. (Bar. 5:8)

> Jerusalem, put on the clothes of your glory, prepare the robe of your holiness. (*Psalms of Solomon* 11.7)
> Put on forever the beauty of the glory from God. Put on the robe of the righteousness that comes from God. (Bar. 5:1b–2)

The author of Bar. 5:1–9 has, of course, supplemented and expanded *Psalms of Solomon* 11 with material chiefly from Isaiah, such as the completion of God's leveling the hills (*Psalms of Solomon* 11.4) with the corresponding raising of the valleys from Isa. 40:4, the source of both images.

It is too easy to dismiss this book as an unoriginal, derivative work (see Moore 1992c: 702), without trying positively to assess its achievement. Baruch offers a creative synthesis of core Jewish traditions, with Deuteronomy 28–32 providing the unifying theme and with the wisdom and prophetic traditions of Israel providing the resources for filling out the details of the whole scheme of confession of sin, repentance, renewed obedience, and reversal of Israel's misfortunes. The reader is immersed in and reconnected to the most relevant parts of the Jewish scriptural tradition as he or she is moved through the book's therapeutic process (see the section on "Genre and Purpose").

Theological Contributions

A commitment to Deuteronomy's theology of history—Israel's national misfortunes result from the nation's departure from wholehearted allegiance to God and God's covenant (Torah), while its restoration would result from heartfelt repentance and wholehearted return to obedience—unites the parts of Baruch.[8] This is evident not only in the prayer, where it dominates (1:15–2:5; 2:27–35), but also in the Wisdom poem (3:10–13; 4:1–3)[9] and the lament of Jerusalem (4:6–8, 12–13, 28–29). This theology is tempered by the idea that God chastens Israel in mercy, rather than destroying it completely (2:27, 31–34; cf. 2 Macc. 6:12–16).

Deuteronomy's theology of suffering provides a framework for understanding national misfortunes, and indeed it has had the effect of motivating the preservation of Jewish culture (through pointing to a return to Torah and its distinctive way of life as the path to recovery) when its national structures falter. It does not, however, provide a consistently helpful framework for personal misfortune, as in fact the Book of Job was written to demonstrate. The starting point of Baruch, however, that God is just (1:15; 2:6) is an important step in coping with any misfortune. After one works through the stages of blaming God and directing one's anger toward God, the rediscovery of the conviction that God is good even in the midst of bad things provides a venue for recovery and reintegration of life.

8. They are not bound together merely by an exilic setting for each part, as in Moore 1977: 259.

9. I disagree with Harrington's (1999: 100) assessment that the Wisdom poem treats "how hard it is for human beings to grasp real (divine) wisdom and to understand the ways of God in allowing the exile to happen." On the contrary, the author regards the answer to this question as obvious (if simplistic) in 3:12–13. Instead, the poem highlights the unique privilege that Israel has been given to have divine Wisdom handed to it, and it alone, in the scroll of the Torah. It is an exhortation to take up the way of Wisdom by living out the covenant, which is the turning point in the fortunes of Israel in the movement of this book.

The conceptualizing of God seems to differ between the various sections. Anthropomorphisms with reference to parts of the body, emotions, and the like abound in 1:1–3:8 but are absent from 3:9–4:4 (Pfeiffer 1949: 424). The titles for God also differ between the two halves of the book. "Lord" and qualifiers of "Lord" (such as "Lord our God") dominate 1:1–3:8, whereas "God," "the Eternal," and "the Holy One" are used in the remainder of the book (Metzger 1957: 90; Moore 1977: 259, 304). This results in a book that fairly reflects the overall biblical witness to God, which vacillates between God's immanence and transcendence, between God depicted as being like the creation and God as being completely other than the creation.

The prayer in particular underscores the peculiar relationship between God and Israel. God's reputation in the world and Israel's fortunes in the world are intimately connected, such that the birth of Israel as an independent people at the exodus was also the birth of God's international reputation (2:11). This means, however, that the disgrace and loss of status that have befallen Israel pose a threat to God's "name," or reputation, in the world as well (2:14–15). Thus, God must not abandon Israel to perdition, if for no other reason than to preserve God's own honor in the world (see the motivation clauses in 2:14–15; 3:5). If the Jews continue in their downward spiral, there will be no one left to acknowledge God's virtue and honor (2:17–18), since the Gentiles had never honored, and were not considered likely ever to honor, the One God, except as a result of witnessing Israel's exaltation again in the world.

Baruch affirms God's persistent commitment to rehabilitate Israel (2:27–35), and its eschatology is wholly focused on the restoration of the national fortunes of Israel, especially focused on Jerusalem, the "mother" of the Jewish people. The second half of the consolation of Jerusalem (4:30–5:9) is, in this regard, extremely similar to Tobit 13 and 14 and strikingly uninfluenced by apocalypticism and thoughts about the world beyond.

In rhythm with the Deuteronomistic pulse of the entire book, the movement of the Wisdom poem should again be underscored. As in Sir. 24:8, 23, the wisdom tradition is falling in line with other movements toward ethnic particularism. Israel alone has received Wisdom, a revelation from God and not something that human beings can discover on their own. That gift of Wisdom is encoded in the Torah and is enacted as, and to the extent that, people embody Torah's precepts.

Influence

The Book of Baruch did not enjoy lasting influence in Jewish circles, having never been so widely used or popularly known and respected as to attain the "classic" status of Scripture. One major difficulty in knowing how far

Baruch may have contributed to later literature lies, of course, in the derivative nature of Baruch itself. Nevertheless, those parts of Baruch that can be readily identified as "original" to the author of one of its constituent parts appear to have influenced only early Christian literature and not Jewish texts of the second century C.E. and beyond. Several scholars believe Baruch to have been read in Jewish synagogues on the ninth or tenth of Ab as part of the lamentation for the loss of the temple, relying on a reference to this practice in the *Apostolic Constitutions* (5.20) (Metzger 1957: 93). Baruch itself enjoins its own public reading at solemn occasions (1:3, 14), but the report in *Apostolic Constitutions* may not be accurate.[10]

There are no clear indications of dependence upon Baruch in the New Testament, although Baruch provides several parallels of thought that are informative for reading specific New Testament texts by way of comparison or contrast. For example, the delegitimation of the Gentiles' worship of idols as service offered to demons (Bar. 4:7; ultimately derived from Deut. 32:16–17 and Ps. 106:37) informs Paul's words in 1 Cor. 10:14–21.[11] The personification of Jerusalem as the mother of all Jews scattered throughout the world provides an informative background to Paul's variations on this theme, in which earthly Jerusalem becomes the mother of slaves and the heavenly Jerusalem the mother of Christians, whether Jew or Gentile (Gal. 4:21–31). Finally, the denunciation of Babylon's pride and insolence and the description of her future as conflagration and inhabitation by demons constitute a precursor in a long history of precursors to Rev. 18:2–8.

It is only with the church fathers of the second and third centuries that one begins to find explicit citations of material from Baruch. The earliest is Athenagoras, who cites Bar. 3:35 ("This is our God; no other can be compared to him") in his *Plea for the Christians* (*Legatio pro Christianis 9*), a defense of Christianity as a rational and pious religion deserving toleration, addressed to the emperor Marcus Aurelius in 177 (Whitehouse 1913: 577; Moore 1977: 260). Irenaeus (*Adversus haereses* 5.35) quotes Bar. 4:36–5.9 as part of his defense of the view that God will establish God's kingdom on earth in the end times, specifically using 5:3 as a refutation of the view that this kingdom will be celestial. Using Baruch as an authority in a theological debate shows that Irenaeus himself regarded the book as authoritative Scripture and that he expected his readers and rivals so to regard it as well. Irenaeus attributes the passage to Jeremiah, as do Clement of Alexandria (*Paedagogus* 1.10.91–92; which cites passages from the Wisdom poem in Bar. 3:9–4:5) and Lactantius (*Divinarum institutionum libri VII* 4.38; citing Bar. 3:36–37) (Whitehouse

10. The possibility that the practice was limited to communities of Jews in Syria, and that they were using the Greek translation, would help to overcome the major obstacle to accepting the report in the *Apostolic Constitutions:* Origen's and Jerome's denial that the Jews of their day possessed any Hebrew version of Baruch. See Schürer 1986: 3.2.739–40.

11. Paul is the first to apply this equation of idols with demons to Gentile worship in toto.

1913: 576, 580), which shows us how Baruch came to be regarded as authoritative. It was regarded as, in effect, preserving more Jeremiah materials, passed on by his scribe, Baruch (who no doubt was regarded as playing a large part in the recording and transmitting of the Book of Jeremiah itself). Jerome later would make a point of separating Baruch from Jeremiah, since the former is not part of the Hebrew scriptural tradition, but by then the association of Baruch as an appendix of Jeremiah had become deeply rooted. Baruch 3:36–37 appears to have been the most widely used passage, lending itself rather easily to a christological reading, especially as a prediction about the incarnation (Origen, *Commentarii in evangelium Joannis;* Cyprian, *Ad Quirinium testimonia adversus Judaeos* 2.6; Tertullian, *Adversus Praxean* 16, refers to Bar. 3:37; Lactantius, *Divinarum institutionum libri VII* 4.38) (Whitehouse 1913: 579–80).

Letter of Jeremiah

9

"They Are Not Gods, So Do Not Fear Them"

The Letter of Jeremiah is a sustained, if poorly organized, polemic against the worship of idols. Writing in the voice of Jeremiah, as if instructing the first exiles deported to Babylon, the author seeks to help Jews sustain commitment to monotheism and to aniconic religion in a world in which polytheism and the use of images in worship surround Jews on every side. Rather than allow them to be swayed from their commitment to a single God whose image cannot be represented, the author seeks to insulate Jewish audiences against any impression that the worship practiced by the Gentile majority is a valid expression of piety. This text is highly dependent on the long history of anti-idolatry polemics known from the Hebrew Scriptures. It stands alongside Bel and the Dragon, Wisdom of Solomon, and *Apocalypse of Abraham* as a specimen of the continuing usefulness throughout the intertestamental period of the ridicule of idolatrous worship as a means of insulating fellow Jews against the dominant culture and preserving their distinctive group culture.

Structure and Contents

After an introduction presenting idolatry as the primary challenge of living in exile (vv. 1–7), the author writes a lengthy refutation of the genuineness of idolatry as an expression of religion. This refutation is divided into ten sections, the termination of each being marked by a negation of the validity of the Gentiles' gods, which serves as a kind of refrain: "From this it is evident that they are not gods; so do not fear them (v. 16; similarly, vv. 23, 29, 65, 69); "Why then must anyone think that they are gods, or call them gods?" (v. 40; similarly, vv. 44, 52, 56, 64).[1] A concluding paragraph closes the tirade

---

1. Verses 64 and 65 function as a double refrain standing at the end of a double section (vv. 57–59, 60–63).

214

with a positive affirmation of the superior honor of the person who abstains from idolatry (v. 73), which corresponds to the positive affirmation of God's unique reality for, and protection of, the Israelites that closed the introduction (vv. 6–7).

Textual Transmission

The Letter of Jeremiah is preserved chiefly in the Septuagint tradition, being present in Codices Alexandrinus and Vaticanus (the end of Sinaiticus having been lost) (see Ziegler 1957). All of the later versions—the Old Latin, Vulgate, Syro-Hexaplar, Syriac, and the Arabic—follow the Septuagint, with the Syriac Peshitta offering perhaps the freest translation (Moore 1977: 330; Mendels 1992: 722). The Letter of Jeremiah was regarded as one of several appendices to Jeremiah (canonical Lamentations and deuterocanonical Baruch being the others). It was, however, originally a separate and independent composition.

In Vaticanus and Alexandrinus (as well as the Syro-Hexaplar), the order of the Jeremiah collection is Jeremiah, Baruch, Lamentations, Letter of Jeremiah; in other Greek texts, the Syriac, and the Latin, the Letter of Jeremiah is placed at the end of Baruch and thus comes to be joined to that book and enumerated as Baruch, chapter 6, in many translations (e.g., the KJV) (Metzger 1957: 95).

Despite the fact that no ancient Semitic manuscript of this text has yet surfaced (not even at Qumran, although a small fragment of a Greek copy was discovered), scholars have tended to favor a Hebrew original (Ball 1913: 597–98; Oesterley 1935: 270; Nickelsburg 1984: 149; Moore 1977: 326–27). Several infelicities in the Greek can be explained as the misreading of, or misvocalization of, an unpointed Hebrew text (a Hebrew text consisting only of consonants, the vowels having to be supplied by the reader). For example, the Greek of v. 12 says that the idols "cannot save themselves from rust and foods"; the Hebrew word for "food" could also mean, if vowels are added differently, "from a devourer," which surely makes better sense. Similarly, in the Greek of v. 68 the wild beasts are said to be able to run for cover and "help themselves," but a revocalization of the Hebrew could yield "to hide themselves," which is more directly in line with the context. Or again, in the Greek of v. 72 the idols' "purple and marble" are said to rot, but this is a result of the homophony of the Hebrew word שׁשׁ, which can mean either "fine linen" or "marble." The former, again, would be a better choice, since marble cannot rot. The fact that the author used the Hebrew version of Jeremiah, rather than the Greek (which lacks the important image of the "scarecrow in a cucumber field" taken from Jer. 10:5 into Let. Jer. 70), lends ancillary support to a Hebrew, rather than a Greek, original (Moore 1977: 323).[2]

Author, Date, and Setting

Jeremiah is the "author" of this text only insofar as Jeremiah provided the primary resource (Jer. 10:2–15) that the actual, anonymous author developed into a lengthier variation on the theme. With regard to the date of composition, Moore's caveat concerning the Additions to Daniel that one must distinguish this carefully from the time of translation into Greek is valid for the Additions to Jeremiah as well (Moore 1977: 128). The translation was accomplished before the end of the second century B.C.E., given the discovery of a Greek fragment of the Letter of Jeremiah at Qumran (7QLXXEpJer).[3] The time of composition is less certain. Several scholars lay great stress on the peculiar internal indication of date: the prediction that the Jews would be in Babylon "for a long time, up to seven generations" (v. 3) before God will bring them back to their ancestral land, which represents an alteration of Jeremiah's seventy years (Jer. 25:11; 29:10; an alteration also occurs in Daniel's "seventy weeks of years" [Dan. 9:24; cf. 9:2]) (Ball 1913: 596; Moore 1977: 328; Mendels 1992: 722; Metzger 1957: 96). These scholars argue that the author must be writing before this period of time had elapsed, for it is difficult to imagine an author deliberately altering Jeremiah's prophecy in such a way that would already have proven false. A date between 317 and 306 B.C.E., or 280 years after either the first or second deportation to Babylon (597 and 586 B.C.E.), is taken as the latest date for the composition of the original Hebrew version. There is in fact no internal evidence to necessitate a later date, although the ambiguity of the length of time covered by a "generation" should make us cautious about being overly precise about the range of dates.

The author appears to have Babylonian religion mainly in mind, as seen from the explicated setting ("in Babylon you will see gods" [v. 4]), the mention of Bel (v. 41), and the incorporation of mourning and other funerary rites in the cult of

2. Torrey (1945: 64–67) found Ball's argument unconvincing, opting instead for an Aramaic original. He questioned the appropriateness of placing the prostitutes "on the roof" in v. 11, suggesting that the Aramaic *'al agrā* ("for hire") was mistakenly vocalized as *'al iggārā* ("on the roof"). The locating of prostitutes *epi tous tegous*, "on the roof," may simply reflect, however, the realities of Eastern living, where rooftops are routinely used as living areas. One thinks immediately of Bathsheba bathing upon the rooftop and Judith living in a tent pitched on the roof of her house. This renders Torrey's arguments unnecessary.

3. Second Maccabees 2:2 has been taken as a reference to the Letter of Jeremiah, particularly since it refers to Jeremiah instructing "those who were led captive" (*metagenomenois*) not to be "led astray in their thoughts on seeing the gold and silver statues and their adornment." The Letter of Jeremiah, however, is itself inspired largely by Jer. 10:2–15, which is all that the author of 2 Macc. 2:2 need have known as well. The Letter of Jeremiah, moreover, adds nothing that could help account for the other Jeremiah traditions found in 2 Macc. 2:1–3 (e.g., the taking of the holy fire from the altar and the scroll of the law). See Pfeiffer 1949: 429 and n. 4.

Tammuz, the deity of fertility in Babylon (vv. 30–32). Certain elements in the description of the women acting as cult prostitutes (vv. 11, 43) resonates with the description of Babylonian worship in Herodotus (*Historiae* 1.199): both speak of the presence of a female "on the roof" or upper level of Bel's temple (*Historiae* 1.181; Let. Jer. 11 may mistake this "bride" of Bel for a group of cult prostitutes), and both speak of cordoned-off women awaiting selection by a male for ritual fornication in honor of the deity (Ball 1913: 596; Pfeiffer 1949: 431; Metzger 1957: 97; Moore 1977: 329). Certainly, there is nothing to suggest specific concern about Egyptian worship, the reference to "cats" in v. 22 notwithstanding (Lee 1968). Here, cats are envisioned not as objects of worship as in Egypt but as pests infesting the temples along with bats, birds, and the like.

The author's interaction with Babylonian idolatry does not, however, immediately clarify the question of provenance. Moore favors Palestine as the most likely provenance, suggesting that the author, although apparently knowing something about Babylonian cult practices, speaks of it "from afar," not mentioning matters of equal or even greater importance for Babylonian religion like astrology and divination (Moore 1977: 329; Pfeiffer 1949: 431). The author's silence on these topics, however, could be equally well explained by the author's thematic focus. The author does not set out to write a polemic against all aspects of Babylonian religion but only against a single, prominent, visible aspect—and one that is most easily debunked—the veneration of idols.[4] On balance, there appear to be no definite clues to deciding whether the work originated in the Jewish community in Babylon or in Palestine. Both communities would have benefited from the kind of ideological insulation provided by the text.[5]

Genre and Purpose

The Letter of Jeremiah is not a letter but a tirade (Moore 1977: 317). It belongs to the genre of polemics, as opposed to apologetics; the latter seeks to demonstrate the worth or validity of one's position, the former to deny validity to another's position. It is very similar in purpose to Bel and the Dragon, Wisdom of Solomon 11–15, and other Jewish "explanations" of the nature of Gen-

---

4. Mendels (1992: 722) argues that Wisdom of Solomon may have used Letter of Jeremiah and that Wisdom of Solomon shows that "idolatry was a central issue in the fight against Hellenism in Palestine from the Diadochi through Roman times." This becomes a sign for Mendels that "there exists no reason to claim that the epistle was written outside Palestine," all the more as the author appears to have used a Hebrew version of the Scriptures (notably Jer. 10:5). This reasoning is problematic in that Wisdom of Solomon is a product of Egyptian Judaism, written in Greek, and thus a witness to ideological warfare in the Jewish community there. Moreover, a Hebrew version of the Scriptures would have been the natural resource for a Jew in the eastern Diaspora as well as for a Palestinian Jew.

5. Oesterley (1935: 269) sees the Jews in Babylon as the primary audience for the tract, which would neither rule out nor necessitate a Palestinian provenance.

tile worship: it aims to keep Jews from being impressed by, and assimilating to, the worship of the other groups of people around them (Ball 1913: 597; Mendels 1992: 722). The growing availability of other forms of religious expression and the earnestness with which many Gentiles pursued their own forms of piety would no doubt have given Jews cause to question the absolute claims they had been taught, and come to accept, about their own religion—a religion in which there was simply no room for "other gods." Polemics here serves the goal of "world legitimation," the preservation of the "self-evident" nature of the truth claims and definitions of reality that stood at the heart of Jewish culture and identity (see Berger 1967: ch. 2). By denying the validity of the alternative, the Jews' commitment to the validity of their own worldview is protected.

Pfeiffer (1949: 432) ventures to suggest that the Letter of Jeremiah was "addressed to the Gentiles as much as to the Jews, if not more," a strong offense being the best defense in the warfare of ideas. This is unlikely for two reasons. First, if the work was in fact composed in Hebrew, few Gentiles would have been able to read it. Second, the offense is far from strong: the approach to Gentile worship is reductionistic and would be easily refuted by Gentiles who knew that the idol was not itself the god being worshiped and that the limitations of a stone statue were no reflection of the power of their gods.

Formative Influences

The author appears to have drawn upon Jeremiah as his primary resource. In terms of content, Jer. 10:2–15 already contains many of the topics expanded in the Letter of Jeremiah: the origin of the idol as the work of craftspersons shaping metal and wood (Jer. 10:3–4, 9; Let. Jer. 4, 8, 11, 39, 45, 50), decked with purple clothing (Jer. 10:9; Let. Jer. 72); the likening of the idol to a scarecrow in a cucumber field (Jer. 10:5; Let. Jer. 70), which cannot speak or walk on its own but is dependent on others for movement (Jer. 10:5; Let. Jer. 8, 26); the claim that idols can neither help nor harm people (Jer. 10:5; Let. Jer. 34–37, 64); the injunction not to fear them (Jer. 10:5; Let. Jer. 16, 23, 29, 65, 69); and the claim that the idolater is put to shame by his or her idols (Jer. 10:14; Let. Jer. 26, 39).[6] The concept of a letter from Jeremiah instructing the exiles stems from Jeremiah 29, Jeremiah's epistle to

6. Several scholars have focused on the single Aramaic verse in Jeremiah, 10:11, as the specific source of inspiration for the Letter of Jeremiah (Torrey 1945: 64–65; Metzger 1957: 96). Torrey (1945: 64, 67) finds in the Letter of Jeremiah (which he takes to have been composed in Aramaic) the explanation for this strange phenomenon: the Letter of Jeremiah was inspired by this verse, which, in turn, was translated from Hebrew into Aramaic in order to authenticate the Letter of Jeremiah. These scholars appear to have been misled by the singularity of the verse appearing in Aramaic; upon closer examination, one finds almost nothing in the Letter of Jeremiah that resonates with the specific content of this verse but much that resonates with the verses that precede Jer. 10:11.

the community of the exile, urging them to submit to Babylon's rule and prepare themselves for seventy years in a foreign land.

The Letter of Jeremiah resonates, of course, with several other texts that treat the topic of idolatry (Torrey 1945: 64–65; Pfeiffer 1949: 428; Roth 1975; Nickelsburg 1984: 146). Deuteronomy 4:27–28 speaks of idols as the work of human hands, fashioned from inanimate material, able neither to "see, nor hear, nor eat, nor smell"—a litany of impotence that is recontextualized and expanded in Ps. 115:3–8; 135:15–16. In addition to this general tradition, the Letter of Jeremiah appears to be particularly indebted to Isa. 46:6–7, which combines the topics of the idol's origins in human handiwork, the inability to move and dependence upon others (being carried on the shoulders, as in Let. Jer. 26), and inability to assist those who cry to it for help (cf. Let. Jer. 36–38).

Ideological Strategy

The primary ideological move made by the author, learned from the Jewish scriptural heritage, is the equation of the pagan deity with its visible representation, the idol. Gentiles would hardly have seen their religion in that way: while the precincts of the idol were sacred, the idol was nothing more than the visual representation of the divinity and not an object of worship in and of itself (Pfeiffer 1949: 428; Harrington 1999: 104). The author makes no attempt to understand pagan religion from the perspective of the Gentile worshipers, for the goal is not to explain but to delegitimate.

Once the identification of stone-cold idol and pagan god is made, however, the author can proceed to interpret the limitations of an inanimate object as the impotence of the pagan deity. The greater part of the Letter of Jeremiah is taken up with claiming that the idol, being inanimate, cannot do what the Living God can do, such as "set up a king . . . or give rain . . . judge their own cause, or deliver one who is wronged" (vv. 53–54), nor even do what ordinary human beings can do, such as speak, walk, or run from a burning building (vv. 8, 26, 55) (Nickelsburg 1984: 147). There is also no advantage to be gained from idol worship, for just as the idol cannot protect or help itself, so it cannot be expected to help its worshipers. Because of the emptiness of idol worship, idolaters are themselves put to shame by their ignorance, whereas the person who refuses to become entangled in such superstition will be above reproach (vv. 26, 39, 72, 73).

A recurring, if minor, theme in the author's debunking of idolatrous cults is the emphasis on the material interests of the priests who officiate at and promote the worship of these idols (vv. 10–11, 28, 33). The priests, who surely know the sham religion they promote (see Bel and the Dragon), dupe the general population so that they and their families may have a constant supply of food and material resources. The author also associates vice with idolatry (though not in the overarching way that one finds in Wis. 14:22–31): the priests themselves steal from the temple, and licentiousness is given an open home in the idol's temple.

In writing v. 29, the author assumes that readers share Jewish cultural sensibilities, for the fact that menstruating or postpartum women are allowed to participate in idolatrous cult is taken as a proof of the cult's emptiness. A "real" god should recognize the encroachment of something unclean or defiling and burst out against it. Or, alternatively, if there was really something holy and other about these idols, the priests and people who worship them should know better than to allow such defilement. Since they are obviously unconcerned, there cannot be any real awareness of their holiness.

The Letter of Jeremiah is not so penetrating or insightful a critique of idolatry as is the Wisdom of Solomon. Although the latter also engages in a certain amount of reductionism, its description of the historical origins of certain kinds of Gentile cults (the emergence of a cult of divinities from the cult of the dead [Wis. 14:15–16]; ruler cult [Wis. 14:17–21]) is actually a helpful contribution to a "history of religions" study of ancient religion. There is no such attempt to enter into the origins of foreign cults in the Letter of Jeremiah, although the critique of pagan religion as the means by which priests retain their material advantage comes closest to what one today would call "ideological criticism."

Influence

The Letter of Jeremiah did not exercise a profound literary influence on later Jewish works. Several later works debunking Gentile idolatry exist, such as *Apocalypse of Abraham*, a work from the early part of the common era, which shares a number of topics with our text: idols are the work of skilled craftspersons and not divine; idols have no power of their own to stand upright when fallen or to escape a fire; idols cannot help themselves, let alone those who call upon them. Its dependence on the Letter of Jeremiah cannot conclusively be demonstrated, however, since it may simply have drawn similar inspiration from the large corpus of Old Testament and other intertestamental anti-idolatry polemics.

Resonances with the New Testament are also of a sort that can be illuminating but not a sign of direct influence. For example, the Corinthians' slogan that "an idol is nothing" is certainly in keeping with the view promoted by the Letter of Jeremiah, as in Jewish polemics in general, although the practical application of that watchword was quite different in the hands of the Corinthian Christians who wanted to justify associating with their old friends and networks of support at pagan banquets. The tension between the claim that an idol is nothing and Paul's response that behind idols lurk Satan and his minions (1 Cor. 10:14–21), the true objects of Gentile cults, is reflected in the same tension between the view of idols in the Letter of Jeremiah and that found in Bar. 4:7, where idol worship is also demon worship.

After the first century, one finds several instances of direct influence as the book came to be viewed as canonical in both East and West as part of the corpus of Jeremiah, not seriously questioned until Jerome (who labeled it a *pseudepigraphon*). The work was used in contexts wherein the folly of traditional religion or the maintenance of the distinctive witness of the Christian religion was the principal theme. The second-century *Apologia* (a "defense" of the Christian religion against pagan critics) of Aristides, for example, appears to have been informed by the Letter of Jeremiah. Speaking of the visible representations of astral phenomena held to be divinities, Aristides writes, "And they shut them up together in shrines, and worship them, calling them gods, even though they have to guard them securely for fear they should be stolen by robbers. . . . If their gods are unfit to look after their own safety, how shall they bestow protection upon others?" (*Apologia* 3; cf. Let. Jer. 18, 49, 57–58). Later, in section 13, Aristides also emphasizes the visible decay of the idols' trappings and the origin of these "gods" in the craftsperson's shop, although these topics would also have been common to the Old Testament anti-idolatry texts. In the fourth century, Firmicus Maternus's attack on pagan religion (*De errore profanarum religionum* 28.4–5) quotes Let. Jer. 5–10, 21–24, 28–31, 50–57 (Metzger 1957: 98; Moore 1977: 324 n. 2).

Tertullian quotes Let. Jer. 4–6 in his defense of martyrdom as a Christian's duty toward God (*Scorpiace* 8). In the midst of a retelling of the story of the three companions of Daniel refusing to worship the idol erected by Nebuchadnezzar, Tertullian quotes this passage as part of the assumed general knowledge of those Jews deported to Babylon, showing no reservations about the attribution of the words to Jeremiah. It was this definition of religious duty—"Say in your heart, 'It is you, O Lord, whom we must worship'"—on which the three were acting when they made their own bold proclamation (Dan. 3:16–18). In a rather different context, Cyprian of Carthage (*De dominica oratione* 5) paraphrases Let. Jer. 6, the same passage to which Tertullian refers.

Additions to Daniel

10

"Let Them Know That You Alone Are God"

The Greek editions of Daniel contain significant material not found in the Hebrew-Aramaic text of Daniel that became canonical for Jews and, later, Protestants. This additional material expands Daniel in two directions. The first is liturgical: Prayer of Azariah and Song of the Three Young Men, added to Daniel 3, greatly enhance the dimension of communication between mortals and God and of praise of this God. The second is legendary: the repertoire of Daniel stories is enhanced by the addition of Susanna, a story about Daniel's timely intervention in a judicial case gone awry, and Bel and the Dragon, a story about Daniel's successful confrontation of false gods in the name of the Living God.

The tales of Susanna and Bel and the Dragon, together with the discovery of other extracanonical Daniel legends found at Qumran, show that the six tales known from Hebrew-Aramaic Daniel were but a portion of a much larger body of independently circulating Daniel stories. Those tales contained in Daniel 1–6 were joined with the visions of Daniel 7–12 and became the standard form of Daniel among Palestinian Jews, but other stories were still told independently of that form of Daniel, while others were inserted in some editions of Daniel (possibly in some Semitic editions and definitely in the Greek editions). The following discussion treats each addition separately after an initial discussion of the textual transmission of all the additions.

Textual Transmission

The longer version of Daniel is known primarily from the Greek, surviving in two rather different editions.[1] The older edition, the "Septuagint" proper,

---

1. English translations of the Septuagint and Theodotion versions can be found in Collins 1993: 195–98, 405–8, 420–25; Bissell 1899: 450–66; Kay 1913: 638–51; Davies 1913: 652–64. Rahlfs 1979 provides the Greek texts of the Septuagint and Theodotion. The preferred critical edition is Ziegler 1954.

survives in its entirety only in a single manuscript, Codex Chisianus from the ninth century (Codex 87; Papyrus 967 contains chs. 5–14), and in the Syriac translation of Origen's edition of the Septuagint (Pfeiffer 1949: 433, 441; Moore 1977: 33). The more recent edition, called "Theodotion" (Θ), displaced the older "Septuagint" edition in the usage of the Christian church by the late third century, so that all the major codices of what we call the Septuagint actually contain the Theodotion edition of Daniel. Most of the versions (the Vulgate, the Peshitta, the Ethiopic, Coptic, Arabic, and Armenian) are based on Theodotion, the Syriac differing mainly through paraphrase; Old Latin versions, extant now only in patristic writings, appear to have existed for both the Septuagint and Theodotion (Bennett 1913: 626; Moore 1977: 34).

The older, Septuagint edition was probably made by the late second century B.C.E., since the Greek translation of 1 Maccabees shows signs of dependence upon it (Hartman and Di Lella 1978: 80–81; Pfeiffer 1949: 440, 442). For example, the order of the names "Hananiah, Azariah, and Mishael" in Sg. Three 66, which differs from the consistent order of "Hananiah, Mishael, and Azariah" (or their Aramaic equivalents, Shadrach, Meshach, and Abednego) in the portions of Daniel found in the Hebrew canon, appears also in 1 Macc. 2:59 and continues to be observed in Greek Jewish literature (see 4 Macc. 16:21; 18:12). Additionally, the term "abomination of desolation" (*bdelygma erēmōseōs*) seems to have been introduced into the Greek translation of 1 Macc. 1:54 from LXX Dan. 11:31.

Theodotion prepared his version in the early second century C.E. but appears to have utilized an earlier Greek text of Daniel that differed markedly from the Septuagint (Grelot 1966). This hypothesis is based on the observation that Theodotionic readings of Daniel appear already in Heb. 11:33 (which agrees with Dan. 6:23 in the Theodotion text tradition, "he closed the mouths of the lions," absent from the Septuagint) and throughout the Book of Revelation, suggesting that there was a version of Daniel substantially like "Theodotion" and unlike the "Septuagint" already in the first century C.E. (Swete 1894: 46–49; Montgomery 1927: 46–50). The fact that Theodotion contains a greater number of Hebraisms than the Septuagint strongly suggests that Theodotion (or the Greek version he used) represents a revision of a current Greek text in light of a Hebrew manuscript. Whether Theodotion or pre-Theodotion also used the Septuagint as a basis for revision is uncertain, but the points of verbatim agreement between Theodotion and the Septuagint suggest that the latter deeply influenced the former at some point (see Moore 1977: 80).

Despite the fact that no Hebrew-Aramaic manuscript of Daniel has been found containing these additions (even among the Dead Sea Scrolls),[2] schol-

2. Gaster (1894–95) believed a fourteenth-century Aramaic version to be an independent witness to the Semitic original of Susanna. Most reject his arguments (e.g., Davies 1913: 656; Moore 1977: 49; Kay [1913: 639–40] regards both the Aramaic and a seventeenth-century Hebrew manuscript merely as signs of the story's ongoing life in Jewish culture). Collins (1993: 202, 205, 410–11), however, suggests that Gaster's Aramaic text should not be dismissed as a retranslation of either Greek version or of the known Syriac versions and should have the status of a premedieval version.

ars nevertheless favor a Hebrew original for the liturgical compositions and a Hebrew or Aramaic original for the additional legends. This is based on the presence of Semitisms in the Greek, but this must be weighed carefully because it could be explained by three different causes: (1) a Greek author is composing in conscious imitation of the Septuagint; (2) an author whose basic linguistic framework is Hebrew or Aramaic is composing a text in Greek; (3) a Greek translator is translating rather woodenly a Semitic original (Bennett 1913: 627). It is not the mere fact of Semitisms but their disproportionately high number that argues most strongly in favor of Hebrew or Aramaic originals for these additions.[3] Moreover, with regard to the liturgical additions, it has been noted that Pr. Azar. 2, 26 and Sg. Three 66 refer to the heroes by their Hebrew names, not the Aramaic names given in chapter 3 of the canonical Hebrew text, suggesting that the Greek version is dependent on a Hebrew *Vorlage*. Moreover, the text can be retroverted into Hebrew with even a distinct poetical meter (Moore 1992d: 19, citing Kuhl 1930: 154–59).[4] The puns in the Greek versions of Susanna, noted as early as a letter of Julius Africanus to Origen, have been used to argue in favor of a Greek original for that tale. This argument is hardly decisive against a Hebrew original, however, since a clever translator could have caught the pun in Hebrew and chosen Greek words to recreate that pun (even if that meant choosing different names for the two trees or different verbs for the action God would take against the elders) (Kay 1913: 642; Moore 1977: 84).

It is highly probable that the Additions to Daniel were present in the Greek versions from the beginning (and not inserted later into the Greek Daniel), as there is stylistic consistency between the various parts of the Greek Daniel (Pfeiffer 1949: 442; Moore 1992d: 19).[5] Moore believes that the additions were already present in the Hebrew manuscripts of Daniel that served as a basis for the Septuagint and Theodotion. The fact that "scholars have never been able to detect syntactical, stylistic, or vocabulary differences between the Greek of the Additions and the Greek of the canonical portions of Daniel" (Moore 1977: 29), however, does not actually re-

---

3. Kay (1913: 641) offers a telling study on this point with regard to the appearance of the *waw*-consecutive as a Semitism underlying the use of *kai* to begin a Greek sentence. Susanna contains more than twice the number of these *kai* equivalents of a *waw*-consecutive than does John in a similar number of verses (and three or more times than Luke or Josephus). Thus, a person whose primary language might be supposed to be Hebrew or Aramaic (John or Josephus) or an author consciously imitating Septuagint style (Luke) would still yield a substantially lower number of this particular Semitism. See Bennett 1913: 628 and Davies 1913: 655 on Semitisms in those additions.

4. The argument that "Hebrew is ipso facto the language of Jewish prayer and worship" (Moore 1992d: 19) is disputable, since a Greek-speaking Jew could pray just as effectively to God in Greek. Although dating a century and a half later, the Song of Mary and the Song of Zechariah in Luke 1 show how Seputagint Greek provides an excellent vehicle for prayer and praise.

5. Steussy (1993: 193) assumes the contrary.

quire this, because the translator might have been responsible for the translation and inclusion of the additions, known from separate sources.[6] Nevertheless, the Dead Sea Scrolls have taught us that different text types could exist in Hebrew and be in use concurrently (e.g., the longer and shorter versions of 1 Samuel and Jeremiah), and so this remains a theoretical possibility for Daniel.

Prayer of Azariah and Song of the Three Young Men

Contents and Structure

These additions were inserted between MT Dan. 3:23, when the three companions of Daniel are cast into the fiery furnace on account of their refusal to worship the idol erected by Nebuchadnezzar, and MT Dan. 3:24, the notice of Nebuchadnezzar's surprise to see four men (rather than three) walking about (rather than being consumed at once) in the furnace. In the prayer, Azariah confesses the nation's transgressions against God's covenant, declares God just in all the calamities that have befallen the Jews, and prays for God's deliverance and vindication of God's people (Pr. Azar. 1–22). Five verses of narrative then connect the two liturgical pieces, telling of the destruction of some Chaldeans who stood too near the furnace and the angel's intervention in the furnace (Pr. Azar. 23–27).[7] This is followed by a psalm of praise blessing God directly and, at greater length, calling upon all creation to bless and honor God (Sg. Three 28–68).

The beginnings of the Prayer of Azariah and the Song of the Three Young Men are strikingly similar (more noticeably so in Greek):

> "Blessed are you, O Lord, God of our ancestors, and worthy of praise;
> and glorious is your name forever!" (Pr. Azar. 3)

> "Blessed are you, O Lord, God of our ancestors,
> and to be praised and highly exalted forever." (Sg. Three 29)

6. Collins (1993: 418, 419, 437 [see also Julius 1903: 15–18]) shows a marked preference for this theory, with which, in the absence of any manuscript evidence for a second-century Hebrew-Aramaic Daniel containing any sign of these additions, I also concur.

7. Kuhl (1930: 161–64) posits that the connecting narrative was composed to introduce the Song of the Three Young Men when it was introduced into the Daniel narrative (and to fill in a perceived gap in MT Dan. 3:23–24, narrating the reason for Nebuchadnezzar's amazement). The Prayer of Azariah was later prefixed to the connecting narrative, a somewhat awkward move since Azariah now gives a leisurely prayer before there is any word about angelic intervention. While this remains possible, the lack of Hebrew-Aramaic manuscripts of Daniel with this addition makes it seem unprofitable to speculate on the stages in development of the hypothetical Hebrew-Aramaic Daniel in terms of the additions.

The prayer in Tob. 8:5–8 begins in the same way, suggesting that this was a typical way of opening a prayer to God in this period. In any event, the fact that both liturgical pieces begin with precisely the same words gives them the structure of a literary diptych, the first presenting the panel before deliverance, the second the panel of exuberance after deliverance (however strained this would be in the "historical" setting of a fiery furnace, when deliverance would be instantaneous or not at all).

The Song of the Three Young Men is quite tightly structured, both in terms of its thematic arrangement in strophes and in terms of the refrain that concludes the second half of every verse (one refrain in vv. 29–34, a second refrain in vv. 35–66):

> 29–34: Benediction addressed directly to God
> 35–68: Invocation to all aspects of creation to bless God
> > 35–41: Celestial phenomena and inhabitants
> > 42–51: Meteorological phenomena
> > 52–59: Terrestrial phenomena and nonhuman inhabitants
> > 60–66: Human beings (first three verses showing concentric circles of Jewish division of humanity: all people, Israel, priests)
> > 67–68: Conclusion

The differences between the Septuagint and Theodotion are minimal in this addition, involving mainly some inversions in the order of verses in the Song of the Three Young Men.

Genre and Purpose

The Prayer of Azariah is a prayer of confession very similar in form and content to Dan. 9:4–19 and Bar. 1:15–2:15. The Song of the Three Young Men is a hymn composed after the manner of Psalm 136 (in terms of form) and Psalm 148 (in terms of content). Both are liturgical pieces that were probably composed for worship and only later inserted into the biblical narrative. Notable examples of this include Exod. 15:1–18 (a psalm of deliverance that clearly derives from a period after the settlement in Canaan but inserted into the Exodus narrative as a means of highlighting the dramatic and decisive deliverance of God's people at the Red Sea), 2 Samuel 22, and Jon. 2:2–9.

Moore (1992d: 19) asserts that the note of confession is "totally inappropriate," since "the three youths are in their present predicament precisely because they *have* been true to God." Although Moore (1977: 40) is correct to exonerate Azariah and his companions from guilt for sin, it is also the case that Jews had a strong sense of corporate identity and thus corporate responsibility. Azariah and his two friends may not have sinned, but Israel sinned against God, and all Israel feels the consequences. That is cause enough for Azariah's literary persona to take up a prayer of confession and cry for deliverance. A similar phenomenon is found in 2 Macc. 7:18, 32–33, 37–38, where seven martyrs, like Azariah, are in their predicament precisely because of their fidelity to God but recognize that their people's sin—their corporate body's sin—stands behind the greater predicament of Gentile domination and religious oppression.

What makes the prayer "inappropriate" for its new literary setting is its vague, general character. There is no hint that the suppliant is standing in a fiery furnace nor would it be possible to pray such a prayer for deliverance in the furnace—either it would have been granted before a word was spoken, or no word would have been spoken at all. Similarly, the general character of the Song of the Three Young Men, linked to the narrative by the mere inclusion of Sg. Three 66, signals that this composition also had a history of liturgical usage before it came to be included in the Daniel cycle.

The purpose for including these additions is not to correct some perceived deficiency in Daniel (unlike the Additions to Esther) but rather to heighten the marvel of the deliverance in the story while at the same time preserving two fine liturgical works from oblivion. Daniel 3 becomes much more a testimony to personal prayer and devotion, as well as a venue for conveying the theology of the poems (the reaffirmation of Deuteronomistic theodicy in the prayer and the majesty of God and the creation theology celebrated in the song).

Author, Date, and Setting

The anonymous author or authors clearly were quite sensitive to and familiar with the liturgical traditions of the intertestamental penitential prayers, as well as the more celebratory hymns among the psalms. The probability of a Hebrew original for the Prayer of Azariah and the Song of the Three Young Men, if not the connecting narrative (Pr. Azar. 23–27), points to a Palestinian provenance. Dating prayers and hymns is notoriously difficult, but there may be a reflection of the Hellenization crisis in Pr. Azar. 9, which speaks of the pious being handed over to apostates and a supremely wicked king (Harrington 1999: 10; Metzger 1957: 103; Moore 1992d: 19). The use of the terms *anomōn* and *apostatōn* in Pr. Azar. 9 makes this suggestion somewhat more plausible. The former may be used of Gentiles, but the latter speaks of those who formerly kept the Torah but "turned away" at some point. The conjunction of lapsed Jews and a foreign king who together act as "enemies" toward the Torah-observant naturally conjures up the period of 175–164 B.C.E. The Song of the Three Young Men, on the other hand, provides no such reminiscences and could be considerably older than the rest of Daniel. As with the other additions, a *terminus ad quem* of 100 B.C.E., the approximate time of translation into Greek (the Septuagint edition), is appropriate (Moore 1977: 29).

Formative Influences

A striking thematic congruity links several prayers of confession composed in the intertestamental period: Prayer of Azariah, Dan. 9:4–19, Bar. 1:15–2:15, and Neh. 9:26–37. Of these, Nehemiah may be presumed to be the oldest and Prayer of Azariah the most recent. The relative dating of Daniel 9 and Baruch 1–2, which are dependent either one on the other or both on a common liturgical source, remains a matter of debate.[8] The Prayer of Azariah surely is shaped and informed by Daniel 9 and, given the possible antiquity of Bar. 1:15–2:15, possibly by that prayer as well.

All four prayers articulate the basic premises of Deuteronomy: Israel's transgression of the covenant with God leads to disaster and corporate misfortune, while fidelity to God's covenant makes for well-being. Prominent in all these prayers is the acknowledgment of God's justice in dealing with Israel by bringing calamity upon it (Neh. 9:33; Dan. 9:7, 14; Bar. 1:15; 2:6; Pr. Azar. 4–5), complemented by an acknowledgment of Israel's sin as the cause of present sufferings (Neh. 9:34; Dan. 9:5–6, 8–11, 14b; Bar. 1:17–18, 21; Pr. Azar. 6–7). The prayers all contain an explicit affirmation of the principle that sinning against God's law leads to God's giving Israel over "into the hands of their enemies," with Daniel and Baruch citing the law of Moses as the place where these terms are laid out (Neh. 9:26–27; Dan. 9:11–13; Bar. 1:20; 2:2; Pr. Azar. 7, 9).

The Prayer of Azariah's resonances with Daniel 9 and Baruch 1–2 continue in the acknowledgment of the shame that has befallen Israel (Dan. 9:7–8; Pr. Azar. 10) and, most notably, in the incentive offered to God to preserve and restore Israel. All three urge God to reach into history and restore Israel for the sake of God's reputation (Dan. 9:15, 17–19; Bar. 2:14–15; Pr. Azar. 11, 20, 22).

The Prayer of Azariah and Baruch both include the detail that Israel's population has been drastically reduced (Bar. 2:13; Pr. Azar. 14). More than a pathetic detail, this is an acknowledgment of the fulfillment of Deut. 28:62, which threatens the radical diminution of the population ("you shall be left few in number"). The Prayer of Azariah further explicates this predicament as endangering the promise God made to Abraham (Pr. Azar. 12–13; cf. Gen. 15:5; 17:6; 22:17), on the basis of which the author hopes for a reversal back toward health and growth for the descendants of Abraham.

Unique among these prayers is the Prayer of Azariah's use of the offering of a contrite heart in place of sacrifices as an effective means of mediation, as encountered also in the penitential Psalm 51, vv. 16–17. By seizing on this

---

8. Moore (1977: 292–93) favors the possibility that Baruch 1–2 is not just an adaptation of Daniel 9 but rather reflects a prayer that could "go back to the late fourth century B.C." The prayer in Daniel 9, moreover, has the character of an interpolation and so could be much older; even if it is the source of Baruch 1–2, this would not then mean that Baruch 1–2 had to have been written after 166 B.C.E., when Daniel was compiled.

intertextual resource, the author of the Prayer of Azariah makes a substantial psychological advance on predecessors, whose prayers are notably devoid of such a vehicle for relief to mediate between the desperate plight and assurance of acceptance before God.

The Song of the Three Young Men appears to have been shaped mainly by the psalms. The "Bless the Lord, so-and-so" formula is prominent in Ps. 103:1, 20–22, which might have provided the basis for the first part of each verse. The content, in which various aspects of creation are adjured to honor God, might have been learned from Psalm 148, which also instructs things though not in such a well-organized or encyclopedic fashion. Finally, Psalm 136 appears to have had a twofold influence upon the Song of the Three Young Men, first in the form of a hymn with a refrain that recurs relentlessly in the second half of every verse and second in the content of vv. 67–68, which are a slightly expanded paraphrase of Ps. 136:1–2.

Theology and Piety

Drawing on sources that articulate the Deuteronomistic theodicy, the Prayer of Azariah, not surprisingly, also articulates this credo. The reaffirmation of the direct relationship between covenant loyalty and the fate of the Jewish people is a recurring theme of intertestamental literature (as in Tob. 3:2–5; 13:5–6; Jdt. 5:17–21; 8:18–20; Bar. 1:15–2:15; 3:10–13; 2 Macc. 7:18, 32–38). Within this framework, the author shares with the author of Daniel 9 and Baruch 1–2 the conviction that God's honor is invested in the fate of the people and the city called by "God's name." Their domination and degradation at the hands of Gentiles, who worship other gods, will not manifest God's honor to those who do not know God. The Prayer of Azariah, like Daniel 9, grounds its plea for deliverance in a plea for God to assert and manifest God's honor in the situation through the deliverance of those claiming God's patronage and protection (deSilva 1995: 190, 293). Ultimately, God's reputation among the nations (Pr. Azar. 22) is bound to the exaltation or degradation of Israel. This link is the source of the psalmist's hope that Israel will be restored to greatness.

The Prayer of Azariah resonates with the moral, ethical, and internal rationalization of sacrifices in many psalms and prophetic texts. The system of animal and produce sacrifices was not left to the realm of externalistic religion by the Israelites but provided a framework by which to give expression to and prioritize the movements of the heart (e.g., toward contrition and repentance, as here in Pr. Azar. 15–17 or in Ps. 51:16–17, or toward adoration of God, as in Ps. 50:23; 141:2), acts of justice in the sphere of human relationships (Prov. 21:3, 27; Hos. 6:6), and obedience to the covenant (1 Sam. 15:22; Ps. 40:6–8). Here the motive for rationalization of sacrifices—the discovery of accessible, yet acceptable, alternatives to the Levitical sacrifices—is the removal of access to the cult center in Jerusalem (one of the reflections in the prayer suggesting composition in the time of Antiochus IV).

The Song of the Three Young Men celebrates God as the Creator of all things, living and inanimate, and calls upon every aspect of creation to acknowledge their debt of gratitude to their Creator (implied in Sg. Three 35). The diverse addressees that form the main content of the song are all held together by this common bond, of being "works," created things, of the Lord, from the angels to Azariah. They are all merely called to take up their duty to revere their Maker.[9] Several concluding rationales for the praise are provided in Sg. Three 66–68, such as are familiar from the canonical Psalter: personal deliverance, God's goodness, and the lasting quality of God's mercy.

Insertion into the Daniel Cycle

The insertion of these liturgical pieces into the Daniel cycle was accomplished with minimal alteration of the originals. The Prayer of Azariah required only a brief prose introduction, with another prose narrative being composed to provide the bridge between petition and praise. In the Song of the Three Young Men, only v. 66 refers to the story of Daniel 3 and thus would seem to be an addition made by the editor who placed this psalm of praise into the story.

The interpolation affects the way that one reads both Daniel and the liturgical compositions. First, the prayer and hymn, quite suitable for use by a wide array of people in an endless number of settings, are given a concrete occasion and setting. They will be read specifically as responses of Daniel's companions to their situation in Daniel 3, which will, in turn, underscore what astounding possibilities are opened up for the individual in need through confession and prayer, as well as suggest a fitting response to God's deliverance: involving the whole cosmos in one's hymn of gratitude to God. The additions dramatically change the character of Daniel 3 as well. Previously, the focus of the story had been on the gold idol and the pompous proclamation calling for its adoration and then on Nebuchadnezzar's responses to the confessors and their unexpected fate. With the additions, the focus turns much more to the God whom the three served, to the worship not around an idol but in the furnace to the One God. The additions may stall the forward movement of the plot, but they also transform the furnace into a place for beautiful, unhurried, ordered worship, which is, after all, the miracle of the plot.

Influence

The primary influence of these additions has been through their use in public worship. Their acceptance into the Daniel story suggests that these li-

---

9. On the universal phenomenon of acknowledging God or the gods for the gift of life and being, see deSilva 2000b: 126–27.

turgical pieces were well respected among the editor's readers. Moreover, these liturgical pieces entered the liturgies of the early church (attested by their inclusion in the Odes in several Septuagint codices) and have remained popular canticles in the Catholic, Anglican, and Episcopal churches.

Susanna

Contents and Structure

The story of Susanna is set in the time of the Babylonian exile, in and around the house of Joakim, a wealthy and honored Jew whose home served as a sort of community center for the exiles in that area. Two elders who had been appointed judges begin to lust after Joakim's wife, Susanna. They offer her an ultimatum: she must indulge their desire or else be charged by them with being caught in the act of adultery with an anonymous young man who escaped them. She chooses to remain faithful to God's law and her husband, even though that would mean losing the reputation of being chaste and even her life. In court, the elders, being judges, are believed, and Susanna is sentenced to death. The Lord hears her cry for vindication and moves Daniel to intervene. Daniel halts the proceedings and catches the two perjurers in an inconsistency in their testimony, with the result that Susanna is spared, the elders executed, and Daniel's reputation increased.

The two Greek versions differ markedly here, with Theodotion providing a richer story line. The differences may be summarized as follows:

1. vv. 14–19: Θ provides an extra scene, as Susanna bathes in the garden, dismisses her servants, and is accosted by the elders. This is absent from the LXX, which instead includes a bare report of the elders' decision to trap Susanna in v. 19.
2. vv. 20–21, 24–27: In Θ, the elders profess their desire and pose their threat, after which Susanna screams, her servants reemerge, and the elders denounce her. The elders' direct speech is absent from LXX.
3. v. 35: LXX shows Susanna praying for deliverance before the elders' testimony in court. Θ delays this prayer until after the sentence of death is passed (vv. 42–43).
4. v. 39: LXX has the elders offer the excuse that the "young man" was wearing a mask and hence could not be identified.
5. vv. 44–45: In LXX, an angel bestows a spirit of discernment on Daniel, who also renders no immediate pronouncement upon the elders. Θ (vv. 44–46) has God stir up Daniel's spirit directly, who opens with a declaration of Susanna's innocence.
6. v. 52: LXX adds an admonition: "Do not think about their status as elders, nor say, 'They can never lie.'"

7. v. 56: LXX reads "Sidon" where Θ reads "Canaan."
8. v. 60: Θ adds "and they blessed God, who saves those who hope in God."
9. v. 62: LXX adds the method of execution and the pouring out of fire upon the elders' corpses by angels.
10. LXX concludes the story with a general praise of sincere young men and exhorts the audience to help train young men to show knowledge and discernment. Θ concludes by narrating the family's relief at Susanna's deliverance and noting Daniel's increased reputation.

Genre and Purpose

Susanna has been called the first "detective story" (Pfeiffer 1949: 448), and its historicity is no longer seriously defended. It has been suggested that the story originated as a reaction against judicial practices of the Sadducees, in line with Simeon ben Shetach's attempts to bring reform by encouraging more stringent cross-examination of witnesses (see vv. 48–49) and by insisting on the Deuteronomic principle of punishing false witnesses in accordance with the potential fate awaiting the accused, independent of whether or not the sentence had already been executed (Brüll 1877; Kay 1913: 643–44). Such a purpose would be far too obscure for the general reader, all the more so as neither Greek version holds this up at the end as the "moral" of the tale, each preferring a different conclusion (Delcor 1971: 277). Moreover, the trial itself is far from a model of justice, and Daniel works by divine inspiration rather than as a jurist (Delcor 1971: 278). While the story should not be regarded, then, as an encoded attempt to promote a particular agenda for the reformation of jurisprudence, it does highlight one of the potential problems of the legal system envisioned by Torah: the potential for two witnesses to conspire to give false testimony and thus the danger that the courts can be manipulated to condemn the innocent.[10]

Like Judith and Tobit, the story of Susanna has pure entertainment value but also reinforces some core values of Judaism. Among these are the importance of remaining loyal to God and God's commandments despite the temporal dangers one might incur in the process (it is never permissible to seek to escape danger by acquiescing to sin), God's vindication of those who walk uprightly, and God's eventual punishment of the sinner.

Author, Date, and Setting

The story of Susanna might represent a Jewish adaptation of an existing tale told outside of the Jewish community. There are many folktales of "the

---

10. Although the historicity of the accounts of Jesus' trial in the Gospels has come under intense fire, the intentional use of false witnesses to gain the verdict that the powers desire is also prominent, and censured, there.

innocent woman falsely accused" and of "the young, intelligent judge" (Delcor 1971: 277). A similar story even appears in the *Arabian Nights* (Pfeiffer 1949: 453). In its present form, the story is completely at home in the Jewish culture and worldview—that is, no evidence of its possible non-Jewish origins remains (Moore 1977: 89). Since the appearance of Daniel is abrupt and rather unnecessary for the story (any unnamed youth would have served just as well), it is possible that the young man who intervenes to bring justice to all was identified as Daniel at a secondary stage (Pfeiffer 1949: 449; Kay 1913: 642).

It is difficult to determine the date of this story. While Daniel's name may only have come to be included later, the story itself resonates well with the condition of Jews throughout most of the Persian and Hellenistic periods. The Jewish community envisioned in the story has a high level of self-governance within Gentile domination, which was true of several Diaspora communities as well as of Judea during much of the intertestamental period. The probability of a Semitic original would also suggest a provenance in Palestine or the eastern Diaspora. The hint of the superiority of a daughter of Judah, who bravely resisted the elders' constraint, to the daughters of Israel (i.e., the northern tribes), who yielded to the elders in the past, suggests that the author would have regarded himself as a Judahite (Collins 1993: 438).

Formative Influences

Aside from the folk motifs that provide major elements of this story, Susanna draws quite heavily on the Hebrew Scriptures for its inspiration and detail. Scholars frequently cite Jer. 29:21–23 as a source, considering Susanna to be a narrative expansion of that tightly compressed oracle. While there are noteworthy motifs shared in common—two men in authoritative positions abusing their position, engaging in adultery with "their neighbors' wives," speaking lies (though as prophets, not judges, in Jeremiah), and coming to a just punishment—there are also significant differences. If Susanna were simply a midrash on Jer. 29:21–23, the author's decision to transform the prophets into judges, the crime of false prophecy into courtroom perjury, and the instrument of justice from Nebuchadnezzar to the Jewish community would represent unnecessary departures from the source (as comparison with a true midrash on Jer. 29:21–23 will show).[11]

The explicit quotation in v. 5 presents difficulties because it is not found in known texts of the Bible. This has been the subject of a well-executed investigation by Marti Steussy (1993: 146–52), who understands the quotation to be a reflection of Jer. 23:15c ("from the prophets of Jerusalem ungodliness has spread throughout the land") read in the light of LXX Jer. 36:21–23 (MT 29:21–23), which situates the ungodly prophets in Babylon. From his postex-

---

11. See *b. Sanhedrin* 93a, quoted in Moore 1977: 85.

ilic setting, the author of the Susanna narrative would see Babylon more naturally as the locale from which ungodliness emerges, whereas Jerusalem is the focus of hope and of holiness (contrary to Jeremiah's presentation of Jerusalem as the place of ungodliness and Babylon as the place of hope and restoration). While there are thus some resonances with Scripture, the author has in large measure crafted his "quotation" to suit his story.[12]

The legal aspects of the story are taken from the Pentateuch with little or no modification. Thus, death is the penalty for adultery in v. 41 (Lev. 20:10; Deut. 22:22). Verse 62 contains a veiled allusion to Deut. 19:18–19: "The judges shall make a thorough inquiry. If the witness is a false witness, having testified falsely against another, then you shall do to the false witness just as the false witness had meant to do to the other." The death penalty is incurred by the elders because they intended that Susanna should incur that penalty through their perjury. This differs from the procedure in place in the early first century in Palestine, when, following Sadducean practice, a false witness could not be executed unless the victim had in fact already been executed.

Finally, in v. 53 Daniel quotes, rather closely, Exod. 23:7b: "Do not kill the innocent and those in the right." The larger context of the Exodus quotation admirably fits the story of Susanna: "Keep far from a false charge . . . for I will not acquit the guilty" (Exod. 23:7a, c). The discovery of the elders' conspiracy to commit murder through perjury, and their fate, affirms God's commitment to justice as expressed in Exod. 23:7.

Theology and Piety

By giving the reader a window into the mental processes of the corrupt elders in vv. 8–11, the author teaches that turning one's mind away from God and hardening one's sense of shame before God's law can lead even trusted judges to become slaves to carnal passions and perjurers (Kay 1913: 646). Susanna, by contrast, embodies the person who "fears the Lord" and hence embodies also the wisdom tradition of Israel, in which "fear of the Lord" is a foundational value (Delcor 1971: 263). The tale reinforces, in the person and ruminations of Susanna, the importance of remaining loyal to God and God's commandments despite the temporal dangers one might incur in the process, a lesson taught also by 2 Macc. 6:26. Ben Sira also had striven to place firmly in the minds and hearts of his pupils the awareness of God, the Divine Judge, who looks upon all actions from beyond and passes the verdict of utmost importance (Sir. 23:18–19; 17:15). This is precisely that which the judges turn away from and that which Susanna keeps foremost in place (vv. 9, 22–23).

Susanna's prayer expresses confidence in God's knowledge of what is buried beneath deceptive appearances, a theme well established in the Hebrew

---

12. This phenomenon is not unique to Susanna, as Matthew also occasionally shapes a Scripture to suit his narrative, as in Matt. 2:23.

Scriptures (see 1 Sam. 16:7; Dan. 2:22) and speaks of God's foreknowledge in a manner that resonates with the fuller expression of this in Jdt. 9:5–6. The story also upholds the conviction that God is absolutely just and would not permit injustice to have the last word in human affairs. God vindicates those who walk uprightly and eventually brings the sinner and oppressor to punishment (Delcor 1971: 278). God not only cares about God's people as a whole but also intervenes on behalf of the individual (Moore 1977:28).

Insertion into the Daniel Cycle

Once the courtroom hero is identified as Daniel, the story is ready to be appended to the Hebrew canonical collection. In Greek versions that place Susanna prior to canonical Daniel 1 (Theodotion traditions), this story becomes an introduction to the wise youth whose career and visions will dominate the remainder of the book. This placement leads to some tension, however, between the presentation of Daniel in the story of Susanna as a member of the community of the exile, long established in Babylon, and the presentation of Daniel as a member of a recently deported people in Daniel 1. Bringing the story into the orbit of the Daniel cycle has the effect of turning the story into a glorification of the intellect of Daniel, the wise person in the service of God. Theodotion's conclusion to the story explicitly makes this the final word of the story.

The older, Septuagint edition placed Susanna between Daniel 12 and 14, giving it more the aura of an appendix than a preface. Its conclusion is also more suited to its preexistence as an independent story than its inclusion in a cycle of Daniel stories, as it encourages the Jewish community to nurture the kind of young man (women would never play such a role in the assemblies) who can discern treachery and ensure justice by the full application of his wits.

Influence

Susanna is not part of the Hebrew canonical Daniel. It has been suggested that Susanna was excluded from the canon because it contradicts a halakhah (*m. Sanhedrin* 5.1): the guilt of a suspected false witness must be confirmed by still other witnesses who can attest that he or she was not even present at the scene of the crime (an opinion cited in Moore 1977: 80). The circumstances of the particular case in Susanna preclude, however, the applicability of this rule (the false witnesses were, in fact, with Susanna; they lied not about their location but about what they saw). Since we have never found or heard a reliable report of a Hebrew Daniel with the additions, it is more likely that Susanna became part of the Daniel cycle too late to have ever been considered an authoritative part of that work and perhaps remained a free-floating Hebrew story unconnected with the Book of Daniel until the Septuagint translation brought the different stories together (Collins 1993: 437). Thus, Susanna probably was not excluded from the canon but merely arose too late to find a place within that body of classical literature.[13]

It has also been suggested that the portrayal of the elders was a stumbling block to canonical acceptance and provides a clue to the church's preference for Theodotion over the Septuagint (which had been even more direct in deconstructing the ethos of the "elder"). Although more learned voices have affirmed this (Moore 1977: 80–81; Collins 1993: 438), I do not assume that, given the choice between ensuring justice by promoting the accountability of elders and protecting one's status by the suppression of that which promotes accountability, an elder would necessarily gravitate toward the latter.

Indeed, an early application of Susanna, according it the authority of inspired Scripture, focuses precisely on this issue. Irenaeus (*Adversus haereses* 4.26.3) quotes vv. 56, 52–53 (in that order and following Theodotion's text) to denounce elders in the church who use their position to "serve their own lusts," thinking to escape human and divine judgment. While Irenaeus expects to find these elders in the camps of the heretics rather than among those who keep to the apostolic teaching, not only purity of thought but also "blameless conduct" are requirements of all elders. He, an elder, is thus perfectly willing to use Susanna as an inspired Scripture calling for absolute norms of thought and conduct to which all elders ought to be held accountable.[14]

The story of Susanna exercised an influence on early Christian art, as evidenced in the catacombs. The image of Susanna, hemmed in by her antagonists, makes her a fitting image for the struggles of the early church to maintain its fidelity to God in the midst of extreme pressures (see Boitani 1996: 7–10). In his commentary on Daniel, Hippolytus read the Susanna story (in Theodotion's version) as an allegory of the contest of the early church against both Jews and pagans, who would denounce and exterminate her (see Boitani 1996: 11–17).[15] John Chrysostom preached a sermon on Susanna, praising her constancy toward God in the face of so many losses and dangers.[16] The story was retold in medieval, Renaissance, and Restoration poems and plays,[17] has inspired scores of artistic representations (see Spolsky 1996),[18] and was set to music in Handel's oratorio *Susanna*.

13. On the ongoing influence of Susanna on Jewish culture and thought, see Lévi 1933.

14. For other patristic references to Susanna, as to the other additions to Daniel, see Julius 1903.

15. Especially striking is Hippolytus's comment on v. 22 as the expression of the plight of every Christian martyr.

16. An excerpt can be found in Metzger 1957: 112. Halpern-Amaru (1996) offers a fine interpretive essay on the reading of Susanna among the early church fathers.

17. Two of these are discussed in Jeffrey 1996 and Kaplan 1996.

18. Metzger (1957: 227–28) includes a catalogue. Spolsky (1996) observes that nothing in the text suggests that Susanna had already undressed when accosted by the elders, even though every painter she canvasses portrays her thus.

Bel and the Dragon

Contents and Structure

The king of Babylon (Cyrus the Persian in Theodotion) asks Daniel why he does not worship Bel, the recipient of lavish cult in Babylon. Daniel replies that he does not worship human-made objects but only the Living God, who made all things. The king objects that Bel consumes massive amounts of food and so must be a living god. Daniel laughs and asserts that Bel never ate any of the food offerings laid before him, as he is only clay and bronze. The king, enraged, poses a challenge: either the priests will prove that Bel is a living god that eats and so escape death, or Daniel will prove that Bel does not eat and so escape death.

The food is laid out before the idol, and the priests are dismissed. Daniel scatters ashes on the floor, shuts the temple, and invites the king to set his seal upon the door. The next morning, the seals are found intact, but the food has disappeared. Daniel points the king to the footprints of men, women, and children in the ashes. The king forces the priests to reveal the trapdoor by which they would enter the temple at night and consume the food, executes them, and authorizes Daniel to destroy Bel and its temple.

The second episode involves a living creature (probably a snake, which is often called a *drakōn*) venerated by the Babylonians. The king invites Daniel to worship it, since obviously it is a living god. Daniel disproves this claim by killing the dragon with a concoction of fat, pitch, and hair. At this point the Babylonians intervene, demanding that the king hand over Daniel to them or else suffer their wrath. Daniel is cast (again) into the den of lions, which, though hungry, do not eat him, even though he is there for a week. On the sixth day, Daniel is miraculously fed by God, who has an angel transport Habakkuk from Palestine, carrying some stew and bread. On the seventh day, Daniel is discovered alive, the king acclaims the One God, and the ringleaders of the revolt are cast to the lions and devoured at once.

Once again, the differences between the two Greek versions, though not nearly as appreciable as in Susanna, merit attention:

1. v. 1: LXX alone presents this story as coming "from the prophecy of Habakkuk," and it leaves the king anonymous, while Θ names the king as Cyrus.
2. v. 5: In LXX, Daniel refuses the king's request merely with a positive profession of monolatry. In Θ, Daniel's refusal includes him saying, "I do not worship idols made with hands."
3. v. 8: In LXX, the priests of Bel actually lie to the king, saying, "It is Bel himself who eats these things," before Daniel accepts the king's challenge.

4. v. 12: Θ gives away the presence of the trapdoor, while LXX leaves this out until the king's discovery at the end of this episode.
5. v. 21: LXX has an extra, brief scene as the king and Daniel surprise the priests at the priests' house, finding Bel's food there.
6. v. 22: In LXX, the king destroys Bel and Daniel kills the priests.
7. v. 25: Θ has Daniel repeat his profession of monolatry.
8. v. 29: In Θ, the people explicitly demand that Daniel be handed over. In LXX, the king does this on his own as a means of placating the mob.
9. v. 32: LXX adds "that he not receive a burial" as part of Daniel's anticipated disgrace.
10. v. 39: LXX adds that "the Lord remembered Daniel."

Some suggest that the stories of Daniel's encounter with Bel and with the dragon originally formed separate and independent narratives. In the current form of the narrative, however, the two episodes are intimately connected and skillfully woven together (at least, the second episode grows organically from the first). The first speaks of a god who cannot eat, the second of a god who eats and dies (Delcor 1971:291). Moreover, there are definite resonances in the second episode of the first episode: (1) the king's opening words to Daniel in the second episode ("You cannot deny that this is a living god" [v. 24]) presuppose Daniel's prior rejection of Bel worship because Bel was merely an inanimate work of human hands (vv. 5–7); (2) the Babylonians revolt against the king in the second episode because he has allowed the destruction of Bel, the dragon, and Bel's priests (v. 28), a prominent reference in the second episode to the denouement of the first (v. 22).[19] Indeed, although the Bel episode may have existed at some point independently of the dragon episode, the opposite is harder to imagine, the dragon episode being a foil to the Bel narrative in so many ways.

Genre and Purpose

Bel and the Dragon falls in line with the plot of the court tales in Daniel 1–6, with which it shares (and perhaps from which it has learned) the following themes: a conflict concerning piety (which is the true God?); a contest in which the One God comes to be acclaimed by the Gentile king; some danger posed to the Jewish hero's life, relieved by divine deliverance. It differs in its more aggressive attack on idolatry initiated by Daniel (in which it resembles the contest initiated by Daniel in Daniel 1 but over the issue of foods there, not deities), whereas in the other tales involving worship the Jewish hero does not initiate the conflict or take direct action against foreign cults.

19. This is more than just a "passing allusion to the Bel incident," as Moore (1977: 121) describes it.

As with Susanna, Bel and the Dragon is no longer regarded as a historical narrative. The main "historical" action mentioned in the narrative—the destruction of Bel and his temple in Babylon—does not even happen during the time of the Babylonian exile. The temple of Bel, along with its statue, is still standing in the time of Xerxes I, who plunders it, although it is found in ruins by Alexander the Great (Delcor 1971: 289). Rather, this narrative is another manifestation of Judaism's polemic against idolatry, a polemic that begins as early as Deut. 4:28, which describes other gods as "objects of wood and stone that neither see, nor hear, nor eat, nor smell," and which is advanced in Jeremiah 10, Hab. 2:18–19, Letter of Jeremiah, and Wisdom of Solomon 13–16 (see Roth 1975).

The fact that authors return repeatedly to the theme of the folly of idolatry suggests the importance of this topic for Jews, particularly in the Diaspora. In Palestine, the question was usually more of an intellectual one: idolatry was taken as a sign of the Gentile's ignorance in the matters of true piety. The more closely Jews interacted with Gentiles and the more involved they became in Gentile circles, the more they would be exposed to idolatry and the invitation—and perhaps expectation—to perform those rites that expressed piety and solidarity with their Gentile comrades. The Jews' failure to worship the local gods figures prominently, for example, in debates over citizenship rights in a variety of cities in the first centuries B.C.E. and C.E. (see Josephus, *Jewish Antiquities* 12.119–126). Beyond these specific instances, there remained the important work of "world maintenance"—legitimating the Jewish worldview and thus the ongoing existence of a distinctive Jewish culture by delegitimating prominently visible aspects of the major alternative worldview.

Author, Date, and Setting

While the author remains anonymous, some scholars have ventured to posit a very specific time and circumstance of composition. Davies (1913: 656), for example, suggests composition in a time of serious religious persecution, as under Antiochus VII Sidetes. The assertion that "the general character of this tract" suggests authorship during a time of bitter persecution is without foundation, arising no doubt from the unwarranted reading of the actions against Daniel in the second part of the story as a reflection of the author's own time. Moreover, the picture of Antiochus VII painted by Josephus (*Jewish Antiquities* 13.236–248) does not support the claim that he was an enemy of the Jewish religion per se. Although he retaliated against Simon's anti-Seleucid actions by invading Judea and even besieging Jerusalem, and although he pressed the siege so hard that many died of famine, he showed himself quite favorably disposed toward Jewish piety, allowing a truce for the week of the Pentecost celebration at John Hyrcanus's request and even providing bulls for sacrifices, winning himself the epithet "Antiochus the Pious."

This display of reverence toward Jewish piety led to a resolution of the dispute shortly thereafter.

The composition of Bel and the Dragon was inspired not by persecution but by the perennial problem of living as a minority, monolatrous culture in an idol-worshiping world. The attack on both idolatry and zoolatry makes Egypt the place where the stories would be most on target with regard to the religious alternatives encountered by God-fearing Jews (see the Egyptian Jewish texts Wis. 11:15–16; 15:18–19; *Letter of Aristeas* 138) (Roth 1975: 43), who could profit from some reinforcement of the unique truth of their own religious heritage despite the lavish expenditures and apparent devotion of their neighbors toward their gods. The main obstacle to this provenance is the fact that no known Egyptian Jewish text was composed in Aramaic or Hebrew (Collins 1993: 419). Thus, while this provenance is not impossible, since not all Egyptian Jews need be supposed to have forgotten their ancestral language, it is more likely that the story originates in Palestine and that idolatry and zoolatry simply are attacked as two well-known forms of Gentile impiety.

Formative Influences

Under the influence of the "history of religions" school, some relationship between Bel and the Dragon and the ancient Babylonian *Enuma Elish* was sought. The identification of Bel as another name for Marduk (the triumphant deity in the *Enuma*) led to the suggestion that the dragon, or serpent, was a living representation of Tiamat, the personification of chaos. Zimmermann (1958b) thought he had traced the development from the "wind" (*sâru*) sent by Bel-Marduk into Tiamat's open mouth, distending and exploding her body, to the "hair" and "barley cakes" (Aramaic: שערא, שערתא) that Daniel fed to the dragon to achieve the same end. Read in this light, Bel and the Dragon would seem to be a parody of the great *Enuma Elish,* in which both the ancient hero and the antagonist are shown to be empty fantasies by the Jewish defender of monotheism. Against this background is the lack of any connection of the snake with Tiamat in the story and the tendency to depict Tiamat as a fantastic "dragon" in our sense of the term (rather than a "snake," befitting the *drakōn* in this story) (Davies 1913: 653–54). It may simply be, then, that the snake is brought into the story as a representative of the zoolatry that Jews knew to be practiced in Egypt alongside idolatry.

Once again, the Hebrew Scriptures offer rich fields for the discovery of the resources mined by the author of this tale. Some scholars read Bel and the Dragon as a midrash on Jer. 51:34–35, 44 (Brüll 1887; Moore 1977: 122). Upon closer inspection, however, Jer. 51:34–35 has only the vaguest of connections with this story. It is Jer. 51:44, which mentions Bel by name in the MT ("I will punish Bel in Babylon, and make him disgorge what he has swallowed"), that really begins a series of resonances with the tale. Verses 47 and 52 of Jeremiah 51 go on to promise God's punishment and destruction of

Babylon's "images" and "idols." Bel and the Dragon might represent, then, a working out of this promised hope in narrative form, God using Daniel as his instrument.

Isaiah 45:1–46:7 has been suggested as a possible source of literary inspiration (Nickelsburg 1984: 39). Indeed, there are many thematic resonances: the uniqueness of the One God who created heaven and earth (Isa. 45:5–6, 12, 18, 21–22; cf. Bel 5, 25); the impotence of idols (Isa. 45:16, 20; 46:1–2, 7; cf. Bel 5, 7); the eventual confession of the One God by the Gentiles (Isa. 45:14, 23; cf. Bel 41). It is noteworthy also that Bel is mentioned by name and said to be humiliated in Isa. 46:1. Theodotion's attribution of the tale to the time of Cyrus (where the Spetuagint merely had left the king anonymous) might also be inspired by Isaiah's unique acclamation of this Gentile and, perhaps, the hope that Isaiah gives that this chosen, God-anointed Gentile king (Isa. 45:1) will come to know the One God who chose and uses him.

The final episode clearly recalls the older and simpler tale in Daniel 6, where the lions' den again provides the conclusion to a debate over worship (Delcor 1971: 291). In Bel and the Dragon, the episode of the lions' den is prolonged to a seven-day stay and is enhanced by the conjunction of the career of the Palestine-based prophet Habakkuk and the Babylon-based Daniel. Habakkuk's being lifted from place to place by an angel grasping the hair of his head recalls Ezek. 8:3, where Ezekiel is thus transported (but in a visionary state only), and the miraculous provision by God for God's prophet recalls the feeding of Elijah in the wilderness by ravens and by an angel (1 Kings 17:4–6; 19:4–8).

These varied threads of tradition have been brought together by the author of Bel and the Dragon in a tale that captures the message of each: God's triumph over idolatry in all its forms and God's provision for and protection of those who bravely witness to the One God who is a "living God."

Theology and Piety

Bel and the Dragon provides a window into Jewish reflection on the God of their ancestors vis-à-vis the gods worshiped by the nations around them. These gods were quite close to home for them—whether in the Diaspora, in the more Hellenized cities in Palestine (notably, the coastland), and in the wake of the introduction of pagan cult into the Jerusalem temple itself for a brief but memorable time—and interpreting their cult in a manner that would support Jewish views about the Divine was an ongoing need. Thus in v. 5 the author poses a stark contrast between the God who created and the created gods/idols. The Jewish author, like most anti-idolatry polemicists, refuses to acknowledge any supernatural reality behind the artifact of the idol: it is just a block of wood or stone or metal and nothing more. The alternative to this among Jewish authors was to acknowledge the spiritual forces of Satan standing behind and profiting from the cult of idols (see Bar. 4:7; *Testament of Job* 2–5).

God is a God who moves, acts, speaks, and works wonders; the idol can do nothing. The author suggests that even their priests know this, but they continue to perpetrate deception upon ruler and people to the priests' own advantage. As for zoolatry, the animal that receives cult, though it is able to eat, see, and move, is found ultimately to be mortal. The story's final scene (the king's confession in v. 41) is a narrative expression of the basic Jewish hope that, eventually, the deviant majority will come to understand the true nature of their so-called gods and the power and reality of the God of Israel.

Bel and the Dragon stands out from the other Daniel stories in the active, aggressive stance that Daniel takes against idolatrous cults. Several other texts from the intertestamental period, however, work out in narrative form the Jewish desire to eradicate the repulsive veneration of idols in their world. What Daniel does to Bel, Job does to an idol's temple in his jurisdiction (*Testament of Job* 2–5) and Abraham does to the idols that his father and family had worshiped out of fear of their neighbors (*Jubilees* 12.1–14) (Nickelsburg 1984: 39 n. 38).

A less prominent theological affirmation of this story is God's mindfulness of those who, being faithful to God, find themselves in distress (v. 38). The effect of this is heightened, however, when this tale is appended to the other Daniel legends in which this theme is so prominent (notably, Daniel 1, 3, 6, and Susanna).

Insertion into the Daniel Cycle

The original independence of Bel and the Dragon from the canonical collection is shown by formal introduction of Daniel in v. 2 (Moore 1977: 121). No modification of the story or of the Hebrew-Aramaic Daniel appears to have been necessary to join the two. It is placed consistently at the end of Greek versions of Daniel. Theodotion adds Cyrus's name to the opening, this being the last-named monarch within whose reign Daniel is said to have been alive. There were tales already for the reigns of Nebuchadnezzar (chs. 1–4), Belshazzar (ch. 5), and Darius (ch. 6), and there were visions for Belshazzar (7:1; 8:1), Darius (9:1), and Cyrus (10:1). Now Theodotion shapes Bel and the Dragon as a tale for the last reign.[20]

We have already noted how joining this tale to Daniel 1–6 would highlight a rather underplayed theological note in the story. Steussy (1993: 192) has suggested a more radical effect that adding this tale would have on the reading of the whole. By ending with a tale, the Greek versions de-emphasize the "apocalyptic and nationalistic tendencies" of Hebrew Daniel (ending, as it

---

20. There is a minor historical problem in v. 1 of Theodotion: Cyrus took the throne by force of arms from his grandfather Astyages, so that "succeeded" is a rather benign word here (see Grabbe 1992: 1.122).

does, with the visions) and return to an emphasis on questions "relevant to ongoing Diaspora life." The end of the story is no longer the glorious vindication of the people of God and the resurrection of the just (Dan. 12:1–3) but the time of waiting and of coping with the realities of life in an idol-ridden, Gentile dominant culture.

Influence

As with Susanna, Bel and the Dragon is not found in the Hebrew canon. Once again, it is less likely to have been a matter of exclusion as much as a matter of the story remaining independent of the canonical Daniel too late into the period for inclusion (Collins 1993: 419). The first-century-C.E. Jewish *Lives of the Prophets* shows an awareness of Habakkuk's visit to Daniel in Babylon (12:1–9), recording this event within Habakkuk's biography. In this text, Habakkuk is a contemporary of Daniel, active in Palestine, and dies two years before the return from the exile. It is thus not likely that the author of the *Lives of the Prophets* regarded the episode as coming from the reign of Cyrus (and so was not reading a text of the pre-Theodotion type).

The story appears to have been accepted as part of the Book of Daniel by the early church, which ensured that it would continue to be read and used in the nurture of the church. Irenaeus (*Adversus haereses* 4.5.2) quotes vv. 4–5, 25, as a witness to God as the "living God" and therefore "God of the living" (cf. Matt. 22:30–32), the God who can give life to the dead. Clement of Alexandria (*Stromata* 1.21) refers to the dragon episode in passing as a proof that Habakkuk was still active in the time of Zedekiah. Tertullian (*De idololatria* 18) refers to Bel and the Dragon as part of his defense that one could wear garments that were occasionally, but not necessarily, connected with idol worship. Although Daniel did not participate in idolatry, he nevertheless did not refuse to wear purple as a mark of his status, even though that color was also worn by idol priests.[21]

21. These three references are listed in Moore 1977: 126.

1 Maccabees

11

"The Family through Which Deliverance Was Given"

First Maccabees recounts how Mattathias and his five sons delivered Israel from the threat posed to the Jewish way of life by Antiochus IV and the renegade Jews and restored political independence to Israel after four and a half centuries of foreign domination. Written by a supporter of the Hasmonean dynasty, the carefully crafted history presents Judas and his brothers as the divinely appointed agents of deliverance and reminds its readers of the enormous debt owed to the house of Mattathias by the nation. The ideology of 1 Maccabees was to shape Jewish nationalism and political messianic hopes through the next three centuries.

Structure and Contents

The story of 1 Maccabees divides neatly into three parts: the crisis and Mattathias's initial response (1:1–2:70), the exploits of Judas (3:1–9:22), and the exploits of Jonathan and Simon (9:23–12:53; 13:1–16:24). The story begins with the introduction of Antiochus IV, a "sinful root" shooting forth from the successors of the arrogant Alexander (1:1–10). Renegade Jews, bent on eliminating the separation between Jew and Gentile and enjoying the benefits of belonging to the dominant Gentile culture, obtain authorization to build a gymnasium and introduce Greek customs into Jerusalem, also erasing the telltale signs of their Jewish heritage (1:11–15). The remainder of chapter 1 tells of Antiochus's robbing of the Jerusalem temple to help finance his Egyptian campaigns and of his plan to unite his kingdom by eliminating the local customs that distinguished one people from another. The author frequently moves into poetic composition to express the sorrow and disgrace that come upon Israel as a result (1:24–28, 36–40). A sharp distinction appears between the renegade Jews, who accept the king's decree, and the loyal Jews, who prefer death to disloyalty toward God and the covenant (1:43–63). The crisis concludes: "Very great wrath came upon Israel" (1:64).

Mattathias, a priest from a distinguished line, steps into the drama lamenting the fate of Jerusalem and Judah (2:1–14). As the program of forced apostasy moves out from Jerusalem into the surrounding villages, Mattathias is confronted by a representative of Antiochus and invited to be the first to offer an unlawful sacrifice and so enter into the king's friendship, honor, and wealth. When Mattathias refuses and another steps in, hoping to receive favor, Mattathias kills both the opportunist Jew and the king's agent in a manner intentionally reminiscent of Phineas's act of zeal in Num. 25:6–15 (2:15–26). He rallies to himself those who are "zealous for the law" and begins to attack the renegade Jews and their Gentile protectors in the hinterlands of Jerusalem (2:27–48). On his deathbed, Mattathias encourages his five sons to continue the tradition of the faithful ancestors in Israel and "show zeal for the law," a zeal manifested through holy war (2:49–70).

Leadership of the revolution falls to Judas, apparently the third-born of the five but the most distinguished warrior. After a poetic encomium praising Judas's exploits (3:3–9), the author tells of his successful campaigns against the Greco-Syrian armies, recapture of the temple, and provision for its rededication after the defilement (3:10–4:61). The author then recounts how Judas, Jonathan, and Simon rescue Jews being oppressed by Gentiles in the surrounding territories (5:1–68). After a respite, the Greco-Syrian kings, embroiled throughout the remainder of the book also in internal strife and power plays between rival claimants for the throne, renew their campaigns against Judas, in the course of which Eleazar, the fourth brother, dies. A temporary peace with Antiochus V results in the decrees proscribing Judaism being repealed (6:55–63), which are not reinstated even after Demetrius I dethrones Antiochus V and renews the war against Judas. At this point, Alcimus, a member of the Zadokites and the high priest appointed by Demetrius, appears on the scene (7:5–25). He is the only non-Hasmonean high priest active in the course of the narrative, and his faithlessness stands in stark contrast to the non-Zadokite Hasmoneans who will inherit the high priesthood within a decade. After some stunning Jewish victories, most notably over Nicanor (7:26–50), and a diplomatic envoy to Rome (8:1–31), Judas himself is killed, and the renegade Jews temporarily regain the upper hand (9:1–27).

In the wake of Judas's death, the people choose to be led by Jonathan, who leads the anti-Seleucid forces to victory against Bacchides, the Greco-Syrian general (9:28–73). This episode ends with the forging of a peace between Bacchides and Jonathan—"Thus the sword ceased from Israel" (9:73). Complete political independence, however, is still some distance away and will hereafter be fully achieved mainly through diplomacy and negotiation, though more fighting will be required to maintain it. The remainder of Jonathan's term of leadership, in fact, is largely taken up with diplomacy, as he plays one rival claimant for the Seleucid throne against another in order to win the greatest concessions for Judea (including the investment of Jonathan with the office of high priest [10:15–21; 11:57–59]). Jonathan himself succumbs to treachery, however, being taken captive by Trypho, one of the Seleucid contenders (12:39–53), and killed shortly afterward.

Now Simon steps forward to offer himself for the people, even as his four brothers have all served—and died in the service of—Israel, and his leadership is confirmed by the people (13:1–9). Still playing one Seleucid claimant off another, Simon wins political independence for Judea (13:10–53), resulting in the removal of the burden of tribute, the authorization to remove the garrison stationed originally by Antiochus IV in the Akra, and the right to mint coins and to adopt a new dating system (no longer based on Seleucid kings' reigns but on Simon's leadership). Chapter 14 consists of various pieces honoring Simon and responding to the benefits he and his house have brought Israel: an encomiastic poem celebrating the golden age that came with Simon's leadership (14:4–15), which nicely complements the poem offered in Judas's honor in 3:3–9; the acknowledgment of the legitimacy of Simon's rule by the foreign powers Rome and Sparta (14:16–24); and the resolution adopted by the people of Israel in gratitude to Simon and his family (14:25–49).

The final chapters tell of Simon and his sons' maintenance of Israel's independence and sovereignty in the face of renewed challenges from Antiochus VII (15:1–16:10); the treacherous murder of Simon and several of his sons by his son-in-law, Ptolemy son of Abubus (16:11–17); and John Hyrcanus I's ascension to the high priesthood and leadership of Judea in his father's stead (16:18–24), thus beginning the history of the hereditary succession of Simon's descendants to the positions of power and prestige held first by Jonathan and then Simon—the dynastic precedent that would be enjoyed by several generations of Hasmoneans.

The literary integrity of the book has occasionally been challenged on two points. First, scholars occasionally suggest that some number of the documents quoted in the text were actually interpolated by an editor after the book's original composition. Second, although this view has long since fallen from favor (Torrey 1945: 74–75), scholars have disputed the authenticity of chapters 14–16 on the basis of Josephus's departure from 1 Maccabees as a source at that point (Tedesche and Zeitlin 1950: 27–33). F.-M. Abel (1949: xiv), however, has given ample evidence that Josephus also knew the remaining chapters of 1 Maccabees and so merely preferred to follow another source for the Hasmonean history after the capture of the Akra, with the result that interpolations would be limited at most to a small number of the "historical documents" found throughout the text (see further discussion later in this chapter).

Textual Transmission

The Septuagint tradition is primarily responsible for the survival of 1 Maccabees and affords us our primary access to the most original version.[1] It is found in Codices Sinaiticus and Alexandrinus, the four books of the Maccabees being absent from Codex Vaticanus. In light of this, Codex Venetus becomes more important as a third principal textual witness. Translations were made from the Greek into Syriac and the Old Latin, the latter being regarded as a valuable witness to the text of the Septuagint before the revisions of Lucian, the scholar and martyr of the third century C.E. (Goldstein 1976: 178; Bartlett 1998: 15). The Syriac texts are based on the Lucianic edition of the Septuagint. An Armenian version was made from the Old Latin and has been of value for confirming the text of the Old Latin (Bartlett 1998: 15).

Despite the absence of surviving manuscript evidence, the majority of scholars affirm that 1 Maccabees was first written in Hebrew (Oesterley 1913: 61; Pfeiffer 1949: 483; Tedesche and Zeitlin 1950: 33; Metzger 1957: 130; Harrington 1999: 123). Translating the book back into Hebrew offers relatively few challenges and has been used to clear up difficulties in the Greek text, a fact that weighs heavily in favor of a Hebrew original standing behind the Septuagint tradition. The Greek translation was in turn deeply influenced by the translator's knowledge of the Septuagint translation of the Jewish Scriptures.[2]

The title of the book comes from the early Christian label for Judas and his brothers, Judas having been nicknamed Maccabeus ("the Maccabee" is used throughout 2 Maccabees to refer to Judas). Prior to the Christian era, Judas and his family were not referred to as "Maccabees," in the plural. The etymology of this name is the subject of much speculation, the favorite choice being "the hammer" or "the hammerer."[3]

Author, Date, and Setting

The author has not left us a name but has given us some clues for a general profile. First, the author reveals a close familiarity with Palestinian geography, suggesting someone who spent considerable time there and perhaps was even a native (Oesterley 1913: 59; Metzger 1957: 130; Torrey 1945: 72). This also correlates well with the evidence that points in the direction of a Hebrew original for the book. The author was a person of means (or at least well supported by literary patrons), educated in Hebrew and Greek, with access to the official archives in Jerusalem (Bartlett 1998: 33). Early attempts to align the author with the Sadducean party on the basis of the author displaying a "tolerant attitude towards the profaning of the Sabbath (ii. 41; ix. 43 ff.)" and a lack of a belief in life after death (Oesterley 1913: 59) failed to consider that the mere

1. The standard critical text is Kappler 1967.
2. For specific examples, see Pfeiffer 1949: 497–98; Tedesche and Zeitlin 1950: 34.
3. Pfeiffer 1949: 462 has a full discussion of various etymologies and explanations.

absence of Pharisaic leanings (life after death, messianic expectations, and the like) does not prove Sadducean tendencies, since not everyone in Judea belonged to one party or another (Pfeiffer 1949: 492).

The book must have been written after the accession of John Hyrcanus in 134 B.C.E., since this event is the last related in the narrative. The author speaks of the Romans highly and emphasizes the Jews' friendly relations with Rome and Rome's faithfulness as allies, necessitating a date of composition prior to 63 B.C.E. (Oesterley 1913: 60; Goldstein 1976: 63; Fischer 1992: 441; Bartlett 1998: 34). The narration of the achievements and character of the Romans in 8:1–16 is an encomium, contrasting sharply with later reflections on Roman conquest and rule as arrogance, insolence, and an affront against God. Pompey's entry into the holy places in 63 B.C.E. would have marred the author's unqualified appreciation of the Romans (as a comparison with the response of *Psalms of Solomon* 2; 8; 17 to that event might show).

There is more debate concerning where in this period to place the book. Torrey (1945: 72–73) places the time of composition nearer the beginning of John Hyrcanus I's high priesthood, but the majority of scholars correctly reject this. The conclusion to the whole (16:23–24), while not necessitating a date after Hyrcanus's death, is certainly more naturally taken that way, given the parallels in the books of Samuel and Kings, on which the author is intentionally drawing (Oesterley 1913: 60; Pfeiffer 1949: 301; Goldstein 1976: 63; Bartlett 1998: 33). More specific suggestions are generally bound up with a theory concerning the book as a piece of pro-Hasmonean propaganda commissioned during one of the known periods of strong anti-Hasmonean sentiments, the most celebrated being under Alexander Janneus. However engaging such theories may be, they remain tenuous at best—suggestions having more to do with when the powers that be would have found 1 Maccabees to be most useful rather than being reliable leads concerning the necessary time of composition. The relationship between 1 and 2 Maccabees also becomes a factor, with arguments concerning which author knew the work of the other, and perhaps even wrote in opposition to the other, coming to the fore. It seems preferable, therefore, to consider 1 Maccabees as having originated sometime after John Hyrcanus's death in 104 B.C.E. and before Roman intervention in the dispute between Hyrcanus II and Aristobulus II in 63 B.C.E.[4]

Genre, Circumstances, and Purpose

First Maccabees presents itself in the form of the historiography that one finds in the Jewish tradition of 1 and 2 Samuel and 1 and 2 Kings. The author has given many signals to the reader that he or she is reading "history" in the

4. Metzger (1957: 130) and Harrington (1999: 123) light upon 100 B.C.E., while Pfeiffer (1949: 491) and Oesterley (1913: 301) suggest 90–70 B.C.E.

use of precise dates, the inclusion of state documents and records, and the general verisimilitude of the events narrated. These signals also mark the historical writings of Josephus and Greek historians. Since history is rarely disinterested and never without context, the circumstances under which this particular version or re-creation of the past was written deserve special consideration.

From the accession of Jonathan to the high priesthood until the collapse of the Hasmonean house under the pressure of its own divisions, Hasmonean rule did not go unopposed. The Qumran community, as it is known from the Dead Sea Scrolls, took shape in reaction against the "Wicked Priest" and the temple cult organized under him. The Wicked Priest typically is identified with Jonathan, the first Hasmonean high priest, which would have been the logical time for a disgruntled Zadokite claimant to make his break with Jerusalem. Other Jews outside the Qumran community might also have found the replacement of the Zadokite line of high priests an unacceptable break with tradition. Another period of high tension and opposition comes during the reign and priesthood of Alexander Janneus after the turn of the century. The Pharisees had questioned Janneus's fitness for the high priesthood on the basis of his pedigree, since his mother had been a captive in a foreign court and might thus have been exposed to certain sexual abuses.[5] Janneus himself would massacre his Pharisaic opponents with barbaric cruelty.

First Maccabees glorifies the founders of the Hasmonean dynasty. It presents Judas and his brothers, including also Simon's descendants, as the legitimate rulers and, starting with Jonathan, high priests over the house of Israel. The author uses biblical precedent and intertexture throughout the narrative as a means by which the Maccabean history can be made to grow out of and continue the sacred history of Israel. The author also uses the models of deliverer and benefactor when presenting Judas, Jonathan, and Simon, thus potentially enhancing the functional legitimation of their dynasty (i.e., seeing their enjoyment of power as the legitimate result of what they have done on behalf of those they now lead). Given the clearly pro-Hasmonean stance of the author of 1 Maccabees, many scholars suggest that the book actually represents Hasmonean propaganda (Harrington 1988: 57), a book written to lend support and legitimation to the dynasty in a period in which that legitimacy is questioned. This possibility is brought to the fore all the more plausibly when 1 Maccabees is set alongside 2 Maccabees and its very different interests: the "achievements of Judas and the later Hasmoneans form the chief topic of the first book; God's care for his Temple and his people are the subject of the second" (Pfeiffer 1949: 482). Not

---

5. See Goldstein (1976: 69), who favors a date in Janneus's reign as the time of composition, since it "fits well the propagandistic thrust" of 1 Maccabees.

all are convinced, however, that the author of 1 Maccabees was a political propagandist of a particular party.[6]

The debate appears to hinge on purpose as opposed to potential function. The author is clearly pro-Hasmonean and considers Israel to owe an enormous debt of gratitude not only to Judas and his brothers but also to their house, the "sons of Simon." The author would have been found among the loyal supporters of their regime. This does not mean, however, that the author wrote this history directly as a reply to open and virulent challenges to the legitimacy of that regime, such as one finds during the reign of Janneus. It would be equally natural for such a history to be written during peak times of prosperity, at the end of Hyrcanus I's reign, for example, as a means by which the readership might be led to recollect how such glorious times came to be enjoyed and to whom the debt of such enjoyment is owed. Even if political propaganda was not the author's conscious intent (or remunerated employment), however, in the environment in which 1 Maccabees was written, the book would certainly have had this effect and have been put to this use in times of challenge to the dynasty's legitimate occupation of the role of high priest or ruler of Judea.

Historical Issues

First Maccabees is of great importance as a source for reconstructing the history of Judea from the accession of Antiochus IV through the reign of Simon.[7] There are, however, a number of problems and issues surrounding the use of 1 Maccabees as a historical source alongside 2 Maccabees, Josephus's

6. Pfeiffer (1949: 493) disputes this reading on the grounds that the author portrays Israel as a whole, or its "great assembly," making important decisions like whether or not to fight on the Sabbath (2:40–41) or the conferral of powers upon Simon (14:25–49). This datum does not militate against the political propagandistic effects of the book, however, for by it the author shows that the Hasmoneans did not impose their will upon the people but rather acted in concert with them and, in fact, were invited by them to lead. Indeed, this helps establish the legitimacy of their regime, distinguishing it from tyranny.

Bartlett (1998: 30) is also reluctant to regard 1 Maccabees as a text written to give "political support" to Simon's successors, since the author does not go on to recount the story of John Hyrcanus. He also points out that the author does not speak of the Hasmoneans as messiahs or as heirs to the throne of David. Again, however, these objections are not strong. With regard to the first, the founding of a dynasty is already in view in 14:25–26 and 16:2–3, and the debts owed the father will certainly be understood to pass to his sons and grandsons. With regard to the second, "messiah" is a term that may not have been particularly meaningful to an author in 100 B.C.E., but as to the quality and nature of Judas's or Simon's achievements, the author leaves no doubt. He colors their encomiums with the hues of the future, restored Israel promised by the prophets. Avoiding the term "messiah" does not make their accomplishments any less "messianic." The use of the title "savior" to describe Judas in 9:21, moreover, may be seen to compensate for the absence of "messiah."

7. See chapter 2 of the present volume.

Jewish Antiquities and *Jewish War,* and Greek historians who refer to the reign and activities of Antiochus IV (notably, Polybius).

First, Maccabean-era chronology represents a basic problem. First Maccabees generally displays an interest in providing reliable dates using the Seleucid system, but a Seleucid year could be reckoned as beginning in April (in the eastern parts of the Seleucid Empire) or October (in the western parts). Complicating this is the likelihood that the author of 1 Maccabees used different sources that themselves used the different starting points for a year (Attridge 1986: 319).[8] This difficulty also emerges when reconstructing the history behind 2 Maccabees and reconciling that history with 1 Maccabees' narrative.

A second issue concerns the nature of Antiochus IV's program, purposes, and procedures. Evidence outside of 1 Maccabees contradicts the presentation of Antiochus IV's agenda, suggesting that the assault on local religion was confined to Judea, "the elimination of a rebellious local group by abolishing the ideological code that sustained it" (Green 1990: 516) and not part of an empire-wide unification program. What was the shape of Antiochus's religious "reforms" in Judea? Here it is difficult to see the reality that the sources describe so elliptically. Was the "abomination of desolation" an actual cult image or merely a pagan altar erected over the original altar of burnt offerings?[9] To what deity or deities was the temple rededicated, and after what customs were sacrificial rites to be offered? Noting the difficulties historians have had aligning the rituals described in 1 and 2 Maccabees with any known Syrian or Greek cultic practices, Goldstein (1983: 106–12) suggests that Antiochus IV attempted to impose a purer, more ancient form of Israelite or Canaanite religion upon the inhabitants of Judea, learned by Antiochus from the syncretistic Jewish mercenaries employed in and manning the Akra, but no single suggestion has ended the debate on this issue.

A third historical concern focuses on reconciling the data in 1 Maccabees with the story of 2 Maccabees, not where these are complementary but where these contradict each other. First, there is the question of how Antiochus's actions in Judea line up with his two Egyptian campaigns in both texts. Second, the two "histories" date the death of Antiochus differently (1 Maccabees places it after the rededication of the temple, 2 Maccabees before). Third, the placement of the campaigns of Judas against neighboring territories differs between the two accounts (1 Maccabees groups them together as a block in chapter 5; 2 Maccabees scatters them throughout the career of Judas). Fourth, the dating and placement of the two campaigns of Lysias differs in the two accounts. Finally, there are notable differences in the tallies of forces involved and casualties in each major battle (Pfeiffer 1949: 476–82). In general, these

8. Bartlett (1998: ch. 3) treats this issue at length.
9. See Bartlett (1998: 65) for an argument in favor of the latter. Wenham 1992 offers a review of the problem and its various solutions.

differences are resolved in favor of 1 Maccabees' version of the story, with the exception of Judas's campaigns to liberate Jews in the territories surrounding Judea, which seem to be grouped together for convenience in 1 Maccabees.

The fourth issue centers on the historical value and authenticity of the diplomatic correspondence and other documents "preserved" in 1 Maccabees.[10] A secondary debate concerning these documents concerns whether the document originally was woven into 1 Maccabees by the author or was introduced by a later editor or copyist. The following is a list of the most important of these documents:[11]

1. Internal Jewish documents
   a. Letter from Jews in Gilead to Judas (5:10–13)
   b. Decree concerning the appointment of Simon and his descendants to the high priesthood (14:27–45)
2. Jews and Rome
   a. Letter from the Roman senate to the Jewish people (8:23–32)
   b. Circular letter from the Romans concerning the Jews (15:16–21)
3. Jews and Sparta
   a. Letter from Jonathan to the Spartans (12:6–18)
   b. Letter from Arius, king of Sparta, to Onias, high priest (12:20–23)
   c. Letter from Sparta to Simon (14:20–23)
4. Jews and Seleucid monarchs
   a. Demetrius I to Jonathan (10:3–6)—10:6 is a report of the contents
   b. Alexander Balas to Jonathan (10:18–20)
   c. Demetrius I to Jonathan (10:25–45)
   d. Demetrius II to Jonathan (11:29–37)
   e. Demetrius II to Simon (13:36–40)
   f. Antiochus VII to Simon (15:1–9)

With regard to the authenticity of these documents, verdicts range from affirming a document as the verbatim text of a record available to the author of 1 Maccabees, to an imaginative expansion on or rewrite of such a text, to a summary of such a text, to a fictitious composition by the author. Some of the factors raised in the discussion include the likelihood that such a document would have been written, preserved, and available for the author's inspection, whether or not the style of the letter conforms to what is known of

10. For extended discussions of this topic, see Oesterley 1913: 61–65; Pfeiffer 1949: 488–90; Tedesche and Zeitlin 1950: 38–48; Bartlett 1998: 81–83, 87–99. It is generally assumed that "messages" sent verbally through ambassadors are invented by the author, as, for example, 10:51–56, 69–73.

11. Taken from Oesterley 1935: 303.

the chancellory styles appropriate for each type (Roman senatorial letters, Seleucid correspondence practices, and the like), and whether or not a document shows signs of being altered in favor of advancing the image or interests the author wishes to project or promote.

In general, the likelihood that the Hasmonean leaders from Judas on kept archives of their dealings with foreign powers and internal resolutions makes it probable that many of these documents contain reliable information, even those that show signs of being summaries or rewritten versions of the document in question.[12] Some, like the letter of Demetrius I to Jonathan (10:25–45), show clear literary signs of expansion on the part of the author. In that letter, the style alternates between impersonal expressions and first-person speech, the latter sections containing the material that is objectionable on other grounds as well. Thus, the version in 1 Maccabees preserves parts of the original interwoven with embellishments made by the author (Murphy-O'Connor 1976). The most widely suspect of the documents is the correspondence with Sparta, although even here the probability that these letters are a literary fiction does not rule out the possibility of real diplomatic relations with Sparta in pre-Maccabean and Hasmonean Judea (Bartlett 1998: 95–97).

Formative Influences

Where did the author of 1 Maccabees get information about the subject of the book? The study of the formative influences on 1 Maccabees naturally inquires first into the sources that the author used in the course of writing. Un-

12. The question certainly is a complex one. Harrington (1988: 58) and Goldstein (1983: 29) regard these documents as mainly authentic sources incorporated into 1 Maccabees, all likely to have been introduced into the text by the author. Oesterley (1913: 61–65) offers a more nuanced verdict upon each: 1a is a summary; 1b genuine but added by a later editor (since some details do not agree with the written history in chapters 12–13); 2a is a report of a genuine document; 2b preserves a basically genuine document but interpolated by a later editor; 3a is a forgery, reflecting, however, a genuine diplomatic relationship with Sparta; 3b is genuine; 3c is a genuine document but inserted by a later editor (as part of a larger interpolation, 14:17–23, embellishing international reactions to Jonathan's death); 4a is not discussed; 4b is a summary of a genuine letter; 4c is a greatly exaggerated rewrite of a genuine letter; 4d elaborates a genuine letter; 4e is genuine; 4f is an exaggeration of a genuine letter. Additionally, 11:57 provides a summary of a genuine communication from Antiochus VI to Jonathan.

Bartlett (1998) provides a similarly detailed examination of each on its own merits: 1b is authentic, coming from the Jerusalem archives (p. 86); 2a is basically authentic, though it is uncertain if this preserves the decree or the actual treaty (p. 83); 2b may be authentic and may date from Simon's reign, although there are difficulties reconciling this account with Josephus's account of a similar embassy and reply placed in the reign of John Hyrcanus II (pp. 93–94); the Spartan correspondence (3a, 3b, 3c) is fictitious, although it is possible to sustain some kind of diplomatic relations with Sparta on other grounds (pp. 95–97). With regard to the Seleucid correspondence, Bartlett is essentially in agreement with Oesterley.

fortunately, apart from the documents discussed above, the author gives few clues about sources available for the composition of this narrative. With regard to the deeds of Judas, the author makes the following statement: "the rest of the acts of Judas, and his wars and the brave deeds that he did, and his greatness, have not been recorded, but they were very many" (9:22). Does this indicate that those deeds that the author does relate had been written down previously and were available in a written source? This has been taken to refer to a "Judas source," although it is ambiguous evidence at best. The author could just be referring to the incomplete nature of 1 Maccabees itself, in which it was impossible to include all the oral information available about Judas's exploits. The book closes with a reference to "the annals of the high priesthood" of John Hyrcanus I (16:23–24). Although the author would not rely on this source for much of the story, the reference suggests that similar annals might have been kept and made available for the term of Jonathan's priesthood and Simon's priesthood.[13]

Scholarship has not limited itself, however, to archival documents, a possible Judas source, and annals of the high priesthood as potential (and already somewhat hypothetical) sources. K.-D. Schunk (1954), for example, adds to these a Seleucid court chronicle, a Mattathias legend source, a Jonathan source, and a Simon source in addition to any official Jewish high-priestly chronicles.[14] Goldstein (1976: 90–103) also posits a history of the Seleucids written from the Gentile perspective and employing the dating system from the western part of the Seleucid Empire, together with a history about the deaths of persecutors, as additional sources. Sources for the exploits of Mattathias, Jonathan, and Simon, which could be oral rather than written, seem necessary; the others, however, are hypothetical at best and fanciful at worst (as in the case of an otherwise unknown Jewish tract celebrating the deaths of oppressors).

The author of 1 Maccabees was also profoundly influenced by the Scriptures of the Jewish people. Biblical expressions appear throughout the narrative, many of which connect this book explicitly with the historical books of the Old Testament. The author also borrows from the broader corpus of the Scriptures, from Genesis in the praise of Judas as a "lion's whelp" (Gen. 49:9; 1 Macc. 3:4) through Daniel in the description of Antiochus's religious reforms as the "abomination of desolation" (Dan. 9:27; 12:11; 1 Macc. 1:54), with the result that the language and style of each part reverberate for the wary listener with echoes of that sacred tradition (see Pfeiffer 1949: 484–85; Bartlett 1998: 31–32). These are far too numerous to be discussed here; the majority of those echoes and recontextualizations that lead us toward an appre-

13. See Oesterley 1913: 61 and Pfeiffer 1949: 302 for similar inventories.
14. Summarized in Bartlett 1998: 22. See also the review and critique of Schunk in G. O. Neuhaus 1974.

ciation of the ideology behind this sequel to biblical history are discussed in the following section.

The "History" That 1 Maccabees Crafts

The author of 1 Maccabees is rightly credited with being a careful and "serious" historian (Bartlett 1998: 101). The author sought to present an orderly account, preserving carefully the dates for major actions, and had used archival materials wherever available to document the history. Where precise information about dating is lacking, the author has inserted the material, as best as was possible, into the more reliable framework created by dated events (Bartlett 1998: 102). For all this, however, the author cannot be credited with being "impartial" or with not "colouring [the facts] with personal observations."[15] It is closer to the truth to say that the author's partiality has been hidden better than that of the main point of comparison, the author of 2 Maccabees, whose own biases and point of view show plainly when they enter the "history."

One manner in which every history reveals its biases and interests is in its selectivity. With regard to 1 Maccabees, the author's selectivity is readily discerned when this work is compared with 2 Maccabees.[16] Second Maccabees includes events under Seleucus IV, God's protection of the temple from Heliodorus's treasury raid during the high priesthood of the pious Onias, the intrigues of Jason and Menelaus and their Hellenization program, and the courage of the nine martyrs. It also includes several battles, maneuvers, and treaties not related in 1 Maccabees. First Maccabees, on the other hand, continues the history down to the accession of John Hyrcanus in his father's place, whereas the author of 2 Maccabees is content to end the story (perhaps following Jason of Cyrene, the author whose work is abridged in 2 Maccabees) with the defeat of Nicanor in 161 B.C.E., even before the death of Judas.

It is at first surprising that the author of 1 Maccabees would have no interest in relating at least the corruption of the high priests Jason and Menelaus, presenting instead a much more succinct and simplified picture of the crisis that invites the Maccabean Revolt. Although the author certainly gives attention to the actions of "certain renegades" from the beginning to the end, they do not appear as principal antagonists in the drama. Instead, Antiochus IV and "the Gentiles" in general are the antagonists against whom Mattathias and his sons do battle. Was the author trying to downplay the role of high

---

15. Metzger (1957: 130) characterizes 1 Maccabees as "obviously the work of a plain and honest chronicler who set down the facts in their historical sequence, with scarcely any attempt to theorize upon them or to emphasize their significance."

16. See Pfeiffer 1949: 474 for a helpful table showing the overlap and discontinuity between the two texts.

priests in leading Israel astray?[17] This is difficult to affirm, since the manner in which the Zadokite Jason disqualified himself in the eyes of history as high priest could have been played up by the author in favor of his Hasmonean successors. Was the author interested in vilifying the Gentiles as the enemy (Pfeiffer 1949: 496)? While hurling a bitter invective against the Syrian forces, the author also goes to great lengths to speak of diplomatic relations with Gentiles, so an absolute "Jew versus Gentile" mentality cannot account for the omissions either. It is perhaps most likely that the author was simply interested in getting to the focus of this history as fast and effectively as possible. Unlike 2 Maccabees, which gives five chapters of prologue to the heroism of Judas (not counting the two chapters of introductory letters and preamble), in 1 Maccabees, Mattathias and his sons emerge as the heroes by the first part of chapter 2 and never leave center stage after that. The author is less interested in giving the details and intrigues that set the stage for the revolt, since the main goal is to recount the achievements of the Hasmonean family on behalf of the people of Israel. The extent of 1 Maccabees, stretching to the accession of John Hyrcanus, also falls in line with this principal interest.

First Maccabees is also a religious history. The prominence of "heaven" or "providence" as the guiding force throughout the narrative affirms God's presence in this history. The fact that God is not mentioned by name or that God does not act directly through angelic intermediaries, as in 2 Maccabees, is no argument for the author's lack of interest in religious matters or God's role in history. Moreover, the conscious sounding of echoes and connections with the sacred Scriptures of Israel shows the author's interest in writing a continuation of sacred history in which the presence and favor of God are mediated through the courage and leadership of a specific family.

The Portrayal of the Crisis

The author regards the activity of the renegades and the developments in Judea under Antiochus IV as a tremendous threat to the well-being of the people of Israel. The renegades are depicted as striving to erase Israel's national identity and thus being false to the basic call of Torah to be a special, distinct people, separate from the nations for the Lord. Antiochus strides onto the scene as an arrogant enemy of Israel, in terms reminiscent of the "little horn" of Daniel's fourth beast that speaks against God, wears down the holy ones, and changes the lawful worship in the temple (Dan. 7:8, 24–25; 1 Macc. 1:10, 21, 24, 41–55). Poetic passages throughout the first two chapters reflect on these developments as a challenge to, and assault upon, the honor of Jerusalem and its temple (1 Macc. 1:24, 28, 37, 39–40; 2:8, 12). A champion of the honor of Israel is desperately needed. Similarly, the poems underscore

---

17. Alternatively, is this an instance of *damnatio memoriae* at work, the erasure of a traitor's or notorious sinner's memory from history, as Goldstein (1983: 67) suggests? The fact that Alcimus is given explicit attention would argue against this explanation.

the removal of joy from Israel. Dwelling on these conditions of disgrace and mourning intensifies the need for a deliverer and makes clear the role that the Hasmonean family will play when Mattathias first steps forward to take up the glove. These conditions will be explicitly reversed at the rededication ceremony under Judas's leadership at 4:58, signaling the first major success of the "family through which deliverance was given to Israel" (5:62).

Missing from 1 Maccabees' understanding of the crisis is any notion of Deuteronomistic theology at work or the requirement for atonement before restoration would be possible, as will be so prominently featured in 2 Maccabees. Second Maccabees 8:1–5, in fact, attributes the turning away of God's wrath to the martyrs, not to Judas, but 1 Maccabees writes a much simpler tale of deliverance and restoration of national honor thanks to the Hasmonean family's efforts, sacrifices, and leadership.

The Hasmonean Family as God's Chosen and Legitimate Agents

One important means of access to the author's own tendencies in this re-creation of the history of the Maccabean Revolt is to observe closely the use of biblical precedents and weaving of intertexture between the history in 1 Maccabees and the sacred history of Israel. The resonances that the author creates make claims on behalf of the Hasmonean house that could not be ignored and reveal how the author regarded that house to be functioning in the plan of God for God's people.

First impressions are important. Mattathias is introduced in 2:1 as a member of a distinguished priestly house (Joarib, listed first among the families of priests in 1 Chron. 24:7) and immediately reveals his passion for the honor, security, and sanctity of Jerusalem in a lament over the crisis of chapter 1 (2:6–13). It is this pious concern that drives him to violence in the first episode of the Maccabean Revolt. When Antiochus's agent comes to Modein to enforce the apostasy, Mattathias kills both that agent and the first Jew who steps forward to submit to the order (2:15–25). Lest any reader miss the connection, the author compares this action and the motivating zeal for the covenant with the very similar action of Phinehas, who won for himself the covenant of an eternal priesthood by killing an Israelite together with his Midianite wife (Num. 25:6–15). The author will return to this episode again at 2:54, there making the connection between zeal against apostates and qualification for priesthood explicit, and in the praise of Judas at 3:8, where Judas's striking down of apostates turns God's wrath away from Israel (as in Num. 25:10), reversing the condition of 1:64. When we first meet Mattathias and his son Judas, therefore, we are meeting Phinehas *redivivus,* and the fact that the Hasmoneans would inherit the title of high priest could not have been far from mind as the author wove the texture of that narrative.

In the immediate sequel to the Phinehas-like episode, Mattathias calls out, "Let everyone who is zealous for the law and supports the covenant come out with me!" (2:27), and those who join him proceed to conduct raids against renegade Jews and their Gentile protectors. Here the author has reconfigured the story of the aftermath of the incident of the golden calf, in which Moses, in response to the idoltary of the people, calls out, "Who is on the Lord's side?" (Exod. 32:26) and then proceeds with a military action in which apostates are the target. This precedent also linked violent zeal against apostasy with ordination to priestly service (Exod. 32:29). Siding with the Hasmoneans, moreover, is presented as the manner in which zeal for Torah is displayed.

Mattathias's deathbed speech also serves to set the deeds of Judas and his brothers in the context of, and as the ongoing story of, the Israelite heroes of faith (2:49–60). Judas and his brothers stand up to enact the faith of their ancestors, to reincarnate their zeal for the covenant, to stand in the gap created by the current crisis. "All who observe the law" will rally to them (2:67).

Although Simon is the titular head of the household after Mattathias's death (2:65), it is Judas whose exploits and military leadership come to occupy center stage. The author introduces Judas to the readers with a poetic encomium in 3:3–9, in which Judas is lauded as being "a lion in his deeds, like a lion's cub roaring for prey" (3:4), similes taken from the description of God's agent in Hos. 5:14 (and reminiscent as well of Jacob's description of Judah's namesake in Gen. 49:9). The claim in 3:6 that deliverance came by means of Judas's hand is a recontextualization of the similar declaration about Samson's victory over the Philistines in LXX Judg. 15:18: "You gave this great salvation by the hand of your slave" (van Henten 1996: 204). By purging the apostates from Israel, "he turned away wrath from Israel" (3:8)—words directly reminiscent of the Phinehas episode (Num. 25:10) already so richly underscored in chapter 2. The first impression of Judas, then, is that of a hero of biblical proportions striding onto the scene, entrusted with extending "the glory of his people" (3:3), the honor that had been so thoroughly assaulted and diminished in chapter 1.

The author also crafts a picture of Judas as a thoroughly pious and Torah-observant individual. His army prays, fasts, and studies the Scriptures before battle (3:44–48); he gathers the offerings, tithes, and Nazirites (3:49–50), all needing to be consecrated in the temple, giving his crusade to retake Jerusalem all the coloration of a "holy war," an attempt to regain access to the sanctuary (having first to cleanse it of the defilements). Judas himself prays on the eve of battle (4:30–33), a prayer rich in biblical allusions to the wars of David and Jonathan. Moreover, Judas's behavior and leadership are shaped by scriptural guidelines. He sets the army in order as Moses ordered the people in Exod. 18:25 (3:55); he releases from his army those groups whose nonparticipation is demanded by Deut. 20:5–8 (3:56); after victory, his army sings hymns of victory reminiscent of the psalms (at 4:24 the author quotes the refrain from Ps. 118:1; 136:1).

The actual campaigns waged by Judas are told in a manner that explicitly connects them with the battles of the judges and the Davidic monarchy. In an early encounter with superior Gentile forces, Judas's soldiers ask how they, so few, could prevail. Judas answers that God can give victory to few as easily as to many (3:18–22), his words reading like a midrash on Jonathan's similar speech to his armor bearer in 1 Sam. 14:6. Judas's battles against the better-equipped and larger armies are like another Red Sea incident (4:9), and Judas's successes are set up to be interpreted as a sign of God's favor upon Israel, the means by which God "remembers his covenant" (4:10). The battles of David and Jonathan against the Philistines (specifically, David's defeat of Goliath in 1 Samuel 17 and Jonathan's routing of the enemy camp in 1 Sam. 14:6–15) are explicitly invoked in 4:30 as paradigms or precedents for Judas's army going up against the Greco-Syrian forces. Jonathan's attack on the Philistine camp is also recalled at 5:40–41, which reconfigures Jonathan's words at 1 Sam 14:8–10 (in both places, it is said that the one who crosses over to engage the enemy first will have victory).

Reenactments of biblical history in the history of the Maccabees continue with Nicanor's threat against the Jerusalem temple (7:33–35). Hearing of Nicanor's threat and preparing for battle, Judas asks God to crush Nicanor's army as God had crushed the 185,000 Assyrian soldiers after Sennacherib, their leader, had spoken arrogantly and dishonorably about the temple and its God (7:40–42). The explicit reference to the episode in 2 Kings 19:8–37 ensures that the hearer will understand 1 Macc. 7:33–50 as a reenactment of that paradigm. In both, a Gentile general speaks haughtily against God and God's temple, prayers are offered to God that God would look upon the arrogance of the Gentiles and defend the temple, and the Gentile offender is disgracefully defeated.

Even in death, Judas's story continues the biblical story. At his passing, "all Israel" laments with the words "How is the mighty fallen, the savior of Israel!" (9:21), which recontextualizes the lament raised by David for Saul and Jonathan (2 Sam. 1:19, 25, 27; adding, however, a significantly different second line). The conclusions to the sections of text dealing with the leadership of Judas (9:19–22) and John Hyrcanus I (16:23–24) are also modeled after the conclusions of regnal histories in 1–2 Samuel and 1–2 Kings. The result of the author's creation of linkages between the history written in 1 Maccabees and the Scriptures is the strong impression that the sacred story of Israel continues to be worked out, and God's age-long purposes for Israel served, in the Maccabean Revolt and its principal players, the members of the house of Mattathias. The choice of intertexture also makes the implicit, yet unmistakable, claim that the Hasmonean household's occupation of the high priesthood and the de facto leadership of Israel (made all the more plain by the assumption in 104 B.C.E. of the title "king" by Judas Aristobulus I, a title retained by his son and grandson) is a legitimate one, the family having risen to that status in precisely the same way as had Phinehas and David: through zeal for the law and through military virtuosity.

The signs of God's choice of the Hasmonean house are to be found not only in the great string of victories and successes achieved under its leadership but also in the failures that attend those who act apart from their leadership. Most noteworthy in this regard is 5:18, 55–62. Joseph and Azariah are left by Judas to defend Judea while Judas takes a specially picked force to assist Jews in neighboring lands. When these men try to win honor for themselves by going out to battle independently of Judas and his brothers, they fail and sustain heavy losses because "they did not belong to the family of those men through whom deliverance was given to Israel" (5:62). The story of the Hasideans who part company with Judas and try to make peace with Alcimus gives a similar impression: it is only in concert with, and under the leadership of, the Hasmonean family that a secure peace for the observance of the law can be established. Military and diplomatic missions undertaken apart from their leadership fail, lacking God's anointing.

Benefaction and Diplomacy: Functional Legitimation of Hasmonean Power

Sociologist Max Weber's study of legitimate authority (authority that was recognized as legitimate by those under that authority) discerned three basic modes by which authority was legitimated. *Charismatic* legitimation underscored the giftedness of the leader or his or her proximity to the divine and to powers not normally accessible to humans. *Traditional* legitimation vests authority in long-established offices rather than individual incumbents. *Functional* legitimation underscores what the authority figure is able to accomplish, or has already accomplished, for those under authority. Although the author regards the Hasmonean house to hold sway in part because of its special charisma, God having selected that family as the agency of deliverance, the third kind of legitimation represents the primary means by which the author seeks to understand and present Hasmonean rule as legitimate rule.

Judas's achievement on behalf of Israel is great indeed. He is credited with the restoration of joy and the removal of the disgrace inflicted upon Israel in the desecration of the temple (4:58), thus answering the need presented in the poems of chapter 1. Reclaiming the temple for the lawful worship of God by covenant-keeping Israelites, coming to the aid of Jews in territories dominated by Israel's historic enemies (the land of the Edomites, the territory of the Ammonites, and Gilead; see chapter 5), and forcing the Seleucid monarch to rescind the edict proscribing Torah and Jewish customs (6:58–60) win for Judas the title "savior of Israel" (9:21), being recognized as the agent of God, the "Savior of Israel" (4:30). The acclamation of Judas as savior encapsulates the enormous debt of gratitude owed him by the Jewish people, all the more as he died in the service of Israel.[18] Thus begins the great debt owed collectively to the Hasmonean house, the storehouse of gratitude that will become its power base.[19]

Jonathan, who is commissioned by the people to lead in his brother's stead (9:29–30), achieves a temporary peace for Israel ("the sword ceased from Israel" [9:73]). Under his leadership, diplomacy becomes an important tool and also a source of political legitimation (Harrington 1988: 75). Jonathan acts, and is recognized by foreign powers, as the legitimate representative of the people of Judea. In a noteworthy twist of fate, Jonathan is given by Alexander Balas the very title, "Friend of the King," that Mattathias had refused decades earlier when offered at the cost of loyalty to the Torah (10:20; cf. 2:18). His rise to leadership is confirmed both by Israel and by the Seleucid king, a rise accompanied by pious zeal for the law at every stage rather than sought through compromise of the covenant (the means by which the renegades sought advancement).

Simon's achievements, however, are far more notable, since the evils of chapter 1—indeed, the evils that befell Israel in the siege of Jerusalem by Nebuchadnezzar four centuries earlier—are completely reversed only under his leadership. Simon has been present since the beginning of the revolt (2:3, 65) and had been active during Jonathan's high priesthood, but his "accession speech" in 13:1–6 is really the first time he emerges as a distinct personality, and, like his brothers and father, Simon (through the author) makes a good impression. He opens with a reminder of the nation's obligation to his family on account of their exceptional service and benefactions (13:3; cf. 16:2), affirms his own generous attitude toward the nation (13:5–6), and is thus acclaimed leader by the people in Judas's and Jonathan's place (13:8–9). The crowning achievement of Simon's leadership is the removal of the "yoke of the Gentiles" (13:41–51), the restoration of political independence to Judea. The Akra had been the thorn in Jerusalem's side from its introduction at 1:33–34 (see also 6:18–21; 11:20, 41), and under Simon that garrison of "sinful people" is removed. The removal of the burden of tribute due the Seleucids and the introduction of a new dating system ("in the first year of Simon" [13:42]) also signal the new independence of Judea.

The author celebrates Simon's achievements in a poetic encomium (14:4–15) that serves very well as a complement to the poem lauding Judas that opened the history of the five brothers (3:3–9). The use of biblical images and resonances is again thick, the chief medium by which the author conveys his message. "The land had rest all the days of Simon" (14:4), as it had in the days

18. Eleazar also contributes by giving "his life to save his people and to win for himself an everlasting name" (6:44), thus in such a way as obligates the beneficiaries, an obligation passed on to surviving members of the family.

19. deSilva (2000b: chs. 3, 4) provides an introduction to a Hellenistic-era and Roman-era understanding of the mutual roles and obligations of benefactors and beneficiaries.

of Solomon (1 Kings 5:4). Simon's reign, moreover, was a period of restoration such as had been promised to Israel since the time of the prophets. First Maccabees 14:8–9 depicts old men sitting at leisure in the streets, people sowing in peace, the vine yielding its fruit, and the ground giving its produce—images from the prophecies of Zech. 8:4, 12; Ezek. 34:27. First Maccabees 14:12 speaks of all the people sitting under their own fig trees and vines with no one to frighten them, a clear recontextualization of Mic. 4:4. The prophecies about a renewed, restored Zion have come to fulfillment under Simon's rule.

The people's response to Simon and his house clearly shows the way in which reciprocity and the ideology of proper response to a benefactor provide the language for the legitimation of Hasmonean power and indeed clue us in to the specific form that the functional legitimation of the dynasty takes. The people ask, "How shall we thank Simon and his sons? For he and his brothers and the house of his father have stood firm; they have fought and repulsed Israel's enemies and established its freedom" (14:25–26). The form of thanks that the people resolve upon is an inscription and public declaration honoring Simon and investing him *and his descendants* with high priesthood and secular powers (14:27–45). These honors and powers were regarded by the people as the only fitting return of gratitude for what the Hasmonean house did and sacrificed for Israel and for the loyalty, firmness, and generosity they maintained toward their nation (14:35 clearly displays the functional legitimation of Simon's power—the things he *did*, for which the people now honor him; see also 14:25–26, 35, 41, 44). The Hasmoneans, then, are no power-hungry tyrants but the duly chosen leaders of the people of Israel whose service had earned them the loyalty and obedience of all Israel.

The Renegades and the Limits of Israel

The author's partisan interests can be seen also in the narrative's treatment of Jews who pursue political and religious agendas contrary to his own. All promoters of Gentile influence and interests in Israel, together with all opponents of the Hasmoneans' revolutionary government, are labeled "renegades" or "sinners" and are excluded from "Israel." That latter, sacred title comes to be the primary label for the Hasmoneans and their supporters throughout the book. Far from being impartial or objective, the author very clearly draws the lines of acceptable and unacceptable policies and behaviors, even going so far as to redefine who constitutes Israel, no longer an ethnic phenomenon, on the basis of one particular response to Gentile influence in the Holy Land and alignment with one particular party. Those driven into hiding during the religious reforms of Antiochus IV constitute Israel, while the renegades follow Antiochus's program (1:43; 1:52–53) (Harrington 1988: 62–63). "All Israel" mourns Mattathias's passing (2:70), thus limiting "Israel" narrowly to those sympathetic to the Hasmonean attacks on apostates and the Gentile occupying forces.

The "renegades," on the other hand, seek to end the separation of Judea from the Gentiles and are said to have "abandoned the holy covenant, joined with the Gentiles, and sold themselves to do evil" (1:11–15). The author highlights the building of a gymnasium and the practice of epispasm (removal of the marks of circumcision, a procedure documented in the writings of Galen), regarding these as signs of the incursion of foreign customs in direct contravention of the Torah. Alongside the renegades stand the soldiers stationed in the Seleucid garrison called the Akra, "a sinful people" (1:34). The description of these soldiers as "renegades" strongly suggests heterodox Jews rather than Gentiles (Goldstein 1983: 106–12). These two parties are found aligned again in 6:18–21, where ungodly Israelites join refugees from the Akra in appealing to Antiochus V for aid in putting down the Maccabean uprising. Behind the author's labels and slurs, it is clear that a significant group of Jews rejected the program of the Hasmoneans and thought Israel's future better and more secure under Seleucid administration.

The champion of the "renegades and godless men of Israel" and "all who were troubling their people" is Alcimus, the "ungodly" high priest (7:5, 9, 21–22). Alcimus has formidable claims to power as a member of the Zadokite priestly family, with the result that even the elusive Hasideans would have broken with Judas in favor of a peaceful settlement under a high priest whom they could regard as a legitimate incumbent of that office. For the author, those Hasideans who thought it possible to live under foreign domination and be safe to keep the law serve as an object lesson promoting the Hasmonean agenda, since they are treacherously murdered by Alcimus. Their demise is actually presented as the fulfillment of a prophecy, the only one that the author explicitly cites as happening "in accordance with the word that was written" (7:16–17; cf. Ps. 79:2–3).

Throughout the remainder of the drama, the "renegades" appear repeatedly, attempting to secure aid from their Seleucid overlords against the growing hold of the Hasmonean regime over Israel (9:23–27, 58, 68–69; 10:61; 11:20–26). This consistent picture reveals clearly the author's conviction that initiatives from within Judaism for Gentile intervention in Jewish affairs constitute a betrayal of the covenant and a forfeiture of one's place in the covenant people. To support the Hasmonean family and political independence, however, is to support the structures under which the covenant can be faithfully and securely observed and thus to show oneself a loyal son or daughter of Israel.

The Gentiles in 1 Maccabees

The attitude of the author toward Gentiles is ambiguous. On the one hand, Alexander the Great and Antiochus IV are characterized as arrogant, acting beyond the measure of what is appropriate for mortals (1:3; 1:21, 24). Antiochus, his generals, and his armies act as enemies toward God and are described as "sinful" and "lawless." Yet, on the other hand, the author regards certain Gentiles as suitable partners for alliances. Clearly, the author is not merely expressing xenophobic prejudices but rather making clear distinctions between ways in which it is suitable for Gentiles to be involved in the life of Israel and ways in which it is not. For the author, Gentile influence, control, and military presence in the land of Israel are all evils to be avoided. These represent threats to Israel's identity as the holy and distinct nation of God, and so Gentiles who enact these forms of relationship with Israel are "arrogant" and "sinful," treading where God would not have them tread.

Alliances with Gentile nations serve the author's purposes by establishing Israel's political autonomy, a prerequisite to the ability to conduct diplomacy and form alliances (Bartlett 1998: 29). The invention of diplomatic correspondence with Sparta, in particular, may show an interest in testifying to the world that "the Jews had no quarrel with the Hellenistic world as such," once their political independence had been won (Bartlett 1998: 95). The choice of Sparta, a city known for strict laws and centrality of military service and values, may be due to a desire to present Judea as a kindred spirit to an ancient and respected Greek city-state (Bartlett 1998: 95). By connecting Judea with Sparta, the author suggests that the militarism of Judas and his armies and the zeal for strict observance of the ancestral laws are not incompatible with the noblest spirits of Greece, these qualities having won for Sparta lasting fame and respect among the Greek city-states.

Influence

First Maccabees may have exercised its greatest influence by nurturing the kind of political ideology that would fuel the messianic movements of the Roman period. Although the book itself avoids the title "messiah," its glorification of a political and military insurgent who leads the people of God as the agent of God appointed to "pay back the Gentiles in full," to restore political independence to Israel, and to drive the foreign power from the homeland has many a counterpart in the abortive uprisings throughout the period of Roman occupation of Judea. The beliefs promoted by 1 Maccabees, that God could bring victory for a grossly outnumbered army and that the prophets foretell a time in which Israel will again enjoy economic prosperity under its own native leadership, would come into play again with each new claimant to the throne of David or would-be liberator of Israel.

The model of political and military messiah fostered by the shining example of Judas Maccabeus and his brothers appears throughout the pages of the New Testament. For example, James and John are portrayed as regarding their association with Jesus as a chance to gain temporal power after the revolution (Mark 10:35–45). In the trial of Jesus, his Jewish accusers and his Roman judge both assume a connection between messianic claims and political subversion. In Acts 1:6, the disciples are still looking for the restoration of Israel's political independence as the result of Jesus' passion and resurrection.

First Maccabees also connects "zeal for the law" with violent action against "renegade" or "apostate" Jews as well as Gentiles invading the sacred land, thus sounding a note that would reverberate throughout the period, from Zealot and Sicarii assaults on Jewish collaborators (not merely on Gentile invaders), to Paul's own zeal for the law manifested in lynching and harassing early Jewish Christians, and later, the persecution faced by Paul and other Jewish Christian teachers from their zealous non-Christian Jewish compatriots.

In terms of literary influence, Josephus uses 1 Maccabees 1–13 as one source for his account of the period in the *Jewish Antiquities,* supplementing it with material from Greek historians. The story of 1 Maccabees is well known to the authors of rabbinic literature and is referred to by early church fathers such as Tertullian and Origen, though its influence there is not extensive, being mainly limited to the examples of courage and zeal that the Maccabees provide. Second Maccabees, with its incipient ideology of martyrdom, would prove to have a much greater impact on the early church, particularly as official persecution in the second and third centuries became more and more pressing an issue.

2 Maccabees

"There Is Some Power of God about the Place"

Second Maccabees also tells the history of the Hellenization crisis under Antiochus IV and the successful resistance movement and restoration of the Jewish way of life but with emphases markedly different from those of 1 Maccabees (with which it was unfamiliar and may even have antedated). Second Maccabees gives far more attention to the role of the Jewish high priests and aristocracy in the promotion of Hellenization and its threat to the ancestral culture of Judaism, introduces the Jerusalem martyrs as major heroes of the resistance movement and as exemplary figures, stresses the direct and miraculous interventions of God, and ends its history with the defeat of Nicanor prior to Judas's own death.

It seeks not to legitimate a dynasty but rather to demonstrate the ongoing legitimacy of Deuteronomy's philosophy of history as can be traced out in recent events, as well as the legitimacy of the Jerusalem temple as the focal point of God's protective care and concern. Like 1 Maccabees, it offers a theological interpretation of history but with a different goal: the promotion of continued or resumed commitment to Jewish cultural values as the path to national security and prosperity.

Structure, Contents, and Textual Transmission

Second Maccabees begins with two letters that have been prefixed to the actual story. The first of these (1:1–9) is actually a brief follow-up letter to a lost letter that invited the Jews in Egypt to join in the celebration of Hanukkah ("the festival of booths in the month of Chislev"), repeating that invitation. The second letter purports to come from the time of Judas himself, issuing the same invitation to the Jewish community in Egypt. It speaks of the necessity of giving gratitude to God for the deliverance God wrought on behalf of the whole Jewish nation in the restoration of the temple (1:11; 2:16–18), gives a gleeful report of the death of Antiochus IV, the persecutor (1:12–17), and attempts to ground the new festival in several obscure eight-day celebrations of the consecration of the Solomonic temple (2:12) and the second temple (1:18).

The history itself begins with the epitomator's (abridger's) prologue, which lays out the major topics, method, and aims in condensing an older, five-volume history by Jason of Cyrene into the more accessible form in which it survives (2:19–32). The narrative opens in the years prior to 175 B.C.E., during the reign of Seleucus IV, with Onias III serving as high priest in Jerusalem, ensuring peace and stability through his careful observance of Torah (3:1–3). An opportunistic Jew named Simon convinces Seleucus to raid the temple treasury, but when Seleucus's emissary, Heliodorus, attempts to enter the Holy Place, he is struck down by divine intervention and barely escapes with his life (3:4–40).

When Antiochus IV ascends the Seleucid throne (175 B.C.E.), Onias's brother Jason obtains the high priesthood from the king with a bribe and sets about founding Greek institutions and promoting Greek customs in Jerusalem, with great support and success (4:1–17). Supported by Simon, Menelaus outbids Jason for the priesthood and relies on raiding the temple treasury for the bribe money he promised to Antiochus, rousing local opposition among the Judeans (4:23–50). Jason, hearing a (false) rumor that Antiochus has been killed in a campaign against Egypt, attempts to retake the high priesthood by force but is repulsed by the inhabitants of Jerusalem. Antiochus takes this as a sign of Judean revolt against his rule and punishes the city mercilessly. He also enters the temple, guided by Menelaus, and plunders it of its wealth as damages (5:1–26). At this time, Judas and a small company leave Jerusalem and go into hiding in the desert so as to avoid "defilement" (5:27).

Antiochus sends an agent to compel the Jews to leave behind their ancestral customs. The temple is defiled with Gentile rites and sacrifices, and Jews are forced to celebrate Dionysiac mysteries. Sabbath observance, circumcision, and observance of dietary regulations of Torah are especially targeted. At this point, Eleazar, a mother, and her seven sons die courageously under torture rather than break faith with the God of Israel (6:1–7:42), bringing an end to God's wrath. Judas now takes center stage and begins his successful campaigns against the Seleucid commanders Nicanor, Timothy, and Bacchides (8:1–29). Antiochus plans to avenge these defeats but is struck down by God and comes to repent of his arrogance and acknowledge the God of the Jews (9:1–29).

Judas and his armies recover the city and rededicate the temple, instituting an annual feast to commemorate the event (10:1–9). After Judas's further victories, Antiochus V grants the Jews the right to observe their ancestral way of life once again (10:10–11:38). Judas still faces trouble, first rescuing Jews living in the cities of Joppa and Jamnia from the assaults of the Gentiles there

(12:1–16), then fighting further against the armies of neighboring Gentile governors (12:17–45). Antiochus V sends Lysias to pacify the land, but Judas's armies again prevail (13:1–26). In an internal power play, Demetrius I seizes the throne from Antiochus V. Demetrius sends Nicanor back to Judea to regain control, and he boastfully advances on Jerusalem, uttering threats against the temple (14:1–36). Here the author provides another scene of "noble death," this time featuring an elder named Razis, who kills himself so as not to fall into the hands of the Seleucid soldiers (14:37–46). In a climactic scene filled with prayer and assurances of divine intervention, including Judas's vision of the dead Onias III praying for his people (an artful link back to 3:1–3), Judas's armies defeat Nicanor's forces, and the temple is spared. A second festival, which came to be known as "Nicanor's Day," is instituted to commemorate this new deliverance (15:1–39). The overall plot of the book focuses on three threats to the temple, each of which is overcome with the help of God, the second episode being rather more complicated by the apostasy led by the high priests.[1]

Second Maccabees, like the history by Jason of Cyrene, was originally composed in Greek. Its style most resembles Septuagint books generally held to have been composed in Greek (like Wisdom of Solomon and 4 Maccabees) rather than translated from Hebrew or Aramaic. Moreover, the text is replete with rhetorical ornaments that would not have been translatable (van Henten 1997: 20–21). Codices Alexandrinus and Venetus are the principal witnesses, but a family of minuscules along with the Old Latin version provide important witnesses to the text of 1 Maccabees before the revisions by Lucian in the third century. The Syriac is too loose to be of real help in textual criticism.[2]

Author, Date, and Setting

Second Maccabees is a unique book among the Apocrypha in that its author is really an editor and abridger of a much longer work, Jason of Cyrene's five-volume history of the Maccabean Revolt (2:23, 26, 28). Because Jason's work did not survive, it is difficult to be sure what belongs to Jason and what was introduced by the epitomator. Having access to the former would help immensely the task of understanding the epitomator's methods, interests, and purposes: Was there complete overlap in contents, or did Jason's work extend

1. Thus, Harrington (1988: 38) speaks of the story in terms of three acts, although others, like Pfeiffer (1949: 510) and van Henten (1997: 26), regard the Heliodorus episode more as a prelude to two major acts (4:7–10:9; 14:1–15:36). These latter episodes do display a marked parallel structure: betrayal of Judaism by high priests; attack on the temple and people by Seleucid forces; display of absolute loyalty to the covenant; deliverance; punishment of enemies; establishment of a festival to commemorate deliverance (van Henten 1997: 26).

2. For detailed discussion, see Habicht 1976a: 191–94; Goldstein 1983: 124–27. Hanhart 1959 provides the standard critical edition of the Septuagint text.

further? If Jason treated more topics than the epitomator included, what pattern was there in the latter's omissions? Did the epitomator introduce events or other material that Jason did not have in his original? Even without the benefit of being able to compare the two, one gets the impression of uneven summarizing. The material in chapters 3–7 seems to be given greater space, proportionally, than the campaigns, some of which are greatly compressed in the telling (see, for an extreme example, 13:18–23). Moreover, the disjunctions in the flow of 2 Maccabees suggest overzealous compressing of those parts of the story that lend themselves less to theologizing and moralizing, two of the epitomator's apparent interests (Pfeiffer 1949: 520–21).

The epitomator's voice, intent, and interests come through most clearly in the preface and epilogue, in the expression of a desire to provide a more accessible version of the history and one more suitable for memorization (and thus oral delivery, perhaps as a new epic for the Jewish people). The epitomator was intent on mixing profit with a pleasant style, which borders on the melodramatic. It is likely that the longer commentaries that intrude upon the narrative (4:16–17; 5:17–20; 6:12–17; 12:43b–45) provide us with the epitomator's interpretation and theological tendencies, which we will further explore below.[3]

Assessing the date of the work is difficult. Jason's original history must postdate 161 B.C.E. and may even have been written just before, or shortly after, Judas's death. Goldstein (1983: 71–83), however, places Jason's work as late as 85 B.C.E., after 1 Maccabees. The epitome is generally held to have been composed prior to 50 C.E., given its influence on 4 Maccabees and Hebrews, and probably before 63 B.C.E., given the positive portrayal of relations with Rome (4:11; 8:10, 36; 11:34–36) (van Henten 1997: 51).[4] Because it is important to consider how the epitome came to be connected with the two prefixed letters, the question of their date often enters the discussion. The later letter (1:1–9) was written in 124/123 B.C.E., a period in which Judea enjoyed prosperity and strength under John Hyrcanus. This was a suitable period in which to invite the translocal Jewish community (yet again) to join in the celebrations of their independence from Greek rule (van Henten 1997: 53).[5] Harrington (1988: 38)

---

3. Even if these comments were Jason's own, the epitomator's decision to include them in an abridgement reveals agreement with, and estimation of the significance of, these interpretative keys.

4. Tedesche and Zeitlin (1954: 27–28) suggest the reign of Agrippa I (41–44 C.E.) on an improbable reading of 2 Macc. 15:37 as an indication that Jerusalem was the capital of Judea at the time of writing (thus ignoring the fact that Jerusalem could not have been considered "in the possession of the Hebrews" during the Roman procuratorships of 6–41 C.E.) and based on the heightened tensions during the reign of Caligula (37–41 C.E.), who proposed to place a statue of himself in the Jerusalem temple, to which 2 Maccabees becomes a spirited response. This event, about which we are well informed by ancient sources, too easily becomes a magnet for scholars who are overly eager to fit every text to known events in the history of the Jewish people.

5. The authenticity of this first letter is defended in Bickermann 1933, though this has not convinced every scholar (see Pfeiffer 1949: 508).

suggests that the epitome was used as support for the request for observance of Hanukkah among the Jews in Egypt, to provide the festal story, as it were.[6] The epitome probably was not composed for this purpose, since the epitomator's prologue itself gives no hint that promoting Hanukkah was part of the agenda but certainly was conducive to it. In this hypothesis, both Jason and his abridger would have completed their work prior to 124 B.C.E.

With regard to location, one scholar considers the epitomator "no doubt an Alexandrian Jew" (Metzger 1957: 140), while to another it is "obvious that 2 Maccabees is of Judean origin" (van Henten 1997: 50). The latter is not ruled out by composition in Greek (Doran 1981: 113) and is all the more likely if the epitome was attached to the letter renewing the invitation to observe Hanukkah.

This leaves the matter of the date and authenticity of the second prefixed, "archival" letter (1:10–2:18). Its authenticity is often rejected on the grounds that the report of the death of Antiochus IV is false, reflecting more the death of Antiochus III, and could not have reached the Judeans in time to be included in a letter being sent before the rededication of the temple after the desecration (winter of 164 B.C.E.) (Wacholder 1978: 91). Wacholder (1978: 102–4) offers an impressive defense of its authenticity, however, suggesting that the letter reflects a situation prior to the *first anniversary* of the rededication of the temple (winter of 163 B.C.E.). God has already "returned the consecration" and "purified the place" (2:17–18), and the letter refers to the observance of the purification rather than to the purification itself (1:18; 2:16). By this time, the Judeans would have heard reports about Antiochus IV's death, but they would have embellished the vague official reports with what they considered plausible details, and one such rumor is recorded in 1:13–16 (Wacholder 1978: 101, 105). Additionally, the author seems intent on legitimating the new festival, something one does not find in the later letter (1:1–9), when the festival is already established in Judea at least.[7] These arguments have not ended debate, but a strong case can be made for claiming that the letter is "the sole authentic surviving record of Judas Maccabeus himself" (Fischer 1992: 444).[8]

Genre and Purpose

Second Maccabees, as it stands, is a mixed composition containing two letters and an epitome of a work of historiography. Abbreviation was a standard

6. See also Collins 2000: 80.

7. The senders connect Hanukkah (called "Purification" at this stage) with Booths and also with a minor "festival of the giving of the sacred fire" known in the postexilic period (Wacholder 1978: 113–15), both of which provide precedents for an eight-day festival.

8. Goldstein (1983: 158) contests Wacholder's suggestion, since Jerusalem was being besieged during 163 B.C.E., and no such letter could have been sent, in his opinion.

literary exercise (epitomes of other histories survive), but it is probably most convenient to consider 2 Maccabees a history as well. It is often labeled a "tragic history," but this is "a label selected by Polybius to vilify a school of historians" rather than an actual generic category (Doran 1981: 87). That said, 2 Maccabees does resemble most those histories that Polybius censured, which sought to rouse emotional responses to the history by presenting "exaggerated pictures," invented moving speeches for the characters, involved dramatic presentation, alleged cause-and-effect relationships between events, and celebrated people getting their just deserts. Doran (1981: 103–4) also helpfully shows that 2 Maccabees treats a well-known topos of histories: the divine providential care for a sacred place or city.

Although some scholars have attempted to define Jason's purpose,[9] most content themselves with investigations of the epitomator's theological agenda, voice, and intent (e.g., Moffatt 1913: 130), lacking, as we do, any external witnesses to Jason's original work. The most notable feature of the epitomator's work is the use of recent history as a narrative demonstration of the Deuteronomistic philosophy of history. This suggests the pastoral goal of dissuading Jews from "converting to an alien way of life," identifying this as the real threat to the nation's well-being, and promoting covenant loyalty with the God who protects God's people and temple (see Doran 1981: 110).[10] The epitomator has preserved those portions of the history that elevate Sabbath observance, circumcision, dietary regulations, and the like as inviolable tenets of the covenant, to be kept even under pain of death rather than violated (Pfeiffer 1949: 513).

The prefixed letters serve a more particular purpose, one that cannot help but also affect the reading of the epitome. The letters' senders seek to gain recognition for their recent history not just as the story of a brilliant military coup but as a sign of God's investment in and acts on behalf of the temple and Jerusalem, which remain thus the center of the Jewish map and conceptual homeland. They also exhibit a strong desire for connection between Palestinian and Egyptian Jews, seen especially in the repeated efforts to get the latter to join in this festival to celebrate the deliverance of their Palestinian sisters and brothers and of the temple for all Jews. The Judean community sent no fewer than *three* letters, if all are authentic: the first was 1:10–2:18, dating

9. Goldstein (1983: 71–83), for example, argues that Jason of Cyrene wrote to correct and counter the Hasmonean propaganda piece called 1 Maccabees. See also the attempt by Pfeiffer (1949: 514–18) to disentangle Jason's voice and interests from the epitomator's.

10. Somewhat more fragile is the further argument of Doran (1981: 112) that the epitomator (or perhaps Jason himself) fashions the history in a way that would be seen as critical of the policies of John Hyrcanus I, who maintained a contingent of mercenaries in his army rather than relying on God, plundered the tomb of David when pressed for funds, and attacked neighboring non-Jewish territories such as Idumea (where Judas fights only to defend Jews). The absence of more pointed commentary on these features of the story by the epitomator suggests not tact but lack of direct interest.

from 163 B.C.E.; the second, sent in 143/142 B.C.E., is not preserved but is mentioned in 1:7; the third is 1:1–9, sent in 124/123 B.C.E. The invitation to make Hanukkah part of the festival calendar of Egyptian Jews would serve both goals.

It is possible that the authors of the earliest letter were aware that some of their Egyptian coreligionists may have regarded the absence of some of the accouterments of the temple as a sign of the second temple's illegitimacy. To uphold its place at the center of the map of sacred spaces, the authors include the traditions that tell how God will restore all things (like the ark) in God's own good time, even as God will restore all Jews to their homeland, as well as connect the second temple with the Solomonic temple through the story of the naphtha, by means of which the continuity of the sacred fire was maintained.[11]

Formative Influences

The primary influence on the shape of 2 Maccabees is, of course, Jason of Cyrene's history.[12] The epitomator appears not to have known 1 Maccabees and may indeed have worked prior to 1 Maccabees (Doran 1981: 13–17). Second Maccabees incorporates several official documents, the origin of which is debated. Antiochus IV's letter of repentance (9:19–27) is almost certainly a product of Jewish wishful thinking, but the letters in 2 Maccabees 11 may well be authentic (Attridge 1986: 323).[13] In their present context, three are misplaced, since they were written under Antiochus IV after the defeat of Lysias but before the accession of Antiochus V (Bartlett 1998: 49–52; Fischer 1992: 444–45). Only 11:22–26 actually comes from the latter's reign. These potentially authentic letters were probably part of Jason's work, their present dislocation being an unfortunate casualty of the abridging process.

Second Maccabees is not so obvious in its dependence on the Jewish Scriptures as is 1 Maccabees, a fact that should give one pause before claiming that 2 Maccabees offers a more "religious" history and 1 Maccabees a "purer" one. Nevertheless, despite the dearth of echoes of Scripture at the level of style and

---

11. Because of the "miracle" of the naphtha, the second temple could still offer holy fire rather than "strange fire" and thus perform acceptable worship to God (cf. Lev. 10:1–3) (Wacholder 1978: 115). Some suggest that the letters, along with 2 Maccabees, serve at least an implicit purpose of countering attraction to, and the continuing function of, the alternative Jewish temple at Leontopolis founded by Onias IV, son of the ousted and murdered Onias III (Habicht 1976: 186), but this would be an oblique aim at best and is not well supported (rightly, Doran 1981: 11–12; Collins 2000: 81).

12. Against the view that the author of 2 Maccabees fabricated this source, see Doran 1981: 81–83.

13. Moffatt (1913: 127) is less affirming, suggesting "at most . . . an historical nucleus" beneath "certainly manufactured documents."

diction, the author has been profoundly influenced by Deuteronomy's philosophy of history: fidelity to the covenant ensures peace, sin against the covenant brings punishment, and repentance and the renewal of obedience leads to restoration. Other theological lessons learned from the Scriptures appear in the history, as, for example, Antiochus IV's unwitting action as agent of divine punishment, himself doomed on account of his hubris,[14] and the comparison of Nicanor's threat and defeat with the story of Sennacherib (15:20–24).

The "History" That 2 Maccabees Crafts

The author of 1 Maccabees is generally preferred as a historian (particularly with regard to chronology) (Dagut 1953), although 2 Maccabees provides critical information about episodes concerning which 1 Maccabees is strangely silent. Many of the differences and anachronisms have already been discussed in the previous chapter,[15] but several of these differences are pertinent now to an exploration of the specific emphases and interests of 2 Maccabees.

The book's interest ends with the victory over Nicanor in 161 B.C.E., leaving the last twenty years of 1 Maccabees' history without parallel. There is no mention of Mattathias, nor is much attention given to Judas's brothers (and Simon, moreover, is not a strong figure when he does appear in 10:18–23). One might go too far in positing 2 Maccabees as an anti-Hasmonean history on the basis of these observations, since, as Collins (2000: 82) rightly points out, Jason's history may have omitted the death of Judas or exploits of his brothers on account of having actually been written before 160 B.C.E. The epitomator's failure to mention these topics may be a function of the commitment to abridge an extant text, not write a supplemented version. Nevertheless, it is also likely that 2 Maccabees was not a Hasmonean-sponsored document (van Henten 1997: 53–56) nor one intent on glorifying a particular family and supporting its political legitimacy.

The prominence of the involvement of God and God's angels in the drama points to the more likely reason that the author is not focused on "the family through which deliverance was given to Israel" (1 Macc. 5:62). Sharing with 1 Maccabees the basic scriptural theme of trusting in God for deliverance rather than force of arms and numbers (2 Macc. 8:18; cf. Ps 20:7), 2 Maccabees departs from the other in its interest in the miraculous, which is announced in the prologue as a major component of the history (2:21). The

14. Compare 2 Macc. 5:17–20; 7:18–19, 33–35; 9:5–12 with Isa. 10:5–19; 47:6–15; Zech. 1:15. See Doran 1981: 92.
15. See also the very helpful synoptic comparisons in Moffatt 1913: 126; Pfeiffer 1949: 474.

prominent role assigned to the heavenly armies (10:29; 11:6–10; 12:17–25) reminds the readers that victory is squarely in God's hands, not those of Judas, who piously relies on divine help in battle and shows it at battle's end (10:38). The book's emphasis falls on God's deliverance through any and all agents God chooses, rather than on the contribution of a particular family to the well-being of Israel. Judas himself seems to be wholly in accord with this viewpoint in the narrative, as seen, for example, in the watchwords he chooses for his army at night: "the help of God" (8:23) and "God's victory" (13:15). The closing acclamation of God's achievement in 15:34—"Blessed is he who has kept his own place undefiled!"—squares well with the emphasis in the letters, too, that gratitude is due God for these acts of deliverance (1:11–12; 2:16–18) and the focus on the festivals in both the letters and the epitome as the pious enactment of this gratitude.[16]

A second, and perhaps more prominent, tendency is the epitomator's demonstration that Deuteronomy's philosophy of history remains an intelligible framework by which to interpret past—and secure future—events. The significantly greater attention given to the prequel to revolt (chapters 3–7), and the epitomator's interpretative comments, admirably effect this proof.

Unlike the author of 1 Maccabees, the epitomator (following Jason, no doubt) begins the history during the reign of Seleucus IV rather than with the archenemy, Antiochus IV. The reason for this is to present the idyllic picture of Jerusalem as governed by Onias III (3:1–3). While the covenant was being observed, the city enjoyed peace, and the temple was honored even by the Gentile rulers. The Heliodorus episode opens the history so as to establish as a foundational premise the conviction that God protects God's temple when the people are governed by Torah and the covenant is scrupulously observed (3:28, 38–39).

There follows a detailed account of the apostasy under Jason and Menelaus,[17] as well as the other offenses committed by these wicked priests, such as Menelaus's use of the temple treasury as his own purse and his serving as guide to Antiochus IV as he defiled the holy places. This elicits the first of a series of interpretative intrusions into the story in which the epitomator connects the disasters to come with the failure to observe Torah and remain distinct

16. Collins (2000: 82) also suggests that the choice of this epitome to accompany the letters reflects an intentional decision to seek common ground between Palestinian Jews and Egyptian (largely pro-Oniad) Jews by focusing on God's restoration of the Jerusalem temple and not focusing on the role of the Hasmoneans who replaced rather than restored the Oniad line of high priests in Jerusalem.

17. There remain historical questions concerning the nature of Jason's reforms and to what extent they would have constituted a setting aside of Torah, since the sacrificial cult continued as before, and Torah still regulated the piety of the Jewish people. It was probably more the introduction of a Greek constitution as the political basis for Jerusalem and the introduction of Greek institutions, cultural customs (such as the athletics in the gymnasium), and the like that constituted the real heart of the apostasy.

from the Gentiles and their way of life (4:16–17). As in Deuteronomy, becoming "like the Gentiles" through apostasy or other forbidden kinds of syncretism leads to the Gentiles themselves becoming whips in God's hands to punish Israel. Antiochus IV's entry into the holy places and unhindered seizure of the funds gives the epitomator an opportunity to remind the readers of the Heliodorus episode, which provides evidence that Antiochus IV's initial successes are due not to God's weakness or the lack of sanctity of the temple but to the disobedience of the people (5:17–20). God's favor and protection of the temple are temporarily removed during a period of apostasy and disobedience.

The epitomator interprets the assaults on Jerusalem by Antiochus and his agents, the proscription of Judaism, and even the execution of the Torah-observant as the nation's experience of chastisement. In 6:12–17 the epitomator articulates a theology of national calamity as punitive, but corrective, discipline rather than destructive judgment (see also 7:16b, 33–35). It is a merciful act by which God motivates timely repentance and return, so that the nation does not reach the "point of no return" in heaping up its sins so high that nothing remains but eradication by the Holy God. The epitomator differs markedly from the author of Wisdom of Solomon on the topic of how God treats the Gentiles. The latter affirms that God also chastens the Gentiles little by little to provoke repentance, hating nothing that God has created (Wis. 11:24; 12:2, 8–10, 20); in 2 Maccabees, the Gentiles do not receive any such care or provision, being left on their own until they are completely destroyed all at once (2 Macc 6:14–15). God's special treatment of Israel and the confidence that God will never forsake Israel utterly stem from the conviction that God's own honor is inextricably linked to the fate of the nation called by God's "holy and glorious name" (8:14–15).

God's chastisement of the nation is collective rather than individual. The righteous consider themselves to suffer justly (although Antiochus IV does not inflict punishment justly) (7:18–19, 32), even though they themselves have not sinned against God as individuals. They suffer as part of the nation; but at the same time, their voluntary surrender of their bodies for the sake of God and God's law becomes an efficacious death on behalf of the nation (7:37–38). The martyrs' obedience unto death is the turning point in 2 Maccabees, the point of reversal: "the wrath of the Lord had turned to mercy" as a result of the martyr's display of covenant loyalty and their appeal to God to have compassion on the nation (7:38; 8:5). Just as the sin of individuals brought collective punishment, so the covenant loyalty of individuals can effect reversal. This is a point at which 2 Maccabees differs significantly from 1 Maccabees, where the violent zeal of Mattathias and Judas (especially against apostate Jews) was what turned away wrath (1 Macc. 3:5–8). The martyrs take their place alongside Judas and his warriors as heroes of the Jewish people, whose courage and dedication contributed something essential to the reestablishment of religious and political independence (van Henten 1997:

243–67, 299–301). Only at this point do Judas's efforts take center stage and bear fruit.

The Nicanor episodes provide a balance to the Heliodorus episode. God and Israel are again in a state of reconciliation productive of the covenant blessings. Once again, "the Jews were invulnerable, because they followed the laws ordained by God" (8:36; this is highly reminiscent of Heliodorus's confession in 3:39). The peace and security in the land with which the history closes mark a return to the conditions under Onias III in 3:1 (van Henten 1997: 31). Several texts in the Apocrypha subscribe explicitly to this philosophy of history (see especially Tobit, Judith, Prayer of Azariah, and Baruch), attesting to its pervasiveness and persistence, as well as to its effectiveness as an ideology that promotes the maintenance of distinctive Jewish cultural values as the path to peace and stability for the commonwealth.

Honor, Shame, and Jewish Cultural Values

Second Maccabees posits an opposition between *allophylismos* ("an alien way of life") and *Hellenismos* ("the Greek way of life"), on the one hand, and *Ioudaismos* ("the Jewish way of life," "Judaism"), on the other. The epitomator promotes Jewish cultural values both by considerations of national advantage, à la Deuteronomy, and also by the social sanctions and codes of honor and dishonor. The story of the Hellenizing high priests and of the loyal martyrs provides an opportunity for a narrative demonstration of the principle that covenant loyalty leads to honor while abandonment of the distinctive Jewish way of life leads to disgrace.

Seeking honor in the eyes of the Greeks and valuing Greek forms of prestige lead to adopting foreign ways. However, those who violate the divine commission to be separate from the nations neglect the honor due God, enacted by keeping God's covenant inviolate. This failure to honor God through covenant loyalty leads to disaster (4:16–17). Jason's mistaken conception of honor leads to the greatest disgrace for him in 5:6–7, 10 and for Menelaus in 13:3–8: to lie unburied after death. The epitomator's joy in relating their just deserts is hardly hidden, pointing out that such life choices as they made lead to dishonor.

On the other hand, the epitomator turns the martyrs' experiences of degradation, mockery, and torture—the utter violation of their personal honor (it is "sport" to the torturers [7:7, 10])—into types of the noble death, worthy of honorable memory and set forward as praiseworthy examples (6:19, 27–28, 31; 7:20). In 2 Maccabees, exemplary Jews dedicate themselves to their own proper way of life (2:21; 8:1; 14:38) and reject any move toward adopting an alien way of life (6:24). It is no accident or coincidence that those values and ancestral customs deemed worth dying for—circumcision, Sabbath keeping,[18] and dietary observances (6:10–11, 18–19)—are also the most visible and widely known markers of Jewish identity, the distinctive customs that most clearly distinguish them from the non-Jewish nations. To this list one should add almsgiving, such as was enacted by the pious Judas on behalf of those widowed, orphaned, or tortured in the Hellenization crisis (8:27–33).

Viewed from this angle, 2 Maccabees strongly supports the maintenance of the distinctive way of life of the Jewish people and recommends insulation against the encroachments, even the defilements, of alien ways of life.[19] Although a minor point, the use of the terms "barbarous" and "barbarian" for the representatives of Hellenistic cultural and political imperialism (2:21; 10:4; 13:9) is a fine example of the epitomator's, and probably Jason's, ideology at work. Rejecting the ideology of Hellenism's cultural imperialism, 2 Maccabees depicts how honorable, "civilized" people live: according to the Jewish way of life.

Eschatology

Second Maccabees makes important contributions in the area of personal eschatology. Here one finds an early witness to the doctrine of the resurrection of the righteous (7:9, 11, 14, 23, 29; 12:43–45; 14:46) and that specifically in bodily form (7:11; 14:46). The emphasis on God's abilities as Creator provides a warrant for the belief that God can also re-create the human person after death (7:28) (van Henten 1997: 178–80).[20] The formulation of a conception of personal survival in the afterlife allows the author to hold to the Deuteronomistic notion of the collective fortunes of Israel (and thus the necessity that faithful Jews suffer alongside ungodly Jews in this life) while still maintaining God's justice toward the individual.

The letters also bear witness to the future gathering together of Israel, the reversal of Diaspora, already encountered in Tobit 13–14. The later letter contains oblique hints of how Palestinian Jews view Diaspora Jews: they are in need of some measure of repentance, renewal of obedience, and reconciliation with God, since they are still living in a state of separation from the

18. Oesterley (1935: 315) rightly observes that Sabbath observance by the pious is stricter in 2 Maccabees (8:26; 12:38; 15:1–4) than in 1 Maccabees, with Nicanor assuming (and the epitomator saying nothing to the contrary) that if he attacks on the Sabbath, he will defeat Judas. In 1 Maccabees, Mattathias and his forces had to come to a conscious decision to defend themselves if attacked on the Sabbath so as not to perish (2:39–41).

19. Clearly, both Jason and the epitomator did not, however, simply reject everything that Greek culture had to offer but rather drew the lines where they felt it counted most—which was obviously not at the level of language or literary production, for example.

20. Second Maccabees 7:28 incidentally promotes a creation *ex nihilo* doctrine, even though that may not have been the meaning of the author (see Winston 1971–72).

homeland (1:4–5). The theme of the eschatological ingathering recurs throughout the earlier letter like a refrain (1:27; 2:7, 18), giving a strongly nationalistic coloring to the eschatology of the book as a whole. The restoration of the people of Israel in their independent homeland is the goal of God's dealings with God's people, which will be realized at some point in the future.

Influence

Perhaps one of the more obvious signs of the influence of 2 Maccabees (together with 1 Maccabees) is the gradual acceptance of Hanukkah into the calendar of Jewish festivals (see John 10:22, where this is one of the festivals included in John's presentation of Jesus as the fulfillment of all those things celebrated in the liturgical cycle). The feast does not owe its existence to these documents, but the literary celebration and promulgation of the festal story would certainly have supported and encouraged its acceptance. The prefixed letters sought to exert a direct influence in this regard on Egyptian Judaism, a purpose that was well served by joining the letters to a narrative that speaks directly of God's intervention on behalf of God's people (something that tends to lie at the heart of a festival, as it does in Passover, Purim, and the unnamed festival created in 3 Maccabees 7) and itself emphasizes the establishing of festivals (Hanukkah in 10:8; "Nicanor's Day" in 15:36). National gratitude requires, in effect, a perpetual commemoration of a new deliverance of Israel by God's hand.

Second Maccabees' greatest direct influence within Judaism was its contribution to Jewish martyrology. These stories became the basis for 4 Maccabees, a philosophical defense of Judaism as a way of life that realized the ethical ideal of the mastery of the passions by (pious) reason (deSilva 1998).[21] Several reincarnations of the "mother and the seven sons" in rabbinic literature, especially recast in a Roman imperial setting, attest to the abiding importance of the martyr stories of 2 Maccabees (Doran 1980).

Second Maccabees exercises an even more profound influence on the martyrology of the early church. First, the idea that righteous individuals can voluntarily give themselves over to torture and death so as to use up the remainder of God's wrath so that their surviving Jewish sisters and brothers may experience mercy may have provided a link between Isaiah 53 and early Christian reflection on the death of Jesus. The motifs of a person who bears the brunt of God's anger so as to free others to be reconciled to God and of an assurance of vindication by God through resurrection are certainly prominent in 2 Maccabees and in New Testament interpretation of Good Friday and Easter.

---

21. Young (1991) offers a study specifically of the mother in 2 and 4 Maccabees.

The martyrs are held up as examples of courage and loyalty worthy of imitation in the early church as early as Heb. 11:35b: "Others were tortured, refusing to accept release, in order to obtain a better resurrection" (see deSilva 2000a: 418–21). Second Maccabees 6–7 is paraphrased at length in both Cyprian's *Exhortation to Martyrdom Addressed to Fortunatus* (*Ad Fortunatum* 11) and Origen's *Exhortation to Martyrdom* (*Exhortatio ad martyrium* 22–27). Eusebius's recollection of the martyrdom of Blandina (*Historia ecclesiastica* 5.1.1–61), who first encouraged a younger Christian to face the torments without denying Christ and then yielded herself to martyrdom, is crafted to reflect the model of the mother and her sons in 2 Maccabees. Augustine regards them as examples of endurance and faith on a par with the three young men in the furnace: "The same God was the God of the three young men as was the God of the Maccabees. The former escaped the fire, the latter were tortured by fire, yet both triumph in the Eternal God."

These martyrs have been commemorated on August 1 in early Catholic and Orthodox calendars, enjoying the distinction of being the only non-Christian saints. The fact that they had "fought for the law of God even to the death" before the coming of Christ (Augustine, *De civitate Dei* 18.36; see also John Chrysostom, *De Eleazaro et septem pueris* 2) made their achievement all the more remarkable and worthy of honorable memory.

The influence of 2 Maccabees also can be detected in areas that became sources of contention between Catholic and Protestant Christians, resulting in the book's unpopularity among the Protestant Reformers. The dream vision of Onias III and Jeremiah interceding on behalf of Israel on the eve of battle in 15:12–16 became a warrant for the doctrine of the intercession of the saints. The practice of offering prayers for the dead, and especially acts of atonement for the sins of the dead, found legitimation in the epitomator's explanation of Judas's collection for a sin offering as an act meant to atone for the sin of the dead soldiers so that they could have a part in the resurrection of the just (12:43–45), even though this was probably a misunderstanding of Judas's intent, which would have been to protect the living soldiers from punishment for the idolatry committed in their midst (Harrington 1988: 51).

1 Esdras

"Leave to Us a Root and a Name"

First Esdras belongs to the genre of literature known as the "Rewritten Bible," which was so important a part of the literary output of the intertestamental period (see, e.g., *Testaments of the Twelve Patriarchs, Apocalypse of Abraham, Jubilees,* and the Qumran *Temple Scroll*). First Esdras retells the story of 2 Chronicles 35–36, Ezra, and Nehemiah 8 but has recast this material so as to include an episode unknown from the canonical literature: the contest of the three bodyguards (1 Esd. 3:1–5:6). Because of this expansion, Zerubbabel, the descendant of King David, moves to center stage as a leader in, and the prime mover of, the restoration of Judah. The text has also thus preserved a court tale that otherwise would not have become part of the Judeo-Christian tradition, one whose praise of the power of truth would become an important resource for the early church.

The titles of the books related to Ezra are often a source of confusion, all the more so as different religious traditions number these books in different ways. What Protestants commonly call Ezra and Nehemiah, following the Hebrew nomenclature, are called 1 Esdras and 2 Esdras in the Latin Vulgate and thus also in many older Catholic translations. These same books, however, are grouped together as 2 Esdras (Esdras B) in the Septuagint tradition. The apocryphal book of Ezra called 1 Esdras in the KJV, RSV, and NRSV is also called 1 Esdras (Esdras A) in the Septuagint tradition but assigned the title 3 Ezra in the Vulgate and its translations. Finally, the apocalypse of Ezra known as 2 Esdras in the RSV and NRSV (and thus also in the present volume) does not appear in the Septuagint at all and is given the title 4 Ezra in the Vulgate.[1]

1. This is further complicated by the fact that 2 Esdras/4 Ezra has been found to be a compilation of three different texts: (1) an original, Jewish apocalypse that retains the title 4 Ezra; (2) an early Christian prologue now referred to as 5 Ezra; (3) a third-century Christian appendix referred to as 6 Ezra.

Structure and Contents

First Esdras begins in the eighteenth year of Josiah's reign with a magnificent celebration of the Passover (1:1–24) and the narration of Josiah's death as he attempted to intervene in foreign affairs (1:25–33). The decline of the Judean state, culminating in the destruction of Jerusalem and its temple by the Babylonian king, Nebuchadnezzar, follows (1:34–58). After Jeremiah's prediction of seventy years of desolation is fulfilled, the narrative continues with the famous edict of Cyrus, king of Persia and conqueror of Babylon, whose policy of repatriation of exiles made him the hero of the exiled Jewish community, the celebrated "Lord's Anointed" of Second Isaiah. Cyrus sends Sheshbazzar at the head of as many Jewish exiles as wish to return, together with the plundered holy vessels of the temple, in order to rebuild the temple and reestablish the cult of the God of Israel (2:1–15). The returnees meet with resistance, however, during the reign of Artaxerxes, with the result that work on the "city, . . . its market places and walls and . . . the foundations for a temple" are halted "until the second year of the reign of King Darius" (2:16–30).

The tone of the book changes now from historiography to court tale, as the reader is brought to a banquet in the court of Darius (3:1–5:6). Three of Darius's bodyguards propose a contest among themselves to see who can best answer and defend their answer to the question "What one thing is strongest?" (3:5). Darius and his courtiers are to be the judges of the responses, and the king is expected to bestow great distinction on the winner. The three bodyguards write down their answers—"wine," "the king," "women, but above all truth"—and slip them underneath the king's pillow (3:4–12). The next day, the king and his court hear the bodyguards' speeches and award victory to the third, whose name is said to be Zerubbabel (3:13–4:41). The favor he requests concerns the fulfillment of an otherwise unknown vow Darius is said to have made at his accession, that he would rebuild Jerusalem and its temple, resettle the exiles in their native land, and restore the plundered vessels to the temple (4:43–46). Darius gives this endeavor his full support, and Zerubbabel, crediting God as the source of his wisdom, sets off to execute the restoration of his native land and its temple (4:47–5:6).

A list of the returnees, organized according to their family groupings, follows. This list is noteworthy for the witness it bears to the care with which genealogy was preserved during the long years of exile, the way in which genealogy regulated the internal life of Israel (particularly membership in the priestly and Levite castes), and the way in which genealogy marked the boundaries of Israel (5:7–46). Zerubbabel immediately restores the altar and celebrates the Festival of Booths (5:47–55), after which construction on the temple begins in earnest and from which the indigenous peoples surrounding Jerusalem are excluded (5:56–71). Once again, construction on the temple is stopped—"as long as King Cyrus lived . . . until the reign of Darius" (5:72–73).

This time, again in the second year of Darius, progress on the temple moves forward through the encouragement provided by the prophets Haggai and Zechariah (the Book of Haggai is especially relevant as a comparative resource here). When the local governors in the areas around Judea send a letter of concern and complaint to Darius, the king searches the royal archives, discovers that Cyrus had indeed authorized the rebuilding of the temple, and orders that the Judeans be allowed to proceed unhindered and with full support, until its completion four years later (6:1–7:9). The occasion is marked by another festival, this time the observance of Passover (7:10–14).

Ezra is now introduced. He is appointed by the Persian king Artaxerxes to make sure that Judea is being regulated by Torah correctly, to take back still more of the temple vessels that had been plundered by Nebuchadnezzar, and to set in order a judicial system in Judea (8:1–27). Many more exiles return with Ezra, again listed with careful attention to their lineage and to the inclusion of certified priests (8:28–67). Upon his arrival in Judea, Ezra is informed about the way in which the "holy race has been mixed with the alien peoples of the land" (8:70). Based on the commandment in Lev. 18:19–30, Ezra leads the responsible males to repudiate their marriages to non-Jews and to disown their children of these marriages, so that the holy seed might remain pure. Those who refuse were to be "expelled from the multitude of those who had returned from the captivity," the body that seems to have taken over the name "Israel" in the postexilic period (8:68–9:36). The book concludes with the reading of the Torah by Ezra and its exposition or paraphrasing by the Levites and with preparations for the celebration of another Festival of Booths (9:37–55).

In its present form, the book does not appear to have an overarching literary design. Rather, it gives the impression of being a truncated part of a larger whole, so much so that most scholars do not believe that 1 Esdras, as we have it, is complete. Torrey (1910: 82) proposed that 1 Esdras originally contained an alternative version of the entire Chronicler's history. Such a suggestion rests on a very weak foundation, however. Eusebius had quoted Eupolemus (a second-century-B.C.E. Jewish historian) quoting 2 Chron. 2:11–13. There are striking differences between this version of 2 Chron. 2:11–13 and the known Septuagint text. Torrey surmised that there was an alternative version of Chronicles available to Eupolemus, and that, since both Eupolemus's version of Chronicles and 1 Esdras use the verb *ktizein* ("to create") instead of *poiein* ("to make") with reference to God's creative activity, Eupolemus's version of Chronicles is probably part of the work of the author of 1 Esdras. This shared choice of a translation hardly establishes common authorship, however, since the context of "creation" naturally suggests *ktizein* to the literate Greek mind.[2]

---

2. See Talshir (1999: 10–12), who also points out that, since Josephus switches from LXX Chronicles to 1 Esdras, it is unlikely that 1 Esdras originally contained Chronicles (if it had, Josephus probably would have preferred it).

Torrey appears to have overstated the case, but it is possible that some material from the beginning was lost. The text starts abruptly in the middle of Josiah's reign with the celebration of Passover. Talshir (1999: 21) rightly observes that the book would have a much better balance and sense of literary structuring if the original began with the start of Josiah's reign and the discovery and reading of the book of the law. The reading of the law, followed by a festival, would then provide a skillful literary frame for the whole, since the closing chapter would also feature the reading of the law and the celebration of a festival. Talshir also rightly admits that such need not be the case; it is a desirable solution only from a literary point of view, as if to say that 1 Esdras would have been better written had it begun this way. The fact that the work begins with "And" (*kai,* followed by a verb) is, of course, no indication that some opening material preceded it, since Joshua, Judges, 2 Chronicles, and Ezra (LXX 2 Esdras) all begin this way as well.

It is more likely that the original ending has been lost. The present ending seems to break off in midsentence: "And they gathered together. . . ." In its original form, 1 Esdras probably went on to include the Festival of Booths as told in Neh. 8:13–18 (Bissell 1899: 71; Talshir 1999: 6–8), a festival to which the last few verses of 1 Esdras already make reference and for which they prepare. It would not be necessary to assume, however, that more has been lost, since this brief story would provide a suitable conclusion to a work in which Passover and Booths would provide the main structuring devices (1:1–22, Passover; 5:47–73, Booths; 7:1–15, Passover; 9:55-[?], Booths). Did the author extend the story further? The Ezra material in Nehemiah does extend through chapter 9, where Ezra offers a lengthy prayer of confession and rededication to the covenant, which is then ratified by the people in chapter 10. This material would have fit 1 Esdras both in terms of its desire to cull the Ezra traditions from the Nehemiah traditions and its interest in the restoration of the covenant under Ezra, which had also been restored under Josiah, but there is no pressing necessity to consider such material to have been included.

Textual Transmission

While there is a growing consensus that 1 Esdras was originally written in Hebrew or Aramaic, this Semitic original has not survived. The Greek translation is preserved in Septuagint Codices Alexandrinus (the preferred text) and Vaticanus. It does not appear in Codex Sinaiticus, although this codex indirectly bears witness to it by listing Ezra-Nehemiah as Esdras B in its table of contents. The existence of Esdras A, or 1 Esdras, is thus presupposed (Cook 1913: 4). There are also several Greek manuscripts representing the Lucianic revision of the Greek Old Testament, which show many emendations of 1 Esdras in the direction of canonical Ezra-Nehemiah (Cook 1913: 4). The Latin, Syriac, and Ethiopic versions appear to have been made from the Septuagint rather than from the Semitic original.

Composition and Purpose

Determining the date of 1 Esdras is difficult, since it is primarily interested in reflecting on past history rather than providing windows into the situation of the author. Determination of date has therefore rested on an examination of the vocabulary of the book, which appears to have much in common with the vocabulary of other second-century-B.C.E. Jewish texts (Goodman 1992: 610; Cook 1913: 5). This has tended to set the composition of the book sometime in the two centuries before the turn of the era. It was used by Josephus as the basis of *Jewish Antiquities* 11.1–158 in preference to the Septuagint translation of Ezra and Nehemiah, though not exclusively, and not without some correction of its historical inaccuracies (Bissell 1899: 70; Schürer 1986: 3.2.714; Cook 1913: 5). It must therefore have been composed prior to the late first century C.E. Egypt has been suggested as a provenance, given the allusions to unveiled women (4:18), sea travel, and piracy (4:15, 23) (Cook 1913: 5; Bissell 1899: 64) but certainty in this matter lies beyond our meager evidence.

The discussion of the purpose of 1 Esdras is intimately bound to the study of its relationship to Ezra-Nehemiah. The correspondences between these books are obvious to the reader of both versions (Coggins and Knibb 1979: 7; Talshir 1999: 4; Myers 1974: 3–4):

1 Esdras 1	2 Chronicles 35–36
1 Esdras 2:1–15	Ezra 1
1 Esdras 2:16–30	Ezra 4:7–24a
1 Esdras 3:1–5:6	—
1 Esdras 5:7–73	Ezra 2:1–4:5
1 Esdras 6:1–9:36	Ezra 4:24b–10:44
1 Esdras 9:37–55	Nehemiah 7:73b–8:13

The extent of overlap suggests that one of the following statements about literary relationship must be true: (1) 1 Esdras was used as a source by the author of Ezra-Nehemiah (Howorth 1901–2); (2) 1 Esdras and Ezra-Nehemiah are both dependent on the original Chronicler's work, which now is accessible only through these two renditions (Torrey 1910:

11–36);[3] (3) 1 Esdras used Ezra-Nehemiah as a source. The third option is most generally held to be true; the first option is seen as the least likely. Indeed, the differences between the two works are most easily explained, and the rationale of the author is most clearly discernible, if Ezra-Nehemiah is given priority as a source for 1 Esdras.

There are a number of important differences between 1 Esdras and Ezra-Nehemiah. First, the material found in Ezra 4:7–24 is now located earlier in the sequence of events (or, as Talshir [1999: 108–9] would put it, the rest of Ezra 2–4 is postponed until after the introduction of Zerubbabel). Second, the episode found in 1 Esd. 3:1–5:6 is unique to this book. Third, the extent of 1 Esdras is different, embracing 2 Chronicles 35–36, Ezra, and Neh. 7:73–8:13 (probably extending to 8:18, the conclusion of the Festival of Booths, and possibly more). First Esdras does not overlap with the Chronicler's work or with Ezra-Nehemiah but chooses its own starting and ending points.

The purpose of 1 Esdras would seem to be linked to the rationale behind these differences. The first step in this enterprise is the search for a rationale for the selection and for the rearrangement of the material. One thing that can be ruled out is that the author wished to provide a more historically accurate version of Ezra-Nehemiah. From what we can know about the Persian period, 1 Esdras actually provides a far more confused sequence of events with more glaring and numerous errors than one finds in Ezra-Nehemiah (which are themselves far from accurate in this regard).[4]

The sequence of Persian kings and their respective dates has been fairly well established: Cyrus (d. 530 B.C.E.) was succeeded by Cambyses, his son (530–522), Darius I (522–486), Xerxes (486–465), and Artaxerxes I (465–424) (see Grabbe 1992: 122–39). Keeping this line of succession in mind, we quite plainly see four chronological errors made by the author:

First, chapter 2 begins with Cyrus's reign (2:1) and concludes with mention of the reign of Darius. This leaves 2:16–30, describing events taking place in Artaxerxes' reign, completely out of place (unless the author mistook Artaxerxes for Cambyses, something that Josephus assumed and corrected in his version of the story).

Second, events taking place in Cyrus's reign (5:7–73) are narrated after we have arrived at Darius's reign (3:1–5:6).

Third, Zerubbabel acts in chapter 5 on Cyrus's authority (5:54–55, 70–73) without any reference to the authority he was granted by Darius, which was the climax of 3:1–5:6. Moreover, 5:70–73 shows the indigenous "peoples of the land" hindering Zerubbabel and Jeshua in Jerusalem during Cyrus's

3. Adopted and modified by Pfeiffer (1949: 245). Pfeiffer does not believe that the contest was part of the common source, later to be excised by rabbis but rather that the shared portions of Ezra-Nehemiah and 1 Esdras represent the contents of the original, each version then supplementing the original in different directions, 1 Esdras with the contest story, Ezra-Nehemiah with Nehemiah's memoirs.

4. Cook (1913: 5–11) and Talshir (1999: 35–59) offer extensive analyses of literary-historical questions.

reign all the way through the second year of Darius's reign, placing Darius's bodyguard in Judea far too early.

Fourth, the hindering of the construction of the temple until the second year of Darius's reign occurs twice (2:30; 5:72–73). Moreover, the way forward in rebuilding the temple is effected by two incompatible means: the success of Zerubbabel in the court of Darius (3:1–5:6) and the exhortation of the prophets Haggai and Zechariah encouraging Zerubbabel, Jeshua, and the people in Jerusalem (6:1–2). This is the most telling internal problem. The author rearranged the original story so as to make room for the court tale of the three bodyguards *and* preserved the original story about the hortatory ministry of the prophets Haggai and Zechariah (who are known both from Ezra and from the prophetic books themselves), instead of choosing one or the other.

In light of its contradictions of other sources and its own internal contradictions, 1 Esdras would not seem to be primarily interested in history, even though it is in the form of historiography. It is instructive that most of the historical problems in 1 Esdras can be explained in connection with the author's desire to make room in the story for the contest of the three bodyguards and to link this story with Zerubbabel and the restoration of the temple. Indeed, the desire to incorporate this court tale into the history of Zerubbabel may have been the primary motivation for the author to undertake writing 1 Esdras. Nevertheless, the literary judgment of Talshir (1999: 46) concerning the success of the author's attempts at a smooth incorporation remains accurate: "The author/ redactor who created this new layout only did half the work: he carefully formed a new outer frame, but failed to notice that the story could not be properly integrated into the surrounding material, as it led the plot forward from the same point of departure and to the same termination as the plot of another literary unit. . . . The Story of the Youths was not properly woven into the fabric of the book; it did not become a natural link in the chain of events."

The goal of making room for the contest of the three bodyguards itself appears to serve another, overarching goal: the elevation of Zerubbabel (with a resulting exclusion or absorption of Nehemiah). The author's use of a court tale (the contest of the three bodyguards) as the means by which to create an episode of Zerubbabel's success at the court of the Persian king may well have been influenced by the story of the benefits Nehemiah gained for Judah from a later Persian king (Artaxerxes) by virtue of being closely located to the king as his cupbearer (Neh. 2:1–8). In this way, the achievement of Nehemiah is attributed to Zerubbabel, notably a figure of the line of David and one celebrated in the writings of the prophets Haggai and Zechariah.[5] Part of the mo-

---

5. Crediting Zerubbabel with laying the foundations of the temple (5:56) may also indicate an authorial desire to magnify this figure. His predecessor, Sheshbazzar, apparently had already done this work (1:18; 6:19). That the author of 1 Esdras would attribute it to Zerubbabel after twice attributing it to Sheshbazzar bears witness not only to an interest in Zerubbabel but also a lack of acuity when it comes to historical fiction.

tivation for elevating Zerubbabel might be—although this remains rather speculative—to give a sense that the Davidic dynasty had not ended, that in Zerubbabel's success there was, in some sense, a restoration of "the booth of David that is fallen" (Amos 9:11). It is possible also that the celebration of this figure would have attracted the early Christians to this version of the story (1 Esdras) in preference to Ezra-Nehemiah, since to magnify Zerubbabel is to render more illustrious one of the ancestors of Jesus (Matt. 1:12–13; Luke 3:27) and thus indirectly add honor to the one who would be born of the house of David.

It is also likely that the author desired to highlight the role of Ezra in this version of the story. The tendency to elevate this figure is apparent in the author's ascription to him of the role of "chief priest" (9:39–40, 49; not in Ezra-Nehemiah). Ezra's reforms and restoration of the law are the climax of the book in its present form, whereas in Ezra-Nehemiah, Ezra must share the stage with, and eventually yield it to, Nehemiah. First Esdras may thus reflect a very different tendency within early Judaism from that found in 2 Maccabees (1:18, 20–21, 31, 36; 2:13) and Wisdom of Ben Sira (49:13), where it is Nehemiah who is remembered and Ezra omitted (Myers 1974: 10).

One more emphasis may be noted in the distinctives of 1 Esdras. The author shows a greater interest in the temple than does the author of Ezra-Nehemiah. This is seen from the cultic emphasis of the book, beginning, in some sense, with the great Passover celebration in the Jerusalem temple under Josiah, focused throughout on the ebb and flow of the progress of the temple's restoration, and concluding in the temple with the reading of the law and the Festival of Booths. This interest is also suggested by the more frequent use of specifically cultic terms for the temple (*hieron* and *naos,* as opposed to the more general *oikos;* the latter is the more common in the Greek translations of Ezra-Nehemiah). In a naturally related manner, this author also emphasizes the holiness of all aspects of the cult at Jerusalem, adding the adjective "holy" in more than a dozen places where Ezra-Nehemiah lacks this descriptor. The use of the term "new moon" instead of "first day of the month" also carries cultic resonances (see Myers 1974: 16).

The Text–Critical Value of 1 Esdras

Because of the close relationship between 1 Esdras and Ezra-Nehemiah, text critics have pondered the value of the former for the textual criticism—the establishing of the original text—of the latter. Exactly how scholars use the Greek 1 Esdras to resolve problems in the Hebrew text of Ezra-Nehemiah depends on the individual scholar's understanding of their relationship, including the language of composition. Four primary options present themselves:

First, 1 Esdras is a Greek translation of an original Hebrew or Aramaic composition that worked by rearranging and revising canonical Ezra and Nehemiah. As such, it might occasionally be of use to correct corruptions in the Masoretic Text of Ezra and Nehemiah.

Second, 1 Esdras is a Greek translation of a Hebrew or Aramaic composition derived from the same source used by the editors of canonical Ezra and Nehemiah. This option would also give 1 Esdras strong leverage in the textual criticism of Ezra and Nehemiah, since it would serve as an independent witness to the *source* of Ezra-Nehemiah.[6] First Esdras becomes a tool by which, in conjunction with Ezra-Nehemiah, one can reconstruct the pre-Masoretic Chronicler's text.

Third, 1 Esdras is a Greek composition based on the Septuagint translation of Chronicles and Ezra-Nehemiah (Esdras B). The text would then serve the textual criticism of Septuagint Ezra-Nehemiah (Esdras B) but not the Hebrew original. This is now considered to be the least likely option, since the translation known from the collection called the "Septuagint" is probably later than, and independent of, 1 Esdras.

Fourth, 1 Esdras is a Greek composition based on a Greek translation of Chronicles and Ezra-Nehemiah that predates or at least differs from the Septuagint tradition. According to this theory, 1 Esdras would serve as an important witness to the pre-Septuagint text of Esdras B, perhaps providing a window into its "precorrected" form.

The difference between some of these is admittedly slight, and the evidence does not permit any firm conclusions on this issue, with the exception of the exclusion of the third option (Schürer 1986: 3.2.710). The tendency is to regard 1 Esdras as a good, flowing translation from a Hebrew-Aramaic original. Recent scholars have regarded the Hebrew-Aramaic Ezra-Nehemiah to be sufficient to provide this original (with variant readings no longer known from the Masoretic Text tradition) (Coggins and Knibb 1979: 6; Talshir 1999: 269–70).

The Greek of 1 Esdras is superior to the wooden translation Greek of the Septuagint version of Ezra-Nehemiah, the translator having sought out proper Greek idioms for Hebrew idioms and having made judicious use of subordinating clauses rather than the paratactic style of Hebrew. Indeed, the result is a smooth, flowing Greek style superior even to most of the Septuagint translations of other books of the Bible (Cook 1913: 3).[7] While this distinguishes the translator in the annals of artistic translating, it actually makes 1 Esdras less useful for the textual criticism of the Hebrew-Aramaic Ezra-Nehemiah.

6. Torrey (1910: 82–87) and Pfeiffer (1949: 249) view 1 Esdras as a fragment of the first Greek translation of the Chronicler's history.

7. Talshir (1999: 181–268) gives a full discussion.

A translator who woodenly brings the Hebrew or Aramaic into Greek makes it easier for text critics to "retrovert" the Greek into Hebrew or Aramaic for the sake of comparison with other manuscripts of the Hebrew Scriptures. The translator of 1 Esdras, however, has made it more difficult to discern the Semitic original. Moreover, many of the "variants" that result between the author's text and Hebrew Ezra-Nehemiah can be attributed to a desire to produce a free, idiomatic Greek translation. Most other variants result from the author's misunderstanding of the Hebrew (including misreadings of the letters *sin* and *shin* or different vocalizations, since none of these marks would have appeared in the Hebrew-Aramaic original from which the author worked), omissions due to lack of knowledge of how to translate certain words, duplications in the provision of several synonyms at once in an attempt to convey the Semitic original, oversights, and, of course, the textual corruption of the Greek text of 1 Esdras itself as it was copied and handed down. In spite of this, a modest twenty variants derived from a retroversion of 1 Esdras into Hebrew and/or Aramaic yield better readings that can correct the Masoretic Text (Pfeiffer 1949: 241).[8] The most that can be said, then, is that 1 Esdras occasionally provides a better original reading than the Masoretic Text type of Ezra-Nehemiah, but its promise in this regard is weaker than one might at first suspect.

1 Esdras and the Forging of Jewish Identity

One of the primary contributions of 1 Esdras to our understanding of postexilic and intertestamental Judaism is the light it sheds on the way in which Israel was reconstructed in the wake of the disasters of 587 B.C.E. A little more than a century after the destruction of Jerusalem, we find once again an Israel with a clearly articulated sense of identity and of group. In the wake of the exile, the Jewish people is rebuilt by means of the resumption of sacrifices at the Jerusalem temple, the rebuilding of the temple, the traditional festivals, the clarification of who truly belonged to Israel, the prohibition of marriages with non-Jews, and the reading of Torah (Harrington 1999: 153).

Especially important for this process is genealogy, both for drawing boundary lines around the group and for constructing internal hierarchy and roles within the group.

Membership in Israel is clearly a matter of genealogy, of linear descent, for the author of 1 Esdras, like the author of Ezra-Nehemiah. The lengthy list of returnees in chapter 5 is marked by attention to the "ancestral houses" to which these returnees belong (5:4, 37). The identity of the generation of returnees is established by linking each to a preexilic ancestor, thus demonstrat-

---

8. Bissell (1899: 65–69), however, offers an extremely negative assessment of the value of 1 Esdras in this regard.

ing their continuity with Israel before the disaster. At the end of the list, we find mention of those who returned with the group "though they could not prove by their ancestral houses or lineage that they belonged to Israel" (5:37). No process is named by which they could be reintegrated into Israel as members in "full standing"; lacking a secure pedigree, they lack a place in Israel.

Lineage is also central to establishing the internal lines of the restored Israel, just as it had been in the preexilic period. The priests and the Levites are carefully identified on the basis of their descent from a preexilic Levite or priest. Indeed, a comparison of the list of returnees in 1 Esdras 5 with the lists in Ezra 2 and Nehemiah 7 shows closest agreement precisely in the lists of priests and Levites, suggesting that special care was taken to preserve these pedigrees intact and beyond doubt. Again, at the close of the list we find those who "had assumed the priesthood but were not found registered" (5:38). After the official registries are checked, "the genealogy of these men was not found," with the result that "they were excluded from serving as priests" and forbidden "to share in the holy things" until their fate could be decided by the casting of the sacred lots, Urim and Thummim, by a qualified high priest (5:39–40).

The way in which lineage establishes and reinforces group boundaries also manifests itself in the designation of potential marriage partners. When Ezra declares all marriages to non-Jewish women to be a violation of the covenant with God and summons the true-blooded male Israelites not only to put away their foreign-born wives but also to disown their children by such marriages, he establishes the importance of pure Jewish bloodlines for the maintenance of a holy Israel. The ideology of kinship articulated in this book, and thus reinforced for its readers, is that those who are descendants of Jacob are holy by virtue of their lineage; it is their genealogy that sets them apart from the rest of the peoples of the earth to be in a special, covenant relationship with the holy God. Intermarriage thus becomes a form of sacral pollution, a defiling of the "holy race" by virtue of it being "mixed with the alien peoples" (8:70), much as it is an abomination to mix two kinds of thread or to yoke together two kinds of animals. The holiness and destiny of Israel depends, therefore, on preserving the holiness of race and bloodline, and Ezra's reforms elevate Deut. 7:1–6 to the status of perpetual ordinance, a guideline for the preservation of Israel for all time.

By entering into this ideology of kinship, we can appreciate more fully Paul's struggles to reform the meaning of membership in Israel and especially its membership requirements. Against this backdrop of a very strong, absolute, and conscious emphasis on the "flesh" and on the qualification of lineage, we can better appreciate how radical and, to many Jewish eyes, revolting was Paul's proclamation of an Israel to which Jew and Gentile alike belonged on the basis of trusting Jesus. We can also appreciate the equation of kinship (descent from Abraham) with assurance of God's favor and covenant relationship, seen, for example, in John 8:33–41 and refuted in Matt. 3:7–10. First

Esdras also supplies helpful background information for the discussion of the qualifications for priesthood as described by the author of the Epistle to the Hebrews. The Levitical priests truly did stand in their office on the basis of a genealogical pedigree; those who lacked this pedigree (whose pedigree could not be confirmed in the official records) had no part in the priesthood or in the portions set aside for the priests (Heb. 7:5, 13–16).

First Esdras also bears witness to the birth of sectarianism within Israel, as does Ezra-Nehemiah (see Cohen 1987: 138–41). The book recounts the history of the "multitude of those who had returned from the captivity" (9:4), but not all Judeans had been deported to Babylon, just as some Israelites remained in the area of the northern kingdom after the Assyrian deportation of 721 B.C.E. What became of these descendants of Jacob? Where do they appear in the story? The prophet Haggai exhorts returnees and "people of the land" to work together to rebuild the temple on the basis of God's promises to them all "when you came out of Egypt" (Hag. 2:4–5). Viewed from the exodus event, both groups enjoy a shared inheritance in God's promises. The "peoples of the land" appear in 1 Esdras only as enemies of "those who had returned from exile" (5:66–73). If those Israelites who had been left behind by Nebuchadnezzar's deportation appear at all in 1 Esdras, it is in a way undifferentiated from the non-Jews who had been resettled there by the Assyrians and Babylonians.

The returnees are thus depicted as the core of true Israel, the "holy seed." It is this group that celebrates the Passover in Jerusalem (7:13): "The people of Israel who had returned from exile ate it, all those who had separated themselves from the abominations of the peoples of the land and sought the Lord." The second part of 1 Esd. 7:13 further describes the returnees and not a second group. Ezra 6:21, however, clearly has two groups in view: the returnees and "all who had joined them and separated themselves from the pollutions of the nations of the land." The Hebrew Ezra certainly is less exclusive but also betrays the sectarian nature of the returnees: it was necessary to join with the returnees to be part of Israel. First Esdras 9:3–4 also reinforces the impression of sectarianism within Israel: all those who failed to divorce their foreign-born wives would be "expelled from the multitude of those who had returned from the captivity." Recall, however, that Ezra arrives on the scene fifty years after the first returnees go back to Judea with Sheshbazzar and, shortly after, Zerubbabel. It is those men who had married women from outside the families of the returnees and who were now being called to account by Ezra and the "ruling elders" (9:4). This gives us the impression that the group designated as "those who had returned from the captivity" (in Hebrew, the *golah*) was a meaningful designation from Sheshbazzar's time. Ezra is, moreover, only concerned to regulate this group and says nothing about the marriages of those descendants of Jacob who had been left in the land all along.

The cumulative impression, therefore, is that the rebirth of Israel in 1 Esdras really concerns the birth of the "congregation of the exile" or the returnees. It is an ideological document that gives no place within Israel, the "holy race," to anyone outside of this group. There is no interest in the Jews among the "peoples of the land"; "real" Jews are to be found in the congregation of the returned exiles. Centuries later, by the time of Jesus, these lines are softened. Nevertheless, that historical situation provided the precedent for several groups that later would emerge within Judaism, each of them claiming its boundaries as the boundaries of "true Israel." The Qumran community and the early church are perhaps the two most prominent such manifestations.

The Contest of the Three Bodyguards

Since the contest does not appear in the parallel history of Ezra-Nehemiah and reflects more the genre of court tale than historiography, scholars have questioned the relationship of this episode to the rest of 1 Esdras. Was this part of the original 1 Esdras, or was it interpolated later? The fact that the displacements of material in 1 Esdras vis-à-vis Ezra, and the resulting infelicities, can be explained mainly in terms of making room for this particular episode suggests strongly that there was never a 1 Esdras without the contest of the bodyguards (Talshir 1999: 42–46).

On the other hand, there might well have been a "contest of the three bodyguards" episode before 1 Esdras. The author of 1 Esdras might well have added the gloss that the winner was Zerubbabel (4:13) and the narration of Zerubbabel's request to Darius in order to merge an older wisdom story/court tale with the story about the restoration of Judah (Pfeiffer 1949: 251; Torrey 1910: 23–25, 50–56). The fact that the story ill fits into the narrative flow of the book also suggests that it was composed earlier and not specifically for its current location in 1 Esdras (Talshir 1999: 46). It is likely that the contest of the three bodyguards was originally written in Aramaic and was known to the author of 1 Esdras (Torrey 1910: 50–51),[9] who then reshaped it so as to provide a flattering introduction for Zerubbabel into the story.

The story resonates with other wisdom tales in which the point is to arrive at what one thing is strongest or hardest or most superior.[10] In its original form, which was most likely Persian (Aramaic would have been the "common language" for an author and audience in that period as well), the point of the story would have been to elevate "cosmic order" (Zimmermann 1963–64: 189–91) or, in the more elegant words of Pfeiffer (1949: 253), "right cosmic order and justice" as the strongest thing. This comes to be translated as "truth"

9. Zimmermann (1963–64: 183) opts for an Aramaic original for the contest of the three bodyguards. See also Talshir 1999: 81–105.

10. Talshir (1999) provides a fine survey of these folktales, beginning with Indian and Sassanid folktales and early Jewish and rabbinic texts (to which could be added *Apocalypse of Abraham* 7).

in Greek, but it is important to recall that Near Eastern deities like Ma'at or Asha could represent truth as well as order and wisdom. This also makes the linking between truth and a personal deity, "the God of truth," far more natural. Cosmic order, then, is more naturally contrasted not with the "wicked" wine, king, and women but with the "ephemeral" or "fleeting" wine, king, and women. When looking for the strongest thing in the universe, then, one must look beyond unstable, ephemeral people and their intoxicants to the cosmic order that guides and rules all phenomena.

Critics of the story have questioned the plausibility of the narrative. How can the guards presume that Darius will grant such honors to the winner of a contest that they, not he, have proposed? How can they (especially the third bodyguard) refer so insolently to the king in their responses and keep their heads? How does the third bodyguard get away with offering two answers instead of naming the one thing that is strongest (Zimmermann 1963–64: 181–82)? Flavius Josephus and Josippon, who used 1 Esdras as a source, also noticed these problems and attempted to amend them. In Josephus's version, for example, an extra scene is created in which the king proposes the contest and names the reward before he goes to sleep. Zimmermann (1963–64: 195–98) includes a discussion of Josephus's and Josippon's versions of the story in order to arrive at the one with the most logical flow of events. He proposes that, in its original form, the setting was not the king's court but a household in which a master poses the question to his slaves. Thus, the words about the king would not be dangerous, the king not being present to hear. Also, there were four respondents, corresponding to the number of answers. Zimmermann's proposals carry weight, however, only if one assumes that the original story was without any inconsistencies or difficulties, and it might be unreasonable to expect a court tale or literary fiction to abide by the canons of historiography.

The most important inconsistency to consider is, however, that the third speaker gives two answers: "women are strongest, but above all things truth is victor" (3:12). In the three speeches that follow, however, the speech on women's strength or power serves an essential rhetorical purpose. It is a topic of refutation to clear the way for the final answer. The second bodyguard's speech actually names "men" and then "the king" as the strongest (although he wrote down only "king" on the paper); Zerubbabel's refutation neatly undermines both by moving from "women" in general to "Apame," the king's concubine, in particular. Indeed, the "women" speech responds both to the "wine" and the "king" speeches because women produce both kings and vintners: even if this is a rather artificial connection, it nevertheless can at least give the impression of refuting the proposal of wine as strongest, and in rhetoric the impression is often what matters (Talshir 1999: 64). Of course, it cannot be presumed that the third bodyguard could know that the second bodyguard would name "the king" and thus be reasonably expected to name "women" as a topic of refutation; but we are probably not dealing with a historical event: the author of the story knew all three answers and thus could name them in the way that would yield a pleasing development in the oratory that would follow.

Clearly, the Jewish author has shaped these speeches to bring them in line with his tradition (either deliberately or unconsciously in passing on the story in the context of the author's assumed values). Zimmermann suggests that an original speech about the power of the "mistress" has been recast in the direction of the "wife" by references to Gen. 2:24 (4:20, 25) in order to make it more acceptable to the Jewish author and audience both.[11] With regard to the climactic speech on truth (4:33–40), Talshir (1999: 75–76) shows through a brilliant intertextual study how this speech has been recast in ways that now resonate broadly with Septuagintal texts speaking of God's relationship to God's works, which now colors all the material on truth and its works. Thus, in its present form, the praise of truth becomes a praise of God's ordering and regulating of the cosmos and God's absolute justice. On account of the intertextuality of the passage, the climactic declaration "Blessed be the God of truth" is not a last-minute Judaizing of the text but the natural conclusion to a speech that has implicated God as the phantom subject from the beginning. The second half of the story reflects that genre seen in the Additions to Daniel and canonical Daniel, Esther, and Nehemiah, in which a Jewish person finds great success at the court of a Gentile monarch (Talshir 1999: 79). This, together with the gloss that the third bodyguard is Zerubbabel (4:13), brings the piece of Aramaic folklore to bear on the story of the restoration of Israel.

The first part of Zerubbabel's speech, on women, provides an interesting window into male perceptions of women in the author's period. Although set in a male-dominated world, this speech frankly acknowledges that the male world of achievement and conquest is entirely dependent on women, who are the source of life (as mothers), sustainers of the quality of life (as wives), and sultry motivators of male activity (as mistresses or wives). From this perspective, a patriarchal culture might question the assumption that men dominate women and even conclude that "women rule over you" (4:22). The author thus acknowledges that even though all formal titles and appearances of domination belong to men, women find alternative means by which to exercise control within that system. It is noteworthy, however, that the speaker does nothing but reinforce the sense of a "woman's place," so that it would be a mistake to regard this as a liberating text in any sense. Moreover, the author attributes to women not only men's positive achievements but also their sins and destruction: "Many have perished, or stumbled, or sinned because of

11. Zimmermann (1963–64: 183–87) offers reconstructions of the original Aramaic of this speech, which he suggests has been misconstrued by its Greek translator. Thus, he reconstructs 4:17 as "Women bring gratification to men and give them children, and without women men cannot come into being," on the basis of reconstructions of the original Aramaic and explanations for how the key words could have been misinterpreted as "garments" and "glory."

women" (4:27) (Schuller 1992: 236). This also curtails any positive contribution the speech might have made to an appreciation of the importance of women in everyday life.

Influence

During the first century before and after the turn of the era, 1 Esdras may have been regarded as an alternative version of Ezra-Nehemiah. In the pre-Masoretic period, several different text traditions of the same work existed side by side. The biblical manuscripts at Qumran show, for example, two different textual traditions of 1 Samuel and Jeremiah, both of which might have functioned as Scripture. This might help to account for Josephus's use of 1 Esdras rather than Ezra when he had previously been following Chronicles as the source material for his *Jewish Antiquities*. Josephus's use of 1 Esdras in his account of the history of the Jewish people is an unmistakable instance of its influence on Jewish literature, although after the fixing of canonical Ezra-Nehemiah one does not see any further Jewish use of 1 Esdras.

In the early church, 1 Esdras appears to have exercised an influence chiefly on account of the episode that it does not share with Ezra-Nehemiah: the contest of the three bodyguards. Zerubbabel's discourse on truth, predictably, is the most frequently quoted part of the book: Clement of Alexandria (*Stromata* 1.21), Origen, Cyprian, Eusebius, Athanasius, Ambrose, Ephrem the Syrian, John Chrysostom, and John of Damascus all refer to or quote this passage; Augustine (*De civitate Dei* 18.36) quotes 1 Esd. 3:12, also for the sake of the reference there to truth being strongest.[12] As far as the early church authors were concerned, it seems that it was the new material in 1 Esdras that was considered most useful; for the rest, they preferred Ezra-Nehemiah. The court tale thus emerges in fact as the primary reason for both the book's composition and its preservation.

Luther and his successors, together with other Reformers, followed Jerome's judgment against the book's value, but Pope Clement reintroduced the book into the Vulgate in an appendix, together with Prayer of Manasseh and 2 Esdras (= 4–6 Ezra). Its preservation was thus assured, even though at the very margins of the Apocrypha.

---

12. See Myers 1974: 17–18 and Schürer 1986: 3.2.714 for full references.

Prayer of Manasseh

14

"The God of Those Who Repent"

Manasseh, king of Judah from 687 to 642 B.C.E.,[1] is remembered by the Deuteronomistic Historians as a uniquely wicked monarch who left behind a singular legacy. Manasseh enthusiastically promoted the worship of Baal, Asherah, and other Canaanite divinities; introduced altars to, and images of, other gods into the Jerusalem temple; and consorted with conjurers and mediums (2 Kings 21:2–9). His sin became the irreversible cause of Judea's destruction (2 Kings 21:10–15; 24:1–4; Jer. 15:1–4). Not even the revival of Torah observance under Josiah, with all his zealous purging of Israel of its idols, could reverse this sentence (2 Kings 23:26–27).

The Chronicler tells the story with a substantial change, which makes Manasseh a model of repentance and self-humbling before God (2 Chron. 33:21–25). After the same catalog of sins, the Chronicler tells of the king of Assyria, God's agent of punishment, taking Manasseh back to Babylon in chains (2 Chron. 33:11). At this point, something astounding occurs, something of which the author of 2 Kings gives no hint. In prison, Manasseh repents, and God, accepting his humble contrition, restores him to Judea and the throne (2 Chron. 33:12–13). The result of this transformation was that Manasseh destroyed all the idols and altars dedicated to other gods and became a devout monotheist (2 Chron. 33:14–16). The Chronicler concludes the review of Manasseh's reign by referring the reader to the (now lost) "Annals of the Kings of Israel," which contain "his prayer to his God." The Chronicler refers, moreover, to the "records of the seers" as another place where one might find "his prayer, and how God received his entreaty" (2 Chron. 33:18–19). Such a reference to the existence of the text of Manasseh's prayer issued an open invitation for some pious Jew to compose a fine penitential psalm in order to fill this gap in the tradition.

---

1. Second Kings 21:1 and 2 Chron. 33:1 record a reign of fifty-five years, which is, however, difficult to harmonize with any known chronology of the kings of Israel and Judah, unless one supposes a ten-year coregency with Hezekiah, Manasseh's righteous father, during his illness (Evans 1992: 496).

The Prayer of Manasseh appears to have been written in Greek, given the resonances with, and recontextualizations of, phrases from the Septuagint. Charlesworth (1985: 627), however, rightly cautions against being dogmatic about this conclusion. The text is too short for a thorough study with a view to deciding whether its Greek is compositional or translational, a question rendered difficult in the best of circumstances on account of the influence of Semitisms on the Septuagint and on later Hellenistic Jewish authors writing in Greek. The date of the text cannot be narrowed down from between 200 B.C.E. and 50 C.E. (Charlesworth 1985: 627). Some scholars (e.g., Metzger 1957: 125) claim that the contents reflect more closely the theology of Palestinian Judaism rather than Diaspora Judaism; but again, an overly strong claim for a specific provenance on such slim evidence is unwise.

The earliest copies of the text are preserved in the expanded retelling of 2 Kings 21 and 2 Chronicles 33 in the late-second- or early-third-century collection called the *Didaskalia*. This early Syriac Christian work was itself preserved as the first six books in the fourth- or fifth-century *Apostolic Constitutions* (see 2.22). Both Greek and Syriac editions of the *Didaskalia* have survived, with the result that the Syriac becomes the most important early translation (called a "version") for text critics.[2] Prayer of Manasseh survives also in Ethiopic, Old Slavonic, Armenian, as well as Latin translations. Jerome did not include it in his Vulgate, but it does appear in Vulgate manuscripts by the medieval period.

The Greek text is preserved not only in the *Apostolic Constitutions* but also in the collection of Odes found in the fifth-century Septuagint codex Alexandrinus and in the seventh-century codex Turicensis.[3] The Odes are a collection of prayers and hymns culled from elsewhere in the Old and New Testaments, including the Songs of Moses (Exodus 15; Deuteronomy 32), Prayer of Hannah (1 Sam. 2:1–10), Prayer of Habakkuk (Hab. 3:2–19), Prayer of Isaiah (Isa. 26:9–19), Prayer of Jonah (Jon. 2:3–9), Prayer of Azariah (Add. Dan. 3:26–45), Song of the Three Young Men (Add. Dan. 3:52–88), Song of Mary (Luke 1:46–55), Song of Zechariah (Luke 1:68–79), Isaiah's Song of the Vineyard (Isa. 5:1–10), Prayer of Hezekiah (Isa. 38:10–20), Prayer of Manasseh, Prayer of Simeon (Luke 2:29–32), and the "Morning Hymn," which is sung in shorter form in many churches as the "Glory to God" or *Gloria*. These liturgical pieces are gathered together as an appendix to the Psalter. This has raised the question as to whether or not Prayer of Manasseh was considered to be Scripture in the communities that used these codices. The answer is likely to be negative. Inclusion in the Odes does not automatically suggest status as Scripture, all the more so as the "Morning Hymn" was certainly known as a composition of the church and not a part of the scriptural canon.

2. Charlesworth (1985) gives the Syriac primary weight in his translation.
3. The prayer does not appear at all in the fourth-century codices Sinaiticus and Vaticanus.

The Odes, then, bear witness to the liturgical usage of Prayer of Manasseh in the Eastern churches rather than its inclusion in the canon.

Prayer of Manasseh appears always to have been attached to Manasseh's name. The "autobiographical" details especially reinforce this impression. In both 2 Chron. 33:3–7 and Pr. Man. 10, the protagonist is guilty of provoking God's anger by setting up idols; in both 2 Chron. 33:11–12 and Pr. Man. 9–11, the protagonist suffers the punishment of "chains" and presents a prayer to God in humility of heart. There are four basic components to this prayer: an invocation to God in praise of God's power in creation and merciful character (1–8); a confession of sin (9–10); a petition for pardon (11–14); and a doxology (15).

The prayer opens with phrases reminiscent of Davidic prayers in 1 Chronicles. "Lord Almighty" echoes the same title in the Septuagint version of 1 Chron. 17:24; "God of our ancestors, of Abraham and Isaac and Jacob," while a frequent way of identifying God, recalls most specifically LXX 1 Chron. 29:18, "God of Abraham, Isaac, and Jacob, our ancestors." The intertexture of the prayer quickly broadens beyond Chronicles to include the wider scriptural tradition. The further identification of this God as the one "who made the heaven and the earth" is frequent in the Jewish Scriptures (Exod. 20:11; 2 Kings 19:15; Neh. 9:6; LXX Ps. 145:6; Isa. 37:16; see also Gen. 1:1; Isa. 45:18; Bel 5). This identification often distinguishes the God of Israel from all other gods, the "gods who did not make the heavens and the earth" (Jer. 10:11), a resonance that might be meaningfully heard in this prayer of an ex-idolater. The recollection of God's power over the waters and the abyss also recalls similar descriptions of God's might in Scripture (see Job 38:8–11; Ps. 104 [LXX 103]:6–9; see also Rev. 20:1–3).

Verses 1–4 dwell on the power of God, especially as seen in the creation and governing of the world; v. 5 brings this power to bear on sinners, who experience it as a grave threat to their existence. The transition is thus begun from the declaration of the power of God, which means destruction and danger for the sinner, to the mercy of God, which sheds a ray of hope into the sinner's heart (6–8). The author now describes God as "tender-hearted, long-suffering, and abounding in mercy," using the language of LXX Exod. 34:6–7, where God self-identifies to Moses as "compassionate, long-suffering, and abounding in mercy." The prayer thus connects with one of the most potent moments of divine self-disclosure in the Torah.

In v. 7, God is said to "repent over the evils of humankind." There is a certain ambiguity here. The word "repent" may refer to being sorrowful at the sins committed by people (as in Gen. 6:5–7, where God's sorrow leads to the eradication of the sinners) or, as the NRSV renders it, relenting in the face of the ills that beset humanity. This certainly is the meaning of God's "repenting" in 1 Chron. 21:14–15. In that passage, David has sinned against God by taking a census of the people. When confronted with the choice of being punished for this sin at the hands of Israel's human enemies or at the hands of

God, David chooses to fall into God's hands, "for his mercy is very great" (1 Chron. 21:13). God responds by decimating the people by means of a plague but "repents/relents" at the suffering of Israel before destroying Jerusalem. The sense of "relenting" is more probable, given the influence of 1 and 2 Chronicles on this prayer more generally and given the parallelism in the situations described in 1 Chronicles 21 and Prayer of Manasseh. Manasseh, afflicted in exile, is now begging God to relent at his suffering, as it is God's character to do.

The word "repentance" affords a transition from God's character of "relenting/repenting at human suffering" to the posture that God has appointed for the sinner to take up toward God. The repetition of the term "repentance" in vv. 7–8 seems intentional,[4] as a means by which the sinner can find a point of common ground with the "God of the righteous" (v. 8). In fact, God has "appointed repentance" as the way for the sinner, so that there can still be a place for the sinner in God's sight, a way provided by God for the sinner to connect with God. Intertexture with Psalm 51 is especially rich in the confession/supplication sections of this prayer (see Charlesworth 1985: 630). In both, the supplicant's acknowledgment of personal sinfulness and the justice or correctness of God's punishment is especially noteworthy, together with the promise that mercy shown now will result in God's praise on the lips of the restored penitent.

The petition for forgiveness (vv. 11–13) begins with a beautiful image of humility of heart: "I bend the knee of my heart." This stands in marked contrast with the hubris that Manasseh displayed in his earlier disregard for God's prohibitions of idolatry. Another acknowledgment of sin, "I have sinned, O Lord, I have sinned," is poetically balanced by the supplication "Forgive me, O Lord, forgive me" (vv. 12–13). The petition concludes by identifying God as the "God of those who repent" (v. 13), which is an original way of describing God, a fine counterpoint to the "God of the righteous" (v. 8) and an expression of the conviction that the God of all does not cease to be God of those who fail to walk in God's way. As their Creator and as the One who stands ready to forgive and restore those who humble themselves and turn aside from sinful ways, God remains "their God."

The petition closes with two "incentives" to God to forgive the sinner. Such incentives are common in the canonical psalms, where praise, fulfilling of vows, and the like are promised to God as a result of God's delivering the psalmist from some threat (see, e.g., Ps. 35:28; 51:12–14). The first incentive—one that is emerging in the intertestamental period—for God to forgive and restore the sinner is that such an act of pardon and kindness will show to the world the generous and gracious character of God. People will be in awe

---

4. Early Greek manuscripts do not include v. 7b, which lessens the prominence of "repentance" words. The NRSV follows the Syriac and Latin versions, which include v. 7b. Charlesworth (1985: 636) considers v. 7b to be original.

of the God who is so magnanimous, so full of favor, as to bestow pardon and favor on so miserable an offender (see, in this regard, 2 Esd. 8:32, 36; Rom. 3:21–26). The second incentive is seen in the promise that the one delivered will praise God continually, will remain mindful of God's generosity and enact appropriate gratitude. In this way, the petitioning sinner claims to be a person upon whom favor would not be wasted but rather would bear its proper fruit. Grace may always be unmerited, but it should never go unre-quited,[5] and it is precisely the latter that Manasseh's literary persona promises to observe should God choose to pardon and restore him.

Prayer of Manasseh teaches the "infinite compassion of the Almighty" and the "efficacy of true repentance" (Ryle 1913: 615; Metzger 1957: 126; Charlesworth 1985: 629). It proclaims that even the worst of offenders can find mercy and forgiveness with God. This provides a perpetual encourage-ment to its readers and users that no sin of theirs is so great as to make for-giveness impossible and thus motivates repentance and hope for a restored re-lationship with God. Although it appears not to have retained a place in Jewish tradition, Prayer of Manasseh became an important liturgical piece in the Eastern churches and continues to be used as a canticle for morning prayer in the *Book of Common Prayer* used by the Episcopal churches in America. Pope Clement VIII's edition of the Vulgate included Prayer of Manasseh, 1 Esdras, and 2 Esdras in an appendix to the New Testament, a tradition that has been followed in most printed Vulgate Bibles (although not in Catholic translations of the Bible, such as the JB and NJB). Luther and the translators of the KJV included it as part of the Apocrypha. Such decisions about inclu-sion were no doubt based on a conviction that Christians would continue to value Prayer of Manasseh's witness to God's mercy as well as to find it a suit-able vehicle for their own expressions of penitence.

5. On the cultural context of grace and giving in the Greco-Roman period, see deSilva 2000b: ch. 3.

Psalm 151

"He Made Me Shepherd of His Flock"

The titles given to many canonical psalms locate them in the life of David. The preface to Psalm 18 links the song to "the day when the Lord delivered him . . . from the hand of Saul," Psalm 34 is linked with the time "when he feigned madness before Abimelech," and Psalm 51 is said to express David's response "when the prophet Nathan came to him, after he had gone in to Bathsheba." The psalms themselves, however, do not contain unambiguous references to those events apart from the secondary titles. Ironically, the psalm "of David" that makes unambiguous reference to events known from David's life is the apocryphal Psalm 151.

This psalm has come down to us in two forms. The Greek form is preserved in the Septuagint codices. Codices Vaticanus and Alexandrinus acknowledge it to be "outside the number," that is, not part of the canonical collection; Sinaiticus, on the contrary, presents it as canonical, calling the whole collection "The 151 Psalms of David." The original Hebrew version is now to be found in the Qumran psalms scroll 11QPs[a],[1] which also necessitates a date of composition prior to 68 C.E. Style alone could suggest a sixth-century date (Pigué 1992: 537), but a number of phrases do not occur in literature until much later, suggesting an intertestamental date. This psalm, along with four others attributed either to David or Hezekiah, is also preserved in the Syriac Peshitta, which follows the Greek version rather than the Hebrew.

---

1. The psalms scrolls found at Qumran (about forty psalters, although some are very fragmentary) contain several extracanonical psalms and poems. 11QPs[a], the fullest example, contains a "Plea for Deliverance," part of the poem from Sirach 51, an "Apostrophe to Zion," a "Hymn to the Creator," the "Last Words of David," a catalogue of David's compositions, and Psalms 151A, 151B, 154, 155. This raises the possibility that the shape of the Book of Psalms was still fluid in the second century B.C.E. and the number of canonical psalms not yet fixed; it is also possible that the Qumran psalms scrolls should be regarded not as specimens of the "Book of Psalms" but of community prayer and hymn books. For translations, see Vermes 1997: 301–18; Abegg, Flint, and Ulrich 1999: 505–89.

The Greek version (the primary text for the NRSV) abridges and conflates two separate Hebrew psalms discovered at Qumran, labeled 151A and 151B. Hebrew Psalm 151A speaks at greater length of David's election by God as king, providing twenty-seven lines compared to the twelve in the first five verses of the Greek version. Little of substance is lost in the Greek version except an objectionable point in v. 3 of the Hebrew. There the psalmist declares that the mountains and the hills do not speak of God's glory, so that David took it up as his own duty. This stands at odds with other psalms that celebrate the natural world's testimony to God's honor and God's deeds (see, e.g., Ps. 19:1–4) and might account for the omission in the Greek. Hebrew Psalm 151B is fragmentary (only the title and first verse are preserved in the Qumran psalms scroll), but its content corresponds to v. 6 in the Greek Psalm 151, and it is likely that it went on to develop at greater length David's triumph over Goliath.[2]

Psalm 151, written as if by David in the first person, recalls David's selection by God to be anointed as king over Israel in Saul's place as well as his first victory for his people in the defeat of Goliath. As such, it is a liturgical retelling and abridgement of 1 Samuel 16–17. In the first five verses, as in the 1 Samuel narrative, a strong emphasis is placed on the stature and fine appearance of David's brothers (1 Sam. 16:6–10; Ps. 151:5) and on the fact that David was the smallest and youngest of them (1 Sam. 16:7, 11; Ps. 151:1); nevertheless, God chose David (1 Sam. 16:12–13; Ps. 151:4b). The role of Samuel, God's messenger who came to anoint a king, is also prominent in both texts (1 Sam. 16:1–5; Ps. 151:4a). The central point of this part of the psalm is thus consonant with the core message of 1 Samuel 16: "Mortals look on the outward appearance, but the Lord looks on the heart" (1 Sam. 16:7) and chooses accordingly.

Verses 2 and 3 speak in a very condensed way (compared with the Hebrew Psalm 151A) of David's commitment to worshiping God, singing hymns celebrating God's works and spreading God's honor out in open fields where he watched over his father's sheep. The suggestion in both the Greek and Hebrew versions is that his commitment to worship—the heart that delights in honoring God—is what made David stand out in the sight of God, who heard all of the boy's songs.

The final two verses recall in brief compass the Philistine giant Goliath's challenge to the Israelites and David's successful meeting of the challenge. The detail that Goliath "cursed [David] by his idols" recontextualizes a phrase from 1 Sam. 17:43. David's actual defeat of Goliath is passed over, but pre-

---

2. Despite the abrupt beginning of Hebrew Psalm 151B ("Then I saw a Philistine"), it is likely that Hebrew Psalm 151A was a complete composition (that is, the Qumran psalter did not divide up what was originally a single psalm), since the opening and closing exhibit an inclusio between v. 1 and v. 5, the second line of these verses containing the same phraseology: "He made me . . . for . . . and ruler of. . . ." (Hebrew: *wysymny . . . l . . . wmwšl b. . . .*).

supposed by the detail that David "drew [Goliath's] own sword" and used it to behead the corpse (v. 7a; cf. 1 Sam. 17:51). The climax of the psalm is the removal of Israel's disgrace, the very thing that David showed himself to be most concerned about when he first arrived on the scene and heard the Philistine's taunts (v. 7b; cf. 1 Sam. 17:26).

Why was it important to remember these aspects of David's life, especially in cultic form? Perhaps it was merely thought strange by a certain Jewish poet that no psalm was preserved celebrating these inaugural episodes in David's life, when so many other psalms were linked by means of their superscriptions to other events, and so the poet composed two psalms to supply suitable hymnic reflections on 1 Samuel 16 and 1 Samuel 17 (which a later poet abridged and combined into one). On the other hand, it is also possible that this part of the story said something about God that inspired the people in their context of domination by foreign powers. David's anointing reminded an Israel that no longer stood tall in stature amidst the nations of the world that God was not impressed with appearances and sought rather a worshipful heart. David's destiny also supplied a historical precedent that a heart that honors God really does make for a grander future than an impressive appearance. The story of Goliath's defeat stood as an important reminder that Israel's honor and future depended not on might of arms or vastness of military power but on the God who chose them. David's defeat of the giant who mocked Israel and their God provided a precedent for the hope that God would again take away the disgrace of Israel and vindicate their faith in God in the sight of the giants around them.

3 Maccabees

"Blessed Be the Deliverer of Israel"

An arrogant and unstable king, a decree of forced conversion, an entire population held captive in an arena awaiting a gruesome death, and miraculous deliverance—these are the main ingredients of this melodramatic story set in Ptolemaic Egypt. Shadows of historical reminiscences are woven together with, and patterned after, more recent literary works to create this rather dark tale of ethnic hatred and misunderstanding, of latent hostilities given free reign, and of a salvation that is somehow less than *shalom*. Third Maccabees cannot fail to make an impact on its reader, however, particularly given the author's talent for playing on the emotions of the audience. It remains as an important literary witness to the suspicions that fostered anti-Judaism in the Greco-Roman period, to the fears of what such animosity might lead to, and to a certain anti-Gentilism on the part of the author that cannot be ignored. The work also gives poignant expression, however, to the conviction that Diaspora Jews are no less connected with the fate and fortunes of the Jerusalem temple than are their Palestinian sisters and brothers and no further removed from God's favor and help.

Structure and Contents

The book begins with Ptolemy IV Philopator's advance against Antiochus III at Raphia, south of Gaza. So abrupt is this start that the original opening must surely have been lost at some point in the textual transmission of the book.[1] A disloyal Theodotus attempts to murder Ptolemy in his sleep, but the plot is thwarted through the timely warning of Dositheus, a Jew who

---

1. The most telling evidence of this is that the book begins with the Greek adversative *de* ("*But* Philopator . . .") and that "those who returned" are introduced without any indication of who these people were, why they had been sent out (or at least the conditions that impelled them to return, if they were refugees). Not more than a few verses need have been lost, however.

has gone over to the Greek way of life. Following his victory over Antiochus III at the battle of Raphia, Ptolemy travels through the cities in Palestine to confirm their loyalty to his throne and to encourage them in the aftermath of the war (1:1–8).

Ptolemy visits the sacred sites of the coastal cities in order to confer gifts to increase morale and a sense of loyalty to himself. This practice becomes a problem when Ptolemy enters Jerusalem and desires to enter the Holy Place of the temple, contrary to local law. Undeterred by the priests, Ptolemy claims it as his kingly right to enter any place in his kingdom (1:9–15). The people take to the streets in protest and prayer, and the high priest successfully arouses divine intervention with a solemn prayer (1:16–2:20). At the last moment, Ptolemy is punished by invisible forces, is dragged out of the temple enclosure by his bodyguards, and, upon recovery, returns to Egypt vowing to inflict vengeance upon the Jewish population there for the repulse he suffered in Jerusalem (2:21–24). This establishes the important connection of the fate of Egyptian Jews with events in Palestine and, in particular, the fortunes of the temple.

Ptolemy now pursues in Egypt a policy similar to what Antiochus IV would enforce in Palestine. Jews who accept initiation into the cult of Dionysus, thus accepting Greek religion, will enjoy full Alexandrian citizenship, a coveted status in Egypt. Those who refuse will be registered in the poll tax and branded as slaves. Those who resist are to be executed (2:25–30). It is noteworthy that those who enjoyed citizenship were expected to take part in the civic life, which included the religious life, of a Greek city. Jewish claims to citizenship were often called into question on precisely this point. From a Gentile point of view, Ptolemy's decree would simply be a means by which the legal status of Jews in Egypt would be clarified. The author, of course, views this plan as a hostile act of anti-Jewish persecution.

About three hundred Jews prefer full citizenship to paying the cost of exclusive commitment to the One God. Most Jews, however, accept loss for the sake of their ancestral covenant, showing open contempt for those who accept the king's offer (2:31–33). Ptolemy regards this as a sure sign of the nation's ill will and so plans to assemble all Egyptian Jews (except for the apostates) in the hippodrome for execution (3:1–30). The author's description of the violent gathering of the Jews from across Egypt plays heavily on the emotions by presenting scenes of piteous distress (4:1–13).

Now God's intervention on behalf of the Jews in Egypt begins. While the lists of Jews slated for execution are being drawn up, the king's agents run out of papyrus and pens, allowing some to escape detection (4:14–21). Those who have been listed and gathered, however, must now face Ptolemy's elephants, gathered for the purpose of trampling the Jews to death. In response to the captives' prayer, God frustrates Ptolemy's plans a first time by making him sleep long past the time appointed for the execution, then a second time by causing the king to forget his plan and accuse his courtiers of plotting this senseless mischief against the Jews to his own hurt (5:1–35). On the third day, however, the king is able to give the order to release the elephants upon the Jews, a sight that fills the victims with a terror depicted with great emotional power by the author (5:36–51). In the midst of chaos, an aged priest named Eleazar calls for silence and offers a public prayer, after which angels frighten the elephants and turn them back to trample Ptolemy's soldiers (6:1–21).

The king tearfully repents of his plan and censures his courtiers for leading him down this self-destructive path. He releases the Jews, provides for a seven-day feast for them (which becomes an annual Jewish festival [6:36]), and issues a decree protecting the rights of Jews in his kingdom (6:22–7:9). Before the Jews disperse to their homes, they receive leave from Ptolemy to execute those of their number who had chosen to apostatize (7:10–16), thus purging "Israel" (see Deut. 13:6–18). Those Jews who were not residents of Alexandria celebrate a second seven-day festival as they begin their journey home (7:17–23). The possessions and prestige that they had lost are restored, and the latter greatly enhanced, at the close of the book (7:21–22).

Author, Date, and Setting

The title of this work is a misnomer, since the events it describes are supposed to have occurred fifty years before the Maccabean Revolt and mostly in Egypt rather than in Israel. Nevertheless, it spins a story so similar to that told in 2 Maccabees and shares so prominently the themes of religious oppression and divine deliverance that its association with the Maccabean literature is readily understandable. An alternative title found in some ancient book lists, *Ptolemaica* ("matters pertaining to Ptolemy"), actually is more appropriate. The book is found in Codices Alexandrinus (fifth century) and Venetus (ninth century) but not the fourth-century codices Sinaiticus and Vaticanus.

The author's name has not come down to us, but clearly this was someone very much at home in the Greek language, sporting a command not only of a broad and educated vocabulary but also of contemporary rhetorical techniques. The most noticeable of these is the author's ability to use vivid description to arouse *pathos*—an emotional response in the audience—especially in the lament at the temple and in the piteous description of the Jews being herded up across Egypt and sent to Alexandria (in terms that cannot help but remind one of the so-called Middle Passage of African slaves en route to the Americas). Another technique is *prosopopoiia:* fashioning speech appropriate to the character one assumes. This is especially evident when one contrasts the Hebraisms and simple style employed for the prayers of Simon and Eleazar, the official tone and form of the decrees of Ptolemy, and the author's own narrative style (otiose and bombastic). The author is also a law-observant

Jew with an unveiled contempt for Gentile religion and for the indigenous Egyptian population's prejudice against Jews.

The book's interest in Egyptian Jewry—something felt all the more as a Palestinian opening scene segues to an Egyptian denouement, as well as in the peculiar social tensions depicted in the book—suggests that 3 Maccabees was written in Alexandria or, at least, some Jewish center in Egypt. It envisions a Jewish, not a Gentile, readership. The presentation of Gentiles in this book would only alienate Gentile readers, who see themselves portrayed as "abominable," "lawless," and "empty-headed" (6:9, 11) (Williams 1995: 18–19).

As to when 3 Maccabees was written, there are no clear answers but only a variety of possibilities. The extreme limits for the date are usually given as 217 B.C.E., when the battle of Raphia took place, and 70 C.E., when the Jerusalem temple was destroyed and which the author does not mention. The latter date is problematic insofar as it is strictly an argument from silence. Many scholars have taken to analyzing the affinities of 3 Maccabees with other Jewish texts as a means of arriving at a more narrowly defined date. Third Maccabees 6:6 remembers the deliverance of the three young men from the fiery furnace with a detail found in the Additions to Daniel (Sg. Three 27) but not in the Hebrew canonical Daniel, namely, that God moistened the fiery furnace as with a dew. This means that 3 Maccabees must postdate the Greek translation of Daniel (itself only compiled, if not entirely composed, in 166 B.C.E.).

Third Maccabees shows even more striking affinities with 2 Maccabees and *Letter of Aristeas*. The fact that both of these are associated with Alexandria (the former having been sent there, the latter originating there) also confirms an Egyptian, even Alexandrian, provenance for 3 Maccabees. The Books of 2 and 3 Maccabees exhibit a striking similarity of vocabulary not shared by, or rarely found in, other Septuagint texts, as well as similar stylistic tendencies, such as crasis of the definite article (when the Greek word for "the" is joined directly to the following word) (Emmet 1913: 156). In this regard, the similarity between 3 Maccabees and *Letter of Aristeas* is also striking, particularly with regard to resemblances in the official letters and decrees but also extending to shared vocabulary and phrases (Emmet 1913: 157). Moreover, as will be noted below, 3 Maccabees gives significant evidence of being patterned after the plot of 2 Maccabees. Both 2 Maccabees and *Letter of Aristeas* tend to be dated in the late second century B.C.E., and it would therefore seem proper to regard this as the earliest possibility for the composition of 3 Maccabees as well.

There are also notable similarities between 3 Maccabees and the Greek version of Esther, especially in the form, content, and flow of the royal decree (3 Macc. 3:12–30; Add. Esth. 13:1–7) (see Moore 1977: 195–99). These decrees contain the same kinds of charges against the Jews and propose the same solution for the preservation of the peace of the kingdom. Hadas (1953: 55) has noted the importance of feasts in both books as the setting where important decisions and reversals occur, as well as the similarities in the descriptions of how Jews receive the news of the king's damning decree (3 Macc. 4:2; Esth. 4:3). In both books, the king's change of mind is given in a second letter, which also blames bad counselors for the plan and praises the services of Jews. Both books begin with a conspiracy against the Gentile king being thwarted by a Jew's timely intervention and end with the institution of an annual festival commemorating the Jews' deliverance. Literary influence is therefore likely, but there is some difficulty in determining the direction of influence, all the more so given the fact that Esther existed first in a Hebrew, then in an expanded Greek, version. Third Maccabees may have been inspired by Hebrew Esther but then in turn influenced the composition of Additions to Esther A and B (Moore 1977: 198–99). The simpler solution, however, would be to posit that the author of 3 Maccabees drew on a variety of resources, such as 2 Maccabees and Greek Esther, in composing a similar saga for Egyptian Judaism.

Study of the Egyptian papyri has shown that the technical language used in the book is accurate and has been taken to favor dating the book to the Ptolemaic rather than the Roman period. Especially noteworthy in this regard is the use of the greeting that begins the official letters as well as the fluctuation between *outheis* and *oudeis* for "neither" or "not" (*oudeis* finally became standard in the first century B.C.E.). "Greetings and good health," the letter opening used at 3:12 and 7:1, appears to have been in vogue only from 160–60 B.C.E. (Emmet 1913: 157–58; Williams 1995: 20). Of course, the author may have adopted this older greeting in an attempt to make the "archival documents" in 3 Maccabees seem less "modern." The term *laographia*, which will figure prominently in arguments favoring a Roman-period date, has been shown also to have existed in the Ptolemaic period as a list of taxable people, most of whom would be native Egyptians rather than Greeks (Emmet 1913: 158, 165).

Scholars who favor a date in the Roman period (i.e., after Rome established its power in the East—one often thinks of 63 B.C.E., the year Pompey established Roman governance over Palestine, as a handy starting point) lean heavily on the importance of the use of the term *laographia* ("registration") and especially the connection of a census or poll tax with the threat of status reduction. This connection, they aver, most closely reflects the census taken by Augustus in 24/23 B.C.E. (Hadas 1953: 3–4; Collins 2000: 124–25). The Greek citizens were exempt from this tax, while the noncitizens were subjected to it; hence, the *laographia* would serve to clarify the legal status of Jews and that not to their advantage. Hadas (1953: 20–21) points to the absence of any receipts for a poll tax amidst the papyri, which do include receipts from many other forms of taxation. He uses this to suggest the lack of any firm evidence that such a poll tax (as would set noncitizens apart from citizens) was actually levied during the Ptolemaic era. Such a tax is, however, known to have been levied in 24/23 B.C.E., and this would have meant a social crisis for those Jews who had enjoyed the privileges of citizenship (such as education in the gymnasium and the like) and who were about to lose them (Parente 1988). This situation is, of course, highly embellished through conflation with memories of other episodes of anti-Jewish acts, such as Ptolemy VIII Physcon's plan to punish the Jews for supporting his sister in a civil war (see below, under "Historical Questions"), and so 3 Maccabees is not to be read as an allegory of Augustan-era Egypt.

Collins (2000: 126) rekindles the view that the crises facing the Jews under Caligula, a time in which the citizenship rights of Alexandrian Jews were notably also in the forefront of debate, "provided the stimulus for putting the story together." The linking of a crisis involving the Jerusalem temple with a crisis facing Alexandrian Jews is, for Collins, also telling on this point, since only during Caligula's reign was there such a confluence. Caligula had resolved to provide the Jews with a cultic image of their invisible God by installing a statue of himself in the Jerusalem temple, a desecration that was forestalled only by Caligula's timely assassination in 41 C.E. It was also under Caligula's reign that anti-Jewish riots broke out in Alexandria.[2] Additionally, Collins finds the portrayal of Ptolemy in his debauchery and fits of madness to be reflective of what is known of Caligula's character.

Objections have been raised to this proposed setting and date, however. Anderson (1985a: 512) finds surprising the lack of any mention of self-deification on the part of the king or the desecration of the temple not merely by entry but by erection of a statue of the monarch—things most notable about the crisis under Caligula. Anderson (1985a: 511) also points to the evidence of Egyptian papyri dating from the Ptolemaic period showing the use of the term *laographia* in the sense of a registry of taxable people, which also involved a class system in which certain elites would be exempted.

The foregoing survey indicates that one cannot be dogmatic about the date of the composition of this book. On the one hand, one need not suppose a crisis setting, such as occurs in Caligula's reign, simply because the book tells the story of a crisis. Its central themes—that loyalty to Torah is always advantageous in the end, that God is the protector of Israelites wherever they live, and that Gentile anti-Judaism is unfounded and reprehensible wherever it appears—would be a suitable message for Diaspora Jews in any decade. The linguistic data do tend to favor composition in the first century B.C.E., but the use of archaic expressions and forms may reflect the intelligence of the author in giving the tale an antique finish. The historical reminiscences, on the other hand, tend to favor a date in the Roman period, particularly in the first half of Augustus's reign. This author can be said to look back at a great series of events—Ptolemy IV's victory at Raphia, Heliodorus's attempted violation of the Jerusalem temple, the aborted act of vengeance perpetrated by Ptolemy VIII, Pompey's successful forced entry into the holy places, and the periodic threat

2. See Philo, *Against Flaccus*, and the analysis in Smallwood 1976.

posed to citizenship rights of Jews in Alexandria—and to weave them together kaleidoscopically into a saga for Egyptian Judaism.

Genre and Purpose

Third Maccabees well suits the genre of "historical romance" (Anderson 1985a: 510) or "Greek Romance" (Hadas 1953: 14). The author was seeking to write not history but an edifying tale loosely anchored in history. Works of this kind start by introducing known characters from history in order to give the story verisimilitude. The climax often happens in a very public place, such as a hippodrome or assembly, involving the protagonist, who is "brought to the very brink of destruction and then by a sudden reversal—through an agency which seems providential—is not only delivered but gains the upper hand" (Hadas 1953: 14–15). These narratives display an interest in religious cults and prayers, use fictive letters and documents, and employ extravagant rhetorical coloring, especially in the heightening of *pathos*. All of these features match 3 Maccabees, but the differences, one must admit, are pronounced. There is in 3 Maccabees no love interest and no central, personal protagonist whose exploits and sufferings provide the central thread of the plot. These differences, however, can be ascribed to the author's particular moral interests, speaking to the place of the people of Israel in God's providence and in Diaspora life. The similarities between 3 Maccabees and other, probably earlier, works of Jewish literature, such as Esther and 2 Maccabees, also point to the genre of romance rather than historiography; the author is weaving together a tale and using other literary models to do so, not reporting a history.

Why did the author write this story? It is widely recognized that 3 Maccabees accomplishes more than entertaining the hearers. One rather straightforward purpose may have been to explain an actual festival held by Egyptian Jews (Hadas 1953: 24; Anderson 1985a: 515), providing in writing a sort of *megillah* for the festival comparable to the books attached to other Jewish festivals (such as Esther to Purim or 2 Maccabees and Judith to Hanukkah). A variation on this theme is offered by Tromp (1995: 324–28), who avers not only that the author wanted to retell the legend but also to do so in such a way as would limit anti-Greek feelings and even actions that might arise from the celebration of this deliverance (a celebration that he rightly notes would have involved wine freely flowing, such as might set off short fuses). Tromp is thus able to account for the exculpation of the Greeks placed so prominently and awkwardly at 3:8–10 as well as the suppression of violent resistance and elevation of prayer and pacifism found at 1:22–24 (as well as in the presentation throughout of the Jews as loyal and orderly citizens).

A rather different purpose is suggested by David Williams (1995: 23–24; following Goldstein 1983: 137–51), who views 3 Maccabees as a defense of Diaspora Jews for a Palestinian Jewish readership. He suggests that this book responds to Palestinian Jewish criticism of Jews in Diaspora, who, according to their purist coreligionists, follow not Torah but an imperfect translation of it (cf. the prologue to Wisdom of Ben Sira), and whose very location in "exile" bears witness to God's lingering displeasure (cf. 2 Macc. 1:1–9). Williams reads the two letters that begin 2 Maccabees as a sign of some estrangement between Palestinian and Diaspora Jews, since the former must urge the latter to accept Hanukkah as a legitimate festival in a second letter after the first request had no effect. The later letter (which actually comes first in 2 Maccabees) also contains some possible criticism of Egyptian Jewry, implying perhaps that the readers need to have their hearts turned back to Torah and experience God's forgiveness.

As attractive as this hypothesis may be, it remains at most a good suggestion. The attempt by Williams (1995: 26–27) to show, for example, that God answers the Egyptian Jews' prayers faster than the Palestinian Jews' prayers is overdrawn. The Egyptian Jews may have experienced a few reprieves, but they were saved at the very last minute, just as their Palestinian counterparts had been in the first episode. Although Williams is correct to point out the presence of some possible tensions between Palestinian and Egyptian Jews in the literature, it is certainly far from clear that the internecine disagreements were hot enough to merit a "defense," especially given the paucity of evidence in so vast a body of literature (Where in Philo or Josephus, for example, do we see this tension?). He is certainly correct to point out the importance of Eleazar's affirmation of the reliability of Lev. 26:44, an assurance of God's presence with and protection of God's people in any land. But whether this is directed to Palestinian Jews as a defense rather than to Egyptian Jews as an encouragement is another matter, which remains tantalizing yet undemonstrated.

We can speak more certainly about the message that the story conveys to an Egyptian Jewish readership. Third Maccabees pointedly affirms (1) that the Diaspora Jews share intimately in the fortunes of the Jerusalem temple, and (2) that God hears the prayers of, and acts to deliver, Jews in the Diaspora just as God does in Israel. The latter is a sure sign of God's acceptance of their performance of Torah and fully restored favor.

The fact that 3 Maccabees is parallel at almost every point to 2 Macc. 3:1–10:9 suggests that the former was composed as a sort of parallel saga for Egyptian Judaism. The plot outlines of the two works are nearly identical: a Gentile leader threatens to violate the temple, resulting in Jewish frenzy (2 Macc. 3:1–21; 3 Macc. 1:1–29); a high priest offers an efficacious prayer (2 Macc. 3:31–34; 3 Macc. 2:1–20);[3] God chastens the insolent Gentile (2 Macc. 3:22–30;

---

3. There is an important difference in the content of the prayer here: in 2 Maccabees, Onias prays for Heliodorus to be spared death after God chastens him; in 3 Maccabees, Simon prays for punishment of Ptolemy before God chastens him.

3 Macc. 2:21–24); a Hellenization crisis follows, resulting in the apostasy of some Jews and danger for faithful Jews (2 Macc. 4:7–17; 6:1–11; 3 Macc. 2:25–33); the faithful Jews are persecuted (2 Macc. 6:12–7:42; 3 Macc. 3:1–5:51); God intervenes in response to the prayer of a steadfast Eleazar and other faithful Jews (2 Macc. 6:26–30; 7:37–38; 8:5; 3 Macc. 6:1–21);[4] God brings victory to God's people, complete with angelic interventions (2 Macc. 8:5–9:29 [angelic activity in 11:6–12; 15:22–24]; 3 Macc. 6:18–21); a festival celebrating deliverance is established to be perpetually observed (2 Macc. 10:1–8 [esp. 10:8]; 3 Macc. 6:30–40 [esp. 6:36]). These parallels suggest a conscious literary imitation of 2 Maccabees with the purpose of providing Egyptian Jews with a similar saga that affirmed their connection with the Holy Place and the fate of the homeland, as well as affirmed the fact that the same providence that protects and delivers Jews in Palestine works to preserve Jews "in the land of their enemies."[5] God's providential care for the Jews in Egypt is manifested in the triple thwarting of the execution attempt; what might seem like a tedious ebb and flow in the plot actually serves to underscore the main theological point of the story.[6]

Third Maccabees accomplishes another result: the reinforcing of boundaries between the Jewish population and their Gentile neighbors. The author speaks bluntly and at length about the prejudices, misunderstandings, and hatred that Gentiles harbor toward Jews and just as freely offers a low opinion of Gentiles, who are lawless, abominable, and alienated from the truth. Moreover, the book holds out the themes of divine election (especially in the prayers of Simon and Eleazar [3 Macc. 2:2–20; 6:2–15]), providence, the dangers of apostasy (3 Macc. 2:31–33; 7:10–16), and the futility of Gentile religion. These themes probably will serve to strengthen the hearers' commitment to their Jewish heritage and to underscore the significance of their ethnic identity—and preserving that identity—in the midst of a pluralistic culture. A special hostility is reserved for Jews who apostatize for the sake of temporal advantage. It is likely that the presentation of apostates in this romance, culminating in their execution at their coreligionists' hands, is meant to rouse feelings of indignation and hostility against the lapsed Jews in the audience's locale and to make this course of action less appealing.

4. The similarity in the descriptions of Eleazar as an aged, respected priest is also quite striking.

5. Tromp (1995: 318–19) documents the parallels between the Heliodorus episode in 2 Maccabees and Ptolemy's attempted violation of the temple. Tromp (1995: 321–22) also notes that the literary parallelism extends beyond this episode to include the ultimatum of assimilation and execution and an Eleazar appearing at a turning point, both of which appear to have been the author's innovations on an earlier legend.

6. While Hadas's proposal for the audience's situation may not be accepted by all scholars, his estimation of the book's purpose is strong: "to reassert the dignity of the Jewish people as the special object of Providence, to raise their self-esteem in the face of political degradation and their faith in ultimate justification, and perhaps also to impress upon Gentile readers that . . . it [is] unjust and possibly even dangerous to molest and injure them" (Hadas 1953: 23).

Historical Questions

One area that has especially occupied scholarly discussion of 3 Maccabees is the degree to which one can safely regard the book as a historical source. The story opens with a remarkable impression of historical accuracy. Ptolemy IV Philopator (222–204 B.C.E.) did, in fact, fight and defeat Antiochus III at the battle of Raphia (217 B.C.E.), after which he visited the coastal cities of Palestine to restore morale and visit local shrines.[7] We learn, from Polybius's *History* (5.40–46, 61–62), that "a certain Theodotus" did, in fact, desert Ptolemy in favor of Antiochus after Raphia (cited in Bissell 1899: 616); Polybius also documents Ptolemy's penchant for debauchery (Emmet 1913: 159), which accords with his portrayal in 3 Maccabees. The author may have used a lost historical source by Ptolemy of Megalopolis, who penned an even more negative account of Ptolemy IV than one finds in Polybius (Emmet 1913: 159). Moreover, Dositheus, son of Drimylus, has emerged from the nonliterary papyrus finds in Egypt as a historical person. As the book opens, then, the author gives every sign of trustworthy reporting.

This has led some to attempt to defend the essential historicity of the book (notwithstanding Hadas's observation that the "Greek Romance" is supposed to start off with a historically plausible scenario for its tale). Modrzejewski (1995: 147–52) reads 3 Maccabees as a true reflection of events under Ptolemy IV Philopator. He points to the accuracy of the presentation of Philopator's character, the existence of Dositheus, the evidence that Philopator did indeed visit local sacred shrines after Raphia, Philopator's devotion to Dionysus,[8] his possession and use of elephants, and the occurrence of censuses in his reign in connection with the levying of armies and financing of the wars against the Syrians. Modrzejewski (1995: 150) suggests the following scenario. Philopator takes a census, which disturbs the Jewish population on account of the dread and danger that has always surrounded the enumeration of the descendants of Abraham (see Exod. 30:12; 2 Samuel 24), who were supposed to be "numberless as the stars in heaven."[9] Philopator did not try to convert Jews forcibly to the Dionysus cult but rather probably regarded their religion as a kind of Dionysus cult, confusing the Lord Sabaoth with Sabazius, another name for Dionysus. His confusion was aided by the tendency of prominent Alexandrian Jews to point up the similarities between Orphic rites

7. This latter detail is corroborated by an inscription on a stela in Pithom (Modrzejewski 1995: 148).

8. Modrzejewski (1995: 149) cites a papyrus that contains a royal decree pertaining to this cult, although the purpose of the decree is much disputed and far from clear. Hadas (1953: 44–45) attests to the fact that several coins were minted in Ptolemy IV's reign showing the head of Dionysus crowned with ivy and that the ivy brand goes back to the Thracian origins of the Dionysus cult (the brand being used to mark initiates like Philopator himself, however, and not slaves).

9. The Jewish response to censuses is discussed more fully in Parente 1988: 176–77.

(Orpheus being closely connected with Dionysus) and Jewish religion. When Philopator attempted to regulate this cult, perhaps by having the Jews present their sacred books to be examined alongside other Dionysiac texts, they protested and took to the streets in a riot. Philopator let loose his elephants as a measure of crowd control (a highly dubious way to quell a riot in one's capital city) but realized his mistake in time to avert disaster.

The view of the majority of scholars, however, is that 3 Maccabees is largely a piece of historical fiction—well-informed historical fiction when it comes to the details that produce verisimilitude, to be sure, but, as concerns an enforced assimilation and persecution of the Jews under Ptolemy IV, not a reliable source. The reasons for this judgment are to be found in the book's being closely patterned after other literary sources (like 2 Maccabees and Esther), as well as in the fact that the elephant episode may have had a very different historical setting, which Josephus places in the reign of Ptolemy VIII Physcon (146/145–117/116 B.C.E.) (see Against Apion 2.50–55 for the full text). Ptolemy Physcon had the Jews who had supported his sister Cleopatra II in an inner-dynastic civil coup rounded up in the hippodrome to be trampled by drugged elephants. The elephants, however, turned on Physcon's soldiers, and Physcon himself was persuaded to make peace with the Jews by his concubine and by disturbing dreams. That Physcon is remembered as a protector of the Jews in the later years of his reign is no obstacle to believing Josephus with regard to hostility early in his reign and in the midst of internecine strife. It is noteworthy that Josephus mentions that the Egyptian Jews hold a festival to commemorate this deliverance (*Against Apion* 2.55), which was surely part of the report he had heard from his source.[10]

Other events may be reflected in 3 Maccabees. Hadas (1953: 37), for example, suggests that Pompey's actual desecration of the temple may be on the author's mind in writing about Ptolemy's attempt, if the book postdates the arrival of Roman power in the East. Similarly, the particular concerns surrounding the *laographia* probably reflect the conditions under Augustus in 24 B.C.E. The author of 3 Maccabees, then, can be said to have combined two events from two different Ptolemaic reigns (not that Ptolemy IV tried to enter the temple sanctuary, but his visit to Jerusalem to confirm the loyalty and morale of his subjects in the wake of the Syrian-Egyptian war is likely enough), as well as other events in the history of the temple and Egyptian Jews in order to achieve the book's purposes, one of which was to tell a story establishing the connection of Egyptian Jewry with the fortunes of the Jerusalem temple (showing that they were in this regard no different from their Palestinian sisters and brothers, particularly in the wake of the 167–164-B.C.E. crisis there). The shaping of this tale, moreover, has been deeply influenced by 2 Macca-

10. Torrey (1945: 81) considers this a literary fiction based on Esther and 2 Maccabees, both of which climax with the establishment of a festival of deliverance, but this judgment is too skeptical in light of Josephus's report, which clearly is independent of 3 Maccabees.

bees and other Jewish literature, such as Esther, to create a new saga for Egyptian Jewry.[11]

3 Maccabees as a Window into Jew–Gentile Tensions

Although 3 Maccabees appears to have had little or no influence on later Jewish or Christian authors, it is a valuable window into the world of Egyptian Judaism and its social tensions, providing essential information on the environment of early Christianity. At the outset, it must be said that not all Gentiles harbored anti-Jewish sentiments. Indeed, among the more philosophically minded Greeks one often finds a sincere admiration for the Jewish way of life, its austerity, and the virtues it produces.[12] It might be fairly said, however, that it was more typical for Gentiles to view Jews with suspicion and even contempt and dislike.[13]

The focus of anti-Jewish polemic was Jewish exclusiveness. Jewish commitment to the One God, and more especially their denial of the reality of any other god, was a unique offense to the sensibilities of their Gentile neighbors. Moreover, this God commanded God's people to "be separate" from the nations around them, and the pious doing of Torah tended to result in limited interaction with, and openness to, non-Jews. Anti-Jewish attitudes during the Greco-Roman period thus coalesce around two main charges: Gentiles perceive the Jewish way of life to enact atheism and misanthropy.[14]

Native Egyptian anti-Judaism was further fueled by the indigenous population's hostility toward Graeco-Macedonian rule.[15] Jews were particularly useful to the Ptolemies in terms of military loyalty and service and were prominent in local "peacekeeping" forces. This made Jews unpopular with the indigenous population (Hadas 1953: 51; Modrzejewski 1995: 136; Gabba 1989: 635–47). Greek anti-Judaism was spurred on by the anomaly of Jewish desire to enjoy the rights of being citizens of Greek cities such as Alexandria while not showing respect for the gods whose favor undergirded civic life (see

11. Tromp (1995: 315–24) speaks cogently and at length about the manner in which the legend of deliverance and 2 Maccabees are used as sources for the present text.

12. See the sources collected in Feldman and Reinhold 1996: 105–46.

13. Feldman and Reinhold (1996: 305–96) are able to collect more than twice as much material on anti-Jewish attitudes as on pro-Jewish attitudes.

14. Jewish apologetics of the period, such as 4 Maccabees and *Letter of Aristeas,* notably focus on demonstrating that the Jewish way of life enacts the purest piety toward the Divine and justice toward other human beings, regardless of their ethnicity. *Letter of Aristeas* 168, for example, presents Torah as a law that trains Jews to show justice and benevolence to all humankind.

15. Seen, for example, in the "Oracle of the Potter," an Egyptian apocalypse that looks forward to a return of Egypt's independence and greatness under a new pharaoh who would expel the foreigners.

Josephus, *Jewish Antiquities* 12.125–126) or solidarity with the non-Jewish citizenry in eating and religious festivals.

An early witness to anti-Jewish sentiments is Hecataeus of Abdera, who had censured Moses for introducing to the Jews "an unsocial and intolerant mode of life" (cited in Modrzejewski 1995: 140). Anti-Jewish prejudice is also reported by Posidonius, according to whom Antiochus Sidetes' courtiers advised him in 132 B.C.E. "to destroy the Jews, for they alone among all peoples refused all relations with other races, and saw everyone as their enemy." These counselors spoke of "the Jews' hatred of all mankind, sanctioned by their very laws, which forbade them to share their table with a Gentile or give any sign of benevolence" (Gabba 1989: 645). An Egyptian named Lysimachus also embodies both the "atheistic" and "misanthropic" sides of anti-Judaism. He plays with the etymology of "Jerusalem" (*Hierosolyma*) to suggest that the Jewish nation is founded on "sacrilege" (*hierosyla*) (see Josephus, *Against Apion* 1.304–311).

Another Gentile critic of Judaism, Apollonius Molon, is preserved for posterity by Josephus (*Against Apion* 2.148): "Apollonius, unlike Apion, has not grouped his accusations together, but scattered them here and there all over his work, reviling us in one place as atheists and misanthropes, in another reproaching us as cowards, whereas elsewhere, on the contrary, he accuses us of temerity and reckless madness." One could also turn to writers of the Roman period, such as Juvenal (*Satirae* 14.96–106), Tacitus (*Historiae* 5.5), and Diodorus of Sicily (*Historical Library* 34/35.1.1–4; 40.3.4) to find the same testimonies. Moses' law is denounced as "an unsocial and intolerant way of life" (Diodorus, *Historical Library* 40.3.4), a set of "outlandish laws" designed to keep Jews apart from other races (Diodorus, *Historical Library* 34/35.1.1). Jews are said to be "extremely loyal to one another, and always ready to show compassion, but toward every other people they feel only hate and enmity. They sit apart at meals, and they sleep apart, and . . . they abstain from intercourse with foreign women" (Tacitus, *Historiae* 5.5).[16]

Within this setting, one can turn to 3 Maccabees 3 with a fuller appreciation for the tensions therein described. The author provides a rather balanced view of the Gentile complaints against Jews (3:3–7). Because of their dietary regulations and exclusive worship of the One God, Jews tended to stand apart from the larger society, neither mingling in everyday intercourse nor appear-

16. An extreme rumor that circulated about Jews concerned charges of ritual murder in the form of the annual sacrifice and cannibalism of a Greek person carried out in the temple (see Josephus, *Against Apion* 2.91–96). This is deeply connected with Gentile perception of Jews as xenophobic, since the sacrifice was connected with an oath of enmity against the Greeks. According to Apion, Antiochus IV broke into the temple just in time to save this Greek citizen from ritual slaughter and on account of this barbaric practice desecrated the temple. Diodorus of Sicily and Tacitus also remember Antiochus IV as a would-be reformer of Jewish misanthropy and barbarism, and both lament his failure.

ing at public festivals (Tracy 1928: 245).[17] This "refusal to mix" (*amixia*) was interpreted as a rejection of the virtue of civic unity and even as a sign of potential seditiousness. The larger community felt that the Jews in their midst were neither fellow citizens concerned about the common good of the city nor reliable friends. Third Maccabees, like the Additions to Esther, adds a new element to the repertoire: the rumor that Jews are disloyal to the king and form a seditious element in the land (3:7; Greek Esther 3:8; 13:4–5)—a danger to the common peace and stability of the government. This development may reflect a new basis for Gentile slander, derived from the Jews' involvement with the losing side in the altercation between Ptolemy VIII and Cleopatra II and from Gentile views of the Maccabean Revolt (Gabba 1989: 641). The First and Second Jewish Revolts would greatly intensify this perception.

The author emphasizes, however, the baselessness of these feelings. In terms of actual practice, the Jews were beneficent, peace-loving, and loyal servants of Ptolemy. It was, according to him, the intolerance of the people of other races, who "gossiped" about the Jews' practices, that led to the ethnic tensions. The paradox in 3 Macc. 3:3–7, that the Jews were held in good repute by "all" while also being maligned on all sides on account of their peculiar customs—a paradox that is simply impossible for the author to resolve—reflects the cognitive dissonance of the Jewish author and, no doubt, his audience. The Jews' commitment to virtue and beneficence *ought* to have resulted in their way of life being accepted as an honorable one by their non-Jewish neighbors; nevertheless, the same way of life that purported to train the Jews in virtue also included elements that undeniably gave the impression of Jewish elitism, rejection of other people, and disrespect for the religious customs of non-Jews.

At another point 3 Maccabees reflects the prominent anti-Jewish tensions of the author's environment: the connection established by Ptolemy between citizenship rights and participation in Gentile cults. When Ptolemy makes the latter a prerequisite to the former in his decree (2:28–30), he reflects the widespread feeling on the part of Gentiles that Jews who wish to have equal part in the life of the city ought also to worship the gods of that city. The repeated refrain of squabbles over "equal citizenship" rights (*isopoliteia*) in Alexandria, Antioch, and the cities of Ionia is this: "If they are citizens, why do they not worship the same gods as us?" (Josephus, *Jewish Antiquities* 12.121–123, 125–126).

When Ptolemy gives his own perspective on Jewish reactions to his acts and decrees, the author of 3 Maccabees allows a Gentile to speak with astounding frankness and clarity about how Jewish responses can be (mis)understood (3:12–24). Ptolemy presents himself as a frustrated benefactor of the

---

17. *Letter of Aristeas* 128–166 and 4 Maccabees 1 and 5 seek, in the face of Gentile puzzlement and misunderstanding, to provide explanations of these dietary laws in terms that Gentiles would be able to appreciate.

Jewish nation. Ptolemy approached the temple as a beneficent patron, one who wished to grace the precincts with worthy gifts. The peculiar customs of the place baffle him, and the refusal of the Jews to allow him access to the Holy Place strikes him as a singular offense, an insult offered to a ruler and patron of the province. This incompatibility of norms and values appears also in the different perspectives on citizenship and the cost of acquiring citizenship (2:27–30; 3:23). Ptolemy regards himself as bestowing the benefaction of the "priceless citizenship," while the Jewish author regards him as "inflicting public disgrace" because his offer involves joining fully in the civic life of an idolatrous culture. He comes to regard the Jews as ungrateful (3:17–19), the worst vice in a society where patronage and benefaction stand at the foundation of the social order, as well as unjust (opposing one they should only obey). In showing contempt for what is good (by rejecting the benefits of full participation in Greek society), the Jews show themselves to be base-minded (3:15–24). These tensions within the narrative world reveal sources of mutual misunderstanding in the real world.

Third Maccabees also allows us to see the other side of anti-Judaism: anti-Gentilism. The presentation of non-Jews is frequently unsympathetic in 3 Maccabees and certainly not free from stereotype and gross generalization. The Gentiles are described, as a whole, as "arrogant" (5:13; cf. 6:4–5), "empty-headed" people worshiping their "empty things" (6:11); as a class, they are "abominable and lawless" (6:9). Ptolemy shows himself to be "alienated from the truth" concerning the One God and true religion (4:16) as he praises his idols, but it is clear that this charge could readily be extended to all Gentiles involved in idolatrous cult. The impression of "arrogance" on the part of the Gentiles, most visible in Ptolemy, is no doubt due to their refusal to honor the One God whom Jews acknowledge, to respect the laws promulgated by that God, and to recognize the special status of Israel.

Within the generally anti-Gentile framework of 3 Maccabees, one noticeable anomaly emerges: the desire to minimize enmity between the Jews and the "Greeks," who are said to console and aid the Jews in their distress (3:8–9) even while the "Gentiles" revel at the Jews' misfortunes, and to maximize the enmity between the native Egyptians and the Jews (4:1). The author wants to foster a sense that the Greek inhabitants of Alexandria are not really the Jews' enemy. Collins (2000: 126–28) points out the similar dynamic at work in Josephus, *Against Apion* 2.68–70, where Josephus claims that the pure-blooded Greeks and Macedonians never acted against the Jews but that when numbers of native Egyptians attained Greek (Alexandrian) citizenship, they used their newfound political clout to injure the Jews. Philo (*In Flaccum* 17; 29; 166–170), likewise, finds the roots of anti-Judaism in the debased "Egyptian" character rather than in the Greek mind. The result is a tension not only in 3 Maccabees but also more broadly in Jewish literature between the sympathy of some Gentiles and hatred of all Gentiles.

The response of 3 Maccabees toward the Gentiles and their anti-Jewish sentiments differs markedly from that found in *Letter of Aristeas*. Tracy has even suggested that *Letter of Aristeas* is a later response to 3 Maccabees or, if not directly in response to the text, at least in response to the inflammation of Jewish anti-Gentilism it promotes. Aristeas is "conciliatory on just those points dealt with unwisely in this earlier document" (Tracy 1928: 246). Aristeas counters the anti-Gentile and overly conservative tendencies of 3 Maccabees with a view of Judaism that can coexist peaceably and respectfully with the Gentile culture. Noteworthy in this regard is the way food is dealt with in *Letter of Aristeas:* the Jewish guests feast *with* Ptolemy, sharing a Gentile's table rather than shunning it. It presents a much more philosophical and gentle education of a Ptolemy in dealing justly with the Jewish people (through the questions and answers posed and given at another seven-day banquet).

One more social dynamic in 3 Maccabees merits closer attention—that is the situation of apostate Jews. Many Jews did in fact find the promises of assimilation more enticing than the rewards of remaining faithful to their ancestral tradition (at least according to a strict interpretation). Third Maccabees accurately reflects this situation when it describes those who preferred not to pay the cost of remaining a fully Torah-observant Jew (although the price was rarely slavery or death, to be sure). The apostate, however, appears to have endured the application of shaming techniques by faithful Jews: "They abhorred those who separated themselves from them, considering them to be enemies of the Jewish nation, and depriving them of companionship and mutual help" (2:33). In short, we see here a narrow window through which to catch a glimpse of pressures that could be applied to apostate Jews, in the first instance, no doubt, to bring them back to a Torah-observant way of life.[18] The interpretation given to these pressures by Ptolemy is illuminating as well: the Jews are so perverse, he reasons, that they even hate "those few among them who are sincerely disposed" toward people of other races (3:22–24). This internecine Jewish tension finally works itself out in the eradication of the lapsed Jews (7:10–16), and one cannot help but recall the similar acts of Judas Maccabeus and his brothers as they, in their first acts of aggression, killed their own who had compromised their loyalty to the Jewish way of life.

The hostility of faithful Jews toward apostate Jews in 3 Maccabees provides important background for the hostility of both Christian Jews and non-Christian Jews toward those perceived to have compromised their covenant loyalty. Prominent among such recipients of social pressure, censure, and even corporal persuasion was Paul, whose mission sought to eliminate centuries-

---

18. Shaming techniques are usually, in the first instance, an attempt to correct the deviant; in the face of a lack of timely repentance (i.e., through conformity), the group may opt for elimination of the deviant as a warning to others and as a cleansing of the group.

old boundaries and prejudices. Paul's relaxation of Torah observance for Jews within the church no doubt appeared as another Hellenizing movement, another threat to the integrity of the covenant people of God.

Theology

The author of 3 Maccabees tells a story that reveals something about God's character and commitments, both through the plot of the book and through the things said about God by the principal characters, such as Simon and Eleazar. The author refers to, or has the priests address, God using a variety of titles unique (or at least very rare) among Septuagint texts. God is thus the sole ruler, the founding ancestor of the Jewish race, the greatly powerful one, a hater of *hybris*, the honored one, the greatly glorified one, the holy one amidst the holy ones (or places), the manifest Lord, the wonder-worker, and the deliverer of Israel (collected in Emmet 1913: 162). God is independent of humanity; the author knows that worship, prayer, and sacrificial offerings do not happen because God experiences any lack that must be filled by God's creatures. God is also acknowledged to be infinite in space, unbounded to any particular locale such as the temple; rather, the idea that the temple is God's house is a sign of God's generous choice of Israel, the special assurance of God's nearness to God's people. This is a development of Solomon's prayer at the dedication of the temple (1 Kings 8:27–30) in directions that would be most congenial to Greek thinking about deity.

Though confessedly the Creator of all, God exhibits a special providential care for Jews, wherever they may be. Eleazar's prayer climaxes with a recitation of Lev. 26:44, which affirms God's care for Jews even "in the land of their enemies" (6:15). This care can be seen in the miraculous but also in what might appear to be merely coincidental or luck in the eyes of those lacking the perception of God's hand at work, such as the exhausting of the paper and ink supply in the registration, which allowed many Jews to escape unnoticed. The author affirms the Deuteronomistic theology of history seen also in 2 Maccabees: the conviction that Gentile oppression and reversals of Jewish fortune are due to sin. Sin is assumed as the prerequisite to adversity, and repentance is assumed as a necessary prerequisite to deliverance (2:13, 19–20).

The dark side of this special care for one people is that all others, as we have seen, tend to become spectators of God's care for the Jews rather than recipients of that care themselves. Thus, the Jews in the stadium pray to God to "show the might of his all-powerful hand to the arrogant Gentiles" (5:13); similarly, Eleazar prays, "Let it be shown to all the Gentiles that you are with *us*, O Lord" (6:15 [emphasis mine]). At the close of the tale, Ptolemy is brought to confess not God's paternal love for all people but rather that "the God of heaven surely defends the Jews, always taking their part as a father does for his children" (7:6; cf. 7:9). One leaves the reading of such passages with Paul's question ringing in the ears: "Is God the God of Jews only? Is he not the God of Gentiles also?" (Rom. 3:29).

Third Maccabees affords a window into Hellenistic Jewish prayer, particularly in the prayers of Simon the high priest (2:2–20) and the priestly Eleazar (6:2–15). Both prayers follow the pattern, common to the psalms, of embedding the story of God's past acts of deliverance as the basis for expecting God's deliverance in the present. These prayers give expression to the conviction that God's past acts express something about God's unchanging character, which provides the basis for understanding what God will do in the present situation. In Simon's prayer, the petition for help is based on the perception that God judges those who act insolently or arrogantly (2:3). This perception is then supported with reference to the punishment of the giants by the flood (2:4; see Gen. 6:1–4 and its developments), the destruction of Sodom (2:5; see Gen. 19:15–29), and the punishment of pharaoh (2:6–8; see Exodus 1–14). In this last example is embedded yet another rationale for God's judgment (and thus the hope of God's help now): it is by means of crushing the arrogant that God makes God's honor known and recognized in the world. The second main premise of this prayer is that God's election of Israel and God's choice of Jerusalem as that special place where God's ubiquitous presence could be accessed by mortals signifies God's protection of both the people and the place. God's character and God's covenant become the anchors for prayer and hope.

Eleazar's prayer follows a similar logic. In the midst of a situation in which Gentile oppressors are threatening the children of Israel, he invokes God's many interventions on behalf of God's special people. Once again, pharaoh appears prominently in the litany of deliverance (6:4), to whom is now added Sennacherib, who boasted that he would destroy God's temple (6:5; see 2 Kings 19) and was cut down for his arrogance. Eleazar then remembers more personal stories of deliverance: the Danielic traditions of the three young men in the furnace (6:6; see Daniel 3; Prayer of Azariah; Song of the Three Young Men) and Daniel in the lions' den (6:7; see Daniel 6), as well as Jonah's deliverance from the belly of the great fish (6:8; see Jonah 2–3). An interesting turn in Eleazar's prayer is when he asks that God, if indeed intent on destroying the Jews for their impieties, do so personally so as not to give the Gentiles occasion to ridicule God (6:10–11). This reveals another important premise behind Israelite prayer: God's own honor in the world is bound up inseparably with the fate of God's people, those few in the world who call upon the name of the One God (see Dan. 9:15–19 for another example of this argument emerging in a Jewish prayer). To Eleazar it is given to recite Lev. 26:44, the ancient authority that provides the moral for this tale: "Not even when they were in the land of their enemies did I neglect them" (6:15). Eleazar prays confidently that God would allow this to remain the testimony of

God's people, even as God promised it would. At this crucial juncture in the narrative, the recitation of Lev. 26:44 provides an important reminder to the audience about their identity even in the Diaspora. Even there they are closely, intimately connected with God and do not cease to be "Israel," the people of God's own choosing.

2 Esdras

"The Mighty One Has Not Forgotten"

The book we know as 2 Esdras is actually three texts in one. The earliest and main part of the book is 4 Ezra (= 2 Esdras 3–14), a Jewish apocalypse written several decades after the devastation of Jerusalem and destruction of the temple by the Roman armies in 70 C.E. Fourth Ezra represents one serious attempt to wrestle with the difficulties of making traditional Jewish convictions meaningful in the light of that devastation and, more especially, of Rome's continued prosperity. The close of the first century C.E. was an important time of reformulation of what it meant to be Jewish, to be faithful to the God of Israel, and to live out the covenant in a world with no temple. The agonized prayers and conversations of 4 Ezra bear witness to the challenge of that period as their author, in the words of John Milton (*Paradise Lost* 1.25–26), seeks to "assert Eternal Providence, and justify the ways of God to men" and women.

Fourth Ezra seeks first to overcome the threat of the collapse of the Jewish worldview under the weight of the conflict between Jewish experience and the basic tenets of Jewish belief. How can Israel's election make sense when Israel is trampled underfoot yet again by the Gentile nations? How can God's justice be affirmed when, having used a grossly sinful nation like Rome to punish Israel, the divinely chosen people who at least *tried* to honor God, God then does absolutely nothing to punish Rome for its greater sins? How can one even make sense of the principle of the covenant itself, when it is clear that Israel has never been able to keep it on account of the power of sin and the evil inclination in human nature? These are the big questions with which the author wrestles in moving from confusion and grief back to confidence in God and commitment to God's law.

The observable world does not provide any hints of a solution to these dilemmas, so the author reaches beyond the visible, the realm of ordinary human experience, in order to regain that "bigger picture" in light of which the present situation will be comprehensible. One of the primary vehicles of an apocalypse's persuasive power is its ability to set everyday realities within a broader context that provides an interpretative lens for those experiences. The disclosure of activity in other realms as well as the revelation of primordial and future history provide the context that lends meaning to present experience, making a threatened world-construct viable once more (see deSilva 1993).

The author's second concern is to reaffirm the observance of the Torah as the path to life and salvation, even in the wake of so many disasters. The author invites readers to gather themselves and their fellow Jews around diligent performance of Torah, to organize their whole lives around that key to salvation, and thus at last to respond wholeheartedly to Deuteronomy's invitation to "choose life" for themselves. Fourth Ezra resonates strongly with *2 Baruch*, another Jewish apocalypse from the end of the first century C.E. In both, providence is affirmed, and the readers or hearers are directed to attend to Torah with all their hearts, souls, bodies, and minds in order to arrive at the honor and favors that God has prepared for the faithful, both in this world and in the age to come. Since God still holds the reins of history and drives it on to its appointed and now revealed end, the conduct prescribed by God remains the honorable and advantageous way of life to preserve in the present.

The first two and last two chapters of 2 Esdras are Christian compositions that have been joined to the older Jewish apocalypse. Fifth Ezra (= 2 Esdras 1–2) affirms the church as the successor to a faithless and disobedient Israel in God's plan and probably was written to Jewish Christians in the wake of the Second Jewish Revolt (132–135 C.E.) and the persecution they endured at the hands of their fellow Jews during that period. Sixth Ezra (= 2 Esdras 15–16) dates from the late third century, exhorting Christians in the eastern Roman Empire to remain faithful to God despite the persecutions and pressures they have faced, and will continue to face, at the hands of Rome. In the discussion that follows, we occupy ourselves wholly with 4 Ezra and return to 5 and 6 Ezra only in the final section on "Influence."

Structure and Contents

Fourth Ezra is composed of seven clearly delimited episodes, each separated by some narration of the seer's ascetic preparation for the next supernatural conversation or visionary experience.

Episode I: 3:1–5:20
Episode II: 5:21–6:34
Episode III: 6:35–9:26
Episode IV: 9:27–10:59
Episode V: 11:1–12:51
Episode VI: 13:1–58
Episode VII: 14:1–48

The author has arranged these episodes in such a way that the reader can discern the growth or movement of Ezra, the explicated author, from doubt and despair to confidence in God and in the value of the law.

Fourth Ezra opens in Episode I with a complaint, "a challenge to God's justice" (Stone 1991: 350). This prayer (3:4–27) articulates the plight of the human being caught between God's commands and the "evil heart" or "evil inclination." Reciting the story of Adam's fall, the multiplication of sin resulting in the flood, and the election of Abraham and his posterity through Jacob, Ezra gives expression to the first vexing problem. While God gave the Torah to Israel, God did not take away the "evil heart" that had burdened Adam, causing him to be "overcome," and that likewise had overcome all of his descendants. Thus, it was impossible for the Torah to bear the fruit that God sought. Despite the raising up of David and the choice of Zion as God's own city, Israel still sinned and brought destruction upon itself. Ezra stops short of blaming God for Israel's failure but clearly regards Israel as trapped in an impossible situation. This is the problematic of human existence, and the angel will affirm the difficulty of the situation but will not allow Ezra to blame God and excuse humanity for transgression.

Ezra moves now to a more precise complaint (3:28–36). Why should Babylon, whose sins are far worse than Israel's and whose neglect of God and God's law far more egregious, prosper in wealth and seem to enjoy divine favor? Where is the justice in punishing Israel for its sins but leaving Babylon unscathed for worse sins? It seems to Ezra that Babylon is being rewarded by God for its sins, while all the labor that Israel had put into following God's law, however imperfectly, "has borne no fruit."

Uriel, Ezra's angelic dialogue partner, does not answer these questions immediately. Posing riddles reminiscent of God's answer to Job, Uriel focuses the conversation on the limits of human comprehension where God is concerned (4:1–25). Ezra laments that nonexistence would be better "than to suffer and not understand why" (4:12). Rejecting any claim to wishing to investigate the secrets of the heavenly world or the unseen places—strikingly, the typical content of apocalyptic literature—Ezra demands only to understand how God works in the observable world of history and everyday life (Stone 1991: 257).

Uriel responds now to Ezra's first complaint, the fact of the evil heart. Uriel points to the cause-and-effect relationship between the seed of sin once sown and the full harvest it must now be permitted to reach. This fact has contaminated the present age, making it impossible for God's promises to be manifested to the righteous within it (4:26–32). The time for the harvest is absolutely set, however. Nothing can hasten or delay it. The angel tells Ezra that he stands near the full measure of time, however, so that the end of wickedness and the reward of the righteous are not far off (4:33–52). Uriel concludes with a list of portents and signs that signal the end of the age and then instructs Ezra to fast and pray for seven days (5:1–20).

Episode II opens with Ezra lamenting the fact that God's chosen people and city have been handed over to the "many" that God did not set apart for God's Self (5:23–30). The complaint is positioned between the doctrine of election that lies at the heart of Jewish identity[1] and the experience of seeing God's chosen trampled by those upon whom God's favor does not rest in any special way. Uriel reproves Ezra for presuming to love Israel more than Israel's Maker does and proceeds again to remind him of the limitations of human understanding (5:31–40). Speaking for God, Uriel states that Ezra's mind is not up to the task of discovering "my judgment, or the goal of the love that I have promised to my people" (5:40). There are signs, however, that the present age is winding down to its close (5:50–55). Uriel announces that, just as creation came into being through God alone, so the end of the age will come through God "alone and not through another" (6:1–6). This claim stands in no small tension with traditions concerning Wisdom as God's partner and agent in creation, as well as with certain eschatological schemes that assign a critical role to the Messiah. While one could argue that the author may consciously be countering such streams of thought, it is more likely that the author merely wishes to stress in this way God's complete sovereignty over creation from beginning to ending.[2] The episode ends with God's own voice giving assurance that the days draw near in which God will exact punishment from those who have sinned against God, thus responding to Ezra's main complaint (the domination of Israel, God's chosen, by more sinful people whom God had not chosen). This will occur "when the humiliation of Zion is complete," which cleverly transforms the present problem (a humiliated Zion) into a sign that the resolution is near at hand (6:13–28).

After another seven days of fasting and grieving, Ezra opens Episode III with another prayer-complaint (6:38–59). A long and beautiful retelling of Genesis 1 ends in Ezra's charge that the purpose of God's creation has been thwarted, since Israel, for whom God created the world (6:55), does not benefit from creation but rather is dominated by the many. If God's word was so effective in creation (see 6:38, 43, 47–48), why has it not proven effective where election is concerned (6:55, 59)? Uriel answers again that this world stands under judgment on account of Adam's sin; the next world, however, holds the inheritance for the righteous, who pass through the difficulties of this world (7:1–16).

The punishment of the many is necessary for the maintaining of the honor of God and God's law, despised by these people (7:17–25; see also 7:60; 8:55–61; 9:9–12). A rather complete end-time agenda is laid out (including

1. See, for example, Lev. 11:44–45; 19:2; 20:24b–26, discussed in deSilva 2000b: ch. 7.
2. Stone (1990: 155) follows the Syriac in interpreting this passage as referring to the beginning and ending of God's visitation to punish the nations, the beginning of which happens by human hands but the end of which by God's hands. The Ethiopic assigns the beginning of judgment to the Messiah, the end to God, which solves the tension between this paragraph and other passages that assign an important role to the Messiah in initiating judgment.

an interim messianic kingdom of four hundred years, rather similar to the millennium in Revelation), culminating in the indictment of those who have denied and despised God (7:26–44). Nevertheless, the paucity of the saved should be of no concern to Ezra, since their number makes them all the more precious in God's sight, while the vast multitude of the damned only shows their inferior value, as gold is rarer than dirt (7:45–61).

Uriel reveals that, after death, the ungodly will immediately be subjected to torments for their failure to honor God and God's law, while the righteous will enjoy the rewards of their contest against the "evil heart," their loyalty, and their obedience for seven days before being gathered to their rest to await the resurrection (7:75–101). There will be no intercession for another person on the day of judgment, since that day is the decisive end of this age and beginning of the next (7:102–115). Ezra laments the condition of those who neglect obedience, and Uriel affirms the importance of taking Torah and the battle against sin seriously in this life, recontextualizing Moses' invitation to "choose life" and live (7:127–129; cf. Deut. 30:19).

Ezra finds the destruction of the many to be incongruous with what he knows from Scripture of God's merciful and gracious character (7:132–140). What, after all, is the purpose of God's gifts and nurture from birth to death if the person is to be lost in the end (8:4–19)? Ezra therefore begs God to look at the righteous, to take no notice of the sins of the sinner, and thus to show divine "righteousness and goodness" by being "merciful to those who have no store of good works" (8:20–36).[3] In response, Uriel merely reaffirms the facts of God's economy. Uriel adds, however, that Ezra cannot love humanity more than its Creator; it is not for lack of divine love that the many will be lost but because of their using God's gift of life wrongly, to dishonor God's name and despise the Giver (8:46–62; 9:9–12, 18–19). The main point of Episode III is the elevation of the need to keep the Torah. This, Uriel avers, is the way to experience God's promises, still securely reserved for the righteous in the age to come.

Episode IV is recognized by all commentators as pivotal in the development of the work and the transformation of Ezra. A change in scene (Ezra moves from his room to a field) and diet (from fasting to eating the plants of the field) marks this off as a new stage. Ezra begins, as before, with a prayer-monologue, but this time there is no complaint—just a lament at the paradox that, while the contents are usually spilt when a container is broken, the Torah abides despite the fact that Israel, its container, has been lost (9:26–37). At this point Ezra sees a woman grieving the loss of her only son, despairing and determined to die (9:38–10:4). Ezra reproaches the woman for considering her own private loss when "Zion, the mother of us all" lies devastated

---

3. This prayer is called the "Confession of Esdras" and appears in Latin prayer books. Apparently, it was used as a prayer for forgiveness, despite the fact that, in its original context, it comes far short of getting a positive response from God.

and when the vast majority of humanity is going to perish in the judgment. He tells her to put her grief in perspective by considering these greater causes for grief but also to trust God's justice so that she may receive a respite from her grief and even receive back her son in the age to come (10:5–24). Ezra now has his first visionary experience. The woman's appearance becomes radiant, and she is transformed into a huge and beautiful city (10:25–28).[4] The angel Uriel explains to Ezra that, because of Ezra's sincere grief over Jerusalem, God has permitted him to see the final state of Jerusalem, Zion as built and reserved by God for the age to come (10:29–59).

After a two-day interval, Ezra has a dream vision on the second night. The whole of this section, Episode V, is patterned very consciously (and even explicitly [see 12:11–12]) on Daniel 7. Ezra sees a three-headed, twelve-winged eagle exercising dominion over the whole earth (11:1–35), each of its body parts representing another in the succession of a kingdom's rulers. This eagle is confronted by a lion, which indicts the eagle for its oppression, deceit, violence, injustices, and persecution of the godly. God has taken notice, the end of the age has come, and the eagle is to be destroyed and the earth refreshed (11:36–46). The lion's indictment of the eagle answers at long last Ezra's first major complaint: the ongoing prosperity of Babylon and the destruction of Israel by its unclean hands, when its own sins were worse than those of Israel. Chapter 12 is largely taken up with the interpretation of the particulars of the vision, placing the real author and audience at the very close of the age, awaiting the coming of the Messiah to destroy the Roman Empire and usher in a new age (12:1–39). When Ezra is visited by the people, he at last is able to assure them, "The Mighty One has not forgotten you" (12:46).

Another seven days of solitude in the field precede Episode VI. Ezra sees a man coming from the sea, flying with the clouds and lighting on a mountain carved out for him. He destroys a multitude that has come to make war against him—which is interpreted as the Messiah's indictment and execution of the lawless (13:1–11, 25–38)—and gathers to himself a peaceful multitude, the Torah-observant from the Diaspora and from Palestine (13:12–13, 39–50). The close of this episode is truly remarkable, for Ezra, questioning

---

4. The woman is thus to be identified with Zion but not, strictly speaking, as heavenly Zion mourning over the destruction of earthly Zion (as in Breech 1973: 272; Longenecker 1995: 68). Rather, the angel's explanation of this figure suggests earthly Zion, since the city is said to have been without the temple for a time and then inhabited and invested with a temple cult in the Solomonic period. This is not heavenly Zion, to be sure, but earthly Zion, who mourns the loss of her temple and its cult, the child for which she had waited. The point of the transformation of the woman is to reveal to Ezra how Jerusalem, even though now mourning and childless, is not bereft of glory. God has prepared an eternal Zion, so that the earthly city, now broken and desolate, is seen by Ezra to have a glorious future (even though, it is true, this is not seen as a rebuilt earthly Zion but more along the lines of John's "new Jerusalem" [Rev. 21:2]). The woman being transformed forges thus a stronger link between earthly Zion and God's eternal Zion: the latter is the future and the restoration of the former, not just a weeping bystander without direct connections.

his convictions for the bulk of the book, is now able to give "praise to the Most High" for his governance of the times (13:57–58).

Finally, Episode VII places Ezra in the role of a new Moses, as God speaks to him from a bush (14:1–3) and uses him to give the Torah anew to the people over a forty-day period (14:23, 36, 42–44).[5] Told that he would soon be taken up to heaven, Ezra asks God to restore the Scriptures (lost in the process of exile) to the people as a guide in Ezra's absence (14:8–22). God consents. Ezra drinks a fiery, heavenly liquid, and for forty days he dictates the twenty-four books of the Jewish Scriptures and another seventy books as well. The former are for the whole people; the latter are to be hidden from the masses and studied only by "the wise" (14:44–47). The fact that both sets of texts are directly inspired by the heavenly source suggests a high view of the inspiration of both canonical and extracanonical works on the part of the author. Ezra's final speech shows his full restoration to faith (14:28–36): God's justice is indeed manifest in Israel's fortunes, and now is the time for Torah observance and disciplining the evil heart, so that one may attain life.

Textual Transmission

During the nineteenth century, scholars debated whether 4 Ezra (= 2 Esdras 3–14) was originally written in Greek or in a Semitic language. At the turn of the century, Julius Wellhausen demonstrated that it was composed originally in Hebrew, a position that generally has won the day.[6] Early on, the book was translated into Greek and from there translated into several other ancient languages by Christian circles. Neither the Hebrew original nor the Greek translation has survived. Fourth Ezra is available only through the secondary translations from the Greek into Latin, Syriac, Arabic, Ethiopic, Armenian, and fragments from Georgian and Coptic translations. The Latin and Syriac versions are universally regarded as the most important (see Coggins and Knibb 1979: 110); some scholars will give more or less weight to the other versions (see Stone 1990: 1–9). Fifth and 6 Ezra (= 2 Esdras 1–2 and 15–16) are to be found only in certain Latin manuscripts.

One important textual problem concerns the omission of 7:36–105 (as enumerated in NRSV and TEV) in the Vulgate manuscripts. It has been suggested that this omission may be due to the impression given in the last

---

5. Ezra had also spent forty days leading up to the opening of Episode VII. Second Esdras 6:35 mentions three weeks of fasting, even though the first week (presumably just before Episode I) is not narrated in chapter 3. Adding to this the seven days before Episodes IV and VI, the two days before Episode V, and the three days before Episode VII, we arrive at a total of forty. See Stone 1990: 35 n. 248.

6. See the discussion of Wellhausen's position in Myers 1974: 115–17, where the Hebraisms discerned behind the Latin translation are laid out at length.

of these verses that prayers on behalf of the dead are prohibited (see Longenecker 1995: 111). Indeed, the passage was used to oppose this practice in the early church, and one could readily see how it would have been advantageous to excise the passage.[7] Nevertheless, if doctrinal censorship did stand behind the omission, then it would have been necessary also to excise 7:106–15, which remains in the Vulgate. Moreover, the text itself speaks not of prayers on behalf of the dead but intercession on the day of judgment.

It is more likely that the omission was accidental. Johann Gildemeister found a ninth-century Vulgate codex with the stub of a page that had been torn out. The missing text corresponded exactly with 7:36–105. Gildemeister concluded that the other Latin manuscripts of 4 Ezra lacking this passage were dependent on this particular codex (Stone 1990: 3–4). The theory of accidental omission is further strengthened by the randomness of the boundaries of the omission, interrupting a perfectly unobjectionable paragraph at 7:35 and omitting only half of the potentially objectionable discussion of intercession on behalf of those facing the judgment. These verses were not available to the translators of the KJV, for example, but had been restored to the text of 2 Esdras in several German translations from the eighteenth century (Bensly 1895) and have appeared in English translations ever since.

The Author and His Setting

The text gives the appearance of having been written by Ezra, thirty years after the destruction of the temple in 587 B.C.E. and after the elites of Judah were taken off to Babylon. Ascribing authorship to Ezra in this instance, however, is a function of the genre of the book, since every Jewish apocalypse uses the technique of pseudonymity to link a recent "revelation" to the name of an ancient and therefore authoritative worthy. The actual author identifies with Ezra, likewise looking back upon Jerusalem's devastation, but in the cataclysm of 70 C.E., when the First Jewish Revolt against Rome was ended with the siege and destruction of Jerusalem by Titus, the Roman general and son of the emperor Vespasian. It is also clear that some time has passed since that event. The thirty years in 3:1 may be a rounded figure, but it is not far from the truth. The author is troubled by the destruction of Jerusalem, to be sure, but even more concerned about the ongoing prosperity of Rome (3:28–36). The author has

7. See Jerome, *Adversus Vigilantium* 6. Jerome's conversation partner brings out 4 Ezra in support of his position against prayers for the dead. Jerome holds such proof from "an apocryphal book" with slight regard, to say the least.

had the opportunity to watch for God's vengeance on Rome for a long while but has seen nothing for a generation.[8]

The eagle vision in Episode V corroborates a date thirty years after 70 C.E. The eagle was Rome's symbol for itself, and so the author's veil is quite thin here. The eagle's heads and wings represent its succession of rulers, with some overlap. The twelve great wings are the twelve emperors from Julius through Domitian (the second emperor, Augustus, did in fact reign twice as long as any of his successors) (11:16–17). The puny wings represent any number of pretenders and rival claimants to the throne, such as fill the pages of Tacitus's *Annals*. The three heads allow for a closer look at the reigns of the last three wings: in the cryptic details of 11:28–35 one sees the fortunes of the Flavian dynasty. The dynasty of Julius Caesar came to an end with Nero's suicide in 68 C.E. Vespasian gained power in 69 C.E. after a disastrous year of civil war between four rivals and their armies (see 12:17–18). He died, in fact, "in his bed" ten years later (12:26) and was succeeded by his elder son, Titus. After two years, Titus died from a fever, but rumor attributed his death to his brother and successor, Domitian, who reigned from 81–96 C.E. (12:22–28).[9]

The focus of the vision, particularly underscored by the Messiah's indictment of the eagle during the reign of the third head, has led most scholars to suggest that the book was written during the last years of Domitian's reign. It is not to be inferred from this, however, that the author expected the end to come during that reign (Longenecker 1995: 13), for the text allows two puny wings to rule the empire in succession after the third head disappears (12:1–3). In fact, Domitian was succeeded by Nerva, an old senator whose reign was "puny" (96–98 C.E.). Here the "prophecy" fails,[10] however, since the second puny wing, Trajan, turns out to be the most successful emperor since Augustus himself, reigning twenty years and expanding the empire's boundaries to their furthest reach. It is therefore quite possible that the author wrote during Nerva's reign or even at the beginning of Trajan's, which would bring us up to 100 C.E., the "thirtieth year" after Jerusalem's destruction (see 3:1). If this

8. A similar situation lies behind *Psalms of Solomon* 2 and 8, which speak of the desecration of the Holy Place by Pompey the Great's entrance therein in 63 B.C.E. and rejoice with relief when God's justice is finally manifested in 48 B.C.E. with Pompey's assassination. While the siege and desecration of Jerusalem in 63 B.C.E. might well have been merited on account of the sins of the Jewish leaders, the agent of God's punishment could not be allowed to escape his own guilt for encroaching upon the Holy Place. For fifteen years, the authors of these psalms watched and waited to see the justice of God work itself out.

9. Stone (1990: 368 n. 47) refers the reader to Dio Cassius, *Roman History* 66.26; Suetonius, *Domitianus* 2; *Sibylline Oracles* 12.120–123; Aurelius Victor, *De Caesaribus* 10, 11.

10. A common feature of apocalypses is the recitation of some portion of world history in the guise of predictive prophecy. From the point of view of a pseudonymous author such as "Ezra" or "Enoch," the events are still future and so can be cast as prophecy; from the point of view of the actual author, most of these events belong to the past, and so the form is called *vaticinium post eventum*, "prophecy after the event." The time of writing is usually the point at which the "prophecy" ceases to reflect the known facts of history.

is true, then it would be quite significant that the author presents the indictment of Rome by God's Messiah as an event already accomplished: the verdict had been rendered, and the sentence will soon be carried out.

"Ezra" writes from "Babylon," which has led some scholars to suggest
Rome (referred to as "Babylon" in Jewish and Christian texts of this period
because of its repetition of Babylon's sins and, particularly, its succession to
Babylon as a destroyer of the temple) as a place of composition. The fact that
the original language was probably Hebrew and the fact that the work stands
in especially close conversation with *2 Baruch* (a Palestinian Jewish apocalypse
from the same decade) suggest instead an origin in the land of Israel.

The author stands within the apocalyptic tradition, considering Daniel to
be a "brother" (12:11), which suggests the close affinity between this author's
work and Daniel. The author is concerned, however, to link the apocalyptic
tradition to the scriptural tradition, especially in Episode VII, where the culmination of "revealed" knowledge is the restored Hebrew text of the Jewish
Scriptures together with the larger collection of esoteric texts (quite possibly
including the apocalyptic works of early Judaism, such as 4 Ezra itself).

Genre and Purpose

Fourth Ezra falls squarely within the genre of apocalypse, a genre that has
received much helpful attention from scholars in the past three decades.[11]
Scholars noted the family resemblances among a wide array of (especially)
Jewish and Christian writings, including Daniel, *1 Enoch*, 4 Ezra, *2 Baruch*,
2 Enoch, *Apocalypse of Abraham*, *Testament of Levi* 2–5, *Jubilees*, Revelation,
and *Shepherd of Hermas*. Drawing up lists of the literary features of these and
similar works, a group of scholars produced the following overall definition
of the genre:

> "Apocalypse" is a genre of revelatory literature with a narrative framework, in
> which a revelation is mediated by an otherworldly being to a human recipient,
> disclosing a transcendent reality which is both temporal, insofar as it envisages
> eschatological salvation, and spatial, insofar as it envisages another, supernatu-
> ral world. (Collins 1986: 346)

The definition is intended at once to provide some limits on what should be
considered an apocalypse as well as to highlight central features (and therefore
audience expectations) of the genre. Fourth Ezra exhibits the mediation of
revelation through an otherworldly being by means of the dialogue form between Ezra and Uriel, as well as through Uriel's interpretations of the vision-

---

11. See the introductions to the modern study of apocalypses in Stone, ed., 1984; Collins
1986; 1987.

ary experiences of the later episodes. The concern with eschatological deliverance dominates 4 Ezra, but interest in the supernatural world is not entirely absent. Both the vision of the Zion that God builds and the appearance of transcendent beings interacting with Ezra (the angel and God) open up the reader in the here and now to otherworldly realities. Fourth Ezra also expresses, along with other apocalypses, the conviction that God is in complete control over history, by emphasizing that the order and succession of kingdoms, their allotted times, and the time of the end have all been decreed by God in advance. Thus, one seed from the Israelite wisdom tradition that was held to be formative for apocalypticism has taken deep root in 4 Ezra in particular (von Rad 1972: 263–86).

The genre itself opens up important avenues to achieving particular purposes. The direct revelation of otherworldly and future realities, allowing the audience to "see" what they had been taught to believe, powerfully reaffirms the worldview of that audience. If Ezra (and the audience) begins the book with the Jewish worldview crumbling around him as present experiences belie what he had held to be true, he nevertheless ends the book completely reassured of that worldview (even if aspects of it have been reshaped in the process). An apocalypse opens up the heavens and allows the audience a glimpse of the "really real," presenting itself as nothing less than a grand intrusion of angels and of God into the mundane world. This goes far toward establishing an impression of factuality for the worldview therein revealed. As a result, the attitudes and behaviors fostered by and promoted within 4 Ezra stand a good chance of being adopted by the audience as an appropriate response to life in the world, given "the way it is."[12] That response, for the author of 4 Ezra, is complete dedication to obey the Torah in gratitude and loyalty to the God who has given the gift of life, who labors alongside the righteous to perfect their way, and who has prepared a glorious reward for those who live now so as to honor God. This is especially highlighted in Episode III, where the consequences of keeping Torah and of despising God through disregarding God's law are laid out at length (Mueller 1982: 262).

The public/private distinction made in 12:37–38 and 14:26, 45–46 also has bearing on determining the purpose of 4 Ezra. The author may have addressed the work to learned circles, given the rich intertexture and allusive nature of the book, the raising of serious questions of theodicy, and the like (Knibb 1982: 72–73). The learned are the audience for the whole book and for other such esoteric books, and they are charged with teaching the public

---

12. The very helpful definition by Longenecker (1995: 17) brings together the formal features while also capturing succinctly the purpose of apocalypses: "An apocalypse is a narrative in which revelation is given to a human being by a divine being in order that earthly circumstances might be interpreted in the light of transcendent, other-worldly and/or eschatological realities, thereby motivating its recipients to adopt certain beliefs and patterns of behavior that are authorised by God."

about the "path" (thus carrying on the work of the learned Ezra).[13] This view has much to commend itself, since the author would have good reason to desire to restrict eschatological speculation to those who could handle it appropriately and not use it to foment revolt. Indeed, apocalyptic eschatology, with its expectation of a violent overthrow of the Gentile overlords at the hands of the righteous, had proved disastrous in the First Jewish Revolt and would again in the Bar Kokhba Revolt of 132–135 C.E. In this way, eschatological knowledge encourages and empowers the leaders of the community, who then can call the community to gather around observance of Torah with complete conviction that this is the path to life and a blessed future.

Formative Influences

For 4 Ezra, as with most apocalypses, the Jewish Scriptures are deeply formative for the new "revelation" of God's acts in history on behalf of God's faithful ones. Principal sources of reflection include Genesis, Job, and Daniel. Ezra's first and third complaint-prayers refer in a concentrated way to the creation and fall stories in Genesis 1–3 and in broader strokes to Genesis 1–11 and 15–17. Fourth Ezra resonates with Job insofar as both works are concerned with questions surrounding God's justice, both proceed in dialogue form (although 4 Ezra is more of a real conversation than Job), are inconclusive at the level of argument, emphasize strongly the limits of human comprehension, and involve divine revelation as the ultimate answer (see Knibb 1982: 70–71). Daniel is explicitly named as a resource in 4 Ezra 12:11–12. The eagle vision is presented by the author as a reconfiguration of Daniel's vision of the fourth kingdom. The author wants the new, eagle vision to be set in the context of Daniel 7, such that the older text lends weight and interpretative force to the newer one. The form of 4 Ezra 11–13 very much resembles the form of Daniel 7–12: the seer is fasting or alone or sleeping and enters into visions; the seer calls upon God to interpret the visions; an angel appears to do just that, also responding to specific questions put forward by the seer. Fourth Ezra 13 draws heavily on the Danielic presentation of the "Son of Man" in Daniel 7 and the "stone . . . cut out not by human hands" in Dan. 2:34–35.

It would be impossible to display here all the ways in which the Jewish Scriptures shaped 4 Ezra, for the very language of almost every verse shows

---

13. Fourth Ezra appears, however, not to have been written within a self-consciously sectarian group that had closed itself off from the majority of Israel, since its author appears to be in conversation with *2 Baruch, Apocalypse of Abraham,* and Pseudo-Philo's *Biblical Antiquities,* all of which are quite mainstream (Longenecker 1995: 101). Moreover, the concern throughout with teaching the people, rather than closing oneself off from the people, also suggests a social setting of vital interaction with the larger population.

some level of intertexture with the sacred writings of Judaism. For but one example of this rich tapestry of influences, we may consider 13:3–11.[14] The repetition of the phrase "and I looked, and behold" (see RSV) in 13:3, 5, 6, 8 is patterned after the same in Dan. 7:2, 6, 7, 13. It is a brief formula that continues to impress upon the hearers' minds the "reality" of the visionary experience, making it more authentic to them as well. That the "man from the sea" rides upon the "clouds of heaven" (13:3) recontextualizes the same from Dan. 7:13. His gaze makes the earth tremble (13:3), as does the gaze of God in Ps. 104:32; those who hear his voice "melt like wax" (13:4), as do the mountains before the approach of God (Ps. 97:5; Mic. 1:3–4). The mountain carved from a mysterious origin (13:6–7) recalls the stone of Dan. 2:34–35, 44–45, which grew into a mountain, and the destruction of the ungodly by the fire of the man's mouth (13:10–11) derives from the attribution of the same to God (Ps. 18:8; 97:3; Isa. 11:4; 66:15–16). Through such thick resonances with the Scriptures, 4 Ezra imbues itself with the authority of the sacred tradition even as it reshapes and renews that tradition to meet the challenges of a new situation.

In addition to Scripture, the author appears to have used oral or written apocalyptic traditions in composing this work. Much of nineteenth- and early-twentieth-century scholarship on this book focused on discerning the sources that went into 4 Ezra, with the result that the whole was dissolved into its constituent parts with very little attention being given to the meaning of the whole formed from the parts. The most ornate source theory was set forward by Richard Kabisch (1889), popularized in English by G. H. Box (1913). The author identifies himself in 3:1 as Salathiel (the Greek form of Shealtiel), which is then awkwardly identified with Ezra (even though Shealtiel elsewhere is the father of Zerubbabel [e.g., Ezra 3:2; Neh. 12:1; Hag. 1:1; 1 Esd. 5:5]). This suggested that the author had actually composed the work by incorporating an earlier "Apocalypse of Salathiel" (Box 1913: 549).

Having discovered one source, Kabisch and Box were emboldened to re-create all the sources that went into this book. The criteria for dissection included literary indications ("I, Salathiel" is the most prominent of these), the alleged incompatibility of various eschatological schemes and concepts, and the identification of traditional forms,[15] resulting in the following:

Salathiel Apocalypse: 3:1–31; 4:1–51; 5:13b–6:10; 6:30–7:25; 7:45–8:62; 9:15–10:57; 12:40–48; 14:28–35
Ezra Apocalypse: 4:52–5:13a; 6:13–29; 7:26–44; 8:63–9:12
Eagle Vision: 11:1–12:51
Son of Man Vision: 13:1–58
Traditional story about Ezra's restoration of Scripture: 14:1–48

14. The references here are drawn from Knibb 1982: 71 and Longenecker 1995: 79.
15. See the review of this endeavor in Stone 1990: 11–12.

An editor was alleged to have put these sources together and to have composed several bridge passages.

Scholars have come to recognize, however, that such an approach does not help us understand the form of the text as we have it, nor to appreciate the movement from beginning to ending created by the person who gave 4 Ezra its final form. The development, growth, and transformation of Ezra (and with him, the readers) is at the heart of this book's achievement, but all this is lost on, and even obscured by, the source critics. The endeavor also proceeds from false assumptions about apocalypses, such as absolute consistency in eschatological predictions and concepts (Stone 1983).

The author probably does use some material from other sources, such as the Son of Man vision (although reinterpreting it), the tale of the mourning woman in 9:43–10:4, and other similar brief paragraphs or blocks of material, but weaves them fully into the new work and puts them to use for new purposes (Stone 1990: 22). It is also difficult to use merely formal grounds when trying to determine whether a passage represents preexisting material or the author's fresh composition, since an author might quite consciously compose material in self-contained blocks with clear openings and closings. Fourth Ezra 7:78–99 is an excellent example. It is set off as a complete unit by its introduction, "Now concerning death, the teaching is" (7:78), and by its conclusion, "This is the order of the souls of the righteous" (7:99), and contains a well-structured and perfectly balanced content. These could be taken to indicate the author's use of a previously independent work, but such a conclusion is far from necessary, let alone probable. Scholars are often too quick to jump to such conclusions when it comes to discerning source material.

Finally, we must give some weight to the possibility that the author draws on personal religious experience as well (so Stone 1990: 33). The fact that the language used to give expression to such experiences is overflowing with allusions to the Jewish Scriptures and other apocalyptic writings does not mean that apocalypticism is a purely literary phenomenon. It merely attests to the depth to which the Scriptures guided and gave content to the visionary's experiences in altered states of consciousness, as well as provided him or her with a language by which to articulate that which stands beyond the realm of everyday experience.

The Persuasive Strategy of 4 Ezra

We noted above that a major purpose of 4 Ezra is the reinforcement of Torah observance as a positive and necessary value among Jews at the close of the first century. This apocalypse was composed to communicate to others the considerations that allowed its author to affirm God's providence and the continuing value of remaining committed to the Jewish way of life. How does the author accomplish this goal?[16]

The first ingredient in persuasion in the Greco-Roman world was establishing the *ethos* of the speaker or author: the audience had to be persuaded first of all that the voice they were hearing was trustworthy, well disposed toward them, and expert in the matter being discussed.[17] Fourth Ezra achieves this by submerging the author's own voice beneath that of otherworldly beings such as God and the angel Uriel and the voice of Ezra. The former are beyond reproach, and the more realistic the account of the author's encounters with otherworldly beings, the more the credibility of their voices enhances the composition. The latter, Ezra, is also presented as a virtuous character (he is repeatedly attested to be righteous by the angel and God: 6:32–33; 7:76–77; 8:48–49; 10:38–39) who bears nothing but good will toward his people (the audience), conveyed by his sympathetic laments for their plight and intercessions on their behalf.[18] As the audience identifies with Ezra, who voices their questions and doubts, they may also participate in his movement from distress to consolation. He articulates the community's own experience of cognitive dissonance and, in his own journey, maps out a pathway for the audience to follow.

Since Ezra's own journey represents the road back to the assurance that the audience also must traverse, the way that Ezra moves from doubt about God's justice (3:28–36) to praising God's governance of the world (13:57–58) merits closer examination. At a very basic level, "the probing questions of Ezra have a cathartic effect. They bring to expression the fears and frustrations of a sensitive and perceptive Jew in the wake of the catastrophe of 70 C.E." (Collins 1987: 168). The articulation of the problem is itself a step toward recovery. But how fully are these questions answered? Scholars frequently critique the angel's speeches for sidestepping the issues, pronouncing platitudes rather than dealing squarely with Ezra's concerns. This approach fails to appreciate, however, the ways in which the author repositions the audience's own focus on issues by means of Uriel's answers. There is a measure of repetition in the angel's discourse: even if the questions change, Uriel may still give the answer he wants Ezra to hear and internalize. The repetition itself has the potential for "calming fear and building trust," eroding doubt "through multiple reassurances" (Collins 1987: 162). Uriel's freedom in his responses, however, in-

---

16. For a more detailed analysis, see deSilva 1999.

17. See, for example, Aristotle's discussion of *ethos* in *Rhetorica* 1.2.4; 2.1.3–5.

18. It is highly unlikely that Ezra represents the author's opponents' position, since the hearers are led to identify and sympathize with Ezra quite deeply. It would seem more prudent to regard Ezra and the angel as two faces of the same authorial persona: the one who knows the correct answers yet struggles with fitting those answers to his everyday experiences and his recollection of the traumatic events of his earlier life (the destruction of Jerusalem thirty years prior to writing). The two come together at last in Episode IV as the mourner becomes the consoler, as personal venting and inquiry give way to pastoral responsibilities.

dicates something of the dynamic of the conversation. The two are not equal conversation partners. Ezra argues from a position of limited knowledge, the limitations themselves being the source of all his complaints and indictments. The angel argues from an intimate knowledge of "the way it is." Thus, it is Uriel who has the authority to guide the conversation and determine its course, and for this reason he does not answer all of Ezra's questions as they arise.

However much Ezra thinks that God should have mercy on the transgressors, especially within Israel, Uriel knows that God will not. However much Ezra thinks that God is at fault for not simply removing the evil inclination so that Torah can be observed easily and readily, Uriel knows that God is not at fault, that human beings are responsible either to fight the good fight or to allow sin to defeat them, and that God labors alongside the righteous to perfect them. Only when Ezra acquiesces to "the way it is" can he hope to find consolation and be empowered to encourage and direct his people along the path. Ezra does make progress in accepting some of the angel's points: the existence of the two ages and the location of rewards and punishments in the second age (even though this prompts new questions or problems, such as the loss of the majority of God's human creatures); the fact that the times and the eschatological events are all predetermined by God, to be neither delayed nor rushed. By the opening of the Episode IV, Ezra has progressed from doubt about God's justice to "bewilderment at divine actions" (Stone 1990: 27), which nonetheless is a considerable step toward resolution.

The full journey cannot be achieved on the basis of rational inquiry alone; it also requires God's revelation, particularly in the form of visionary experiences that allow "Ezra" to "see" beyond the disconfirming realities of the present, visible world to the faith-affirming realities of the unseen future. The vision of the mourning woman's transformation into an awe-inspiring city is widely regarded as the critical step in this pilgrimage (see Longenecker 1995: ch. 5; Stone 1990: 24–33). When Ezra speaks to the mourning woman in the role of adviser or consoler (in a "tough love" sort of way), he shows first that he has accepted much of what Uriel revealed to him (see 10:10, 16), and it is possible that the pastoral necessity of the moment moved him to identify more fully with Uriel's positions.[19] The vision of the city is the first vision of hope that responds to Ezra's initial complaint about the ascendancy of Rome

19. Stone (1990: 32–33) offers a very plausible analysis of the transformation, even if the ancient author would not have understood the psychological nature of the analysis: "The weeping woman whom he sees in the fourth vision is also an aspect of his own experience—she is his pain and distress over Zion. In comforting her, the seer undergoes a dramatic change, a shift, a conversion. That which had been outside him, as 'God' or 'the angel', suddenly became dominant; instead he sees his pain and distress as externalized. . . . The significance of that sudden shift can be appreciated only when it is perceived not as the result of deliberate 'authorial' policy, designed to advance certain views to the disadvantage of others, but as the result of profound religious experience."

and the devastation of Zion. The latter still has a glorious future in God's plan, and Ezra's vision of that future eliminates in a stroke all his doubts about God's faithfulness to God's people and to the city of God's name. The dream visions, especially the eagle and the lion, will continue to answer the problem of Jews under Roman rule: God has determined when and how to hold Rome accountable for its sins, just as God had done with Jerusalem. Part of the problem in assessing the angel's answers to Ezra has been the tendency to limit one's discussion to the dialogues. In an apocalypse, however, the visions are the more persuasive answers to those questions.

The apocalyptic genre opens up other persuasive strategies as well. First, the convention of pseudonymity allows the author to set the realities of 90–100 C.E. in the interpretative context of past history—specifically, the aftermath of the first destruction of Jerusalem and its temple in 587 B.C.E. The Jewish people had faced this kind of crisis before and had discovered the resources to persevere in their commitment to God and God's law. Moreover, the Jewish people had survived through seven centuries since 587 B.C.E., but Babylon, their destroyer, did not. Casting one eye to Ezra and the exilic and postexilic experiences of the Jews, therefore, already begins to introduce hope into the post–70 C.E. situation. God is still able to preserve the Jewish people and bring down their destroyer.

Second, apocalypse allows the author to place current circumstances in the interpretative context of Scripture, Daniel in particular (explicitly named as a resource for the interpretation of the eagle vision [12:11–12]). Setting the present in light of Daniel 7 makes a claim about the position of Rome vis-à-vis God's "end of the times," creating the expectation that Rome would be replaced by the messianic kingdom rather than yet another Gentile empire. An especially important feature of Daniel is the emphasis on God's sovereignty over the Gentile kingdoms, allotting to each its turn and time to rule (see, e.g., Dan. 4:17, 32; 5:18–28). This aspect of Daniel is specifically recalled in 4 Ezra 11:39, affirming that Rome's ascendancy over Israel is part of God's design for bringing about the "end of the times" that God had appointed long ago.

Third, the genre permits the author to interpret the present moment in the context of God's forthcoming interventions in history. The revelations of God's coming judgment, the destruction of the wicked, and the reward of the righteous continue to provide a meaningful frame of reference for the author's experience. In this regard, apocalypses provide exactly what standard rhetorical forms (like sermons and letters) cannot. Aristotle writes, "In deliberative oratory narrative is very rare, because no one can narrate things to come" (*Rhetorica* 3.6.11), but things to come are precisely what an apocalypse is able to narrate. Looking to the future, the author enables the audience to see vividly the resolution of the dissonance between their worldview and their experiences.

It is also by narrating the future, and by introducing authoritative figures such as the angel Uriel, or other supernatural channels of knowledge such as dream visions, that the author is able to promote continued, even redoubled, observance of Torah as the advantageous, honorable course of action. The chief question that Ezra poses at the outset of this work is, in effect, whether Torah observance (or failure to observe Torah) is really determinative for the enjoyment of reward or suffering of punishment. If Torah is the absolute norm laid out by God, then why should those who give absolutely no thought to God's law (i.e., the Gentiles, especially Rome) fare well while those who at least tried to keep the commandments (the Jewish people), however fallibly, are cast down? Uriel is able to describe authoritatively and graphically exactly what consequences will follow honoring or despising God's law (see, e.g., 7:31–44, 70–73, 78–99), thus reaffirming the advantage of the former course of action. Although Ezra cannot see these consequences in his circumstances, if one grasps the larger picture of the two ages that God has prepared, and if one could see beyond the veil of death (and Uriel allows Ezra and the audience briefly to see), then the answer to Ezra's question becomes clear.

Beyond the presentation of the consequences and the use of the topic of advantage, the author employs (through Uriel) the topics of justice and honor to promote Torah observance as the core value for the audience. It was universally regarded as a just, and therefore virtuous and good, action to repay one's benefactors with gratitude.[20] As giver of all life and creator of all things, God merits gratitude from those whom God has benefited. Such a gift engenders complete obligation on the part of the recipients to do all within their power to show their thanks by honoring and offering themselves in service to God. Those who neglect God's law dishonor and insult the very one whom they should honor and serve (see 7:21–24; 8:60–61). Those who obey God's law, on the other hand, act justly and virtuously, returning to their Patron what is due. By means of Torah observance, "they have made my glory to prevail now, and through them my name has now been honored" (7:60), with the result that the faithful bring God joy and continue to experience God's favor.

Moreover, Torah observance is the one quality that ultimately gives a person value or worth (as in Sir. 10:19–24). Those who are unmindful of the commandments are compared to lead and clay, while the godly are like precious stones; it is precisely the scarcity of the latter that makes them more valuable (hence, possessing more honor in God's sight) than the mass of evil-doers (7:52–58; 8:1–3). From the perspective of their visible circumstances, then, the Jewish audience might be viewed as the least valuable of nations or

20. See Anaximenes of Lampsacus, *Rhetorica ad Alexandrum (Ars rhetorica)* 1421.b37–1422.a2; Pseudo-Cicero, *Rhetorica ad Herennium* 3.3.4; Seneca, *De beneficiis* 1.3.2–3; 1.4.4; 2.25.3; 3.1.1; 3.17.1–2; Dio Chrysostom, *Rhodiaca (Oration 31)* 31.7, 37–38, 65. For more detailed discussion, see deSilva 2000b: chs. 3–4.

people. In actuality, however, God regards them as treasure in the midst of dirt and sand. The nobility of those who observe Torah in God's estimation is reinforced by the praiseworthy example of the Jews who, in response to exile, keep themselves apart from the Gentile nations so as to observe "their statutes [Torah] that they had not observed in their own land" (13:39–42). It is these who enjoy God's approval and experience God's deliverance and restoration in the end times. These considerations will help the audience to identify themselves as Torah-observant people and to connect their diligent obedience to the commandments with the reaffirmation of their own worth.

In Episode VII, the Jewish Scriptures are placed center stage as the locus of divine revelation and guidance (along with supporting, esoteric books like 4 Ezra), and Torah is commended by God's own voice as the "path" to "live in the last days" (14:22). Thus, Torah is commended as the way to survive the dangers of this age and enter upon the rewards of the age to come (or the rewards of the messianic kingdom that closes this age and refreshes God's people until the judgment [12:34]). Ezra's final speech to the people (and thus the audience) reinforces an earlier position articulated by Uriel. Ezra teaches, "If you, then, will rule over your minds and discipline your hearts, you shall be kept alive, and after death you shall obtain mercy" (14:34). With these words, Ezra shows his acceptance of Uriel's succinct statement of the "meaning of life" in 7:127–29. This life is a contest in which the human being wins by submitting to God's law or loses by submitting to the evil inclination. Uriel's quotation of Deut. 30:19, "Choose life for yourself, so that you may live" (7:129), affirms that the worldview of Deuteronomy remains true in the midst of the hearers' present circumstances. Significantly, this quotation comes from the concluding speech of Moses that also affirms the possibility of doing Torah (Deut. 30:11, 14), of which context the audience would also be aware. Uriel will not concede that the evil inclination necessitates defeat in the contest, as Ezra lamented. Instead, he overturns that position by affirming the possibility, indeed the necessity, of dedicating oneself to doing Torah with the rigor of an athletic contestant.

Neusner (1984: 93) is correct to contrast 4 Ezra's accomplishment for a postdestruction Judaism with that of a Yohanan ben Zakkai insofar as the latter sought to provide very practical guidance "for the repair of the Jewish soul and reconstruction of the social and political life of the Land of Israel," while clearly the former did not offer the kind of detail that would be helpful for day-to-day living. Nevertheless, Neusner (1984: 90) draws too sharp a dichotomy between apocalypticism and early rabbinic Judaism: "Out of preoccupation with the sufferings of the past came neurotic obsession with the secret of future redemption. From stubborn consideration of present and immediate difficulties came a healthy, practical plan by which Israel might in truth hold on to what could be saved from the disaster." Fourth Ezra does not fit so simply into the first of these categories, for the author seeks "the secret of future redemption" or, better, the mystery of God's faithfulness, in order to make a practical plan for survival possible in the first place. For the author of 4 Ezra, like Yohanan ben Zakkai and the author of *2 Baruch* (notably, another apocalypse), continuing to do Torah is the practical plan for the preservation of the covenant and the hope of redemption. It is thus not the case that one must choose between "eschatological vision" and "concrete actions in the workaday world" in order to transcend the problems of the historical moment (Neusner 1984: 94); the former can also serve as the sacred canopy under which the latter can be performed with confident assurance.

Theological Importance

Fourth Ezra engages in a redefinition of the covenant theology inherited from the Old Testament. The doctrine of God's election of Israel retains its meaningfulness, but Israel now includes not all ethnic Jews but "those who stored up treasures of faith" (6:5) with God by faithful performance of the Torah (Longenecker 1991: 150). The redefinition of Israel during the second half of the first century was also a deep concern in the early church. Paul also had moved in the direction of affirming that "not all Israelites truly belong to Israel" (Rom. 9:6), looking to the Jewish Christians as the remnant of Israel (Rom. 11:1–6). For Paul and the author of 4 Ezra, redefining the boundaries of Israel became the means by which to understand how God remained faithful to God's covenant people.[21]

Even though 4 Ezra emphasizes the keeping of Torah as the determinative factor for salvation or damnation, it would be a mistake to conclude that 4 Ezra exhibits the degeneration of a covenant religion into a legalistic religion (Longenecker 1991: 153 n. 1). Longenecker (1991: 152) writes, "Divine grace is, for all purposes, absent in his scheme, except as an eschatological reflex to those who have saved themselves anyway by their works." This position is overdrawn. Here, grace is being defined as the divine pardon for sins, divine mercy at judgment; the meaning of grace is being unduly limited to the divine "cover up" or "looking the other way" when it comes time to judge or exact punishment.

Rather than letting Protestant notions of grace determine whether or not grace is present in 4 Ezra, one should start by observing how God's generosity and assistance are present and how people are called to respond to God on the basis of God's gifts. God's favor is operative in the gift of life and the sustenance of the human person (8:4–14, 60). Throughout one's lifetime one receives God's benefits (9:10), and the responsibility now falls to the recipients

---

21. Longenecker (1995: 31) captures 4 Ezra's negation of ethnic privilege well: "4 Ezra redefines traditional covenantalism, narrowing the scope of divine grace and thereby limiting covenant membership to include only a remnant, a much smaller group than the whole of Israel."

of these gifts to respond nobly and gratefully. People who respond by honoring God's name and law will enjoy God's future favors as well—life in the age to come (7:60). Those who deny their Divine Benefactor, despise his law, and dishonor his name (7:22–24; 8:55–61; 9:10–12) respond ignobly and can only expect punishment at the hands of the slighted Patron.

Grace is alive and well in 4 Ezra, though the author may place more emphasis on human responses to God and responsibility before God than some, perhaps, find comfortable. The law itself is a gift (3:19), outlining the proper response to divine benefits (graces) already received and promising to cultivate "fruit" in those who heed it (3:20), fruit that will ripen unto eternal life. Finally, one must also hear the words of the angel in 9:21–22 (which is really the speech of God, since properly the "I" does not represent the angel's actions but God's) as an inbreaking of God's favor. The human being is not asked to achieve perfect Torah observance on his or her own but learns that it is God who has "perfected" those who are saved. This is a sign of the mercy and help for which Ezra calls—not the complete removal of the evil inclination but the knowledge that God is working alongside the human being to defeat it, as the human being's partner in the "contest that all who are born on earth shall wage" (7:127).[22] Uriel does not negate covenantal theology or the place of grace in God's economy; rather, the angel negates any position that would regard ethnicity without Torah observance as a claim on God's beneficence. Fourth Ezra can assist readers of the New Testament to ponder whether or not the early Christian leaders also called the recipients of God's favor in Christ to take their obligation to respond in kind with equal seriousness.

The first three episodes express the age-old dilemma about the God of the Scriptures: the God of mercy and the God of justice. Ezra begins by screaming for the God of justice, who will trounce Babylon because it is a worse sinner than its victim, Israel. When he begins to discover exactly how just God is, he screams for the God of mercy, who will overlook transgressions and give deliverance to the sinner along with the righteous. In the midst of this dilemma, lest the reader sympathize too much with Ezra in his grief over Israel and over humanity, Uriel twice reminds Ezra that no human can love God's creation more than God does (5:33; 8:47). Within God's own being stands the unresolvable tension between love and justice, between compassion and righteousness. God cannot choose between justice and mercy, as Ezra would have God do (8:26–36); instead, Ezra must learn that it is in the nature of God that God's love cannot express itself unjustly.

The text also speaks to the mystery of evil in a world ruled by a loving and good God. The position of this text is that evil has to play itself out. The sin once sown in the present age must produce its full harvest. God is not responsible for sin or its consequences; these were sown by humankind in their de-

---

22. This is very similar to what one finds at Qumran. Compare 1QH 7.29–32.

cisions to transgress the commandment, beginning with Adam. God appears as a parent who chooses not to shield children from the consequences of their choices but rather to allow them to experience the full impact of those choices, to allow the consequences to take their course. In the midst of all that, however, God, like a good parent, still provides clear direction (in the Torah) in the midst of those untoward consequences and even works together with those children to help them pursue that path and persevere in their contest. God is still generous, however, insofar as God has prepared not one age but two. Precisely because the good things that God wanted the righteous to enjoy cannot be enjoyed in this age, God prepared another age in which the righteous will receive those good things.

Of course, we may still wish, along with Ezra, that God would act differently, that God would simply remove from us the negative consequences of the actions of our whole race and "make everything all right." The author calls us, even as he calls himself, to submit our limited wisdom to the unlimited wisdom of God. While this may be unappealing, especially to the Western mind, it is finally the only path to consolation and empowerment that the author has discovered.

Fourth Ezra has perhaps its greatest appeal in the way it connects grief with the theological enterprise. Ezra provides a model for how one might move through various stages of grief, particularly with regard to wrestling with God. Ezra begins by blaming God and questioning God's justice, given his experiences in the "real" world. He moves through this period of questioning to a point where the distance between his experiences and the answers he knows to be true begins to close, such that he can still grieve but in the context of trusting God's justice and God's provision for a better future for the faithful. This is especially evident in his consolation to the mourning woman. As he continues avidly to seek to ascertain greater knowledge of God's ways—Ezra's intentionality in this regard cannot be missed, since he devotes forty days to fasting and prayer or to seeking God in places of solitude—he eventually arrives at a point where he can again wholly affirm God's justice in governing the world (13:57–58). This is a model of hope for those who wrestle with grief like Ezra's, whether over national or personal misfortune.

Taken as such, 4 Ezra offers these counsels: not every question can be answered, but receiving assurance of God's goodness and justice does not depend on getting all the answers; one cannot expect to make it through the difficult time of questioning and grieving if one is not committed to seeking God in serious, intentional ways; it is important to give expression in prayer to what is truly on one's heart and mind, especially in those challenging situations of grief and despair; it is equally important not to leave the place of prayer without listening for the voice of the divine conversation partner. Even if the answers merely reaffirm what we already know about God and appear to sidestep the questions we may raise in grief and anger, they are still answers that point us to recovery, as they did for Ezra.

This text offers several considerations of interest to the study of the theologies of early Judaism. It has, for a start, a well-developed concept of the Messiah (even if there are some inconsistencies between Episode III and the later visions). In 7:28–29 we find the expectations of a temporary messianic kingdom, said to last four hundred years and to conclude with the Messiah's death and the reversion of the cosmos to primeval silence before the new creation seven days later. This resonates with several other Jewish texts, including the Jewish-Christian apocalypse Revelation, that seek to make a place for a messianic kingdom of limited duration before the inception of the eternal kingdom of God (see Bailey 1934).

The activity of the Messiah receives more attention in Episodes V and VI (see 11:37–12:1; 12:31–34; 13:3–13, 25–52). Since one of the main concerns of the book is the justice of God where history is concerned, specifically the apparent injustice of allowing Rome to continue to prosper despite its sins against God and humankind, it is not surprising that the author presents the Messiah as a legal figure who indicts Rome for its injustice, pronounces sentence, and then executes that sentence.[23] More commonly, messianic expectations centered on the restoration of the Davidic monarchy, or at least of Israel's political hegemony among, and even over, the Gentile nations. Fourth Ezra shows how messianic hopes were shaped by the specific concerns and problems for which eschatology provided a solution.[24] The Messiah is the agent by whom the concerns of Ezra voiced in chapter 3 are worked out on the stage of history prior to the final resolution, the last judgment, which is God's purview alone, indicting and sentencing wicked Babylon and restoring the righteous remnant of Israel.

The work of the Messiah opens up another important feature of this apocalypse, one shared by the Revelation to John. An apocalypse, as a claim to present "the way things really are" from a perspective beyond and more reliable than the limited perspective of the visible world, is a powerful vehicle for expressing an ideology and also for opposing other available ideologies. In 4 Ezra 11:36–46, the author directly counters Roman imperial ideology not in the voice of a powerless protester in a province but in the voice of God's end-time agent of justice. The public ideology of Rome's significance is encapsulated in Plutarch's essay "On the Fortune of Rome": "With God's help, Time founded her, using the special powers both of Fortune and Virtue to make for all humankind a holy and prosperous home, a reliable mooring rope, a secure foundation, an anchor in the ebbs and flows of this changing

23. Stone (1987: 213–14) proposes that the vision in Episode VI probably comes from an older source taken up by the author and given a new interpretation, moving the focus away from political rule and the Messiah as "Divine Warrior" toward the legal/judicial role of the Messiah; see especially 13:37–38.

24. A similar situation appertains at Qumran, where the dual messiahs of Israel and Aaron, a king and a high priest, reveal the centrality of the restoration of a pure temple cult to that community.

world" (*Moralia* 317A). All the essential elements of the ideology are here: Rome's founding by the will of God (or Jupiter),[25] Rome's function as the vehicle for stability, rule of law, and peace,[26] and the fruits of divine favor manifested in temporal prosperity. Fourth Ezra refuses to whitewash Rome's methods in order to sanctify the prosperity it has achieved: the violence, the suppression of those who "speak the truth" where this counters the dominant ideology, and the burden of Rome's oppression will be neither forgotten nor swept to the side. Rather, it will all be remembered by God and, thanks to the author, by the readers. The author does not allow Rome to represent itself as a benign goddess who has ushered in the golden age but rather uses the resources of Daniel 7 (as do its contemporaries *2 Baruch* 39–40, Revelation 13, and Josephus, *Jewish Antiquities* 10.276) to present Rome as the last obstacle to the golden age. Apocalypticism is no opiate for the author but a powerful vehicle of political critique.

Fourth Ezra is also of interest as a witness to several other theological developments in the late Second Temple period, such as the depiction of Abraham and Moses as visionaries to whom the secrets of the end of the times were revealed (3:14; 14:5), which is shared with other Jewish texts such as *Jubilees* and *Apocalypse of Abraham;* the belief that Eden and the things pertaining to the last judgment were made before the world was created;[27] and, of course, the reflection on the relationship between Adam's sin and the evil heart that is replicated in every human being (e.g., 3:7, 20–22, 26).

Influence

Fourth Ezra was kept alive not in Jewish circles but in Christian ones. It was read and quoted by Clement of Alexandria, Cyprian, Tertullian, the *Apostolic Constitutions,* Commodianus, and most extensively by Ambrose. The translation of the book into many languages by Christians for the use of Christians and the preservation of the work in several different streams of Christianity also attest to its estimation in the eyes of the early church.[28]

The situation with 4 Ezra is not so different from that of other Jewish apocalypses, such as *1 Enoch* or *Apocalypse of Abraham,* that fell into disuse among Jews while being taken up and read by Christians. In its reformulation, early

25. Cf. Virgil, *Aeneid* 1.234–237, where Venus says to Jupiter of the survivors of Troy, "Surely from these the Romans are to come . . . to rule the sea and all the lands about it, according to your promise."

26. Cf. Virgil, *Aeneid* 4.231–232, where Jupiter summarizes Aeneas's mission as to "bring the whole world under law's dominion."

27. See Stone 1990: 68 n. 46 for a list of Targumim and rabbinic texts developing this notion.

28. For details on quotations and echoes in writings of the early church fathers, see Myers 1974: 131–34.

Judaism became less and less a religion with interests in the end times. Indeed, such speculations were associated with the First and Second Jewish Revolts and their disastrous consequences. Fourth Ezra itself gives evidence of this association when it seeks to channel the eschatological, esoteric mysteries to the learned and keep such mysteries from the populace, who might misuse it. Christianity, on the other hand, had a deep apocalyptic imprint from the beginning and continued to produce and read apocalypses throughout the first centuries of its development (and, indeed, on to the present).

There is a clear affinity between 4 Ezra and New Testament eschatology more broadly (such as the expectation of a heavenly city and rest in Hebrews) that would have made 4 Ezra agreeable to the early church. Christians also would have appreciated its redefinition of who constitutes Israel. Fourth Ezra's rejection of ethnicity as the assurance of inclusion is in keeping with New Testament emphases on the same point. The actual position of the author, that only those who do Torah faithfully belong, could easily be overlooked and the relevant passages understood through a Pauline lens that would regard Christians as those who fulfill the Torah by following Jesus and his teachings (see Rom. 8:2–4). Finally, 4 Ezra's emphasis on the "evil heart" that spread from Adam to the rest of the race like a "disease" would have been viewed as consonant with Paul's teaching on the corporate nature of Adam's fall (see Rom. 5:12–21). Despite its popularity, 4 Ezra achieved canonical status only in the Slavonic churches. It was also included as an appendix in manuscripts of the Latin Vulgate but only to ensure its preservation, not to suggest its canonical authority.

The influence of 4 Ezra on the early church can also be seen from the existence of the texts now called 5 and 6 Ezra. The author of 5 Ezra, although perhaps intending this work to circulate independently of 4 Ezra, nevertheless took from 4 Ezra the choice of pseudonym for the visionary persona of the book. Fifth Ezra survives only in Latin. Since it is hard to reconstruct a critical text, it is also difficult to be dogmatic about scriptural allusions and quotations (Stanton 1997: 69). The book presents a Jewish-Christian response to the destruction of Jerusalem at the close of the Second Jewish Revolt (also called the Bar Kochba Revolt) in 135 C.E. and appears especially to remember the persecutions against Jewish Christians in Judea during that period (Stanton 1997: 70, 72).[29] Stanton (1997: 70–71) argues that a mid-second-century date is likely given the lack of evidence of an acquaintance with a broader sampling of New Testament texts, the emphasis on the church's replacement of Israel rather than stress on the difference between the two (the former being more typical of early Christian apologetics), the expectation that Christian prophets will be active (these become rather rare after the second century), and the emphasis on eschatology and an imminent end rather than speculation on the antichrist and heaven and hell (the latter being more common in

---

29. See Justin Martyr, *Apologiai* 31.6.

later Christian apocalypses). Moreover, the depiction of the ravaging of Mother Jerusalem seems to be so vivid and harsh as to suggest proximity to the events of 135 C.E. Fifth Ezra provides, then, a Christian interpretation of the final destruction of Jerusalem.

The main theme of 5 Ezra is the final rejection of Israel by God and the transfer of God's promises and Israel's privileges to "other nations" upon whom God will set God's name and who will keep God's statutes (1:24). The work shows early Christian use and development of Matthew's Gospel, especially Matthew 21 and 23, where the same theme is articulated (see Stanton 1997: passim). It is particularly instructive to compare Matthew's parable of the wicked tenants (Matt. 21:33–43, esp. 21:40, 43) with the declaration of transfer in 5 Ezra 1:24; the lament of Jesus over Jerusalem in Matt. 23:37–38 with God's lament over Israel in 5 Ezra 1:30, 33; and Jesus' prediction of the Jewish leaders' rejection and murder of his prophets in Matt. 23:34–35 with God's indictment of Israel for the same in 5 Ezra 1:32.[30]

The basis for God's charge against Israel is ingratitude, which includes disobedience. In 5 Ezra 1:4–32, the author calls to mind God's generous provision and care for Israel manifested in the exodus, wilderness, and conquest traditions, culminating in the sending of prophets to warn Israel and call them back into a right response to God.[31] In the context of this narration of God's "great benefits" (1:9), God holds up the incongruity of Israel's disobedience to God's law (1:8–9) and Israel's forgetting God (1:14) when the enjoyment of God's gifts should have kept them mindful of their Divine Benefactor. When God asks, "Where are the benefits that I bestowed on you?" (1:17), it is a reproach to them for not living in a manner consonant with having received those benefits, a manner that honors God's name and displays trust in God (1:15–16), among other things. Furthermore, it is the Christian community's gratitude that will stand as a witness against the first people of God (1:37),[32] justifying God's reproach and rejection of Israel and transfer of God's beneficence to "other nations" (1:24).

Stanton (1997: 76) appears to suggest that these Jewish Christians were concerned to keep the whole of Torah, given such descriptions of the saved as those who "have fulfilled the law of the Lord" (2:40); however, Paul also uses phrases such as "so that the just requirements of the law might be fulfilled in us" (Rom. 8:4), where clearly he does not include large blocks of Mosaic leg-

---

30. Other Matthean echoes can be heard in 5 Ezra 2:13, which recalls the command to "keep watching" in Matt. 24:42 and 25:13, and in the title "little ones" (NRSV, "children"; Latin, *parvuli*) in 5 Ezra 1:37, which recalls the Matthean designation for the members of the kingdom at 18:6, 10 (for the latter, see Stanton 1997: 82).

31. The first section of 5 Ezra uses the form of the *rib*, or "lawsuit," learned from the preexilic prophets. In this form, God brings a formal indictment against God's people for their failure to live out their covenant obligations.

32. There is an obvious hortatory purpose in this statement, calling the hearers to manifest gratitude properly, learning from Israel's story.

islation (particularly the purity and dietary laws). Stanton is correct, however, to see 5 Ezra as standing "at the opposite end of the theological spectrum from Marcion," who would have been its contemporary, in its emphasis on the complete continuity between the Old Testament people of God and the Christian community (as well as between the Old Testament revelation and that of the New Testament).

The theme of the transfer from Israel to the church is underscored by the use of the figure of the mother, perhaps to be seen as Jerusalem. In 2:1–7, the mother bears witness to the sin of Israel and laments that she must now be bereaved of them as they are scattered and "their names . . . blotted out from the earth"; in 2:15–24, however, the mother is enjoined to embrace and rejoice together with her children, the "others" who have entered into God's favor and promises (2:10–14). Within this story of transfer is set a brief summary of covenant requirements (2:20–24), reminiscent of the social principles of Deuteronomy and the preexilic prophets. These are representative of the aspects of Torah that figure prominently in Jesus' teachings and were taken up as binding in the church as well.

Fifth Ezra concludes with Ezra's summons to the nations to look for their shepherd and the arrival of the kingdom (2:33–48). They are called to "see" a final vision with Ezra: the company of "those who have been sealed at the feast of the Lord" (2:38). Zion receives again its full number in the church, particularly in the triumphant confessors and witnesses of God, who "stood valiantly for the name of the Lord" (2:47). The author has in mind particularly those who have been persecuted for their faith, a growing concern in the second-century church.

This vision clearly shows the imprint of Rev. 7:4–17. The invitation to "see the number of those who have been sealed" (2:38) recalls Rev. 7:4, "And I heard the number of those who were sealed." "I . . . saw on Mount Zion a great multitude that I could not number" (2:42) recontextualizes Rev. 7:9, "I looked, and there was a great multitude that no one could count." In both texts, this multitude is characterized by singing songs of praise to the Lord. Fifth Ezra 2:39–40 speaks of "glorious garments" and "people who are clothed in white," which recalls the important motif of white clothing in Rev. 3:4–5; 7:9. Palm branches in 2:45 recall the same detail in Rev. 7:9. Finally, the form of 2:44–45 is reminiscent of Rev. 7:13–17. In both, the question "Who are these?" (5 Ezra 2:44; Rev. 7:13) is followed by the angel's answer, which concerns both the triumph of these souls over persecution and their reward (5 Ezra 2:45, 47b; Rev. 7:14–17).[33] Fifth Ezra thus becomes a valuable witness to the use of Matthew and Revelation in the second century.

Sixth Ezra is an even later Christian addition. The transition from the end of 4 Ezra to the beginning of 6 Ezra is rather smooth: no new characters

---

33. Additionally, 5 Ezra 2:14 ("I am the Living One") recontextualizes Jesus' self-designation in Rev. 1:18.

are introduced, and one gets a sense of continuity in the fact that God is still commissioning Ezra to speak and to write down the words that God is delivering. This suggests that the author of 6 Ezra had 4 Ezra in hand and wrote these chapters consciously as an appendix to 4 Ezra. The author did not, however, continue in the genre of apocalypse but rather in the form of the prophetic oracles of the Old Testament. This addition was probably made in the late third century C.E. in the eastern regions of the Roman Empire. Scholars have seen in the allusions to famine and plagues recently visited upon Egypt (15:10–11) a reflection of the famine during the reign of Gallienus (260–268 C.E.). Similarly, 15:28–33 is taken to refer to the Parthian invasion of Syria under King Shapur I (240–273 C.E.) (Metzger and Murphy, eds., 1991: 336–37).

The book is a series of oracles spelling doom for the unbelieving nations of the Mediterranean, starting with Egypt (15:11–13), the empire in general (15:14–28), the eastern provinces, Asia in particular (15:28–63), and then the whole empire again (16:1–34). The appendix concludes with an exhortation to God's people, the church, to understand the nature of the times in which they live, to conduct themselves as strangers on the earth, and to be ready to endure many forms of repression and persecution for the sake of loyalty to God (16:35–78). Like 5 Ezra, 6 Ezra exhibits a clear awareness of both the Old and New Testament writings.[34]

Persecution of the church is a matter of record (15:22, 52–53) as well as a present and forthcoming reality (15:3, 10; 16:68–75), which is also very much in keeping with a post-Decian setting. Sixth Ezra speaks of plots laid out against the Christians (15:3) by an angry society, plots that do not stop short of massacre (15:10). The author speaks of their neighbors attempting to force conformity with the dominant culture through eating "what was sacrificed to idols" (16:68). The author anticipates riots and pogroms against the Christians, the plundering and destruction of their property, the complete dispossession of believers at the hands of unbelievers. The purpose of the addition is, of course, to encourage the Christians to persevere in their loyalty to God, all the more so as it is specifically this loyalty that has brought them into conflict with their neighbors. Renunciation of God and the Messiah could lead to relief in this life; the author must make that course of action as unappealing as possible. The whole is, in a way, a narrative amplification of

34. Compare 6 Ezra 15:15 ("nation shall rise up to fight against nation") with Matt. 24:7; 6 Ezra 15:35 ("there shall be blood from the sword as high as a horse's belly") with Rev. 14:20; 6 Ezra 16:18 ("the beginning of sorrows") with Matt. 24:8; 6 Ezra 15:10 ("see, my people are being led like a flock to the slaughter") with Ps. 44:22. In addition, 6 Ezra 15:11 refers to the plagues visited upon Egypt during the exodus; 6 Ezra 16:40–42 is modeled after 1 Cor. 7:29–31, even down to the eschatological context of the "as if not" lifestyle; 6 Ezra 16:73 interprets trials as the process by which the quality of the elect, like pure gold, is made known, as in 1 Pet. 1:6–7; 6 Ezra 15:46–48 presents Babylon as a whore (and thus those who imitate her as prostitutes), revealing an acquaintance with Revelation 17–18.

this saying of Jesus: "Do not fear those who kill the body but cannot kill the soul; rather fear him who can destroy both soul and body in hell" (Matt. 10:28). Thus, the climax of 6 Ezra is "God is the judge; fear him! Cease from your sins, and forget your iniquities" (16:67).

Speaking in the voice of God, therefore, the author summons Christians to remain separate from, and uncontaminated by, the works of the society around them (16:50–52). They are called to live "like strangers on the earth," unattached to the everyday affairs of this world, the fortunes of which might turn at any moment (16:40–48). They must remain thus at a distance from all those things that might become incentives to apostatize—free, in effect, to let go of whatever the society would take from them in its attempt to "rehabilitate" them. The author promises recompense upon the heads of the persecutors, however, and the vindication of the faithful (15:4, 21–22, 52–53; 16:67, 74–75).

It is curious that the author chose, by all appearances, to offer this exhortation as an appendix to a Jewish apocalypse. The author may have believed that these words would be heard more powerfully and make a greater impact in the context of the larger work rather than on their own. Fourth Ezra's struggles with discerning God's justice and sovereignty in the midst of Roman oppression would no doubt have resonated with the author and audience of 6 Ezra. Fourth Ezra's assurance that the Messiah (whom the author of 6 Ezra would now look back upon and give the name Jesus) would indict Rome and execute judgment upon it, and vision of the Messiah's triumph over the nations and restoration of the "peaceful people," certainly provided a context of hope for Christians in their contest as well. Thus, despite the fact that the events described in 6 Ezra 15–16 have no place in the eschatological scheme of 4 Ezra 11–13, the latter could still be regarded as complementary to, and supportive of, Christian hope in a new context long after the eagle's three heads and two puny wings had been replaced by yet more of the same through the centuries.

4 Maccabees

"Noble Is the Contest"

Once again a Jewish author returns to the Hellenization crisis and the violent suppression of Torah observance and Jewish particularism, but this time not for the purpose of legitimating a dynasty of Jewish kings or promoting the observance of a new festival. Rather, this is a "most philosophical discussion" of the thesis that "devout reason is sovereign over the emotions" (1:1), for which the martyrs under Antiochus IV provide the most conclusive proof. Fourth Maccabees, however, is much more than a philosophical treatise. It presents an eloquent defense of the Jewish way of life as an honorable pursuit, since it leads to the perfection of those virtues that even Greek and Roman critics recognize as indispensable. In this way, the author encourages hearers and readers to remain loyal to their ancestral law and their Divine Benefactor even in the face of hostile opposition from those who regard Jews with suspicion and contempt.

Structure and Contents

The author begins by announcing the book's thesis: "devout reason is sovereign over the emotions" (1:1). This is a topic worth the hearers' attention, the author asserts, since mastery of the emotions is necessary if one is to live a life of virtue. Left to their own devices, the emotions and passions would hinder justice, courage, and temperance. While there are many examples that might be used to prove the case, the author declares that the Jews who "died for the sake of virtue" (1:8) under Antiochus IV (2 Macc. 6:1–7:42) provide the most irrefutable evidence. The author begins this demonstration with the claim that reason is the faculty that chooses wisdom, and this wisdom is the direct result of education in Torah, which produces the fruit of the four cardinal virtues lauded by Greek moralists: prudence, justice, courage, and temperance (1:15–18). The mind thus equipped can master the *pathē*, a complex term involving emotions, passions, and all sensory experiences (1:19–30).

The author goes on to show from Old Testament stories and specific regulations of Torah how those who have honored the God of Israel and submitted to God's law have risen above vice and displayed virtuous behavior (1:31–3:18), which brings us up to the episode on which the author wishes to focus the audience's attention.

The author recounts the events that led up to the martyrdoms, familiar from 2 Maccabees 3–6 (cf. 4 Macc. 3:21–5:3), to set the stage. The first victim (or contestant, in the author's view) was the aged priest Eleazar. The author expands the account of this martyrdom given in 2 Macc. 6:18–31, mainly by giving speeches to Antiochus and Eleazar. Antiochus urges Eleazar to give up his empty philosophy, which despises the gifts permitted by nature; nature should teach what is truly shameful or permissible, not the local and lesser law of a particular ethnic group (5:5–13). Eleazar replies that he may not violate Torah in even those things that the Greeks deem trivial. Torah trains its adherents in self-control, courage, justice, and piety and has been given by the Creator of nature, who is a better judge of what is suitable for human beings. He announces his willingness to die for the sake of the divine law (5:14–38). In an attempt to compel him to yield, he is stripped and beaten, but his courageous spirit outlasts his torturers' stamina. When some members of the king's court suggest an alternative way out—eating some cooked meat that resembles pork—he courageously refuses lest he encourage the young to give in to impiety as well. He urges his fellow Jews, "Die nobly for your religion!" and is tortured to death. His last words are a prayer that God would accept his life as a ransom for the Jewish people and that God would turn aside the wrath they had provoked by turning aside from Torah under Jason (6:1–30; cf. 4:19–21). The author pauses for an encomiastic reflection on Eleazar's courage, commitment, and endurance, stating that already the book's thesis is proved: all who train themselves in Torah equip their reason to endure any hardship for the sake of virtue (6:31–7:23).

In the next section, Antiochus turns his attention to seven brothers (cf. 2 Maccabees 7). He shows his clear preference for assimilating them into Greek culture rather than killing them, offering to be their personal patron—a greater political and economic good than even most Greeks could ever wish for. If they refuse his offer of a pleasurable life, there remains nothing for them but an excruciating, degrading death at the hands of his officers. Again he suggests that even their God would excuse them for transgression under such compulsion (8:1–14). The author heightens the dramatic effect by including here a hypothetical speech, one that the brothers *might* have spoken had they been of a cowardly disposition (8:15–26). They, however, are true sons of Abraham, and they tell the tyrant that his offer of safety through transgression is more distressing than death. They spurn his offer and invite him to prove their mettle, that they are indeed the equals of the aged Eleazar (8:27–9:9). Enraged at them for their ingratitude, Antiochus tortures each to death in turn by the most grievous contrivances, during which process the brothers assure themselves of God's vindication: rewards for those who die for the sake of God's laws, punishments for the tyrant for his inhumane, unjust, and impious acts (9:10–13:18). One, indeed, goes so far as to thank Antiochus for the favor of giving them an opportunity to demonstrate their endurance for the law and thus to achieve honor in the sight of God (11:12). The author once more pauses to reflect on the martyrdoms, pointing out that dedication to Torah (that is, pious reason) has mastered even the good and natural emotions of fraternal affection. Not even the brothers' feelings for one another could draw them away from commitment to virtue (loyalty, courage, and piety) but rather they were perfected in their harmony as they stood side by side encouraging one another to endure for the sake of God (13:19–14:10).

The most powerful example is the mother of the seven brothers, whom the author has reserved for the end. She is given only a few verses in 2 Maccabees 7 but here is the primary focus of four chapters. Nature teaches all parents, but mothers especially, sympathy for their young and care for their preservation at any cost. Again the author interposes a hypothetical speech, what the mother *might* have said had she been "unmanly." This mother, however, although she felt strongly the natural emotions and longings for her children as they were cruelly tortured to death, did not seek to preserve their lives in this world at the cost of their exclusion from the blessedness promised for the faithful. She overcame her maternal passions in order to preserve her children for a better life (14:11–15:28). The author praises the mother and declares that the book's thesis is more than amply demonstrated by her courage and steadfastness. Indeed, in both the brothers' and the mother's cases we find that Torah is a better guide to virtue than nature. Where nature would have failed to empower the virtuous course but actually rather fought against it, training in Torah and piety enabled victory. The author includes another speech by which the mother encouraged her sons to endure the torments out of loyalty and gratitude to the God who was their Benefactor and who had a complete claim on their lives that must be honored. She dies by her own hand before her body can be violated by a Gentile's touch (15:29–17:6).

The author closes by describing the benefits of the martyrs' deaths. Through their endurance, they defeated the tyrant, who after this was unable to enforce his plan—their noble example had stirred up too much native courage and resistance. Their deaths were rendered honorable not only because they died for the sake of virtue but also because they died on behalf of the whole people, like soldiers defending a city against a foreign power. God accepted their deaths as an atonement for the people's sins (again, cf. 4:19–21). The audience is encouraged to emulate the commitment of these noble athletes and devote themselves to Torah as the path to virtue and honor (17:7–18:5). The work concludes with a strikingly different picture of the domestic life of the family of the seven brothers: how their mother maintained her female virtue of continence and how their father instructed them in the Torah and its many exemplars of faith and divine deliverance (18:6–24).

Author, Date, and Setting

The complete text is found in a number of important manuscripts (Codices Sinaiticus, Alexandrinus, and Venetus) but without any hints of authorship. Several manuscripts of the works of Josephus include 4 Maccabees under the title "On the Supremacy of Reason," but Josephan authorship is almost universally rejected (Townshend 1913: 656–57; Anderson 1985b: 533). The anonymous author was a devout Jew who regarded Torah as inviolable and who promotes such a view among peers. Nevertheless, the author was thoroughly immersed in the Hellenistic environment, to the extent of displaying a keen interest in, and familiarity with, tenets of Greek philosophy. Although probably lacking a formal education in any particular Hellenistic philosophical school, the author (whose philosophy was *Judaism*) was quite conversant in the "philosophical *koinē*" of the time and had more than a passing acquaintance with Stoic and Platonic ethics. The author writes artful and flawless Greek and displays an uncommon rhetorical ability.

Discerning the time of composition is a matter of deduction and invention. The author has most likely used 2 Maccabees directly, rather than borrowed from a common source, and so must be placed later than that book. Some have argued for a date in the early second century C.E., perhaps around the time of the Second Jewish Revolt (115–117 C.E.) or during Hadrian's suppression of Judaism in Judea (130–135 C.E.).[1] It is not necessary to suppose, however, that the oration was composed during a time of extraordinary hostility against the Jewish community. The choice of the martyrs as exemplars of the virtuous and honorable person does not necessitate the renewed possibility of martyrdom or physical persecution for the first audience. Rather, the author calls for emulation not of the martyrs' noble end but of their commitment to Torah—a timely message for a Jewish audience throughout the Greco-Roman period.

Bickerman (1976) has produced the most enduring evidence for dating the work. First, he notes the presence of two Greek words (*thrēskeia*, "religion"; *nomikos*, "skilled in the law") that do not come into common use until the Roman period, specifically Augustus's reign (30 B.C.E.–14 C.E.). He further observes that Apollonius, the Seleucid-appointed administrator, is said to govern "Syria, Phoenicia, and Cilicia" (4:2), which is a change from the description of his jurisdiction in 2 Macc. 3:5, where he is styled the "governor of Coelesyria and Phoenicia." The linking of Syria, Phoenicia, and Cilicia into a single administrative unit occurred only under Roman rule, from about 19 to 72 C.E., so that we are left with a date somewhere in the middle half of the first century (van Henten 1997:

---

1. See the survey of these views in deSilva 1998: 15–18, and, in general, the bibliography provided therein.

74).[2] Given the points of contact between 4 Maccabees and the New Testament documents and the popularity of the book among the fathers of the early church, a date in the first half of the first century C.E. is most likely.

The place of composition is still more difficult to determine. Because much is known about the large Jewish community in Alexandria, Egypt, and because Philo and other authors connected with Alexandria show an impressive awareness of Greek philosophical thought, there is always an urge to locate 4 Maccabees there as well (Grimm 1857: 293; Townshend 1913: 654; Pfeiffer 1949: 215). There was hardly an urban center in the Mediterranean world, however, that was not frequented by sophists and philosophers declaiming in the public places, and our author does not appear to have a more in-depth knowledge of Greek philosophy than could have been made available to attentive ears through the orations and conversations in the market places and colonnades of any significant city. Syrian Antioch is an attractive suggestion due to its connection with the relics of the martyrs, venerated by the early church (Dupont-Sommer 1939: 67–68). Indeed, the form of the speech, in part similar to a commemorative eulogy, has led some to believe that it was composed for delivery at the site of the martyrs' grave as part of an annual festival of remembrance. Against this more specific suggestion, veneration of the dead went contrary to standard Jewish practice. Van Henten (1994) provides the helpful observation that the epitaph for the martyrs in 17:9–10 closely resembles Jewish inscriptions on tombs in Cilicia, suggesting a provenance in that region. The most that one can say with certainty is that 4 Maccabees was a product of the eastern Diaspora, probably somewhere between Asia Minor (where the florid style was most at home) and Syria (the traditional site of the martyrs' graves), in an urban center with a significant Jewish community. This audience would have welcomed the exhortation to remain loyal to Torah but needed to see that Torah observance led to a life that could be understood as virtuous and honorable even by Greek ethical standards, even if the religious differences would never permit rapprochement between the two cultures.

Genre and Purpose

What type of literature is 4 Maccabees, and what clues does its literary form give regarding its author's purpose and the work's intended effect? The book belongs to the rhetorical genre called epideictic, or demonstrative ora-

---

2. Others narrow this down further to the reign of Caligula, who threatened to desecrate the temple in a manner reminiscent of Antiochus IV and provoked demonstrations of resistance comparable to the protests in 2 Macc. 3:14b–21 and 3 Macc. 1:16–29. This, however, caters more to our desire to know more than the evidence will allow.

tory. This category is the least well defined and, indeed, became a sort of catch-all category for speeches that were not clearly deliberative (advisory) or forensic (judicial). The author's own language points to this category: language of demonstration (*epideiknysthai* [1:1]; *apodeixis* [3:19]; *apodeiknymi* [16:2]), which matches the concern to demonstrate a philosophical proposition, stated conspicuously at the outset; and language of praise, appropriate for a funeral oration, commemorative speech, or simply a piece of moral exhortation (*epainos* [1:2]; *epainein* [1:10]).

Fourth Maccabees shares much in common with ancient funeral orations or commemorative speeches (Lebram 1974). Such speeches set out to praise some figure by showing him or her to be the exemplar of a specific virtue or cluster of virtues. The speech was meant not only to honor the dead but also to promote the imitation of those virtues by the living; indeed, ancient orators knew that the praise of the dead would be believed and accepted only to the extent that the hearers could imitate the exemplars' virtues and attain an honorable remembrance themselves. Funerary speeches often concluded with direct exhortations to fix one's gaze upon the noble life just praised and set as one's goal the embodiment of the same virtues in a way appropriate to one's sphere of life (see, e.g., Thucydides, *Peloponnesian War* 2.43–44; Dio Chrysostom, *Melancomas [Oration 29]* 21). Our author, too, concludes with such an exhortation: "O Israelite children, offspring of the seed of Abraham, obey this law and exercise piety in every way" (18:1).

Nevertheless, the oration is in fact framed as a philosophical demonstration of a thesis (e.g., 1:1, 13), of which the martyrs are the best proofs (1:7–9). A strong mixture of philosophical argument and encomiastic reflection on specific individuals' lives is not without parallel in the first century C.E. Seneca, the Stoic author and tutor to Nero, wrote a treatise called "That the Wise Man Receives Neither Injury Nor Insult" (*De constantia sapientis*), in which he presents numerous arguments for his thesis but depends most heavily on the examples of Cato the Younger and Stilbo of Megara, who show how the philosophy was effective in life situations. The recollection of their particular triumphs over injury and degradation through holding to Stoic philosophy makes that philosophy all the more appealing to Seneca's readership.

Perhaps the best way to describe 4 Maccabees, then, is as a sort of philosophical protreptic discourse, which mingles philosophical argumentation and vivid examples of the philosophy at work, delivering what it promises, all for the purpose of making that philosophy more credible (see 7:9), appealing, and worth wholehearted commitment. Such a work is not necessarily an invitation to outsiders to join the "way of life" (see 2:8; 4:19) outlined by the philosophy. Those who have already started along such a road (or have been born into that way of life, as were Jews) need frequent encouragement to persevere, particularly when the dominant culture does not accept such a way of life as honorable or reasonable (see 5:7–11). Fourth Maccabees seeks to strengthen the commitment of Jews to the Jewish way of life, making that way of life credible, reasonable, and honorable through the double presentation of argument and example.

Returning to the issue of occasion, which the text itself raises with its references to the appropriateness of the speech to a specific day (1:10) and season (3:19), we may venture some suggestions. Several scholars think that the oration was composed for a festival commemorating the martyrs (Dupont-Sommer 1939: 67–73; Hadas 1953: 103–7). This would be a suitable occasion, if such an occasion existed in the first century, but there is no evidence for such a festival in Jewish sources, although it came to be celebrated in the Christian liturgical calendar.

One suggestion that has gained some support is that 4 Maccabees was composed for delivery during the festival of Hanukkah, which celebrated the liberation and purification of the Jerusalem temple by Judas Maccabeus and his forces. The martyrdoms occurred, of course, during the Hellenization crisis that Judas, in effect, ended, and so the celebration of the restoration of Judaism in Israel would also recommend some remembrance of those who died during the oppression. A frequently raised objection is that 4 Maccabees fails to refer to the Hasmonean heroes or their victory over Antiochus's forces, which tended to occupy center stage during Hanukkah (Townshend 1913: 667). Dissatisfaction with the Hasmonean dynasty, particularly with its later representatives, however, might discourage Jewish communities from celebrating the founders of that dynasty and hence continuing to legitimate, in effect, a rule that came to be regarded with mixed feelings. Any mention of the military exploits of Judas and his brothers, moreover, would run counter to the author's own interpretation of that crisis. It was the martyrs, not the warriors, who defeated the tyrant and compelled him to leave the land (1:11; 17:20–22; 18:4–5). Their self-sacrifice for the sake of Torah was essential for the liberation of Israel from Antiochus's armies, for it turned away God's wrath and secured God's renewed favor and deliverance (4:19–21; 6:27–29; 17:21–22; cf. 2 Macc. 4:13–17; 5:17–20; 6:12–17; 7:32–33, 37–38; 8:5). The faithful martyrs become, therefore, the essential heroes of the Hellenization crisis. Hanukkah remains, therefore, a fitting occasion for such a "narrative demonstration" of fidelity to Torah and to the patron-client bond between God and the Jewish people.

A second, though perhaps less appropriate, occasion might be one of the festivals focused on the giving of Torah, such as Shavuoth (Pentecost) or Simchath Torah (Joy of Torah). The protreptic thrust of 4 Maccabees is that Torah ought to be kept as the surest, and only perfect, path to virtue and eternal honor, no matter what the cost in terms of life in a Gentile-dominated world (see 18:1–2). The choice of examples is not as inappropriate to these festivals as it may seem at first: a day to celebrate Torah and the virtues of following its way of life would be a suitable occasion to speak of those who died rather than abandon that way of life.

4 Maccabees and Greco–Roman Philosophy

This oration stands out from other books in the Apocrypha in its depth of interaction with Hellenistic philosophy. Wisdom of Solomon, to be sure, shows many points of contact with the language of the Greek philosophers but does not begin to approach 4 Maccabees for breadth of contact and conversation with Stoic and Platonic philosophical discourse, particularly in the area of ethics. Here we will hold 4 Maccabees up to the light of Stoic, Platonic, and Peripatetic thought (see Renehan 1972) to illumine better its argument and its recasting of Jewish ethnic particularism as a true philosophy, fit to compete with (and overmatch!) the best Greece has to offer.

The author's thesis, that "devout reason is sovereign over the emotions" (1:1; 6:31; 13:1; 16:1; 18:2), resonates with the frequent discussions in Greek and Latin authors of the relationship between reason and the *pathē*, the complex of emotions, feelings, desires, and sensory experiences connected with the irrational, physical nature of humanity. Orthodox Stoicism asserted that reason should aim to destroy or root out the emotions, rather than simply control and moderate them (see Cicero, *Tusculanae disputationes* 4.57, 83–84). Other Stoics (like Poseidonius and, later, Galen), Peripatetic philosophers, and eclectic ethicists such as Plutarch argued that the emotional and appetitive side of human nature should, rather, be controlled, guided to an Aristotelian "mean" and kept from excess rather than extirpated completely. This is the position also of 4 Maccabees: God implanted the "emotions and inclinations" in humanity (2:21) but enthroned the mind as governor. Humans are therefore not to destroy part of God's creation but live a well-ordered life with reason's dominion over the emotions and feelings.

Why were the *pathē* thus targeted by ethicists? These were the natural hindrances to living in full accordance with virtue. Fear (an emotion of the soul, as it were), if allowed to overpower right reasoning, could undermine the determination to act courageously and lead one into cowardice (seeking safety above honor). Anger might destroy the virtue of prudence, leading one to do what right reasoning would disallow. The physical sensations, too, ranged their forces against reason's commitment to virtue. Pain could make one desist from pursuing the courageous course or cause one to violate the virtue of justice by compelling one to violate loyalty. Pleasure is equally dangerous, leading people into intemperance with regard to food or sexuality or luring them away from their commitments by the promise of greater enjoyment of life. The virtues of justice, courage, temperance, and prudence were hailed as cardinal because society, for its continued survival, depended on its individual members acting in particular ways and avoiding certain behaviors. Reason aided this endeavor; the passions were held suspect for their tendency to jeopardize commitment to virtue. Thus, while philosophers disagreed with regard to the extent of reason's purview (mastery or extirpation), they were in essential agreement as to the need for its primacy.

The author of 4 Maccabees, however, introduces something new into the equation: it is not merely reason that is able to overcome the emotions but "pious" or "devout" reason (*eusebēs logismos*). Reason is fully equipped to master the emotions only when it has been trained in the law of God—not the law of nature cherished by the Stoics (cf. 5:8–9) but the Torah given by God to the Jewish people. The author walks alongside Stoic philosophers in definitions of reason and wisdom: "Reason is the mind that with sound logic prefers the life of wisdom. Wisdom, next, is the knowledge of divine and human matters and the causes of these" (1:15–16; cf. Cicero, *Tusculanae disputationes* 4.26.57). The author parts company with them, however, in the assertion that follows: "This, in turn, is education in the law, by which we learn divine matters reverently and human affairs to our advantage" (1:17). In this, our author follows the lead of Jewish Wisdom tradition, particularly as developed by Ben Sira. Wisdom in all its fullness is found in obedience to Torah (cf. Sir. 19:20; 1:14–18, 26–27).

Turning to examples, the author draws solely from the Old Testament Scriptures, pointing out both specific stories and specific commandments within the Jewish law that show the restraining power of Jewish piety over the forces within people that lead to vice and away from virtue. Thus, Jewish dietary laws, often the target of Gentile ridicule, actually exercise the obedient in the virtue of temperance or self-control (*epikrateia*) (1:31–35); the laws governing lending and leaving the gleanings of a harvest for the poor check greed (2:8–9); the law restrains the excess of wrath even in enmity relationships (2:14). Moreover, the heroes of Scripture show how dedication to God's law overcomes sexual desire (Joseph [2:1–4]), anger (Moses [2:16–20]), and irrational desire (David [3:6–18]). The martyrs themselves, of course, demonstrate pious reason's mastery over the most powerful enemies of virtue—physical agony—and manifest the extreme self-control, courage, and justice (in not violating the bond of loyalty to the Divine Patron, even under the direst compulsion) that dedication to Torah engenders in both sexes and all age groups.

The author's claims for Torah's power to enable virtue increase as the oration proceeds. It is the Torah that allows the mind to exercise its divinely appointed governance over the emotions and appetites (see 2:21–23). This promise, however, becomes a more exclusive claim after the narration of Eleazar's steadfastness. The extreme agonies that he withstood and his staunch refusal to have his mind swayed by external compulsions lead the author to declare, "As many as attend to religion with a whole heart, these alone are able to control the passions of the flesh, since they believe that they, like our patriarchs Abraham and Isaac and Jacob, do not die to God, but live in God" (7:18–19). The general term "religion" is made specific by the reference to the Jewish patriarchs: it is the devout Jew who alone has been equipped to walk in virtue with complete consistency, above all assaults on his or her reason through the emotions, passions, and sensory experiences. This claim appears again on the lips of the eldest brother: "Through all these tortures I will convince you that children of the Hebrews alone are invincible where virtue is concerned" (9:18).

These are, indeed, extraordinary claims for the Jewish law in philosophical discourse. A Stoic believed that the many ethnic and national laws were inferior to the law of nature, giving but a skewed vision of what a virtuous life should look like. Dio Chrysostom, an orator who thrived at the turn of the first century, is representative when he chides people for slavishly observing human-made laws and customs but giving no heed to the universal laws that lead to a virtuous life (see *De libertate [Oration 80]* 80.5–6). Antiochus IV is made to say what any Stoic would have said about the Jewish law: as a law code peculiar to one ethnic group—and one that appeared to contravene nature at many points—it did not appear to be any better than slavery or superstition and certainly not on equal footing with true philosophy. Spurning nature's gifts, such as the succulent meat of the pig, is censured by him as ingratitude and senselessness. In his eyes, Eleazar holds "a vain opinion concerning the truth" and will bring suffering on his own head if he stubbornly persists in a "foolish philosophy" (5:7–11).

Eleazar's response is a significant counterattack. Torah's value as a philosophy is proven by the fruits it bears in the individual: living by the four cardinal virtues (5:23–24). Moreover, its source is superior to the Stoic law of nature. The Stoic goal was to live *kata physin,* "in accordance with nature's law." The Jew could claim, however, a higher authority. The One who created nature and ordered it is the same One who gave Torah to human beings; therefore, Torah is indeed the surer guide to virtue, since it came from nature's own Lawgiver.

The author dwells at length on the affection of siblings for one another and of a mother for her children, in order to prove further that Torah alone, and not nature, empowers the perfection of virtue and absolute mastery of the passions. After narrating their martyrdoms one by one and their mutual encouragement to endure death for the sake of God, the author speaks at some length of the forces that aroused great sympathy and unity of spirit among the seven: being nurtured in the same womb, sharing the same blood, nursing at the same breasts, and growing from "common nurture and daily companionship, and from both general education and our discipline in the law of God" (13:19–22). These topics (except for Torah) belong to the common stock of Hellenistic ethical reflection on the various types of friendship, of which fraternal affection (*philadelphia*) is a particularly strong species. Aristotle (*Ethica nichomachea* 9.4.1161.b30–35) invokes these topics to show that brothers are "in a sense the same thing, though separate individuals" (see also Xenophon, *Cyropaedia* 8.7, 14). Nature thus arranges for siblings to love one another and to seek each other's well-being, survival, and enjoyment. Fourth Maccabees asserts, however, that the seven brothers overcame the affection that nature had implanted (13:27), preferring the preservation of loyalty to Torah to the preservation of one another's lives.

The example of the mother, a story told in briefest scope in 2 Maccabees, is here expanded to become the climax of the author's demonstration, for in her one sees the ultimate triumph of pious reasoning over the emotions, since maternal love was held to be the strongest emotion. The author writes about maternal love as any other ethical philosopher of the period might (striking parallels are found in Plutarch, *On Affection for Offspring*), noting how nature itself teaches us in the example of unreasoning animals how parents are to behave toward their children (14:13–20). Nature counsels animals to preserve the lives of their children at any cost, even at the cost of their own well-being, and the voice of nature was one counselor who spoke into the mother's ear (15:25), tempting her to urge her sons to give in to the king and so save their lives. Her faculty of reason, however, educated by observance of Torah, chose the path of loyalty and justice for her children rather than the path of preservation from harm. Indeed, she encouraged them to face agony and death for the sake of keeping faith with God (16:18–19). The author shows that nature itself is an imperfect guide to virtue, being insufficient to empower the reason to conquer fraternal love and parental affection for the sake of choosing virtue. The Jewish Torah is superior even to the guide claimed by the most thoughtful of Gentiles.

Stoic ethicists were very interested in how people face adversity. This is where philosophy is put to the test, and the genuine philosopher parted company with the play-actor or fair-weather devotee of virtue. The true wise person, as defined by Stoics especially, was above compulsion. No outward force or threat could shake his or her resolution to remain dedicated to virtue alone and unconcerned about all external things (property, reputation, even life itself). Thus, Epictetus (50–120 C.E.) declares truly free and above all compulsion, "the person over whom pleasure has no power, nor evil, nor fame, nor wealth, and who, whenever it seems good, can spit his whole paltry body into some oppressor's face and depart from this life" (*Diatribai [Dissertationes]* 3.24.71). Caesar can threaten and inflict loss with regard to property, status, and life but cannot enslave the will of the wise person, who considers all these things as "foreign" to his or her interest (*Diatribai [Dissertationes]* 4.1.60, 87). Thus, the tyrant is robbed of all power to compel a person to act against the dictates of reason.

So also the martyrs are depicted as perfect examples of the wise person in their ability to overcome even the most fearsome of coercive measures. Antiochus twice assures the objects of his energies that transgression through compulsion is not liable to judgment (5:13; 8:14), but the martyrs refuse to accept the dishonorable course, even if it can be excused. They refuse to allow their moral principles to be bullied by the tyrant (see 5:38) and so "nullified his tyranny" (8:15; 11:24). The Jewish martyr-philosophers become the conquerors of the tyrant, even though beaten in body and tortured to death, since the tyrant is unable to achieve his objective and separate the martyrs from their religious commitment (11:25–27). Stoic philosophers taught that one could overcome by enduring. Philo (*Quod omnis probus liber sit* 26–27) borrows this notion when he writes about two competitors in the arena, one inflicting every manner of blow, the other receiving these blows but withstanding them on account of his firm body and enduring spirit, winning at last when the attacker is exhausted. "The virtuous man appears to me very much to resemble this person. For having thoroughly fortified his soul with strong and powerful reasoning, he so compels the man who is offering him violence to desist from weariness, before he himself can be compelled to do any thing contrary to his opinion of propriety." Just so, the martyrs in 4 Maccabees conquer their oppressors through endurance, an endurance made possible only through their training in piety and Torah (1:11; 6:10; 7:4; 9:30).

Seneca's *De constantia sapientis* elaborates another basic tenet of Stoic ethics: "the wise person can receive neither injury nor insult." The wise person knows that one's only sure possession is virtue; all else is at the mercy of forces beyond one's control. Physical harm is no injury, for the body is, by nature, subject to pain and death; loss of property or status is no injury, for these, too, nature has not placed under our control. As long as the wise person remains constant in virtue, his or her possessions are safe, and he or she is beyond all harm. The martyrs reflect such a stance when they challenge Antiochus: "If you take our lives because of our religion, do not suppose that you can injure us by torturing us. For we, through this severe suffering and endurance, shall have the prize of virtue and shall be with God, on whose account we suffer" (9:7–8). The possession of virtue and the hope of its prize (here, of course, notably different from the Stoic view) make injury impossible. Their true welfare is secure, since the path of virtue leads to the enjoyment of honor in the presence of God (17:18).

Indeed, the martyrs make use of the tortures as an opportunity to show their endurance for the sake of the Torah (11:12) and thus prove their virtue. The hardships become a gracious gift by which the martyrs may demonstrate their worthiness of God and be welcomed into their reward. This, too, is a clear echo of Stoic authors' descriptions of the wise and virtuous person. Thus, Seneca (*De constantia sapientis* 9.3) writes that the wise person "counts even injury profitable, for through it he finds a means of putting himself to the proof and makes trial of his virtue." So the brothers' virtue is proven by the tortures (9:7), and Eleazar is able to have this important effect for the author and audience: "You, father, strengthened our loyalty to the law through your glorious endurance, and . . . by your deeds you made your words of divine philosophy credible" (7:9).

In the ancient world, physical assault attacked the honor of a person. A slap was an insult, and physical punishment was a disgrace inflicted in order to label certain behavior as deviant and unacceptable. The tortures suffered by the martyrs were aimed at bringing them into conformity with the values of the dominant Greek culture and expressed that culture's negative evaluation of the Jewish way of life. The author, however, takes up an argument familiar to both Stoic and Platonic philosophers that nullifies the dishonor. Plato, for example, emphasizes that inflicting abuse upon a person unjustly is far more disgraceful than suffering insult and abuse undeservedly (*Gorgias* 508C–E). Doing injustice is always more shameful than suffering injustice. Seneca (*De constantia sapientis* 16.3) echoes Plato when he advises the one being victimized to ask himself or herself: "Do I, or do I not, deserve that these things befall me? If I do deserve them, there is no insult—it is justice; if I do not deserve them, he who does the injustice is the one to blush."

The author of 4 Maccabees notes quite pointedly that the sufferings inflicted upon the martyrs were not just. The tyrant (an "enemy of heavenly justice" [9:15]), being alienated from the One God, did not even understand what actions were truly honorable and what actions ought to be punished (11:4–6). Indeed, the tortures manifest Antiochus's own shamelessness, treating people of flesh and blood like himself so cruelly, and his own injustice, abusing the servants of the God who gave him his kingdom (12:11–14). Here one returns to the fact that the author is not simply engaged in philosophical debate but seeks to create a discourse that will sustain commitment among the audience to the Jewish way of life in the face of a dominant culture that does not value Torah or the One God, that often responds to the Jewish people with hostility and suspicion because of their commitment to these exclusive values. The author assures the audience, however, using the very language of the dominant culture's own conscience, that such opposition is never a sign of Jewish disgrace but rather shows the opponents' alienation from virtue.

The Rhetorical Situation and Strategy of 4 Maccabees

The author's philosophical arguments serve a more basic purpose: to assure Jews that their way of life is the path that preserves virtue and self-respect and to encourage them to persevere in that way as the means to attain honor and a praiseworthy remembrance. Jewish authors frequently felt the need to defend the nobility and validity of Judaism for their own compatriots, since the attitudes of Gentile Greek and Latin authors were often unfavorable and since anti-Jewish prejudice frequently erupted into anti-Jewish action.[3] While the Jewish religion was generally declared tolerable by authorities, many among the Greco-Roman population still regarded Jews with suspicion and ill will.

Greco-Roman religion was fairly accommodating; new gods could always be assimilated into the old pantheon, often through being identified as some

---

3. See also the discussions in the chapters on "Additions to Esther" and "3 Maccabees" on anti-Jewish prejudice in the Hellenistic and Roman periods.

local manifestation of one of the better-known Homeric gods. Participation in civic cults, showing oneself to be a pious worshiper of the gods, was prerequisite to being regarded as a reliable member of Greco-Roman society. Someone who paid the gods what was owed them, and who supplicated their favor toward the city along with everyone else, was "one of us," someone who could be counted on to do his or her part for the general welfare.

Jews were dedicated to the One God and neglected—even denied—all others. This religious exclusivism was seen to be reflected in their social interactions. The dietary regulations and purity laws of Torah enforced a high degree of separateness between Jews and their neighbors in the Hellenistic city. The Jews' tendency to interact closely with other Jews and to restrict the closeness of their interaction with people of other races led to their gaining a reputation for *misanthrōpia*, "hatred of the human race" and *misoxenia*, "hatred of outsiders." This is the complaint against the Jewish people that reverberates throughout the Greek and Latin literature. Diodorus of Sicily (*Historical Library* 34.1–4; 40.3.4), Tacitus (*Historiae* 5.5), Juvenal (*Satirae* 14.100–104), and Apion (*apud* Josephus *Against Apion* 2.121) all accuse the Jewish people of supporting their fellow Jews but showing no good will to those who are not of their race. The dietary laws and restrictions on social intercourse practiced by Jews loyal to Torah, while an effective means of maintaining group boundaries and cohesion, gave rise to anti-Jewish slander from outsiders.

The anti-Jewish actions described in 4 Maccabees might well have been seen by the perpetrators as attempts to correct or reform a deviant people, to bring them into a healthy relationship with the larger social entity of the Hellenistic, global culture. Antiochus speaks for many when he questions the reasonableness of the Jewish way of life (5:7). The restrictions that Judaism placed on diet (the prohibition against pork was a frequent target of Gentile ridicule and speculation), on purity, and on worship were so foreign and strange that it might have seemed to a Gentile ruler an act of deliverance to bring these people out of a strange superstition into the light of cosmopolitan Hellenism. When Hellenization offered such obvious advantages as gaining access to a larger political and trade network, to wider arenas of recognition and fame, and to more powerful patrons, Jewish resistance must have seemed incomprehensible indeed. Third Maccabees, we saw, provides a window into the thought world of the Gentile: the things that are most prized by Greeks are despised by the Jews, who prefer to cling to their ancestral and regional ways than embrace the advance of civilization (3 Macc. 3:21–23). This made the Jews themselves appear strange and dishonorable in Gentile eyes. We catch a glimpse of this again in 4 Maccabees as Antiochus offers not only release from torture and execution but also the best that Greek life can offer to the seven brothers—high office in government, the invaluable resource of a king for a personal patron (4 Macc. 8:5–7)—and they reject these, which are the greatest goods in Greek eyes, for the sake of loyalty to local laws and customs.

Fourth Maccabees speaks to a tension-filled sociocultural situation. Jews are faced with an imposing, dominant culture that may tolerate their religion but certainly does not respect their way of life. In the face of society's praise of Greek values and those who show loyalty to the traditional gods and fulfill their duty through full participation in the life of the city, how can a Jew resist the desire to be well regarded by Gentiles and remain loyal to a way of life that brings suspicion and misunderstanding rather than approval and honor? Our author provides a badly needed response to this question.

To whom does the author address the defense? Some have suggested that Gentiles were the target audience: the author wished to demonstrate to outsiders that Judaism was a reasonable philosophy that could match Greek philosophical discourse point for point. Gentiles, however, would not be much convinced by the document. They would not, for the most part, accept the exclusive commitment to one local deity that Judaism presupposes and could not therefore accept a particular ethnic legal code as the revelation of God Most High. The author seeks, rather, to direct the defense to fellow Jews, those who would in essence agree with the author's presuppositions, even while faltering in their commitment to the way of life based on those presuppositions. This is the audience that the author holds explicitly in view when writing, "You, father, strengthened our loyalty to the law . . . and by your deeds you made your words of divine philosophy credible" (7:9). It is this loyalty to the Torah, already in existence in the audience, that requires the strength born of the remembrance of the martyrs. Similarly, the final exhortation addresses fellow Israelites: "O Israelite children, offspring of the seed of Abraham, obey this law and exercise piety in every way, knowing that devout reason is master of all emotions, not only of sufferings from within, but also of those from without" (18:1–2). The philosophical proof (18:2) has as its goal not the persuasion of Gentile detractors but the confirmation of Jews whose observance of Torah must not waver in the face of Gentiles' failure to honor their way of life.

Fourth Maccabees thus sets out to promote a way of life for those who already have been set on that track, making continued obedience to Torah and separateness from Gentile culture seem reasonable, honorable, and sensible. It seeks to show that loyalty to Judaism does in fact result in advantage, while transgression of loyalty to the ancestral ways, although apparently advantageous in light of the pressures (subtle and forceful) that Gentiles leveled against Jews, would certainly result in disadvantage. Here the relationship of epideictic and deliberative rhetoric shows itself to be very close—a fact often noted by ancient rhetoricians. Aristotle (*Rhetorica* 1.9.35–36), for example, said that "praise and counsels have a common aspect; for what you might suggest in counseling becomes encomium by a change in the phrase. . . . Accordingly, if you desire to praise, look what you would suggest; if you desire to suggest, look what you would praise." What our author praises as honorable and sensible becomes—if the writing is successful—a sort of general policy that the audience will adopt due to their desire to live honorably and sensibly.

The author seeks to demonstrate that those who possess "devout reason" will achieve the highest honor. Pious reason overcomes the obstacles to the cardinal virtues of courage, justice, and temperance—virtues that bring praise to those who embody them. The martyrs are chosen as exemplars of virtue (1:8) and are, as such, praiseworthy (1:10); those who are similarly committed to living in accordance with devout reason will attain comparable honor and a similar praiseworthy remembrance. Apart from the cultivation of devout reason, all other forms of claiming and pursuing honor are but "vainglory," "arrogance," and "boastfulness" (1:26; 2:15).

Devout reason, we have seen, is none other than the mind that has been educated and exercised by observing the Torah, which bridles the passions and empowers virtuous conduct. Victory over the emotions that hinder the practice of justice comes "as soon as one adopts a way of life in accordance with the law" (2:8). Similarly, in unfolding God's provisions in the creation of humanity for a life of virtue, the author states, "To the mind he gave the law; and one who lives subject to this will rule a kingdom that is temperate, just, good, and courageous" (2:23). The more exclusive claim that the author makes for Torah, that only those who attend to Judaism with a full heart will truly master the emotions and attain the perfection of virtue (7:18–19; 9:18), adds to the protreptic aim of the work. The extravagant promises for those who pursue this way of life, and the exclusive claims for Judaism as the means to achieve honor and virtue, aid the hearers to commit themselves more fully to Torah.

While 4 Maccabees is a work of epideictic rhetoric, holding up a set of values and way of life as worthy of praise and therefore worthy of imitation, the author weaves several significant deliberative elements into the narrative. These heighten the protreptic nature of the work, providing further exhortations to strengthen commitment to Torah and dealing with objections (i.e., from the Gentile world in the person of Antiochus and from Jewish apostates in the hypothetical speeches of the seven brothers and the mother) ahead of time.

First, the author directly exhorts the audience to "pay earnest attention to philosophy" (1:1) because of the ethical fruits it promises. This is a standard protreptic invitation; an audience is being invited to consider a particular way of life for the sake of virtue. This "philosophy," however, is none other than observance of Torah. Because of this, the initial encouragement to pay attention to philosophy can be transformed into the concluding exhortation (18:1–2). The author's goal is to secure the audience's loyalty to Torah as the policy upon which all other actions are based.

Second, within the narrative the author creates a deliberative world. There are two counselors vying for the martyrs' approval, just as in the assembly hall two orators would stand and make speeches urging one or the other opposite courses of action as the more advantageous. The brothers declare their allegiance to "the law and to Moses our counselor," rejecting the advice of Antiochus, the "counselor of lawlessness" (9:2–3). Antiochus's appeals may be taken as representative of the sort of internal deliberations going on in the minds of the audience, who are assaulted on the one hand with Gentile contempt for Judaism and on the other with the promise of approval, honor, and advancement for those who are willing to compromise or even abandon Torah observance in order to form essential relationships with Gentile benefactors (see 8:5–7). The martyrs are praised for their decision to accept the divinely appointed counsel of Moses and Torah, approving these counselors rather than Antiochus. So also the audience should place their hope for honor and security in following Torah rather than listening to the voices urging disloyalty to God. By creating alternative, or hypothetical, responses by the seven brothers and the mother in 8:16–26 and 16:5–11, the author heightens the deliberative atmosphere of the piece. Presenting these speeches, however, allows the author to cast such capitulation to the pressures of the Hellenistic culture as dishonorable, "cowardly and unmanly" (8:16). Such censure would cause the audience to think twice before adopting a course that might be construed as disgraceful.

A third deliberative element appears in the exhortations that the martyrs address to one another. Because the whole speech is addressed to the audience, however, and the audience has been led at every point to identify with the martyrs, these exhortations are also in part addressed to the audience. Eleazar concludes his speech of refusal to fake the eating of food offered to idols with the exhortation "Therefore, O children of Abraham, die nobly for your religion!" (6:22). This is a general invitation that of necessity involves the audience (who are all "offspring of Abraham" [18:1]). The mother's final words of exhortation to her sons cannot fail to have an impact on her extended family as well: "My sons, noble is the contest to which you are called to bear witness for the nation. Fight zealously for our ancestral law. . . . Remember that it is through God that you have had a share in the world and have enjoyed life, and therefore you ought to endure any suffering for the sake of God" (16:16, 18–19). No doubt the book's auditors, also hearing such exhortations, would at least have had to consider the applicability of such advice to their own situations.

The author uses epideictic rhetoric to present the choice of absolute loyalty to Torah and the One God as the noble choice, the only choice aligned with the highest virtues and a noble character. Those who yield to the pressure to assimilate to Gentile culture, or who seek honor in those foreign values, will not achieve true honor in the sight of God. Rather, they, like Simon (4:1–5) and Jason (4:19), are remembered as traitors, enemies of the public harmony (3:21), and disloyal clients of their Divine Benefactor. Seeking advancement in Gentile society at the cost of obedience to Torah and honor toward God provokes the wrath of God and brings judgment upon the nation (4:21) and eternal torment upon individuals (9:9, 32; 10:21; 11:23; 12:12, 14, 18; 13:15; 18:5, 22). Not only is such a course "cowardly and unmanly" (8:16), but also it is opposed to the course of virtue (by which the Torah leads the subject mind to "rule a kingdom that is temperate, just, good, and courageous" [2:23]) and dishonors the One who is able to bring down both temporal and eternal tribulation on the heads of the disobedient and disrespectful (4:21; 13:15).

Only those who resist courageously are found to be committed to nobility (*kalokagathia,* a word denoting the highest level of noble character [1:10; 11:22; 13:25; 15:9]) and virtue (*aretē,* "excellence" [1:8; 7:21–22; 9:8; 10:10; 11:2]). The virtues of piety (which Gentiles claim Jews lack in their neglect of the traditional gods) and courage (most extravagantly praised in Greek culture) are the possession of the martyrs for Torah and all who would follow in their commitment (*eusebeia,* "piety" [5:31; 7:16; 9:6, 24; 13:8, 10; 15:1, 3]; *andreia,* "courage," and its cognates [1:11; 7:23; 15:23, 30; 17:23–24]).

While their opponents viewed the martyrs dying for folly (8:5; 10:13; 12:3) in a most degrading manner, in the author's encomium they are praised as dying nobly (6:30; 9:24; 10:1, 15; 11:12; 12:1, 14; 15:32; 16:16). The Gentiles' opinion of them is based on error, failure to honor God (9:32; 10:11; 12:11), and lack of virtue (10:17; 11:4) and is therefore not worth consideration. For a Jew to be dishonored by a Gentile, therefore, reflects more upon the Gentile's honor. By such means, the author is able to separate the audience from concern over their reputation in Greek eyes and focus their attention back toward their reputation in the eyes of God (17:5) and of the community of faith throughout the ages (including the patriarchs, who do not die but continue to form an important body of significant others [13:17]). This is the court whose verdict is eternal, such that honor in God's sight is of much greater value than honor in the sight of Gentile society (9:8; 17:5, 17–19; 18:23). This is meant to relieve the pressure under which the audience finds itself, freeing them to remain loyal to their ancestral identity and preserve their culture and religion in the face of an unsympathetic world.

Fourth Maccabees devotes its full attention to assisting Jews to remain committed to a particular way of life. It allows them to reject the Gentile society's lack of regard and to hold fast to Judaism as the true means of attaining honor—honor based on virtues that even Greeks should recognize. The criticism from without is turned back against the detractors, as Jews are now equipped to see in their religion the fulfillment of the virtues that Greek culture lauds as honorable. They may ask themselves why the Gentiles fail to recognize their worth, but they will not be as sorely tempted to seek Gentile validation of their worth.

4 Maccabees and the Environment of Early Christianity

Because 4 Maccabees has a mid-first-century date, any direct literary dependence between it and the New Testament is difficult to demonstrate. Rather than argue for influence on the New Testament here, then, we will consider how 4 Maccabees illumines the first-century environment of Judaism and Christianity and particularly some theological, social, and rhetorical features of New Testament texts, their settings, and their purpose.

Theological Context

God as Patron

Patronage was a fundamental social institution in the first-century Mediterranean world, with specific roles and obligations known to every inhabitant of that world; the giving and receiving of benefactions was "the practice that constitutes the chief bond of human society" (Seneca, *De beneficiis* 1.4.2) (see deSilva 2000b: chs. 3–4). Human beings were held together in networks of allegiance and favor, relationships that were long-lasting because the accounts could never be precisely settled. Patrons gave access to material goods, entertainment, and advancement; success, even survival, depended upon cultivating a powerful patron. One who received a benefit accepted the obligation to augment the patron's reputation through publicizing the favor and to augment the patron's power through pledging absolute loyalty and obedience to whatever the patron asked as a return. In this society, gratitude was an essential virtue and ingratitude indeed a gross offense. A client showed gratitude, and thus continued to enjoy favor, by living to increase the patron's honor (certainly never to bring the patron into dishonor) and by holding firm his or her allegiance to the patron. This allegiance could be costly, as Seneca (*Epistulae morales* 81.27) notes:

> No man can be grateful unless he has learned to scorn the things which drive the common herd to distraction; if you wish to make a return for a favour, you must be willing to go into exile, or to pour forth your blood, or to undergo poverty, or, . . . even to let your very innocence be stained and exposed to shameful slanders.

Gratitude such as Seneca describes involved an intense loyalty to the person from whom one has received beneficence, such that one would place a greater value on service to the benefactor than on one's place in one's homeland, one's physical well-being, one's wealth, and one's reputation. The bond between client and patron, or, we should add, between friends who share mutual beneficence, was thus an inviolable bond in Greco-Roman society.

The author of 4 Maccabees uses this social relationship prominently in the oration. The martyrs remain obedient and loyal to God because they understand the debt of gratitude they owe God as their Divine Patron. They cannot abandon their Patron, or bring his name into dishonor before his enemies (cf. Rom. 2:24), by disobeying his commands. Thus, the mother urges her sons on to death in obedience to God's law based on God's beneficence: "Remember that it is through God that you have had a share in the world and have enjoyed life, and therefore you ought to endure any suffering for the sake of

God" (16:18–19; cf. 13:13). The martyrs hope thus to gain future benefits from their Benefactor, both for the nation in the form of deliverance from political oppression (6:27–28) and for themselves as individuals in the form of eternal life in the presence of God (7:19; 9:8; 15:2–3, 8; 16:13, 25; 17:18–19). As honorable clients, therefore, they set their hope in this Benefactor (16:25; 17:4).

In this context, the word "faith" (*pistis*) takes on a specific meaning that continues to be important for New Testament authors. Here it means not simply "belief" but "loyalty" to their divine Patron such as Daniel and his three companions demonstrated (16:21–22). Another aspect of this faith is found in 8:5–7 in Antiochus's offer of patronage for those who are willing to abandon Torah (the offer that the brothers must refuse out of loyalty to God). Here, Antiochus speaks of trusting the benefactor's good will and ability to deliver the promised benefits (8:7). Faith, then, expresses the proper stance of a client toward a benefactor and the proper return for benefits conferred.

In the New Testament, God continues to be known as the Patron and Benefactor; Jesus has, indeed, become the mediator who secures access to God's favor, that is, to God as Patron (Heb. 4:14–16). As such, the whole complex of a client's obligations to a patron enter into the picture, especially trust and loyalty ("faith"). God's benefits are to be sought above those of any human patron (e.g., the emperor or any of his agents), and loyalty to God cannot be breached for the sake of gaining the favor of some lesser patron. The Maccabean martyrs become examples of this sort of faith (as loyalty to, and trust in, the Divine Benefactor) for the audience of Hebrews (11:35; cf. 11:6), a document that comes closest to exhibiting literary dependence on 4 Maccabees.[4]

4. Hebrews echoes several verses from 4 Maccabees in content and form. In 4 Macc. 6:9, the author speaks of Eleazar thus: "But he endured the torments and despised compulsion" (ὁ δὲ ὑπέμενεν τοὺς πόνους καὶ περιεφρόνει τῆς ἀνάγκης). This bears a striking resemblance to Heb. 12:2, where Jesus, persevering in obedience to God, "endured a cross, despising shame" (ὑπέμεινεν σταυρὸν αἰσχύνης καταφρονήσας). Similarly, in 4 Macc. 17:4, the author interjects an apostrophe encouraging the mother to persevere, "holding firm toward God the hope of perseverence" (τὴν ἐλπίδα τῆς ὑπομονῆς βεβαίαν ἔχουσα πρὸς τὸν θεὸν), which bears a certain likeness in thought and vocabulary to Heb. 3:6, ἐάν[περ] τὴν παρρησίαν καὶ τὸ καύχημα τῆς ἐλπίδος κατάσχωμεν, and Heb. 3:14, ἐάνπερ τὴν ἀρχὴν τῆς ὑποστάσεως μέχρι τέλους βεβαίαν κατάσχωμεν.

Finally, the author of Hebrews gives the detail of these martyrs "refusing to accept release" from their torments (Heb. 11:35), so that they might attain the better resurrection. In 2 Maccabees, the torments of Eleazar and the brothers commence only after they refuse to obey the tyrant. Once begun, they are uninterrupted. In 4 Macc. 9:16, however, we find the guards making the offer "Agree to eat so that you may be released from the tortures," and the third brother refusing this offer and urging the torturers to do their worst. Also, Eleazar is given a brief respite between tortures in which some members of the king's retinue seek to persuade him to eat and so save himself, likewise an offer that is refused (6:12–23).

Torah as the Path to Virtue

The line of reasoning found in 4 Maccabees, that the passions and emotions that hinder righteousness and other virtues may be overcome through following a life in accordance with Torah, may also stand behind Paul's difficulties in Galatia. The last two chapters of Galatians are not a mere appendix but rather provide an important corrective, or remedy a certain deficiency, that left the Gentile Galatian Christians susceptible to Judaizing Christians. In addition to providing scriptural arguments for the necessity of circumcision and Torah observance, the rival teachers may have argued that Torah provides what was lacking in the Galatians' initial evangelization: a reliable means of making progress in virtue and the righteousness that God seeks in God's people (Barclay 1991, esp. chs. 2, 4). Thus, the Galatian believers, while making a good beginning by faith, may move on to perfection of God's work in them (righteousness) through Torah (see Gal. 3:3). Paul specifically posits the Spirit as that which overcomes "the passions of the flesh" (5:16–17) in a way that Torah cannot, contrary to his opponents' view (righteousness cannot come through the Torah [2:21]; the law cannot make alive [3:21]). While it would be too much to suggest that Paul's opponents used 4 Maccabees itself, it does seem likely that 4 Maccabees develops a line of argumentation that was taken over for Judaizing "evangelism," the specifics of which are reflected in Galatians.

Fourth Maccabees contributes greatly to our understanding of Jews in a Gentile world and for the strong need felt within that community for bolstering commitment to Torah, even while using the language of the dominant culture. Sensitivity to what is going on within the Jewish community assists our interpretation of Jewish resistance to the gospel, particularly as put into practice by Paul. Paul's gospel weakens dedication to Torah and relaxes its strict observance for the sake of demonstrating unity with the Gentile believers in the new Israel, the body of Christ. Jews had defended Torah, and its governance of Jewish-Gentile relations, with their lives in periods of high tension and were unable to permit such an affront to a primary identity marker of their community. Indeed, to many it may have seemed that Paul was just another Hellenizer seeking ways to accommodate to Gentile culture and facilitate Jewish-Gentile interaction through breach of Torah. As such, their responses to his mission are not the product of malice but of a desire to maintain the essential values of their community against the continuing erosion of Hellenization—a venture that, for them, was an act of loyalty to God. This same zeal for doing Torah as an expression of loyalty to God may also be seen to stand behind the pressure put upon Jewish Christians (by other Jewish Christians and by non-Christian Jews both) to keep Torah themselves and thus behind the situations that Paul encounters in Antioch and Galatia.

Fourth Maccabees also poses a striking contrast to Rom. 7:7–24. The Jewish orator declares that the fact that the "law says, 'You shall not covet your neighbor's wife or anything that is your neighbor's'" proves that "reason is able to control desires" (2:4–6). The commandment is seen to empower resistance to the particular sin of coveting. The very fact of the command is taken to mean that God has equipped the devout mind to overcome sinful passions and choose righteousness. Paul, however, makes a completely different claim with regard to this same commandment: he finds the command "You shall not covet" awakening the knowledge of sin and allowing the power of sin to wreak "in me all kinds of covetousness. . . . The very commandment that promised life proved to be death to me" (Rom. 7:7–10). For one author, the commandment establishes reason's domination over the passions (i.e., the victory of the will over sin); for the other, the commandment gives sin the opportunity to gain the upper hand and fails to deliver its promise of life. The text from 4 Maccabees assists us in ruling out certain interpretations of Romans 7–8, in particular the assertion that the decisive difference in the Christian life is that now sin finds resistance whereas before it exercised free rein, together with the assertion that the struggle is all that matters for one to fulfill the just requirement of the law (see Rom. 8:4). All of this is already possible in the life of the devotee of Torah apart from Christ.

Substitutionary Atonement

One final contribution of 4 Maccabees to the theological milieu of the early church is its use of the language of vicarious atonement as a metaphor for the effects of the deaths of the martyrs (de Jonge 1988). It thus represents a development of the thought of the Servant Song of Isa. 52:13–53:12 very similar to early Christian reflection on the death of Jesus such as one finds in Rom. 3:25; Heb. 1:3; 9:11–15; 1 Pet. 1:19; 1 John 1:7. Most intriguing is the linking of a martyr's absolute obedience with the efficacy of the ransom. The wrath of God is occasioned in 4 Maccabees by the transgression of (indeed the setting aside of) the covenant by the Hellenizing Jerusalem aristocracy (4:21). Disobedience leads to judgment. When Eleazar, then, remains loyal to God to the point of death (indeed, "obedient even unto death"), it is this obedience that, he hopes, will arouse God's forgiveness of the whole people, covering their sins in his righteousness:

> You know, O God, that though I might have saved myself, I am dying in burning torments for the sake of the law. Be merciful to your people, and let our punishment suffice for them. Make my blood their purification, and take my life in exchange for theirs. (6:27–29)

The term "purification" (*katharismos*) appears also in Heb. 1:3, speaking of Jesus' ministry "having made purification for sins." The author of 4 Maccabees goes on to interpret the martyrs' deaths by means of the metaphor of an efficacious sacrifice, a blood sacrifice that atones for the sins of the many, and by means of another term that becomes important for New Testament soteriology, *hilastērion:* "They became, as it were, a ransom for the sin of our nation. And through the blood of those devout ones and their death as an atoning sacrifice [*hilastērion*], divine Providence preserved Israel that previously had been mistreated" (17:21–22; cf. Rom. 3:25).

The possibility that the death of a righteous person for the sake of loyalty and obedience to God might effect atonement for the sins of the people who stand under God's wrath is, of course, developed fully in the New Testament with regard to the execution of Jesus at the hands of the Romans. Like the martyrs, his death was not a shameful death but rather one that brought benefit to many—the benefit of reconciliation with God. Reflection on Jesus' death, therefore, has more in common with the interpretation of the Maccabean martyrs' deaths than with ancient practices of human sacrifice or even the animal sacrifice of the Old Testament (although, of course, both are developments of this). It is not simply "blood" or "a death" but specifically the obedience shown in the death of the righteous person out of loyalty to God that moves God to accept and deliver God's people (see Heb. 10:4–10) (van Henten 1993: 101).

Rhetorical Context

Athletic Imagery

The athletic arena in the Hellenistic and Greco-Roman periods was a place where individuals could win great honor and fame. It was a place where courage and endurance could be exercised and demonstrated and the only such place in times of peace when the military arena was closed to seekers of repute. Participants in all manner of athletic competitions (boxing, running, wrestling, weaponry) would strain their sinews or endure painful blows in order to win recognition for their skill, prowess, or simply their ability to endure longer than an adversary.

The language of the arena quickly became an important metaphor for other sorts of demonstrations of courage and endurance. It was used in such a way as to give nobility to pursuits that the majority or dominant culture might not recognize as praiseworthy or, indeed, might ridicule or censure. Philosophers, for example, took up the metaphor in order to impress upon their hearers that the only competition worth fighting and winning was the competition for virtue and the mastery over things that detract from achieving that prize. In an oration on virtue, Dio Chrysostom (*De virtute [Oration 8]* 11–18) tells of Diogenes of Sinope, who went up to the Isthmian games near Corinth and proclaimed himself to be engaged in the one contest worth striving to win: the contest against hardships and pleasures. This was a contest undertaken not to win a mere sprig of laurel but for "happiness and virtue all of one's days." The virtuous person squares off with hardships, disclosing no weakness even though he must endure the lash or give his body to be cut or burned. Hunger, exile, loss of reputation, and the like have no terrors for him; nay, he holds them as mere trifles. . . . If we accept our hardships in a spirit of contempt for them and approach them cheerfully, they avail very little against us.

Endurance of pain and bodily assault, far from being a source of disgrace, is transformed into a noble competition for honor and victory, just as it is in the athletic arena.

This is a primary image used by the author of 4 Maccabees to describe the events in the "arena of sufferings" (11:20) in which the martyrs compete for holiness and virtue (12:14). Their endurance of torture to the point of death, without yielding to the tyrant's demands, means for them an honorable victory. Even though under the most extreme physical distress, they gain victory over the tyrant: "My sons, noble is the contest to which you are called to bear witness for the nation. Fight zealously for our ancestral law" (16:16). The author lauds the martyrs as the contestants who defeated Antiochus their antagonist before the world as spectator. "Reverence for God was victor and gave the crown to its own athletes. Who did not admire the athletes of the divine legislation? Who were not amazed?" (17:15–16).

New Testament authors also make extensive use of athletic imagery as a means of turning endurance of the unbelieving society's hostility and opposition, and single-minded pursuit of the prize of the gospel, into a noble and honorable venture, one that should give the contestants self-respect even in the face of bitter reproach and shame:

> Therefore, since we are surrounded by so great a cloud of witnesses, let us . . . run with perseverance the race that is set before us, looking to Jesus the pioneer and perfecter of faith. . . . In your contest against sin (*antagōnizomenoi*) you have not yet resisted to the point of shedding blood. (Heb. 12:1–4 [translation mine])

> Do you not know that in a race all the runners compete, but only one receives the prize? So run that you may obtain it. Every athlete exercises self-control in all things. They do it to receive a perishable wreath, but we an imperishable. Well, I do not run aimlessly, I do not box as one beating the air; but I pommel my body and subdue it. (1 Cor. 9:24–27 RSV; see also Phil. 3:12–14).

Fourth Maccabees is one of a number of Hellenistic Jewish channels for this sort of appropriation of an important metaphor. As in 4 Maccabees, so also in the New Testament a way of life that is suspect, held in contempt, and often subjected to trial and hostility is cast as a noble contest for virtue in which there are many antagonists. Victory lies, however, not in making peace with the antagonists by yielding to their blows but in enduring their hostility and persevering unto the prize that God has announced for the victors.

Military Imagery

A similar effect is achieved by the use of military language in 4 Maccabees. The martyrs are compared to soldiers who refuse to desert their post but rather hold their ground and fight (9:23–24) and to a city withstanding siege warfare (7:4). Even the mother is lauded as a "soldier of God in the cause of religion" (16:14). The battlefield is perhaps the most traditional locale for winning distinction and honor. Courage and endurance there are most extravagantly praised because the well-being of the culture most immediately depends on virtuous soldiers who hold their ground and prefer death to safety with disgrace. This image is taken up by our author in order to praise these Jews who held their ground and preferred violent death to personal safety for the sake of preserving their culture, a minority culture within the Hellenistic world. Their resistance, though to the onlooker appearing perhaps most pathetic and dishonorable, actually struck a powerful blow for the nation, conquering the tyrant through their courageous deaths (1:11; 9:30; 11:24–27; 18:4).

The model of achieving a military victory by holding out (as in the renowned case of the Spartans at Thermopylae) appears again very prominently in the Revelation to John. Looking ahead to a time in his near future when Christians would be called to choose between absolute loyalty to the One God and the Lamb and submission to the demands of the political powers, John prepares Christians to achieve victory through remaining loyal in the face of the sentence of death. Martyrdom becomes a victory over the system that has set itself against God, because the martyr does not capitulate to that system's demands. In so doing, the martyr "conquers" the adversaries of God and of his or her own soul (Rev. 12:10–11; 15:2). This model appears also in John's interpretation of the death of Jesus, for the Lamb overcomes his enemies by dying. What is in the world's eyes the shameful defeat of the cross is transformed into a mighty conquest over God's enemies (Rev. 5:5–6) and the ransoming of God's people (5:9–10), blending two central images from 4 Maccabees: death as victory and death as atoning sacrifice.

Temporary versus Eternal Advantage

A third rhetorical feature of 4 Maccabees that appears also in the rhetoric of New Testament documents is the comparison of temporary advantage versus eternal advantage. In deliberative rhetoric, two (or more) orators would present two different courses of action, each arguing for one course as the more advantageous for the audience and thus hoping to win them to that course of action. Belief in an unending afterlife led to the strategy of setting two courses available to people in this life in light of its eternal consequences. Plato portrays Socrates doing this in *Gorgias,* where Socrates urges that justice, piety, and virtue be pursued—courses of action that will be of eternal advantage even if they bring temporary disadvantage. Even though the philosopher will not be as well equipped with friends and money for defense and protection in this life, he or she will be infinitely better off in the next world than those who have occupied themselves with worldly matters to the neglect of their souls.

So also in 4 Maccabees, we find a Jewish author capitalizing on this rhetorical strategy. The brothers accept temporary disadvantage, the pain from torture and deprivation of life, in order to avoid eternal disadvantage, the dangers that accrue from betraying God (13:14–15). This theme is developed with greater effect in the encomium on the mother:

> Two courses were open to this mother, that of religion, and that of preserving her seven sons *for a time*, as the tyrant had promised. She loved religion more, the religion that preserves them for *eternal* life according to God's promise. . . . Because of the fear of God she disdained the *temporary* safety of her children. . . . She did not approve the deliverance that would preserve the seven sons *for a short time*. (15:2–3, 8, 27 [emphasis added])

This rhetorical strategy, like the use of athletic and military metaphors, makes the endurance of temporary disgrace and deprivation reasonable and noble for those enduring it, since it sets the present distress in the context of the eternal benefit and honor that will follow. Choosing release and resolution of tension with the dominant culture is no longer so attractive an option, for really it deprives one of the greater good to be gained by endurance now.

Not surprisingly, New Testament authors also found this a useful form of argumentation for the shoring up of the believers' commitment. Paul, for example, weighs his own endurance of hardship for the gospel against the eternal rewards:

> We do not lose heart. . . . For this slight momentary affliction is preparing for us an eternal weight of glory beyond all measure, because we look not at what can be seen but at what cannot be seen; for what can be seen is temporary, but what cannot be seen is eternal. (2 Cor. 4:16–18)

Paul's loss of status and esteem among the Jewish people, and his endurance of a life of wandering and shameful treatment at the hands of unbelievers, constitute a temporary disadvantage worth enduring in light of the eternal advantage he gains for his loyalty to Christ.

The author of Hebrews makes perhaps the most extensive use of such comparisons. The virtue of faith is clarified through a series of examples (cf. 4 Macc. 16:20–22), among which stands Moses, "choosing rather to share ill-treatment with the people of God than to enjoy the fleeting pleasures of sin" because he was "looking to the reward" (11:25–26). Faith weighs the eternal benefactions promised by God ("better and abiding possessions" [10:34]; "a better country, that is, a heavenly one" [11:16]; "a better resurrection" [11:35]) against the temporary advantages to be gained by separating from the people of God and conforming to the life of unbelieving society. Faith perceives the great value of the former and willingly suffers the loss of the latter in order to acquire it (see 10:34). This author is not reticent about speaking about the eternal disadvantages that befall those who show contempt for God's gifts by choosing society's approval and promises over God's (6:4–8; 10:26–31, 35–39).

Fourth Maccabees provides many useful insights into the first-century environment of early Christianity. Besides being a text that speaks powerfully of faith, loyalty, and overcoming every obstacle to responding to God in obedience, it also shines a helpful light into the theology and rhetorical strategy of the New Testament documents.

Influence

As the church went on to face ever stronger opposition from the Roman authorities, the examples of the Maccabean martyrs became increasingly important to those who now faced similar terrors for the sake of the "same faith toward God" (16:22). The literature of the Jewish martyrs became increasingly important as a resource for the church to prepare itself for the ultimate contest. One of the earliest celebrated Christian martyrs was Ignatius, the bishop of Antioch, who died sometime near 110 C.E. Since his episcopal see was within the region where 4 Maccabees probably was composed, it is quite possible that the work exercised some direct influence upon him. As he faces his own martyrdom, he considers it a "favor" and a "sweet" death, as do the martyrs in 4 Maccabees (see 9:29; 11:12) (Frend 1967: 152). Ignatius speaks of his own death as occurring on behalf of the lives of other Christians (*To the Ephesians* 21.1; *To the Smyrnaeans* 10.2; *To Polycarp* 2.3; 6.1), a concept he was more likely to borrow from martyr ideology than from Christology. The mid-second-century *Martyrdom of Polycarp* also possibly shows awareness of 4 Maccabees, particularly in the language used by the proconsul to dissuade Polycarp from persisting in a course that leads to execution (*Martyrdom of Polycarp* 9.2–3) and in Polycarp's reasons for refusing this invitation: "You threaten that fire which burns for a season and after a little while is quenched, for you are ignorant of the fire of the future judgment and eternal punishment, which is reserved for the ungodly" (*Martyrdom of Polycarp* 11.2). The consideration of temporal versus eternal advantage, as we have seen, was an important feature in the Jewish text. The martyr's death is described as a new birth (*Martyrdom of Polycarp* 18.3; Ignatius, *To the Romans* 6.1; cf. 4 Macc. 16:13); the martyr wins the prize (*Martyrdom of Polycarp* 17.1; cf. 4 Macc. 9:28; 15:29; 17:12); the reward of the martyr's witness is a "crown of immortality" (*Martyrdom of Polycarp* 17.1, 19.2; cf. 4 Macc. 17:12, 15).

As persecution sharpened and broadened, the influence of this literature becomes even more noticeable. Origen's *Exhortation to Martyrdom,* written to two deacons in Caesarea during the persecution of Christian clergy by Maximin in 235 C.E., is a homiletical retelling of the martyrdoms recounted in 2 Maccabees 6–7 and in 4 Maccabees 5–18. When Origen's language is closely observed, however, it becomes readily apparent that he is mainly influenced by the latter text, particularly in his use of athletic imagery and his focus on dying for "virtue" or "piety." The logic of the mother's speech in 4 Macc. 16:18–19, moreover, is taken up by Origen, who asserts that the virtuous recipient of God's favors looks for ways in which to repay the favor, the most perfect return being martyrdom.

Fourth Maccabees continued to enjoy popularity among Christians even after the threat of state persecution was virtually eliminated by Constantine's conversion and decrees (after which it would be heretics who faced persecution from the church). Sermons by both Gregory of Nazianzen and John Chrysostom praise these martyrs and recommend their example to the congregation, and Gregory makes it clear that he has 4 Maccabees in mind, since he refers to "the Book which philosophizes about Reason being supreme over the passions." This text, and the stories it preserved, continued to encourage Christians to fight nobly in contest for virtue against "the passions that wage war on the soul" and also continued to remind readers of the dignity that could still be enjoyed even while one's body was ravaged by persecutors and one's name cast out as evil. The person whose reason is informed by God has the wherewithal to resist any compulsion to violate the conscience or one's testimony to God's truth.

Reference List

Abegg, M., P. Flint, and E. Ulrich. 1999. *The Dead Sea Scrolls Bible.* San Francisco: HarperSanFrancisco.

Abel, F.-M. 1949. *Les livres des Maccabées.* Paris: Gabalda.

Ackroyd, P. R., and C. F. Evans, eds. 1970. *The Cambridge History of the Bible.* Vol. 1, *From the Beginnings to Jerome.* Cambridge: Cambridge University Press.

Anderson, G. W. 1970. "Canonical and Non-canonical." Pp. 113–59 in Ackroyd and Evans, eds., 1970.

Anderson, H. 1985a. "3 Maccabees (First Century B.C.): A New Translation and Introduction." Pp. 509–29 in Charlesworth, ed., 1985.

———. 1985b. "4 Maccabees (First Century A.D.): A New Translation and Introduction." Pp. 531–64 in Charlesworth, ed., 1985.

Attridge, H. W. 1986. "Jewish Historiography." Pp. 311–44 in Kraft and Nickelsburg, eds., 1986.

Baars, W. 1972. "Apocryphal Psalms." Vol. 4.6 of *The Old Testament in Syriac according to the Peshitta.* Leiden: Brill.

Bailey, J. W. 1934. "The Temporary Messianic Reign in the Literature of Early Judaism." *JBL* 53: 170–87.

Bailey, K. E. 1972. "Women in Ben Sirach and in the New Testament." Pp. 56–73 in *For Me to Live: Essays in Honor of James Leon Kelso,* edited by R. A. Coughenour. Cleveland: Dillon/Liederbach.

Ball, C. J. 1888. "Judith." Pp. 241–360 in Wace, ed., 1888, vol. 1.

———. 1913. "The Epistle of Jeremy." Pp. 599–611 in Charles, ed., 1913, vol. 1.

Bar-Kochva, B. 1989. *Judas Maccabeus: The Jewish Struggle against the Seleucids.* Cambridge: Cambridge University Press.

Barclay, J. M. G. 1991. *Obeying the Truth: Paul's Ethics in Galatia.* Minneapolis: Fortress.

———. 1996. *Jews in the Mediterranean Diaspora from Alexander to Trajan (323 B.C.E.—117 C.E.).* Edinburgh: Clark.

Bartlett, J. R. 1998. *1 Maccabees.* Sheffield: Sheffield Academic Press.

Beckwith, R. 1985. *The Old Testament Canon of the New Testament Church and Its Background in Early Judaism.* Grand Rapids: Eerdmans.

Beentjes, P. C. 1997. *The Book of Ben Sira in Hebrew.* Leiden: Brill.

Bennett, W. H. 1913. "Prayer of Azariah and Song of the Three Children." Pp. 625–37 in Charles, ed., 1913, vol. 1.

Bensly, R. L. 1895. *The Fourth Book of Ezra.* Texts and Studies 3.2. Cambridge: Cambridge University Press.

Berger, P. L. 1967. *The Sacred Canopy: Elements of a Sociological Theory of Religion.* Garden City, N.Y.: Doubleday.

Bergren, T. A. 1990. *Fifth Ezra: Text, Origin, and Early History.* Atlanta: Scholars Press.

Bickerman, E. J. 1933. "Ein jüdischer Festbrief vom Jahre 124 v. Chr. (2 Makk 1, 1–9)." *Zeitschrift für die neutestamentliche Wissenschaft und die Kunde der älteren Kirche* 32: 233–53.

———. 1944. "The Colophon of the Greek Book of Esther." *JBL* 63: 339–62.

———. 1950. "Notes on the Greek Book of Esther." *Proceedings of the American Academy of Jewish Research* 20: 101–33.

———. 1976. *Studies in Jewish and Christian History.* Arbeiten zur Geschichte des antiken Judentums und des Urchristentums 9. Leiden: Brill.

———. 1979. *The God of the Maccabees: Studies on the Meaning and Origin of the Maccabean Revolt.* Translated by H. R. Moehring. Studies in Judaism in Late Antiquity 32. Leiden: Brill.

Bissell, E. C. 1899. *The Apocrypha of the Old Testament.* New York: Scribner.

Blenkinsopp, J. 1995. *Wisdom and Law in the Old Testament.* Oxford: Oxford University Press.

Boccaccini, G. 1991. *Middle Judaism: Jewish Thought 300 B.C.E. to 200 C.E.* Minneapolis: Fortress.

Boitani, P. 1996. "Susanna in Excelsis." Pp. 7–19 in Spolsky, ed. 1996.

Bow, B., and G. W. E. Nickelsburg. 1993. "Patriarchy with a Twist: Men and Women in Tobit." Pp. 127–43 in *"Women Like This": New Perspectives on Jewish Women in the Greco-Roman World,* edited by A.-J. Levine. Atlanta: Scholars Press.

Box, G. H. 1913. "4 Ezra." Pp. 542–624 in Charles, ed., 1913, vol. 2.

———. 1917. *The Apocalypse of Ezra.* London: SPCK.

Box, G. H., and W. O. E. Oesterley. 1913. "The Book of Sirach." Pp. 268–517 in Charles, ed., 1913, vol. 1.

Breech, E. 1973. "These Fragments I Have Shored against My Ruins: The Form and Function of 4 Ezra." *JBL* 92: 267–74.

Brownlee, W. H. 1966. "Le livre grec d'Esther et la royauté divine." *Revue biblique* 73: 161–85.

Brüll, N. 1877. "Das apokryphische Susanna Buch." *Jahrbuch für jüdische Geschichte und Literatur* 3: 1–69.

———. 1887. "Die Geschichte von Bel und dem Drachen." *Jahrbuch für jüdische Geschichte und Literatur* 8: 28–29.

Burke, D. G. 1982. *The Poetry of Baruch: A Reconstruction and Analysis of the Original Hebrew Text of Baruch 3:9–5:9.* Chico, Calif.: Scholars Press.

Callaway, M. C. 1997. "The Apocrypha/Deuterocanonical Books: An Anglican/Episcopal View." Pp. xxxv–xxxix in Kohlenberger, ed., 1997.

Camp, C. V. 1991. "Understanding a Patriarchy: Women in Second-Century Jerusalem through the Eyes of Ben-Sira." Pp. 1–39 in *"Women Like This": New Perspectives on Jewish Women,* edited by A.-J. Levine. Atlanta: Scholars Press.

Caponigro, M. S. 1992. "Judith, Holding the Tale of Herodotus." Pp. 47–60 in VanderKam, ed., 1992.

Carson, D. A. 1997. "The Apocrypha/Deuterocanonicals: An Evangelical View." Pp. xliv–xlvii in Kohlenberger, ed., 1997.

Charles, R. H., ed. 1913. *The Apocrypha and Pseudepigrapha of the Old Testament in English.* 2 vols. Oxford: Oxford University Press.

Charlesworth, J. H. 1985. "The Prayer of Manasseh (Second Century B.C.–First Century A.D.): A New Translation and Introduction." Pp. 625–38 in Charlesworth, ed., 1985.

———, ed. 1983. *The Old Testament Pseudepigrapha.* Vol. 1, *Apocalyptic Literature & Testaments.* Garden City, N.Y.: Doubleday.

———, ed. 1985. *The Old Testament Pseudepigrapha.* Vol. 2, *Expansions of the "Old Testament" and Legends, Wisdom and Philosophical Literature, Prayers, Psalms and Odes, Fragments of Lost Judeo-Hellenistic Works.* Garden City, N.Y.: Doubleday.

Charlesworth, J. H., and J. A. Sanders. 1985. "More Psalms of David (Second Century B.C.–First Century A.D.): A New Translation and Introduction." Pp. 609–15 in Charlesworth, ed., 1985.

Cheon, S. 1997. *The Exodus Story in the Wisdom of Solomon: A Study in Biblical Interpretation.* Sheffield: Sheffield Academic Press.

Chroust, A. H. 1964. *Aristotle: Protrepticus. A Reconstruction.* South Bend, Ind.: University of Notre Dame Press.

Clarke, E. G. 1973. *The Wisdom of Solomon.* Cambridge: Cambridge University Press.

Clines, D. J. A. 1984. *The Esther Scroll: The Story of the Story.* Journal for the Study of the Old Testament: Supplement Series 30. Sheffield: JSOT Press.

Coggins, R. J. 1998. *Sirach.* Sheffield: Sheffield Academic Press.

Coggins, R. J., and M. A. Knibb. 1979. *The First and Second Books of Esdras.* Cambridge: Cambridge University Press.

Cohen, S. J. D. 1987. *From the Maccabees to the Mishnah.* Philadelphia: Westminster.

Collins, J. J. 1984. "Apocalyptic Literature." Pp. 383–442 in Stone, ed., 1984.

———. 1986. "Apocalyptic Literature." Pp. 345–70 in Kraft and Nickelsburg, eds., 1986.

———. 1987. *The Apocalyptic Imagination: An Introduction to the Jewish Matrix of Christianity.* New York: Crossroad.

———. 1993. *Daniel.* Hermeneia. Minneapolis: Fortress.

———. 1997a. "The Apocryphal/Deuterocanonical Books: A Catholic View." Pp. xxxi–xxxiv in Kohlenberger, ed., 1997.

———. 1997b. *Jewish Wisdom in the Hellenistic Age.* Louisville: Westminster/John Knox.

———. 2000. *Between Athens and Jerusalem: Jewish Identity in the Hellenistic Diaspora.* 2nd ed. Grand Rapids: Eerdmans.

Constantelos, D. 1997. "The Apocryphal/Deuterocanonical Books: An Orthodox View." Pp. xxvii–xxx in Kohlenberger, ed., 1997.

Coogan, M. D., ed. 1998. *The Oxford History of the Biblical World.* Oxford: Oxford University Press.

Cook, H. J. 1969. "The A-Text of the Greek Versions of the Book of Esther." *Zeitschrift für die alttestamentliche Wissenschaft* 81: 369–76.

Cook, S. A. 1913. "I Esdras." Pp. 1–58 in Charles, ed., 1913, vol. 1.

Cowley, A. E. 1913. "The Book of Judith." Pp. 242–67 in Charles, ed., 1913, vol. 1.

Craven, T. 1983. *Artistry and Faith in the Book of Judith.* Chico, Calif.: Scholars Press.

Crenshaw, J. L. 1975. "The Problem of Theodicy in Sirach: On Human Bondage." *JBL* 94: 47–64.

———. 1981. *Old Testament Wisdom.* Atlanta: John Knox.

Dagut, M. J. 1953. "2 Maccabees and the Death of Antiochus IV Epiphanes." *JBL* 72: 149–57.

Davies, T. Witton. 1913. "Bel and the Dragon." Pp. 652–64 in Charles, ed., 1913, vol. 1.

Davies, W. D., and L. Finkelstein, eds. 1984. *The Cambridge History of Judaism.* Vol. 1, *The Persian Period.* Cambridge: Cambridge University Press.

———, eds. 1989. *The Cambridge History of Judaism.* Vol. 2, *The Hellenistic Period.* Cambridge: Cambridge University Press.

de Jonge, M. 1988. "Jesus' Death for Others and the Death of the Maccabean Martyrs." Pp. 142–51 in *Text and Testimony: Essays on New Testament and Apocryphal Literature in Honor of A. F. J. Klijn,* edited by T. Baarda et al. Kampen, Netherlands: Kok.

de Lange, N. 1978. *Apocrypha: Jewish Literature of the Hellenistic Age.* New York: Viking Press.

Delcor, M. 1971. *Le livre de Daniel.* Paris: Gabalda.

———. 1989. "The Apocrypha and Pseudepigrapha of the Hellenistic Period." Pp. 409–503 in Davies and Finkelstein, eds., 1989.

Deselaers, P. 1982. *Das Buch Tobit: Stuiden zu seiner Entstehung, Komposition, und Theologie.* Göttingen: Vandenhoeck & Ruprecht.

deSilva, D. A. 1992. "The Revelation to John: A Case Study in Apocalyptic Propaganda and the Maintenance of Sectarian Identity." *Sociological Analysis* 53: 375–95.

———. 1993. "The Construction and Social Function of a Counter-Cosmos in the Revelation of John." *Forum* 9: 47–61.

———. 1995. *Despising Shame: Honor Discourse and Community Maintenance in the Epistle to the Hebrews.* Society of Biblical Literature Dissertation Series 152. Atlanta: Scholars Press.

———. 1996. "The Wisdom of Ben Sira: Honor, Shame, and the Maintenance of the Values of a Minority Culture." *CBQ* 58: 433–55.

———. 1998. *4 Maccabees.* Sheffield: Sheffield Academic Press.

———. 1999. "Fourth Ezra: Reaffirming Jewish Cultural Values through Apocalyptic Rhetoric." Pp. 123–39 in *Vision and Persuasion: Rhetorical Dimensions of Apocalyptic Discourse,* edited by G. Carey and L. G. Bloomquist. St. Louis: Chalice Press.

———. 2000a. *Perseverance in Gratitude: A Socio-Rhetorical Commentary on the Epistle "to the Hebrews."* Grand Rapids: Eerdmans.

———. 2000b. *Honor, Patronage, Kinship, and Purity: Unlocking New Testament Culture.* Downers Grove, Ill.: InterVarsity Press.

———. 2000c. "Why Did God Choose Abraham?" *Bible Review* 16: 16–21, 42–44.

Di Lella, A. A. 1966a. *The Hebrew Text of Sirach: A Text-Critical and Historical Study.* The Hague: Mouton.

———. 1966b. "Conservative and Progressive Theology: Sirach and Wisdom." *CBQ* 28: 139–54.

———. 1979. "The Deuteronomistic Background of the Farewell Discourse in Tob 14:3–11." *CBQ* 51: 380–89.

———. 1992. "Wisdom of Ben-Sira." Pp. 931–45 in Freedman, ed., 1992, vol. 6.

————. 1995. "Women in the Wisdom of Ben Sira and the Book of Judith: A Study in Contrasts and Reversals." Pp. 39–52 in *Congress Volume: Paris 1992,* edited by J. A. Emerton. Vetus Testamentum Supplements 61. Leiden: Brill.

————. 1996. "The Wisdom of Ben Sira: Resources and Recent Research." *Currents and Trends in Research* 4: 161–81.

Doran, R. 1980. "The Martyr: A Synoptic View of the Mother and Her Seven Sons." Pp. 189–222 in *Ideal Figures in Ancient Judaism,* edited by J. J. Collins and G. W. E. Nickelsburg. Chico, Calif.: Scholars Press.

————. 1981. *Temple Propaganda: The Purpose and Character of 2 Maccabees.* Catholic Biblical Quarterly Monograph Series 12. Washington, D.C.: Catholic Biblical Association.

Downing, J. 1963. "Jesus and Martyrdom." *JTS* 14: 279–93.

Dubarle, A. M. 1966. *Judith: Formes et sens des diverses traditions.* 2 vols. Analecta biblica 24. Rome: Pontifical Biblical Institute.

du Boylay, J. 1976. "Lies, Mockery, and Family Integrity." Pp. 389–406 in *Mediterranean Family Structures,* edited by J. G. Peristiany. Cambridge: Cambridge University Press.

Duesberg, H., and P. Auvray. 1958. *Le livre de L'Ecclésiastique.* Paris: Cerf.

Dupont-Sommer, A. 1935. "Les impies du livre de la Sagesse sont-ils des Épicuriens?" *Revue de l'histoire des religions* 111: 90–112.

————. 1939. *Le quatrième livre des Machabées.* Paris: Champion.

Eissfeldt, O. 1964. *The Old Testament: An Introduction.* Translated by P. R. Ackroyd. New York: Harper & Row.

Emmet, C. W. 1913. "The Third Book of Maccabees." Pp. 155–73 in Charles, ed., 1913, vol. 1.

Enns, P. 1997. *Exodus Retold.* Atlanta: Scholars Press.

Enslin, M., and S. Zeitlin. 1972. *The Book of Judith.* Leiden: Brill.

Eron, L. J. 1991. "'That Women Have Mastery over Both King and Beggar' (T. Jud. 15.5)—The Relationship of the Fear of Sexuality to the Status of Women in the Apocrypha and Pseudepigrapha: 1 Esdras (3 Ezra), Ben Sira, and the Testament of Judah." *Journal for the Study of the Pseudepigrapha* 9: 43–66.

Esler, P. F. 1994. "The Social Function of 4 Ezra." *Journal for the Study of the New Testament* 53: 99–123.

Evans, C. A., and S. E. Porter, eds. 2000. *Dictionary of New Testament Background.* Downers Grove, Ill.: InterVarsity Press.

Evans, C. D. 1992. "Manasseh, King of Judah." Pp. 496–99 in Freedman, ed., 1992, vol. 6.

Feldman, L. H. 1986. "How Much Hellenism in Jewish Palestine?" *Hebrew Union College Annual* 57: 83–111.

Feldman, L. H., and M. Reinhold, eds. 1996. *Jewish Life and Thought among Greeks and Romans.* Minneapolis: Fortress.

Fischer, T. 1992. "Maccabees, Books of." Pp. 439–50 in Freedman, ed., 1992, vol. 4.

Fitzmyer, J. A. 1995a. "The Aramaic and Hebrew Fragments of Tobit from Cave 4." *CBQ* 57: 655–75.

————. 1995b. *Tobit.* Discoveries in the Judean Desert 19. Oxford: Oxford University Press.

Freedman, D. N., ed. 1992. *The Anchor Bible Dictionary.* 6 vols. Garden City, N.Y.: Doubleday.

Frend, W. H. C. 1967. *Martyrdom and Persecution in the Early Church: A Study of Conflict from the Maccabees to Donatus.* New York: New York University Press.

Gabba, E. 1989. "The Growth of Anti-Judaism or the Greek Attitude towards the Jews." Pp. 614–56 in Davies and Finkelstein, eds., 1989.

Gardner, A. E. 1984. "The Relationship of the Additions to the Book of Esther to the Maccabean Crisis." *JSJ* 15: 1–8.

Gaster, M. 1894–95. "The Unknown Aramaic Original of Theodotion's Additions to the Book of Daniel." *Proceedings of the Society for Biblical Archaeology* 16: 280–90, 312–17; 17: 75–94.

Gerould, G. H. 1950. "The Words of Ahiqar." Pp. 427–30 in Pritchard, ed., 1950.

Gilbert, M. 1973. *La critique des dieux dans le livre de Sagesse (Sg 13–15).* Analecta biblica 53. Rome: Biblical Institute Press.

———. 1984. "Wisdom Literature." Pp. 301–13 in Stone, ed., 1984.

Glasson, T. F. 1959. "The Main Source of Tobit." *Zeitschrift für die alttestamentliche Wissenschaft* 71: 275–77.

Goldstein, J. 1984. "The Origins of the Doctrine of Creation Ex Nihilo." *Journal of Jewish Studies* 35: 127–35.

———. 1987. "Creation Ex Nihilo: Recantations and Restatements." *Journal of Jewish Studies* 38: 187–94.

Goldstein, J. A. 1976. *I Maccabees.* AB 41. Garden City, N.Y.: Doubleday.

———. 1983. *II Maccabees.* AB 41A. Garden City, N.Y.: Doubleday.

Goodman, W. R. 1992. "Esdras, First Book of." Pp. 609–11 in Freedman, ed., 1992, vol. 2.

Grabbe, L. L. 1991. "Maccabean Chronology: 167–164 or 168–165 B.C.E." *JBL* 110: 59–74.

———. 1992. *Judaism from Cyrus to Hadrian.* Vol. 1, *The Persian and Greek Periods.* Vol. 2, *The Roman Period.* Minneapolis: Fortress.

———. 1997. *Wisdom of Solomon.* Sheffield: Sheffield Academic Press.

———. 2000. "Jewish History: Roman Period." Pp. 576–80 in Evans and Porter, eds., 2000.

Grant, R. M. 1967. *After the New Testament.* Philadelphia: Fortress.

Green, P. 1990. *Alexander to Actium: The Hellenistic Age.* London: Thames and Hudson.

Gregg, J. A. F. 1913. "The Additions to Esther." Pp. 665–84 in Charles, ed., 1913, vol. 1.

Grelot, P. 1966. "Les versions grecques de Daniel." *Bib* 47: 381–402.

Grimm, C. L. W. 1857. "Das zweite, dritte und vierte Buch der Maccabäer." Pp. 283–370 in *Kurzgefasstes exegetisches Handbuch zu den Apokryphen des Alten Testaments,* edited by O. Fritzsche. Part 4. Leipzig: Weidmann.

———. 1860. *Das Buch der Weisheit.* Leipzig: Hirzel.

Habicht, C. 1976a. *2 Makkabäerbuch.* JSHRZ 1.3. Gütersloh: Mohn.

———. 1976b. "Royal Documents in II Maccabees." *Harvard Studies in Classical Philology* 80: 1–18.

Hadas, M. 1953. *The Third and Fourth Books of Maccabees.* New York: Harper.

———. 1959. *Hellenistic Culture: Fusion and Diffusion.* New York and London: W. W. Norton & Co.

Hallo, W. W., ed. 1997. *The Context of Scripture: Canonical Compositions from the Biblical World.* Vol. 1. Leiden: Brill.

Halpern-Amaru, B. 1996. "The Journey of Susanna among the Church Fathers." Pp. 22–41 in Spolsky, ed., 1996.

Hanhart, R. 1959. *Maccabaeorum liber II.* Septuaginta 9.2. Göttingen: Vandenhoeck & Ruprecht.

———. 1966. *Esther.* Septuaginta 3. Göttingen: Vandenhoeck & Ruprecht.

———. 1974. *Esdrae liber I.* Septuaginta 8.1. Gottingen: Vandenhoeck & Ruprecht.

———. 1979a. *Iudith.* Septuaginta 8.4. Göttingen: Vandenhoeck & Ruprecht.

———. 1979b. *Text und Textgeschichte des Buches Judith.* Göttingen: Vandenhoeck & Ruprecht.

———. 1983. *Tobit.* Septuaginta 8.5. Göttingen: Vandenhoeck & Ruprecht.

———. 1984. *Text und Textgeschichte des Buches Tobit.* Göttingen: Vandenhoeck & Ruprecht.

Harrington, D. J. 1988. *The Maccabean Revolt: Anatomy of a Biblical Revolution.* Wilmington, Del.: Michael Glazier.

———. 1994. "Sirach Research since 1965: Progress and Questions." Pp. 164–76 in *Pursuing the Text: Studies in Honour of Ben Zion Wacholder on the Occasion of His Seventieth Birthday,* edited by J. C. Reeves and J. Kampden. Journal for the Study of the Old Testament: Supplement Series 184. Sheffield: Sheffield Academic Press.

———. 1999. *Invitation to the Apocrypha.* Grand Rapids: Eerdmans.

Harris, R. 1915–16. "A Quotation from Judith in the Pauline Epistles." *Expository Times* 27: 13–15.

Harrison, R. 1994. "Hellenization in Syria-Palestine: The Case of Judea in the Third Century B.C.E." *Biblical Archaeologist* 57: 98–110.

Hartman, L. F., and A. A. Di Lella. 1978. *The Book of Daniel.* AB 23. Garden City, N.Y.: Doubleday.

Harwell, R. R. 1915. "The Principal Versions of Baruch." Ph.D. diss., Yale University.

Hayes, J. H., and S. R. Mandell 1998. *The Jewish People in Classical Antiquity: From Alexander to Bar Kochba.* Louisville: Westminster/John Knox.

Hengel, M. 1974. *Judaism and Hellenism.* 2 vols. Philadelphia: Fortress.

———. 1980. *Jews, Greeks, and Barbarians.* Philadelphia: Fortress.

Holmes, S. 1913. "The Wisdom of Solomon." Pp. 518–68 in Charles, ed., 1913, vol. 1.

Howorth, H. H. 1901–2. "Some Unconventional Views on the Text of the Bible." *Proceedings of the Society of Biblical Archaeology* 23: 147–49, 305–25; 24: 147–72, 332–40.

Jacob, B. 1890. "Das Buch Esther bei dem LXX." *Zeitschrift für die alttestamentliche Wissenschaft* 10: 241-98.

Jansen, H. L. 1937. "La composition du Chant de Judith." *Acta orientalia* 15: 63–71.

Jeffrey, D. L. 1996. "False Witness and the Just Use of Evidence in the Wycliffite Pistel of Swete Susan." Pp. 57–72 in Spolsky, ed., 1996.

Jobes, K. H., and M. Silva. 2000. *Invitation to the Septuagint.* Grand Rapids: Baker.

Julius, C. 1903. "Die griechischen Danielzusätze und ihre kanonische Geltung." Biblische Studien (Frieburg, 1895–). 6: 1–183.

Kabisch, R. 1889. *Das vierte Buch Esra auf seine Quellen untersucht.* Göttingen: Vandenhoeck & Ruprecht.

Kaplan, M. L. 1996. "Sexual Slander and the Politics of the Erotic in Gartner's Susanna." Pp. 73–84 in Spolsky, ed., 1996.

Kappler, W. 1967. *Maccabaeorum liber I.* Septuaginta 9.1. Göttingen: Vandenhoeck & Ruprecht.

Kay, D. M. 1913. "Susanna." Pp. 638–51 in Charles, ed., 1913, vol. 1.

Klauck, H.-J. 1989. *4 Makkabäerbuch. JSHRZ* 3.6. Gütersloh: Mohn.

Kloppenberg, J. S. 1982. "Isis and Sophia in the Book of Wisdom." *Harvard Theological Review* 75: 57–84.

Knibb, M. A. 1982. "Apocalyptic and Wisdom in 4 Ezra." *JSJ* 13: 56–74.

Kohlenberger, J. R., III, ed. 1997. *The Parallel Apocrypha.* New York: Oxford University Press.

Kolenkow, A. B., and J. J. Collins. 1986. "Testaments." Pp. 259–86 in Kraft and Nickelsburg, eds., 1986.

Kraft, R. A., and G. W. E. Nickelsburg, eds. 1986. *Early Judaism and Its Modern Interpreters.* Philadelphia: Fortress; Atlanta: Scholars Press.

Kuhl, C. 1930. *Die drei Männer im Feure. Beihefte zur Zeitschrift für die alttestamentliche Wissenschaft* 55. Giessen: Töpelmann.

Larcher, C. 1969. *Études sur le livre de la Sagesse.* Paris: Gabalda.

Lebram, J. C. H. 1974. "Die literarische Form des vierten Makkabäerbuches." *Vigiliae christianae* 28: 81–96.

Lee, G. M. 1968. "Apocryphal Cats: Baruch 6:21." *Vetus Testamentum* 18:488–93.

Lee, T. R. 1986. *Studies in the Form of Sirach 44–50.* Society of Biblical Literature Dissertation Series 75. Atlanta: Scholars Press.

Lehmann, M. R. 1961. "'Yom Kippur' in Qumran (and Ben Sira)." *Revue de Qumran* 3: 117–24.

Leon, H. J. [1960] 1995. *The Jews of Ancient Rome.* Rev. ed. Peabody, Mass.: Hendrickson.

Lévi, I. 1933. "L'histoire de 'Suzanne et les deux vieillards' dans la littérature juïve." *Revue des études juives* 95: 157–71.

Levine, A.-J. 1991. "Tobit: Teaching Jews How to Live in the Diaspora." *Bible Review* 8: 42–51, 64.

———. 1992. "Sacrifice and Salvation: Otherness and Domestication in the Book of Judith." Pp. 17–30 in VanderKam, ed., 1992.

———. 1998. "Visions of Kingdoms: From Pompey to the First Jewish Revolt." Pp. 467–516 in Coogan, ed., 1998.

Levison, J. 1985. "Is Eve to Blame? A Contextual Analysis of Sirach 25:24." *CBQ* 47: 617–23.

Lindenberger, J. M. 1985. "Ahiqar (Seventh to Sixth Century B.C.): A New Translation and Introduction." Pp. 479–507 in Charlesworth, ed., 1985.

Longenecker, B. W. 1991. *Eschatology and the Covenant: A Comparison of 4 Ezra and Romans 1–11.* Sheffield: JSOT Press.

———. 1995. *2 Esdras.* Sheffield: Sheffield Academic Press.

Mack, B. L. 1973. *Logos und Sophia.* Göttingen: Vandenhoeck & Ruprecht.

———. 1985. *Wisdom and the Hebrew Epic: Ben Sira's Hymn in Praise of the Fathers.* Chicago: University of Chicago Press.

———. 1989. "Sirach." Pp. 65–86 in *The Apocrypha and the New Testament,* vol. 2 of *The Books of the Bible,* edited by B. W. Anderson. New York: Scribner.

MacKenzie, R. A. F. 1983. *Sirach.* Wilmington, Del.: Michael Glazier.

Mantel, H. 1976. "Hsydwt Qdwmh [Ancient Hasidim]." *Studies in Judaism* 60–80.

Martin, R. A. 1975. "Syntax Criticism of the LXX Additions to the Book of Esther." *JBL* 94: 65–72.

Mendels, D. 1992. "Jeremiah, Epistle of." Pp. 721–22 in Freedman, ed., 1992, vol. 3.

Metzger, B. M. 1957. *An Introduction to the Apocrypha.* Oxford: Oxford University Press.

Metzger, B. M., and Roland Murphy, eds. 1991. *The New Oxford Annotated Apocrypha.* New York: Oxford University Press.

Meurer, S., ed. 1991. *The Apocrypha in Ecumenical Perspective.* Translated by Paul Ellingworth. United Bible Societies Monograph Series 6. New York: United Bible Societies.

Middendorp, T. 1973. *Die Stellung Jesus ben Siras zwischen Judentum und Hellenismus.* Leiden: Brill.

Modrzejewski, J. M. 1995. *The Jews of Egypt from Ramses II to Emperor Hadrian.* Philadelphia: Jewish Publication Society.

Moffatt, J. 1913. "2 Maccabees." Pp. 125–54 in Charles, ed., 1913, vol. 1.

Momigliano, A. 1982. "Biblical Studies and Classical Studies: Simple Reflections about Historical Method." *Biblical Archaeologist* 45: 224–28.

Montgomery, J. A. 1927. *A Critical and Exegetical Commentary on the Book of Daniel.* International Critical Commentary. New York: Scribner.

Montley, P. 1978. "Judith in the Fine Arts: The Appeal of the Archetypal Androgyne." *Anima* 4: 37–42.

Moore, C. A. 1967. "A Greek Witness to a Different Hebrew Text of Esther." *Zeitschrift für die alttestamentliche Wissenschaft* 79: 351–58.

———. 1973. "On the Origins of the LXX Additions to Esther." *JBL* 92: 382–93.

———. 1977. *Daniel, Esther, and Jeremiah: The Additions.* AB 44. Garden City, N.Y.: Doubleday.

———. 1982. "Prolegomenon." Pp. xix–xcix in *Studies in the Book of Esther,* edited by C. A. Moore. New York: Ktav Publishing House.

———. 1985. *Judith.* AB 40. Garden City, N.Y.: Doubleday.

———. 1989. "Scholarly Issues in the Book of Tobit Before Qumran and After: An Assessment." *Journal for the Study of the Pseudepigrapha* 5: 65–81.

———. 1992a. "Why Wasn't the Book of Judith Included in the Hebrew Bible?" Pp. 61–72 in VanderKam, ed., 1992.

———. 1992b. "Esther, Additions to." Pp. 626–33 in Freedman, ed., 1992, vol. 2.

———. 1992c. "Jeremiah, Additions to." Pp. 698–706 in Freedman, ed., 1992, vol. 3.

———. 1992d. "Daniel, Additions to." Pp. 18–28 in Freedman, ed., 1992, vol. 2.

———. 1992e. "Judith, Book of." Pp. 1117–25 in Freedman, ed., 1992, vol. 3.

———. 1996. *Tobit.* AB 40A. Garden City, N.Y.: Doubleday.

Mueller, J. R. 1981. "A Prologemenon to the Study of the Social Function of 4 Ezra." Pp. 259–68 in *Society of Biblical Literature 1981 Seminar Papers,* edited by K. H. Richards. Chico, Calif.: Scholars Press.

Murphy-O'Connor, J. 1976. "Demetrius I and the Teacher of Righteousness (1 Macc. x.25–45)." *Revue biblique* 83: 400–420.

Myers, J. M. 1974. *I and II Esdras.* AB 42. Garden City, N.Y.: Doubleday.

Nestle, E. 1899. "Zum Buche Tobias." Pp. 22–35 in *Septuagintastudien,* vol. 3. Stuttgart: Maulbronn.

Neuhaus, G. O. 1974. "Quellen im 1. Makkabäerbuch?" *JSJ* 5: 162–75.

Neusner, J. 1984. "Judaism beyond Catastrophe: The Destruction of the Temple and the Renaissance of Torah." Pp. 89–99 in *Judaism in the Beginning of Christianity*, edited by J. Neusner. London: SPCK.

Neyrey, J. H. 1993. "Deception." Pp. 38–42 in *Biblical Social Values and Their Meanings*, edited by J. J. Pilch and B. J. Malina. Peabody, Mass.: Hendrickson.

Nickelsburg, G. W. E. 1972. *Resurrection, Immortality, and Eternal Life in Intertestamental Judaism*. Cambridge: Harvard University Press.

—. 1984. "Stories of Biblical and Early Post-biblical Times" and "The Bible Rewritten and Expanded." Pp. 33–156 in Stone, ed., 1984.

Oesterley, W. O. E. 1913. "1 Maccabees." Pp. 59–124 in Charles, ed., 1913, vol. 1.

—. 1935. *An Introduction to the Books of the Apocrypha*. London: SPCK.

Oikonomos, E. 1991. "The Significance of the Deuterocanonical Writings in the Orthodox Church." Pp. 16–32 in Meurer, ed., 1991.

Orlinsky, H. L. 1974. "The Canonization of the Hebrew Bible and the Exclusion of the Apocrypha." Pp. 227–84 in *Essays in Biblical Culture and Bible Translation*. New York: Ktav Publishing House.

O'Fearghail, F. 1978. "Sir 50,5–21: Yom Kippur or the Daily Whole-Offering?" *Bib* 59: 301–16.

Parente, F. 1988. "The Third Book of Maccabees as Ideological Document and Historical Source." *Henoch* 10: 143–82.

Paton, L. 1908. *A Critical and Exegetical Commentary on the Book of Esther*. International Critical Commentary. New York: Scribner.

Perry, B. E. 1967. *The Ancient Romances: A Literary-Historical Account of Their Origins*. Berkeley: University of California Press.

Petrie, W. M. F. 1909. *Personal Religion in Egypt before Christianity*. London and New York: Harper & Brothers.

Pfeiffer, R. H. 1949. *History of New Testament Times, with an Introduction to the Apocrypha*. New York: Harper & Brothers.

Pigué, S. 1992. "Psalms, Syriac [Apocryphal]." Pp. 536–37 in Freedman, ed., 1992, vol. 6.

Pilch, J. J. 1992. "Lying and Deceit in the Letters to the Seven Churches: Perspectives from Cultural Anthropology." *Biblical Theology Bulletin* 22: 126–35.

Pitt-Rivers, J. 1966. "Honour and Social Status." Pp. 21–77 in *Honour and Shame: The Values of Mediterranean Society*, edited by J. G. Peristiany. Chicago: University of Chicago Press.

Pohlmann, K. F. 1980. *3. Esra-Buch. JSHRZ* 1.5. Gütersloh: Mohn.

Pritchard, J. B., ed. 1950. *Ancient Near Eastern Texts Relating to the Old Testament*. Princeton: Princeton University Press.

Purdie, E. 1927. *The Story of Judith in German and English Literature*. Paris: Champion.

Purinton, C. E. 1928. "Translation Greek in the Wisdom of Solomon." *JBL* 47: 276–304.

Rahlfs, A. [1935] 1979. *Septuaginta*. Stuttgart: Deutsche Bibelgesellschaft.

Reese, J. M. 1965. "Plan and Structure in the Book of Wisdom." *CBQ* 27: 391–99.

—. 1970. *Hellenistic Influence on the Book of Wisdom and Its Consequences*. Rome: Biblical Institute Press.

———. 1993. "Wisdom of Solomon." Pp. 803–5 in *The Oxford Companion to the Bible,* edited by B. M. Metzger and M. D. Coogan. Oxford: Oxford University Press.

Reider, J. 1957. *The Book of Wisdom.* New York: Harper & Brothers.

Renehan, R. 1972. "The Greek Philosophic Background of Fourth Maccabees." *Rheinisches Museum für Philologie* 115: 223–38.

Ringgren, H. 1947. *Words and Wisdom.* Lund: Ohlsson.

Roiron, F. X. 1916. "Les parties deutérocanoniques du livre d'Esther." *Recherches de science religieuse* 6: 3–16.

Roitman, A. D. 1992. "Achior in the Book of Judith: His Role and Significance." Pp. 31–46 in VanderKam, ed., 1992.

Roth, C. 1952. "Ecclesiasticus in the Synagogue Service." *JBL* 71: 171–78.

Roth, W. 1975. "For Life, He Appeals to Death (Wisd 13:18): A Study of Old Testament Idol Parodies." *CBQ* 37: 21–47.

———. 1980. "On the Gnomic-Discursive Wisdom of Jesus Ben Sirach." Pp. 59–79 in *Gnomic Wisdom,* edited by J. D. Crossan. *Semeia* 17. Chico, Calif.: Society of Biblical Literature.

Ryle, H. E. 1913. "The Prayer of Manasses." Pp. 612–24 in Charles, ed., 1913, vol. 1.

Sanders, J. T. 1979. "Ben Sira's Ethics of Caution." *Hebrew Union College Annual* 50: 73–106.

———. 1983. *Ben Sira and Demotic Wisdom.* Society of Biblical Literature Monograph Series 28. Chico, Calif.: Scholars Press.

Sanders, J. A. 1965. *The Psalms Scroll of Qumran Cave 11.* Discoveries in the Judean Desert 4. Oxford: Oxford University Press.

Saracino, F. 1982. "Resurrezione in Ben Sira?" *Henoch* 4: 185–203.

Sauer, G. 1981. *Jesus Sirach.* Gütersloh: Mohn.

Schaberg, J. 1982. "Major Midrashic Traditions in Wisdom 1,1–6,25." *JSJ* 8: 75–101.

Schechter, S. 1891. "The Quotations from Ecclesiasticus in Rabbinic Literature." *Jewish Quarterly Review* 3: 682–706.

Schuller, E. M. 1992. "The Apocrypha." Pp. 235–43 in *The Women's Bible Commentary,* edited by C. A. Newsome and S. Ringe. Louisville: Westminster/John Knox.

Schunk, K.-D. 1954. *Die Quellen des I und II Makkabäerbuches.* Halle: Niemeyer.

———. 1980. *1 Makkabäerbuch. JSHRZ* 1.4. Gütersloh: Mohn.

Schürer, E. 1986. *The History of the Jewish People in the Age of Jesus Christ (175 B.C.– A.D. 135).* 3 vols. in 4. Revised and edited by G. Vermes, F. Millar, and M. Goodman. Edinburgh: Clark.

Semler, C. 1943. "Traces of the 'Sayings of the Seven Sages' in the Liber Ecclesiasticus." *CBQ* 5: 264–74.

Siebeneck, R. T. 1959. "May Their Bones Return to Life!—Sirach's Praise of the Fathers." *CBQ* 21: 411–28.

———. 1960. "The Midrash of Wisd. 10–19." *CBQ* 22: 176–82.

Simpson, D. C. 1913a. "Tobit." Pp. 174–241 in Charles, ed., 1913, vol. 1.

———. 1913b. "The Chief Recensions of the Book of Tobit." *JTS* 14: 516–30.

Skehan, P. W. 1962. "Why Leave Out Judith?" *CBQ* 24: 147–54.

———. 1963a. "The Hand of Judith." *CBQ* 25: 94–109.

———. 1963b. "Didache 1,6 and Sirach 12,1." *Bib* 44: 533–36.

————. 1971. *Studies in Israelite Poetry and Wisdom.* Catholic Biblical Quarterly Monograph Series 1. Washington: Catholic Biblical Association.

Skehan, P. W., and A. A. Di Lella. 1987. *The Wisdom of Ben Sira.* AB 39. New York: Doubleday.

Smallwood, E. M. 1976. *The Jews under Roman Rule.* Leiden: Brill.

Snaith, J. G. 1974. *Ecclesiasticus.* Cambridge: Cambridge University Press.

Soll, W. 1988. "Tobit and Folklore Studies, with Emphasis on Propp's Morphology." Pp. 39–53 in *Society of Biblical Literature 1988 Seminar Papers,* edited by David Lull. Atlanta: Scholars Press.

Sparks, H. F. D. 1970. "Jerome as Biblical Scholar." Pp. 510–41 in Ackroyd and Evans, eds., 1970.

Speiser, E. A. 1923–24. "The Hebrew Origin of the First Part of the Book of Wisdom." *Jewish Quarterly Review* 14: 455–87.

Spolsky, E. 1996. "Law or the Garden: The Betrayal of Susanna in Pastoral Painting." Pp. 101–18 in Spolsky, ed., 1996.

————, ed. 1996. *The Judgment of Susanna: Authority and Witness.* Society of Biblical Literature Early Judaism and Its Literature 11. Atlanta: Scholars Press.

Stanton, G. N. 1997. "5 Ezra and Matthean Christianity in the Second Century." *JTS* 28: 67–83.

Steinmann, J. 1953. *Lecture de Judith.* Paris: Gabalda.

Steussy, M. J. 1993. *Gardens in Babylon: Narrative and Faith in the Greek Legends of Daniel.* Society of Biblical Literature Dissertation Series 141. Atlanta: Scholars Press.

Stone, M. E. 1983. "Coherence and Inconsistency in the Apocalypses: The Case of 'The End' in 4 Ezra." *JBL* 102: 229–43.

————. 1987. "The Question of Messiah in 4 Ezra." Pp. 209–25 in *Judaisms and Their Messiahs,* edited by J. Neusner et al. Cambridge: Cambridge University Press.

————. 1990. *Fourth Ezra.* Hermeneia. Minneapolis: Fortress.

————. 1991. *Selected Studies in Pseudepigrapha and Apocrypha.* Leiden: Brill.

————, ed. 1984. *Jewish Writings of the Second Temple Period.* Assen: Van Gorcum; Philadelphia: Fortress.

Stone, N. 1992. "Judith and Holofernes: Some Observations on the Development of the Scene in Art." Pp. 73–94 in VanderKam, ed., 1992.

Stuhlmacher, P. 1991. "The Significance of the Old Testament Apocrypha and Pseudepigrapha for the Understanding of Jesus and Christology." Pp. 1–15 in Meurer, ed., 1991.

Suggs, M. J. 1957. "Wisdom of Solomon 2:10–5: A Homily Based on the Fourth Servant Song." *JBL* 76: 26–33.

Sundberg, A. C. 1964. *The Old Testament of the Early Church.* Cambridge: Harvard University Press.

Swete, H. B. 1894. *The Old Testament in Greek According to the Septuagint.* 3 vols. Cambridge: Cambridge University Press.

Talshir, Z. 1999. *I Esdras: From Origin to Translation.* Society of Biblical Literature Septuagint and Cognate Studies 47. Atlanta: Society of Biblical Literature.

Tcherikover, V. [1959] 1999. *Hellenistic Civilization and the Jews.* Peabody, Mass.: Hendrickson.

Tedesche, S., and S. Zeitlin. 1950. *The First Book of Maccabees.* New York: Harper & Brothers.

———. 1954. *The Second Book of Maccabees.* New York: Harper & Brothers.

Thackeray, H. St. John. 1903. "Notes and Studies: The Greek Translators of Jeremiah." *JTS* 4: 245–66.

Thompson, A. L. 1977. *Responsibility for Evil in the Theodicy of IV Ezra.* Missoula, Mont.: Scholars Press.

Torrey, C. C. 1910. *Ezra Studies.* Chicago: University of Chicago Press.

———. 1944. "The Older Book of Esther." *Harvard Theological Review* 37: 1–40.

———. 1945. *The Apocryphal Literature: A Brief Introduction.* New Haven: Yale University Press.

Tov, E. 1975. *The Book of Baruch, Also Called I Baruch (Greek and Hebrew): Edited, Reconstructed, and Translated.* Society of Biblical Literature Texts and Translations 8. Missoula, Mont.: Scholars Press.

———. 1976. *The Septuagint Translation of Jeremiah and Baruch: A Discussion of an Early Revision of the LXX of Jeremiah 29–52 and Baruch 1:1–3:8.* Harvard Semitic Monographs 8. Missoula, Mont.: Scholars Press.

Townshend, R. B. 1913. "The Fourth Book of Maccabees." Pp. 653–85 in Charles, ed., 1913, vol. 2.

Tracy, S. 1928. "III Maccabees and Pseudo-Aristeas: A Study." *Yale Classical Studies* 1: 241–52.

Trebilco, P. R., and C. A. Evans. 2000. "Diaspora Judaism." Pp. 281–96 in Evans and Porter, eds., 2000.

Trenchard, W. C. 1982. *Ben Sira's View of Women: A Literary Analysis.* Chico, Calif.: Scholars Press.

Tromp, J. 1995. "The Formation of the Third Book of Maccabees." *Henoch* 17: 311–28.

van Henten, J. W. 1993. "The Tradition-Historical Background of Romans 3.25: A Search for Pagan and Jewish Parallels." Pp. 101–28 in *From Jesus to John: Essays on Jesus and New Testament Christology in Honour of Marinus de Jonge,* edited by M. C. De Boer. Journal for the Study of the New Testament: Supplement Series 84. Sheffield: Sheffield Academic Press.

———. 1994. "A Jewish Epitaph in a Literary Text: 4 Macc. 17:8–10." Pp. 44–69 in *Studies in Early Jewish Epigraphy,* edited by J. W. van Henten and P. W. van der Horst. Leiden: Brill.

———. 1995. "Judith as Alternative Leader: A Rereading of Judith 7–13." Pp. 224–52 in *A Feminist Companion to Esther, Judith and Susanna,* edited by Athalya Brenner. Sheffield: Sheffield Academic Press.

———. 1996. "The Song of Praise for Judas Maccabaeus: Some Remarks on I Maccabees 3:3–9." Pp. 199–206 in *Give Ear to My Words: Psalms and Other Poetry in and around the Hebrew Bible,* edited by J. Dyk. Kampen, Netherlands: Kok Pharos.

———. 1997. *The Maccabean Martyrs as Saviours of the Jewish People: A Study of 2 & 4 Maccabees.* Leiden: Brill.

VanderKam, J. C., ed. 1992. *"No One Spoke Ill of Her": Essays on Judith.* Atlanta: Scholars Press.

Vermes, G. 1997. *The Complete Dead Sea Scrolls in English.* New York: Allen Lane/Penguin.

von Rad, G. 1972. *Wisdom in Israel*. London: SCM.

Wace, Henry, ed. 1888. *The Holy Bible according to the Authorized Version (A.D. 1611)*. 2 vols. London: John Murray.

Wacholder, B. Z. 1978. "The Letter from Judah Maccabee to Aristobulos: Is 2 Maccabees 1:10b–2:18 Authentic?" *Hebrew Union College Annual* 49: 89–133.

Wambacq, B. N. 1959. "Les prières de Baruch (i 15—ii 19) et de Daniel (ix 5–19)." *Bib* 40: 463–75.

———. 1966. "L'unité de livre de Baruch." *Bib* 47:574–76.

Weisengoff, J. P. 1949. "The Impious in Wisd. 2." *CBQ* 11: 40–65.

Weitzman, G. 1996. "Allusion, Artifice, and Exile in the Hymn of Tobit." *JBL* 115: 49–61.

Wenham, D. 1992. "Abomination of Desolation." Pp. 28–31 in Freedman, ed., 1992, vol. 1.

White, S. A. 1992. "In the Steps of Jael and Deborah: Judith as Heroine." Pp. 5–16 in VanderKam, ed., 1992.

Whitehouse, O. C. 1913. "The Book of Baruch." Pp. 569–95 in Charles, ed., 1913, vol. 1.

Williams, D. S. 1994. "The Date of Ecclesiasticus." *Vetus Testamentum* 44: 563–65.

———. 1995. "3 Maccabees: A Defense of Diaspora Judaism?" *Journal for the Study of the Pseudepigrapha* 13: 17–29.

Winslow, D. F. 1974. "The Maccabean Martyrs: Early Christian Attitudes." *Judaism* 23: 78–86.

Winston, D. 1971–72. "The Book of Wisdom's Theory of Cosmogony." *History of Religion* 11: 185–202.

———. 1979. *The Wisdom of Solomon*. AB 43. Garden City, N.Y.: Doubleday.

———. 1986. "Creation Ex Nihilo Revisited: A Reply to Jonathan Goldstein." *Journal of Jewish Studies* 37: 88–91.

Wright, A. G. 1965. "The Structure of Wisdom 11–19." *CBQ* 27: 28–34.

———. 1967. "The Structure of the Book of Wisdom." *Bib* 48: 165–84.

Wright, B. G., III. 1989. *No Small Difference: Sirach's Relationship to Its Hebrew Parent Text*. Atlanta: Scholars Press.

———. 1999. "'Put the Nations in Fear of You': Ben Sira and the Problem of Foreign Rule." Pp. 77–93 in *Society of Biblical Literature 1999 Seminar Papers*. Atlanta: Scholars Press.

Wright, R. B. 1985. "Psalms of Solomon." Pp. 639–70 in Charlesworth, ed., 1985.

Wylen, S. M. 1996. *The Jews in the Time of Jesus: An Introduction*. New York: Paulist.

Yadin, Y. 1965. *The Ben Sira Scroll from Masada*. Jerusalem: Israel Exploration Society.

Young, R. D. 1991. "The 'Woman with the Soul of Abraham': Traditions about the Mother of the Maccabean Martyrs." Pp. 67–82 in *"Women Like This": New Perspectives on Jewish Women in the Greco-Roman World*, edited by A.-J. Levine. Society of Biblical Literature Early Judaism and Its Literature 1. Atlanta: Scholars Press.

Ziegler, J. 1954. *Susanna, Daniel, Bel et Draco*. Septuginta 16.2. Göttingen: Vandenhoeck & Ruprecht.

———. 1957. *Ieremias, Baruch, Threni, Epistula Ieremiae*. Septuaginta 15. Göttingen: Vandenhoeck & Ruprecht.

———. 1980. *Sapientia Salomonis.* Septuaginta 12.1. 2nd ed. Göttingen: Vandenhoeck & Ruprecht.
Zimmermann, F. 1958a. *The Book of Tobit.* New York: Harper & Brothers.
———. 1958b. "Bel and the Dragon." *Vetus Testamentum* 8: 438–40.
———. 1963–64. "The Story of the Three Guardsmen." *Jewish Quarterly Review* 54:
179–200.

Index of Authors

Index of Subjects

Index of Scripture and Other Ancient Writings

Apocrypha

Old Testament

New Testament

Old Testament Pseudepigrapha

Jewish Sources

Christian Sources

Classical Sources

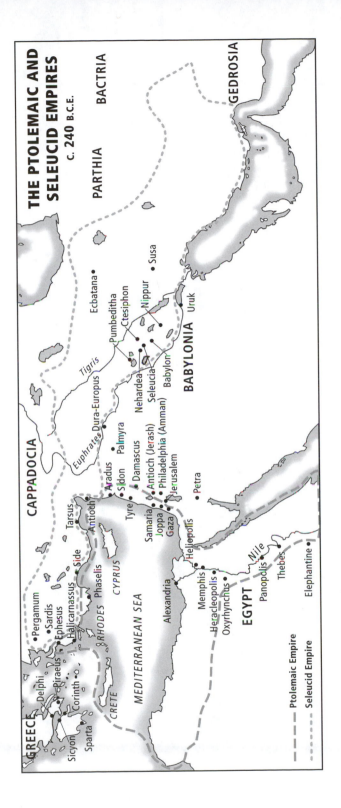

THE PTOLEMAIC AND SELEUCID EMPIRES

c. 240 B.C.E.

GEDROSIA

BACTRIA

PARTHIA

CAPPADOCIA

Susa

Ecbatana

Pumbeditha
Ctesiphon
Nippur

Uruk

Tigris

Nehardea
Seleucia
Babylon

BABYLONIA

Dura-Europus

Euphrates

Palmyra

Aradus

Sidon
Damascus

Antioch (Jerash)
Philadelphia (Amman)
Jerusalem

Petra

Antioch

Tarsus

Tyre

Samaria
Joppa
Gaza

Heliopolis

Side

Phaselis

CYPRUS

RHODES

Halicarnassus

Ephesus
Sardis

Pergamum

Nile

Thebes

Elephantine

Panopolis

Memphis
Heracleopolis
Oxyrhynchus

EGYPT

Alexandria

MEDITERRANEAN SEA

CRETE

Sparta

Sicyon

Corinth

Piraeus

Delphi

GREECE

— — — Ptolemaic Empire

· · · · · · Seleucid Empire

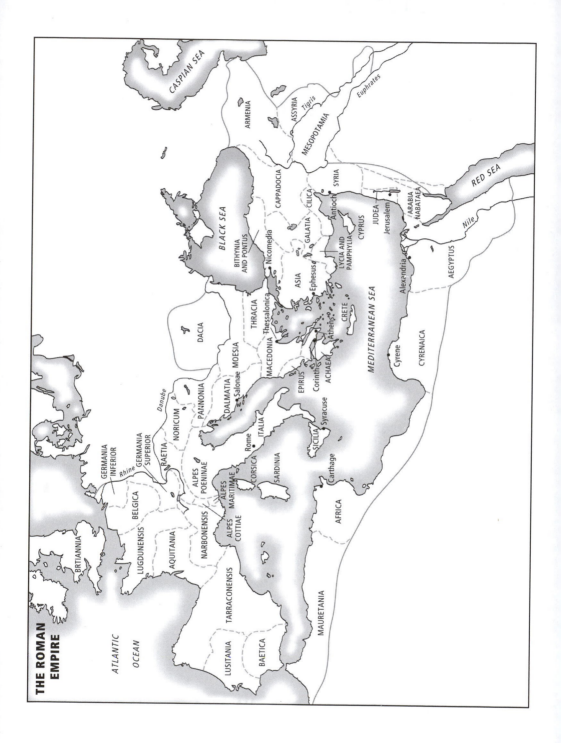

THE ROMAN
EMPIRE

ATLANTIC
OCEAN

BRITANNIA

BELGICA

GERMANIA
INFERIOR

GERMANIA
SUPERIOR

LUGDUNENSIS

Rhine

RAETIA

NORICUM

PANNONIA

Danube

DACIA

BLACK SEA

CASPIAN SEA

ARMENIA

ASSYRIA

Tigris

Euphrates

MESOPOTAMIA

CAPPADOCIA

BITHYNIA
AND PONTUS

Nicomedia

GALATIA

CILICIA

SYRIA

Antioch

LYCIA AND
PAMPHYLIA

CYPRUS

JUDEA

Jerusalem

ARABIA
NABATAEA

RED SEA

Nile

AEGYPTUS

Alexandria

Ephesus

ASIA

THRACIA

Thessalonica

MACEDONIA

MOESIA

DALMATIA

Salonae

EPIRUS

Corinth

ACHAEA

CRETE

Athens

Syracuse

SICILIA

Carthage

MEDITERRANEAN SEA

Cyrene

CYRENAICA

AQUITANIA

NARBONENSIS

ALPES
POENINAE

ALPES
MARITIMAE

ALPES
COTTIAE

CORSICA

SARDINIA

Rome

ITALIA

AFRICA

LUSITANIA

TARRACONENSIS

BAETICA

MAURETANIA